Expert C# 5.0

with .NET 4.5 Framework

Mohammad Rahman

Apress®

Expert C# 5.0: with .NET 4.5 Framework

Copyright © 2013 by Mohammad Rahman

ISBN-13 (pbk): 978-1-4302-4860-6

ISBN-13 (electronic): 978-1-4302-4861-3

President and Publisher: Paul Manning
Lead Editor: Ewan Buckingham
Developmental Editors: Jonathan Hassel and James Markham
Technical Reviewer: Todd Meister
Editorial Board: Steve Anglin, Ewan Buckingham, Gary Cornell, Louise Corrigan, Morgan Ertel, Jonathan
    Gennick, Jonathan Hassell, Robert Hutchinson, Michelle Lowman, James Markham, Matthew
    Moodie, Jeff Olson, Jeffrey Pepper, Douglas Pundick, Ben Renow-Clarke, Dominic Shakeshaft,
    Gwenan Spearing, Matt Wade, Tom Welsh
Coordinating Editor: Katie Sullivan
Copy Editor: Mary Bearden
Compositor: Bytheway
Indexer: SPi Global
Artist: SPi Global
Cover Designer: Anna Ishchenko

Distributed to the book trade worldwide by Springer Science+Business Media New York, 233 Spring Street, 6th Floor, New York, NY 10013. Phone 1-800-SPRINGER, fax (201) 348-4505, e-mail orders-ny@springer-sbm.com, or visit www.springeronline.com.

For information on translations, please e-mail rights@apress.com, or visit www.apress.com.

Apress and friends of ED books may be purchased in bulk for academic, corporate, or promotional use. eBook versions and licenses are also available for most titles. For more information, reference our Special Bulk Sales–eBook Licensing web page at www.apress.com/bulk-sales.

Any source code or other supplementary materials referenced by the author in this text is available to readers at www.apress.com. For detailed information about how to locate your book's source code, go to www.apress.com/source-code.

Contents at a Glance

Contents

About the Author

 **Mohammad Rahman** is a computer programmer. He has been a programmer since 1998 and for the past seven years he has been designing desktop and web-based systems for private and government agencies using C# language in Microsoft .NET. Currently he is working as a computer programmer and earning his doctorate as a part-time student at the University of Canberra, Australia.

About the Technical Reviewer

 **Todd Meister** has been working in the IT industry for over 15 years. He's been the technical editor on over 75 titles, ranging from SQL Server to the . NET Framework. Besides technical editing titles, he is the senior IT architect at Ball State University in Muncie, Indiana. He lives in central Indiana with his wife, Kimberly, and their five riveting children.

Acknowledgments

It has been a long journey writing this book, and I want to thank many people, especially my acquisition editor, Ewan Buckingham, from Apress, who made publication of this book possible. Every person at Apress who was involved with this book did an excellent job, and I thank them all. I would especially like to express my appreciation to my development editor, Jonathan Hassell, as well as James Markham, who gave me many great suggestions and improved the quality of the book. I also thank my copy editor, Mary Bearden, who did a great job editing this book. I also express my thanks to my coordinating editor, Katie Sullivan. Lastly and most importantly, I thank my technical editor, Todd Meister, who did a fabulous job and provided many excellent suggestions.

Looking back on this year, when I was writing articles for the codeproject.com, a few members suggested that I should write a book. Especially Sander Rossel, who recommended I get in touch with Apress. Marcelo Oliveira is another member from codeproject.com who inspired me to write this book. My thanks to both Sander and Marcelo.

I also give special thanks to my parents for their support and best wishes through this process. I also thank my sister and sister-in-law. Lastly, I am grateful to my wife for her support, passion, and understanding and for letting me work late nights and over weekends.

CHAPTER 1

■ ■ ■

Reintroducing C#:-A Detailed Look at the Language We All Know

This chapter will discuss the basics of the C# language. It begins with an example of a square number generator program to explain the basic structure of a C# program, how the C# compiles a C# program, and then explains Just-in-Time compilation. You will learn about the lexical element of the C# language, different types such as value and reference types, variables, parameters, and statements, and about the `interface`, `enum`, and `delegate` classes.

Square Number Using the C#

Listing 1-1 shows a simple program that calculates the square of a given number and displays the squared number as output.

Listing 1-1. Square Number Program

```
using System;                            /* importing namespace */

namespace Ch01                           /* namespace declaration */
{
    class Program                        /* class declaration*/
    {
        static void Main(string[] args)  /* method declaration */
        {
            PowerGenerator pg = new PowerGenerator();
            pg.ProcessPower();
        }                                /* end of method declaration */
    }                                    /* end of class declaration */

    public class PowerGenerator
    {
        const int limit = 3;             /* constant declaration */
        const string
                original = "Original number",
```

```
            square    = "Square number";

    public void ProcessPower()
    {
        Console.WriteLine("{0,16}{1,20}",
                original, square);        /* statement*/
        for (int i = 0; i <= limit; ++i)    /* iteration statement*/
        {
            Console.Write("{0,10}{1,20}\n", i, Math.Pow(i, 2));
        }
    }
  }
}                                        /* end of namespace declaration */
```

A C# program consists of statements, and each of these statements executes sequentially. In Listing 1-1, the Pow method from the Math class processes the square of a number, and the Write method from the Console class displays the processed square number on the console as output. When Listing 1-1 is compiled using the C# compiler csc.exe and executes the executable, it will produce the output:

```
Original number      Square number
      0                    0
      1                    1
      2                    4
      3                    9
```

Listing 1-1 contains a class called a *program* inside the namespace Ch01. A *namespace* is used to organize classes, and *classes* are used to organize a group of function members, which is called a method. A *method* is a block of statement defined inside curly braces {}, such as {statement list} inside a class, for example:

```
static void Main( string[] args ){……}
```

An int literal 3 and the string literals "Original number" and "Square number" are used in the program to define three variables. In Listing 1-1, the iteration statement for is used to iterate through the processing. A local variable i is declared in the for loop as a loop variable. The following section will explore the compilation process of a C# program.

Compilation of a C# Program

The C# compiler compiles the C# source code into the module, which is finally converted into the assembly. The *assembly* contains the Intermediate Language (IL) code along with the metadata information about the assembly. All of this happens in the compile time of the program. Figure 1-1 demonstrates the compilation process of a C# program.

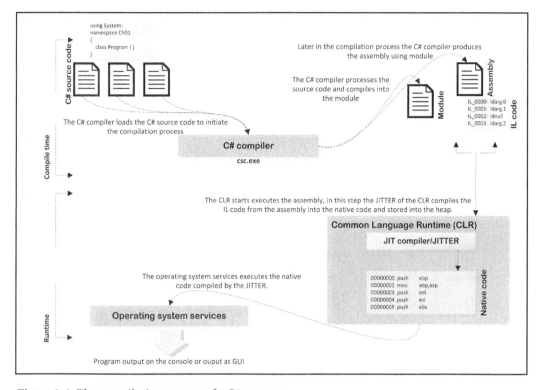

Figure 1-1. The compilation process of a C# program

The common language runtime (CLR) works with the assembly. It loads the assembly and converts it into the native code to execute the assembly, as demonstrated in Figure 1-1.

When the CLR executes a program, it executes the program method by method, and before it executes any method (unless the method has already been Jitted), the JITTER needs to convert it into the native code. The compiler refers to the Just-in-Time (JIT) compiler of the CLR, which is responsible for compiling the IL code into the native instructions for execution. The CLR retrieves the appropriate metadata information of the method from the assembly, extracts the IL code for the method, and allocates a block of memory onto the Heap, where the JITTER will store the JITTED native code for that method. The following section will explore the Jitting process to convert IL code into the native code.

Jitting a C# Program

Figure 1-1 shows that in runtime the JIT compiler, which is part of the CLR, compiles the IL code into the native code. Let's analyze Listing 1-1 to see how the IL code of the method is converted into the native code.

1. *Step 1*: When the CLR loads the assembly produced from Listing 1-1, the methods of the Program class and PowerGenerator class will not yet be Jitted by the JITTER. In Figure 1-2, you can see that the Main method of the Program class and ProcessPower method of the PowerGenerator class has not yet been JITTED, as shown by its Not JITTED yet status. Sometime later, the JITTER converts the IL code of the Main method into the native code, and the status of the method

3

description table of the Main method shows the JITTED address stored in the Heap. The contents of this address will contain the JITTED native code for the Main method.

2. *Step 2*: The JITTER still has not generated the native code for the ProcessPower method because the status of the ProcessPower method shows Not JITTED yet as the status and the status of the ProcessPower method shows NONE for JIT status, as described in Figure 1-2.

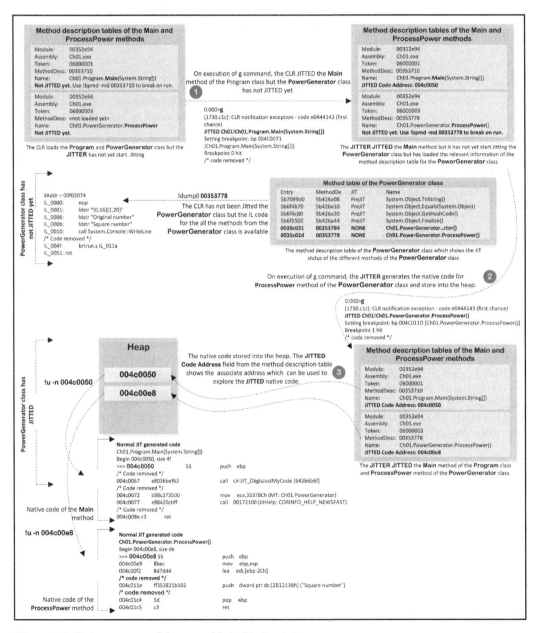

Figure 1-2. Jitting process of the assembly in Listing 1-1

3. *Step 3*: Sometime later, the JITTER converts the IL code of the `ProcessPower` method into the native code and the native code is stored in the Heap. The method description table of the `ProcessPower` method in Figure 1-2 shows the address of the native code for the `ProcessPower` method. The contents of the native code that are stored in the Heap, as shown in Figure 1-2, were extracted using the following commands:

```
!u –n 004c0050
!u –n 004c00e8
```

■ **Note:** The IL code shown in Figure 1-1 was decompiled using the `ildasm.exe`. The `windbg.exe` was used to explore different runtime information while the executable from Listing 1-1 executes. You can explore more detail about the `ildasm.exe` and `windbg.exe` tools in Chapter 15. In Figure 1-2, a different debugging command used, which is also discussed in Chapter 15. In addition to the `ildasm.exe` and `windbg.exe` tools, the .NET Reflector tool is used to explore the IL/C# code for the assembly.

Understanding the C# Language

This section explores the C# language. You will learn the syntax and usage of the identifiers, keywords, and literals. You will explore the different types used in C#, such as value type and reference type, how to declare a variable, and how many different types of variables can be used in a program. You will also learn about different types of statements that can be declared in C#, and, finally, you will learn about classes, types of classes, constructors, fields, and methods.

Identifiers

Identifiers are names used in the application to identify a namespace, class, method, variable, delegate, interface, and so on. Figure 1-3 demonstrates the possible forms of the identifiers.

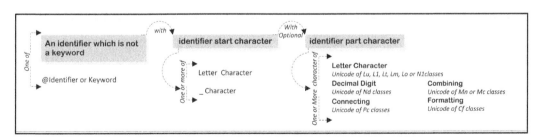

Figure 1-3. *Possible forms of the identifier declaration*

Figure 1-3 demonstrates the possible combination of the characters and digits used to define an identifier.

- An identifier is composed of the Unicode characters or it can start with an underscore character or characters (_) along with other characters, such as _ identifier or _iden77tifier, or \u005F\u005FIdentifier (compiled as __Identifier).

- An identifier can start with the at sign (@) as its prefix, such as @int (as used in Listing 1-2), and it is referred to as the verbatim identifier. To use a keyword as an identifier, the @ needs to be the prefix for the keyword.

- Unicode escape is used to define an identifier, such as "cl\u0061ss," when the C# compiler compiles "cl\u0061ss" as a class.

Listing 1-2 shows the usage of the identifier in a program.

Listing 1-2. Example of the Identifier

```
using System;

/* Ch01 is the identifier to name the namespace*/
namespace Ch01
{
    /* Program is the identifier to name the class */
    class Program
    {
        /* Main is the identifier to name the method */
        static void Main(string[] args)
        {
            /* a and _a is the identifier to name the variable */
            int a =  10, _a = 20;
            /* Verbatim identifier - start with an @ prefix */
            int   @int = 10;

            Console.WriteLine("{0}\t{1}\t{2}", a,_a, @int);
        }
    }
}
```

This program will produce the output:

```
10      20      10
```

The decompiled IL code (decompiled using the ildasm.exe) of Listing 1-2 shows how the variable names, such as a, _a, and @int, are compiled by the C# compiler:

```
.method private hidebysig static void Main(string[] args) cil managed
{
    .entrypoint
    .maxstack 4
    .locals init (
        [0] int32      a,              /* a compiled as a */
        [1] int32      _a,             /* _a compiled as _a */
        [2] int32      int)            /* @int compiled as int */
    /* Code removed */
}
```

The IL code shows that the variables a and _a are compiled as they are defined in the C# source code, but the @int is compiled as int, where the C# compiler eliminates the @ character from the verbatim identifier.

Keywords

A *keyword* is a sequence of characters, such as identifiers, but it is used as reserved by the C# compiler except that it can be used as the identifier when prefixed with the @ character. The C# language supports the @ character to prefix a variable name, but it is not common practice to use it. Listing 1-3 shows the usage of the keywords in a method.

Listing 1-3. Example of the Keywords

```
static void Main(string[] args)
{
    int a = 100, @int = 100;              /* int is keyword and @int used
                                           * as identifier */
    try {                                  /* try is keyword */
        Console.Write(a / @int);
    }
    catch {
        throw;
    }                                      /* catch and throw is keyword */
}
```

In Listing 1-3, the int keyword is prefixed with @, which makes int the identifier. The decompiled IL code (decompiled using the ildasm.exe) of Listing 1-3 shows how the C# compiler compiles keywords:

```
.method private hidebysig static void Main(string[] args) cil managed
{
    .entrypoint
    .maxstack 2
    .locals init (
        [0] int32      a,       /* Code removed */
        [1] int32      int)     /* @int translates as int */
    /* Code removed */
}
```

The IL code shows that the variable a is compiled as it is defined in the C# source code, but the @int is compiled as int, and the C# compiler eliminates the @ character from the variable name. Table 1-1 lists the keywords available for use in C#.

Table 1-1. Keywords for C#

abstract	as	base	bool	break
byte	case	catch	char	checked
class	const	continue	decimal	default
delegate	do	double	else	enum
event	explicit	extern	false	finally
fixed	float	for	foreach	goto
if	implicit	in	int	interface
internal	is	lock	long	namespace
new	null	object	operator	out
override	params	private	protected	public

readonly	ref	return	sbyte	sealed
short	sizeof	stackalloc	static	string
struct	switch	this	throw	true
try	typeof	uint	ulong	unchecked
unsafe	ushort	using	virtual	void
volatile	while			

The C# also has a few contextual keywords besides the keywords shown in Table 1-1. The following section discusses the contextual keywords in C#.

Contextual Keywords

A *contextual keyword* is not a reserved word in C#, but it is used to provide specific meaning in the code. Table 1-2 shows the list of contextual keywords available in C#.

Table 1-2. Contextual Keywords

add	ascending	async	await	by	dynamic	descending
equals	from	get	global	group	in	into
join	let	on	orderby	partial	remove	set
select	value	var	where	where (constraints to a generic declaration)		yield

Literals

In C#, a *literal* is used to represent the value in source code, or a literal can be a piece of data embedded into the source code, such as:

```
string book    = "Expert C# 5.0";    /* "Expert C# 5.0" represents a string
                                       * literal in source code */
int chapters   = 14;                 /* 14 is the int literal used for the
                                       * chapters variable */
```

Table 1-3 lists six types of literal used in C# language.

Table 1-3. Types of Literals

Literal	Values
boolean	**true** **false**
integer	decimal integer hexadecimal integer
real	**float** **double** **decimal**
character	'M' /* any single character */'
String	regular string literals verbatim string literals
Null	**null**

Boolean Literal

Two types of Boolean literal values can be used in C#:

```
bool myBoolAsTrue      = true;
bool myBoolAsFalse     = false;
```

Integer Literal

Integer literals are use to represent the values of int, uint, long, and ulong:

```
long one          = 30l;        /* long literal 30l with suffix l */
uint two          = 0x2u;       /* uint literal 0x2u in Hexadecimal
                                 * format (starts with 0x) */
int three         = 3;          /* int literal 3 */
ulong hundred     = 100;        /* ulong literal 100 which has more
                                 * than one decimal digit */
```

Figure 1-4 demonstrates the possible forms of the integer literals.

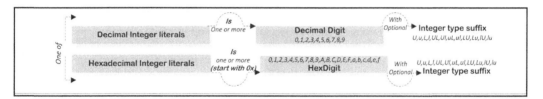

Figure 1-4. *Possible forms of the integer literals declaration*

From Figure 1-4, you can see that integer literals can be either a decimal integer literal or a hexadecimal integer literal. These are discussed in the next sections.

Decimal Integer Literals

A decimal integer literal starts with one or more decimal digits (depending on the type size where it is going to be stored) along with one of the integer type suffixes, for example, 7, 77, 77u, 77l. As Figure 1-4 demonstrates, an integer type suffix is optional to define the decimal integer literals.

Hexadecimal Integer literals

A hexadecimal integer literal starts with 0x to denote it as the hexadecimal format along with one or more (depending on the type size where it is going to be used) hex digits along with one of the integer type suffixes, for example, 0x7, 0x77, 0x77l. As Figure 1-4 demonstrates, the integer type suffix is optional to define hexadecimal integer literals.

Real Literal

Real literals are use to represent the values of float, double, and decimal:

```
double one          = 30.1;        /* double literal 30.1 */
float two           = 30;          /* float literal 30 */
double three        = 30.1e+1;     /* double literal with exponent
                                    * part e+1, 30.1e+1 */
double hundred      = 100.12E-1;   /* double literal with E-1, 100.12E-1 */
```

The possible forms of the real literals are demonstrated in Figure 1-5.

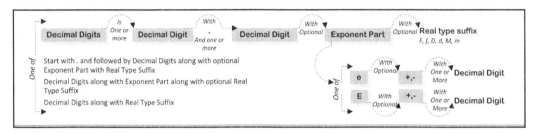

Figure 1-5. *Possible forms of the real literal declaration*

Character Literal

A *character literal* represents a single character and consists of a character in single quotes:

'a character'

For example:

'M'
'R'

When declaring a character literal that contains a backslash character (\), it must be followed by one of the escape sequence characters, as shown in Table 1-4.

Table 1-4. *Escape Sequences*

Escape sequence	Character name
\'	Single quote
\"	Double quote
\\	Backslash
\0	Null
\a	Alert
\b	Backspace
\f	Form feed
\n	New line
\r	Carriage return
\t	Horizontal tab
\v	Vertical tab

For example:

```
/* declare a char variable */
char charLiteral;

/* assign variety of the escape characters on multiple lines.
 * Each of the escape character will produce respective output as
 * describes on the above table.*/

charLiteral = '\'';   /*        \ character follows by '      */
charLiteral = '\"';   /*        \ character follows by "      */
charLiteral = '\\';   /*        \ character follows by \      */
charLiteral = '\0';   /*        \ character follows by 0      */
charLiteral = '\a';   /*        \ character follows by a      */
charLiteral = '\b';   /*        \ character follows by b      */
charLiteral = '\f';   /*        \ character follows by f      */
charLiteral = '\n';   /*        \ character follows by n      */
charLiteral = '\r';   /*        \ character follows by r      */
charLiteral = '\t';   /*        \ character follows by t      */
charLiteral = '\x4';  /*        \ character follows by x      */
charLiteral = '\v';   /*        \ character follows by v      */

/* If you declare a character literal as shows below, the C# compiler
 * shows compile time error as \ does not follows any escape character. */

//char charLiteral       = '\';
```

Null Literal

In C#, the null literal is used for the reference type, and it cannot be used in the value type unless the value type is used as a nullable type. Listing 1-4 shows the use of the null literal in a program.

Listing 1-4. Example of the Null Literal

```
using System;
namespace Ch01
{
    class Program
    {
        static void Main(string[] args)
        {
            Book aBook          = null; /* Reference type can be set with
                                         * null literal */
            int chapters        = null; /* Compiler error for value type
                                         * when set with null literal*/
            Nullable<int> pages = null; /* null can be set in value type
                                         * when it is a type of Nullable */
        }
    }
    class Book { }
}
```

String Literal

A string literal is used to represent a series of characters in the source code. The C# compiler supports two forms of the string literals: regular string literals and verbatim string literals.

A string literal is used in source code as shown in the code:

```
string address  = "Zero Point, Prometheus";        /* Regular string literal */
string source   = @"J:\Book\ExpertC#2012\Ch01";    /* Verbatim string literal
                                                    * with @*/
string bookName = @"Expert C# 5.0
                  : with the .NET 4.5 Framework";  /* Verbatim string literal
                                                    * in multiple lines */
string regularString   = "One\tTwo";               /* One      Two */
string verbatimString  = @"One\tTwo";              /* One\tTwo */
```

Figure 1-6 shows the possible forms of the string literals.

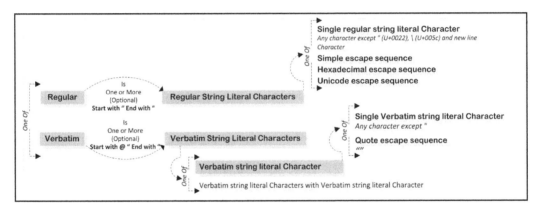

Figure 1-6. *Possible forms of the string literals declaration*

Figure 1-6 demonstrates that a regular string literal character needs to be declared inside double quote marks (""), and inside the double-quoted string literal it is not possible to use a character, such as " (U+0022 - Unicode representation of "), \ (U+005c – Unicode representation of the \ ), or a new line character, such as CR (carriage return) or LF (line feed).

When declaring a string literal that contains a backslash character in regular string literal, the character must be followed by one of the ', ", \, 0, a, b, f, n, r, t, x, v characters, which is demonstrated in Table 1-4. For example:

```
/* declare a string variable */
string stringLiteral;

/* assign variety of the escape characters on multiple lines.
 * Each of the escape character will produce respective output as
 * describes on the Table 1-4.*/

stringLiteral = "A String Literal with  \' "; /* \ character follows by '    */
stringLiteral = "A String Literal with  \" "; /* \ character follows by "    */
stringLiteral = "A String Literal with  \\ "; /* \ character follows by \    */
```

```
stringLiteral = "A String Literal with  \0 "; /* \ character follows by 0      */
stringLiteral = "A String Literal with  \a "; /* \ character follows by a      */
stringLiteral = "A String Literal with  \b "; /* \ character follows by b      */
stringLiteral = "A String Literal with  \f "; /* \ character follows by f      */
stringLiteral = "A String Literal with  \n "; /* \ character follows by n      */
stringLiteral = "A String Literal with  \r "; /* \ character follows by r      */
stringLiteral = "A String Literal with  \t "; /* \ character follows by t      */
stringLiteral = "A String Literal with  \x4 ";/* \ character follows by x      */
stringLiteral = "A String Literal with  \v "; /* \ character follows by v */

/* If you declare a string literal as shows below, the C# compiler
 * shows compile time error as \ does not follows any escape character. */

//stringLiteral= "A String Literal with \ "; /*  Compiler error */
```

Comments

C# language supports comments in the source code in the following forms:

- *Single line*: Single line comment starts with // followed by characters except for the new line character.

- *Multiline*: Multiline comment starts with /* and ends with */. In between the /* and */, it contains characters that are treated as comments by the C# compiler.

For example:

```
int daysInStandardYear    = 365;     // When the year is not a leap year.
int daysInLeapYear        = 366;     /* When the year is
                                      * a leap year. */
```

The C# compiler skips all the comments used in the C# source code while it compiles the source into the IL code. For example, when the C# compiler compiles the following program, it will eliminate comments used in the program when compiled into IL code:

```
namespace Ch01
{
    class Program
    {
        static void Main(string[] args)
        {
            int daysInStandardYear  = 365; // When the year is not a leap year.
            int daysInLeapYear      = 366; /* When the year is
                                            * a leap year. */
        }
    }
}
```

The decompiled (decompiled using the .NET Reflector tool) IL for this program is:

```
.class private auto ansi beforefieldinit Program extends [mscorlib]System.Object
{
    .method public hidebysig specialname rtspecialname instance
            void .ctor() cil managed
```

```
    {
        .maxstack 8
        L_0000: ldarg.0
        L_0001: call instance void [mscorlib]System.Object::.ctor()
        L_0006: ret
    }

    .method private hidebysig static void Main(string[] args) cil managed
    {
        .entrypoint
        .maxstack 1
        .locals init (
            [0] int32 daysInStandardYear,
            [1] int32 daysInLeapYear)
        L_0000: nop
        L_0001: ldc.i4 0x16d
        L_0006: stloc.0
        L_0007: ldc.i4 0x16e
        L_000c: stloc.1
        L_000d: ret
    }
}
```

The decompiled IL code shows that the C# eliminates the comments used in the C# source code while it is compiled into the IL code.

Types

In C#, types are divided into two main categories: value types and reference types. These are discussed in the sections that follow.

Value Types

The variables of the value types directly contain their value. Listing 1-5 shows an example of value type int (10), struct (Book), and enum (Planets). Listing 1-5 shows how we can determine the usage of the value type in a program.

Listing 1-5. Example of Value Types

```
using System;
namespace Ch01
{
    class Program
    {
        static void Main(string[] args)
        {
            int a            = 10;              /* int type */
            Book book        = new Book();      /* struct type */
            Planets planets  = Planets.Earth;   /* enum type */
        }
```

```
    }

    struct Book          { }             /* struct type declaration */
    enum Planets         { Earth = 0 }   /* enum type declaration*/
}
```

Figure 1-7 demonstrates the possible different value types.

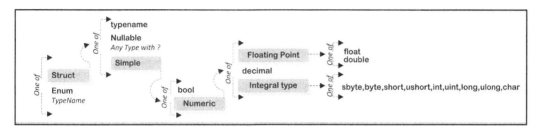

Figure 1-7. *Possible forms of the value types declaration*

Figure 1-7 demonstrates that in C# the value type is categorized into two main categories, such as `struct` and `enum`. The `struct` type is further divided into `simple` and `nullable` types and so on.

Simple Types

Tables 1-5 through 1-9 list the different types of integrals, their ranges, and the precision information.

Table 1-5. *Signed Integral*

Size in bits	Type	Range/Precision
8	sbyte	−128...127
16	short	−32,768...32,767
32	int	−2,147,483,648...2,147,483,647
64	long	−9,223,372,036,854,775,808...9,223,372,036,854,775,807

Table 1-6. *Unsigned Integral*

Size in bits	Type	Range/Precision
8	byte	0...255
16	ushort	0...65,535
32	Uint	0...4,294,967,295
64	ulong	0...18,446,744,073,709,551,615

Table 1-7. *IEEE Floating Point*

Size in bits	Type	Range/Precision
32	float	-3.402823E+38 to 3.402823E+38, 7-digit precision
64	double	-1.79769313486232E+308 to 1.79769313486232E+308, 15-digit precision

Table 1-8. High Precision Decimal

Size in bits	Type	Range/Precision
128	decimal	-79228162514264337593543950335 to 79228162514264337593543950335, 28-digit precision

Table 1-9. Others Value Types

Value type	Value
Boolean	bool
Unicode characters:	char
enum types	User-defined types of the form enum E {...}
struct types	User-defined types of the form struct S {...}
nullable types	Extensions of all other value types with a null value

Default Constructor of Value Types

The *default constructor* is the value type implicitly declared by a public parameterless instance constructor, which sets the default value for that value type. Table 1-10 shows the default values for the different value types.

Table 1-10. Default Constructor of Value Types

Default value set by default constructor of value types						
simple types	sbyte, byte, short, ushort, int, uint, long, and ulong	char	float	double	decimal	bool
	0	'\x0000'	0.0f	0.0d	0.0m	false
enum type	The default value is 0, converted to the type E.					
struct type	The default value for the struct type is the value produced by initializing: All value type fields to their default value All reference type fields to null					
nullable type	The default value for the nullable type is an instance for which the HasValue property is false and the Value property is undefined.					

Reference Types

In C#, the reference type is either the class type, an interface type, an array type, or a delegate type. Listing 1-6 shows the usage of these reference types.

Listing 1-6. Example of the Reference Types

```
using System;
namespace Ch01
{
    class Program
    {
        static void Main(string[] args)
        {
```

```
        IBook book = new Book();    /* book is an instance of the Book */
    }
}

interface IBook { }

class Book : IBook { }
}
```

Figure 1-8 shows the possible different reference types.

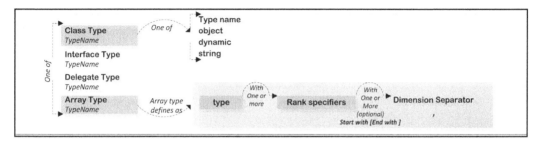

Figure 1-8. *Possible forms of the reference type declaration*

The value of the reference types is the instance of that type, which is known as its *object*. Table 1-11 lists the different reference types that are shown in Figure 1-8.

Table 1-11. *Different Reference Types*

Reference types	Description
class	Ultimate base class of all other types: object Unicode strings: string User-defined types of the form class C {...}
interface	User-defined types of the form interface I{...}
array	Single and multidimensional, for example, int[] and int[,]
delegate	User-defined types of the form, for example, delegate int D(...)

The This Keyword and Reference Type

The this keyword is a special keyword used in a class. It is a reference to the current instance of a type. The this keyword cannot be used in any static function member of a type since the static members are not part of an instance. The this keyword can be used in the following class members:

- Instance constructors
- Instance methods
- Instance accessors of properties and indexers

Listing 1-7 demonstrates the use of the this keyword.

Listing 1-7. Example of the Usage of the This Keyword

```
using System;
namespace Ch01
{
    class Program
    {
        static void Main(string[] args)
        {
            AClass aClass = new AClass();
            Console.WriteLine(aClass.MethodA(10));
            Console.ReadLine();
        }
    }

    public class AClass
    {
        public int MethodA(int a) { return a * MethodB(); }
        public int MethodB() { return 10; }
    }
}
```

Listing 1-7 produces the output:

100

The body of the MethodA from the AClass can be writing as:

```
public int MethodA(int a)
{
    return a * this.MethodB(); /* this refers to the instance of the
                                * AClass in runtime */
}
```

In this version of the MethodA, the this keyword is used to access MethodB. It is the same for MethodB, but the Main method of the Program class cannot use the this keyword because it is a static member of the Program class.

In Listing 1-7, the this keyword has not been used directly because the C# compiler can take care of it without including it in the C# source code. Let's analyze the decompiled IL code from Listing 1-7:

```
.method public hidebysig instance int32 MethodA(int32 a) cil managed
{
    .maxstack 2
    .locals init (
        [0] int32 CS$1$0000)
    L_0000: nop
    L_0001: ldarg.1

    /* Points to the this parameter whose value passed by the CLR
     * and it will be explored in the Figure 1-9.*/
    L_0002: ldarg.0

    L_0003: call instance int32 Ch01.AClass::MethodB()
```

```
    L_0008: mul
    L_0009: stloc.0
    L_000a: br.s L_000c
    L_000c: ldloc.0
    L_000d: ret
}
```

The decompiled IL code shows how the CLR passed the value of the this keyword as part of the method call. In L_0002 the ldarg.0 IL instruction loads the value of the first argument passed when the MethodA is called. Figure 1-9 illustrates in detail the use of the this keyword.

When the CLR calls MethodA from the Main method of the Program class and MethodB from the MethodA of the AClass in Listing 1-7, the CLR passes an extra argument to the method (which belongs to the instance of the type) as input for the this parameter. In this circumstance, the keyword this will refer to the object (instance of the AClass, instantiated in the Main method). Figure 1-9 demonstrates how the CLR passes value for the this parameter when it calls MethodA and MethodB.

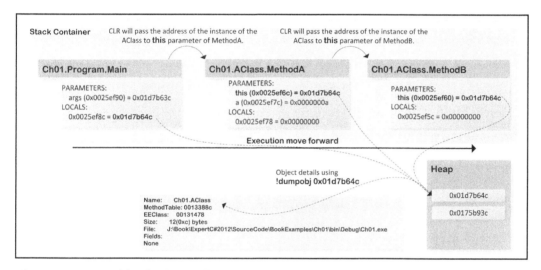

Figure 1-9. *Usage of the this keyword in runtime*

Figure 1-9 shows that MethodA and MethodB have an extra parameter this in the PARAMETERS section of the Method state description table for MethodA and MethodB. This extra parameter is filled with the instance of AClass when the CLR calls MethodA from the Main method and MethodB from the MethodA. The this keyword is only visible in the instance method.

Finally, the this keyword can also be used:

- To distinguish between class members and local variables or parameters in a class

- When calling a method, as an actual parameter, as shown in Figure 1-9

■ dumpobj: Command used in the windbg.exe program to explore the status of an object stored onto the Heap.

Array

Arrays are data structures that store collections of data and allow access to the elements by using simple index operations. Some of the characterizations of the C# array are:

- C# arrays are zero indexed; the array index starts at zero.
- All of the array elements must be of the same type.
- Array elements can be of any type, including an array type.
- An array can be a single-dimensional array or a multidimensional array.
- Array types are reference types derived from the abstract base type `System.Array`.

In C#, arrays can be one dimensional, multidimensional, rectangular, variable length, or associative. The next section explores these types of arrays.

One-Dimensional Arrays

One-dimensional arrays are declared by stating their element type followed by empty square brackets, as shown in the code:

```
int[] arr1;
char[] characters      = { 'a', 'b', 'c' };
double[] arr3   = new double[5];

string[] arr4 = new string[]
{
    "Galactic Centre", "Great Rift", "Interstellar Dust"
};

Console.WriteLine(arr1.Length);         /* Compile time error:
                                         * unassigned variable */
Console.WriteLine(characters.Length);   /* 3 */
Console.WriteLine(arr3.GetLength(0));    /* 5 */
```

Multidimensional Arrays

Multidimensional arrays can be jagged or rectangular. Jagged arrays hold reference to other arrays:

```
double [][]     arr = new double [2][];
                arr[0] = new double [] {1.3, 2.4, 4.5, 6.6};
                arr[1] = new double [] {6.7, 1.1, 3.5};

Console.WriteLine(arr[0].Length);       /* 4 */
Console.WriteLine(arr[1].Length);       /* 3 */
Console.WriteLine(arr.Rank);            /* 1 (1 dimension) */
Console.WriteLine(arr.GetLength(0));    /* 2 */
Console.WriteLine(arr.GetLength(1));    /* Runtime error: Index was outside
                                         * the bounds of the array */
```

Rectangular arrays are more compact and efficient for indexing:

```
double [,] a    = new double[2, 3];
string[, ,] b   = new string[3, 2, 4];
double[,] arr   =
{
        { 1.3, 2.4, 4.5 },
        { 6.6, 1.2, 3.2 }
};
Console.WriteLine(arr.Length);          /* 6 */
Console.WriteLine(arr.Rank);            /* 2 (2 dimensions) */
Console.WriteLine(arr.GetLength(0));    /* 2 */
Console.WriteLine(arr.GetLength(1));    /* 3 */
```

Variable-Length Arrays

Jagged or rectangular arrays have fixed lengths after declaration. The ArrayList (discussed in detail in Chapter 11) class in the namespace System.Collections provides arrays of variable length, as shown in Listing 1-8.

Listing 1-8. An Example of the Variable Length Arrays

```
using System;
using System.Collections;

namespace Ch01
{
    class MainClass
    {
        static void Main(string[] args)
        {
            ArrayList al = new ArrayList();
            al.Add("C#");
            Console.WriteLine(al.Count);        /* 1 */
            Console.WriteLine(al[0]);           /* C# */
        }
    }
}
```

This program will produce the output:

```
1
C#
```

Associative Arrays

Arrays can be indexed by strings if they are created by the class Hashtable (discussed in detail in Chapter 11) in the namespace System.Collections, as shown in Listing 1-9.

Listing 1-9. Example of the Associative Arrays

```
using System;
using System.Collections;
```

```csharp
namespace Ch01
{
    class MainClass
    {
        static void Main(string[] args)
        {
            Hashtable htArray    = new Hashtable();
            htArray["1"]        = "Milky way";
            htArray["2"]        = "Galaxy";
            Console.WriteLine(htArray.Count);        /* 2 */
            Console.WriteLine(htArray["1"]);         /* Milky way */
            Console.WriteLine(htArray["2"]);         /* Galaxy */
        }
    }
}
```

This program will produce the output:

```
2
Milky way
Galaxy
```

Variables

In C#, *variables* represent the storage locations that contain the value. The type of value can be stored in the variable determined by the variable type. For example:

```csharp
/* a string type variable */
string bookName         = " Expert C# 5.0: with the .NET 4.5 Framework";
/* a int type variable */
int publishedYear       = 2012;
```

The C# compiler guarantees that values stored in variables are always of the appropriate type as it defined.

Default Values for the Variables

All the type instances have a default value. Table 1-12 shows the default values for the different types.

Table 1-12. Default Value for the Variables

Type	Default value
All reference types	null
All numeric and enum types	0
char type	'\0'
bool type	false

Listing 1-10 shows the usage of the default keyword, which is used in C# to return the default value of a type.

Listing 1-10. Example of the Default Values for Different Types

```
using System;
namespace Ch01
{
    class Program
    {
        static void Main(string[] args)
        {
            Book book   = default(Book);      /* null */
            int i       = default(int);       /* 0 */
            float f     = default(float);     /* 0.0 */
            char c      = default(char);      /* '\0' */
            bool b      = default(bool);      /* false */
            Planets p   = default(Planets);   /* Earth */
        }
    }

    class Book      { }             /* a reference type Book declaration */
    enum Planets    { Earth=0 }     /* enum declaration */
}
```

Listing 1-10 shows how you can use the default keyword to initialize the default values for the type, otherwise you can explicitly set the default value for the type when it is initialized.

Variable Storage

There are two kinds of variable storage used in the C#: the Stack and the Heap. These are discussed in the following sections.

Stack

The Stack is used to store local variables and parameters and other information. Let's see how the CLR maintains the Stack when it executes the Main method, as shown in Listing 1-11.

Listing 1-11. Example of the Stack and Heap

```
using System;
namespace Ch01
{
    class Program
    {
        static void Main(string[] args)
        {
            Converter converter = new Converter();
            converter.ConvertAndIncrease(10);
        }
    }

    public class Converter
    {
```

```
    public int ConvertAndIncrease(int baseValue)
    {
        int increaseFactor = 10;
        return baseValue + increaseFactor;
    }
  }
}
```

When the CLR calls the ConvertAndIncrease method of the converter object, it will create a block of memory to store arguments, local variables, and others, which it refers to as the Stack for that method. Figure 1-10 shows the Stack information for the Main method while the CLR executes the ConvertAndIncrease method.

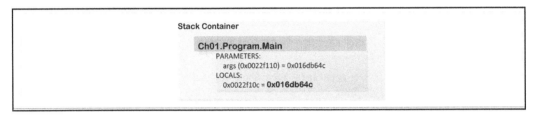

Figure 1-10. Stack state of the Main method

Heap

The C# stores objects of the reference type into the Heap (i.e., when you instantiate an instance of a reference type, the CLR allocates that instance in the Heap and returns the reference of that object). When the program in Listing 1-11 is executed by the CLR, it will instantiate an instance of the Converter class onto the Heap and pass the reference of that instance back to the Main method Stack, as demonstrated in Figure 1-11.

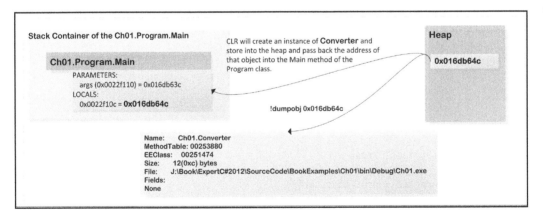

Figure 1-11. Heap state when instantiates an instance of the reference type

The Stack and the Heap are discussed in greater detail in Chapter 2.

Types of Variables

C# defines seven categories of variables: `static` variables, instance variables, array elements, value parameters, reference parameters, output parameters, and local or global variables. The following sections explore these variables in detail.

Static Variables

The `static` variables are declared with the `static` keyword. It comes to life before execution of the `static` constructor for the type in which it is defined. The life of the `static` variable loses its existence when the associated application domain loses its existence. The initial value of a `static` variable is the default value of the variable's type. Listing 1-12 shows the usage of the `static` variables in a program.

Listing 1-12. Example of the Static Variables

```
using System;
namespace Ch01
{
    class Program
    {
        public static int X=100;           /* Static variable */

        static void Main(string[] args)
        {
            Console.Write("{0}\t", X);        /* 100 */
            Program.X = 200;                  /* This change affect globally */
            Console.Write("{0}\t", X);        /* 200 */
            Show();
        }

        static void Show()
        {
            Console.Write("{0}\t", Program.X);   /* 200 */
        }
    }
}
```

This program will produce the output:

```
100     200     200
```

If you debug Listing 1-12 using the `windbg.exe` tool, you will be able to see that the scope of the `static` variable is class wide. It does not require the compiler to instantiate an instance of the containing class, for example, X variable of the `Program` class will be accessible without instantiating the `Program` class:

```
0:000> !name2ee Ch01.exe Ch01.Program
Module:         00232e94
Assembly:       Ch01.exe
Token:          02000002
MethodTable:    00233760
EEClass:        00231264      /* This address used to explore about the
                              * static class such as Program */
Name:           Ch01.Program
```

Let's look at the details of the static variable of the Program class using the EEClass address of the program:

```
0:000> !dumpclass 00231264
Class Name:             Ch01.Program
mdToken:                02000002
File:                   J:\Book\ExpertC#2012\SourceCode\BookExamples\Ch01\bin\Debug\
Ch01.exe
Parent Class:           55094f7c
Module:                 00232e94
Method Table:           00233760
Vtable Slots:        4
Total Method Slots:  6
Class Attributes:    100000
Transparency:        Critical
NumInstanceFields:   0
NumStaticFields:     1
MT        Field     Offset Type          VT Attr   Value Name
5548cfc8  4000001   20     System.Int32  1  static  100   X
```

The output shows that a class is not required to instantiate access to its static variables.

Instance Variables

A field declared without the static modifier is called an *instance variable*. Listing 1-13 shows an example of the instance variable.

Listing 1-13. Example of the Instance Variables

```csharp
using System;
namespace Ch01
{
    class Program
    {
        static void Main(string[] args)
        {
            AClass anObject = new AClass();
            Console.ReadLine();
        }
    }
    public class AClass
    {
        public int X;
        public AClass()
        {
            Console.WriteLine("Initial value of the X :{0}", X);
            X = 100;
            Console.WriteLine("Updated value of the X :{0}", X);
            MethodA();
        }
        public void MethodA() { }
```

```
    }
}
```

This program will produce the output:

```
Initial value of the X :0
Updated value of the X :100
```

Instance Variables in Classes

An instance variable of a class comes to life when a new instance of that class is instantiated. In addition, it will no longer exist when there are no references to that instance and the instance's destructor (if any) has executed.

Instance Variables in Structs

An instance variable of a struct has exactly the same lifetime as the `struct` type variable to which it belongs.

Array Elements

The elements of an array come into existence when an array instance is created and it ceases to exist when there are no references to that array instance:

```
int[] myArray = new int[]{1,2,3,4,5};   /* An array of int  */
```

Value Parameters

A parameter declared without a `ref` or `out` modifier is a *value parameter*.

```
MethodA(10,10);                      /* MethodA calls with 10,10 */
...
void MethodA( int a, int b){}        /* MethodA has two parameters a, b */
```

Reference Parameters

A parameter declared with a `ref` modifier is a *reference parameter*.

```
object myObject = new object();
ProcessObject(ref  myObject);
...
static void ProcessObject(ref object aObject)   {}
```

Output Parameters

A parameter declared with an out modifier is an *output parameter*. Listing 1-14 shows the use of the output parameter.

Listing 1-14. Example of Output Parameters

```
using System;

namespace Ch01
{
    class Program
    {
        static void Main(string[] args)
        {
            int x;
            WithOutInParameter(out x);
            Console.WriteLine(x);           /* 100 */
        }

        static void WithOutInParameter(out int a)
        { a = 100; }
    }
}
```

This program will produce the output:

```
100
```

Local Variables

A local variable would be declared as:

typeName variableName   = variable initializer or
var variableName   = variable initializer

It may occur in a block, in a for statement, in a switch statement, or in a using statement. It can also occur in a foreach statement or a specific catch clause for a try statement:

```
void MethodA()
{
        int a=10;                /* Example of the local variable */
}
```

Listing 1-15 demonstrates the use of the local variable.

Listing 1-15. Example of the Local Variable Usage

```
using System;
using System.IO;
namespace Ch01
{
    class Program
    {
        static void Main(string[] args)
        {
            AClass aClass = new AClass();
            aClass.MethodA();
```

```
            Console.ReadLine();
        }
    }

    public class AClass
    {
        public void MethodA()
        {
            int a = 10;
            switch (a)
            {
                case 7:
                    Console.WriteLine("...");
                    break;
                case 10:
                    int b = 10;
                    Console.WriteLine(b);
                    break;
                default: Console.WriteLine("Default"); break;
            }
            for (int i = 0; i < 5; ++i) ;
            using (MemoryStream ms = new MemoryStream())
            {
                ;    /*Doing nothing*/
            }
        }
    }
}
```

This program produces the output:

```
10
```

Local Variable in Compile Time

When the C# compiler compiles the program shown in Listing 1-15 into IL, it will add a local variable section for the Main method of the Program class and the same for the MethodA of the ACLass, as shown in Listing 1-16 and Listing 1-17.

Listing 1-16. Decompiled IL Code of the Main Method for Listing 1-15

```
.method private hidebysig static void Main(string[] args) cil managed
{
    .entrypoint
    .maxstack 1

    /* Local section of the MethodA which will hold all the local
     * variable used in the MethodA*/
    .locals init (
        [0] class        Ch01.AClass aClass)
    /* code removed */
}
```

Listing 1-17. IL Code of the MethodA of the ACLass for Listing 1-15

```
.method public hidebysig instance void MethodA() cil managed
{
    .maxstack 2

    /* Local section of the MethodA which will hold all the local variable
     * used in the MethodA*/
    .locals init (
        [0] int32        a,
        [1] int32        b,
        [2] int32        i,
        [3] class        [mscorlib]System.IO.MemoryStream ms,
        [4] int32        CS$4$0000,
        [5] bool         CS$4$0001)
    /* Code removed */
}
```

Listing 1-16 and Listing 1-17 show that for the `.locals` section of the `Main` method of the `Program` class, there is a variable for the instance of the `AClass`, and `MethodA` of the `AClass` has the six local variables:

- The variables a and b are used to hold the value of 10.

- The variable i is used in the `for` statement as a loop variable. The variable is declared in the `for` statement, but the C# is compiled by storing it in the local variable section of the `MethodA`. The same is true for the `ms` variable, which is used in the `using` statement.

- In the `.locals` section, there are two extra variables used in positions 4 and 5, such as CS$4$0000 and CS$4$0001. The CS$4$0000 variable is used to store the value for the case label used in the `switch` block. For example, for the case label value of 7 or 10, the C# complier will generate IL code such as `ldc.i4.7` to load 7 in the CS$4$0000 variable or for the case label value 10 the IL instruction will be `ldc.i4.s 10` to load the value into CS$4$0000. The variable CS$4$0001 is used to store the results of the condition `i<5` (used in the statement in Listing 1-15).

Local Variable in Runtime

If you debug the executable of Listing 1-15 using the `windbg.exe` tool, the CLR will keep the value of the local variable in the `LOCALS` section of the `MethodA` stack, as shown in Figure 1-12.

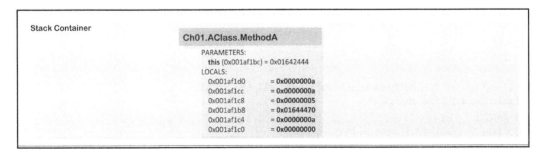

Figure 1-12. Local variable in the method

Figure 1-12 shows that in the stack of the MethodA, the CLR stores 0x0000000a (10) in the 0x001af1d0 and b in the 0x001af1cc address. The address 0x001af1c8 is used for the i variable used in the for statement and 0x001af1b8 for the MemoryStream class. The 0x001af1c4 address for the case variable and 0x001af1c0 address are used to store the bool value of the result of the condition (i<5) used in the for statement.

Parameters

Parameters are used in the .NET to pass data into the method as values or variable references. The parameters of a method get their actual values from the arguments that are specified when the method invokes:

```
public class AClass
{
    public int MethodA(int a)  /* a is the parameter for the MethodA*/
    { return a * 10; }
}
```

MethodA of the AClass has the parameter a, from which it gets its value, as shown in the code:

```
static void Main(string[] args)
{
    AClass aClass = new AClass();
    aClass.MethodA(10);          /* 10 is the argument for the MethodA*/
}
```

In runtime of a method, the CLR stores all the values for the parameter used in that method, in addition to the extra value for the this keyword in the PARAMETERS section of the method Stack, as demonstrated in Figure 1-12.

Types of Parameter Passing

The sections that follow explain the different types of parameter passing:

- Passing arguments by value
- Ref modifier
- Out modifier
- Implications of passing by reference
- Params modifier
- Optional parameters
- Named arguments

Passing Arguments by Value

A value parameter is used for input parameter passing. A value parameter corresponds to a local variable that gets its initial value from the argument that is passed for the parameter. Modifications to a value parameter do not affect the argument that is passed for the parameter. Listing 1-18 provides an example of parameter passing.

Listing 1-18. *Passing Arguments by Value*

```csharp
using System;
namespace Ch01
{
    class Program
    {
        static void Main(string[] args)
        {
            /* Initializes with 100 */
            int x = 100;
            Console.WriteLine("Before method call :\t{0}", x);

            /* pass as value to the Increment method*/
            Increment(x);
            Console.WriteLine("After  method call :\t{0}", x);
        }

        /* a is the parameter for the MethodA*/
        static void Increment(int a)
        {
            ++a;
            Console.WriteLine("Incremented  value :\t{0}",a);
        }
    }
}
```

This program produced the output:

```
Before method call  :     100
Incremented  value  :     101
After  method call  :     100
```

The call of the Increment method will be passed with the value type; as a result, the increment of the value of parameter a in the Increment method does not update the original value of the X in the Main method.

Ref Modifier

A reference parameter is used for both input and output parameter passing, and during execution of the method, the reference parameter represents the same storage location as the argument variable. A reference parameter is declared with the ref modifier. The example in Listing 1-19 shows the use of the ref parameter.

Listing 1-19. *Example of the Ref Parameter*

```csharp
using System;
namespace Ch01
{
    class Program
    {
        static void Main(string[] args)
```

```
        {
            int x = 100;           /* Needs to initialize x */
            Console.WriteLine(x); /* 100 */
            Increment(ref x);      /* pass the location (0x052de8b4) of the x */
            Console.WriteLine(x); /* 101 */
        }
        static void Increment(ref int a) /* a pointing to the same memory
                                          * location as x (0x052de8b4)
                                          * of Main method */

        { ++a; }
    }
}
```

This program will produce the output:

```
100
101
```

Out Modifier

An output parameter is used for output parameter passing. An output parameter is similar to a reference parameter except that the initial value of the caller-provided argument is not necessary. An output parameter is declared with the out modifier. Listing 1-20 provides an example of the use of an out modifier.

Listing 1-20. Example of the Out Modifier

```
using System;
namespace Ch01
{
    class Program
    {
        static void Main(string[] args)
        {
            int x;                     /* Does not need to initialize x */
            SetInitialValue(out x);
            Console.WriteLine(x);      /* 1 */
        }

        static void SetInitialValue(out int a)
        { a = 1; }
    }
}
```

This program will produce the output:

```
1
```

Implications of Passing by Reference

When an argument passes by reference to a method, the same storage location is used to access that variable. In Listing 1-20, x and a refer to the same location.

Params Modifier

A parameter array permits a variable number of arguments to be passed to a method. A parameter array is declared with the params modifier. Only the last parameter of a method can be a parameter array, and the type of a parameter array must be a single dimensional array type. Listing 1-21 provides an example of the use of the params modifier.

Listing 1-21. Example of the Params Modifier

```csharp
using System;
namespace Ch01
{
    class Program
    {
        static void Main(string[] args)
        {
            string[] planets = { "Jupiter", "\n", "Pallas" };
            Console.WriteLine("{0}", ConcatStrings(planets));
        }

        static string ConcatStrings(params string[] items)
        {
            string result = default(string);
            foreach (string item in items)
            {   result = string.Concat(result, item);   }
            return result;
        }
    }
}
```

This program will produce the output:

```
Jupiter
Pallas
```

Optional Parameters

A parameter can be optional if the default value for the parameter is specified in its declaration, as shown in Listing 1-22.

Listing 1-22. Example of the Optional Parameters

```csharp
using System;
namespace Ch01
{
    class Program
    {
        static void Main(string[] args)
        {
            Show();                 /* Please specify message */
            Show("Message set");    /* Message set */
        }
```

```
        static void Show( string message="Please specify message")
        {
            Console.WriteLine(message);
        }
    }
}
```

This program will produce the output:

```
Please specify message
Message set
```

Named Arguments

A named argument is used to identify the argument by name instead of its position. Listing 1-23 provides an example of the named argument.

Listing 1-23. Example of the Named Arguments

```
using System;
namespace Ch01
{
    class Program
    {
        static void Main(string[] args)
        {
            Add(a: 10, b: 10);          /* 20 */
            Add(10, b: 10);             /* 20 */
            //Add(a: 10, 10);           /* Compile time error, position */
        }

        static void Add(int a, int b)
        {
            Console.WriteLine(a + b);
        }
    }
}
```

This program will produce the output:

```
20
20
```

Kinds of Operators

There are three kinds of operators:

- *Unary operators*: The unary operators take one operand and use either prefix notation (such as -x) or postfix notation (such as x++).

- *Binary operators*: The binary operators take two operands and they all use infix notation (such as x - y).

- *Ternary operator*: Only one ternary operator, ?:, exists; it takes three operands and uses infix notation (condition? whenTrue: whenFalse).

Expressions are constructed from operands and operators. Table 1-13 summarizes the operators used in C#, listing the operator categories in order of precedence from highest to lowest. Operators in the same category have equal precedence.

Table 1-13. Kinds of Operators in C#

Category	Expression	Description
Primary	x.m	Member access
	x(...)	Method and delegate invocation
	x[...]	Array and indexer access
	x++	Postincrement
	x--	Postdecrement
	new T(...)	Object and delegate creation
	new T(...){...}	Object creation with initializer
	new {...}	Anonymous object initializer
	new T[...]	Array creation
	typeof(T)	Obtain System.Type object for T
	checked(x)	Evaluate expression in checked context
	unchecked(x)	Evaluate expression in unchecked context
	default(T)	Obtain default value of type T
	delegate {...}	Anonymous function (anonymous method)
Unary	+x	Identity
	-x	Negation
	!x	Logical negation
	~x	Bitwise negation
	++x	Preincrement
	--x	Predecrement
	(T)x	Explicitly convert x to type T
Multiplicative	x * y	Multiplication
	x / y	Division
	x % y	modulus
Additive	x + y	Addition, string concatenation, delegate combination
	x - y	Subtraction, delegate removal
Shift	x << y	Shift left
	x >> y	Shift right
Relational and type testing	x < y	Less than
	x > y	Greater than
	x <= y	Less than or equal
	x >= y	Greater than or equal
	x is T	Return true if x is a T, false otherwise
	x as T	Return x typed as T, or null if x is not a T

Category	Expression	Description
Equality	x == y	Equal
	x != y	Not equal
Logical AND	x & y	Integer bitwise AND, boolean logical AND
Logical XOR	x ^ y	Integer bitwise XOR, boolean logical XOR
Logical OR	x | y	Integer bitwise OR, boolean logical OR
Conditional AND	x && y	Evaluates y only if x is true
Conditional OR	x || y	Evaluates y only if x is false
Null coalescing	X?? y	Evaluates to y if x is null, to x otherwise
Conditional	x? y : z	Evaluates y if x is true, z if x is false
Assignment or anonymous function	x = y	Assignment
	x op= y	Compound assignment; supported operators are *= /= %= += -= <<= >>= &= ^= |=
	(T x) => y	Anonymous function (lambda expression)

Statements

The operations of a program are expressed using statements. C# supports several kinds of statements, a number of which are defined in terms of embedded statements. A block permits multiple statements to be written in contexts where a single statement is allowed.

A block consists of a list of statements separated using the delimiters (;):

```
{ list of statement }
```
Or,
```
{
    statement ;
    statement ;
    statement ;
    statement ;
}
```

Figure 1-13 demonstrates the possible different statements used in the C#.

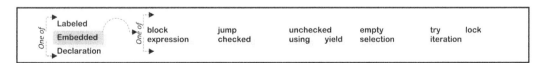

Figure 1-13. Possible forms of the statements used in C#

The following sections will explore the labeled, embedded, and declaration statements in more detail.

Labeled Statements

A statement prefix with a label is denoted as a Label statement. A label statement can be declare as:

An identifier following by : with statement or statements.

It is used in a block rather than as an embedded statement. The goto statement can transfer control within blocks and out of blocks, but never into blocks. Let's look at the following example:

```
public void MethodA()
{
    int i = 0;
    while (++i < int.MaxValue)
    {
        if (i == int.MaxValue / 2)
            goto Display;          /* Program control will transfer to the label
                                    * Display when the condition meets. */
    }
    Display: Console.WriteLine(i);
}
```

The Display label can be written as:

```
Display:
    {
        Console.WriteLine("Labeled statement");
        Console.WriteLine(i);
        Console.WriteLine("End Labeled statement");
    }
```

The Label statement is used in C# code to transfer the program control from one place to another. In IL code of the MethodA, the Label statement is translated using the instruction br, as demonstrated in Listing 1-24.

Listing 1-24. Decompiled IL Code for MethodA

```
.method public hidebysig instance void MethodA() cil managed
{
    .maxstack 2
    .locals init (
        [0] int32 i,
        [1] bool CS$4$0000)
    L_0000: nop
    L_0001: ldc.i4.0
    L_0002: stloc.0
    L_0003: br.s L_0018
    L_0005: nop
    L_0006: ldloc.0
    L_0007: ldc.i4 0x3fffffff
    L_000c: ceq
    L_000e: ldc.i4.0
    L_000f: ceq
    L_0011: stloc.1
    L_0012: ldloc.1
    L_0013: brtrue.s L_0017

    /* The program control will transfer to L_0028 to execute the statements
     * define for the Display label in C#. It will skip the execution of the
```

```
 * statements from L_0017 to L_0026 the CLR will execute the statement
 * from L_0028 to L_0052.*/
L_0015: br.s L_0028

L_0017: nop
L_0018: ldloc.0
L_0019: ldc.i4.1
L_001a: add
L_001b: dup
L_001c: stloc.0
L_001d: ldc.i4 0x7fffffff
L_0022: clt
L_0024: stloc.1
L_0025: ldloc.1
L_0026: brtrue.s L_0005

/* Display labeled start from here and end at L_0045 */
L_0028: nop
L_0029: ldstr "Labeled statement"
L_002e: call void [mscorlib]System.Console::WriteLine(string)
L_0033: nop
L_0034: ldloc.0
L_0035: call void [mscorlib]System.Console::WriteLine(int32)
L_003a: nop
L_003b: ldstr "End Labeled statement"
L_0040: call void [mscorlib]System.Console::WriteLine(string)
L_0045: nop
L_0046: nop
L_0047: ldstr "Continue with the rest of the statements in the method"
L_004c: call void [mscorlib]System.Console::WriteLine(string)
L_0051: nop
L_0052: ret
}
```

Declaration Statements

A *declaration statement* is used to declare a local variable (which discussed earlier) or a constant. The following section further explains the constant variable declaration.

Constant Declarations

In a constant declaration, one or more constants can be declared. The following line of code shows that a constant variable book has been declared:

```
public const string book = "Expert C# 5.0";
```

Embedded Statement

The following sections will explore the different embedded statements, such as the empty statement, expression statement, selection statement, iteration statement, jump statement, try statement, lock statement, using statement, and yield statement.

Empty Statement

An empty statement does nothing but is used when there are no operations to perform. An empty statement can be declared as:

```
;
empty statement defined by ;
```

The following example is provided to explain the empty statement:

```
public void MethodA()
{
    int i = 0;
    while (++i < int.MaxValue)
        ;                           /* ; Does nothing in here except elapsed
                                     * time to execute the looping until
                                     * int.MaxValue reached*/

    Console.WriteLine(i);
}
```

Expression Statements

An expression statement evaluates an expression. Expression statements will be one of the following:

- Invocation expression
- Object creation expression
- Assignment expression
- Post- or preincrement or post- or predecrement expression

The example in Listing 1-25 shows the usage of the different expressions.

Listing 1-25. Example of the Expression Statement

```
using System;
namespace Ch01
{
    class Program
    {
        static void Main(string[] args)
        {
            int x, y;               /* Declaration statement */
            x = 10;                 /* Assignment expression */
            y = 12;                 /* Assignment expression */
            ++x;                    /* Increment expression */
            --y;                    /* Decrement expression */
            Show(x, y);             /* Method call expression which will
```

```
                                       * show 22 as output*/
        string message =
                new string('.', 10);    /* object instantiation expression */
        Console.WriteLine(message);     /* Method call expression which will
                                         * show method */
    }

    static void Show(int a, int b)
    {
        Console.WriteLine(a + b);
    }
  }
}
```

This program will produce the output:

```
22
..........
```


Selection Statements

Selection statements are used in C# to select possible statements for execution based on a given condition. In C#, there are two kinds of selection statements: `if` and `switch`. The declaration of the `if` statement would be:

```
if  ( boolean expression )  embedded statement
```
or
```
if  ( boolean expression )  embedded statement else embedded statement
```
The declaration of the `switch` statement would be:
```
switch ( expression )
{
   One or more switch block which consists of the switch label along with the statement or
statements.
}
```

The switch label would be:

```
case constant expression: statements
default: statements
```

The following example shows the usage of the `if` and `switch` statements:

```
public static void MethodA(int a)
{
    if (a < 10)
    {
        switch (a)
        {
            case 1:
            case 2:
            case 3:
            case 4:
                /* Following statement will execute when a is in range
```

```
                * of {1,2,3,4} */
             Console.WriteLine(a);
             break;

        case 5:
            /* Following statement will execute when a is 5 */
            Console.WriteLine(a);
            break;

        default:
            /* otherwise */
            Console.WriteLine("Input < 10");
            break;
        }
    }
    else
    {
        Console.WriteLine("Input > 10");
    }
}
```

MethodA will produce the following output for the value set {1, 4, 5, 7} when used in a program:

```
1
4
5
Input < 10
```

Iteration Statements

To execute repeated statements in C#, the while, do, for, and foreach statements would be used. The declaration of the while statement would be:

```
while  ( boolean expression )   embedded statement
```

The declaration of the do statement would be:

```
do embedded statement while  ( boolean expression ) ;
```

The declaration of the for statement would be:

```
for (
     local variable declaration or statement expression;
     boolean expression;
     statement expression or statement expression list along with comma (,)
     separated statement expression
     )
        embedded statement
```

The declaration of the foreach statement would be:

```
foreach (
     local variable type follows by an identifier and this follows
     in
```

along with an expression
)
embedded statement

The following is an example of the use of these statements:

```
public static void MethodA(int a)
{
    do
    {
        /* Iterate through the Enumerator and extract each of the item from
         * the data source*/
        foreach (char ch in "Expert C# 5.0" + Environment.NewLine)
            Console.Write(ch);

        /* loop through until does not meet the condition */
        for (int i = 0; i <= 2; ++i)
            ++a;
    } while (a <= 10);    /* loop through until does not meet the condition */
}
```

MethodA will produce the following output for the value 1 when used in a program:

```
Expert C# 5.0
Expert C# 5.0
Expert C# 5.0
Expert C# 5.0
```

Jump Statements

To transfer the control of the program execution in C#, one of the jump statements, such as break, continue, goto, return, and throw, can be used. The declaration of the while statement would be:

break ;

The declaration of the continue statement would be:

continue ;

The declaration of the goto statement would be:

goto identifier ;

The declaration of the return statement would be:

return expression ;

The declaration of the throw statement would be:

throw expression ;

The following example explains the use of statements:

```
public static void MethodA(int a)
{
    do
    {
```

43

```
        foreach (char ch in "Expert C# 5.0\t" + Environment.NewLine)
        {
            if (Environment.NewLine.Contains(ch.ToString()))
                break;
            Console.Write(ch);
        }
    } while ((a = MethodB(a)) <= 10);
}

public static int MethodB(int a)
{
    if (a == 100)
        throw new Exception("Error: a>10");
    return ++a;
}
```

MethodA and MethodB will produce the following output for the value 1 when used in a program:

```
Expert C# 5.0    Expert C# 5.0    Expert C# 5.0    Expert C# 5.0    Expert C# 5.0
Expert C# 5.0    Expert C# 5.0    Expert C# 5.0    Expert C# 5.0    Expert C# 5.0
```

Try Statement

The try statement provides a mechanism for catching exceptions that occur during execution of a block. Furthermore, the try statement provides the ability to specify a block of code that is always executed when control leaves the try statement:

```
public static int MethodB(int a)
{
    try
    {
        return Int16.MaxValue / a;
    }
    catch (DivideByZeroException dbze)
    {
        Console.WriteLine(dbze.Message);
    }
    finally
    {
        Console.WriteLine("Execute always");
    }
    return -1;
}
```

MethodB will produce the following output for the value 0 when used in a program:

```
Attempted to divide by zero.
Execute always
-1
```

Lock Statement

The lock statement obtains the mutual exclusion lock for a given object, executes a statement, and then releases the lock. The lock statement can be declared as in the following example:

```
 lock   (   expression   )   embedded-statement
```

A lock statement of the form of

```
lock(x) {/*  some code */ }
```

is compiled by the C# compiler, as shown in the following pseudo code:

```
System.Threading.Monitor.Enter(x);
try     { /*  some code */ }
finally { System.Threading.Monitor.Exit(x); }
```

Listing 1-26 shows an example of the lock statement.

Listing 1-26. *Example of Lock Statement Using Value Type*

```
using System;
namespace Ch01
{
    class Program
    {
        static void Main(string[] args)
        {
            int a = 0;
            lock (a)
            {
                Console.WriteLine(a);
            }
        }
    }
}
```

When you compile Listing 1-26, the C# compiler will generate the following compile-time error:

```
'int' is not a reference type as required by the lock statement
```

The reason for the compile-time error is because the lock statement can be used for the reference type, not for the value type, as demonstrated in Listing 1-27.

Listing 1-27. *Example of the Lock Statement Using the Reference Types*

```
using System;
namespace Ch01
{
    class Program
    {

        static void Main(string[] args)
        {
            AClass anObject = new AClass();
            lock (anObject)
```

```
        {
            Console.WriteLine(anObject.ToString());
        }
    }
    class AClass { }
    }
}
```

This program produces the output:

```
Ch01.Program+AClass
```

Let's look at the IL code of Listing 1-27 to see how the C# compiler compiles the lock statement. Listing 1-28 shows how the C# compiler handles the lock statement behind the scenes.

Listing 1-28. *IL Equivalent of Listing 1-27*

```
.method private hidebysig static void  Main(string[] args) cil managed
{
  .entrypoint
  // Code size       54 (0x36)
  .maxstack  2
  .locals init ([0] class Ch01.Program/AClass anObject,
           [1] bool '<>s__LockTaken0',
           [2] class Ch01.Program/AClass CS$2$0000,
           [3] bool CS$4$0001)
  IL_0000:  nop
  IL_0001:  newobj      instance void Ch01.Program/AClass::.ctor()
  IL_0006:  stloc.0
  IL_0007:  ldc.i4.0
  IL_0008:  stloc.1

  /* try..finally block added to the code */
  .try
  {
    IL_0009:  ldloc.0
    IL_000a:  dup
    IL_000b:  stloc.2
    IL_000c:  ldloca.s   '<>s__LockTaken0'

    /* Instance of the AClass is now Enter into the Threading Monitor and from
     * IL_0013 to IL_0021 the CLR will work with it whatever it requires to.*/
    IL_000e:  call       void [mscorlib]System.Threading.Monitor::Enter(object,
                                                                        bool&)
    IL_0013:  nop
    IL_0014:  nop
    IL_0015:  ldloc.0
    IL_0016:  callvirt   instance string [mscorlib]System.Object::ToString()
    IL_001b:  call       void [mscorlib]System.Console::WriteLine(string)
    IL_0020:  nop
    IL_0021:  nop
```

```
  /* leave.s instruction will execute the closest finally  block which
   * will release the instance of the AClass and '<>s__LockTaken0'
   * will be released.*/
  IL_0022:  leave.s    IL_0034
} // end .try
finally
{
  IL_0024:  ldloc.1
  IL_0025:  ldc.i4.0
  IL_0026:  ceq
  IL_0028:  stloc.3
  IL_0029:  ldloc.3
  IL_002a:  brtrue.s   IL_0033
  IL_002c:  ldloc.2

  /* Release the lock of the anObject instance.*/
  IL_002d:  call       void [mscorlib]System.Threading.Monitor::Exit(object)
  IL_0032:  nop
  IL_0033:  endfinally
} // end handler
IL_0034:  nop
IL_0035:  ret
}
```

Using Statement

The using statement obtains one or more resources, executes a statement, and then disposes of the resource. The declaration statement of the using statement is:

```
using  (   resource-acquisition   )    embedded-statement
resource-acquisition:
        local-variable-declaration
expression
```

Listing 1-29 shows the usage of the using statement.

Listing 1-29. *Example of the Using Statement*

```
using System;
using System.IO;
using System.Text;

namespace Ch01
{
    class Program
    {
        static void Main(string[] args)
        {
            MethodB();
        }
```

```
public static void MethodB()
{
    using (MemoryStream ms =
            new MemoryStream(Encoding.ASCII.GetBytes("Expert C# 5.0")))
    {
        int i = 0;
        do
        {
            int current = ms.ReadByte();
            Console.Write("{0}\t{1}\n", current, (char)current);
        } while (++i < ms.Length);
    }
}
}
```

This program will produce the output:

```
69      E
120     x
112     p
101     e
114     r
116     t
32
67      C
35      #
32
53      5
46      .
48      0
```

The using statement is discussed in detail in Chapter 13.

Yield Statement

The yield statement is used in an iterator block to yield a value to the enumerator object or enumerable object. The yield statement can be used in one of the following forms:

```
yield return <expression>;
yield break;
```

There are a few restrictions on use of the yield statement:

- It cannot be used outside the method body.

- It cannot be used in the anonymous function.

- It cannot be used in the finally block of the try block.

- It cannot be used in the try statement that contains any catch statement.

If you do any of the above, the C# compiler will complain. Listing 1-30 shows the usage of the yield statement.

Listing 1-30. *Example of Yield Statement*

```
using System;
using System.Collections;

namespace Ch01
{
    class Program
    {
        static void Main()
        {
            foreach (int i in GeneratePower(2, 4))
            {
                Console.Write("{0} ", i);
            }
        }

        public static IEnumerable GeneratePower(int initialValue, int range)
        {
            int result = 1;
            for (int counter = 0; counter < range; ++counter)
            {
                result = result * initialValue;
                yield return result;
            }
        }
    }
}
```

This program will produce the output:

```
2  4  8  16
```

The yield statement and it iterator are discussed in Chapter 9.

Namespaces

In C#, a namespace is used to organize a program. A namespace declaration starts with the keyword namespace and it is followed by the name and body of the namespace. An optional ; (semicolon) can be used to declare a namespace. Listing 1-31 presents an example of the use of the namespace.

Listing 1-31. *Example of the Namespace*

```
namespace Ch01
{
    class A { }
    class B { }
}
```

The declaration of the namespace starts with a qualified identifier, which can be a single identifier or multiple identifiers separated with dot (.) tokens. As a result, the following two namespace declarations, as declared in Listing 1-32 and Listing 1-33, will be treated the same by the C# compiler.

Listing 1-32. *Namespace Declaration with Multiple Identifier Separator (.)*

```
namespace Ch01Level3.Ch01Level2.Ch01Level1
{
    class ClassA { }
}
```

Listing 1-33. *Namespace Declaration with Multiple Identifier Separator (.)*

```
namespace Ch01Level3
{
    namespace Ch01Level2
    {
        namespace Ch01Level1
        {
            class ClassA { }
        }
    }
}
```

The namespace declared in Listing 1-32 and Listing 1-33 is compiled as shown in Listing 1-34.

Listing 1-34. *Namespace with Multiple Identifier*

```
namespace Ch01Level3.Ch01Level2.Ch01Level1
{
    internal class ClassA
    {
        /* Methods */
        public ClassA();
    }
}
```

When two namespaces are declared with the same fully qualified name, the C# compiler combines those declarations of the namespace inside one qualified name, as shown in Listing 1-35.

Listing 1-35. *Multiple Namespace with Same Fully Qualified Name*

```
namespace Ch01
{
    class ClassA { }
}

namespace Ch01
{
    class ClassB { }
}
```

Listing 1-35 is compiled as shown in Listing 1-36 to combine same namespace declarations.

Listing 1-36. *Combined Namespace*

```
namespace Ch01
{
```

```
    internal class ClassA            {}
    internal class ClassB            {}
    public class Person              {}
    internal class Program           {}
}
```

The using directive is used to import a namespace, as shown in Listing 1-37.

Listing 1-37. *Usage of the Using Directive*

```
namespace Ch01.Using
{
    using Ch01;                     /* using statement imports the namespace
                                     * defined in the Listing 1-36 */
    using One=Ch01;                 /* using alias directives One refers to
                                     * the Ch01 */
    class ClassC
    {
        private ClassB classB;
        private One.ClassA classA;
    }
}
```

Class

Class is the most fundamental of all of the types in C#. A *class* is a data structure that combines state (properties) and actions (methods) in a single block. A class provides a definition for dynamically created instances of the class, also known as *objects*. A class will support:

- Inheritance

- Polymorphism

- A mechanism in which derived classes can extend and specialize base classes

Figure 1-14 shows the possible ways to declare a class.

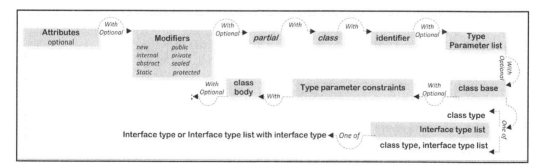

Figure 1-14. *Possible forms of the class declaration*

An example of the class declaration is shown in Listing 1-38.

Listing 1-38. Example of the Class Declaration

```
using System;
namespace Ch01
{
    class Program
    {
        static void Main(string[] args)
        {
            Person person = new Person()
            {
                Name            = "Person A",
                Address         = "Address of Person A"
            };
            Console.WriteLine(person.ToString());
        }
    }

    public class Person
    {
        public override string ToString()
        {
            return string.Format("Name: {0}\nAddress:{1}", Name, Address);
        }

        public string Name { get; set; }
        public string Address { get; set; }
    }
    public class Address {};               /* ; is optional and it used in here
                                            * to show the usage of it.*/
}
```

This program will produce the output:

```
Name: Person A
Address: Address of Person A
```

In Listing 1-38, a class Person is declared with public accessibility using the accessibility modifier as public. It has two properties—Name, Address (declared using the automatic property declaration)—and this class overrides the ToString method of the base class (for all the classes in C#) or object class.

Object

The type object is the root of the entire type hierarchy in C#, so all types are compatible with it, for example:

```
object person         = new Person();
Person anotherPerson  = (Person) person;
```

The class System.Object contains the following methods inherited by all classes and structs:

- Equals

- ToString

- GetHashCode

Instances of classes are created using the new operator, which:

- Allocates memory for a new instance

- Invokes a constructor to initialize the instance

- Returns a reference to the instance

The following statements create two Point objects and store references to those objects in two variables—p1 and p2:

```
Point p1 = new Point(0,0);
Point p2 = new Point(20,30);
```

The memory occupied by an object is automatically reclaimed when the object is no longer in use. It is neither necessary nor possible to explicitly reallocate objects in C#.

Class Members

The members of a class are either static members or instance members. Static members belong to classes, and instance members belong to objects (instances of classes). Table 1-14 provides an overview of the different kinds of members a class can contain.

Table 1-14. Class Members

Member	Description
Constants	Constant values associated with the class
Fields	Variables of the class
Methods	Computations and actions that can be performed by the class
Properties	Associated with reading and writing named properties of the class
Indexers	Actions associated with indexing instances of the class like an array
Events	Notifications that can be generated by the class
Operators	Conversions and expression operators supported by the class
Constructors	Actions required to initialize instances of the class or the class itself
Destructors	Actions to perform before instances of the class are permanently discarded
Types	Nested types declared by the class

Accessibility

A class can have one of the five forms of accessibility:

- Public: There is no limit of access.

- Protected: It is accessible within the containing type.

- Protected internal: It defines the access is limited to the containing class or types derived from the containing class.

- Internal: It defines the access is limited to the program.

- Private: It defines the access is limited to the program or types derived from the continuing class.

There are some pros and cons of these modifiers, such as, you cannot use the modifiers private, protected, or protected internal when a class is defined in a namespace. Use of these modifiers by the C# compiler generates compile-time error:

```
namespace Ch01
{
    private class ClassA                {}
    protected class ClassB              {}
    protected internal class ClassC     {}
}
```

The C# compiler complains when compiling this code and shows the following error message:

```
Elements defined in a namespace cannot be explicitly declared as private, protected, or protected
internal
```

On the other hand, use of the private, protected, or protected internal is valid in nested class, as shown in the following code:

```
namespace Ch01
{
    class Program
    {
        static void Main(string[] args) {}
    }
    public class ClassA         {}
    internal class ClassB       {}

    /* Nested classes allowed protected, private or protected internal
     * modifiers for class declaration */
    public class ClassC
    {
        protected class ClassD              {}
        private class ClassE                {}
        protected internal class ClassF {}
    }
}
```

The modifier internal is the default accessibility for any class when the accessibility has not been specified explicitly:

```
class Planets { };                      /* a class declaration without
                                         * specifying accessibility */
```

This will be compiled as follows:

```
internal class Planets                  /* The C# compiler sets internal as
                                         * the accessibility */
```

```
{
    public Planets(){}                    /* default constructor provided by
                                           * the C# compiler */
}
```

The derived class cannot have greater accessibility than the base class, as shown in the following code:

```
namespace Ch01
{
    internal class ClassA               {}
    public class ClassB:ClassA          {}
}
```

The C# compiler produces the following compile-time error while it compiles this code:

```
Inconsistent accessibility: base class 'Ch01.ClassA' is less accessible than class 'Ch01.ClassB'
```

In the access modifier usage, union of modifiers is not allowed except for the protected internal. Listing 1-39 presents an example of this.

Listing 1-39. Example of Access Modifiers Usage

```
namespace Ch01
{
    class Program
    {
        static void Main(string[] args)      {}
        protected   internal void MethodA() {}   /*  Valid use of access modifiers
                                                   * combination */
        public      internal void MethodA() {}   /*  Invalid use of access
                                                   * modifiers combination */
        private     internal void MethodA() {}   /*  Invalid use of access
                                                   * modifiers combination */
    }
}
```

Listing 1-39 produced the following exception due to the multiple protection modifiers:

```
Error   11     More than one protection modifier       J:\Book\ExpertC#2012\SourceCode\
BookExamples\Ch01\Program.cs    7      16      Ch01
Error   12     More than one protection modifier       J:\Book\ExpertC#2012\SourceCode\
BookExamples\Ch01\Program.cs    8      17      Ch01
```

Types of Classes

There are three types of classes: abstract classes, sealed classes, and static classes. The following sections discuss each of these in detail.

Abstract classes

The abstract class is intended to be used only as a base class, and it can only be used as the base class of another class. You cannot create instances of an abstract class, and an abstract class is declared using the abstract modifier. An abstract class can contain abstract members or regular, nonabstract members. The members of an abstract class can be any combination of abstract members and normal members with implementations. An abstract class can itself be derived from another abstract class. For example, the code in Listing 1-40 shows a class derived from an abstract class. Any class derived from an abstract class must implement all the abstract members of the class by using the override keyword, unless the derived class is itself abstract.

Listing 1-40. *Example of Abstract Class*

```
using System;
namespace Ch01
{
    class Program
    {
        static void Main(string[] args)
        {
            StandardCalculator sc = new StandardCalculator();
            Console.WriteLine(sc.Add(10, 10));    /* 20 */
            Console.WriteLine(sc.Sub(10, 10));    /*  0 */
        }
    }

    public abstract class Calculator
    {
        public abstract int Add(int a, int b);
        public int Sub(int a, int b) { return b - a; }
    }

    public class StandardCalculator : Calculator
    {
        public override int Add(int a, int b) { return a + b; }
    }
}
```

This program will produce the output:

```
20
0
```

Sealed Classes

The sealed modifier is used to prevent derivation from a class. Listing 1-41 presents an example of the sealed class.

Listing 1-41. *Example of Sealed Class*

```
using System;
namespace Ch01
{
    class Program
    {
        static void Main(string[] args)
        {
```

```
            Person person = new Person
            {
                Age = 30
            };
        }
    }

    public sealed class Person
    {
        public int Age { get; set; }
    }
}
```

A sealed class cannot be used as the base class of another class, otherwise a compile-time error occurs, for example, if the Person class is used as a base class, as in the code that follows:

```
public sealed class Person
{
    public int Age { get; set; }
}

public class Alien : Person { }
```

The C# compiler will throw the following compile-time error:

```
'Ch01.Alien': cannot derive from sealed type 'Ch01.Person'
```

A sealed class cannot also be an abstract class. The sealed class gives certain runtime optimizations, for example, the C# complier could possibly transform the virtual function member invocations on sealed class instances into nonvirtual invocations. Most often, sealing a class makes the best sense when you are designing a utility class. For example, the System namespace defines numerous sealed classes.

Static Classes

The static modifier is used to mark the class declared as a static class. A static class has following characteristics:

- It cannot be used to instantiate.

- It can contain only the static members, otherwise it produces a compile-time error, for example: "cannot declare instance members in a static class".

- The extension method can be declared only in the static class.

- A static class may not include a sealed or abstract modifier.

- The access modifiers protected or protected internal cannot be used to define members in a static class, otherwise it produces a compile-time error, for example, for protected: "static classes cannot contain protected members".

- An instance constructor cannot be declared in the static class, otherwise it produces a compile-time error, for example: "Static classes cannot have instance constructors".

Listing 1-42 shows an example of the static class.

Listing 1-42. *Example of Static Class*

```
using System;
namespace Ch01
{
    class Program
    {
        static void Main(string[] args)
        {
            Console.WriteLine("{0}", Calculator.Add(10, 10));
        }
    }

    public static class Calculator      /* A static class declaration */
    {
        /* A static method declaration */
        public static int Add(int a, int b) { return a + b; }
    }
}
```

This program will produce the output:

```
20
```

A static class does not contain any default constructor, for example, the IL version of the Calculator class, as demonstrated in the following code:

```
.class public abstract auto ansi sealed beforefieldinit Calculator
    extends [mscorlib]System.Object
{
    .method public hidebysig static int32 Add(int32 a, int32 b) cil managed{}
}
```

The IL code shows that the static class does not contain any default constructor unless you define the static constructor.

Constructor

C# supports both instance and static constructors. An *instance constructor* is a member that implements the actions required to initialize an instance of a class. A *static constructor* is a member that implements the actions required to initialize a class itself when it is first loaded. The following code shows an example of the instance constructor of a class:

```
public class Person
{
    private string name;
    public Person()                           /* Constructor for the Person class */
    {
        name=string.Empty;
    }
}
```

Default Constructors

If a class contains no instance constructor declarations, a default instance constructor is provided automatically by the C# compiler. That default constructor simply invokes the parameterless constructor of the direct base class. If the direct base class does not have an accessible parameterless instance constructor, a compile-time error occurs. If the class is abstract, then the declared accessibility for the default constructor is protected.

Listing 1-43. Example of Default Constructors

```
using System;
namespace Ch01
{
    class Program
    {
        static void Main(string[] args)
        {
            Person person = new Person();
        }
    }

    public class Person
    {
        /* Empty class, there hasn't been declared any explicit constructor,
         * property or method. After compiling C# compiler will add a
         * default constructor*/
    }
}
```

When compiling the program in Listing 1-43, the C# compiler adds the default constructor to the Person class as shown in the code:

```
.class public auto ansi beforefieldinit Person  extends [mscorlib]System.Object
{
    /* Default constructor .ctor generated by the C# compiler for the
     * Person class. */
    .method public hidebysig specialname rtspecialname instance
    void .ctor() cil managed {}
}
```

■ **Note:** Chapter 15 discusses the .ctor and .cctor constructors.

Private Constructors

When a class C declares only private instance constructors, it is not possible for classes outside of C to be derived from C or to directly create instances of C, as shown in the code that follows:

```
public class Person
{
    private string name;
```

```
private Person()                        /* private constructor */
{
    name = string.Empty;
}
}
```

The Person class will be inaccessible while trying to instantiate an instance of the Person class, and the C# compiler will show following message:

```
Ch01.Person.Person()' is inaccessible due to its protection level
```

If a class contains only static members and you do not want it to be instantiated, you can prevent instantiation of that class by adding a private constructor. In addition, if you have a class that does not have an instance field or instance method, a private constructor can be used to prevent instantiation of that class. If you have a class that contains only constants, you can use a private constructor to prevent instantiation, because accessing constants from the class does not require you to have an object of the class.

Optional Instance Constructor Parameters

The this(...) form of constructor initializer is commonly used in conjunction with overloading to implement optional instance constructor parameters.

Static Constructor

A static constructor is a member that implements the actions required to initialize a closed class type. Listing 1-44 presents an example of the static constructor.

Listing 1-44. Possible Forms of the Static Constructors

```
using System;

namespace Ch01
{
    class Program
    {
        public static int Y = StaticClass.X + 1;    /* StaticClass.X= 1 */
        static Program() { }
        static void Main()
        {
            Console.WriteLine("X = {0}, Y = {1}", StaticClass.X, Program.Y);
        }
    }

    class StaticClass
    {
        public static int X;                         /*0*/
        static StaticClass()
        {
            X = Program.Y + 1;                       /* Program.Y = 0 */
        }
```

```
    }
}
```

This program will produce the output:

```
X = 1, Y = 2
```

Field

A *field* is a variable that is associated with a class or with an instance of a class. The initial value of a field, whether it is a static field or an instance field, is the default value of the field's type. Figure 1-15 demonstrates the declaration of the field.

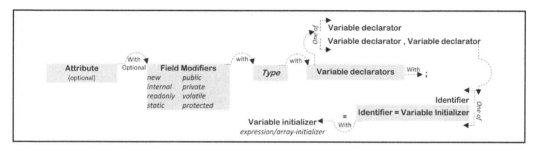

Figure 1-15. Possible forms of the field declaration

The following code indicates two fields—Name and FirstTwoDigitOfDob—have been declared:

```
public class Person
{
    public string Name       = "Mohammad Rahman";  /* A field of type string */
    public int FirstTwoDigitOfDob = 19;            /* A field of type int   */
    public int a = 0, b = 1, c = 2;          /* Multiple variable declarator */
}
```

Figure 1-15 shows that when you declare a field, you can use the new modifier to suppress the warning when the same member name was used in the derived class, as demonstrated in the code:

```
public class AClass
{
    public string Name;
}

public class BClass : AClass
{
    public string Name;           /* Same field name used in the derived class */
}
```

This code produced the following compile-time warning:

```
Warning 150     'Ch01.BClass.Name' hides inherited member 'Ch01.AClass.Name'. Use the new
keyword if hiding was intended.
```

Usage of the new modifier in the Name field declaration in the BClass will eliminate this warning. As a modifier, you can also use the volatile keyword, which indicates that the field declared with the volatile keyword might be modified by concurrent threads execution.

There are four kinds of fields in C#: static field, instance field, readonly field, and volatile field. Each of these is discussed in the sections that follow.

Static Field

A field declared with the static modifier defines a static field. A *static field* identifies exactly one storage location. No matter how many instances of a class are instantiated, there is only ever one copy of a static field, as shown in the following code:

```
public static int FirstTwoDigitOfDob = 19; /* A static field of type int */
```

Instance Field

A field declared without the static modifier defines an *instance field*, as shown in the following code:

```
public int FirstTwoDigitOfDob = 19;        /* An instance field of type int */
```

The instance variable comes into existence when an instance of that class is instantiated, and every instance of a class contains a separate copy of all the instance fields of that class. The initial value for the instance fields is the default value of the variable's type.

When you initialize an instance field, you cannot reference the instance field being created, as shown in the following code:

```
public class AClass
{
    public int a = 0;
    public int b = a + 1;  /* The C# compiler complains about this line
                            * of statement */
}
```

In the AClass, the instance field b tries to access the value of a, which was just created, but the C# compiler raised the following compile-time error:

```
A field initializer cannot reference the non-static field, method, or property 'Ch01.AClass.a'
```

Readonly Field

When a field declaration includes a readonly modifier, the fields introduced by the declaration are readonly, as shown in the following code:

```
/* An readonly field of type int */
public readonly int FirstTwoDigitOfDob = 19;
```

Volatile Field

When a field declaration includes a volatile modifier, the fields introduced by that declaration are volatile fields, as shown in the following code:

```
/* An volatile field of type int */
public static volatile int FirstTwoDigitOfDob = 19;
```

Methods

A *method* is a member that implements the operations that can be performed by an object or class. A method has a (possibly empty) list of parameters, which represent values or variable references passed to the method, and a return type, which specifies the type of the value computed and returned by the method. Figure 1-16 demonstrates the possible forms of the method declaration.

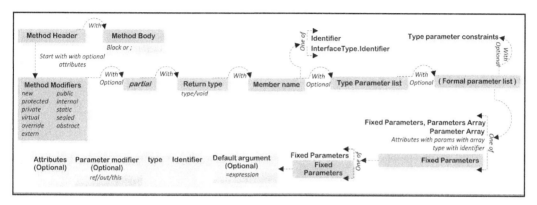

Figure 1-16. *Possible forms of the method declaration*

Listing 1-45 presents an example of the method declaration in C#.

Listing 1-45. Example of the Method Declaration

```
using System;
namespace Ch01
{
    class Program
    {
        /* A static method */
        static void Main(string[] args)
        {
            AClass anInstanceOfAClass = new AClass();
            anInstanceOfAClass.Display();
        }
    }

    public class AClass
    {
        /* An instance method */
        public void Display()
        {
            Console.WriteLine("Hello world! from the Main method");
            /* Hello world! from the Main method */
        }
    }
}
```

This program will produce the output:

```
Hello world! from the Main method
```

When you derive a class called BClass from AClass and implement a method with the same name as Display, as shown in the code:

```
public class BClass:AClass
{
    /* An instance method */
    public  void Display()
    {
        Console.WriteLine("Hello world! from the Main method");
        /* Hello world! from the Main method */
    }
}
```

the C# compiler will raise a warning, as follows:

```
Warning 150    'Ch01.BClass.Display()' hides inherited member 'Ch01.AClass.Display()'. Use the
new keyword if hiding was intended.
```

To eliminate that warning, we need to add the new modifier in the method header, as shown in Figure 1-16. The Display method of the BClass requires the new modifier, as shown in the following code:

```
public new void Display()
{
    Console.WriteLine("Hello world! from the Main method");
    /* Hello world! from the Main method */
}
```

Types of Methods

There are several types of methods: static methods, instance methods, virtual methods, override methods, sealed methods, abstract methods, external methods, partial methods, and extension methods. These are discussed in the sections that follow.

Static Method

A static method cannot be used on a specific instance and can only directly access static members. Listing 1-46 presents an example of the static method.

Listing 1-46. Example of the Static Method

```
using System;

namespace Ch01
{
    class Program
    {
        static void Main()
        {
            AClass.Method1();        /* Call Method1 but Method2 is not
```

```
                                    * accessible outside of the AClass*/
            Console.ReadLine();

        }
    }
    public static class AClass
    {
        public static void Method1()
        {
            Console.WriteLine("Method 1");
            Method2();
        }
        private static void Method2()
        {
            Console.WriteLine("Method 2");
        }
    }
}
```

This program will produce the output:

```
Method 1
Method 2
```

In a static class, it is an error to refer to the this keyword in a static method, so the compiler will generate a compile-time error:

```
"Keyword 'this' is not valid in a static property, static method, or static field initializer"
```

Instance Method

The instance method operates on a specific instance and can access both static and instance members. The this keyword can be used in the instance on which an instance method was invoked. Listing 1-47 presents an example of the instance method.

Listing 1-47. Example of the Instance Method

```
using System;
namespace Ch01
{
    class Program
    {
        static void Main()
        {
            AClass anObjectOfAClass = new AClass();
            anObjectOfAClass.Method1();
            Console.ReadLine();
        }
    }
    public class AClass
    {
        public void Method1()
```

```
        {
            Console.WriteLine("Method 1");
            this.Method2();          /* this keyword used to invoke Method2 */
        }
        private void Method2()
        {
            Console.WriteLine("Method 2");
            Method3();                /* this keyword can not be used to
                                       * static Method3 */
        }
        public static void Method3()
        {
            Console.WriteLine("Method 2");
        }
    }
}
```

This program will produce the output:

```
Method 1
Method 2
Method 2
```

Virtual Method

The actual virtual method implementation is determined based on the runtime type of the instance for which the invocation takes place, whereas the compile-time type is used for the nonvirtual method. A derived class D can override the virtual method defined in the base class B (D:B). The override modifier overrides an inherited virtual method. A new implementation can provide for the virtual method defined in the base class. Listing 1-48 presents an example of the virtual method.

Listing 1-48. Example of the Virtual Method

```
using System;
namespace Ch01
{
    class Program
    {
        static void Main()
        {
            D anObjectOfDClass = new D();
            anObjectOfDClass.Method1();
            Console.ReadLine();
        }
    }

    public class B
    {
        public virtual void Method1()
        {
            Console.WriteLine(ToString());
```

```
        }
    }

    public class D : B
    {
        public override void Method1() /* virtual method overriden */
        {
            Console.WriteLine(ToString());
        }
    }
}
```

This program will produce the output:

```
Ch01.D
```

Abstract Method

An abstract method is declared with the abstract modifier and is permitted only in a class that is also declared abstract. An abstract method is a virtual method with no implementation. An example would be if Method2 is defined as abstract in the nonabstract class AClass, as shown in the following code:

```
public abstract class BaseClass
{
    public abstract void Method1();
}

public class AClass : BaseClass
{
    public override void Method1()
    {
        Console.WriteLine(ToString());
    }

    public abstract void Method2();          /* The C# compiler complain about
                                              * the Method2 */
 }
```

The C# compiler raised a compile-time error:

```
'Ch01.AClass.Method2()' is abstract but it is contained in non-abstract class 'Ch01.AClass'
```

An abstract method must be overridden in every nonabstract-derived class. Listing 1-49 shows an example of the abstract method.

Listing 1-49. *Example of the Abstract Method*

```
using System;
namespace Ch01
{
    class Program
    {
        static void Main()
```

```
        {
            AClass anObjectOfAClass = new AClass();
            anObjectOfAClass.Method1();
            Console.ReadLine();

        }
    }
    public class AClass : BaseClass
    {
        public override void Method1()
        {
            Console.WriteLine(ToString());
        }
    }

    public abstract class BaseClass
    {
        public abstract void Method1();
    }
}
```

This program will produce the output:

```
Ch01.AClass
```

Sealed Method

When an instance method declaration includes a sealed modifier, that method is said to be a sealed method. If an instance method declaration includes the sealed modifier, it must also include the override modifier (the Method2 method from the AClass), as shown in Listing 1-50.

Listing 1-50. Example of the Sealed Method

```
using System;
namespace Ch01
{
    class Program
    {
        static void Main()
        {
            AClass anObjectOfAClass = new AClass();
            anObjectOfAClass.Method1();
            anObjectOfAClass.Method2();

            BClass anObjectOfBClass = new BClass();
            anObjectOfBClass.Method1();
            Console.ReadLine();
        }
    }

    public class BaseClass
```

```
    {
        public virtual void Method1() { Console.WriteLine(ToString()); }
        public virtual void Method2() { Console.WriteLine(ToString()); }
    }

    public class AClass : BaseClass
    {
        public override void Method1() { Console.WriteLine(ToString()); }
        public sealed override void Method2()
        { Console.WriteLine(ToString()); }
    }

    public class BClass : AClass
    {
        public override void Method1() { Console.WriteLine("Overriden"); }
    }
}
```

This program will produce the output:

```
Ch01.AClass
Ch01.AClass
Overriden
```

A sealed method defined in the base class is not overridden in the derived class; for example, further overriding of Method2 of the AClass from the BClass, as shown in the code that follows, will throw a compile-time error:

```
public class BClass : AClass
{
    public override void Method1()
    {
        Console.WriteLine("Overriden");
    }
    public override void Method2()
    {
        Console.WriteLine("Overriden");
    }
}
```

The compile-time error would be:

```
'Ch01.BClass.Method2()': cannot override inherited member 'Ch01.AClass.Method2()' because it is
sealed
```

External Method

When a method declaration includes an extern modifier, that method is said to be an external method. To use a method to define externally typical language other than C#, the extern modifier is used. For example, if you want to use a Win32 method Beep in a C# application, you need to use the extern modifier. The extern modifier is used in DllImport as an attribute. The DllImport needs to mention in which Dynamic Link Libraries (DLL) it implemented the relevant method, for example, the Beep method defined in the

User32.dll. In addition, a static modifier must be included when accessing the external method via extern. Listing 1-51 shows an example of the external method.

Listing 1-51. *Example of the External Method*

```
using System;
using System.Runtime.InteropServices;
namespace Ch01
{
    class Program
    {
        [DllImport("User32.dll")]
        static extern Boolean MessageBeep(UInt32 beepType);

        static void Main()
        {
            MessageBeep((UInt32)BeepTypes.MB_ICONEXCLAMATION);
        }
        enum BeepTypes
        {
            MB_ICONASTERISK = 0x00000040,
            MB_ICONEXCLAMATION = 0x00000030
        }
    }
}
```

Override Method

When an instance method declaration includes an override modifier, the method is said to be an override method. An override method overrides an inherited virtual method with the same signature. The overridden base method is a virtual, abstract, or override method. A sealed base method cannot be declare as overridden. Listing 1-52 shows an example of the override method.

Listing 1-52. *Example of the Override Method*

```
using System;
namespace Ch01
{
    class Program
    {
        static void Main()
        {
            AClass anObjectOfAClass = new AClass();
            anObjectOfAClass.Method1();
            anObjectOfAClass.Method2();
            Console.ReadLine();
        }
    }

    public abstract class BaseClass { public abstract void Method1();}
```

```
    public class BaseClass2 : BaseClass
    {
        public override void Method1()
        {
            Console.WriteLine(
                    "Method1 of the BaseClass overridden in the BaseClass2");
        }

        public virtual void Method2()
        { Console.WriteLine("Method2 define as virtual in the BaseClass2"); }

    }
    public class AClass : BaseClass2
    {
        public override void Method1()
        { Console.WriteLine("Method1 of the AClass overridden"); }
        public override void Method2()
        { Console.WriteLine("Method2 of the AClass overridden"); }
    }
}
```

This program will produce the output:

```
Method1 of the AClass overridden
Method2 of the AClass overridden
```

If you do not use the overridden Method2 in the AClass, as shown in the following code:

```
public class AClass : BaseClass2
{
    public override void Method1()
    {
        Console.WriteLine("Method1 of the AClass overridden");
    }
    /* Method2 removed from the AClass */
}
```

and instead use the following code:

```
AClass anObjectOfAClass = new AClass();
anObjectOfAClass.Method1();
anObjectOfAClass.Method2();
Console.ReadLine();
```

it will produce the output:

```
Method1 of the AClass overridden
Method2 define as virtual in the BaseClass2
```


Partial Method

A partial method has its signature defined in one part of a partial type, and its implementation is defined in another part of the type. The partial method enables class designers to provide method hooks, similar to event handlers, that developers can decide whether or not to implement. If the developer does not supply an implementation, the compiler removes the signature at compile time. The following conditions apply to partial methods:

- Signatures in both parts of the partial type must match.

- The method must return void.

- No access modifiers or attributes are allowed. Partial methods are implicitly private.

Listing 1-53 provides an example that shows a partial method defined in two parts of a partial class.

Listing 1-53. *Example of the Partial Method*

```
using System;
namespace Ch01
{
    class Program
    {
        static void Main()
        {
            A anObject = new A();
        }
    }

    public partial class A
    {
        public A() { MethodOfA("Partial method"); }
        partial void MethodOfA(string s);
    }

    /* This part can be in a separate file. */
    public partial class A
    {
        partial void MethodOfA(String s) { Console.WriteLine("{0}", s); }
    }
}
```

This program will produce the output:

```
Partial method
```

Extension and Anonymous Methods

The extension and anonymous methods will be discussed in detail in Chapter 4.

Properties

Properties are a natural extension of fields. Both are named members with associated types, and the syntax for accessing fields and properties is the same. However, unlike fields, properties do not denote storage locations. Instead, properties have accessors that specify the statements to be executed when their values are read or written. Figure 1-17 demonstrates the possible forms of the properties declaration.

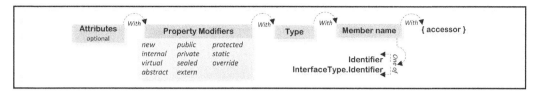

Figure 1-17. Possible forms of the properties declaration

The following code is presented as an example:

```csharp
public class Person
{
    private string address;
    public string Name                      /* Implicit property declaration */
    {
        get;
        set;
    }
    public string Address
    {
        get { return address; }             /* get accessor*/
        set { address = value; }            /* set accessor*/
    }
}
```

Indexers

An *indexer* is a member that enables objects to be indexed in the same way as an array. An indexer is declared like a property except that the name of the member is this followed by a parameter list written between the delimiters [and]. Figure 1-18 demonstrates the possible forms of the index declaration.

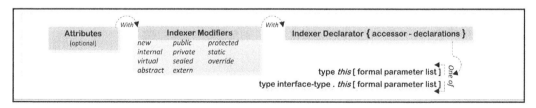

Figure 1-18. Possible forms of the indexers declaration

Listing 1-54 presents an example of the use of the indexer.

Listing 1-54. Example of the Indexer

```csharp
using System;
namespace Ch01
{
    public delegate void EventHandler(string name);
```

```
class Program
{
    static void Main(string[] args)
    {
        Planets planets = new Planets();
        for (int i = 0; i <= 8; ++i)
            Console.Write("{0}\t",planets[i]);
        Console.ReadLine();
    }
}

public class Planets
{
    private string[] nameOfThePlanets =
        { "Sun", "Mercury", "Venus", "Earth", "Mars", "Jupiter",
          "Saturn", "Uranus", "Neptune" };

    public string this[int index]
    {
        get
        {
            return nameOfThePlanets[index];
        }
        set
        {
            nameOfThePlanets[index] = value;
        }
    }
}
```

This program will produce the output:

Sun   Mercury Venus   Earth   Mars   Jupiter Saturn Uranus Neptune

Automatically Implemented Properties

When a property is specified as an automatically implemented property, a hidden backing field is inserted by the C# compiler for the property, and the accessors are implemented to read from and write to that backing field. Listing 1-55 presents an example that shows the automatic implemented properties.

Listing 1-55. Example of the Automatic Implemented Properties

```
namespace Ch01
{
    class Program
    {
        static void Main(string[] args)
        {
            Book aBook = new Book
```

```
            {
                Name = "Expert C# 5.0: with the .NET 4.5 Framework"
            };
        }
    }
    public class Book
    {
        public Book()
        { Name = default(string); }

        public string Name

        { get; set; }
    }
}
```

When the C# compiler compiles the code in Listing 1-55, it will add the extra field <Name>k_BackingField for the Name property. This will be explored in depth in Chapter 5.

Struct

Structs are data structures that can contain data members and function members, but unlike classes, they are value types and do not require Heap allocation. A variable of a struct type directly stores the data of the struct. Figure 1-19 demonstrates the possible struct declarations in C#.

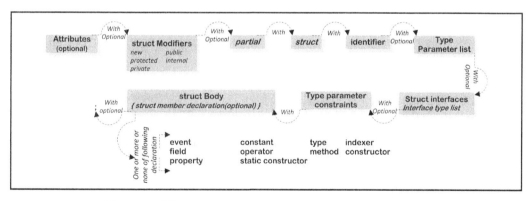

Figure 1-19. *Possible forms of the struct declaration*

Listing 1-56 presents an example of the struct.

Listing 1-56. *Example of the Struct*

```
public struct Point
{
    public const int ZeroPoint = 0;    /* Constant declaration */
    public int X;                      /* Field declaration */
```

```
public int Y;                      /* Field declaration */
private int length;
public Point(int x, int y)         /* Non-parameterless constructor */
{
    X = x; Y = y;
    length = X + Y;
}
public string ToString()           /* Method declaration */
{
    return "X" + X + "\n Y:" + Y;
}
public int PointLength             /* Read only Property declaration */
{
    get { return length; }
}
}
```

Event

An *event* is used as a member to provide notification to an object or class. Figure 1-20 demonstrates the possible declaration of an event.

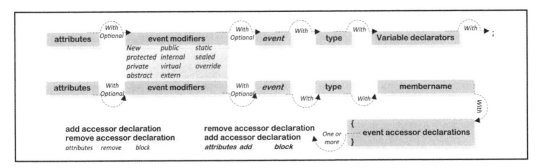

Figure 1-20. *Possible forms of the interface declaration*

Listing 1-57 presents an example of the event in C#.

Listing 1-57. *Example of the Event*

```
using System;

namespace Ch01
{
    public delegate void EventHandler(string name);
    class Program
    {
        static void Main(string[] args)
        {
            Book book = new Book();
```

```csharp
            book.ShowBookName += new EventHandler(book_ShowBookName);
            book.Name = "Expert C# 5.0 with .NET Framework 4.5";
            Console.WriteLine(book.Name);
        }

        static void book_ShowBookName(string name)
        {
            Console.WriteLine(name);
        }
    }

    public class Book
    {
        public event EventHandler ShowBookName;
        private string name;

        public string Name
        {
            set
            {
                BookEventArgs eventArgs = new BookEventArgs()
                {
                    BookName = "Book name updated...."
                };
                name = value;
                OnNameChanged(eventArgs);
            }
            get
            {
                return name;
            }

        }

        protected virtual void OnNameChanged(BookEventArgs args)
        {
            EventHandler handler = ShowBookName;
            if (handler != null)
            {
                handler(args.BookName);
            }
        }
    }
    public class BookEventArgs : EventArgs
    {
        public string BookName { get; set; }
    }

}
```

In Listing 1-57, the event keyword is used to define an event and produces the following output:

```
Book name updated....
Expert C# 5.0 with .NET Framework 4.5
```

Chapter 8 will explore in detail the event.

Interfaces

An *interface* defines a contract or specification rather than an implementation for its members. When a class or struct implements an interface, it must implement all of its members. Figure 1-21 demonstrates the possible declaration of an interface.

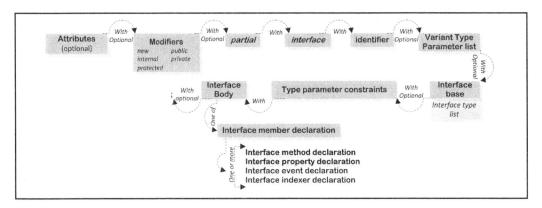

Figure 1-21. *Possible forms of the interface declaration*

Listing 1-58 shows an example of the interface.

Listing 1-58. *Example of the Interface*

```csharp
using System;
namespace Ch01
{
    class Program
    {
        static void Main(string[] args)
        {
            Calculator calculator = new Calculator();
            Console.WriteLine(calculator.Add(10, 10));      /* 20 */
            Console.WriteLine(calculator.Sub(10, 10));      /* 0 */
            Console.WriteLine(calculator.Mul(9, 7));        /* 63 */
        }
    }

    /* interface definition*/
    interface IAddition  { int Add(int a, int b);} /* Interface declaration */
    interface IExAddition{ int Add(int a, int b);} /* Interface declaration */
    interface ISubtraction{ int Sub(int a, int b);}/* Interface declaration */
```

```
    interface IMultiplication :IAddition                    { int Mul(int a, int b);  }
/* Extending Interface declaration */


    /* interface implementation*/
    public class Calculator :
        IAddition,
        ISubtraction,
        IMultiplication,
        IExAddition
/* Multiple interface implementation */
    {
        public int Add(int a, int b) { return a + b; }

        int IExAddition.Add(int a, int b)
/* Explicit interface implementation */
        { return 100 + a + b; }

        public int Sub(int a, int b) { return a > b ? a - b : b - a; }

        public int Mul(int a, int b)
        {
            var result = 0;
            for (int i = 0; i < a; ++i)
                result += Add(0, b);
            return result;
        }
    }
}
```

This program will produce the output:

```
20
0
63
```

In Listing 1-58, the IAddition, IExAddition, ISubtration, and IMultiplication interfaces are defined. The IMultiplication interface is derived from the IAddition interface, and this concept is called "extending an interface in C#." The Calculator class implements the IAddition, IExAddition, ISubtration, and IMultiplication interfaces. The Calculator class explicitly implements the IExAddition method due to the collision between IAddition and IExAddition interface for the Add method. When a class implements an interface by default, interface members are sealed. To override any member, you need to mark that member as virtual or abstract. Listing 1-59 presents an example of this.

Listing 1-59. *Example of Virtual Member*

```
using System;
namespace Ch01
{
    class Program
    {
        static void Main(string[] args)
        {
```

```
                Calculator calculator = new ScientificCalculator();
                Console.WriteLine(calculator.Add(10, 10));          /* 120 */
            }
        }

    /* Interface declaration */
    interface IAddition { int Add(int a, int b); }

    /* Interface implementation */
    public class Calculator : IAddition
    {
        public virtual int Add(int a, int b) { return a + b; }
    }

    public class ScientificCalculator : Calculator
    {
        public override int Add(int a, int b) { return 100 + a + b; }
    }
}
```

This program will produce the output:

120

Enum

An enum type contains a set of named constants. Figure 1-22 demonstrates the possible declaration of an enum.

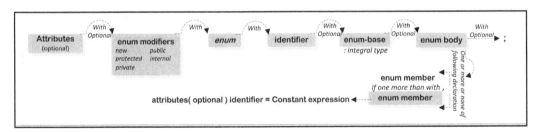

Figure 1-22. *Possible forms of the enum declaration*

The example in Listing 1-60 declares an enum type named Planets with nine constant values, such as Sun, Mercury, Venus, Earth, Mars, Jupiter, Saturn, Uranus, and Neptune.

Listing 1-60. *Example of Enum Usage*

```
using System;
namespace Ch01
{
    class Program
    {
        public enum Planets
```

```
    {
        Sun,
        Mercury,
        Venus,
        Earth,
        Mars,
        Jupiter,
        Saturn,
        Uranus,
        Neptune
    }
    static void Main()
    {
        DisplayInformation(Planets.Earth);
        DisplayInformation(Planets.Mars);
        DisplayInformation(Planets.Jupiter);
    }
    static void DisplayInformation(Planets planets)
    {
        switch (planets)
        {
            case Planets.Earth:
                Console.WriteLine("Third planet from the Sun");
                break;
            case Planets.Mars:
                Console.WriteLine("The fourth planet from the Sun");
                break;
            default:
                Console.WriteLine("Please provide valid Planet name");
                break;
        }
    }
  }
}
```

This program will produce the output:

```
Third planet from the Sun
The fourth planet from the Sun
Please provide valid Planet name
```

Chapter 6 will explore the details about the enum.

Delegates

A delegate type represents references to methods with a particular parameter list and return type. Delegates make it possible to treat methods as entities that can be assigned to variables and passed as parameters. Figure 1-23 demonstrates the possible declaration of a delegate.

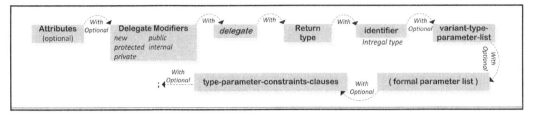

Figure 1-23. *Possible forms of the delegate declaration*

Delegates are similar to the concept of function pointers found in some other languages, for example, C, C++, but unlike function pointers, delegates are object oriented and type safe. Listing 1-61 declares and uses a delegate type named function.

Listing 1-61. *Example of the Delegate*

```csharp
using System;
namespace Ch01
{
    /* A delegate which will encapsulate a method which accept two parameter
     * and return int */
    delegate int BinaryOperation(int x, int y);

    class Program
    {
        static void Main(string[] args)
        {
            Calculate(Add, new Tuple<int, int>(10, 10));    /* 20 */
            Calculate(Sub, new Tuple<int, int>(10, 10));    /*  0 */
            Calculate(Sub, new Tuple<int, int>(1, 10));     /*  9 */
        }

        static void Calculate(
                    BinaryOperation binaryOperation, Tuple<int, int> data)
        {
            Console.WriteLine(binaryOperation(data.Item1, data.Item2));
        }

        static int Add(int x, int y)
        {
            return x + y;
        }

        static int Sub(int x, int y)
        {
            return x > y ? x - y : y - x;
        }
    }
}
```

This program will produce the output:

20
0
9

Chapter 7 will explore the details about the delegate. In Listing 1-61, a class Tuple has been used to represent a set of values. The *tuple*, introduced in C# 4.0, is a data structure that has a specific number and sequence of elements. It is used to represent a set of values or to return multiple values from a method.

Exception

A program consists of a sequence of instructions that are to execute a specific operation based on the given data (if any) to produce an expected outcome of the operation. In the execution time, if the instruction cannot do its operation based on the provided data, it will raise an exception for that operation to let the user know about this unexpected behavior. Listing 1-62 shows an example that throws an exception when the system cannot do the divide operation.

Listing 1-62. *Example of Division Operation*

```
using System;

namespace Ch01
{
    class Program
    {
        static void Main(string[] args)
        {
            int a = 10, b = 0;
            Division div = new Division();
            Console.WriteLine("{0}/{1}={2}", a, b, div.Divide(a, b));
        }

        public class Division
        {
            public int Divide(int a, int b)
            {
                return a / b;
            }
        }
    }
}
```

The program in Listing 1-45 is intended to do a divide operation based on the data passed via parameter a, b. The divide operation for the a = 10, b = 0; will produce an exception:

Unhandled Exception: System.DivideByZeroException: Attempted to divide by zero. at Ch01.Program. Division.Divide(Int32 a, Int32 b) in J:\Book\ExpertC#2012\SourceCode\BookExamples\Ch01\Program. cs:line 18 at Ch01.Program.Main(String[] args) in J:\Book\ExpertC#2012\SourceCode\BookExamples\ Ch01\Program.cs:line 11

The exceptions are handled in a program using the try, catch, and finally statements. Chapter 13 will explore the details about the exception.

Summary

In this chapter we have learned about the C# compilation process and how the JITTER works to JIT the IL code into the native code to make the program understandable by the operating system. You have explored the lexical elements of the C# language such as identifiers, keywords, and comments. You have learned value types and reference types and how you can use these types, and you have explored the parameters and how many different way these can be used in a program to pass data between method calls. The this keyword was analyzed in detail to understand how the CLR passes value for the this keyword as part of parameter passing.

You have learned about the different types of statements used in the C# program, such as the empty statement, expression statement, selection statement (such as, if, switch), iteration statement (such as while, do, for, and foreach), jump statement (such as break, continue), goto statement, and also try, using, lock, and yield statements.

This chapter also explored classes, types of classes, fields in classes, methods, properties, index, struct, event, interface, delegate, and exception. With this foundation in place, we move into the next chapter and examine in detail C# objects in memory.

CHAPTER 2

C# Objects in Memory

This chapter examines the C# object and the relation between it and the stack and heap of the memory. The life of the value type stays in the stack, whereas the reference type stays in the heap. I will explain about these using the windbg.exe program and discuss the different sections of the memory while the CLR executes any .NET application.

Finally, this chapter will discuss boxing and unboxing by examining the stack and heap memory while executing a program.

Memory in .NET Applications

In .NET, when an application is run, the CLR uses two kinds of memory—stack and heap—to store value types and reference types. The CLR uses stack memory to store method-related information, which is called the *Method state* while executing a method, and it uses heap memory to store application-wide information. In the method state section, the CLR stores local variables, parameters, and method return addresses when it is finished executing it. In the heap memory, CLR stores all the objects (large and small objects) used by the application and Jitted code (the code compiled by the Just in Time [JIT]). The CLR allocates four sections of heap memory for storage while executing a managed application in .NET:

- *Code heap*: The code heap stores the actual native code instructions after they have been JIT compiled.

- *Small object heap* (SOH): The CLR stores allocated objects that are less than 85kB in size in the SOH.

- *Large object heap* (LOH): The LOH stores allocated objects greater than 85kB.

- *Process heap*: The process heap stores process-related information.

When the CLR starts executing a program, it allocates to the process heap, JIT code heap, garbage collector (GC) heap, and LOH, which is being structured into the system, shared, and default app domains. Figure 2-1 illustrates the memory CLR allocated while executing a .NET application, as given in Listing 2-1.

Listing 2-1. An Example of a C# Program

```
using System;

namespace Ch02
{
```

```csharp
class Program
{
    static void Main(string[] args)
    {
        Person aPerson = new Person()
        {
            Name = "A"
        };
    }
}
public class Person
{
    public string Name { get; set; }
}
}
```

When the CLR executes the program, as shown in Listing 2-1, it is required to maintain a stack for the methods of the Program class, heap to store the reference objects, and so on. So the CLR will allocate the memory for the program in Listing 2-1 at runtime, as shown in Figure 2-1.

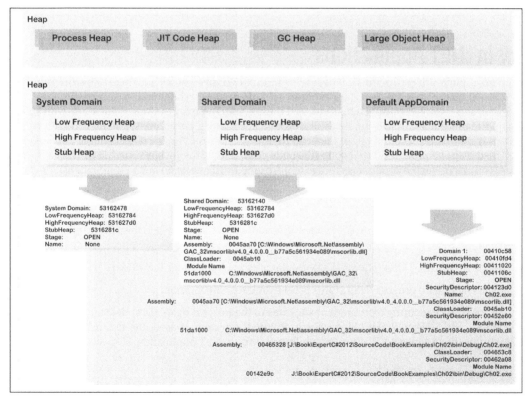

Figure 2-1. *Memory sections in .NET application*

In .NET heap, the CLR manages a series of addresses to keep track of the execution of the program by storing the instances of the reference type needed by the application and the state of the application. In a C# class, when you define methods for executing those methods, the CLR stores local variables to process its task, parameters (if any) to get data from the caller, and return data, which is the output of the method to the caller. It also needs to keep information to return back to the execution point (by address). The .NET uses a data structure called *Stack* to keep track of all of this information.

▨ The memory information extracted via `windbg.exe` might be different when you run it locally.

The Stack

The Stack is the local or native storage table for a method, while the CLR executes that method. The lifetime of the Stack begins when the CLR instructs a particular method to execute. The CLR populates the Stack table with data passed as parameter sections of the Stack and stores the address of the object reference (where the calling method belongs) in this variable (provided by the CLR as part of the method call) in the Parameters section except for the static class. It stores local variables of the method in the Local section of the method stack. In addition to these, the CLR stores the return address when it finishes the execution of the method.

Here is an example that will help explain the concept of the stack. In Listing 2-2, Program class instantiates an instance of the TestClass and calls the TestMethod from the instance of the TestClass. So there will be two method calls that will take place while the CLR executes the following code, which we will call the Main method and the TestMethod derived from the Main method.

Listing 2-2. An Example of Stack Container Used in a Program

```
namespace Ch02
{
    class Program
    {
        static void Main(string[] args)
        {
            TestClass testClass = new TestClass();
            testClass.TestMethod(10);
        }
    }

    public class TestClass
    {
        public int TestMethod(int a)
        {
            return a + a;
        }
    }
}
```

The CLR has to keep track of the information for the Main method and TestMethod of the TestClass, so it will create a stack while it starts executing the Main method. When execution moves on and sees the

```
testClass.TestMethod(10);
```

line of code, the CLR will create another stack to keep related information for the TestMethod method on top of the stack of the Main method. The stacks of the Main and TestMethod will be stacked together, and the stack for the Main method will be at the bottom of that stack as it was called first and so on.

If you debug Listing 2-2 using the windbg.exe tool and execute the clrstack command, you can see the Stack information for the Main and TestMethod. Figure 2.2 explains the use of the Stack container of the Program class while in the execute mode.

■ clrstack: It uses in the windbg.exe tool to determine the stack trace method in the managed application.

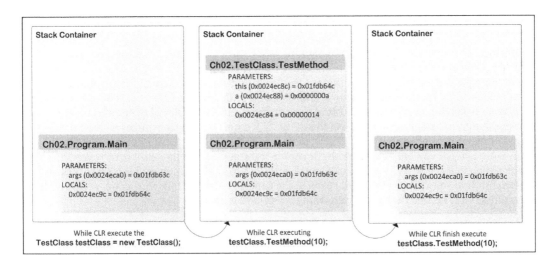

Figure 2-2. *Stack container of the Program class while in execute mode*

From Figure 2-2, you can easily see the stack state of the Main method when the CLR starts to execute the program. In the Stack of the Main method, the CLR maintains the arguments passed to the Main method in the Parameters section and address (0x0024ec8c), holding the testClass (0x01fdb64c) instance of the TestClass in the LOCALS section.

The lifetime of the TestMethod has not yet begun, as it hasn't been called by the CLR to execute. The CLR has not yet created a stack for the TestMethod. As soon as the CLR starts executing TestMethod, it will create a stack and put that on the top of the Main method's stack, as shown in Figure 2-2. In the stack of the TestMethod method, CLR stores the value of a and this parameters stored in the Parameters section and the results of the operation (a+a=20 (in hex 0x14)) into the LOCALS section of the method stack. While the CLR finishes the execution of the TestMethod, the stack of the TestMethod will end and the CLR passes the program pointer back to the Main method. If the application has multiple threads, then each thread will have its own stack.

The lifetime of the stack for a method ends when the method execution ends, or the CLR keeps the stack of the method alive if the method calls another method from itself. Until that method finishes, the CLR keeps the stack alive for the caller method. For example, if the CLR executes method A and A then calls method B, until B finishes the execution the CLR will keep alive the stack life for method A. A practical example of this is recursion. An example of the factorial calculation using the recursion algorithm is presented in Listing 2-3.

Listing 2-3. *Example of the Factorial Recursion Algorithm*

```
namespace Ch02
{
    class Program
    {
        static void Main(string[] args)
        {
            Math fc = new Math();
            var result = fc.Factorial(3);
        }
    }

    public class Math
    {
        public int Factorial(int a)
        {
            if (a <= 1)
                return a;
            else
                return a * Factorial(a - 1);
        }
    }
}
```

Figure 2.3 demonstrates the execution model and the stack creation and lifetime.

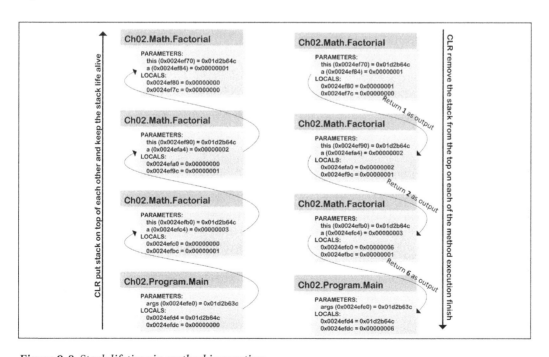

Figure 2-3. *Stack lifetime in method invocation*

From Figure 2-3 you can see that the CLR allocates Stack for the Main method as well as for the Factorial method on each call of this method. These stacks will be placed on top of each other. The CLR keeps this Stack alive until it finishes with the respective methods. Figure 2-3 also shows that the CLR removes the Stack of the relevant method from the top of the stack container as soon as it finishes with the method.

The Heap

The heap in .NET is used to store all the reference types, such as:

- Classes
- Interfaces
- Delegates
- Strings
- Instances of objects

The CLR stores the instances of the reference types in either the LOH or SOH (depending on the size of the objects). When the CLR instantiates any reference type, it instantiates on the heap and it assigns an address to it that refers to the stack or the place from where this instance of the reference type is referenced. Listing 2-4 is an example of a reference type instantiation and the related heap while executing the program.

Listing 2-4. An Example of TestClass Object into the Heap

```
namespace Ch02
{
    class Program
    {
        static void Main(string[] args)
        {
            TestClass testClass = new TestClass();
        }
    }

    public class TestClass
    {
    }
}
```

Although the CLR executes the above program in the Main method, it creates the instance (testClass) of the TestClass and stores that in the heap and assigns an address, for example, 0x0184b64c (address might be different on your machine while debug via windbg.exe) to it, as demonstrates in Figure 2-4.

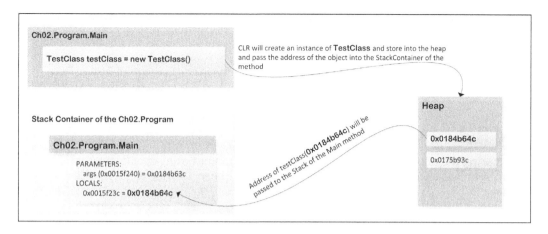

Figure 2-4. *The stack and heap combination showing how the CLR stores an object in the heap*

The address (0x0184b64c) is used later to access the object from the application, for instance, from the Main method. Figure 2-4 demonstrates that while CLR is executing the statement

```
TestClass testClass= new TestClass();
```

it creates an instance of the TestClass on the heap and assigns an address (0x0184b64c) to that instance into the heap while putting the address into the stack of the Main method for access. To explore this further, you can debug the executable produced by the above code listing in the windbg.exe and run the clrstack command, which will give the following information (address might be different when you debug locally) about the stack and memory address stored in the local variables of the Main method stack:

```
0:000> !clrstack -a
OS Thread Id: 0x158c (0)
Child SP IP        Call Site
0015f238 003d00a9 Ch02.Program.Main(System.String[]) [J:\Book\ExpertC#2012\SourceCode\
BookExamples\Ch02\Program.cs @ 8]
    PARAMETERS:
        args (0x0015f240) = 0x0184b63c
    LOCALS:
        0x0015f23c = 0x0184b64c /* Address of the TestClass */

0015f474 540121db [GCFrame: 0015f474]
```

From this code you can see the address 0x0015f23c in the LOCALS section of the stack is storing the address (0x0184b64c) of an instance of a reference type, in this case it is TestClass. To find out more about this object in windbg.exe, you can use the dumpobj command along with the address 0x0184b64c, which will give the following information (again the address might be different when you debug locally) as output about the TestClass:

```
0:000> !dumpobj 0x0184b64c
Name:          Ch02.TestClass
MethodTable:   00343884
EEClass:       00341494
Size:          12(0xc) bytes
```

```
File:              J:\Book\ExpertC#2012\SourceCode\BookExamples\Ch02\bin\Debug\Ch02.exe
Fields:
None
```

This demonstrates that the CLR instantiates a reference type on the heap and uses the address of that object from the stack to access it.

Value and Reference Types

In .NET, the CLR stores the value type in the stack unless you perform the boxing operation for the value type, under which circumstance the boxed type will be stored in the heap. The reference type will always store into the heap.

Let's examine this in depth, as shown in Listing 2-5, where byte, int, float, long, bool, char, IntPtr, and string are used to declare value type variables. The ReferenceType class is used to declare a reference type variable to show where the CLR stores this type in runtime.

Listing 2-5. Example of the Value and Reference Types

```csharp
using System;

namespace Ch02
{
    class Program
    {
        static void Main(string[] args)
        {
            byte        aByte           = 1;
            int         aInt            = 10;
            float       aFloat          = 10.5f;
            long        aLong           = 10;
            bool        aBool           = true;
            char        aChar           = 'C';
            IntPtr      aIntPtr         = IntPtr.Zero;
            string      aString         = "string literal";

            ReferenceType referenceType = new ReferenceType();

            Console.WriteLine("Finish the execution");
        }
    }

    public class ReferenceType { }
}
```

Based on Listing 2-5, the CLR allocates all the value types of the Main method into the stack, and the instance of the ReferenceType class (which instantiates on the heap) stores this in the stack of the Main method, which is used from the Main method when needed.

Let's explore the stack and heap status while executing the above program using windbg.exe. In this test you can use the clrstack -a command in the windbg.exe tool, which will produce the following output (address might be different when you debug locally):

```
0:000> !clrstack -a
OS Thread Id: 0x1148 (0)
Child SP IP      Call Site
001af084 002e0123 Ch02.Program.Main(System.String[]) [J:\Book\ExpertC#2012\SourceCode\
BookExamples\Ch02\Program.cs @ 20]
    PARAMETERS:
        args (0x001af0b0) = 0x01f9b63c
    LOCALS:
        0x001af0ac = 0x00000001 // 1
        0x001af0a8 = 0x0000000a // 10
        0x001af0a4 = 0x41280000 // 10.5f
        0x001af09c = 0x0000000a // 10
        0x001af098 = 0x00000001 // true
        0x001af094 = 0x00000043 // 'C'
        0x001af090 = 0x00000000 // IntPtr.Zero
        0x001af08c = 0x01f9b64c // instance of the String
        0x001af088 = 0x01f9b6b0 // instance of the ReferenceType

001af2e4 52b721db [GCFrame: 001af2e4]
```

From this output, all of the value types are stored as literal values of the respective types in the stack of the Main method, such as 0x00000001 for the 1, 0x0000000a for the 10, 0x41280000 for the 10.5f, 0x0000000a for the 10, 0x00000001 for the true, 0x00000043 for the C, 0x00000000 for the IntPtr.Zero stored as a literal value of the relevant type into the stack. The reference type instance, for example, the string and ReferenceType object, is stored in the stack with the address 0x01f9b64c for the aString variable and 0x01f9b6b0 for the ReferenceType.

In the next step, we will find details about information the object stored in the 0x01f9b64c and 0x01f9b6b0 addresses on the heap. If you explore the 0x01f9b64c address from the heap, you can see that the heap maintains object information in the heap with the following information (address might be different when you debug locally):

```
0:000> !dumpobj 0x01f9b64c
Name:        System.String
MethodTable: 520bf9ac
EEClass:     51df8bb0
Size:        42(0x2a) bytes
File:        C:\Windows\Microsoft.NET\assembly\GAC_32\
             mscorlib\v4.0_4.0.0.0__b77a5c561934e089\mscorlib.dll
String:      string literal
Fields:
MT       Field    Offset   Type            VT  Attr     Value   Name
520c2978 40000ed  4        System.Int32    1   instance 14      m_stringLength
520c1dc8 40000ee  8        System.Char     1   instance 73      m_firstChar
520bf9ac 40000ef  8        System.String   0   shared   static  Empty
    >> Domain:Value  00380c58:01f91228 <<

0:000> !dumpobj 0x01f9b6b0
Name:        Ch02.ReferenceType
MethodTable: 00233884
EEClass:     002314a4
Size:        12(0xc) bytes
```

```
File:            J:\Book\ExpertC#2012\SourceCode\BookExamples\Ch02\bin\Debug\Ch02.exe
Fields:
None
```

So the address 0x01f9b64c points to the instance of the string object and 0x01f9b6b0 to the instance of the ReferenceType from the heap.

Instantiating an Object

When you instantiate a type in .NET, it becomes an object that is the memory representation of that type. You can use the new keyword in .NET to instantiate an instance of the reference type. From the following program, you can find out how a class, interface, or struct type is instantiated by the CLR, as shown in Listing 2-6.

Listing 2-6. Example of Instantiation

```
namespace Ch02
{
    class Program
    {
        static void Main(string[] args)
        {
            int aInt = 2012;
            TestClass aTestClass = new TestClass();
            AInterface aInterfaceImplementation = new InterfaceImplementation();
            AStruct aAStruct = new AStruct();
        }
    }

    public class TestClass
    {
        public void TestMethod() {/*Code removed*/}
    }

    public interface AInterface
    {
        void AMethod();
    }

    public class InterfaceImplementation : AInterface
    {
        public void AMethod() {/*Code removed*/}
    }

    public struct AStruct
    {
        public int ANumber { get; set; }
    }
}
```

We can decompile this code into IL code using ildasm.exe, as demonstrated in Listing 2-7.

Listing 2-7. IL Code of Program

```
.class private auto ansi beforefieldinit Program
    extends [mscorlib]System.Object
{
    /* Code removed */
    .method private hidebysig static void Main(string[] args) cil managed
    {
        .entrypoint
        .maxstack 1
        .locals init (
            [0] int32 aInt,
            [1] class Ch02.TestClass aTestClass,
            [2] class Ch02.AInterface aInterfaceImplementation,
            [3] valuetype Ch02.AStruct aAStruct)

        L_0000: nop
        L_0001: ldc.i4 0x7dc
        L_0006: stloc.0

        /* CLR creates an instance of TestClass on the heap and
         * store the address of the instance into local stack location
         * 1 of this Main method */

        L_0007: newobj instance void Ch02.TestClass::.ctor()
        L_000c: stloc.1

        /* CLR creates an instance of InterfaceImplementation on the heap and
         * store the address of the instance into local stack location
         * 2 of this Main method */

        L_000d: newobj instance void Ch02.InterfaceImplementation::.ctor()
        L_0012: stloc.2

         /* CLR will load the local address of the aAStruct using ldloca
          * instruction and initialize the default value for that address
          * using initobj instruction */

        L_0013: ldloca.s aAStruct
        L_0015: initobj Ch02.AStruct
        L_001b: ret
    }
}
```

From the code in Listing 2-7, L_0007, CLR uses **newobj** IL instruction:

- It allocates a new instance of the class associated with .ctor and initializes all the fields in the new instance to 0 for the value type or null for the reference type.

- The CLR calls the constructor with the given arguments along with the newly created instance and the initialized object reference is pushed on the stack.

■ .ctor: This refers to the constructor in IL. In the Explore .ctor and .cctor using ildasm.exe section of Chapter 15, there is a discussion about .ctor and .cctor.

So while the above code executes through the CLR, it instantiates the reference type on the heap and assigns an address to it. The CLR then assigns that address back to the stack for later access. Let's explore the heap for the TestClass and InterfaceImplementation, as shown in this code:

```
0:000> !dumpheap -type TestClass
 Address        MT              Size
01d2b91c        00133938        12
total 0 objects
Statistics:
MT              Count      TotalSize      Class Name
00133938        1          12             Ch02.TestClass
Total 1 objects

0:000> !dumpheap -type InterfaceImplementation
 Address        MT      Size
01d2b928 00133a10        12
total 0 objects
Statistics:
MT              Count      TotalSize   Class Name
00133a10        1          12          Ch02.InterfaceImplementation
Total 1 objects
```

The TestClass and InterfaceImplementation are on the heap, and the CLR assigns address 01d2b91c for the instance of the TestClass and 01d2b928 for the InterfaceImplementation class. Figure 2-5 shows that the CLR stores the instances of the TestClass and InterfaceImplementation at the 01d2b91c and 01d2b928 addresses on the heap and stores these addresses to the stack of the Main method.

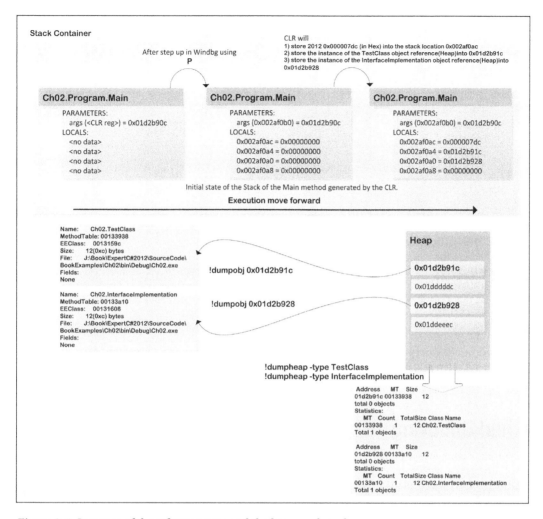

Figure 2-5. Instance of the reference type and the heap and stack

When we examine the stack of the Main method, you can see that 0x01d2b91c and 0x01d2b928 have been stored as local variables.

```
0:000> !clrstack -a
OS Thread Id: 0x7b8 (0)
Child SP IP      Call Site
002af098 003800e1 Ch02.Program.Main(System.String[]) [J:\Book\ExpertC#2012\SourceCode\
BookExamples\Ch02\Program.cs @ 13]
    PARAMETERS:
        args (0x002af0b0) = 0x01d2b90c
    LOCALS:
        0x002af0ac = 0x000007dc  /* literal of int 2012 */
        0x002af0a4 = 0x01d2b91c  /* Address of the TestClass */
        0x002af0a0 = 0x01d2b928  /* Address of the InterfaceImplementation */
```

```
        0x002af0a8 = 0x00000000
```

```
002af2e4 673621db [GCFrame: 002af2e4]
```

And the Object information,

```
0:000> !dumpobj 0x01d2b91c
Name:           Ch02.TestClass
MethodTable:    00133938
EEClass:        0013159c
Size:           12(0xc) bytes
File:           J:\Book\ExpertC#2012\SourceCode\BookExamples\Ch02\bin\Debug\Ch02.exe
Fields:
None
```

```
0:000> !dumpobj 0x01d2b928
Name:           Ch02.InterfaceImplementation
MethodTable:    00133a10
EEClass:        00131608
Size:           12(0xc) bytes
File:           J:\Book\ExpertC#2012\SourceCode\BookExamples\Ch02\bin\Debug\Ch02.exe
Fields:
None
```

And from this experiment you can see that struct does not instantiate on the heap (unless you box the struct), so there is no reference of it. You can see from the IL that it is created using the initObj instruction, which initializes the address of the struct local variable with a default value.

Boxing and Unboxing

Boxing is the process where the CLR uses the value type, such as int, float, long, and so forth, to wrap into an instance of the system.object type or more specifically into the related type. For example, the value of the int into the System.Int32 and the reverse will give a value, and this process is called *unboxing*. Listing 2-8 presents an example where the variable aInt of the type int has been declared.

Listing 2-8. An Example of Boxing and Unboxing

```
using System;

namespace Ch02
{
    class Program
    {
        static void Main(string[] args)
        {
            int aInt = 2012;
            string aStringLiteral = "Expert C# 5.0: with the .NET 4.5 Framework";
            TestClass testClass = new TestClass();

            Console.WriteLine("{0} {1}.",
                testClass. CastingString(aStringLiteral),
```

```
                    testClass.BoxInt(aInt));
        }
    }

    public class TestClass
    {

        public int BoxInt(object aInt)
        {
            int unboxedInt = 0;
            unboxedInt = (int)aInt;
            return unboxedInt;
        }

        public string CastingString(object aStringLieteral)
        {
            string unboxedString = string.Empty;
            unboxedString = (string)aStringLieteral;
            return unboxedString;
        }
    }
}
```

This program will produce the following output.

```
Expert C# 5.0: with the .NET 4.5 Framework.
```

In the TestClass the BoxInt method will accept an object type input. While executing the

```
testClass.BoxInt(aInt);
```

statement, the CLR will convert the aInt variable into an instance of the System.Int32 type, which will hold the value of the 2012, and passes this object to the BoxInt method. Listing 2-9 presents the IL code produced for Listing 2-8, extracted via **ildasm.exe**.

Listing 2-9. IL Code of the Program Class

```
.class private auto ansi beforefieldinit Program
    extends [mscorlib]System.Object
{
    /* Code removed */

    .method private hidebysig static void Main(string[] args) cil managed
    {
        .entrypoint
        .maxstack 4
        .locals init (
            [0] int32 aInt,
            [1] string aStringLiteral,
            [2] class Ch02.TestClass testClass)

        /* Code removed */
        L_001f: ldloc.2
```

```
            /* load the value from the local variable location
             * 0 into the evaluation stack*/
            L_0020: ldloc.0

            /* CLR will instantiate the type of the System.Int32
             * and store the top value from the evaluation stack
             * due to the box instruction.*/
            L_0021: box int32

            L_0026: callvirt instance int32 Ch02.TestClass::BoxInt(object)
            L_002b: box int32
            L_0030: call void [mscorlib]System.Console::WriteLine(string, object, object)
            L_0035: nop
            L_0036: ret
        }
}
```

From the IL code in Listing 2-9, you can see that in the runtime the CLR will load the value from the local variable section of the Main method stack into the evaluation stack in the L_0020 label. In the execution of the IL instruction in L_0021, the CLR will instantiate an instance of the System.Int32 with a top value from the evaluation stack. Figure 2-6 illustrates the boxing process.

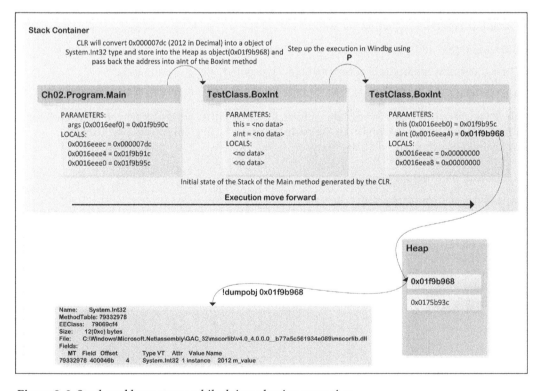

Figure 2-6. *Stack and heap status while doing a boxing operation*

From Figure 2-6, you can see that in the stack of the BoxInt method the aInt variable is holding an address (0x01f9b968) of the object from the heap that is being created by the IL instruction box and holding the value 2012. If you explore the address 0x01f9b968 in windbg.exe, you will find the memory information about the object, for example:

```
0:000> !dumpobj 0x01f9b968
Name:         System.Int32
MethodTable:  79332978
EEClass:      79069cf4
Size:         12(0xc) bytes
File:         C:\Windows\Microsoft.NET\assembly\GAC_32\
              mscorlib\v4.0_4.0.0.0__b77a5c561934e089\mscorlib.dll
Fields:
MT       Field      Offset  Type          VT  Attr      Value  Name
79332978 400046b    4       System.Int32  1   instance  2012   m_value
```

The stack information for the Main method will show that the aInt variable in the LOCALS section holds the address of 0x01f9b968.

```
0:000> !clrstack -a
OS Thread Id: 0x1618 (0)
Child SP IP        Call Site
0016eea4 003e0244 Ch02.TestClass.BoxInt(System.Object) [J:\Book\ExpertC#2012\SourceCode\
BookExamples\Ch02\Program.cs @ 22]
    PARAMETERS:
        this (0x0016eeb0) = 0x01f9b95c
        aInt (0x0016eea4) = 0x01f9b968 /* a object stored onto the Heap */
    LOCALS:
        0x0016eeac = 0x00000000
        0x0016eea8 = 0x00000000

0016eebc 003e010d Ch02.Program.Main(System.String[]) [J:\Book\ExpertC#2012\SourceCode\
BookExamples\Ch02\Program.cs @ 12]
    PARAMETERS:
        args (0x0016eef0) = 0x01f9b90c
    LOCALS:
        0x0016eeec = 0x000007dc /* 2012 */
        0x0016eee4 = 0x01f9b91c
        0x0016eee0 = 0x01f9b95c

0016f120 673621db [GCFrame: 0016f120]
```

While unboxing, the CLR will get the value from the boxed object and initialize a literal value for the same boxed type. For example, as in Listing 2-8, the unboxing type for the aInt will be **int32**. The decompiled IL code of the **TestClass** is shown in Listing 2-10.

Listing 2-10. IL Code for the TestClass

```
.class public auto ansi beforefieldinit TestClass
    extends [mscorlib]System.Object
{
    /* Code removed*/
    .method public hidebysig instance int32 BoxInt(object aInt) cil managed
```

```
    {
        .maxstack 1
        .locals init (
            [0] int32 unboxedInt,
            [1] int32 CS$1$0000)

        /* CLR will load the argument 1 which is the boxed value
         * of the aInt variable passed from the Main method.*/
        L_0003: ldarg.1

        /* CLR will convert the value of aInt object into the value
         * of the int32 and store into the local variable location 0
         * for the unboxedInt variable */
        L_0004: unbox.any int32
        L_0009: stloc.0

        L_000a: ldloc.0
        L_000b: stloc.1
        L_000c: br.s L_000e
        L_000e: ldloc.1
        L_000f: ret
    }

    .method public hidebysig instance string CastingString(
        object aStringLieteral) cil managed
    {
        .maxstack 1
        .locals init (
            [0] string unboxedString,
            [1] string CS$1$0000)
        L_0000: nop
        L_0001: ldsfld string [mscorlib]System.String::Empty
        L_0006: stloc.0
        L_0007: ldarg.1
        L_0008: castclass string
        L_000d: stloc.0
        L_000e: ldloc.0
        L_000f: stloc.1
        L_0010: br.s L_0012
        L_0012: ldloc.1
        L_0013: ret
    }
}
```

So in the process of unboxing, CLR will unbox the value from the object referred by 0x01f9b968 into its value and store it in the local variable 0x0016eeac, as demonstrated in Figure 2-7.

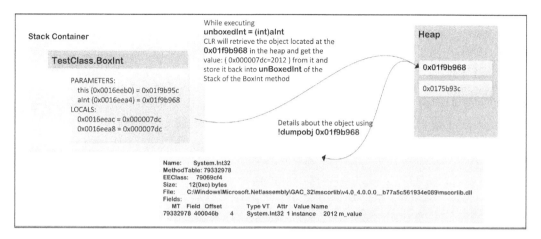

Figure 2-7. Stack and heap status while doing an unboxing operation

Let's explore this in the runtime using windbg.exe program to see the stack information while the CLR is executing the BoxInt method of the TestClass shown in Listing 2-8. In the windbg.exe command prompt, if you run clrstack -a you will get the following memory information (address might be different when you debug locally):

```
0:000> !clrstack -a
OS Thread Id: 0x1618 (0)
Child SP IP       Call Site
0016eea4 003e0271 Ch02.TestClass.BoxInt(System.Object) [J:\Book\ExpertC#2012\SourceCode\
BookExamples\Ch02\Program.cs @ 25]
    PARAMETERS:
        this (0x0016eeb0)      = 0x01f9b95c
        aInt (0x0016eea4)      = 0x01f9b968 /* a object stored onto the Heap */
    LOCALS:
        0x0016eeac      = 0x000007dc /* 2012 */
        0x0016eea8      = 0x000007dc

0016eebc 003e010d Ch02.Program.Main(System.String[]) [J:\Book\ExpertC#2012\SourceCode\
BookExamples\Ch02\Program.cs @ 12]
    PARAMETERS:
        args (0x0016eef0) = 0x01f9b90c
    LOCALS:
        0x0016eeec = 0x000007dc
        0x0016eee4 = 0x01f9b91c
        0x0016eee0 = 0x01f9b95c

0016f120 673621db [GCFrame: 0016f120]
```

In the BoxInt method, CLR stores the unboxed value (0x000007dc equivalent decimal is 2012) to get from the boxed type instance located on the heap at 0x01f9b968 into the 0x0016eeac address of the LOCALS section of the BoxInt method stack. In day-to-day programming, you use boxing and unboxing without noticing, for example, in the following code using boxing and unboxing underneath:

```
ArrayList aListOfNumbers = new ArrayList();
aListOfNumbers.Add(1);
aListOfNumbers.Add(2);
int result = (int)aListOfNumbers[1];
```

The decompiled IL code for this code demonstrates how the CLR uses the boxing and unboxing operation for the item to go in and out of the ArrayList:

```
.method private hidebysig static void Main(string[] args) cil managed
{
    /* Code removed */

    /* The CLR does the boxing in the insertion into the
     * ArrayList while executing the Add method of the ArrayList.
     */
    L_0009: box int32
    L_000e: callvirt instance int32
            [mscorlib]System.Collections.ArrayList::Add(object)
    /* Code removed */

    /* The CLR does the boxing in the insertion into the
     * ArrayList while executing the Add method of the ArrayList.
     */
    L_0016: box int32
    L_001b: callvirt instance int32
            [mscorlib]System.Collections.ArrayList::Add(object)
    /* Code removed */

    L_0023: callvirt instance object
            [mscorlib]System.Collections.ArrayList::get_Item(int32)
    /* The CLR unbox the return value from the get_Item while executing
     * (int)aListOfNumbers[1] line of code.
     */
    L_0028: unbox.any int32
    L_002d: stloc.1
    L_002e: ret
}
```

Performance in Boxing and Unboxing Operation

Boxing and unboxing are time-consuming processes that might affect the performance of an application. The boxing operation can take up to 20 times more time than the assignment operation. The right use of the boxing operation is important when the performance is the key factor for your application. Let's find out how boxing and unboxing operations affect the performance of an application. In Listing 2-11, a list of int is stored in the instance of the List<int> type. And Listing 2-12 uses ArrayList for storage.

Listing 2-11. List Creation

```
using System;
using System.Collections.Generic;
namespace Ch02
```

```
{
    class Program
    {
        static void Main(string[] args)
        {
            IList<int> ll = new List<int>();
            for (int i = 0; i <= Int16.MaxValue * 2; ++i)
                ll.Add(i);
            foreach (int st in ll) ;
        }
    }
}
```

Listing 2-12. *ArrayList Creation*

```
using System;
using System.Collections;

namespace Ch02
{
    class Program
    {
        static void Main(string[] args)
        {
            ArrayList ll = new ArrayList();
            for (int i = 0; i <= Int16.MaxValue * 2; ++i)
                ll.Add(i);
            foreach (int st in ll) ;
        }
    }
}
```

Figure 2-8 profiles Listings 2-11 and 2-12 using the ClrProfiler.exe tool to find out how much memory the ArrayList consumes while adding items into it compared to using List<int>.

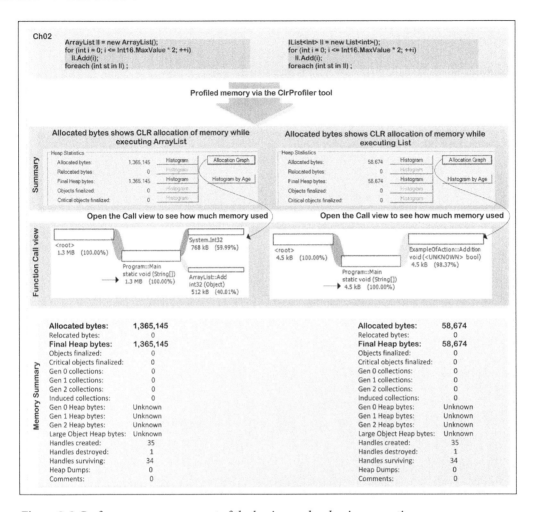

Figure 2-8. Performance measurement of the boxing and unboxing operation

Figure 2-8 demonstrates that the ArrayList consumes about 1,365,145 bytes, whereas the List class consumes only 58,674 bytes for the same number of items. As you saw earlier, the ArrayList uses the boxing and unboxing operation to move items in and out of it, which requires a lot of memory. The List class does not use the boxing and unboxing operation, which makes it more effective in performance compared with using ArrayList.

Garbage Collection

When you create an instance of a type in .NET, for example, a reference type, using the new keyword, the CLR takes care of the rest. For example, it will instantiate it onto the heap, allocate extra memory if required, and deallocate the memory when you finish with that object. The CLR takes care of this memory reclaim process using the GC. The GC maintains information about object usage and uses this information to make memory management decisions, such as where in the memory to locate a newly created object, when to relocate an object, and when an object is no longer in use or inaccessible.

In .NET, automatic memory cleanup is achieved using the GC algorithm. The GC algorithm looks for the allocated objects on the heap and tries to determine if that object is being referenced by anything; if it is not, it will allocate it for collection or to the cleanup cycle. There are several possible sources of these references:

- Global or static object references

- Central processing unit (CPU) registers

- Object finalization references (more later)

- Interop references (.NET objects passed to Component Object Model (COM)/ Application programming interface (API) calls)

- Stack references

To clean up the objects, GC needs to traverse a number of objects to determine whether they can be collected for cleanup. The CLR uses the concept of longibility of the object in the memory. For example, when the object is in use for a long time, it is less likely to lose the reference, whereas a newly created object is more likely to be cleaned up.

In GC, three generations of object groups are used:

- Generation 0

- Generation 1

- Generation 2

Generation 0

Generation 0 (Gen 0) is the youngest group and it contains short-lived objects. An example of a short-lived object is a temporary variable. GC occurs most frequently in this generation. Newly allocated objects form a new generation of objects and are implicitly Gen 0 collections, unless they are large objects, in which case they go on the LOH in a Gen 2 collection. Most objects are reclaimed for GC in Gen 0 and do not survive to the next generation.

Generation 1

Gen 1 contains short-lived objects and serves as a buffer between short-lived objects and long-lived objects.

Generation 2

Gen 2 contains long-lived objects. An example of a long-lived object is a server application that contains static data that are live for the duration of the process.

The life of an object starts in Gen 0. If the objects in Gen 0 survive, GC promotes them to Gen 1, and likewise for Gen 1 objects to Gen 2. The objects in Gen 2 stay in Gen 2. Gen 0 objects are collected frequently, so short-lived objects are quickly removed. Gen 1 objects are collected less frequently, and Gen 2 objects even less frequently. So the longer an object lives, the longer it takes to remove from memory once it has lost all references. When Gen 1 objects are collected, the GC gathers Gen 0 objects as well. In addition, when Gen 2 objects are collected, those in Gen 1 and Gen 0 are also collected. As a result, higher generation collections are more expensive.

A GC has the following phases to clean up the objects:

- A marking phase that finds and creates a list of all live objects.

- A relocating phase that updates the references to the objects that will be compacted.

- A compacting phase that reclaims the space occupied by the dead objects and compacts the surviving objects. The compacting phase moves objects that have survived GC toward the older end of the segment.

The Gen 2 collections can occupy multiple segments; objects that are promoted into Gen 2 can be moved into an older segment. Both Gen 1 and Gen 2 survivors can be moved to a different segment, because they are promoted to Gen 2.

The LOH is not compacted, because this would increase memory usage over an unacceptable length of time.

Summary

In this chapter we have learned about the usage of the memory by the CLR when it executes an managed application. We have examined the stack and the heap, how they are used by the CLR to store data for the value type and reference type in the application, and the steps in boxing and unboxing operations. We also saw how the boxing and unboxing operation affects the performance of the application. In the next chapter, we will learn how the parameter in .NET sets the value and reference type parameter, what happens when you pass the parameter using the out and ref keywords, and how CLR takes care of the named parameter.

CHAPTER 3

■ ■ ■

Parameters

This chapter will discuss the parameters in C#. The focus will be to show different ways of passing parameters to a method, such as pass by value, pass by reference, and pass default value of the parameter. You will find explanations of these in detail and see how CLR handles these behind the scene.

Parameter

The parameter is the mechanism used to accept input to a method from the caller of that method. In a method signature, you can define the parameter or parameters to accept the input. These parameters could be any type, such as value types, for example, Int32, string, or reference type for an instance object, a person object of Person type, and so forth.

Figure 3-1 shows the parameters used in the method signature definition.

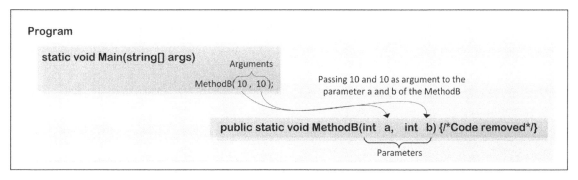

Figure 3-1. *Parameter and arguments in C#*

When you are accepting value from the caller of the method, the caller can pass just the value to the parameter or pass the reference of the variable and so on. Table 3-1 shows the different types of parameter accepting strategies you can use in a method declaration.

Table 3-1. Parameter Passing Conventions

Type of data	Pass by	How data are sent
Built-in value type (int, float, etc.)	Value	The data are copied to the called method; the type is statically known at both sides.
	Reference	The address of a variable is sent to the called method; the type is statically known at both sides.
	Typed reference	The address of a variable is sent along with the type of information to the called method.
User-defined value type	Value	The called method receives a copy; the type is statically known at both sides.
	Reference	The address of the reference type is sent to the called method; the type is statically known at both sides.
	Typed reference	The address is sent along with the type information to the called method.
Object	Value	The reference to data is sent to the called method; the type is statically known and the class is available from the reference.
	Reference	The address of the reference is sent to the called method; the type is statically known and the class is available from the reference.
	Typed reference	The address of the reference is sent to the called method along with static type information; the class (i.e., dynamic type) is available from the reference.

Method State Description Table

Method state describes the environment within which a method executes, and the method state description table is the temporary storage where CLR keeps information relating to a method while executing that method. Figure 3-2 shows different components of the method state table.

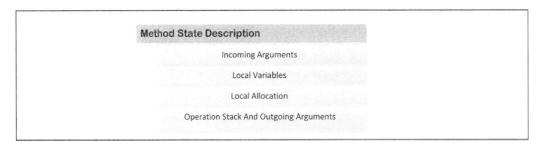

Figure 3-2. Method state description table

Let's examine the details for the different components of the method state description table.

An Instruction Pointer

The instruction pointer (IP) is used to point to the next Common Intermediate Language (CIL) instruction to be executed by the Common Language Infrastructure (CLI) in the present method.

An Evaluation Stack

In .NET, the method in runtime contains an evaluation stack. The stack is empty upon method entry. The contents of the stack are local to the method and preserved across call instructions. The addresses in the evaluation stack are not addressable.

A Local Variable Array

An array of local variables will start at index 0. The values of local variables are preserved across calls (in the same sense as for the evaluation stack). A local variable can hold any data type. The address of an individual local variable can be taken using the `ldloca` instruction.

An Argument Array

The argument array will hold the values of the current method's incoming arguments and will start at index 0. This argument array can be read and written by the logical index. The `ldarga` IL instruction can be used to take the address of an argument.

A Method Info Handle

The method info handle holds the signature of the method, the types of its local variables, and data about its exception handlers. This contains read-only information about the method.

A Local Memory Pool

The CLI includes instructions for dynamic allocation of objects from the local memory pool (`localloc`). Memory allocated in the local memory pool is addressable and is reclaimed upon method context termination.

A Return State Handle

The return state handle is used to restore the method state on return from the current method. Typically, this would be the state of the method's caller.

A Security Descriptor

The security descriptor is not directly accessible to the managed code but is used by the CLI security system to record security overrides.

Value Type

This section will describe how the CLR takes care of the value type parameter during the method call.

Parameter by Value

Parameter by value is one of the common ways to pass the value type. The CLR will pass a copy of the value as an argument to the method. In Listing 3-1, you can see that in the BuiltInValuePassingAsValue class, MethodB accepts two parameters, a and b, of the built-in value type, such as int. MethodA calls the MethodB method with int value 10 and 10 as an argument, as shown in Figure 3-3.

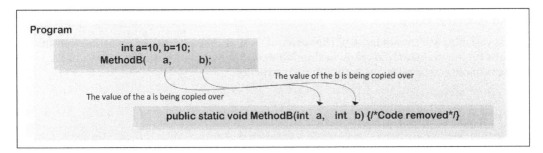

Figure 3-3. Parameter passing by value for the value type

When the program in Listing 3-1 executes, the CLR will call MethodB(a,b) from the MethodA. It will copy the value of a and b to the MethodB, so the MethodB will have the copy of the value a and b as demonstrated in Figure 3-3. Listing 3-1 presents where the built-in value is used to pass parameters.

Listing 3-1. An Example of the Built-In Value Type Parameter as a Value

```
using System;

namespace Ch03
{
    class Program
    {
        static void Main(string[] args)
        {
            BuiltInValuePassingAsValue temp = new BuiltInValuePassingAsValue();
            temp.MethodA();
        }
    }

    public class BuiltInValuePassingAsValue
    {
        public BuiltInValuePassingAsValue()
        { Console.WriteLine("Built in value type passing as value"); }

        public void MethodA()
        {
```

```
        int a = 10, b = 10;
        MethodB(a, b);
        Console.WriteLine("Method A: {0},{1}", a, b);
    }

    public void MethodB(int a, int b)
    { Console.WriteLine("Method B: {0},{1}", a, b);  }
    }
}
```

The program in Listing 3-1 will produce the following output:

```
Built in value type passing as value
Method B: 10,10
Method A: 10,10
```

Let's explore more about the program in Listing 3-1 by examining the stack and heap while the program in Listing 3-1 is being executed.

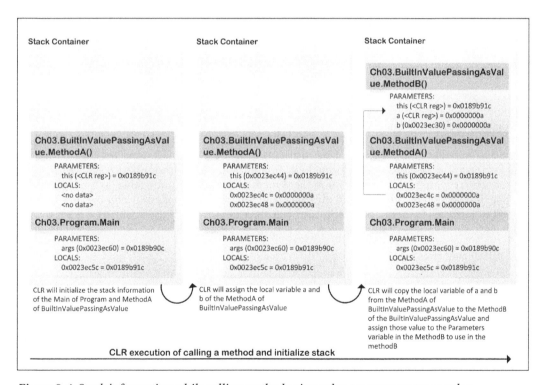

Figure 3-4. Stack information while calling method using value type parameter as value

In Figure 3-4, you can see that while CLR calls the MethodB from the MethodA method it passes the value of the a(10=0xa) and b(10=0xa), and these values get stored in the LOCALS section of the MethodB method. As a result, any change of those values will not affect the value of the a and b in MethodA.

Let's see the IL code generated using the .NET Reflector tool for the MethodA from Listing 3-1, as shows in Listing 3-2, to explore more about the parameter pass by value of the value type.

Listing 3-2. *IL Code for the MethodA() of the BuiltInValuePassingAsValue*

```
.method public hidebysig instance void MethodA() cil managed
{
    .maxstack 3
    .locals init (
        [0] int32 a,
        [1] int32 b)

    L_0000: ldc.i4.s 10      /* The CLR push numeric constant 10 onto the stack */
    L_0002: stloc.0          /* Pop the value 10 from stack into local variable
                              * at position 0.*/
    L_0003: ldc.i4.s 10      /* The CLR push numeric constant 10 onto the stack */
    L_0005: stloc.1          /* Pop the value 10 from stack into local variable
                              * at position 1.*/
    L_0006: ldarg.0
    L_0007: ldloc.0          /* Load local variable at position 0 from the Local
                              * section of the MethodA onto stack.*/
    L_0008: ldloc.1          /* Load local variable at position 1 from the Local
                              * section of the MethodA onto stack.*/

    L_0009: call instance void Ch03.BuiltInValuePassingAsValue::MethodB(int32, int32)
    //Code removed
    L_0024: ret
}
```

From Listing 3-2 you can see that, in L_0007 and L_0008, ldloc.0 and ldloc.1 IL instruction has been used that will load the local variable's value from the Local variable section of the MethodA's method state description table at location 0 and 1, which will be 10 and 10, onto the evaluation stack. The call instruction in the L_0009 passes those values from the evaluation stack to the method MethodB. The CLR copies those values to the argument array of the MethodB method state description table (as the incoming arguments' array has been set by the CLR from the caller with the related values), and later in the MethodB, those values will be retrieved for the parameters a and b by the CLR.

---

ldc.<type>: Load numeric constant

stloc: Pop value from stack to local variable

ldloc: Load local variable onto the stack

maxstack: Does not represent the size of the stack at runtime but is related to analysis of the program specially for the IL verification.

.locals init: Used to define a variable in the current method. The init keyword means the local variables will be initialized at runtime before the method executes.

To explore this more, see the generated IL code for the MethodB from Listing 3-1 as shown in Listing 3-3.

Listing 3-3. IL Code for the MethodB() of the BuiltInValuePassingAsValue

```
.method public hidebysig instance void  MethodB(int32 a, int32 b) cil managed
{
    .maxstack 8
    L_0000: ldstr "Method B: {0},{1}"

    L_0005: ldarg.1      /* ldarg.1 load the argument at position 1 onto the
                          * evaluation stack */
    L_0006: box int32

    L_000b: ldarg.2      /* ldarg.2 load the argument at position 2 onto the
                          * evaluation stack */
    L_000c: box int32

    /* Get the values from the evaluation stack and pass as argument of the WriteLine method */
    L_0011: call void [mscorlib]System.Console::WriteLine(string, object, object)
    L_0016: ret
}
```

From Listing 3-3, you can see that in L_0005 and L_000b, CLR loads the values from the argument array at positions 1 and 2, which will be 10 and 10, onto the evaluation stack. Those values will be used to pass an argument in L_0011 to call the WriteLine method of the Console class.

Parameter by ref

Let's see how the built-in value type works while passing as a reference using the ref keyword. The program as shown in Listing 3-4 passes the built-in value type as a reference to a method, which accepts a built-in value type as the reference. When the CLR calls the MethodB(ref a, ref b) from the MethodA, it copies the address of the a and b to the MethodB. So the MethodB will have the address of a and b variables as demonstrated in Figure 3-5.

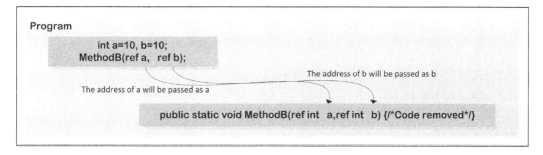

Figure 3-5. Parameter passing as ref

In the program in Listing 3-4, MethodB accepts two int-type parameters as references using the ref keyword.

Listing 3-4. Parameter Passing by ref for the Value Type

```
using System;

namespace Ch03
{
    class Program
    {
        static void Main(string[] args)
        {
            BuiltInValuePassingAsRef temp = new BuiltInValuePassingAsRef();
            temp.MethodA();
        }
    }

    public class BuiltInValuePassingAsRef
    {
        public BuiltInValuePassingAsRef()
        {
            Console.WriteLine("Built in value type passing as ref");
        }

        public void MethodA()
        {
            int a = 10, b = 10;
            MethodB(ref a, ref b);
            Console.WriteLine("Method A: {0},{1}", a, b);
        }

        public void MethodB(ref int a, ref int b)
        {
            Console.WriteLine("Method B: {0},{1}", a, b);
            a *= 2; b *= 2;
        }
    }
}
```

The program in Listing 3-4 produces the following output:

```
Built in value type passing as ref
Method B: 10,10
Method A: 20,20
```

To explore this more, see the generated IL code for the MethodA from Listing 3-4 and as shown in Listing 3-5.

Listing 3-5. IL Code for the MethodA of the BuiltInValuePassingAsRef

```
.method public hidebysig instance void MethodA() cil managed
{
    .maxstack 3
    .locals init (
        [0] int32 a,
```

```
        [1] int32 b)

    L_0000: ldc.i4.s 10          /* The CLR push numeric constant 10 onto the
                                   * stack */
    L_0002: stloc.0              /* Pop the value 10 from stack into local variable
                                   * at position 0.*/
    L_0003: ldc.i4.s 10          /* The CLR push numeric constant 10 onto the
                                   * stack */
    L_0005: stloc.1              /* Pop the value 10 from stack into local variable
                                   * at position 1.*/
    L_0006: ldarg.0

    L_0007: ldloca.s a           /* Load the address of the a variable from the
                                   * Local section of the method stack */

    L_0009: ldloca.s b           /* Load the address of the b variable from the
                                   * Local section of the method stack */

    /* Pass the address of the a and b as argument to the MethodB call */
    L_000b: call instance void Ch03.BuiltInValuePassingAsRef::MethodB(int32&, int32&)

    //Code removed
    L_0026: ret
}
```

---

ldloca.<length>: Load local variable address. The ldloca instruction pushes the address of the local variable number index onto the stack, where local variables are numbered 0 upward.

In Listing 3-5, you can see the ldloca.s instruction used in L_0007 and L_0009, which loads the addresses of the local variables a and b onto the evaluation stack and are later used to call the MethodB method in L_000b. The CLR copies the addresses of a and b into the argument array of the method state description table of the MethodB, which are later used to retrieve the value of the a and b variables.

To explore this more, see the generated IL code for MethodB from Listing 3-4 as shown in Listing 3-6.

Listing 3-6. IL Code for the MethodB to Process Built-In Value Type ref Parameter

```
.method public hidebysig instance void  MethodB(int32& a, int32& b) cil managed
{
    .maxstack 8
    L_0000: ldstr "Method B: {0},{1}"

    /* ldarg.1 load the argument at position 1 onto the evaluation stack */
    L_0005: ldarg.1

    /* Get the address of the a from the top of the stack (loaded in L_0005) and
     * using that address the CLR load the value of the variable located at
     * that address.*/
    L_0006: ldind.i4
    L_0007: box int32
```

```
    /* ldarg.2 load the argument at position 2 onto the evaluation stack */
    L_000c: ldarg.2

    /* Get the address from the top of the stack (loaded in L_000c) and using
     * that address the CLR load the value of the variable located at that address.*/
    L_000d: ldind.i4
    L_000e: box int32

    L_0013: call void [mscorlib]System.Console::WriteLine(string, object, object)

    L_0018: ldarg.1
    L_0019: dup
    L_001a: ldind.i4
    L_001b: ldc.i4.2
    L_001c: mul

    /* Store the value from the evaluation stack to the specified address */
    L_001d: stind.i4

    L_001e: ldarg.2
    L_001f: dup
    L_0020: ldind.i4
    L_0021: ldc.i4.2
    L_0022: mul
    L_0023: stind.i4
    L_0024: ret
}
```

ldind.<type>: Loads value indirectly onto the stack. It indirectly loads a value from address addr onto the stack.

stind.<type>: Stores the value indirect from the stack. The stind instruction stores value val at address addr.

In Listing 3-6, the IL instruction ldarg.1 is used in the L_0005 to load the first argument value (i.e., the address of variable a of the MethodA method) from the argument array of the method state description table of the MethodB method onto the evaluation stack. The next instruction ldind.i4 in L_0006 will load a value from the address (which just pushed onto the stack using IL instruction in L_0005). The same technique is used in L_000c to L_000e to load the variable b of MethodA. These values are later used to write output in L_0013.

As you know, if you change the contents of variable a or b from this method, this will update the contents of variable a and b, which can be seen from the MethodA. In the L_0018 to L_001c, the contents of the variable a of the MethodA have been modified, later using stind.i4 in the L_001d, which will store the new updated value into the relevant address. The same techniques are used to update the value of variable b of MethodA in the L_001e to L_0024.

Let's explore this more by examining the stack and heap while we are executing the program in Listing 3-4.

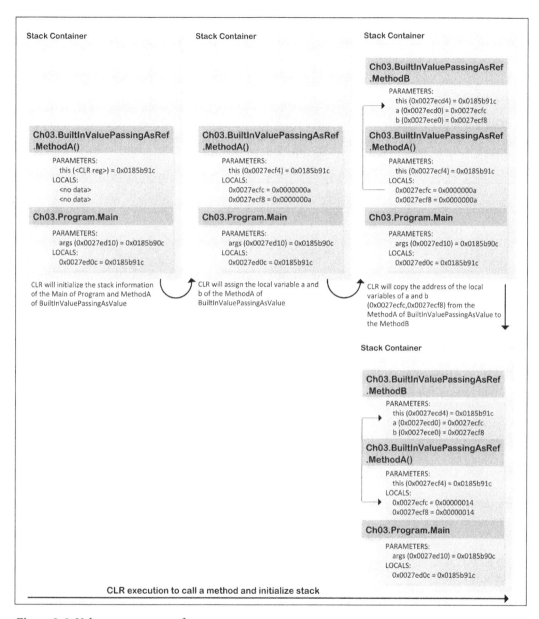

Figure 3-6. *Value type pass as reference*

In Figure 3-6, you can see that while CLR calls the MethodB from the MethodA method, it passes the addresses of the variables a(0x0027ecfc) and b(0x0027ecf8), and these addresses get stored in the PARAMETERS section of the MethodB method. As a result, any change of those values affects the original value of the a and b in MethodA.

Reference Type

This section will explain how the CLR takes care of the reference type parameter during the method call.

Parameter by Value

This section describes how CLR deals with the reference type when it passes a value. In Listing 3-7, in the ObjectAsValue class, MethodB is accepting a parameter of Person type from the MethodA, the MethodB is called with an instance of the Person type as an argument, as shown in Figure 3-7.

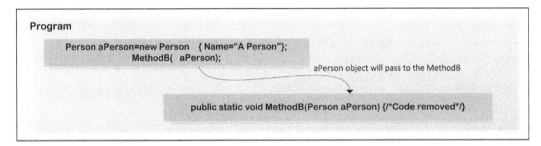

Figure 3-7. *Parameter passing with object as value type*

When the CLR calls the MethodB(Person aPerson) from MethodA, it will copy the aPerson object to the argument array of the method state description table of the MethodB so the MethodB will have the aPerson object, as shown in Listing 3-7.

Listing 3-7. *Object Passing as Value in Parameter Passing*

```
using System;

namespace Ch03
{
    class Program
    {
        static void Main(string[] args)
        {
            ObjectAsValue temp = new ObjectAsValue();
            temp.MethodA();
        }
    }

    public class ObjectAsValue
    {
        public ObjectAsValue()
        {
            Console.WriteLine("Object as value");
        }
        public void MethodA()
        {
            Person aPerson = new Person()
```

```
        {
            Name = "APerson"
        };
        MethodB(aPerson);
        Console.WriteLine("Method A: {0}", aPerson.Name);
    }
    public void MethodB(Person aPerson)
    {
        Console.WriteLine("Method B: {0}", aPerson.Name);
        aPerson.Name = "Updated" + aPerson.Name;
    }
}

public class Person
{
    public string Name
    { get; set; }
}
}
```

The program in Listing 3-7 produces the following output:

```
Object as value
Method B: APerson
Method A: UpdatedAPerson
```

To explore this more, let's see the generated IL code for MethodA from Listing 3-7 as shown in Listing 3-8.

Listing 3-8. IL Code of the Program in Listing 3-7

```
.method public hidebysig instance void MethodA() cil managed
{
    .maxstack 2
    .locals init (
        [0] class Ch03.Person aPerson,
        [1] class Ch03.Person <>g__initLocal0)

    L_0000: newobj instance void Ch03.Person::.ctor()
    L_0005: stloc.1
    L_0006: ldloc.1
    L_0007: ldstr "APerson"
    L_000c: callvirt instance void Ch03.Person::set_Name(string)
    L_0011: ldloc.1
    L_0012: stloc.0

    L_0013: ldarg.0
    L_0014: ldloc.0
    L_0015: call instance void Ch03.ObjectAsValue::MethodB(class Ch03.Person)

    L_001a: ldstr "Method A: {0}"
    L_001f: ldloc.0
```

```
        L_0020: callvirt instance string Ch03.Person::get_Name()
        L_0025: call void [mscorlib]System.Console::WriteLine(string, object)
        L_002a: ret
}
```

In this IL code, two local variables have been stored at positions 0 and 1, such as aPerson and <>g__ initLocal0, which is an instance of the Person type. In L_0000 to L_0011, an instance of the Person type will be created and the CLR will load that instance to the local variable at position 1, which will later store it at position 0, which is the aPerson object.

In L_0013, the IL code ldarg.0 will load the argument value from the position 0 and in L_0014 the IL code ldloc.0 will load the current local variable at position 0, which will be used as the argument of the method call for MethodB in the L_0015. Therefore, you can see that this is passed as a value to the method call MethodB. Figure 3-8 shows the stack–heap relationship in the memory while executing the code in Listing 3-7.

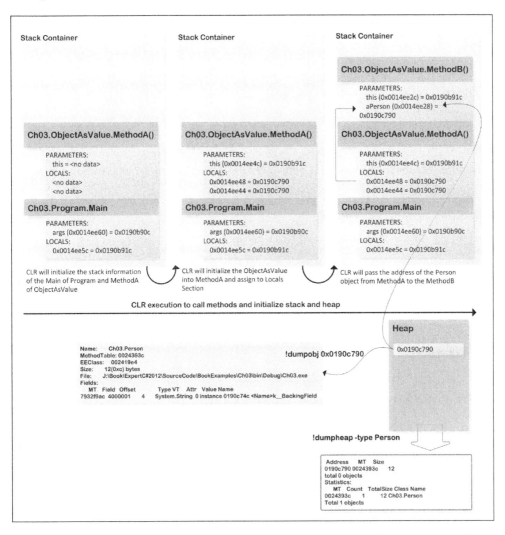

Figure 3-8. Stack and heap information while passing the parameter of an object as a value

You can see the IL code in Listing 3-9 for the MethodB, and you can see that in L_0005, ldarg.1 is used to load the argument value of aPerson and later on to call the get_Name() method from the aPerson object passed from MethodA.

Listing 3-9. IL Code of MethodB

```
.method public hidebysig instance void  MethodB(class Ch03.Person aPerson) cil managed
{
    .maxstack 8
    L_0000: ldstr "Method B: {0}"

    L_0005: ldarg.1
    L_0006: callvirt instance string Ch03.Person::get_Name()

    L_000b: call void [mscorlib]System.Console::WriteLine(string, object)

    L_0010: ldarg.1
    L_0011: ldstr "Updated"
    L_0016: ldarg.1
    L_0017: callvirt instance string Ch03.Person::get_Name()
    L_001c: call string [mscorlib]System.String::Concat(string, string)

    L_0021: callvirt instance void Ch03.Person::set_Name(string)

    L_0026: ret
}
```

In L_0021, the set_Name(string) method of the Person class has been called to update the value of the Name property, and get_Name() and set_Name(string) are the internal methods for the property Name of the aPerson object. When you pass an object of reference type as an argument of method call (which accepts an object of the related type), you can modify the value of the public property of that object. But if you try to update the object itself (i.e., replace the existing contents of the aPerson object with the new instance of the Person object), as demonstrated in Listing 3-10, it will not be visible in MethodA.

Listing 3-10. Updated Code in MethodB

```
public void MethodB(Person aPerson)
{
    Console.WriteLine("Method B: {0}", aPerson.Name);
    aPerson = new Person()
    {
        Name = "New name"
    };
}
```

To explore this more, see the generated IL code for MethodB from Listing 3-10 as shown in Listing 3-11.

Listing 3-11. IL Code for Listing 3-10.

```
.method public hidebysig instance void MethodB(class Ch03.Person aPerson) cil managed
{
    .maxstack 2
    .locals init (
```

```
          [0] class Ch03.Person <>g__initLocal1)
    L_0000: ldstr "Method B: {0}"
    L_0005: ldarg.1
    L_0006: callvirt instance string Ch03.Person::get_Name()
    L_000b: call void [mscorlib]System.Console::WriteLine(string, object)
    L_0010: newobj instance void Ch03.Person::.ctor()

    L_0015: stloc.0
    L_0016: ldloc.0
    L_0017: ldstr "New name"
    L_001c: callvirt instance void Ch03.Person::set_Name(string)

    L_0021: ldloc.0

    L_0022: starg.s aPerson

    L_0024: ret
}
```

The IL instruction ldloc.0 in L_0021 will load the local variable at position 0, which is <>g__ initLocal0, onto the evaluation stack and, using the starg.s aPerson instruction, CLR will load this new <>g_initLocal0 object into the argument, which holds the aPerson object. However, this new value will never come across to MethodA. Therefore, the contents of the original object will never be replaced, but to do this you will need to pass the reference of the object to the method call, as discuss in the next section.

---

starg.s: The starg instruction pops a value from the stack and places it in the argument slot at a specific position.

Parameter by ref

The reference of a type passes as a reference to the method call. In ObjectAsValue class, MethodB is accepting a parameter of Person type as a reference, and the MethodB is being called from MethodA with an instance of the Person type by passing the address of that Person instance as an argument, as shown in Figure 3-9.

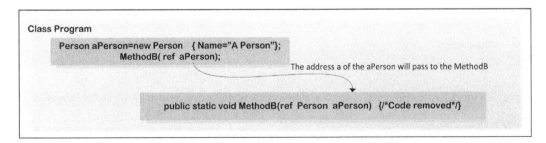

Figure 3-9. Reference type used as ref

When the CLR executes the MethodB(ref Person aPerson) from the MethodA, it will copy the address of the aPerson object to the argument array of the method state description table of the MethodB, so the MethodB will have the address of aPerson object, as shown in Listing 3-12.

Listing 3-12. Passing Object Type as ref

```
using System;

namespace Ch03
{
    class Program
    {
        static void Main(string[] args)
        {
            ObjectAsValue temp =  new ObjectAsValue();
            temp.MethodA();
        }
    }

    public class ObjectAsValue
    {
        public ObjectAsValue()
        {
            Console.WriteLine("Object as value");
        }

        public void MethodA()
        {
            Person aPerson = new Person()
            {
                Name = "APerson"
            };
            MethodB(ref aPerson);
            Console.WriteLine("Method A: {0}", aPerson.Name);
        }

        public void MethodB(ref Person aPerson)
        {
            Console.WriteLine("Method B: {0}", aPerson.Name);
            aPerson = new Person()
            {
                Name = "New name"
            };
        }
    }

    public class Person
    {
        public string Name
```

```
            { get;  set; }
        }

}
```

The program in Listing 3-12 produces the following output:

```
Object as value
Method B: APerson
Method A: New name
```

To explore this more, see the generated IL code for MethodA from Listing 3-12 as shown in Listing 3-13.

Listing 3-13. IL Code of the MethodA Method

```
.method public hidebysig instance void MethodA() cil managed
{
    .maxstack 2
    .locals init (
        [0] class Ch03.Person aPerson,
        [1] class Ch03.Person <>g__initLocal0)

    L_0000: newobj instance void Ch03.Person::.ctor()
    L_0005: stloc.1
    L_0006: ldloc.1
    L_0007: ldstr "APerson"
    L_000c: callvirt instance void Ch03.Person::set_Name(string)
    L_0011: ldloc.1
    L_0012: stloc.0

    L_0013: ldarg.0

    /* Load the address of the local variable aPerson onto the Stack. */
    L_0014: ldloca.s aPerson

    /* The CLR will use the address of the aPerson object from the Stack and
     * pass as argument of the MethodB call.*/
    L_0016: call instance void Ch03.ObjectAsValue::MethodB(class Ch03.Person&)

    L_001b: ldstr "Method A: {0}"
    L_0020: ldloc.0
    L_0021: callvirt instance string Ch03.Person::get_Name()
    L_0026: call void [mscorlib]System.Console::WriteLine(string, object)
    L_002b: ret
}
```

The CLR instantiates an instance of the Person using newobj instruction in L_000. The ldloca.s aPerson instruction in the L_0014 label will push the address of the local variable aPerson onto the stack. This address will be copied to the argument array of the method state description table of the MethodB while initializing the MethodB call, MethodB(class Ch03.Person&) in L_0016. The MethodB, on the other hand, is accepting an address of the Person type object. When you update the aPerson object with the new instance of the Person, this change will be visible from the MethodA method, as shown in Listing 3-14.

Listing 3-14. IL Code of the MethodB Method

```
.method public hidebysig instance void  MethodB(class Ch03.Person& aPerson) cil managed
{
    .maxstack 3
    .locals init (
        [0] class Ch03.Person <>g__initLocal1)
    L_0000: ldstr "Method B: {0}"

    /* Load the address passed via the aPerson parameter onto the stack */
    L_0005: ldarg.1

    /* Load the contents of the aPerson object indirectly */
    L_0006: ldind.ref

    L_0007: callvirt instance string Ch03.Person::get_Name()
    L_000c: call void [mscorlib]System.Console::WriteLine(string, object)

    L_0011: ldarg.1
    L_0012: newobj instance void Ch03.Person::.ctor()
    L_0017: stloc.0

    L_0018: ldloc.0

    L_0019: ldstr "New name"
    L_001e: callvirt instance void Ch03.Person::set_Name(string)

    /* Load the value of the local variable at position at 0 on the stack */
    L_0023: ldloc.0

    /* It will store the object from the stack on to the memory object which actually
     * replace the original aPerson passed as argument. */
    L_0024: stind.ref

    L_0025: ret
}
```

The IL instruction `ldind.ref` in L_0006 will load the object onto the stack. The IL instruction `ldloc.0` in the L_0018 will load the local object aPerson stored into the position at 0 and set the new value for the Name field of the aPerson object. This updated aPerson will be stored in the address of the aPerson object of the MethodA using the `stind.ref` in L_0024. This `stind.ref` instruction will store the new object instance at the given address as passed by the caller. The address passed from the MethodA to the MethodB, `stind.ref` will store this new instance of Person object from the evaluation stack to that location. As a result, this updated Person object will be visible from the MethodA.

Default Parameter Value

Default parameter value is a way to declare an optional parameter in a method declaration. In other words, when you define a method with a parameter, you can also set the default value for the parameter. Then the caller of the method does not have to pass the value for the parameter while calling the method.

When CLR handles any method that has a parameter with the default value set, it treats these methods in two ways:

- If you do not set any value for the parameters when you call the method, then CLR grabs the default values from that method signature and passes those values as arguments for that method call.

- On the other hand, if you set the value for the parameters from the calling method, then CLR will take these values as arguments to call that method.

An example is given in Listing 3-15, where the default value has been set to the method parameter and that method has been called twice, with and without passing a parameter value.

Listing 3-15. An Example of Default Value for the Parameter of the Value Type

```
using System;
namespace Ch03
{
    class Program
    {
        static void Main(string[] args)
        {
            int result = GetTotalPrice();          /* Test scenario 1- with the value */
                result = GetTotalPrice(55);         /* Test scenario 2 - with the value*/
        }
        public static int GetTotalPrice(int basePrice = 40)
        {
            return basePrice - (basePrice * 10) / 100;
        }
    }
}
```

The program in Listing 3-15 will produce approximately the following stack information, as demonstrates in Figure 3-10, while executing.

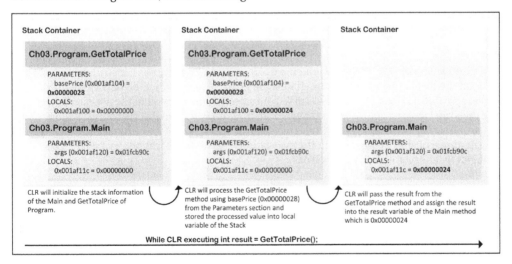

Figure 3-10. Executing GetTotalPrice method without passing value for the parameters

As you can see, the PARAMETERS section of the GetTotalPrice method's stack basePrice has been initialized with the default value 0x00000028(40). While CLR moves the program control into the GetTotalPrice, it will use the value of the basePrice variable stored in the PARAMETERS section of the stack, and after finishing the processing it will return the result 0x00000024(36) of the expression basePrice (basePrice * 10)/100.

To understand more in depth about the default value parameter, let's look at the decompiled IL code for Listing 3-15 as shown in Listing 3-16.

Listing 3-16. IL Code for Listing 3-15

```
.class private auto ansi beforefieldinit Program  extends [mscorlib]System.Object
{
    .method public hidebysig specialname rtspecialname instance void .ctor() cil managed
    {
        /* code removed */
    }

    .method public hidebysig static int32 GetTotalPrice([opt] int32 basePrice) cil managed
    {
        .param [1] = int32(40)
        .maxstack 3
        .locals init (
            [0] int32 CS$1$0000)
        L_0000: nop

    /* ldarg will load the argument at position 0 from the arguments array of this method's
     * method state description table. These arguments have been passed from the
     * caller which is Main method and the argument at position 0 is 40. */
        L_0001: ldarg.0
        L_0002: ldarg.0
        L_0003: ldc.i4.s 10
        L_0005: mul
        L_0006: ldc.i4.s 100
        L_0008: div
        L_0009: sub
        L_000a: stloc.0
        L_000b: br.s L_000d
        L_000d: ldloc.0
        L_000e: ret
    }

    .method private hidebysig static void Main(string[] args) cil managed
    {
        .entrypoint
        .maxstack 1
        .locals init (
            [0] int32 result)
        L_0000: nop

    /* Push numeric constant 40 onto the evaluation stack. The C# compiler will take the
     *constant value 40 from the signature of the method GetTotalPrice */
```

```
    L_0001: ldc.i4.s 40

    /* Get the top value from the evaluation stack, use as the parameter value and
     * call the GetTotalPrice method */
    L_0003: call int32 Ch03.Program::GetTotalPrice(int32)

    /* Store the result return from the IL code L_0003. */
    L_0008: stloc.0

    /* Push numeric constant 0x37(55) onto the evaluation stack. */
    L_0009: ldc.i4.s 0x37

    /* Get the top value from the evaluation stack, use as the parameter value and
     * call the GetTotalPrice method */
    L_000b: call int32 Ch03.Program::GetTotalPrice(int32)

    /* Store the result return from the IL code L_0003. */
    L_0010: stloc.0
    L_0011: ret
  }
}
```

The IL code in Listing 3-16 demonstrates that:

- When the CLR Jits the Main method, it will get the default value set for the GetTotalPrice method and embed that numeric constant into the IL instruction in L_0001 of the Main method, as shown in Listing 3-16.

- The CLR will use this numeric constant 40 in the Main method to call the GetTotalPrice.

- From the GetTotalPrice method, CLR will access the arguments from the method state description table of the GetTotalPrice method and get the value for the parameter basePrice. The value of the basePrice has been passed to the GetTotalPrice method by the CLR in runtime as GetTotalPrice has been called without any argument value for the parameter basePrice.

---

ldc.<type>: It loads a numeric constant on the stack.

ldc.i4.s N: It pushes N onto the stack as int32.

Figure 3-11 shows that GetTotalPrice is executing using the argument value 55 (0x37). While the CLR executes as in Listing 3-15, it will use the parameter value for the basePrice, which is 55 (0x37), instead of the default value 40.

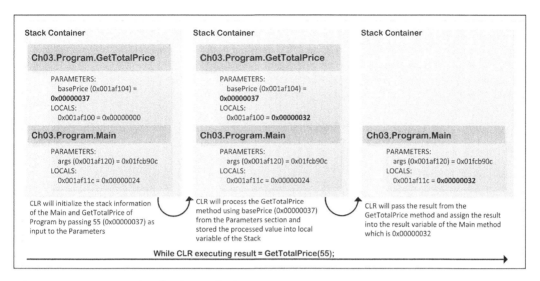

Figure 3-11. *CLR executing the GetTotalPrice(55)*

In C#, the reference type can be set as the default value for the parameter using the `default` keyword or setting null as the default value. You can try to set the default value for the reference type, as shown in Listing 3-17.

Listing 3-17. *Reference Type as the Default Value of a Parameter*

```
using System;

namespace Ch03
{
    class Program
    {
        static void Main(string[] args) { }

        /* The C# compiler complain in here as reference type Person used for the default
value.*/
        public static string GetPersonDetails(Person aPerson = new Person())
        { return aPerson.ToString(); }
    }

    public class Person { }
}
```

In the compile time, the C# compiler will throw an exception as shown:

```
Error   11      Default parameter value for 'aPerspon' must be a compile-time constant
            J:\Book\ExpertC#2012\SourceCode\BookExamples\Ch03\Program.cs   10   65   Ch03
```

However, if you define the `GetPersonDetails` method, as below, you will be able to set the default value for the reference type:

```
public static string GetPersonDetails(Person aPerspon = null)
{ return aPerspon.ToString(); }
```
Or it is defined as:
```
public static string GetPersonDetails(Person aPerspon = default(Person))
{ return aPerspon.ToString(); }
```
You can use string as the default value of a parameter, as shown in Listing 3-18.

Listing 3-18. An Example of Named Parameter in C#

```
using System;

namespace Ch03
{
    class Program
    {
        static void Main(string[] args)
        {
            GetNameWithDefaultValue();
            GetNameWithDefaultValue("Expert C# 5.0 by Mohammad Rahman", "C#");
        }

        /* Default value has been set as of string type */
        public static void GetNameWithDefaultValue(
            string name = "Expert C# 5.0: with the .NET 4.5 Framework",
            string language = ": C#")
        {
            Console.WriteLine("{0} {1}", name, language);
        }
    }
}
```

In the above code, the GetNameWithDefaultValue method defined with the two parameters name and language of string type with its default value "Expert C# 5.0: with the .NET 4.5 Framework" and ": C#". The caller of this method, for example, Main method, does not have to pass any value for the name and address parameters or they could be. To explore this more, see the generated IL code for Listing 3-18 as shown in Listing 3-19.

Listing 3-19. IL Code for GetNameWithDefaultValue Method

```
.class private auto ansi beforefieldinit Program extends [mscorlib]System.Object
{
    /* Code removed */
    .method public hidebysig static void
        GetNameWithDefaultValue([opt] string name, [opt] string language) cil managed
    {
        .param [1] = string('Expert C# 5.0: with the .NET 4.5 Framework')
        .param [2] = string(': C#')
        .maxstack 8
        L_0000: nop
        L_0001: ldstr "{0} {1}"

        /* Load the argument value at position 0 and 1 from the argument values
```

```
    * of the Method state description table into the evaluation stack and
    * execute the following IL instruction using those values from the
    * evaluation stack.*/
   L_0006: ldarg.0      /* refers to the name */
   L_0007: ldarg.1      /* refers to the language */

   L_0008: call void [mscorlib]System.Console::WriteLine(string, object, object)
   L_000d: nop
   L_000e: ret
}


.method private hidebysig static void Main(string[] args) cil managed
{
    .entrypoint
    .maxstack 8
    L_0000: nop

    /* In the compile time the C# compiler extract the default values set for the parameter
     * name and language from the GetNameWithDefaultValue method and
     * embed into the IL instruction L_0001 and L_0006.
     * The CLR load the given string into the heap as result those string will have
     * memory address on the heap. The CLR use memory addresses as the parameter
     * value for the GetNameWithDefaultValue method call.*/
    L_0001: ldstr "Expert C# 5.0: with the .NET 4.5 Framework"
    L_0006: ldstr ": C#"

    L_000b: call void Ch03.Program::GetNameWithDefaultValue(string, string)
    L_0010: nop

    /* The CLR load the given string into the heap as result those string will have
     * memory address on the heap. The CLR use memory addresses as the parameter
     * value for the GetNameWithDefaultValue method call.*/
    L_0011: ldstr "Expert C# 5.0 by Mohammad Rahman"
    L_0016: ldstr "C#"

    L_001b: call void Ch03.Program::GetNameWithDefaultValue(string, string)
    L_0020: nop
    L_0021: ret
  }
}
```

You can see in L_0001 and L_0006 that CLR loads the "Expert C# 5.0: with the .NET 4.5 Framework" and ":C#" from the parameter's array of the GetNameWithDefaultValue method to the Main method using the ldstr instruction. This will be used as an argument to call the GetNameWithDefaultValue method, as you can see in the IL instruction from L_0001 to L_000b of the Main method. On the other hand, for the L_0011 and L_0016, CLR does not load a parameter value from the GetNameWithDefaultValue method while executing GetNameWithDefaultValue("Expert C# 5.0 by Mohammad Rahman", "C#") from the Main method. Figure 3-12 shows stack and heap information that is formed while executing the GetNameWithDefaultValue method without any default values.

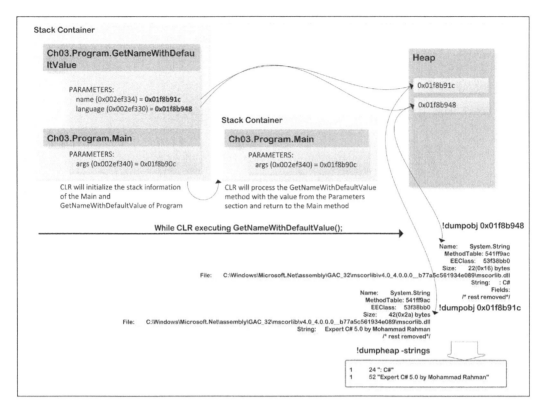

Figure 3-12. *CLR Executes GetNameWithDefaultValue();*

From Figure 3-12 you can see that all the values of the related string have been stored into the heap, and CLR just used the memory reference to access those values. This exemplifies executing the GetNameWithDefaultValue method while no value for the parameter has been set. However, in Figure 3-13, you can see that CLR handles the GetNameWithDefaultValue method call the same way, but this time the argument value has been set to the GetNameWithDefaultValue method instead of CLR getting values from the GetNameWithDefaultValue method signature.

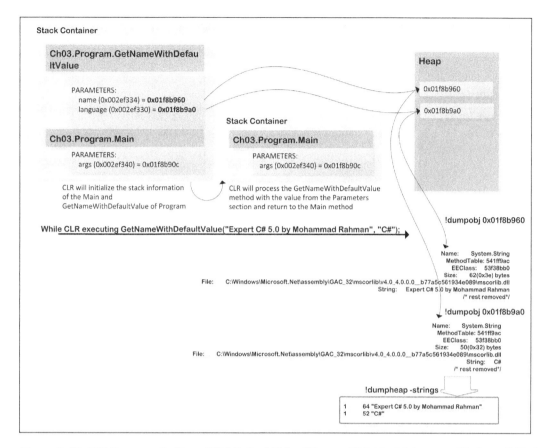

Figure 3-13. *CLR Executes GetNameWithDefaultValue("Expert C# 5.0 by Mohammad Rahman", "C#");*

Summary

This chapter presented information about parameters, including value type and reference type. The CLR has some special mechanisms when you use the `ref` and `out` keywords for value types and reference types, which is seen in the debugging information produced by the `windbg.exe` tool. In the next chapter, we will explore the methods used in C#.

CHAPTER 4

Methods

This chapter will discuss the following C# methods: instance, static, anonymous, and extension. In doing so, you'll learn how the this keyword relates to these methods and how the CLR passes value for the this keyword used as parameter in runtime by examining data on the stack.

You will also explore how the anonymous method works when there is external variable reference in it and when there is no external variable referenced from it. Additionally, you will find out how the this keyword is used in both circumstances.

Finally, you will learn about the compile time and runtime behavior of the extension methods and how the C# compiler eliminates the this keyword from the extension method signature.

Instance and Static Method with this Keyword

The this keyword refers to the current instance of the class, and it is permitted only in the block of an instance constructor, an instance method, or an instance accessor (all of these were covered in Chapter 1). When the this keyword is used in the instance constructor or in an instance method, the CLR treats it as the value of the object for which the constructor, instance method, or the accessor was invoked. For example, if you have a type T and it has an instance method M or instance constructor C that uses the this keyword, in runtime this this keyword from the M and C refers to the object O which is the instance of the type T for that time and from where M and C tried to access this keyword.

This is only possible in the instance method or instance constructor. However, it is not possible to use the this keyword with the static method because you cannot instantiate an instance of the static class. In runtime, for the instance method or instance constructor, the CLR passes an extra value for the invocation, which is the value of the this parameter. The value of the this refers to the instance of the type for which the method or constructor is being invoked. In the following section, you will learn more about this by looking into the runtime stack information for an instance and static method of a type.

The program in Listing 4-1 uses an instance and static method to do an add operation of two int values to show how C# compiler includes the this keyword as a parameter to the instance method behind the scenes. Static method does not have the this keyword as a parameter.

Listing 4-1. An Example of the Instance and Static Methods

```
using System;

namespace Ch04
{
    class Program
```

```
    {
        static void Main(string[] args)
        {
            int valueOfA = 10, valueOfB = 20;
            Calculator calculator = new Calculator();

            Console.WriteLine("The sum using instance method \t{0} \nand using static method
\t{1}",
                calculator.Add(valueOfA, valueOfB),
                CalculatorAsStatic.Add(valueOfA, valueOfB));
        }
    }

    public class Calculator
    {
        public int Add(int a, int b)          /* An extra this parameter will be added in behind the
                                               * scene to the Parameters section of Add
                                               * methods stack */

        {
            return a + b;
        }
    }

    public static class CalculatorAsStatic
    {
        public static int Add(int a, int b) /* No extra this parameter will be added to the
                                             * Parameters section of Add methods
                                             * stack */

        {
            return a + b;
        }
    }
}
```

This program will produce the following output:

```
The sum using instance method       30
and using static method             30
```

Memory Information while Running an Instance Method

Figure 4-1 shows that in the PARAMETERS section of the Add method's stack there is an extra this parameter that holds the object reference where the Add method belongs. The value of the this parameter is passed by the Main method. For example, the address 0x0180b6dc from the LOCALS section of the Main method refers to the instance of the Calculator class.

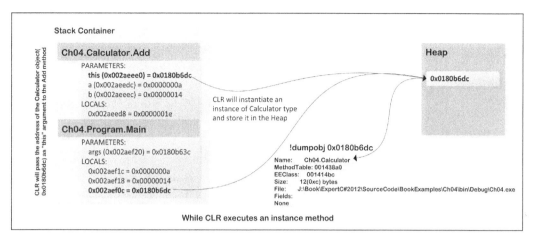

Figure 4-1. *Instance* method and this keyword

Let's see the stack information of the Main method of the Program class and Add method of the Calculator class while debugging Listing 4-1 using the windbg.exe tool:

```
0:000> !clrstack -a
OS Thread Id: 0x434 (0)
Child SP IP       Call Site
002aeed8 004201b9 Ch04.Calculator.Add(Int32, Int32) [J:\Book\ExpertC#2012\SourceCode\
BookExamples\Ch04\Program.cs @ 21]
    PARAMETERS:
        this (0x002aeee0) = 0x0180b6dc        /* refers to the Calculator object as this*/
        a (0x002aeedc)    = 0x0000000a
        b (0x002aeeec)    = 0x00000014
    LOCALS:
        0x002aeed8        = 0x0000001e

002aeef0 004200db Ch04.Program.Main(System.String[]) [J:\Book\ExpertC#2012\SourceCode\
BookExamples\Ch04\Program.cs @ 11]
    PARAMETERS:
        args (0x002aef20) = 0x0180b63c
    LOCALS:
        0x002aef1c        = 0x0000000a
        0x002aef18        = 0x00000014
        0x002aef0c        = 0x0180b6dc        /* refers to the Calculator object */

002af154 5a8a21db [GCFrame: 002af154]
```

Memory Information while Running a Static Method

In Figure 4-2, you can see that in the PARAMETERS section of the Add method there is not an extra this parameter. The Add method of the CalculatorAsStatic class has only a and b parameters in the PARAMETERS section.

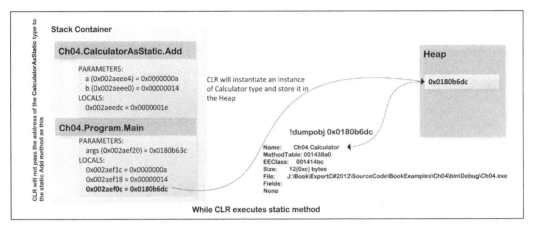

Figure 4-2. Static method and the this keyword

Let's see the stack information of the Main method of the Program class and Add method of the CalculatorAsStatic class while debugging Listing 4-1 using the windbg.exe tool:

```
0:000> !clrstack -a
OS Thread Id: 0x434 (0)
Child SP IP        Call Site
002aeedc 00420209 Ch04.CalculatorAsStatic.Add(Int32, Int32) [J:\Book\ExpertC#2012\SourceCode\
BookExamples\Ch04\Program.cs @ 29]
    PARAMETERS:
        a (0x002aeee4)  = 0x0000000a
        b (0x002aeee0)  = 0x00000014
    LOCALS:
        0x002aeedc      = 0x0000001e

002aeef0 00420106 Ch04.Program.Main(System.String[]) [J:\Book\ExpertC#2012\SourceCode\
BookExamples\Ch04\Program.cs @ 11]
    PARAMETERS:
        args (0x002aef20)       = 0x0180b63c
    LOCALS:
        0x002aef1c              = 0x0000000a
        0x002aef18              = 0x00000014
        0x002aef0c              = 0x0180b6dc

002af154 5a8a21db [GCFrame: 002af154]
```

You have now learned about the instance and static methods in relation to the this keyword. Instance and static are the common kinds of methods used in the program. This sometimes requires writing a method that does not do much. Therefore, instead of writing separate methods, you can use an anonymous method that gives you the option to write an inline method that does not have any valid names. In the next section, you will learn more about this and explore how the this keyword relates to the anonymous method.

Anonymous Method

An *anonymous function* is an expression that represents an inline method definition in a type. It is convertible to a compatible `delegate`.

The conversion of an anonymous function depends on the target type, for example:

- If it is a *delegate type*, the conversion evaluates to a `delegate` value, referencing the method that the anonymous function defines.

- If it is an *expression tree type*, the conversion evaluates to an expression tree that represents the structure of the method as an object structure.

You can use anonymous functions in two ways:

- Lambda expressions

- Anonymous method

The *anonymous method* offers a simple and elegant solution in many situations, such as when using `Array.ForEach<T>`. Typically when you see a method that accepts a `delegate` as a parameter, you could use the anonymous method. The lambda expression is an anonymous function can be used to create delegates or expression tree types. Listing 4-2 provides an example of the anonymous method.

Listing 4-2. An Example of the Anonymous Method

```csharp
using System;

namespace Ch04
{
    class Program
    {
        static void Main(string[] args)
        {
            int valueOfA    = 10,
                valueOfB    = 20,
                increment   = 2;                /* Used as the external or captured variable
                                                 * for the anonymous method */
            Calculator calculator = new Calculator();

            Console.WriteLine("The sum is \t:{0}", calculator.Add
                (delegate(int a, int b)         /* Anonymous method declaration */
                    {
                        return a + b + increment;   /* increment is the outer variable */
                }, valueOfA, valueOfB));
        }
    }

    public class Calculator
    {
        public delegate int Adder(int a, int b);

        public int Add(Adder adder, int a, int b)
        {
```

```
            return adder(a, b);
        }
    }
}
```

This program will produce the following output:

```
The sum is     :32
```

In Listing 4-2, the `Calculator` class has a method `Add`, which takes `Adder`, a type of delegate, along with two other `int` type parameters. The `Adder` is declared as a `delegate`, which takes two `int` type inputs and returns an `int`. The `Main` method of the `Program` class is called the `Add` method of the `Calculator` class by passing an anonymous method defined by using the `delegate`.

In Compile Time

You can see in Listing 4-2 that the anonymous method is defined using the `delegate` type. The `Add` method of the `Calculator` class accepts a `delegate` input, and the `Main` method of the `Program` class passes a block of code as input to the `Add` method. This block of code is the anonymous method used in C#.

The C# compiler compiles the anonymous method as follows:

- When an external variable or capture variable is used in the anonymous method body, the C# compiler generates a type with a method that contains the original body of the anonymous method.

- If the anonymous method does not use a capture variable, the C# compiler generates a method using the code used for the anonymous method in the same class where the original anonymous method was defined.

These two scenarios are detailed in the following sections.

External Variable Referenced from the Anonymous Method

If you access any variable defined outside the anonymous method body, the C# compiler then compiles the anonymous method as follows:

- It generates a new class, for example, `<>c__DisplayClass1`, as in Listing 4-2.

- It generates a method that contains the body of the anonymous method, as defined in Listing 4-2.

- It adds the external variable (accessed from the anonymous method) as the field of the `<>c__DisplayClass1` class.

- The caller of the anonymous method instantiates an instance of the `<>c__DisplayClass1` class and loads the function pointer of the autogenerated method of the anonymous method block defined in the `<>c__DisplayClass1` class. The function pointer of the anonymous method is defined in the `<>c__DisplayClass1` used to instantiate the instance of the `Adder` delegate and passes it as an argument to the `Add` method of the `Calculator` class.

Figure 4-3 demonstrates the anonymous method compilation using the C# compiler. You can see that the C# compiler compiles the anonymous method into a class `<>c__DisplayClass1`, which contains a method `<Main>b__0` that contains the body of the anonymous method you defined in the `Main` method of the `Program` class.

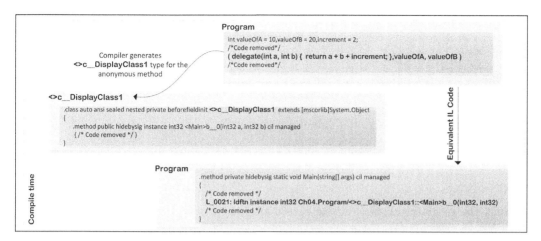

Figure 4-3. *Anonymous method in compile time*

The C# compiler generates the Program class in a way that it can use the <Main>b__0 method it generates in the <>c__DisplayClass1 class.

To explore more about this, let's examine the coding in Listing 4-3, which is the decompiled IL version of Listing 4-2. It was decompiled using the *.NET Reflector* tool.

Listing 4-3. *Decompiled IL of Listing 4-2*

```
.class private auto ansi beforefieldinit Program
    extends [mscorlib]System.Object
{
    .method public hidebysig specialname rtspecialname instance void .ctor() cil managed
    {
        .maxstack 8
        L_0000: ldarg.0
        L_0001: call instance void [mscorlib]System.Object::.ctor()
        L_0006: ret
    }
    .method private hidebysig static void Main(string[] args) cil managed
    {
        .entrypoint
        .maxstack 5
        .locals init (
            [0] int32 valueOfA,
            [1] int32 valueOfB,
            [2] class Ch04.Calculator calculator,
            [3] class Ch04.Program/<>c__DisplayClass1 CS$<>8__locals2)

        /* Instantiates an instance of the <>c__DisplayClass1 class */
        L_0000: newobj instance void Ch04.Program/<>c__DisplayClass1::.ctor()
        L_0005: stloc.3
        L_0006: nop
        L_0007: ldc.i4.s 10
        L_0009: stloc.0
```

```
        L_000a: ldc.i4.s 20
        L_000c: stloc.1
        L_000d: ldloc.3
        L_000e: ldc.i4.2

        /* Adds the value for the outer variable increment*/
        L_000f: stfld int32 Ch04.Program/<>c__DisplayClass1::increment
        L_0014: newobj instance void Ch04.Calculator::.ctor()
        L_0019: stloc.2
        L_001a: ldstr "The sum is \t:{0}"
        L_001f: ldloc.2
        L_0020: ldloc.3

        /* Loads the function pointer for the method <Main>b__0 generated
         * by the C# compiler for the anonymous method block */
        L_0021: ldftn instance int32 Ch04.Program/<>c__DisplayClass1::<Main>b__0(int32, int32)

        /* Instantiates an instance of the Adder delegate using the
         * function pointer loads in L_0021 */
        L_0027: newobj instance void Ch04.Calculator/Adder::.ctor(object, native int)
        L_002c: ldloc.0
        L_002d: ldloc.1

        /* Calls the Add method of the Calculator class by passing the delegate instance
         * instantiated in L_0027 and the value stored at position 0 (valueOfA) and
         * 1 (valueOfB) in the Locals section of the Main method  */
        L_002e: callvirt instance int32 Ch04.Calculator::Add(class Ch04.Calculator/Adder, int32,
int32)
        L_0033: box int32
        L_0038: call void [mscorlib]System.Console::WriteLine(string, object)
        L_003d: nop
        L_003e: nop
        L_003f: ret
    }

    /* The C# compiler automatically generates the anonymous method block as method
     * embedded into the auto generated class <>c__DisplayClass1 */
    .class auto ansi sealed nested private beforefieldinit <>c__DisplayClass1
        extends [mscorlib]System.Object
    {
        { /* Code removed */  }
        .method public hidebysig specialname rtspecialname instance void .ctor() cil managed
        { /* Code removed */  }

        .method public hidebysig instance int32 <Main>b__0(int32 a, int32 b) cil managed
        {
            .maxstack 2
            .locals init (
                [0] int32 num)
            L_0000: nop
            L_0001: ldarg.1
```

```
        L_0002: ldarg.2
        L_0003: add
        L_0004: ldarg.0
        L_0005: ldfld int32 Ch04.Program/<>c__DisplayClass1::increment
        L_000a: add
        L_000b: stloc.0
        L_000c: br.s L_000e
        L_000e: ldloc.0
        L_000f: ret
    }
    .field public int32 increment

  }
}
```

Memory Information with External Variable Referenced from the Anonymous Method

Listing 4-3 demonstrates that the C# compiler automatically generates the <>c__DisplayClass1 class for the anonymous method. Inside this class it defined a method <Main>b__0 with the same body as the original anonymous method defined in the Main method of the Program class. In L_0000 of Listing 4-3, an instance of the <>c__DisplayClass1 has been instantiated. The CLR loads the function pointer of the <Main>b__0 method from the instance of the <>c__DisplayClass1 class in L_0021. This function pointer will use L_0027 to instantiate an instance of the Adder delegate to pass it as a parameter to the Add method of the instance of Calculator class instantiated in L_0014. Figure 4-4 demonstrates how the CLR handles the anonymous method in runtime.

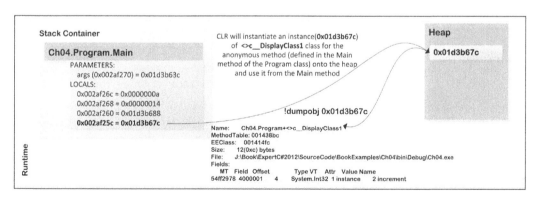

Figure 4-4. Anonymous Method in Runtime

Let's examine the stack information while debugging Listing 4-2 using the windbg.exe tool, where you can see the stack information of the Add and Main methods:

```
0:000> !clrstack -a
OS Thread Id: 0x1358 (0)
Child SP IP       Call Site
```

```
002af234 003901f0 Ch04.Calculator.Add(Adder, Int32, Int32) [J:\Book\ExpertC#2012\SourceCode\
BookExamples\Ch04\Program.cs @ 26]
    PARAMETERS:
        this (<CLR reg>) = 0x01d3b688
        adder (<CLR reg>)= 0x01d3b694          /* Which contains reference of the
                                                      * 0x01d3b67c  in the _target field*/

        a (0x002af23c)   = 0x0000000a
        b (0x002af238)   = 0x00000014
    LOCALS:
        <no data>


002af240 00390127 Ch04.Program.Main(System.String[]) [J:\Book\ExpertC#2012\SourceCode\
BookExamples\Ch04\Program.cs @ 13]
    PARAMETERS:
        args (0x002af270) = 0x01d3b63c
    LOCALS:
        0x002af26c        = 0x0000000a
        0x002af268        = 0x00000014
        0x002af260        = 0x01d3b688
        0x002af25c        = 0x01d3b67c          /* Instance of the <>c__DisplayClass1  */


002af4a8 5a8a21db [GCFrame: 002af4a8]
```

Let's see the object information located in the 0x01d3b67c of the heap used in the LOCALS section of the Main method, which is the address of the <>c__DisplayClass1 class:

```
0:000> !dumpobj 0x01d3b67c
Name:           Ch04.Program+<>c__DisplayClass1
MethodTable:    001438bc
EEClass:        001414fc
Size:           12(0xc) bytes
File:           J:\Book\ExpertC#2012\SourceCode\BookExamples\Ch04\bin\Debug\Ch04.exe
Fields:
      MT       Field     Offset                  Type   VT  Attr       Value      Name
54ff2978    4000001        4           System.Int32    1   instance   2          increment
```

The address 0x01d3b694 is used for the Adder variable of the Add method of the Calculator class, which refers to the instance of the delegate Adder from the Calculator class, as shown below:

```
0:000> !dumpobj 0x01d3b694
Name:           Ch09.Calculator+Adder
MethodTable:    002438ac
EEClass:        002413c8
Size:           32(0x20) bytes
File:           J:\Book\ExpertC#2012\SourceCode\BookExamples\Ch09\bin\Debug\Ch09.exe
Fields:
      MT       Field     Offset   Type             VT  Attr       Value        Name
5654bba8    400002d    4       System.Object     0   instance   0x01d3b67c   _target
5654bba8    400002e    8       System.Object     0   instance   00000000     _methodBase
5654ac2c    400002f    c       System.IntPtr     1   instance   24c088       _methodPtr
5654ac2c    4000030    10      System.IntPtr     1   instance   0            _methodPtrAux
5654bba8    4000031    14      System.Object     0   instance   00000000     _invocationList
5654ac2c    4000032    18      System.IntPtr     1   instance   0            _invocationCount
```

The CLR also passes the value for the this parameter to the anonymous method, For example, if you explore the stack information of the <Main>b__0 method from the Program+<>c__DisplayClass1 class in runtime you will see that the CLR passes the value of the this parameter to the <Main>b__0 method in addition to the other parameters. To do so, a breakpoint needs to be set using the windbg.exe tool while debugging Listing 4-2, using the following commands:

```
!bpmd Ch04.exe Ch04.Program.Main
!bpmd Ch04.exe Ch04.Program+<>c__DisplayClass1.<Main>b__0
```

After setting the breakpoint, execute the !clrstack -a command in the windbg.exe tool, which will show you the detailed stack information of the <Main>b__0 method from the Program+<>c__DisplayClass1 class:

```
0:000> !clrstack -a
OS Thread Id: 0x11ec (0)
Child SP       IP Call Site
0022eda4 00510257 Ch04.Program+<>c__DisplayClass1.<Main>b__0(Int32, Int32) [J:\Book\
ExpertC#2012\SourceCode\BookExamples\Ch04\Program.cs @ 17]
    PARAMETERS:

        /* this pointing to the instance of the  Ch04.Program+<>c__DisplayClass1*/
        this (0x0022eda4)      = 0x01d3b67c

        a (0x0022edac)  = 0x0000000a
        b (0x0022edb8)  = 0x00000014
    LOCALS:
        0x0022eda8 = 0x00000000


0022edbc 0051020e Ch04.Calculator.Add(Adder, Int32, Int32) [J:\Book\ExpertC#2012\SourceCode\
BookExamples\Ch04\Program.cs @ 29]
    PARAMETERS:
        this (0x0022edc8)      = 0x01682480
        adder (0x0022edbc)     = 0x0168248c
        a (0x0022edd8)  = 0x0000000a
        b (0x0022edd4)  = 0x00000014
    LOCALS:
        0x0022edc4 = 0x00000000


0022eddc 00510119 Ch04.Program.Main(System.String[]) [J:\Book\ExpertC#2012\SourceCode\
BookExamples\Ch04\Program.cs @ 15]
    PARAMETERS:
        args (0x0022ee0c) = 0x01682434
    LOCALS:
        0x0022ee08      = 0x0000000a
        0x0022ee04      = 0x00000014
        0x0022edfc      = 0x01682480
        0x0022edf8      = 0x01682474


0022ef9c 53a43dd2 [GCFrame: 0022ef9c]
```

The stack information of the `<Main>b__0` method from the `Program+<>c__DisplayClass1` class shows that the CLR passes the value for the `this` parameter exactly the same as in the instance method we explored earlier.

The following section will examine the anonymous method, which does not have any external variable references. You will also learn how the CLR passes the value for the `this` parameter for the anonymous method.

External Variable Not Referenced from the Anonymous Method

Let's modify the anonymous method body defined in Listing 4-2, as shown in Listing 4-4. In this modified version, the anonymous method does not use any external or captured variable.

Listing 4-4. Modified Anonymous Method

```
static void Main(string[] args)
{
    int valueOfA = 10, valueOfB = 20;
    Calculator calculator = new Calculator();

    Console.WriteLine("The sum is \t:{0}", calculator.Add
        (delegate(int a, int b)
        {
            return a + b;
        }, valueOfA, valueOfB));
}
```

If you do not access any variable defined outside the anonymous method body, the C# compiler compiles the anonymous method, as demonstrated here:

- It generates a method `<Main>b__0` (for example, based on Listing 4-4), which contains the body of the anonymous method defined in Listing 4-4.

- The caller of the anonymous method will load the function pointer for the anonymous method `<Main>b__0,` and using this function pointer, the CLR instantiates an instance of the delegate `Adder` and passes it to the `Add` method of the `Calculator` class.

To explore more about this, Listing 4-5 presents the decompiled IL version of Listing 4-4 using the .NET Reflector tool.

Listing 4-5. Decompiled IL Version of Listing 4-4

```
.class private auto ansi beforefieldinit Program
    extends [mscorlib]System.Object
{
    /* Code removed */
    /* The C# compiler generates the anonymous method block as method  */
    .method private hidebysig static int32 <Main>b__0(int32 a, int32 b) cil managed
    {
        /* Code removed */
        .maxstack 2
        .locals init (
```

```
        [0] int32 CS$1$0000)
    L_0000: nop
    L_0001: ldarg.0
    L_0002: ldarg.1
    L_0003: add
    L_0004: stloc.0
    L_0005: br.s L_0007
    L_0007: ldloc.0
    L_0008: ret
}

.method private hidebysig static void Main(string[] args) cil managed
{
    .entrypoint
    .maxstack 5
    .locals init (
        [0] int32 valueOfA,
        [1] int32 valueOfB,
        [2] class Ch04.Calculator calculator)
    L_0000: nop
    L_0001: ldc.i4.s 10
    L_0003: stloc.0
    L_0004: ldc.i4.s 20
    L_0006: stloc.1

    /* Instantiates an instance of the Calculator class */
    L_0007: newobj instance void Ch04.Calculator::.ctor()
    L_000c: stloc.2
    L_000d: ldstr "The sum is \t:{0}"
    L_0012: ldloc.2

    L_0013: ldsfld class Ch04.Calculator/Adder Ch04.Program::
            CS$<>9__CachedAnonymousMethodDelegate1
    L_0018: brtrue.s L_002d
    L_001a: ldnull

    /* Loads the function pointer for the method <Main>b__0 generates
     * by the C# compiler for the anonymous method block */
    L_001b: ldftn int32 Ch04.Program::<Main>b__0(int32, int32)

    /* Instantiates an instance of the Adder delegate using the
     * function pointer load in L_0021 */
    L_0021: newobj instance void Ch04.Calculator/Adder::.ctor(object, native int)

    L_0026: stsfld class Ch04.Calculator/Adder Ch04.Program::
            CS$<>9__CachedAnonymousMethodDelegate1
    L_002b: br.s L_002d
    L_002d: ldsfld class Ch04.Calculator/Adder Ch04.Program::
            CS$<>9__CachedAnonymousMethodDelegate1
    L_0032: ldloc.0
    L_0033: ldloc.1
```

```
        /* Calls the Add method using the delegate instance instantiated
         * in the L_0027 and the value stored at position 0 and 1 in the
         * Locals section of the Main method  */
        L_0034: callvirt instance int32 Ch04.Calculator::Add(class Ch04.Calculator/Adder, int32,
int32)
        L_0039: box int32
        L_003e: call void [mscorlib]System.Console::WriteLine(string, object)
        L_0043: nop
        L_0044: ret
    }
    .field private static class Ch04.Calculator/Adder CS$<>9__CachedAnonymousMethodDelegate1
    { /* Code removed */  }
}
```

Listing 4-5 demonstrates that C# compiler automatically generates a method <Main>b__0 with the contents of the anonymous method defined in Listing 4-4. The CLR loads the function pointer of <Main>b__0 in L_001b and passes this function pointer as an argument to the Adder delegate in L_0021. The CLR uses this delegate instance in L_0026 to store this into the CS$<>9__CachedAnonymousMethodDelegate1 field of the Program class. The CLR passes the value of the CS$<>9__CachedAnonymousMethodDelegate1 along with the other two arguments of the Add method of the instance of the Calculator class instantiated in L_0007.

Listing 4-5 also shows that the anonymous method in this circumstance is compiled as a static method. As a result, there will not be any this parameter for the anonymous method; for example, in this circumstance it is the <Main>b__0 method, as shown in Listing 4-5.

So far we have examined the instance method, extension method, and anonymous method, but when you define these methods for a type, they all have to reside in the same assembly where the type was defined. The extension method does not require defining the method in the same assembly for which you will write the method.

Extension Method

In .NET, extension methods provide a mechanism by which you can add functionality to a type without modifying it to avoid the risk of breaking code in existing applications. You can also add additional methods in the interface without altering the existing class libraries.

So the extension method allows you to extend the existing compiled types to have a new functionality without needing to directly update the type. It is quite helpful when you need to inject new functionality into types where you do not have an existing code base. It can also be useful when you need a class to support a set of members, but it cannot modify the original type declaration. Using the extension method, you can add functionality to compiled types while providing the illusion that these methods were there all along.

To extend a type's functionality using the extension method technique provided by the C#, you need to do the following:

- Make a static class.

- Add a static method in this static class with the appropriate functionality. In the parameter list of this new method, add an extra parameter this along with the type name for which this method will extend the functionality. For example, GetLastCharacter method in Listing 4-6 extends functionality for the string type.

In Listing 4-6, an extension method is defined for the string type. This extension method is used to determine the last character of a word whose type is string.

Listing 4-6. An Example of the Extension Method

```
using System;

namespace Ch04
{
    class Program
    {
        static void Main(string[] args)
        {
            string data = "abcd";
            Console.WriteLine("{0}", data.GetLastCharacter());    /* Calls extension defined for
the string type. */
        }
    }
    public static class Ch04_ExtensionMethods                     /* A Static class defined */
    {
        public static string GetLastCharacter(this string data)
                                        /* A static method with the parameter
                                         * this along with the type name string */
        {
            if (data == null || data == string.Empty)
                return string.Empty;
            return data[data.Length - 1].ToString();
        }
        public static Int32 GetNum(this Int32 dd)
        {
            return dd;
        }
    }
}
```

The program will produce the following output:

d

The GetLastCharacter extension method determines the last character from the input data if the data are not null or do not contain an empty value. In Listing 4-6, a static class Ch04_ExtensionMethods is defined and a static method GetLastCharacter is added. The first parameter contains the this keyword along with a parameter of the type that is going to be extended, in this case it is string.

When you define any extension method for a type, it shows Visual Studio's IntelliSense along with the standard methods of that type. In Figure 4-5, you see that the GetLastCharacter extension method for the string type shows Visual Studio's IntelliSense along with other standard methods of the string type.

```
        static void Main(string[] args)
        {
            string data = "abcd";
            Console.WriteLine("{0}",
                data.Get);
        }
    }
    public static cla
    {
        public static
        {
            if (data == null || data == string.Empty)
```

🔹 GetEnumerator	
🔹 GetHashCode	
🔹 GetLastCharacter	(extension) string string.GetLastCharacter()
🔹 GetType	(this string data)
🔹 GetTypeCode	

Visual studio's IntelliSense window

Figure 4-5. *Extension methods in Visual studio's IntelliSense*

You have seen how to design an extension method, and in the following sections you will explore more about the internal working of the extension method, for example, how the C# compiler translates the definition of the extension method into a static method and what happens if the this keyword is used to define the extension method.

Internal Work of the Extension Method

The C# compiler rewrites the extension methods by removing the this keyword from the extension methods signature and adding an ExtensionAttribute to it. The compiler also changes the extension method's caller code with the same syntax as that of the static method call.

Figure 4-6 demonstrates the C# compiler's compilation process in the extension method and calling convention.

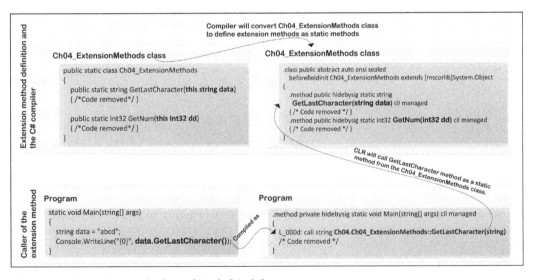

Figure 4-6. *Extension methods working behind the scenes*

You can see from Figure 4-6 that the C# compiler compiles the Ch04_ExtensionMethods class as a static class that contains all the extension methods defined in the original class except for the this keyword from the methods parameter list, which is eliminated by the C# compiler in the compile time.

To explore more about this, let's examine Listing 4-7, which is the decompiled IL version of Listing 4-6.

Listing 4-7. IL Code of the Extension Methods and Calling Class

```
.class public abstract auto ansi sealed
    beforefieldinit Ch04_ExtensionMethods
    extends [mscorlib]System.Object
{
    /* Code removed */
    /* The Original GetLastCharacter decompiled as a static method and removed the
     * this keyword from the parameter list*/
    .method public hidebysig static string GetLastCharacter(string data) cil managed
    {
        .custom instance void [System.Core]System.Runtime.CompilerServices.ExtensionAttribute::.
ctor()
        .maxstack 3
        .locals init (
            [0] string CS$1$0000,
            [1] bool CS$4$0001,
            [2] char CS$0$0002)
        /* Code removed */
    }

     /* The Original GetLastCharacter decompiled as a static method and removed the
      * this keyword from the parameter list*/
    .method public hidebysig static int32 GetNum(int32 dd) cil managed
    {
        .custom instance void [System.Core]System.Runtime.CompilerServices.ExtensionAttribute::.
ctor()
        .maxstack 1
        .locals init (
            [0] int32 CS$1$0000)
        /* Code removed */
    }

}
```

In Listing 4-7, you can see that the C# compiler removed the this keyword from the GetLastCharacter method signature and declares a static method, which accepts a string type input and also defines inside a static class, as shown in Listing 4-7.

The C# compiler also changed the code from where the extension method GetLastCharacter is called. From Listing 4-8 you can see that the GetLastCharacter method from the Main method is called as Ch04.Ch04_ExtensionMethods::GetLastCharacter(string), which is the syntax of the static method call.

Listing 4-8. Decompiled IL code of the Main Method from Listing 4-6 Using the .NET Reflector Tool

```
.method private hidebysig static void Main(string[] args) cil managed
{
    .entrypoint
```

```
        .maxstack 2
        .locals init (
            [0] string data)
        L_0000: nop
        L_0001: ldstr "abcd"
        L_0006: stloc.0
        L_0007: ldstr "{0}"
        L_000c: ldloc.0

        /* GetLastCharacter method is called as a static method */
        L_000d: call string Ch04.Ch04_ExtensionMethods::GetLastCharacter(string)

        L_0012: call void [mscorlib]System.Console::WriteLine(string, object)
        L_0017: nop
        L_0018: ret
    }
```

In L_000d of Listing 4-8, GetLastCharacter method is called as the static method. In L_000c, the CLR loads the local variable stored at the position 0 from the method state description table to the evaluation stack. In L_000d, CLR calls a static method GetLastCharacter of the Ch04_ExtensionMethods class by passing the data (in L_000c) from the evaluation stack as the argument value. The extension method is another design-time syntactic sugar to make the development easier, but in runtime, it behaves exactly like the static class and static method.

Extension Method and Resolution

When you use an extension method from a different namespace, it needs to define the namespace specifically, as demonstrates in Listing 4-9.

Listing 4-9. Extension Method and Resolution

```
namespace Ch04
{
    using System;

    /* CH04_Extensions has to declare here otherwise compiler-time error occurred. */
    using Ch04_Extensions;

    class Program
    {
        static void Main(string[] args)
        {
            string data = "abcd";
            Console.WriteLine("{0}", data.GetLastCharacter());
        }
    }
}

/* Extension method defined in the  Ch04_ExtensionMethods class which reside
 * in the Ch04_Extensions namespace */
namespace Ch04_Extensions
```

```
{
    public static class Ch04_ExtensionMethods
    {
        public static string GetLastCharacter(this string data)
        {
            if (data == null || data == string.Empty)    return string.Empty;
            return data[data.Length - 1].ToString();
        }
    }
}
```

This program will produce following output:
d

Extension Method and Custom Class

You can also extend a custom-defined type. For example, in Listing 4-10, Calculator class has been extended in the Ch04_ExtensionMethods class. The extended functionality using extension method is named Sub. Let's see how this works, as shown in Listing 4-10.

Listing 4-10. *Extending Custom Class*

```
using System;

namespace Ch04
{
    class Program
    {
        static void Main(string[] args)
        {
            Calculator calculator = new Calculator();
            Console.WriteLine(calculator.Sub(10, 5));
        }
    }
    public static class Ch04_ExtensionMethods                    /* A Static class defined */
    {
        public static int Sub(this Calculator calculator, int a, int b)
        {
            return a > b ? a - b : b - a;
        }
    }

    public class Calculator
    {
        public int Add(int a, int b)
        {
            return a + b;
        }
    }
}
```

The Listing 4-10 produces the following output:

5

Summary

In this chapter we have learned about the instance method, static method, anonymous method, and extension method in C# by examining the stack information. You explored how the anonymous method works when there is or is not an external variable referenced in the anonymous method. In addition, you learned how the this keyword is used in both circumstances. Finally, you learned about the extension method by looking into the compile time and runtime behavior of the extension methods. Learning the internal mechanism of these methods will give you a solid understanding of how these methods work behind the scenes and also help you to write better code.

CHAPTER 5

Automatic Property Declaration

This chapter will discuss automatic property declaration, which is a simplified syntax to declare a property for a class. I will also discuss the implicit variable declaration using the var keyword and show how var is handled by the C# compiler in design and runtime. Finally, I will discuss the anonymous type declaration and how the C# compiler compiles it.

Automatic Property

You can use the class of a real-world object to encapsulate its characteristics. For example, if you think about a real-life object, such as a book of class Book as demonstrated in Listing 5-1, you can see it has a name, a publication year, and the author field to define it.

Listing 5-1. A Class of the Book

```
namespace Ch05
{
    public class Book
    {
        private string name;                    /* name field to define Book*/
        private int publishedYear;              /* publishedYear field to define Book*/
        private string author;                  /* author field to define Book*/

        public Book()
        {
            name            = default(string);
            publishedYear   = default(int);
            author          = default(string);
        }

        public Book(string nameOfTheBook, int publishedYearOfTheBook, string authorOfTheBook)
        {
            name            = nameOfTheBook;
            publishedYear   = publishedYearOfTheBook;
            author          = authorOfTheBook;
        }
```

```
    /* A method to get the value of name field */
    public string GetName() { return name; }

    /* A method to set the value of name field */
    public void SetName(string nameOfTheBook) { name = nameOfTheBook; }

    /* A method to get the value of publishedYear field */
    public int GetPublishedYear() { return publishedYear; }

    /* A method to set the value of publishedYear field */
    public void SetPublishedYear(int publishedYearOfTheBook)
    { publishedYear = publishedYearOfTheBook; }

    /* A method to get the value of author field */
    public string GetAuthor() { return author; }

    /* A method to set the value of author field */
    public void SetAuthor(string authorOfTheBook) { author = authorOfTheBook; }
    }
}
```

The Book class from Listing 5-1 has three fields, and these are accessible to the outside of the Book class via get and set accessors. Using the get and set methods, you can expose private fields to the consumer of the Book class. You can make the field read only, write only, or read-write only by using only the get method or the set method or get-set both to make it read writable. In .NET, you can also use the concept called Property to encapsulate private fields and to replace the get and set methods used in Listing 5-1, as shown in Listing 5-2.

Listing 5-2. The Book Class with Property

```
namespace Ch05
{
    public class Book
    {
        private string name;
        private int publishedYear;
        private string author;

        public Book()
        {
            name            = default(string);
            publishedYear   = default(int);
            author          = default(string);
        }

        public Book(string nameOfTheBook, int publishedYearOfTheBook, string authorOfTheBook)
        {
            name            = nameOfTheBook;
            publishedYear   = publishedYearOfTheBook;
            author          = authorOfTheBook;
        }
```

```
    public string Name                              /* Name property */
    {
        get { return name; }
        set { name = value; }
    }

    public int PublishedYear                        /* PublishedYear property */
    {
        get { return publishedYear; }
        set { publishedYear = value; }
    }

    public string Author                            /* Author property */
    {
        get { return author; }
        set { author = value; }
    }
  }
}
```

The Book class in Listing 5-2 defined the properties Name, PublishedYear, and Author for the private fields name, publishedYear, and author. These properties will eliminate the need to define the get and set methods manually in the type; behind the scenes the C# compiler takes care of that when you use a property to expose the private fields. When the C# compiler compiles the Book class, as defined in Listing 5-2, it implements the get and set method automatically to expose private fields used for the properties, for example, the name field for the Name property. This is a wrapper for the get and set methods to expose the fields from the type.

Let's decompile the Book class as shown in Listing 5-2 into IL to find out more about the Property definition defined by the C# compiler, as shown in Listing 5-3.

Listing 5-3. ILCode of the Book Class.

```
.class public auto ansi beforefieldinit Book extends [mscorlib]System.Object
{
    /* Code removed */
    .property instance string Author
    {
        .get instance string
        Ch05.Book::get_Author()            /* C# Compiler generates the get_Author method */
        .set instance void
        Ch05.Book::set_Author(string)      /* C# Compiler generates the set_Author method */
    }

    .property instance string Name
    {
        .get instance string
        Ch05.Book::get_Name()              /* C# Compiler generates the get_Name method */
        .set instance void
        Ch05.Book::set_Name(string)        /* C# Compiler generates the set_Name method */
    }
```

```
    .property instance int32 PublishedYear
    {
        .get instance int32
        Ch05.Book::get_PublishedYear()          /* C# Compiler generates the get_PublishedYear
                                                 * method */

        .set instance void
        Ch05.Book::set_PublishedYear(int32)     /* C# Compiler generates the set_PublishedYear
                                                 * method */

    }
    .field private string author                            /* Private field*/
    .field private string name                              /* Private field*/
    .field private int32 publishedYear                      /* Private field*/
}
```

In Listing 5-3, you can see that the C# compiler generates the get and set method for the private fields, for example, for the Author property it implements two new methods such as get_Author and set_Author to encapsulate the author field. This is also done for the Name and PublishedYear property, for which the C# compiler implements get_Name and set_Name and get_PublishedYear and set_PublishedYear.

If you examine the get_Author and set_Author method in IL implementation, as shown in Listing 5-4, you will understand how a C# compiler implements these get and set methods.

Listing 5-4. Implementation of the get_Author() and set_Author(string)

```
.method public hidebysig specialname instance string get_Author() cil managed
{
    .maxstack 1
    .locals init (
        [0] string CS$1$0000)
    L_0000: nop
    L_0001: ldarg.0
    L_0002: ldfld string Ch05.Book::author          /* It loads the value of the private field
                                                     * author */

    L_0007: stloc.0
    L_0008: br.s L_000a
    L_000a: ldloc.0
    L_000b: ret
}


.method public hidebysig specialname instance void set_Author(string 'value') cil managed
{
    .maxstack 8
    L_0000: nop
    L_0001: ldarg.0
    L_0002: ldarg.1
    L_0003: stfld string Ch05.Book::author          /* It replace the value of the field author
                                                     * with the given value */

    L_0008: ret
}
```

In Listing 5-4, the get_Author method loads the value of the author field and returns to the caller of the Author property as output. The set_Author method loads the argument value at position 1 from the argument array of the Method state description table defined for the set_Author (by the C# compiler) onto the evaluation stack using the instruction ldarg.1 in L_0002. The value of the author field of the Book class is stored using the stfld instruction in L_0003.

- ldfld field - Push the value of field of object (or value type) aObject, onto the stack

- stfld field - Replace the value of field of the object aObject with value.

The property declaration in C# reduces the task of defining get and set methods in a class. The property declaration concept has been abstracted a step further to make it easier by introducing the Automatic property declaration concept. In this concept you do not need to define any private fields for the class, just declare the property for the class with the get; and set; statements in it. The CLR will take care of the rest (i.e., it will define private fields for the relevant property as well as define the get and set methods for which CLR-generated private fields to expose via the relevant property).

In Listing 5-5, the Book class defines three automatic properties: Name, PublishedYear, and Author.

Listing 5-5. Automatic Property in C#

```
namespace Ch05
{
    public class Book
    {
        /* Assigning default value to the Property */
        public Book()
        {
            Name                = default(string);
            PublishedYear       = default(int);
            Author              = default(string);
        }

        /* Assigning value to the Property */
        public Book(string nameOfTheBook, int publishedYearOfTheBook, string authorOfTheBook)
        {
            Name                = nameOfTheBook;
            PublishedYear       = publishedYearOfTheBook;
            Author              = authorOfTheBook;
        }

        /* Automatic property declaration for the Name */
        public string Name {get; set;}

        /* Automatic property declaration for the PublishedYear */
        public int PublishedYear { get;  set; }

        /* Automatic property declaration for the Author */
        public string Author{get; set; }
    }
}
```

The Book class in Listing 5-5 has not declared any private fields for the Name, PublishedYear, and Author properties, and these properties do not have the implementation code inside the get and set accessors (i.e., it has not explicitly mentioned which field to expose, and this is the beauty of the automatic property concept). When you declare any automatic property in a type, the C# compiler:

- Adds a private field for that property, such as for Name, Author, and PublishedYear, and the CLR adds the private fields <Name>k__BackingField, <Author>k__ BackingField, and <PublishedYear>k__BackingField.

- Implements the get and set method for the private field to get and set values from that property, such as get_Name and set_Name for the Name property and so on.

Let's decompile the Book class defined in Listing 5-5 into IL code to find out how the C# compiler adds private fields and get and set methods for the automatic property, as shown in Listing 5-6.

Listing 5-6. IL Code for the Automatic Property

```
.class public auto ansi beforefieldinit Book  extends [mscorlib]System.Object
{
    /* Code removed */
    .property instance string Author
    {
     /* C# Compiler generates the get_Author method */
       .get instance string Ch05.Book::get_Author()
     /* C# Compiler generates the set_Author method */
       .set instance void Ch05.Book::set_Author(string)
    }
    .property instance string Name
    {
    /* C# Compiler generates the get_Name method */
       .get instance string Ch05.Book::get_Name()
    /* C# Compiler generates the set_Name method */
       .set instance void Ch05.Book::set_Name(string)
    }
    .property instance int32 PublishedYear
    {
    .get instance int32
    Ch05.Book::get_PublishedYear()                  /* C# Compiler generates the get_PublishedYear
                                                     * method */


    .set instance void
    Ch05.Book::set_PublishedYear(int32)             /* C# Compiler generates the set_PublishedYear
                                                     * method */

    }
    .field private string        <Author>k__BackingField          { /* Code removed*/ }
    .field private string        <Name>k__BackingField            { /* Code removed*/ }
    .field private int32         <PublishedYear>k__BackingField   { /* Code removed*/ }
}
```

The CLR adds three private fields: <Author>k__BackingField, <Name>k__BackingField, and <PublishedYear>k__BackingField for the Author, Name, and PublishedYear properties, respectively, in the Book class. It implements the get and set methods for those private fields, such as, for the Author property the CLR adds get_Author and set_Author method and likewise for the Name and PublishedYear property.

Let's examine the get_Author and set_Author, get_Name and set_Name, get_PublishedYear and set_PublishedYear method, as implemented in Listing 5-7, from the generated IL code in Listing 5-5.

Listing 5-7. IL Code for the get and set Methods

```
/* To read value from the Author property about the author  */
.method public hidebysig specialname instance string get_Author() cil managed
{
    /* Code removed */
    L_0001: ldfld string Ch05.Book::<Author>k__BackingField     /* It loads the value of the field
                                                                  * <Author>k__BackingField */
    /* Code removed */
}


/* To write value about the author via the Author property. The Author property is read-
writeable */
.method public hidebysig specialname instance void set_Author(string 'value') cil managed
{
    /* Code removed */
    L_0002: stfld string Ch05.Book::<Author>k__BackingField      /* It replaces the value of the
                                                                  * field <Author>k__BackingField
                                                                  * with the given value */
    /* Code removed */
}


/* To read value from the Name property about the name  */
.method public hidebysig specialname instance string get_Name() cil managed
{
    /* Code removed */
    L_0001: ldfld string Ch05.Book::<Name>k__BackingField        /* It loads the value of the field
                                                                  * <Name>k__BackingField */
    /* Code removed */
}


/* To write value about the name  via the Name property. The Name property is read-writeable */
.method public hidebysig specialname instance void set_Name(string 'value') cil managed
{
    /* Code removed */
    L_0002: stfld string Ch05.Book::<Name>k__BackingField        /* It replaces the value of the
                                                                  * field <Name>k__BackingField
                                                                  * with the given value */
    /* Code removed */
}


/* To read value from the PublishedYear property about the published year  */
.method public hidebysig specialname instance int32 get_PublishedYear() cil managed
{
    /* Code removed */
    L_0001: ldfld int32 Ch05.Book::<PublishedYear>k__BackingField  /* It loads the value of the
                                                                    * field < PublishedYear>k__
                                                                    * BackingField */
```

```
        /* Code removed */
}


/* To write value about the published year  via the PublishedYear property. The PublishedYear
 * property is read-writeable */
.method public hidebysig specialname instance void set_PublishedYear(int32 'value') cil managed
{
    /* Code removed */
/* It replaces the value of the field <PublishedYear>k__BackingField with the given value */
 L_0002: stfld int32 Ch05.Book::<PublishedYear>k__BackingField
    /* Code removed */
}
```

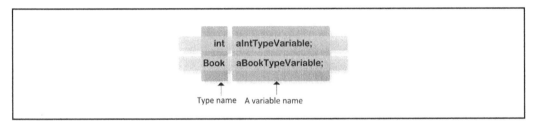

Figure 5-1. Variable declaration in C#

var Implicitly Typed Local Variable

In C#, you can declare a variable using a type name and then the variable name followed by **;**, as shown in Figure 5-1. The C# compiler will then know what type of variable it is and what the name of the variable is.

To declare a variable you need a type name, which will tell the CLR to allocate appropriate memory based on the type name, assign that memory an address, and associate it with the variable name. This is an explicit variable declaration in .NET, which you can define by using the keyword var in your program to define a variable. An example of the usage of the var keyword is shown in Listing 5-8.

Listing 5-8. Implicit Type Declaration Using var Keyword

```
using System;

namespace Ch05
{
    class Program
    {
        static void Main(string[] args)
        {
            var person     = new Person                                /* type of Person */
            {
                Name       = "A Person"
```

```
        };
        var personAge  = 30;                                     /* type of int */
        var authorOf   = "Expert C# 5.0: with the .NET 4.5 Framework"; /* type of string */

        Console.WriteLine("Name:{0}\nAge: {1}\nBook: {2}",
                        person.Name, personAge, authorOf);
    }
}

public class Person
{
    public string Name
    {
        get;
        set;
    }
}
}
```

This program will produce the following output:

```
Name: A Person
Age:  30
Book: Expert C# 5.0: with the .NET 4.5 Framework
```

In Listing 5-8, Program class defines three variables—person, personAge, and authorOf—using the var keyword. Let's explore how the CLR deals with the var keyword.

var in Runtime

The C# compiler infers the type of the variable from the right-hand-side expression. For example, the type for the person is inferred from the type of the right-hand-side expression new Person{....}, which makes person a type of Person in the same way as for personAge as int and authorOf as string.

Let's explore more about this by examining the decompiled IL code for Listing 5-8, as shown in Listing 5-9.

Listing 5-9. IL Code of the C# code in Listing 5-8

```
.method private hidebysig static void Main(string[] args) cil managed
{
    .entrypoint
    .maxstack 4
    .locals init (
        [0] class Ch05.Person person,
        [1] int32 personAge,
        [2] string authorOf,
        [3] class Ch05.Person <>g__initLocal0)
    L_0000: nop

    /* newobj instantiates an instance of the Person type onto the Heap.*/
    L_0001: newobj instance void Ch05.Person::.ctor()
```

```
/* Stores the heap address reference of the Person object instantiated in L_0001 into the
 * Locals section of
 * the stack at position 3.*/
L_0006: stloc.3

/* Loads the Person object <>g__initLocal0 */
L_0007: ldloc.3
L_0008: ldstr "A Person"

/* Sets the value for the Name property of the Person object*/
L_000d: callvirt instance void Ch05.Person::set_Name(string)
L_0012: nop

/* Loads the Person object <>g__initLocal0 */
L_0013: ldloc.3

/* The Person object (<>g__initLocal0) at the position 3 (Load in L_0013) will be stored
 * into the Locals section of the Main method stack at position 0.*/
L_0014: stloc.0
L_0015: ldc.i4.s 30
L_0017: stloc.1
L_0018: ldstr "Expert C# 5.0: with the .NET 4.5 Framework"
L_001d: stloc.2
L_001e: ldstr "Name:{0}\nAge:{1}\nBook: {2}"
L_0023: ldloc.0

/* get the Name property value of the Person object*/
L_0024: callvirt instance string Ch05.Person::get_Name()
L_0029: ldloc.1
L_002a: box int32
L_002f: ldloc.2
L_0030: call void [mscorlib]System.Console::WriteLine(string, object, object, object)
L_0035: nop
L_0036: ret
}
```

The C# compiler sets the type for the person object as Ch05.Person, personAge as int32, and authorOf as string. In Listing 5-9, there is another variable, <>g__initLocal0 type of Ch05.Person, that has been defined. In L_0001 the newobj instruction instantiates an instance of Person type and stores it in the local variable at position 3 (<>g__initLocal0) and sets the value for the Name property in L_000d. In L_0013, the <>g__initLocal0 object will be stored in the local variable at position 0 (person). The C# compiler sets the instruction to load the value 30 (0x1E) into the local variable at position 1 of the Local section of the Main method for personAge. Finally, it sets the instruction to load the string literally "Expert C# 5.0: with the .NET 4.5 Framework" into the local variable authorOf at position 2 of the Local section of the Main method.

In C#, the variables declared with var keyword are strongly typed and the compiler makes sure to associate those with the appropriate type before they get executed. The approximate C# code shown in Listing 5-10 is for the Main method of Listing 5-8 after compilation,

Listing 5-10. *Compiler Modified Code for Listing 5-8*

```
private static void Main(string[] args)
{
    Person <>g__initLocal0 = new Person {                            /* change var to Person */
        Name           = "A Person"
    };
    Person person    = <>g__initLocal0;
    int personAge    = 30;                                           /* change var to int */
    string authorOf  = "Expert C# 5.0: with the .NET 4.5 Framework"; /* change var to string */


    Console.WriteLine("Name:{0}\nAge:{1}\nBook: {2}", person.Name, personAge, authorOf);
```

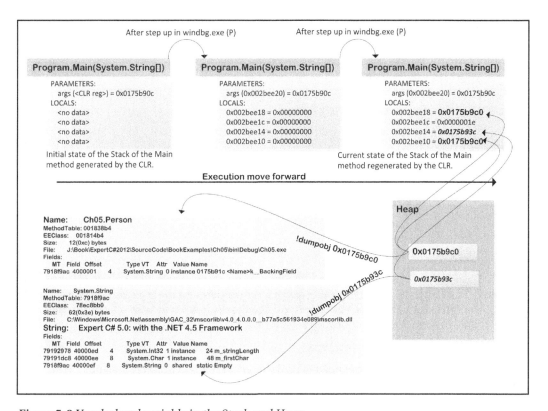

Figure 5-2.*Var declared variable in the Stack and Heap*

}

In Listing 5-10, you can see that the C# compiler sets the appropriate types for the relevant statement where the variable is declared using the var keyword. In the runtime, CLR will take care of all the variables declared with var the same as normal in respect to the stack and heap. Let's explore more about this by examining the memory (stack and heap) status when CLR deals with using the var keyword in the Program class, as shown in Listing 5-8.

Figure 5-2 shows that the LOCALS section of the Main method's Method state description table contains a Heap reference of the Person instantiated on the Heap at 0x0175b9c0, an object of a string instantiated on the Heap at 0x0175b93c and int value 0x1e (30).

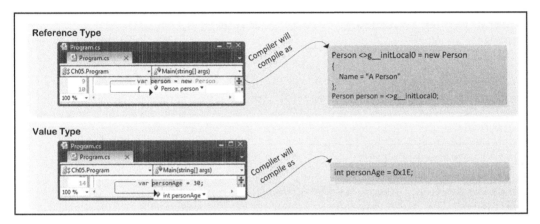

Figure 5-3. *Implicit variable declaration in design time*

var in Design Time

In the design time, the C# compiler sets the appropriate type for those var declared variables. The variable declared using var keyword will be a strongly typed variable, and the C# compiler sets the type in design time as well. Figure 5-3 shows how the compiler sets the type for the variable declared using the keyword var.

Anonymous Type

The anonymous type is a way to declare a type that contains the property for the type, without any functionality in it. You can use anonymous type where you need to declare a type with only properties. There are several things you can do using anonymous type:

- It can define only properties for the type.

- The type of the property does not need to be declared, as it infers from the assigned value at runtime.

- You cannot define any method inside the anonymous type.

- Once the type is defined with the value, it is not possible to change the value of the properties.

Listing 5-11 shows an anonymous type anObjectOfAnonymousType that has been defined, which contains four properties, such as Name, Language, PublishedOn, and Description, with the value assign to it in declaration time.

Listing 5-11. *An Anonymous Type Declaration*

```
using System;

namespace Ch05
{
    class Program
    {
        static void Main(string[] args)
        {
/* Anonymous type definition*/
    var anObjectOfAnonymousType = new
    {
     /* a string  type */
      Name                   = "Expert C# 5.0: with the .NET 4.5 Framework",
     /* a string  type */
                Language     = "C#",
     /* a int   type */
                PublishedOn = 2012,
     /* a DescriptionAboutBook type */
                Description = new DescriptionAboutBook("This book is about C#")
            };

            Console.WriteLine("{0}\n{1}\n{2}\n{3}",
                anObjectOfAnonymousType.Name,
                anObjectOfAnonymousType.Language,
                anObjectOfAnonymousType.PublishedOn,
                anObjectOfAnonymousType.Description.Description);
        }
    }
    public class DescriptionAboutBook
    {
        public DescriptionAboutBook(string data)
        {
            Description = data;
        }
        public string Description { get; set; }
    }
}
```

This program produces the following output:

```
Expert C# 5.0: with the .NET 4.5 Framework
C#
2012
This book is about C#
```

This anObjectOfAnonymousType object will hold an object of an anonymous type, which has the properties and their associated values as shown in Table 5-1.

Table 5-1. Property of the Anonymous Types

Property name	Types	Value	Editable
Name	string	Expert C# 5.0: with the .NET 4.5 Framework	×
Language	string	C#	×
PublishedOn	Int32	2012	×
Description	DescriptionAboutBook	An object of the type DescriptionAboutBook	×

When the C# compiler finds the code shown in Listing 5-11, it will do the following:

- Define new type, which encapsulates the Name, Language, PublishedOn, and Description field inside it.

- Create an instance of that type and store it into the variable anObjectOfAnonymousType.

- The rest of the code in the Main method will then be able to access the values stored in this anonymous type field through this anObjectOfAnonymousType object.

The <>f__AnonymousType0 accepts four generic types:

```
<Name>j__TPar
<Language>j__TPar
<PublishedOn>j__TPar
<Description>j__TPar>
```

The <>f__AnonymousType0 class also defines four fields based on the above types, as shown in Table 5-2.

Table 5-2. Types in the Anonymous Type Declaration

Field name	Type
<Name>i__Field	<Name>j__TPar
<Language> i__Field	<Language>j__TPar
<PublishedOn> i__Field	<PublishedOn>j__TPar
<Description> i__Field	<Description>j__TPar>

This <>f__AnonymousType0 class has a constructor that takes four parameters, such as Name, Language, PublishedOn, and Description of type <Name>j__TPar, <Language>j__TPar, <PublishedOn>j__TPar, and <Description>j__TPar>, which will be used to initialize the <Name>i__Field, <Language>i__Field, <PublishedOn>i__Field, and <Description>i__Field fields of the <>f__AnonymousType0 class.

The actual type for these <Name>j__TPar, <Language>j__TPar, <PublishedOn>j__TPar, and <Description>j__TPar> will be provided by the consumer of this <>f__AnonymousType0 anonymous type. The consumer of these anonymous types can only read values of the fields from the instance of this type because the property of this anonymous type has been defined as read only (i.e., only the get methods defined for the fields). Listing 5-12 shows the decompiled IL for the anonymous type defined in Listing 5-11.

Listing 5-12. Decompiled Code for the <>f__AnonymousType0 Type

```
.class private auto ansi sealed beforefieldinit <>f__AnonymousType0<
    <Name>j__TPar,                      /* Generic type for the Name*/
    <Language>j__TPar,                  /* Generic type for the Language*/
    <PublishedOn>j__TPar,               /* Generic type for the PublishedOn*/
    <Description>j__TPar>               /* Generic type for the Description*/
    extends [mscorlib]System.Object
{
  /* Constructor */
  .method public hidebysig specialname rtspecialname instance void .ctor
        (!<Name>j__TPar         Name,      /* Name type of  !<Name>j__TPar */
         !<Language>j__TPar      Language,  /* Language type of !<Language>j__TPar */
         !<PublishedOn>j__TPar   PublishedOn, /* PublishedOn type  of !<PublishedOn>j__TPar */
         !<Description>j__TPar   Description) /* Description type of !<Description>j__TPar */
         cil managed                { /* Code removed*/     }

  .property instance !<Description>j__TPar Description
  { .get instance !<Description>j__TPar  <>f__AnonymousType0'4::get_Description() }

  .property instance !<Language>j__TPar        Language
  { .get instance !<Language>j__TPar           <>f__AnonymousType0'4::get_Language() }

  .property instance !<Name>j__TPar        Name
  { .get instance !<Name>j__TPar           <>f__AnonymousType0'4::get_Name() }

  .property instance !<PublishedOn>j__TPar PublishedOn
  { .get instance !<PublishedOn>j__TPar        <>f__AnonymousType0'4::get_PublishedOn() }

  .field private initonly !<Description>j__TPar <Description>i__Field  { /* Code removed*/ }
  .field private initonly !<Language>j__TPar    <Language>i__Field     { /* Code removed*/ }
  .field private initonly !<Name>j__TPar        <Name>i__Field         { /* Code removed*/ }
  .field private initonly !<PublishedOn>j__TPar <PublishedOn>i__Field  { /* Code removed*/ }
}
```

The <>f__AnonymousType0 class defines the get method to access the fields of this anonymous type, but this class does not have any set method. As a result, the value of the field or property cannot be changed (i.e., read only). The caller of this anonymous type, which is the Main method of the Program class, shown in Listing 5-13, calls the newobj IL instruction in L_001a by passing the <>f__AnonymousType0 type name with the associated generic parameter type, for example, the string for <Name>j__TPar, string for <Language>j__TPar, int32 for the <PublishedOn>j__TPar, and Ch05.DescriptionAboutBook for the <Description>j__TPar>.

In the Main method of Listing 5-13, the instructions from L_0001 to L_0015 initialize the related data to make an instance of the <>f__AnonymousType0 type.

Listing 5-13. Decompiled IL Code for the Main Method from Listing 5-11

```
.class private auto ansi beforefieldinit Program extends [mscorlib]System.Object
{
    .method public hidebysig specialname rtspecialname instance void .ctor() cil managed
    {
        /* Code removed */
    }
    .method private hidebysig static void Main(string[] args) cil managed
    {
        .entrypoint
        .maxstack 5
        .locals init (
            [0] class <>f__AnonymousType0'4
                <string,                              /* The Type for the <Name>j__TPar */
                 string,                              /* The Type for the  <Language>j__TPar */
                 int32,                               /* The Type for the  <PublishedOn>j__TPar */
                 class Ch05.DescriptionAboutBook>     /* The Type for the <Description>j__TPar> */
                                                      anObjectOfAnonymousType,
            [1] object[] CS$0$0000)

        L_0000: nop
        L_0001: ldstr "Expert C# 5.0: with the .NET 4.5 Framework"
        L_0006: ldstr "C#"
        L_000b: ldc.i4 0x7dc
        L_0010: ldstr "This book is about C#"
        L_0015: newobj instance void Ch05.DescriptionAboutBook::.ctor(string)

        /* Instantiates an instance of the <>f__AnonymousType0'4 type*/
        L_001a: newobj instance void <>f__AnonymousType0'4
                <string,                              /* The Type for the <Name>j__TPar */
                 string,                              /* The Type for the  <Language>j__TPar */
                 int32,                               /* The Type for the  <PublishedOn>j__TPar */
                 class Ch05.DescriptionAboutBook>     /* The Type for the <Description>j__TPar> */
                 ::.ctor(!0, !1, !2, !3)
        L_001f: stloc.0
        L_0020: ldstr "{0}\n{1}\n{2}\n{3}"
        L_0025: ldc.i4.4
        L_0026: newarr object
        L_002b: stloc.1
        L_002c: ldloc.1
        L_002d: ldc.i4.0

        /* Loads the instance of the <>f__AnonymousType0'4 type stored at position 0 of
         * Locals section */
```

```
L_002e: ldloc.0

/* To read the field value from the instance of the <>f__AnonymousType0'4 type*/
L_002f: callvirt instance !0 <>f__AnonymousType0'4
        <string,                        /* The Type for the <Name>j__TPar */
        string,                         /* The Type for the  <Language>j__TPar */
        int32,                          /* The Type for the  <PublishedOn>j__TPar */
        class Ch05.DescriptionAboutBook> /* The Type for the <Description>j__TPar> */
                                        ::get_Name()
L_0034: stelem.ref
L_0035: ldloc.1
L_0036: ldc.i4.1

/* Loads the instance of the <>f__AnonymousType0'4 type stored at position 0 of Locals
 * section */
L_0037: ldloc.0

/* To read the field value from the instance of the <>f__AnonymousType0'4 type*/
L_0038: callvirt instance !1 <>f__AnonymousType0'4
        <string,                        /* The Type for the <Name>j__TPar */
        string,                         /* The Type for the  <Language>j__TPar */
        int32,                          /* The Type for the  <PublishedOn>j__TPar */
        class Ch05.DescriptionAboutBook>  /* The Type for the <Description>j__TPar> */
                                        ::get_Language()
L_003d: stelem.ref
L_003e: ldloc.1
L_003f: ldc.i4.2

/* Loads the instance of the <>f__AnonymousType0'4 type stored at position 0 of Locals
 * section */
L_0040: ldloc.0

/* To read the field value from the instance of the <>f__AnonymousType0'4 type*/
L_0041: callvirt instance !2 <>f__AnonymousType0'4
        <string,                        /* The Type for the <Name>j__TPar */
        string,                         /* The Type for the  <Language>j__TPar */
        int32,                          /* The Type for the  <PublishedOn>j__TPar */
        class Ch05.DescriptionAboutBook> /* The Type for the <Description>j__TPar> */
        ::get_PublishedOn()
L_0046: box int32
L_004b: stelem.ref
L_004c: ldloc.1
L_004d: ldc.i4.3

/* Loads the instance of the <>f__AnonymousType0'4 type stored at position 0 of Locals
section */
L_004e: ldloc.0

/* To read the field value from the instance of the <>f__AnonymousType0'4 type*/
L_004f: callvirt instance !3 <>f__AnonymousType0'4
        <string,                          /* The Type for the <Name>j__TPar */
```

```
            string,                       /* The Type for the  <Language>j__TPar */
            int32,                        /* The Type for the  <PublishedOn>j__TPar */
            class Ch05.DescriptionAboutBook>  /* The Type for the <Description>j__TPar> */
            ::get_Description()
L_0054: callvirt instance string Ch05.DescriptionAboutBook::get_Description()
L_0059: stelem.ref
L_005a: ldloc.1
L_005b: call void [mscorlib]System.Console::WriteLine(string, object[])
L_0060: nop
L_0061: ret
      }
}
```

The rest of the IL code will access this instance of the <>f__AnonymousType0 type and access the related property, for example:

- The instruction ldloc.0 in L_002e loads the local variable stored onto the position 0, which is anObjectOfAnonymousType, into the evaluation stack.

- On the following IL instruction, L_002f will call the method get_Name of the DescriptionAboutBook type to get the value of the Name field of the DescriptionAboutBook type.

Code from the L_0037 to L_0054 will be used to get the values of the different fields. Finally, this value will be displayed on the console as output.

As you saw earlier, the value of the anonymous type's property is read only, and you can define the value of the different properties of the type while you define it but you cannot change the value of the property after the instantiation of the anonymous type. The property of the anonymous type only implements the get method, and as a result it will not be able to change the value after it is instantiated. The C# compiler shows an error message when you build Listing 5-11 by adding the line of code shown in Listing 5-14 to update the Name field from the anonymous type instantiated.

Listing 5-14. To Modify the Name Property of the Anonymous Type

```
anObjectOfAnonymousType.Name = "Try to add new name";
```

When you try to assign a new value of the Name property of the anonymous type, the C# compiler raises the following error:

```
Error   1      Property or indexer 'AnonymousType#1.Name' cannot be assigned to -- it is read
only
```

Summary

In this chapter we have explore how the C # compiler implements the automatic property behind the scenes. You also explored the implicitly typed local variable using the var keyword as well as the anonymous type. In the next chapter, you will learn about the enum in C#.

CHAPTER 6

Enum

This chapter will discuss one of the nice features of the C# language: enumerated type or enum for short. I will show you how the enum type is defined in the .NET Framework, how you can get symbolic names and values from the enum, and how enum parses in C#.

Enum and .NET

Enum in C# is a type, which is a set of symbolic names and values (given by you or the C# compiler) pair. For example:

```
public enum Planets
{
    Sun = 0,
    Earth,
}
```

Or with the explicit type:

```
public enum Planets : int      /* int is the underlying type which C# compiler will use to set
                                * the values */
{                              /* for each of the symbolic names such as Sun, Earth. */
    Sun = 0,
    Earth,
}
```

Or you can also define it as shown here, which is the most common way to declare an enum:

```
public enum Planets
{
    Sun,                       /* The C# compiler sets the values */
    Earth,
}
```

Planets is an Enum type, which contains two symbolic names—Sun and Earth—with value 0 (given) and 1 (assigned by the C# compiler). You can use this Planets Enum as shown in this example:

```
Planets whereYouLive = Planets.Earth;            /* assign Earth to the whereYouLive variable */
bool liveInEarth = whereYouLive == Planets.Earth; /* produced true as result */
```

Enumerated type is derived from the System.Enum, as shown in Figure 6-1.

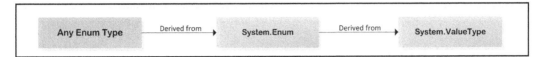

Figure 6-1. Enum in .NET

The Enum type has been defined in the System namespace of the mscorlib.dll (located in C:\WINDOWS\ Microsoft.NET\Framework\v4.0.30319\mscorlib.dll), which is derived from System.ValueType, as shown in Figure 6-2.

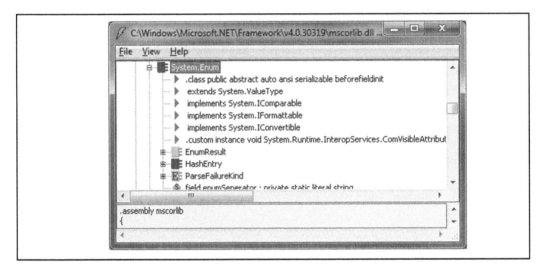

Figure 6-2. System.Enum in .NET Framework

The class definition of the Enum would be:

```
public abstract class Enum : ValueType, IComparable, IFormattable, IConvertible
```

Listing 6-1 presents an example of an enum to show how .NET deals with the Enum type.

Listing 6-1. An Example of Planets Enum

```
namespace Ch06
{
    class Program
    {
        public enum Planets
        {
            Sun = 0,            /*  Otherwise compiler will assign default value */
            Mercury,            /*  C# compiler will assign 1 */
            Venus,              /*  C# compiler will assign 2 */
            Earth,              /*  C# compiler will assign 3 */
            Mars,               /*  C# compiler will assign 4 */
```

```
        Jupiter,                /* C# compiler will assign 5 */
        Saturn,                 /* C# compiler will assign 6 */
        Uranus,                 /* C# compiler will assign 7 */
        Neptune                 /* C# compiler will assign 8 */
    }

    static void Main(string[] args)
    {
        Planets planets = new Planets();
        planets = Planets.Earth;
    }
}
}
```

In Listing 6-1, an Enum type Planets has been defined that has nine symbolic names with an initial value of 0 for the first item. You do not need to set the initial value for the Enum item explicitly; the C# compiler can take care of that. Listing 6-1 will be compiled and then the C# compiler will assign a value for the rest of the items in the Planets Enum, as the initial value for the first item has already been given. Listing 6-2 shows the decompiled IL code for Listing 6-1 (decompiled using the .Net Reflector tool), which will show how the C# compiler makes each of the items of the Enum static and assigns a value to it.

Listing 6-2. Decompiled IL Code of the Planets Enum

```
.class auto ansi sealed nested public Planets
    extends [mscorlib]System.Enum
{
    .field public static literal valuetype Ch06.Program/Planets Sun         = int32(0)
    .field public static literal valuetype Ch06.Program/Planets Mercury     = int32(1)
    .field public static literal valuetype Ch06.Program/Planets Venus       = int32(2)
    .field public static literal valuetype Ch06.Program/Planets Earth       = int32(3)
    .field public static literal valuetype Ch06.Program/Planets Mars        = int32(4)
    .field public static literal valuetype Ch06.Program/Planets Jupiter     = int32(5)
    .field public static literal valuetype Ch06.Program/Planets Saturn      = int32(6)
    .field public static literal valuetype Ch06.Program/Planets Uranus      = int32(7)
    .field public static literal valuetype Ch06.Program/Planets Neptune     = int32(8)
    .field public specialname rtspecialname int32 value__
}
```

From Listing 6-2 you can see that Planets Enum has been derived from the System.Enum class and the compiler assigned each of the items in the enum a value of type int32 (default type given by the C# compiler), where the value started at 0 and then incremented unless otherwise defined, such as shown in Listing 6-3.

Listing 6-3. Value Assigned for the Enum Items

```
public enum Planets
{
    Sun        = 10,     /* C# compiler will assign 10 */
    Mercury    = 12,     /* C# compiler will assign 12 */
    Venus      = 14,     /* C# compiler will assign 14 */
    Earth      = 16,     /* C# compiler will assign 16 */
    Mars       = 20,     /* C# compiler will assign 20 */
```

```
    Jupiter   = 24,      /* C# compiler will assign 24 */
    Saturn    = 32,      /* C# compiler will assign 32 */
    Uranus    = 16,      /* C# compiler will assign 16 */
    Neptune   = 99       /* C# compiler will assign 99 */
}
```

Let's decompile Listing 6-3 using the .Net Reflector tool, which shows that the C# compiler assigned the given value for each of the Enum items, as shown in Listing 6-4. For example, 10 for the Sun, 12 for the Mercury, and so on. You don't need to set values for the enum item unless it's required for your application.

Listing 6-4. Decompiled IL Code of Listing 6-3 using the .Net Reflector Tool

```
.class auto ansi sealed nested public Planets
    extends [mscorlib]System.Enum
{
    .field public static literal valuetype Ch06.Program/Planets Sun          = int32(10)
    .field public static literal valuetype Ch06.Program/Planets Mercury      = int32(12)
    .field public static literal valuetype Ch06.Program/Planets Venus        = int32(14)
    .field public static literal valuetype Ch06.Program/Planets Earth        = int32(0x10)
    .field public static literal valuetype Ch06.Program/Planets Mars         = int32(20)
    .field public static literal valuetype Ch06.Program/Planets Jupiter      = int32(0x18)
    .field public static literal valuetype Ch06.Program/Planets Saturn       = int32(0x20)
    .field public static literal valuetype Ch06.Program/Planets Uranus       = int32(0x10)
    .field public static literal valuetype Ch06.Program/Planets Neptune      = int32(0x63)
    .field public specialname rtspecialname int32 value__
}
```

If you dive in to find out more about the enum, you will find that:

- The C# compiler adds the given Enum values to the Constant section of the Metadata Info of the executable file. Each of the constant items from the Constant section will be linked with the Blob section of the Metadata Info, as shown in Figure 6-3. For example, the first row of the Constant section (1) refers to the blob#1b of the Blob section; the second row of the Constant section (2) refers to the blob#20 of the Blob section, and so on.

- Each of the blob items will contain a value for the enum item, for example, blob item 1b contains 0x0a, which is 10 in decimal for the Sun, blob item 20 contains 0x0c, which is 12 in decimal for Mercury, and so on.

Figure 6-3 demonstrates the Metadata Info relating to the enum in C# for the Enum defined in Listing 6-3.

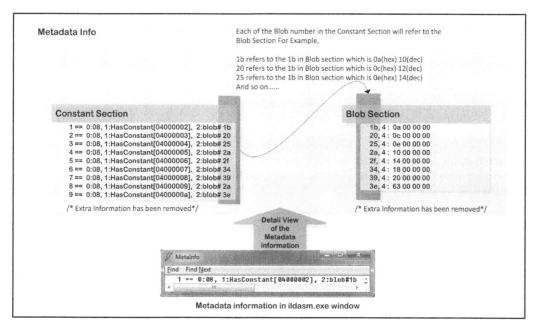

Metadata Info

Each of the Blob number in the Constant Section will refer to the Blob Section For Example,

1b refers to the 1b in Blob section which is 0a(hex) 10(dec)
20 refers to the 1b in Blob section which is 0c(hex) 12(dec)
25 refers to the 1b in Blob section which is 0e(hex) 14(dec)
And so on......

Constant Section

```
1 == 0:08, 1:HasConstant[04000002], 2:blob# 1b
2 == 0:08, 1:HasConstant[04000003], 2:blob# 20
3 == 0:08, 1:HasConstant[04000004], 2:blob# 25
4 == 0:08, 1:HasConstant[04000005], 2:blob# 2a
5 == 0:08, 1:HasConstant[04000006], 2:blob# 2f
6 == 0:08, 1:HasConstant[04000007], 2:blob# 34
7 == 0:08, 1:HasConstant[04000008], 2:blob# 39
8 == 0:08, 1:HasConstant[04000009], 2:blob# 2a
9 == 0:08, 1:HasConstant[0400000a], 2:blob# 3e
```

/* Extra Information has been removed*/

Blob Section

```
1b, 4 : 0a 00 00 00
20, 4 : 0c 00 00 00
25, 4 : 0e 00 00 00
2a, 4 : 10 00 00 00
2f, 4 : 14 00 00 00
34, 4 : 18 00 00 00
39, 4 : 20 00 00 00
3e, 4 : 63 00 00 00
```

/* Extra Information has been removed*/

Detail View of the Metadata information

MetaInfo

Find   Find Next

```
1 == 0:08, 1:HasConstant[04000002], 2:blob#1b
```

Metadata information in ildasm.exe window

Figure 6-3. *Enum value in the Metadata Info*

How to Get Names and Values from the Enum

When you define an enum, you might need to get all the names or the values defined in the enum. The program in Listing 6-5 shows how to get all of the names from the enum.

Listing 6-5. *Get Names of the Enum*

```csharp
using System;
using System.Linq;

namespace Ch06
{
    class Program
    {
        public enum Planets
        {
            Sun = 0,            /* Otherwise compiler will assign default value  */
            Mercury,            /* compiler will assign 1  */
            Venus,              /* compiler will assign 2  */
            Earth,              /* compiler will assign 3  */
            Mars,               /* compiler will assign 4  */
            Jupiter,            /* compiler will assign 5  */
            Saturn,             /* compiler will assign 6  */
            Uranus,             /* compiler will assign 7  */
            Neptune             /* compiler will assign 8  */
        }
```

```
        static void Main(string[] args)
        {
            Enum.GetNames(typeof(Planets)).ToList().ForEach(name => Console.Write(name + "\t"));
        }
    }
}
```

The program in Listing 6-5 will produce the following output:

```
Sun     Mercury Venus   Earth   Mars    Jupiter Saturn  Uranus  Neptune
```

Let's find out how the GetNames works internally in C#.

The first step is where the GetNames method internally calls the GetEnumNames method of the RuntimeType class:

```
.method public hidebysig static string[] GetNames(class System.Type enumType) cil managed
{
    /* Code removed */
    L_0015: callvirt instance string[] System.Type::GetEnumNames()
    L_001a: ret
}
```

In addition, the GetEnumNames method internally calls the InternalGetNames method to retrieve the names from the given Enum and returns it as an array of string, as demonstrated in the following implementation of the GetEnumNames method:

```
public override string[] GetEnumNames()
{
    string[] names = Enum.InternalGetNames(this); /* Get all the symbolic names define in the
given Enum. */
    string[] destinationArray = new string[names.Length];
    Array.Copy(names, destinationArray, names.Length);
    return destinationArray;
}
```

The InternalGetNames method calls the GetHashEntry method to get the data. This method wraps all the names and associated values into a HashEntry object. The HashEntry class has been defined in the Enum class, as shown in Figure 6-4.

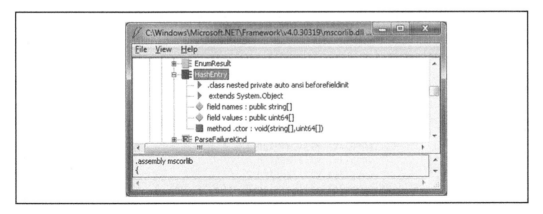

Figure 6-4. *HashEntry Class of the Enum*

The implementation of the HashEntry class is:

```
private class HashEntry
{
    public string[] names;        /* Used to hold the Symbolic name defined in a Enum */
    public ulong[] values;        /* Used to hold the associate values for the symbolic names
                                   * defined in a Enum */

    public HashEntry(string[] names, ulong[] values)
    {
        this.names = names;
        this.values = values;
    }
}
```

The implementation of the GetHashEntry method would be:

```
private static HashEntry GetHashEntry(RuntimeType enumType)
{
    HashEntry entry = (HashEntry) fieldInfoHash[enumType];
    /*Code removed*/
    ulong[] o = null;
    string[] strArray = null;
    GetEnumValues(
        enumType.GetTypeHandleInternal(),
        JitHelpers.GetObjectHandleOnStack<ulong[]>(ref o),
        JitHelpers.GetObjectHandleOnStack<string[]>(ref strArray));
    entry = new HashEntry(strArray, o);
    fieldInfoHash[enumType] = entry;
    return entry;
}
```

The GetHashEntry method returns the instance of the HashEntry, which holds symbolic names and values. Finally, GetEnumNames method returns the names' array from the HashEntry object.

Listing 6-6 shows that Listing 6-5 has been modified to get only the values from the given Enum.

Listing 6-6. GetValues from the Enum

```
using System;
using System.Linq;

namespace Ch06
{
    class Program
    {
        public enum Planets
        {
            Sun = 0,            /* Otherwise compiler will assign default value */
            Mercury,            /* compiler will assign 1 */
            Venus,              /* compiler will assign 2 */
            Earth,              /* compiler will assign 3 */
            Mars,               /* compiler will assign 4 */
            Jupiter,            /* compiler will assign 5 */
```

```
            Saturn,          /* compiler will assign 6 */
            Uranus,          /* compiler will assign 7 */
            Neptune          /* compiler will assign 8 */
        }

        static void Main(string[] args)
        {
            Enum.GetValues(typeof(Planets)).Cast<int>().ToList().ForEach(
        name => Console.Write(name + "\t"));
        }
    }
}
```

This program will produce the following output:

0   1   2   3   4   5   6   7   8

The CLR will call the GetValues method of the Enum class to retrieve all the values from the given Enum. The implementation of the GetValues is shown below:

```
public static Array GetValues(Type enumType)
{
  return enumType.GetEnumValues();
}
```

The GetValues method calls the GetEnumValues method of the RuntimeType class. Internally this GetEnumValues method will call the InternalGetValues method of the Enum class. InternalGetValues will call the GetHashEntry method in the same way it works for the GetNames method described above, except this method will return values instead of names as output from the HashEntry instance returned from the GetEnumValues method.

Determining Whether an Item Is Defined

In many circumstances, we need to find out if a particular item is defined in an enumerated type. For example, the code in Listing 6-7 shows Jupiter is defined in the Planets enum.

Listing 6-7. Item Finding from the Enum

```
using System;
using System.Linq;

namespace Ch06
{
    class Program
    {
        public enum Planets
        {
            Sun = 0,           /* Otherwise compiler will assign default value */
            Mercury,           /* compiler will assign 1 */
            Venus,             /* compiler will assign 2 */
            Earth,             /* compiler will assign 3 */
            Mars,              /* compiler will assign 4 */
```

```
    Jupiter,             /* compiler will assign 5 */
    Saturn,              /* compiler will assign 6 */
    Uranus,              /* compiler will assign 7 */
    Neptune              /* compiler will assign 8 */
}

static void Main(string[] args)
{
    string enumItemToFind = "Jupiter";
    Console.WriteLine(
        "Is {0}, has been defined in the Planets enum? {1}",
        enumItemToFind,
        Enum.IsDefined(typeof(Planets), enumItemToFind));
}
}
}
```

This program will produce the following output:

```
Is Jupiter, has been defined in the Planets enum? True
```

Let's find out how this IsDefined method works in C#.

The IsDefined method calls the IsEnumDefined method of the RuntimeType class:

```
public static bool IsDefined(Type enumType, object value)
{
    return enumType.IsEnumDefined(value);
}
```

The IsDefined method then calls the InternalGetNames from the Enum class. InternalGetNames method will return all the names defined in the given enum and, using the IndexOf method from the Array class, CLR finds out whether the given item (input to the IsDefined method) has been defined in the specified enum. The implementation of the IsEnumDefined method is demonstrated below:

```
public override bool IsEnumDefined(object value)
{
    /* Code removed*/
    return (Array.IndexOf<object>
                (Enum.InternalGetNames(this),          /* Return all the names in the Enum */
                value) >= 0);
    /* IndexOf will find value(name) from the names of the enum */
    /* Code removed*/
}
```

If you want to find the item based on the value instead of the name, for example:

```
Enum.IsDefined(typeof(Planets), Planets.Neptune) /* Planets.Neptune refers to 9 */
```

CLR will find the item based on the following code:

```
public override bool IsEnumDefined(object value)
{
    /* Code removed */
    ulong[] values = Enum.InternalGetValues(this);
    ulong num = Enum.ToUInt64(value);
```

```
        return (Array.BinarySearch<ulong>(values, num) >= 0);
}
```

Parsing

Listing 6-8 presents an example to help us understanding how CLR handles enum parsing.

Listing 6-8. Parsing an Item into an Enum

```
using System;
using System.Linq;

namespace Ch06
{
    class Program
    {
        public enum Planets
        {
            Sun = 0,            /* Otherwise compiler will assign default value */
            Mercury,            /* compiler will assign 1 */
            Venus,              /* compiler will assign 2 */
            Earth,              /* compiler will assign 3 */
            Mars,               /* compiler will assign 4 */
            Jupiter,            /* compiler will assign 5 */
            Saturn,             /* compiler will assign 6 */
            Uranus,             /* compiler will assign 7 */
            Neptune             /* compiler will assign 8 */
        }

        static void Main(string[] args)
        {
            string enumItemToFind = "Jupiter";
            Planets result;
            bool isParsable = Enum.TryParse<Planets>(enumItemToFind, true, out result);
        }
    }
}
```

The code in Listing 6-8 will try to find out whether enumItemToFind is parsable into the Planets Enum and return the parsed Enum into the result. If the parse operation is successful, CLR will return the appropriate Enum item into the result, otherwise it will return the default item (value with 0 or the item with lowest value) from the Enum as a result. In Listing 6-8, the result will hold Jupiter, otherwise it will be Sun, as Sun is the default of the Planets Enum. Let's find out how this works.

To do the parsing operation, the CLR will call the TryParse method of the Enum class. This method will initialize an instance of the EnumResult struct, as shown in Figure 6-5. Note that you can get this view when you check the Show Member Types option in ildasm.exe tool.

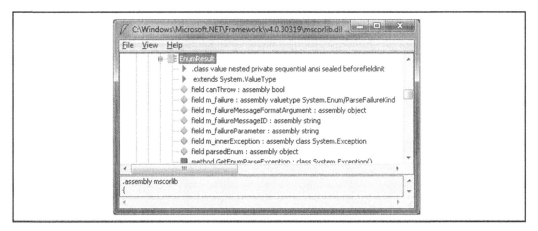

Figure 6-5. EnumResult Struct in the System.Enum

In the TryParse method, CLR will call the TryParseEnum method with the instance of the EnumResult struct. The CLR will parse the given item into Enum, wrap the result into the EnumResult object, and pass back the instance of the EnumResult to the TryParse method. The EnumResult object will hold the relevant Enum in it and return the Boolean to the caller, as demonstrated in the following implementation of the TryParse method:

```
public static bool TryParse<TEnum>(string value, bool ignoreCase, out TEnum result)
    where TEnum : struct
{
    bool flag;
    result = default(TEnum);
    EnumResult parseResult = new EnumResult();
    parseResult.Init(false);
    if (flag = TryParseEnum(typeof(TEnum), value, ignoreCase, ref parseResult))
    {
        result = (TEnum)parseResult.parsedEnum;
    }
    return flag;
}
```

Summary

In this chapter, we have learned that enumerated types are strongly typed. For example, if a method requires a value of Planets.Neptune and you send Universe enumerated type, the C# compiler throws a compilation error. Enumerated types make the program easy to write, read, and maintain instead of using hard-coded value in the program. We also learned how the C# compiler takes care of the enum, how you can get values and names from an enum, and how the CLR parses an enum. In the next chapter, you will explore the delegate in C#.

CHAPTER 7

Delegate

This chapter will discuss delegates. First, we will examine the C# delegate compared to the function pointer in C language, which will give you a basic idea of the similarity between the function pointer in C and delegate in .NET. This will also build a background knowledge about the function pointer, which will help you understand the internal working of delegates. Finally, you will explore generic delegates such as Func and Action in .NET by examining how the C# compiler takes care of the Func and Action delegates.

Understanding Delegates

In .NET, a *delegate* defines a reference type that can be used to encapsulate a method such as static or an instance method with a specific signature. When you declare a variable of delegate type, the CLR stores a method pointer in it as the method pointer value, and through that variable of delegate type, you can invoke the assigned method from the appropriate places. The CLR maintains the method pointer behind the scenes for the delegate type, so before diving deeper into the workings of the delegate, let's revisit the pointer concept.

The *pointer* is nothing but a memory address stored in a variable that points back to the value the address is pointing to and is also used to point to a method. The pointer is all about accessing or updating the value of a variable or function by accessing the address of that variable or function using the & and * symbols in a program.

The pointer can hold a variable's memory location, such as:

Variable Pointer (VP) =a memory location P store in a variable V then V is called the pointer of P or V is pointing to P

It can also hold the location of a function or method as a value. A function pointer declared with a syntax would be:

Function Pointer (FP) = ReturnType (*NameOfFunctionPointer) (InputType)

This function pointer holds an address of a function whose signature matches the function pointer signature defined as FP. When it stores the variable location defined as VP, you can call it a variable pointer, and when it stores the function's location, you can call it a function or method pointer. Figure 7-1 demonstrates variable and function pointers.

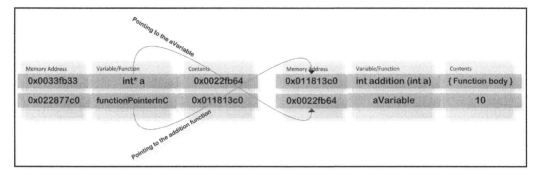

Figure 7-1. *Pointer and memory location*

To explore more about the variable and function pointers, let's examine the code in Listing 7-1, where a variable pointer and a function pointer are declared, using C programming language, to describe the pointer concept of a variable and a function.

Listing 7-1. *Example of the Function Pointer in C*

```c
#include "stdafx.h"

int addition( int a )
{
      return a+10;
}

int pointerTest( int* a )
{
      *a=100;                  /* change the value of the pointer variable a pointing to*/
      return *a;               /* return the value of the pointer variable a pointing to*/
}

int _tmain(int argc, _TCHAR* argv[])
{

      int aVariable =10;                        /* declare a variable aVariable of type  int */
      printf("%d\n", pointerTest(&aVariable)); /* aVariable's address pass to the pointerTest
                                                * function */
      int (*functionPointerInC)(int);          /* declare a Function Pointer which accept and
                                                * return int.*/
      functionPointerInC = &addition;          /* Assign a function's
                                                * address to the Function Pointer */
      printf("%d",(*functionPointerInC)(1) );  /* Invoke the Function pointer */
      return 0;
}
```

This program produces the following output:

```
100
11
```

In Listing 7-1, three functions, addition, which takes an input, pointerTest, which takes a variable pointer as input, and _tmain, which takes two inputs, execute the program. In the _tmain method, a variable called aVariable of type int with value 10 is declared and the pointerTest function is called by passing the address of the aVariable variable.

The addition method is used in Listing 7-1 to assign the function pointer functionPointerInC by assigning the address of addition function (&addition refers to the address or location of the addition function).

In runtime, the contents or value and address or location of the variable aVariable in the _tmain and pointerTest method will be as shown as in Table 7-1.

Table 7-1. Variable Addresses

&aVariable (The address of aVariable)	Int* a or a (The address a point to)	&a (The address of the pointer)
0x0022fb64	0x0022fb64	0x0022fa84

As with the variable pointer a, functionPointerInC will hold the address of the addition method as a value in runtime, as shown in Table 7-2.

Table 7-2. Function Addresses

Address of functionPointerInC	functionPointerInC pointing to	&addition
0x0118111d	0x011813c0	0x011813c0

■ **Note:** The address will vary when you execute Listing 7-1 in your environment.

Encapsulating Memory Handling with Delegates

From the above discussion and C code, you saw how you need to handle the memory addresses when using a function pointer. In .NET, C# introduces a new way to encapsulate all the memory handling of the method pointer in an object-oriented manner, which is called *delegate*. The delegates are conceptually similar to the function pointer in C/C++ as described earlier, but they are more easy to use and they provides the type safety.

Listing 7-2 provides an example that will help you understand delegate. The DelegateOfTheCalculator is declared as the type of delegate to store a method, which takes two inputs and returns a type of int. In the DelegateHandler method, an instance of the DelegateOfTheCalculator type has been instantiated and assigned the Add method, and in addition the Sub method was added and removed from the delegateOfTheCalculator.

Listing 7-2. Example of the Delegate in C#

```
using System;

namespace Ch07
{
    class Program
    {
        /* declare a delegate type. */
```

189

```
delegate int DelegateOfTheCalculator(int a, int b);

static void Main(string[] args)
{
    DelegateHandler();
}

static void DelegateHandler()
{
    StandardCalculator standardCalculator = new StandardCalculator();

    DelegateOfTheCalculator delegateOfTheCalculator =
                        new DelegateOfTheCalculator(standardCalculator.Add);
    delegateOfTheCalculator += standardCalculator.Sub;
    delegateOfTheCalculator -= standardCalculator.Sub;

    /* Execute the Add method */
    Console.WriteLine("Sum of a and b is:{0}", delegateOfTheCalculator(10, 10));
    }
}

public class StandardCalculator
{
    public int Add(int a, int b) { return a + b; }
    public int Sub(int a, int b) { return a > b ? a - b : 0; }
    public int Mul(int a, int b) { return a * b; }
}
}
```

This program will produce the following output:

```
Sum of a and b is:20
```

In Listing 7-2, you can see how delegate makes accessing the method easy in comparison to using the function pointer, as shown in Listing 7-1. You can also add multiple methods into one delegate type and remove multiple methods from the delegate without even handling any of the pointer functions. In the next section, you will explore more about the delegates in .NET.

Delegate in .NET

The Delegate and MulticastDelegate classes, defined in the mscorlib.dll assembly, as demonstrated in Figure 7-2, are responsible for taking care of the underlying function pointer in C#.

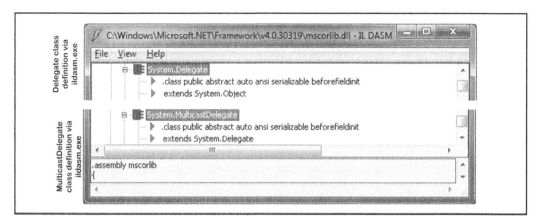

Figure 7-2. Delegate and MulticastDelegate class in the .NET

This `MulticastDelegate` class encapsulates the assigned methods inside it and provides functionality to execute those methods stored inside the `MulticastDelegate` class. The `Delegate` and `MulticastDelegate` classes' declaration is shown in Listing 7-3.

Listing 7-3. The MulticastDelegate and Delegate Class Definition in IL

```
.class public abstract auto ansi serializable beforefieldinit MulticastDelegate
    extends System.Delegate
{
    /* Code removed */
    .field private       native int       _invocationCount
    .field private       object           _invocationList
}

.class public abstract auto ansi serializable beforefieldinit Delegate
    extends System.Object
    implements System.ICloneable, System.Runtime.Serialization.ISerializable
{
    /* Code removed */
    .field assembly      object           _methodBase
    .field assembly      native int       _methodPtr              { /* Code removed */ }
    .field assembly      native int       _methodPtrAux           { /* Code removed */ }
    .field assembly      object           _target                 { /* Code removed */ }
}
```

Fields

Table 7-3 describes the important fields used in the `Delegate` and `MulticastDelegate` classes.

Table 7-3. *Fields from Delegate and MulticastDelegate Classes*

Field	Description
_methodPtr	It holds the address of the method where it is going to store the delegate or the method, it is going to point at.
_target	The related type where the method belongs and is going to store the delegate or the type in which the method belongs or is going to point at.
_invocationCount	Total number of the method stored into the delegate object or the total number of the method currently pointed at.
_invocationList	It holds all the delegate objects that encapsulate the method information.

Internal Work of the Delegate

While the C# compiler compiles the code as shown in Listing 7-2, it will do the following:

1. Convert the delegate declaration into a class, which inherits from the MulticastDelegate class, and MulticastDelegate class inherits from the Delegate class. As a result the C# compiler compiles delegate int DelegateOfTheCalculator(int a, int b) into a class that inherits from the MulticastDelegate class, as shown in Listing 7-4.

2. Instantiate the delegate class (generates for DelegateOfTheCalculator) and pass the initial method for which this delegate class has been instantiated. For Listing 7-2, the Add method is passed to the instance of the DelegateOfTheCalculator class as the initial method.

3. To add or remove a method from the delegate, CLR instantiates a new instance of the related delegate class and combines with the initial delegate instance to add a new method to the delegate object. As in Listing 7-2, the new instance of the DelegateOfTheCalculator will be instantiated and combined with the initial delegate instance as well as removing the stored delegate from the initial delegate instance.

Let's find out more details about the delegate.

Decompiled Delegate Class

Listing 7-4 shows the decompiled IL code from Listing 7-2 using ildasm.exe.

Listing 7-4. *Decompiled IL Code of Listing 7-2*

```
.class auto ansi sealed nested private DelegateOfTheCalculator
    extends [mscorlib]System.MulticastDelegate
{
    .method public hidebysig specialname rtspecialname instance void
        .ctor (object 'object', native int 'method') runtime managed    /* Constructor */
    { /* code removed */ }

    /* To asynchronously invoke the method stored into the delegate */
    .method public hidebysig newslot virtual instance class [mscorlib]System.IAsyncResult
        BeginInvoke
```

```
        (int32 a, int32 b, class [mscorlib]System.AsyncCallback callback, object 'object')
runtime managed
    { /* code removed */ }


    /* This method will invoke when the delegate execution */
    .method public hidebysig newslot virtual instance int32
        EndInvoke
        (class [mscorlib]System.IAsyncResult result) runtime managed
    { /* code removed */ }


    /* To synchronously invoke the method stored into the delegate */
    .method public hidebysig newslot virtual instance int32
        Invoke
        (int32 a, int32 b) runtime managed
    { /* code removed */ }
}
```

Instantiate, Combine, and Remove in Delegate

Let's decompile the DelegateHandler from Listing 7-2 using the .NET Reflector tool, which shows delegate instantiation, and combine and remove multiple delegate instances for multiple methods, as shown in Listing 7-5.

Listing 7-5. DelegateHandler Method

```
.method private hidebysig static void DelegateHandler() cil managed
{
    .maxstack 4
    .locals init (
        [0] class Ch07.StandardCalculator standardCalculator,
        [1] class Ch07.Program/DelegateOfTheCalculator delegateOfTheCalculator)
    L_0000: nop
    L_0001: newobj instance void Ch07.StandardCalculator::.ctor()
    L_0006: stloc.0

    /* Loads the standardCalculator object (which has methods Add, Sub, Mul) onto the stack */
    L_0007: ldloc.0

    /* Loads the function pointer of the Add method from the standardCalculator onto the
     * stack */
    L_0008: ldftn instance int32 Ch07.StandardCalculator::Add(int32, int32)

    /* CLR passes the standardCalculator object and the function pointer loaded in L_0008
     * to the DelegateOfTheCalculator class which eventually call the constructor
     * of the Delegate class.*/
    L_000e: newobj instance void Ch07.Program/DelegateOfTheCalculator::.ctor(object, native int)
    L_0013: stloc.1
    L_0014: ldloc.1
    L_0015: ldloc.0
```

```
    /* Loads the function pointer of the Sub from standardCalculator onto the stack */
    L_0016: ldftn instance int32 Ch07.StandardCalculator::Sub(int32, int32)

     /* CLR passes the standardCalculator object and the function pointer loaded in L_0016
     * to the DelegateOfTheCalculator class which eventually calls the constructor
     * from the Delegate class.*/
    L_001c: newobj instance void Ch07.Program/DelegateOfTheCalculator::.ctor(object, native int)

    /* CLR passes delegate object instantiated in the L_001c and retrieved in L_0014
     * to the Combine method of the Delegate class*/
    L_0021: call class [mscorlib]System.Delegate [mscorlib]System.Delegate::
                   Combine(class [mscorlib]System.Delegate, class [mscorlib]System.Delegate)
    L_0026: castclass Ch07.Program/DelegateOfTheCalculator
    L_002b: stloc.1
    L_002c: ldloc.1

    /* Loads the standardCalculator object into the stack */
    L_002d: ldloc.0

    /* Loads the function pointer of the Sub method onto the stack */
    L_002e: ldftn instance int32 Ch07.StandardCalculator::Sub(int32, int32)

    /* CLR passes the standardCalculator object and the function pointer loaded in L_002e
     * to the DelegateOfTheCalculator class which calls the constructor
     * of the Delegate class.*/
    L_0034: newobj instance void Ch07.Program/DelegateOfTheCalculator::.ctor(object, native int)

    /* CLR passes delegate object instantiated in the L_0034 and retrieved in L_002c
     * to the Remove method of the Delegate class*/
    L_0039: call class [mscorlib]System.Delegate [mscorlib]System.Delegate
                       ::Remove(class [mscorlib]System.Delegate, class [mscorlib]System.
Delegate)
    L_003e: castclass Ch07.Program/DelegateOfTheCalculator
    L_0043: stloc.1
    L_0044: ldstr "Sum of a and b is:{0}"
    L_0049: ldloc.1
    L_004a: ldc.i4.s 10
    L_004c: ldc.i4.s 10
    L_004e: callvirt instance int32 Ch07.Program/DelegateOfTheCalculator::Invoke(int32, int32)
    L_0053: box int32
    L_0058: call void [mscorlib]System.Console::WriteLine(string, object)
    L_005d: nop
    L_005e: ret
}
```

The C# compiler uses the memory address to locate the method but wraps all these underneath the pointer of the method, the type it belongs to, and into the different fields defined in the delegate and MulticastDelegate classes.

Let's find out more about this by analyzing the following:

- *Instantiate*: In the DelegateHandler method of Listing 7-5, in L_0008 the CLR loads the function pointer of the Add method onto the evaluation Stack and instantiates an instance of the DelegateOfTheCalculator in L_000e.

- *Combine*: In Listing 7-2, Add method has been added to the delegate using the + operator. The CLR will use the Combine method of the Delegate class internally to add a method into the delegate object. From Listing 7-5, in L_0016, the CLR loads the function pointer of Sub onto the evaluation Stack and instantiates an instance of the DelegateOfTheCalculator class in L_001c using the function pointer loaded in L_0016. In L_0021, the CLR calls the Combine method from the Delegate class to combine the original delegate object and the instance instantiated in the L_001c.

- *Remove*: In Listing 7-2, the Sub method has been removed from the delegate using the - operator. The CLR will use the Remove method of the Delegate class to remove the method stored in the delegate object. From Listing 7-5, in L_002e, the CLR loads the function pointer of the Sub method onto the evaluation Stack and instantiates an instance of the DelegateOfTheCalculator class in L_0034 using the function pointer loaded in L_002e. In L_0039, the CLR calls the Remove method of the Delegate class to remove this instance of the DelegateOfTheCalculator class instantiated in L_0034.

■ **ldftn method_name:** Pushes an unmanaged pointer (type native int) to a method referenced by method, on the Stack.

Examine the Memory

In .NET, delegate maintains the assigned or combined method information into fields such as _invocationList, _invocationCount, _methodPtr, _methodPtrAux, and _target. Let's find out the initial information that CLR maintains in the delegate class while it initiates the DelegateOfTheCalculator class (using the Add method as the initial method), as shown in Table 7-4.

Table 7-4. Function Pointer Details

_methodPtr	_Method	_target
0x4442160	Int32 Add(Int32, Int32)	Ch07.StandardCalculator

Table 7-4 shows that the CLR stored method Add of the StandardCalculator address information into _methodPtr field of delegate. CLR adds more methods into the delegate object, for example, if the instance of the DelegateOfTheCalculator class stores Add, Sub, and Mul methods from the StandardCalculator class, as shown in Listing 7-6.

Listing 7-6.Stores methods to the DelegateOfTheCalculator class

```
DelegateOfTheCalculator delegateOfTheCalculator = new DelegateOfTheCalculator(standardCalculat
or.Add);
delegateOfTheCalculator += standardCalculator.Sub;
delegateOfTheCalculator += standardCalculator.Mul;
```

In this case, the CLR will keep the method information in the delegate object, as shown in Table 7-5.

Table 7-5. Function Pointer Details

_methodPtr	Method	_target
0x04442160	Int32 Add(Int32, Int32)	Ch07.StandardCalculator
0x04442168	Int32 Sub(Int32, Int32)	Ch07.StandardCalculator
0x04442176	Int32 Mul(Int32, Int32)	Ch07.StandardCalculator

In addition to the information shown in Table 7-5, CLR also keeps count of the number of methods added into the delegate, as shown in Table 7-6.

Table 7-6. Number of Method

_invocationList	_invocationCount
{object[0x00000004]}	0x00000003

To prove this, let's get the address for the Add, Sub, and Mul methods from the StandardCalculator class by adding the following code block into the Main method of Listing 7-2.

```
StandardCalculator standardCalculator = new StandardCalculator();
var addressOfAddMethod = typeof(StandardCalculator).GetMethod("Add").MethodHandle.
GetFunctionPointer();
var addressOfSubMethod = typeof(StandardCalculator).GetMethod("Sub").MethodHandle.
GetFunctionPointer();
var addressOfMulMethod = typeof(StandardCalculator).GetMethod("Mul").MethodHandle.
GetFunctionPointer();
```

It will return the memory information, as shown in Table 7-7.

Table 7-7. Function Pointer Details of the StandardCalculator Class

Variable	Memory address	Type	Method name
addressOfAddMethod	0x04442160	StandardCalculator	Add
addressOfSubMethod	0x04442168	StandardCalculator	Sub
addressOfMulMethod	0x04442176	StandardCalculator	Mul

From Table 7-7, you can see that .NET delegate is all about the method addresses and managing those addresses in an object-oriented way using different data structures defined in the Delegate and MulticastDelegate classes.

■ **Note:** The memory address shown in Table 7-7 might be different when you run this locally.

Func and Action

The Func and Action delegates are a set of generic delegates that can work for methods of any return type (for Func) and reasonable number of arguments. These delegates are defined in the System namespace. The Action represents any function that may accept up to 16 parameters and returns void, for example, Action<T1>, where T1 refers to the input parameters and can be of any data type. Func is the same as Action but it has a return value of any type, for example, Func<T1, TResult> where T1 input parameters can be of any type and TResult is a returned value of any type. The only difference between Action and Func is the return value. In the following sections, we will explore more about Func and Action.

Func

The Func class is used to encapsulate method information in C#. The Func class is defined in the mscorlib. dll (C:\Windows\Microsoft.NET\ Framework\v4.0.30319), as shown in Figure 7-3, using the ildasm.exe.

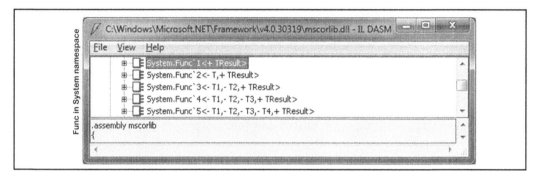

Figure 7-3. Func in .NET

The signature of the Func<TResult> class is shown in Listing 7-7.

Listing 7-7. Signature of the Func<TResult>

```
.class public auto ansi sealed Func<+ TResult> extends System.MulticastDelegate
```

The Func class declaration is shown in Listing 7-8.

Listing 7-8. Func Class Definition in IL Format

```
.class public auto ansi sealed Func<+ TResult> extends System.MulticastDelegate
{
    .method public hidebysig specialname rtspecialname instance void
        .ctor(object 'object', native int 'method') runtime managed
    {}

    .method public hidebysig newslot virtual instance class System.IAsyncResult
        BeginInvoke(class System.AsyncCallback callback, object 'object') runtime managed
    {}

    .method public hidebysig newslot virtual instance !TResult
        EndInvoke(class System.IAsyncResult result) runtime managed

    {}

    .method public hidebysig newslot virtual instance !TResult
```

```
        Invoke() runtime managed

    {}
}
```

Func<TResult> is a generic type, which inherits from the MulticastDelegate class and later inherits from the delegate class, as shown in Figure 7-4.

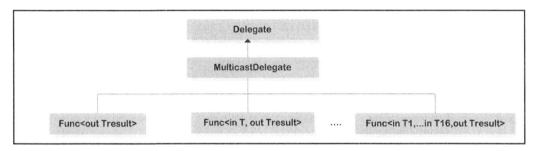

Figure 7-4. *Func and Delegate relationship*

The Func<TResult> class will have all the functionality and properties of the MulticastDelegate and Delegate types due to the inherent relationship between Func<TResult> and MulticastDelegate and the Delegate classes. The Func class has BeginInvoke, EndInvoke, and Invoke as well as the constructor method. The Func has _methodPtr, _target, _methodPtrAux, and Method properties functions, as described in Table 7-3.

The Func class can take up to 16 inputs and returns per type. Listing 7-9 shows an overloaded Func.

Listing 7-9. *Func Signature*

```
Func<TResult>
Func<ISource,TResult>
Func<ISource1,ISource2,TResult>
Func<ISource1,ISource2,ISource3,TResult>
Func<ISource1,ISource2,ISource3,ISource4,TResult>
Func<ISource1,ISource2,ISource3,ISource4,ISource5,TResult>
Func<ISource1,ISource2,ISource3,ISource4,ISource5,ISource6,TResult>
Func<ISource1,ISource2,ISource3,ISource4,ISource5,ISource6,ISource7,TResult>
Func<ISource1,ISource2,ISource3,ISource4,ISource5,ISource6,ISource7,ISource8,TResult>
Func<ISource1,ISource2,ISource3,ISource4,ISource5,ISource6,ISource7,ISource8,...,ISource16,TResu
lt>
```

Internal Work of the Func

Let's examine the example given in Listing 7-10 that is used to explain Func.

Listing 7-10. *An Example of Func<TResult> Type*

```
using System;

namespace Ch07
```

```
{
    class Program
    {
        static void Main(string[] args)
        {
            ExampleOfFunc exampleOfFunc = new ExampleOfFunc();

            Console.WriteLine("{0}", exampleOfFunc.Addition(exampleOfFunc.Add));
            Console.WriteLine("{0}", exampleOfFunc.Addition(
        () =>
                {
                    return 100 + 100;
                }));
        }
    }

    public class ExampleOfFunc
    {
        public int Addition(Func<int> additionImplementor)
        {
            if (additionImplementor != null)
                return additionImplementor();
            return default(int);
        }

        public int Add()
        {
            return 1 + 1;
        }
    }
}
```

This program will produce the following output:

2
200

The C# compiler compiles the Func declaration as below:

- The CLR instantiates an instance of the Func<TResult> using the method passed to it.

- In the instantiation time, Func<TResult> calls the constructor of the MulticastDelegate, which initializes a set of variables using the method-related information (which is passed to it), such as method pointer, name, and so forth.

- The CLR passes this instance of Func back to the place, for example, as shown in Listing 7-10. Addition method accepts Func, and the CLR passes this newly instantiated Func<TResult> object to it.

- When the Func<TResult> object will be executed, the CLR will call the invoke method of that Func<TResult> object, which will execute the containing method inside the Func<TResult> object.

Figure 7-5 demonstrates the Func instantiation process.

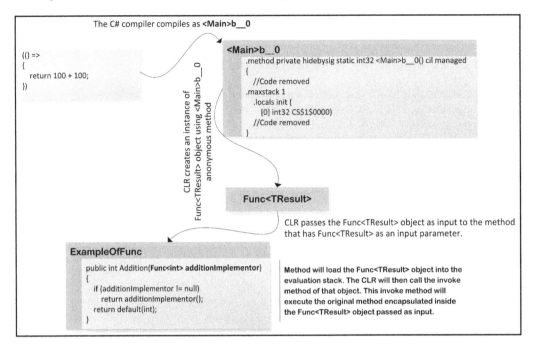

Figure 7-5. Func instantiation process in CLR

Listing 7-11 provides the decompiled IL, using the .NET Reflector tool, from Listing 7-10 to explain the Func instantiation process described in Figure 7-5.

Listing 7-11. IL Code for the Func<TResult> Example

```
.class private auto ansi beforefieldinit Program extends [mscorlib]System.Object
{
    .method public hidebysig specialname rtspecialname instance void .ctor() cil managed
    { /* Code removed */ }

    .method private hidebysig static int32 <Main>b__0() cil managed
    {
        .custom instance void [mscorlib]System.Runtime.CompilerServices.
CompilerGeneratedAttribute::.ctor()
        .maxstack 1
        .locals init (
            [0] int32 CS$1$0000)
        L_0000: nop
        L_0001: ldc.i4 200         /*  100 + 100 = 200*/
        /* Code removed */
    }

    .method private hidebysig static void Main(string[] args) cil managed
    {
```

```
.entrypoint
.maxstack 5
.locals init (
    [0] class Ch07.ExampleOfFunc exampleOfFunc)
L_0000: nop
L_0001: newobj instance void Ch07.ExampleOfFunc::.ctor()
L_0006: stloc.0
L_0007: ldstr "{0}"

/* Load the instance of the ExampleOfFunc from the locals section at position 0.  */
L_000c: ldloc.0
L_000d: ldloc.0

/* It loads the method pointer of the Add method on the stack*/
L_000e: ldftn instance int32 Ch07.ExampleOfFunc::Add()

/* Using the method pointer an instance of System.Func'1<int32> */
L_0014: newobj instance void [mscorlib]
               System.Func'1<int32>::.ctor(object, native int)

/* Instance of the System.Func'1<int32> will be pass to the Addition method call */
L_0019: callvirt instance int32
               Ch07.ExampleOfFunc::Addition(class [mscorlib]System.Func'1<int32>)
L_001e: box int32
L_0023: call void [mscorlib]System.Console::WriteLine(string, object)
L_0028: nop
L_0029: ldstr "{0}"
L_002e: ldloc.0

/* CLR load the CS$<>9__CachedAnonymousMethodDelegate1 field on to the stack */
L_002f: ldsfld class [mscorlib]
               System.Func'1<int32> Ch07.Program::CS$<>9__CachedAnonymousMethodDelegate1
L_0034: brtrue.s L_0049
L_0036: ldnull

/* It loads the method pointer of the <Main>b__0 anonymous method on the stack */
L_0037: ldftn int32 Ch07.Program::<Main>b__0()

/* Using the method pointer an instance of System.Func'1<int32> instantiated onto
 * the Heap */
L_003d: newobj instance void
               [mscorlib]System.Func'1<int32>::.ctor(object, native int)
/* CLR will store the instance of System.Func'1<int32> on the
 * CS$<>9__CachedAnonymousMethodDelegate1 field */
L_0042: stsfld class [mscorlib]
            System.Func'1<int32> Ch07.Program::CS$<>9__CachedAnonymousMethodDelegate1
L_0047: br.s L_0049

/* CLR load the CS$<>9__CachedAnonymousMethodDelegate1 field on to the stack */
L_0049: ldsfld class [mscorlib]
        System.Func'1<int32> Ch07.Program::CS$<>9__CachedAnonymousMethodDelegate1
```

```
    /* CLR will call the Addition method by passing
     * the CS$<>9__CachedAnonymousMethodDelegate1 field */
    L_004e: callvirt instance int32
                  Ch07.ExampleOfFunc::Addition(class [mscorlib]System.Func'1<int32>)


    L_0053: box int32
    L_0058: call void [mscorlib]System.Console::WriteLine(string, object)
    L_005d: nop
    L_005e: ret
}


.field private static class [mscorlib]System.Func'1<int32> CS$<>9__
CachedAnonymousMethodDelegate1
    { /* Code removed */ }
}
```

Let's analyze the IL code in Listing 7-11 to understand how the Func was handled by the CLR while executing the code in Listing 7-10.

Anonymous Method and Func

The C# compiler compiles the anonymous method from the Main method of the Program class as shown below:

```
() =>
{
  return 100 + 100;
}
```

Into a method block <Main>b__0 and using this <Main>b__0, the CLR instantiates an instance of the Func'1<int32> type. To instantiate Func'1<int32>, CLR loads the function pointer for the <Main>b__0 using the ldftn IL instruction in L_0037 and, using the newobj IL instruction in L_003d, instantiates the Func'1<int32>. This instance will later store into the field CS$<>9__CachedAnonymousMethodDelegate1 (type of Func'1<int32>) in L_0042, as shown below:

```
/* It loads the method pointer of the <Main>b__0 anonymous method on the stack */
L_0037: ldftn int32 Ch07.Program::<Main>b__0()


/* Using the method pointer an instance of System.Func'1<int32>  instantiated onto the Heap*/
L_003d: newobj instance void
            [mscorlib]System.Func'1<int32>::..ctor(object, native int)


/* CLR will store the instance of System.Func'1<int32> on the
 * CS$<>9__CachedAnonymousMethodDelegate1 field */
L_0042: stsfld class [mscorlib]
            System.Func'1<int32> Ch07.Program::CS$<>9__CachedAnonymousMethodDelegate1
```

In L_0049 the CLR loads the CS$<>9__CachedAnonymousMethodDelegate1 field and passes an argument to the Addition method in L_004e, and in the Addition method CLR will execute the <Main>b__0 method.

Instance Method and Func

In the Main method of Listing 7-11, in L_000e the CLR loads the function pointer of the Add method onto the evaluation stack and instantiates an instance of the Func'1<int32> in L_0014 and passes this instance of the Func'1<int32> to the Addition method, from where the Add method will be executed.

In Func, you can assign a method or an anonymous method as input to it, and that embedded method will be executed when the CLR executes the Func object. Let's see another example of the Func that accepts five inputs and returns an output as Func<TSource1, TSource2, TSource3, TSource4, TSource5, TResult>, as shown in Listing 7-12.

Listing 7-12. Example of Func<TSource1, TSource2, TSource3, TSource4, TSource5, TResult>

```
using System;

namespace Ch07
{
    class Program
    {
        static void Main(string[] args)
        {
            ExampleOfFunc exampleOfFunc = new ExampleOfFunc();

            Console.WriteLine("{0}", exampleOfFunc.Addition(
                exampleOfFunc.Add,                         /* Pass method name */
                1, 2, 3, 4, 5));

            Console.WriteLine("{0}", exampleOfFunc.Addition(
                (a, b, c, d, e) =>
                {
                    return a + b + c + d + e;
                },                                         /* Pass anonymous method */
                1, 2, 3, 4, 5));
        }
    }

    public class ExampleOfFunc
    {
        public int Addition(
            Func<int, int, int, int, int, int> additionImplementor,
            int a,
            int b,
            int c,
            int d,
            int e)
        {
            if (additionImplementor != null)
                return additionImplementor(a, b, c, d, e);

            return default(int);
        }
```

```
        public int Add(int a, int b, int c, int d, int e)
        {
            return a + b + c + d + e;
        }
    }
}
```

This program will produce the following output:

```
15
15
```

The Func is a generic delegate that can be used to pass an argument of a method, which accepts an instance of the Func. The Func is defined in the .NET Framework so you do not need to worry about defining a generic delegate (as long as the number of input parameters in the Func support meets your requirement). If you need a generic delegate, which does not need to return any type other than void, the .NET Framework provides you with the Action delegate. Action is another generic delegate you can use in your program, and the next section will explore this further.

Action

The Action class is used to encapsulate the method information in C#. The Action class is defined in the mscorlib.dll (C:\Windows\Microsoft.NET\ Framework\v4.0.30319), as shown in Figure 7-6 using the ildasm.exe.

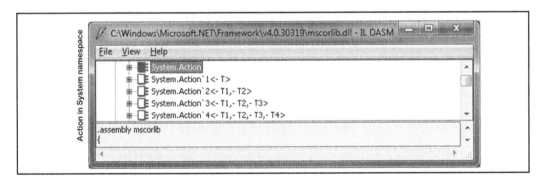

Figure 7-6. Action in .NET

The signature of the Action<T> class is shown in Listing 7-13.

Listing 7-13. *Signature of the Action<T>*

```
.class public auto ansi sealed Action<- T> extends System.MulticastDelegate
```

The Action class declaration is shown in Listing 7-14.

Listing 7-14. *Action Class Definition in IL Format*

```
.class public auto ansi sealed Action<- T1, - T2>
    extends System.MulticastDelegate
```

```
{
    .method public hidebysig specialname rtspecialname instance void
        .ctor(object 'object', native int 'method') runtime managed
    {}

    .method public hidebysig newslot virtual instance class System.IAsyncResult
        BeginInvoke(!T1 arg1, !T2 arg2, class System.AsyncCallback callback, object 'object')
        runtime managed
    {}

    .method public hidebysig newslot virtual instance void
        EndInvoke(class System.IAsyncResult result) runtime managed
    {}

    .method public hidebysig newslot virtual instance void
        Invoke(!T1 arg1, !T2 arg2) runtime managed
    {}
}
```

Action is a generic type, which is inherited from the MulticastDelegate class, and it inherits from the delegate class, as shown in Figure 7-7.

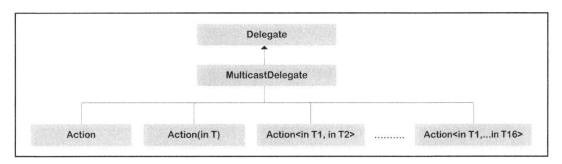

Figure 7-7. *Action and Delegate relationship*

The Action class will have all the functionality and properties of the MulticastDelegate and Delegate types due to the inherent relationship between Action and the MulticastDelegate and Delegate classes. The Action class has BeginInvoke, EndInvoke, and Invoke and the constructor method. Action also has _methodPtr, _target, _methodPtrAux, and Method properties, which work as described in Table 7-3.

Action class can take up to 16 inputs, but it does not return anything. In .NET, Action has been implemented, as 17 overloaded Action with a different number of inputs, as shown in Listing 7-15.

Listing 7-15. *Action Signature*

```
Action
Action<T>
Action<T1, T2>
Action<T1, T2, T3>
Action<T1, T2, T3, T4>
Action<T1, T2, T3, T4, T5>
```

```
Action<T1, T2, T3, T4, T5, T6>
Action<T1, T2, T3, T4, T5, T6, T7>
Action<T1, T2, T3, T4, T5, T6, T7, T8>
Action<T1, T2, T3, T4, T5, T6, T7, T8, T9>
Action<T1, T2, T3, T4, T5, T6, T7, T8, T9, T10>
Action<T1, T2, T3, T4, T5, T6, T7, T8, T9, T10, T11>
Action<T1, T2, T3, T4, T5, T6, T7, T8, T9, T10, T11, T12>
Action<T1, T2, T3, T4, T5, T6, T7, T8, T9, T10, T11, T12, T13>
Action<T1, T2, T3, T4, T5, T6, T7, T8, T9, T10, T11, T12, T13, T14>
Action<T1, T2, T3, T4, T5, T6, T7, T8, T9, T10, T11, T12, T13, T14, T15>
Action<T1, T2, T3, T4, T5, T6, T7, T8, T9, T10, T11, T12, T13, T14, T15, T16>
```

Internal Works of Action

Listing 7-16 provides an example to explain Action.

Listing 7-16. An Example of Action<T1,T2> Type

```csharp
using System;
namespace Ch07
{
    class Program
    {
        static void Main(string[] args)
        {
            ExampleOfAction exampleOfAction = new ExampleOfAction();
            exampleOfAction.Addition(exampleOfAction.Add, 10, 10);
            exampleOfAction.Addition(
                (a, b) =>
                {
                    Console.WriteLine("{0}", a + b);
                }, 20, 20);
        }
    }

    public class ExampleOfAction
    {
        public void Addition(Action<int, int> additionImplementor, int a, int b)
        {
            if (additionImplementor != null)
                additionImplementor(a, b);
        }

        public void Add(int a, int b)
        {
            Console.WriteLine("{0}", a + b);
        }
    }
}
```

This program produces the following output:

20
40

The C# compiler compiles the Action declaration as below:

- The CLR instantiates an instance of the Action<T1, T2> using the input method to pass to it.

- In the instantiation time Action<T1, T2> calls the constructor of the MulticastDelegate, which initializes a set of variables based on the method-related information (which is passed to it), such as method pointer, name, and so forth.

- The CLR passes this instance of the Action back to the place, for example, in Listing 7-16 the Addition method accepts Action<int,int>, so the CLR passes this newly instantiated Action<T1, T2> object to it.

- When the Action<T1, T2> object will be executed, CLR will call the invoke method of that Action<T1, T2> object, which will execute the containing method inside the Action<T1, T2> object.

Figure 7-8 illustrates the Action instantiation process.

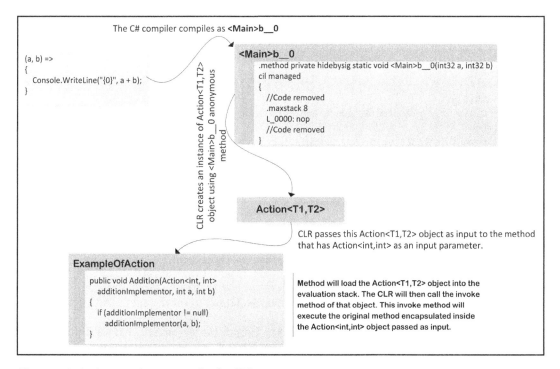

Figure 7-8. *Action creation process in the CLR*

Let's decompile the IL code, as shown in Listing 7-17, using the .NET Reflector tool, for Listing 7-16 to understand the Action instantiation process demonstrated in Figure 7-8.

Listing 7-17. IL Code for the Action<T1,T2> Example

```
.class private auto ansi beforefieldinit Program extends [mscorlib]System.Object
{
    .method public hidebysig specialname rtspecialname instance void .ctor() cil managed
    { /* Code removed */ }

    .method private hidebysig static void <Main>b__0(int32 a, int32 b) cil managed
    {
        .custom instance void [mscorlib]System.Runtime.CompilerServices.
CompilerGeneratedAttribute::.ctor()
        .maxstack 8
        L_0000: nop
        L_0001: ldstr "{0}"
        L_0006: ldarg.0
        L_0007: ldarg.1
        L_0008: add
        L_0009: box int32
        L_000e: call void [mscorlib]System.Console::WriteLine(string, object)
        L_0013: nop
        L_0014: ret
    }

    .method private hidebysig static void Main(string[] args) cil managed
    {
        .entrypoint
        .maxstack 4
        .locals init (
            [0] class Ch07.ExampleOfAction exampleOfAction)
        L_0000: nop
        L_0001: newobj instance void Ch07.ExampleOfAction::.ctor()
        L_0006: stloc.0

        /* It loads the instance of the ExampleOfAction
         * from the locals section at position 0.  */
        L_0007: ldloc.0
        L_0008: ldloc.0

        /* It loads the method pointer of the Add method on the stack*/
        L_0009: ldftn instance void Ch07.ExampleOfAction::Add(int32, int32)

        /* Using the method pointer an instance of System.Action'2<int32, int32> */
        L_000f: newobj instance void
                    [mscorlib]System.Action'2<int32, int32>::.ctor(object, native int)

        L_0014: ldc.i4.s 10
        L_0016: ldc.i4.s 10

        /* Instance of the System.Action'2<int32, int32> will be passed
         * to the Addition method call */
```

```
    L_0018: callvirt instance void
            Ch07.ExampleOfAction::Addition(class [mscorlib]System.
                .Action'2<int32, int32>, int32, int32)
    L_001d: nop
    L_001e: ldloc.0

    /* CLR load the Ch07.Program::CS$<>9__CachedAnonymousMethodDelegate1
     * field on to the stack */
    L_001f: ldsfld class
                [mscorlib]System.Action'2<int32, int32> Ch07.Program::
            CS$<>9__CachedAnonymousMethodDelegate1
    L_0024: brtrue.s L_0039
    L_0026: ldnull

    /* It loads the method pointer of the <Main>b__0 anonymous method on the stack */
    L_0027: ldftn void Ch07.Program::<Main>b__0(int32, int32)

    /* Using the method pointer loaded in L_0027, an instance
     * of System.Action'2<int32, int32> will be instantiated*/
    L_002d: newobj instance void
                [mscorlib]System.Action'2<int32, int32>::.ctor(object, native int)

    /* CLR will store the instance of System.Action'2<int32, int32> on the
     * CS$<>9__CachedAnonymousMethodDelegate1 field */
    L_0032: stsfld class
                [mscorlib]System.Action'2<int32, int32> Ch07.Program::
                CS$<>9__CachedAnonymousMethodDelegate1
    L_0037: br.s L_0039

    /* CLR load the CS$<>9__CachedAnonymousMethodDelegate1 field on to the stack */
    L_0039: ldsfld class
                [mscorlib]System.Action'2<int32, int32> Ch07.Program::
                CS$<>9__CachedAnonymousMethodDelegate1
    L_003e: ldc.i4.s 20
    L_0040: ldc.i4.s 20

    /* CLR will call the Addition method by passing
     * the CS$<>9__CachedAnonymousMethodDelegate1 field */
    L_0042: callvirt instance void
            Ch07.ExampleOfAction::Addition(class
                [mscorlib]System.Action'2<int32, int32>, int32, int32)
    L_0047: nop
    L_0048: ret
}

.field private static class
        [mscorlib]System.Action'2<int32, int32> CS$<>9__CachedAnonymousMethodDelegate1
{ /* Code removed */ }
}
```

Let's analyze the IL code in Listing 7-17 to understand the underlying method of how the `Action` was handled by the CLR while executing the code in Listing 7-16.

Anonymous Method and Action

The C# compiler compiles the anonymous method from the `Main` method of the `Program` class as shown below:

```
(a, b) =>
{
    Console.WriteLine("{0}", a + b);
}
```

Into a method block `<Main>b__0` and using this `<Main>b__0`, it instantiates an instance of the `System.Action'2<int32, int32>` type. To instantiate `System.Action'2<int32, int32>` CLR loads the function pointer of the `<Main>b__0` using `ldftn` IL instruction in `L_0027`, and using the `newobj` IL instruction in `L_002d` it instantiates the `System.Action'2<int32, int32>` in Listing 7-17. This instance will later store into the field `CS$<>9__CachedAnonymousMethodDelegate1` (type of `System.Action'2<int32, int32>`) in `L_0032`, as shown here:

```
/* It loads the method pointer of the <Main>b__0 anonymous method on the stack */
L_0027: ldftn void Ch07.Program::<Main>b__0(int32, int32)

/* Using the method pointer an instance of System.Action'2<int32, int32> */
L_002d: newobj instance void
            [mscorlib]System.Action'2<int32, int32>::.ctor(object, native int)

/* CLR will store the instance of System.Action'2<int32, int32> on the
 * CS$<>9__CachedAnonymousMethodDelegate1 field */
L_0032: stsfld class
            [mscorlib]System.Action'2<int32, int32> Ch07.Program::CS$<>9__
CachedAnonymousMethodDelegate1
```

In `L_0039`, CLR loads `CS$<>9__CachedAnonymousMethodDelegate1` and passes an argument to the `Addition` method in `L_0042`, and in the `Addition` method CLR will execute the `<Main>b__0` method.

Instance Method and Action

In the `Main` method of Listing 7-17, in `L_0009`, the CLR loads the function pointer of the `Add` method onto the evaluation stack and instantiates an instance of the `System.Action'2<int32, int32>` in `L_000f` and passes it to the `Addition` from where the `Add` method will be executed.

So by using `Action` you can pass a method or an anonymous method as input to another method, such as the function pointer showed in Listing 7-1. The only difference with `Func` is that `Func` returns a value, whereas `Action` does not return any value.

Summary

In this chapter, we have learned about the delegate types in C#. First, we looked at the C# delegate in comparison to the function pointer in C, which shows you the basic similarity between the function pointer in C and `delegate` in .NET. We also explored how the C# compiler delegates pointer handling from developers. Finally, we explored the generic delegates `Func` and `Action` in .NET. You also learned how the C# compiler handles the `Func` and `Action` delegates. And the chapter concluded with a discussion about the use of the anonymous method in `Func` and `Action`. The next chapter will examine about the event in C#.

CHAPTER 8

Event

This chapter will discuss the event program. A type that defines an event member allows other types to subscribe for the notification when something happened in the type. We start by designing a type, which, when exposed to the event where subscribers are to subscribe, implements the code to handle the event and explains the concept of the event in C# language. We will then explore the behind the scenes workings of the event, for example, how C# compiler translates an event member to implement, add, and remove a method. We also examine how the subscription operator, for example, += and -=, will be translated to use the add and remove method compiled for the event member by the C# compiler. Finally, we will also explore how different pieces of the event program fit together in runtime.

Understanding the Event

In .NET, an event is a mechanism for a class, for example, if you consider a class named EC, that provides notifications to the subscribers of that class when something happens to an object of that EC. The most common use for events is in graphical user interfaces. Typically the classes that represent controls in the interface have events that are notified, for example, when the user clicks a button control. In Figure 8-1, you can see an event that is typically exposed for the subscription (S1, S2....Sn, where n is a valid range of subscribers) where subscribers subscribe to be notified. When the event is raised from the event handler class, it will notify the subscribers by sending the notification, as demonstrated in Figure 8-1.

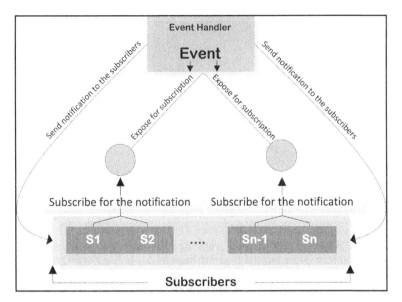

Figure 8-1. *Example of a basic event.*

Figure 8-1 shows the basics of the event in C#. It can be used to provide a generally useful way for objects, for example, the event handler, to notify clients of the state changes, which may be useful for the subscribers of that object.

Events are declared using delegates (Chapter 7). A delegate object encapsulates a method (typically called the callback method) so that it can be called on later from the appropriate places when needed. In C#, the event provides a way for a class to allow subscribers to provide delegates that should be called when the event occurs. When the event occurs, the event handler executes the delegate(s) given to it by its subscribers.

In the following sections, we will explore how to design a type with an event, how the C# compiler takes care of the event, and how the CLR executes an event in runtime.

Designing a Type with the Event

Defining a type that exposes one or more event member requires a few steps. First, define a field in a type with EventHandler or EventHandler<TEventArgs> type followed by the event keyword. This requires defining a handler method in that type that exposes events. This handler will execute when an event is raised by another method from the event handler class. In Listing 8-1, NewsManager type exposes an event member NewsEvent that will be used by the subscribers to subscribe for the notification by adding relevant methods with it as the callback method. This callback will be executed by the event handler when there is any event raised in the NewsManager type. So the subscribers will be notified when the event is raised in the NewsManager type. The subscriber of the event adds relevant method(s) to the event.

Listing 8-1 presents an example of the event declaration in a program. In the example, NewsManager class exposes an event and implements a method, OnNewsArrival, that is used to handle the event raised by the PublishNews. We will explore this in greater detail shortly. Two subscriber classes—Reviewer and Publisher—are used to show subscribers that used subscribed for the notification in the NewsEvent event of the NewsManager class.

Let's look at the skeleton of a program, which declares an event, a subscriber, and an event argument class to pass additional information to the subscriber as part of the event notification.

Listing 8-1. Skeleton of the Event Declaration

```
namespace Ch08
{
    /* Event initialization and setup */
    class Program
    {
        static void Main(string[] args)                    {}
    }

    /* Subscribers of the event. When these classes subscribed to the
     * event, it passes an instance of the EventHandler instantiated
     * using the relevant function pointer of
     * the method it uses as callback.*/
    public class Reviewer                                  {}
    public class Publisher                                 {}

    /* This is the class which exposes the event that contains all
     * the subscribed methods for the event, handle the event when
     * it occurs and send the notification the
     * subscribed methods to notify them about the event. */
    public class NewsManager
    {
        public event EventHandler<NewsEventArgs> NewsEvent;
        public void PublishNews(string name, string detail)    {...}
        protected virtual void OnNewsArrival(NewsEventArgs args){...}
    }

    /* It is the event argument which uses to pass additional information
     * from the event to subscribers.*/
    public class NewsEventArgs : EventArgs                 {}
}
```

In the following sections, you will learn more about the steps mentioned in Listing 8-1 that were used to define the event in a program.

EventHandler Declaration

The C# event keyword is used to define an event member in a type by giving the accessibility as public to expose the other types to consume it. A type of delegate, for example, EventHandler<TEventArgs> (derived from the delegate), comes after the event keyword to indicate the prototype of the method(s) and any valid identifier used as a name of the event. The event member NewsEvent is defined for the NewsManager class, as shown in the code:

```
public event EventHandler<NewsEventArgs> NewsEvent;
```

The name of the event is NewsEvent with the type of EventHandler<NewsEventArgs>. The subscribers of the event (to be notified) must provide a callback method whose prototype matches that of the EventHandler<NewsEventArgs> delegate type. The EventHandler<NewsEventArgs> is the generic System. EventHandler delegate defined as follows:

```
public delegate void EventHandler<TEventArgs>(object sender, TEventArgs e);
```

The EventHandler<TEventArgs> type is defined in the System namespace in the mscorlib.dll assembly, as shown in Figure 8-2.

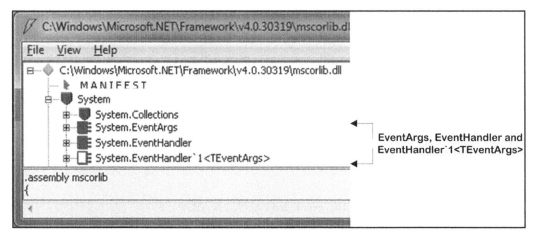

Figure 8-2. *EventArgs, EventHandler, and EventHandler`1<TEventArgs>*

UNDERSTANDING `, !, AND !! SYMBOL IN THE TYPE NAME

---

1.   If a type C has one or more generic parameters, the C# compiler compiles the name of the type C with the suffix `n, where n is a decimal integer constant (without leading zeros) representing the number of generic parameters that C has.

2.   The generic parameters of a generic type definition are referred to by their index. Generic parameter zero is referred to as !0, generic parameter one as !1, and so on.

3.   In the body of a generic method definition, its generic parameters are referred to by their index; generic parameter zero is referred to as !!0, generic parameter one as !!1, and so on.

For example in C#:

```
public class GenericType<T, R>
{
    public T Method1(T a, R b)                    { return a; }
    public N GenericMethod<M, N>(M c, N d)        { return d; }
    public N GenericMethod<M, N, P>(M c, N d, P e) { return d; }
}
public class GenericType<T, R, S>                 { }
```

The GenericType<T,R> and GenericType<T, R, S> classes are compiled into IL as:

```
/* '2 - ' symbol postfix with the number of parameter (2) defined in
 * the C# code */
.class public auto ansi beforefieldinit ConsoleApplication2.GenericType'2<T,R>
      extends [mscorlib]System.Object
{
  .method public hidebysig instance !T   Method1(!T a,!R b)                    cil
managed       {..}
```

```
    .method public hidebysig instance !!N  GenericMethod<M,N>(!!M c,!!N d)            cil
managed       {..}
    .method public hidebysig instance !!N  GenericMethod<M,N,P>
        (!!M c,!!N d,!!P e)    cil managed {..}
}

/* '3 - ' symbol postfix with the number of parameter (3) defined
 * in the C# code */
.class public auto ansi beforefieldinit
        ConsoleApplication2.GenericType'3<T,R,S>
        extends [mscorlib]System.Object {..}
```

The EventHandler<TEventArgs> is derived from the MulticastDelegate class, and it has the definition as shown in Listing 8-2.

Listing 8-2. The IL Definition of the EventHandler<TEventArgs> Class

```
/* The EventHandler< TEventArgs> derived from the MulticastDelegate
 * class which derived from the Delegate class. */
.class public auto ansi serializable sealed EventHandler<TEventArgs>
    extends System.MulticastDelegate
{
    .method public hidebysig specialname rtspecialname instance void
        .ctor(object 'object', native int 'method') runtime managed      {}

    .method public hidebysig newslot virtual instance class System.IAsyncResult
        BeginInvoke
      (object sender, !TEventArgs e, class System.AsyncCallback callback,
                    object 'object')  runtime managed            {}

    .method public hidebysig newslot virtual instance void
        EndInvoke(class System.IAsyncResult result) runtime managed      {}

    /* The Invoke method will be used to start executing the methods
     * subscribed to the event to get the notification from the event.
     * This method will be called from the handler method of
     * the NewsManager.*/
    .method public hidebysig newslot virtual instance void
        Invoke(object sender, !TEventArgs e) runtime managed             {}
}
```

Listing 8-2 shows an Invoke, which is used by the event handler to send notification to the subscriber when an event is raised.

Event Argument

If you want to pass additional information from the object that raised the event to the subscribers object, you need to define a type, which encapsulates this additional information. This type is typically called the event argument class. When you define this type, you add private fields to encapsulate the additional information you want to pass and expose this additional information to the subscribers via the read-only public fields.

A class that holds additional information to pass to the event handler should be derived from System. EventArgs, which is defined in the System namespace of the mscorlib.dll assembly, as shown in Figure 8-2. Listing 8-3 shows the definition of the EventArgs class.

Listing 8-3. The Class Definition of the EventArgs

```
public class EventArgs
{
    public static readonly EventArgs Empty;
    static EventArgs();
    public EventArgs();
}
```

The name of the event argument class should be suffixed with EventArgs. In this example, the NewsEventArgs class has fields identifying the title of the news (Title) and the details of the news (Detail), as shown in Listing 8-4.

Listing 8-4. Example of the NewsEventArgs Class

```
public class NewsEventArgs : EventArgs
{
    /*  Declared few private fields */
    private string title;
    private string detail;

    public NewsEventArgs(string TitleOfTheNews, string DetailOfTheNews)
    {
        title = TitleOfTheNews;
        detail = DetailOfTheNews;
    }

    /* ReadOnly fields */
    public string Title        { get { return title; }  }
    public string Detail       { get { return detail; } }
}
```

Event Handler

The class that defines and exposes an event is responsible to define an event handler for the event to handle when an event is raised. This method will be executed in response to an event, for example, in Listing 8-5, the OnNewsArrival method is responsible for handling the event for the NewsManager class when an event is raised by the PublishNews method.

In general, the event handler method can be defined as a protected, virtual method that is called by code internally within the class and its derived classes when the event is to be raised. This method takes one parameter, a NewsEventArgs object, as the event argument, which includes the additional information passed to the objects receiving the notification. The default implementation of this method simply checks if any objects have registered interest in the event and, if so, the event will be raised, thereby notifying the registered methods that the event has occurred. Let's look at the event handler class, NewsManager class, as shown in Listing 8-5.

Listing 8-5. Example of the Event Handler Class

```
public class NewsManager
{
    /* An container of the subscribed method to the event. Clients
     * can subscribe for the notification via NewsEvent event.*/
    public event EventHandler<NewsEventArgs> NewsEvent;

    public void PublishNews(string name, string detail)
    {
        NewsEventArgs na = new NewsEventArgs(name, detail);

        /* If news arrived and ready to publish then call OnNewsArrival
         * method which will execute subscribed methods.*/
        OnNewsArrival(na);
    }

    /* If anyone subscribe for the notification then this method will
     * invoke each of the subscribed method and execute all. */
    protected virtual void OnNewsArrival(NewsEventArgs args)
    {
        EventHandler<NewsEventArgs> newsHandler = NewsEvent;
        if (newsHandler != null)
        {
            newsHandler(this,args);
        }
    }
}
```

In the NewsManager class, the OnNewsArrival method is called from the PublishNews method to indicate that a new news message has arrived in the NewsManager class. The PublishNews method accepts information about the message and constructs a NewsEventArgs object, passing the message information to its constructor, and NewsManager's own virtual OnNewsArrival method is then called to formally notify the NewsManager object of the new news message. Typically this is called the event raised, and it notifies all of the subscribed methods that need to be notified.

Subscriber

This section will explore the subscriber, who has asked for subscription of the NewsEvent of the NewsManager class. The Reviewer class subscribes to the event in the constructor by providing the callback method ReviewOnArrivedNews. It also implements the UnSubscribe method to allow the subscriber to unsubscribe from the event.

In Listing 8-6, the Reviewer class subscribed to the event using the += operator from the constructor by passing the ReviewOnArrivedNews method as the callback method. The ReviewOnArrivedNews method has the same prototype as the NewsEvent event defined in the NewsManager class, shown in Listing 8-5. As mentioned earlier, the NewsEvent is the type of EventHandler<NewsEventArgs> delegate whose signature shows that it accepts two input parameters, such as sender as the type of object and e as the type of TEventArgs. In addition, the ReviewOnArrivedNews method has the same signature as the EventHandler<NewsEventArgs>, so it can be added or removed from the NewsEvent event.

Listing 8-6. Example of the Subscribers Class

```
public class Reviewer
{
    public Reviewer(NewsManager nlm)
    {
        /* Subscribe to the NewsManager for the notification.*/
        nlm.NewsEvent += ReviewOnArrivedNews;
    }

    /* When news arrived if subscribe then execute this method.*/
    private void ReviewOnArrivedNews(object sender,NewsEventArgs na)
    {
        Console.WriteLine("Reviewed:\n{0},\t{1}", na.Title, na.Detail);
    }

    /* To unsubscribe from the NewsEvent */
    public void UnSubscribe(NewsManager nlm)
    {
        nlm.NewsEvent -= ReviewOnArrivedNews;
    }
}
```

Listing 8-6 also shows the UnSubscribe method, which uses the -= operator to unsubscribe the ReviewOnArrivedNews method from the NewsEvent event. And in the Reviewer constructor, the ReviewOnArrivedNews method was subscribed using the += operator to the NewsEvent event. As described earlier, when we want to add and remove a callback method from the NewsEvent event, the callback method has to have the same signature as EventHandler<NewsEventArgs>. The ReviewOnArrivedNews method has the same signature as EventHandler<NewsEventArgs>, so it can be removed from the NewsEvent. Listing 8-6 shows the Reviewer class to indicate the subscriber implementation. The Publisher class will have almost the same implementation, as shown in Listing 8-8.

Execute the Defined Event

The Program class instantiates an instance of the NewsManager class and passes it to the subscriber's class to let subscribers subscribe for the notification. The Program class then calls the PublishNews method of the NewsManager class to raise two events, as shown in Listing 8-7.

Listing 8-7. Example of the Event Executor

```
class Program
{
    static void Main(string[] args)
    {
        NewsManager nlm = new NewsManager();
        /* Initialize the client of the news manager event. The
         * clients will subscribe to the event in the initialization time.*/
        /* Reviewer class defined in the Listing 8-8 */
        Reviewer subscriberOne = new Reviewer(nlm);

        /* Publisher class defined in the Listing 8-8 */
```

```
        Publisher subscriberTwo = new Publisher(nlm);

        /* Some news arrived to the NewsManager to publish and notify
         * to the subscribers.*/
        nlm.PublishNews("Higgs particle",
                        "The Higgs particle is named after Peter Higgs.");
        nlm.PublishNews("Expert C# 5.0 with .NET Framework 4.5",
                        "A about the C# language.");

        /* Finished job so UnSubscribe the events */
        subscriberOne.UnSubscribe(nlm);
        subscriberTwo.UnSubscribe(nlm);

        /* Publishing new news but it not going to be notified as
         * subscriberOne and subscriberTwo already unsubscribes
         * by calling the UnSubscribe method */
        nlm.PublishNews("10th Dimensional world",
                        "Still under investigation so don't publish.");
    }
}
```

In Listing 8-7, the UnSubscribe method is called twice for the subscribers—subscriberOne and subscriberTwo—to unsubscribe for the notification. We saw earlier the different pieces of the program that are used to explain the event. In Listing 8-8, the full listing of the program is shown.

Listing 8-8. Full Listing of the Event Program

```
using System;

namespace Ch08
{
    class Program
    {
        static void Main(string[] args)
        {
            NewsManager nlm = new NewsManager();
            /* Initialize the client of the news manager event. The
             * clients will subscribe to the event in the
             * initialization time.*/
            Reviewer subscriberOne = new Reviewer(nlm);
            Publisher subscriberTwo = new Publisher(nlm);

            /* Some news arrived to the NewsManager to publish and
             * notify to the subscribers.*/
            nlm.PublishNews("Higgs particle",
                    "The Higgs particle is named after Peter Higgs.");
            nlm.PublishNews("Expert C# 5.0 with .NET Framework 4.5",
                            "A about the C# language.");

            /* Finished job so UnSubscribe the events */
            subscriberOne.UnSubscribe(nlm);
```

```
                subscriberTwo.UnSubscribe(nlm);

                /* Publishing new news but it not going to be notified */
                nlm.PublishNews("10th Dimensional world",
                                "Still under investigation so don't publish.");
        }
    }

    public class Reviewer
    {
        public Reviewer(NewsManager nlm)
        {
            /* Subscribe to the NewsManager for the notification.*/
            nlm.NewsEvent += ReviewOnArrivedNews;
        }

        /* When news arrived if subscribe then execute this method.*/
        private void ReviewOnArrivedNews(object sender, NewsEventArgs na)
        {
            Console.WriteLine("Reviewed:\n{0},\t{1}", na.Title, na.Detail);
        }

        /* To unsubscribe from the NewsEvent */
        public void UnSubscribe(NewsManager nlm)
        {
            nlm.NewsEvent -= ReviewOnArrivedNews;
        }
    }

    public class Publisher
    {
        public Publisher(NewsManager nlm)
        {
            /* Subscribe to the NewsManager for the notification.*/
            nlm.NewsEvent += PublishArrivedNews;
        }

        /* When news arrived if subscribe then execute this method.*/
        private void PublishArrivedNews(object sender, NewsEventArgs na)
        {
            Console.WriteLine("Published:\n{0} news.", na.Title);
        }

        public void UnSubscribe(NewsManager nlm)
        {
            nlm.NewsEvent -= PublishArrivedNews;
        }
    }

    public class NewsManager
    {
```

```
        /* An container of the subscribed method to the event.
         * Clients can subscribe for the notification via
         * NewsEvent event.*/
        public event EventHandler<NewsEventArgs> NewsEvent;

        public void PublishNews(string name, string detail)
        {
            NewsEventArgs na = new NewsEventArgs(name, detail);

            /* If news arrived and ready to publish then call OnNewsArrival
             * method which will execute subscribed methods.*/
            OnNewsArrival(na);
        }

        /* If anyone subscribe for the notification then this method will
         * invoke each of the subscribed method and execute all. */
        protected virtual void OnNewsArrival(NewsEventArgs args)
        {
            EventHandler<NewsEventArgs> newsHandler = NewsEvent;
            if (newsHandler != null)
            {
                newsHandler(this, args);
            }
        }
    }

    public class NewsEventArgs : EventArgs
    {
        /*  Declared few private fields */
        private string title;
        private string detail;

        public NewsEventArgs(string TitleOfTheNews, string DetailOfTheNews)
        {
            title = TitleOfTheNews;
            detail = DetailOfTheNews;
        }

        /* ReadOnly fields */
        public string Title  { get { return title; } }
        public string Detail { get { return detail; } }
    }
}
```

This program will produce the following output:

```
Reviewed:
Higgs particle, The Higgs particle is named after Peter Higgs.
Published:
Higgs particle news.
Reviewed:
```

```
Expert C# 5.0 with .NET Framework 4.5,  A about the C# language.
Published:
Expert C# 5.0 with .NET Framework 4.5 news.
```

Behind the Scenes

When the C# compiler compiles the code presented in Listing 8-8, it will regenerate the NewsManager class and event subscribers Publisher and Reviewer classes. The event member of the NewsManager class will be implemented to contain add_<EventName> and remove_<EventName> (<EventName> will be replaced with the relevant event name, for example, add_<EventName> will be add_NewsEvent and the remove_<EventName> method will be remove_NewsEvent) methods to add and remove subscribed method to and from the event.

The subscriber's += and -= operators will be replaced with the add_<EventName> and remove_<EventName> method in the Publisher and Reviewer classes. In the following sections, we will explore more about these by looking into the decompiled IL code (decompiled using the .NET Reflector tool) for the code given in Listing 8-8.

In Compile Time

The C# compiler compiles the NewsManager class to generate the add_<EventName> and remove_<EventName> methods for the event member NewsEvent declared in the NewsManager class. These methods are also used by the subscribers to subscribe for the notification of the event, which you will see later in Listing 8-10. Listing 8-9 shows the decompiled IL version of the NewsManager class.

Listing 8-9. IL Version of the NewsManager

```
.class public auto ansi beforefieldinit NewsManager extends [mscorlib]System.Object
{
    /* The C# compiler translates NewsEvent into two methods add_NewsEvent
     * and remove_NewsEvent which will used by the CLR to add subscribed
     * method into the event using the add_NewsEvent method and also methods
     * can be unsubscribed from the event using the remove_NewsEvent method */
    .event [mscorlib]System.EventHandler'1<class Ch08.NewsEventArgs> NewsEvent
    {
        /* to add subscribed method to the event */
        .addon instance void Ch08.NewsManager::add_NewsEvent
            (class [mscorlib]System.EventHandler'1<class Ch08.NewsEventArgs>)

        /* removed unsubscribed method from the event */
        .removeon instance void Ch08.NewsManager::remove_NewsEvent
            (class [mscorlib]System.EventHandler'1<class Ch08.NewsEventArgs>)
    }

    /* Execute the subscribed method to send the notification of
     * the event from the NewsEvent */
    .method family hidebysig newslot virtual instance void OnNewsArrival
        (class Ch08.NewsEventArgs args) cil managed
    {
        .maxstack 3
        .locals init (
```

```
        [0] class [mscorlib]System.EventHandler'1<class Ch08.NewsEventArgs>
                 newsHandler,
        [1] bool CS$4$0000)
    L_0000: nop
    L_0001: ldarg.0

    /* Load the NewsEvent field on the evaluation stack */
    L_0002: ldfld class [mscorlib]System.EventHandler'1<class
                    Ch08.NewsEventArgs> Ch08.NewsManager::NewsEvent

    /* and store into the local variable section at position 0. */
    L_0007: stloc.0

    /* Load the NewsEvent object stored at local variable section
     * at position 0.*/
    L_0011: ldloc.0

    /* Load the object passed as this to this method call*/
    L_0012: ldarg.0

    /* Load NewsEventArgs object passed as args*/
    L_0013: ldarg.1

    /* Call the Invoke method from the object loaded in L_0011 to
     * start handling the event.*/
    L_0014: callvirt instance void [mscorlib]System.EventHandler'1<class
            Ch08.NewsEventArgs>::Invoke(object, !0)

    L_0019: nop
    L_001a: nop
    L_001b: ret
}

.method public hidebysig instance void PublishNews (string name, string
        detail) cil managed
{
    /* Call the OnNewsArrival method on any news send to the
     * NewsManager to publish. It calls the OnNewsArrival due to
     * send notification to the subscribers */
    L_001b: callvirt instance void Ch08.NewsManager::OnNewsArrival
            (class Ch08.NewsEventArgs)
    L_0020: nop
    L_0021: ret
}

/* The event in where the subscriber add the method which will
 * be execute later on to send the notification of the event.*/
.field private class [mscorlib]System.EventHandler'1<class
                        Ch08.NewsEventArgs> NewsEvent


}
```

Let's explore the add_NewsEvent and remove_NewsEvent methods, presented in Listing 8-10, to see how the C# compiler generates these methods to add and removed callback method to and from the subscribers to the event.

Listing 8-10. add_NewsEvent and remove_NewsEvent Methods

```
public void add_NewsEvent(EventHandler<NewsEventArgs> value)
{
    EventHandler<NewsEventArgs> handler2;
    EventHandler<NewsEventArgs> newsEvent = this.NewsEvent;
    do
    {
        handler2 = newsEvent;
        EventHandler<NewsEventArgs> handler3 =
            (EventHandler<NewsEventArgs>) Delegate.Combine(handler2, value);
        newsEvent = Interlocked.CompareExchange<EventHandler<NewsEventArgs>>
                    (ref this.NewsEvent, handler3, handler2);
    }
    while (newsEvent != handler2);
}


public void remove_NewsEvent(EventHandler<NewsEventArgs> value)
{
    EventHandler<NewsEventArgs> handler2;
    EventHandler<NewsEventArgs> newsEvent = this.NewsEvent;
    do
    {
        handler2 = newsEvent;
        EventHandler<NewsEventArgs> handler3 =
            (EventHandler<NewsEventArgs>) Delegate.Remove(handler2, value);
        newsEvent = Interlocked.CompareExchange<EventHandler<NewsEventArgs>>
                    (ref this.NewsEvent, handler3, handler2);
    }
    while (newsEvent != handler2);
}
```

The add_NewsEvent method is used by the subscribers to subscribe to the event and the remove_NewsEvent method is used to remove the subscription from the event. The OnNewsArrival method from Listing 8-9 is another important method the C# compiler uses for the Invoke method from the NewsManager class to trigger the handler to handle the raised event in the NewsManager class.

The C# compiler regenerates the code for the subscribers class, for example, the Publisher and Reviewer classes, to add necessary code to add and remove callback method(s) to and from the event for subscription and un-subscription. As you saw in the C# implementation of the Publisher and Reviewer classes, it uses += and -= operators to subscribe and unsubscribe to the event, which will be translated to use the add_NewsEvent and remove_NewsEvent method generated for the event NewsEvent by the C# compiler.

Let's look at the decompiled IL code for the Publisher class, shown in Listing 8-11, to see how the Publisher class uses the add_NewsEvent and remove_NewsEvent methods.

Listing 8-11. *The Decompiled IL Code of the Publisher Class*

```
.class public auto ansi beforefieldinit Publisher
    extends [mscorlib]System.Object
{
    .method public hidebysig specialname rtspecialname instance void
            .ctor(class Ch08.NewsManager nlm) cil managed
    {
        /* Code removed */

        /* It loads the function pointer for the PublishArrivedNews
         * method onto the evaluation stack.*/
        L_000a: ldftn instance void Ch08.Publisher::PublishArrivedNews
                (object, class Ch08.NewsEventArgs)

        /* It instantiates an instance of the EventHandler and use
         * in the L_0015 to add into the event to get notification.*/
        L_0010: newobj instance void
                    [mscorlib]System.EventHandler'1<class
                        Ch08.NewsEventArgs>::.ctor(object, native int)

        /* The add_NewsEvent is translation for the += and will be
         * used to add the subscribed method (created in L_0010)
         * into the event.*/
        L_0015: callvirt instance void Ch08.NewsManager::
                add_NewsEvent(class [mscorlib]System.EventHandler'1<class
                                            Ch08.NewsEventArgs>)

        L_001a: nop
        L_001b: nop
        L_001c: ret
    }

    .method private hidebysig instance void
            PublishArrivedNews(object sender, class Ch08.NewsEventArgs na)
            cil managed
    { /*code removed*/ }

    .method public hidebysig instance void
            UnSubscribe(class Ch08.NewsManager nlm) cil managed
    {
        /* Code removed */

        /* It loads the function pointer for the PublishArrivedNews
         * method onto the evaluation stack.*/
        L_0003: ldftn instance void Ch08.Publisher::PublishArrivedNews
                (object, class Ch08.NewsEventArgs)

        /* It instantiates an instance of the EventHandler and use
         * in the L_0015 to add into the event to get notification.*/
        L_0009: newobj instance void
                [mscorlib]System.EventHandler'1<class
```

```
            Ch08.NewsEventArgs>:::.ctor(object, native int)

    /* The add_NewsEvent is translation for the += and will be
     * used to add the subscribed method
     * (created in L_0010) into the event.*/
    L_000e: callvirt instance void Ch08.NewsManager::
            remove_NewsEvent(class [mscorlib]
                    System.EventHandler'1<class Ch08.NewsEventArgs>)
    L_0013: nop
    L_0014: ret
    }
}
```

In Listing 8-11, you can see that in the constructor (.ctor) of the Publisher class, the add_NewsEvent method is used in L_0015 to add the instance of the EventHandler<NewsEventArgs> instantiated in L_0010 using the function pointer of the PublishArrivedNews shown in L_000a. If you examine the UnSubscribe method shown in Listing 8-11, you will see that it loads the function pointer of the PublishArrivedNews shown in L_0003, instantiates an instance of EventHandler<NewsEventArgs> in L_0009, and uses this to call the remove_NewsEvent method in L_000e to unsubscribe the PublishArrivedNews method from the event. The C# compiler compiles the Reviewer class the same the Publisher class does.

In Runtime

While the subscriber, for example, Publisher or Reviewer classes, tries to subscribe for the notification, it calls the add_NewsEvent method from the NewsEvent, which internally calls the Combine method from the Delegate class, which internally called the CombineImpl method from the MulticastDelegate class, as shown in Listing 8-12.

Listing 8-12. Implementation of the Combine Method

```
public static Delegate Combine(Delegate a, Delegate b)
{
    if (a == null)
    {
        return b;
    }
    return a.CombineImpl(b);
}
```

As we saw earlier, the NewsEvent is derived from the EventHandler class, and it is derived from the Delegate class. Therefore, when subscribers call the add_NewsEvent from the NewsEvent, it passes the instance of the EventHandler instantiated using the callback method, for example, PublishArrivedNews for the Publisher and ReviewOnArrivedNews for the Reviewer class, as arguments to the add_NewsEvent method. The CombineImpl method will combine the original NewsEvent with the EventHandler instance and pass it to the add_NewsEvent method. It returns the combined Delegate as MulticastDelegate using the NewMulticastDelegate method, as shown in Listing 8-13, and stores it back in the NewsEvent field of the NewsManager.

Listing 8-13. Implementation of the NewMulticastDelegate Method

```
private MulticastDelegate NewMulticastDelegate(
        object[] invocationList, int invocationCount,
      bool thisIsMultiCastAlready)
{
    MulticastDelegate delegate2 = Delegate.InternalAllocLike(this);
    if (thisIsMultiCastAlready)
    {
        delegate2._methodPtr = base._methodPtr;
        delegate2._methodPtrAux = base._methodPtrAux;
    }
    else
    {
        delegate2._methodPtr = base.GetMulticastInvoke();
        delegate2._methodPtrAux = base.GetInvokeMethod();
    }
    delegate2._target = delegate2;
    delegate2._invocationList = invocationList;
    delegate2._invocationCount = (IntPtr) invocationCount;
    return delegate2;
}
```

Figure 8-3 shows that when the CLR tries to subscribe a method in Step A1, it calls the add_NewsEvent from the event by passing an instance of EventHandler instantiated using the PublishArrivedNews or ReviewOnArrivedNews method. In Step A2, the CLR calls the Combine method from the Delegate class to combine this instance of the EventHandler with the NewsEvent field declared in the NewsManager class. In Step A3, the Delegate class returns the combined delegate and it is stored back in the NewsEvent field.

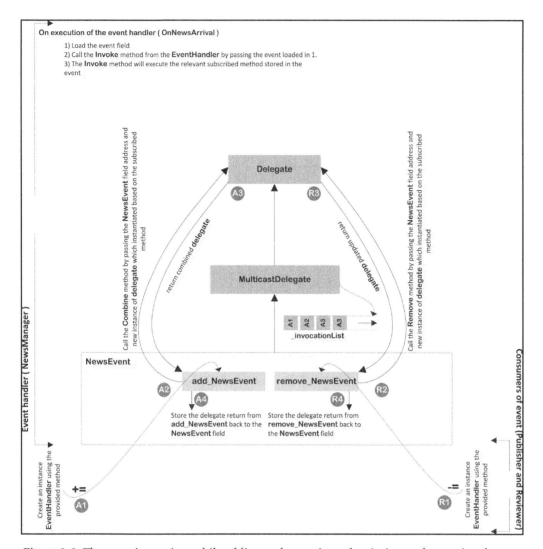

Figure 8-3. *The event in runtime while adding and removing subscription and executing the event.*

While the subscribers tries to unsubscribe (-=) in Step R1, for the notification, for example, from the Publisher class, it calls the remove_NewsEvent method of the NewsEvent event, which calls the Remove method from the Delegate class in Step R2, which internally calls the RemoveImpl method from the MulticastDelegate class to update the NewsEvent, as shown in Listing 8-14.

Listing 8-14. *Implementation of the Remove Method from the Delegate Class*

```
public static Delegate Remove(Delegate source, Delegate value)
{
    /* Code removed*/
    return source.RemoveImpl(value);
}
```

The CLR passes back the updated Delegate from the RemoveImpl method as MulticastDelegate using the NewMulticastDelegate method in Step R3, and it is stored back in the NewsEvent field in Step R4, as demonstrated in Figure 8-3.

While the CLR executes the OnNewsArrival method, it loads the NewsEvent and calls the Invoke method from the EventHandler. The Invoke method will execute all the methods stored in the _invocationList array. The _invocationList maintains the method pointers of all methods subscribed to the event, as shown in Figure 8-4: method pointer of ReviewOnArrivedNews method 1492808 and method pointer of the PublishArrivedNews method 1492848.

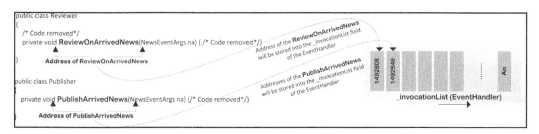

Figure 8-4. The memory information while executing the event.

The addresses shown in the Figure 8-4 will vary when you execute Listing 8-8 in your environment.

Summary

In this chapter, we have learned about the event, how to design a type that exposes the event to the subscribers to subscribe to be notified, implemented the code to handle the event, and explained the concept of the event in C#. We also explored the behind the scenes workings of the event by looking into the decompiled IL code for the respective event member, event handler, and subscribers code. We also learn how the event works in runtime.

This chapter wraps up by examining a simple Windows application, shown in Listing 8-15, to help you understand how event works in the Windows application. This application will generate a Guid when you click the Generate button. The Button class exposed the Click event, and if you subscribe to this event by providing an event handler and then clicking the instance of the Button, it will execute the subscribed event handler. Listing 8-15 shows the partial code for the event in this Windows application.

Listing 8-15. Sample Windows Application

```
using System;
using System.Windows.Forms;
namespace Ch08_GUI
{
    public partial class frmMain : Form
    {
        public frmMain()
        {
            InitializeComponent();
        }
```

```
                /* This method used to subscribe to the Click event of the
                 * Button class */
                private void btnGenerate_Click(object sender, EventArgs e)
                {
                    lblGuid.Text = Guid.NewGuid().ToString("N");
                }
            }
        }

namespace Ch08_GUI
{
        partial class frmMain
        {
            /* code removed */
            private void InitializeComponent()
            {
                this.btnGenerate = new System.Windows.Forms.Button();
                /* code removed */
                /* Subscribe to the Click event of the Button class using
                 * the  btnGenerate_Click  method*/
                this.btnGenerate.Click += new
                    System.EventHandler(this.btnGenerate_Click);
                /* code removed */
            }
            private System.Windows.Forms.Button btnGenerate;
            private System.Windows.Forms.Label lblGuid;
        }
}
```

Listing 8-15 produces the output shown in Figure 8-5.

Figure 8-5. *Sample windows application to show the usage of the event.*

The next chapter will examine Iterator in .NET using C#.

CHAPTER 9

Foreach and Iterator

This chapter will discuss the foreach statement and iterators block. The foreach statement is used to iterate an array or an object collection that implements the System.Collections.IEnumerable or System. Collections.Generic.IEnumerable<T> interface. The iterators block is also used to iterate through an array or an object collection based on the state machine generated automatically by the C# compiler.

State Machine

Throughout this chapter, you will explore how the C# compiler generates the state machine for an iterator block, what the states are that the state machine contains, and how the state transition takes place in the iterator sections. Therefore, it's important to begin this chapter with a brief overview of state machines.

The C# compiler automatically generates a state machine for the iterator code block when an iterator method is defined in a program. A *state machine* is a model by which an object alters its behavior when its internal state changes in response to events. A *state* is a unique condition in which a state machine does some specific action in its lifetime. An *event* in context of the state machine is something that triggers the state machine to do a transition, and a *transition* demonstrates the actions when a state machine receives an event depending on its current state. An *action* refers to what a state machine performs during a transition.

In .NET, the C# compiler generates the state machine for the iterator block used in a program and maintains its state on each of the transitions of the state based on an event (called the MoveNext method, which we will explore later in this chapter). For each of the transitions in the state machine, the CLR does some action, for example, process the iterated item that was defined in the respective state and return it to the caller.

Foreach Statement

The foreach statement iterates over each of the elements in a collection and associated statements will process each of the elements it retrieves from the collection on iteration. The following section explains how to declare a foreach statement in a program, and later you will explore how the C# compiler compiles the foreach statement used in a program and also how the CLR handles it in runtime.

Declaration

The foreach statement declared in the program will have the following syntax:

```
foreach ( local_variable_type(LT) iteration_variable(IV) in an_expression(E)  )
{
    Statement or Statements (S)
}
```

The local variable type (LT) defines the type of the iteration variable (IV) but if var is used for the LT, it is said to be an implicitly typed iteration variable and its type is the element type of the Enumerator object that we get from the expression E. The iteration variable can't be updated from the Statement or Statements (S) used for the foreach block or a compile-time error occurs, as shown below, while trying to update the iteration variable number from the statement block of the foreach statement, as shown in Listing 9-1.

```
Error   19      Cannot assign to 'number' because it is a 'foreach iteration variable'
```

Listing 9-1. An Example of a Foreach Statement

```
using System;
using System.Collections.Generic;

namespace Ch09
{
    class Program
    {
        static void Main(string[] args)
        {
            IList<int> numbers = new List<int>
            {
                1,2,3,4,4,6,7,8,9,10
            };

            foreach (int number in numbers)
            {
                Console.Write("{0}\t", number);
            }
        }
    }
}
```

The program in Listing 9-1 produces the following output:

```
1      2      3      4      4      6      7      8      9      10
```

Internal of the Foreach

In the following sections, we will explore how the C# compiler treats a foreach statement in compile time and also how the CLR takes care of it in runtime when there is a foreach statement used in a program.

In Compile Time

The C# compiler determines the collection type of the expression E (in foreach declaration), enumerator type (get the enumerator type from the E), and element type (type for the iteration variable for the foreach declaration) for the foreach statement before it starts iterating the collection. To determine the collection type, enumerator type, and element type, the C# compiler completes various checks, as outlined in the following sections.

Array Type

If the type T of expression (E) is an array type, then there is an implicit reference conversion from T to the IEnumerable interface (since System.Array implements this interface). The collection type is the IEnumerable interface, the enumerator type is the IEnumerator interface, and the element type is the element type of array type T. The IEnumerable and IEnumerator are defined in the System.Collections namespace.

Dynamic Type

If the type T of expression (E) used in the foreach statement is dynamic, then there is an implicit conversion from expression to the IEnumerable interface.

Other

If the collection type can't be determined in the array and dynamic type check stage, then the C# compiler determines whether the type T has an appropriate GetEnumerator method, and if the GetEnumerator is found, then it does the following:

- Checks whether the return type E of the GetEnumerator method is a class, struct, or interface type or otherwise terminates the operation.

- Performs a member lookup on E for the property Current and method MoveNext. If the lookup returns true, then the operation will continue or otherwise terminates the operation.

After determining the collection type T, the enumerator type E, and the element type, the CLR starts iterating the collection.

In Runtime

From Listing 9-1, you can see that the C# compiler found the collection type of the numbers, which is System.Collections.Generic.IEnumerable'1<int32>, and retrieved the Enumerator object System.Collections.Generic.IEnumerator'1<int32> from the numbers. It iterates through the Enumerator object to get the value from the numbers and assigns it to the iteration variable number. Figure 9-1 demonstrates how the foreach statement works in runtime based on the example in Listing 9-1.

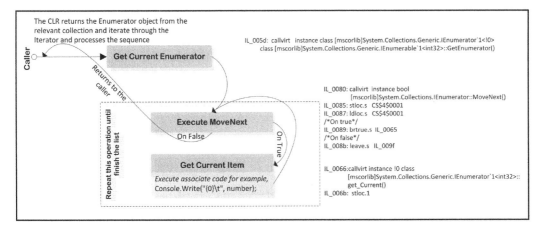

Figure 9-1. Foreach in runtime

Figure 9-1 shows that:

- The CLR gets the Enumerator object from the numbers collection by calling the GetEnumerator method of the collection type determined against the numbers (used in Listing 9-1).

- The CLR calls the MoveNext method of the Enumerator, and if the return of MoveNext method is true, it calls the get_Current method to get the current item from the collection and processes the element if there is any.

The CLR keeps calling the MoveNext method of the Enumerator object until the MoveNext method return false.

Internal of the Foreach Execution

Let's decompile Listing 9-1 using the ildasm.exe tool to understand how the CLR handles the foreach statement, as shown in Listing 9-2.

Listing 9-2. IL Code for the Foreach Statement

```
.method private hidebysig static void  Main(string[] args) cil managed
{
  .entrypoint
  // Code size       161 (0xa1)
  .maxstack  2
  .locals init (
          [0] class [mscorlib]System.Collections.Generic.IList'1<int32>
              numbers,
          [1] int32 number,
          [2] class [mscorlib]System.Collections.Generic.List'1<int32>
              '<>g__initLocal0',
          [3] class [mscorlib]System.Collections.Generic.IEnumerator'1<int32>
              CS$5$0000,
          [4] bool  CS$4$0001)
```

```
IL_0000:  nop
IL_0001:  newobj instance void class
          [mscorlib]System.Collections.Generic.List'1<int32>::.ctor()
IL_0006:  stloc.2
IL_0007:  ldloc.2
IL_0008:  ldc.i4.1
IL_0009:  callvirt   instance void class
          [mscorlib]System.Collections.Generic.List'1<int32>::Add(!0)
/* Rest of the Add method call removed */


/* Get Enumerator*/
/* CLR loads the Enumerator object from the collection instantiated
 * in IL_0001 on to the evaluation stack*/
IL_005d:  callvirt   instance class
          [mscorlib]System.Collections.Generic.IEnumerator'1<!0> class
          [mscorlib]System.Collections.Generic.IEnumerable'1<int32>::
          GetEnumerator()


/* Store the Enumerator object returned from the IL_005d into the Local
 * variable CS$5$0000 at position 3. */
IL_0062:  stloc.3


/* Compiler wrap the foreach iteration block into the try block when use a
 * foreach statement*/
.try
{
  /* Transfer the program control in IL_007f to load the Enumerator
   * object CS$5$0000 from the local variable at position 3 and continue
   * the operation from there.*/
  IL_0063:  br.s      IL_007f

  /* CLR loads the Enumerator object from the collection type instantiated
   * in IL_0001 on to the evaluation stack*/
  IL_0065:  ldloc.3

  /* get_Current method of the Enumerator returns the Current element. */
  IL_0066:  callvirt instance !0 class
            [mscorlib]System.Collections.Generic.IEnumerator'1<int32>::
            get_Current()

  /* Store the value return from IL_0066 in the Local variables section
   * at position 1 and do related operation*/
  IL_006b:  stloc.1
  IL_006c:  nop
  IL_006d:  ldstr     "{0}\t"
  IL_0072:  ldloc.1
  IL_0073:  box       [mscorlib]System.Int32
  IL_0078:  call      void [mscorlib]System.Console::Write(string, object)
  IL_007d:  nop
  IL_007e:  nop
```

```
    /* CLR loads the Enumerator object from the collection type instantiated
     * in IL_0001 on to the evaluation stack*/
    IL_007f:  ldloc.3

    /* Execute the MoveNext method to find out whether it is
     * possible to iterate the collection any further. The MoveNext
     * method returns a boolean value , on true it will iterate
     * through the list or otherwise  on false it will
     * execute the finally block to terminate the iteration.*/
    IL_0080:  callvirt  instance bool
                  [mscorlib]System.Collections.IEnumerator::MoveNext()
    IL_0085:  stloc.s   CS$4$0001
    IL_0087:  ldloc.s   CS$4$0001

    /* Transfer the program control to the IL_0065 to continue the iteration.
     * If the MoveNext return true from IL_0080.*/
    IL_0089:  brtrue.s  IL_0065
    IL_008b:  leave.s   IL_009f
  }  // end .try

  finally /* Finally block will execute regardless to dispose the iterator */
  {
    IL_008d:  ldloc.3
    IL_008e:  ldnull
    IL_008f:  ceq
    IL_0091:  stloc.s   CS$4$0001
    IL_0093:  ldloc.s   CS$4$0001
    IL_0095:  brtrue.s  IL_009e
    IL_0097:  ldloc.3
    IL_0098:  callvirt   instance void [mscorlib]System.IDisposable::Dispose()
    IL_009d:  nop
    IL_009e:  endfinally
  }  // end handler

  IL_009f:  nop
  IL_00a0:  ret
}
```

■ **Note:** br.s target: Branch to target.

brtrue.s target: Branch to target if value is nonzero (true).

Let's analyze Listing 9-2 to understand the underlying foreach execution.

Get Enumerator

In IL_005d, the CLR retrieves the Enumerator object by calling the GetEnumerator method of the collection type List'1<int32> instantiated in IL_0001. On a successful return of the GetEnumerator method, the CLR stores the iterator object in CS$5$0000 in the Local variable section of the Main Method.

Execute MoveNext

When the program control moves in IL_0063, it transfers the program control to the IL_007f to call the MoveNext method of the Enumerator object returned from the GetEnumerator method in IL_005d. The CLR loads the Enumerator object CS$5$0000 stored at the local variable section at position 3 and calls the MoveNext method of that Enumerator object to make sure the iteration is possible over the collection. On return of true from the MoveNext method, the CLR processes the associated embedded statement with the foreach statement using the current iterated item.

To get the current item, the CLR transfers the program control in IL_0065 and loads the Enumerator object stored in the Local section at position 3. It gets the current item from the Enumerator object by calling the get_Current method of the Enumerator object in IL_0066. In IL_006b to IL_007e, the CLR processes the iterated item, for example, by display on the console as output.

End of Iteration

When the CLR calls the MoveNext method in IL_0080 and on return of true, the CLR continues, as discussed in the "Execute MoveNext" section. On return of false, the CLR executes the leave instruction in IL_008b, which will execute the nearest finally block defined in IL_008d to IL_009e. After finishing the execute instruction in IL_008d to IL_009e, the CLR transfers the program control to the IL_009f and from IL_00a0 it will return from this method.

The false return from the MoveNext method denotes that there are no more items to iterate through in the collection object and this is the end of the operation.

So far we have explored how the foreach statement works in C#; now we will see how to use the foreach statement in the iterator block and explore in detail how the iterator is used in C#.

Iterators

When a function member is implemented using an iterator block (a block that contains one or more yield statements), it is referred to as an *iterator*. When the C# compiler finds any yield statement in a method, it generates a class, which is a state machine used to implement the behavior that is expressed in the iterator block. On each yield statement, control is returned to the caller, but the CLR maintains the state of the callee into the state machine the compiler generated for it. The iterator block can be declared as shown in Figure 9-2.

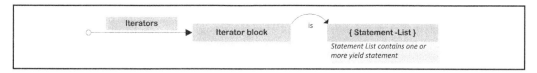

Figure 9-2. *Iterators declaration*

The return type of the iterator block is one of the following:

- *Enumerator*: System.Collections.IEnumerator or System.Collections.Generic. IEnumerator<T>.

- *Enumerable*: System.Collections.IEnumerable or System.Collections.Generic. IEnumerable<T>.

Let's look at the example provided in Listing 9-3 where an iterator block is defined for the Power method using the yield keyword. The Power method calculates the power of a number based on a given exponent and returns the current iterated item, which results in the power of the number to the caller. It will continue iteration until it reaches the termination condition (counter++< exponent).

Listing 9-3. *An Example of the Iterator*

```
using System;
using System.Collections;

namespace Ch09
{
    class Program
    {
        static void Main(string[] args)
        {
            int currentExponent = 0;
            int iterationPhase = 0;
            Console.WriteLine("{0,10}\t{1,10}\t{2,10}",
                    "Iteration Phase", "Power", "Next Power will be");
            foreach (int i in Power(2, 4))
            {
                currentExponent = i;
                Console.Write("{0,9}\t{1,9}",
                    ++iterationPhase, currentExponent);
            }
        }

        public static IEnumerable Power(int number, int exponent)
        {
            int counter = 0;
            int result = 1;
            while (counter++ < exponent)
            {
                result = result * number;
                yield return result;
                Console.WriteLine("\t{0,9}x{1}\t\u25BC", result, number);
            }
        }
    }
}
```

This program will produce the following output:

```
Iteration Phase        Power                Next Power will be
            1            2                2x2            ▼
            2            4                4x2            ▼
            3            8                8x2            ▼
            4           16               16x2            ▼
```

Listing 9-3 shows that the CLR calls the Power method from the foreach statement and calculates the power of a number. The Power method will be called as long as the condition specified in the while statement (counter++< exponent) is valid. On each iteration, behind the scenes the CLR maintains the state of the Power method in a C# compiler–generated state machine <Power>d__0. The state stored in the state machine is used to iterate through the collection. On each iteration, the CLR loads the state from the state machine and changes the state to the running state to continue the operation. It checks the condition (the condition specified in while statement) whether or not the next iteration is valid to continue, stores back the state and related information in the state machine, and returns to the caller. The CLR will continue this operation as long as the call of the MoveNext method of the state machine returns the true result.

The <Power>d__0 state machine is extracted from the executable, which is produced from Listing 9-3 using the ildasm.exe tool, as shown in Figure 9-3.

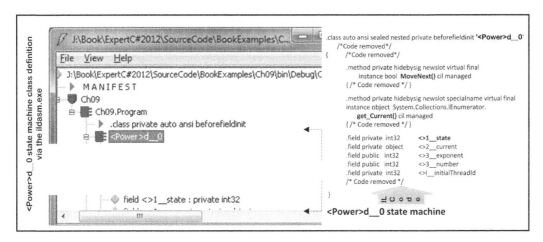

Figure 9-3. *<Power>d__0 state machine explored via the ildasm.exe tool*

This state machine implements the MoveNext method, which is used to control the state transition of the state machine. On a successful true return of the MoveNext method, iteration will continue; but upon a false return, the iteration will terminate.

Iterator Internal

In Figure 9-3, we saw that the C# compiler generated the <Power>d__0 state machine for Listing 9-3. In the following section, we will explore in depth the <Power>d__0 state machine.

Iterator and State Machine

The <Power>d__0 state machine has four states that maintain the state of the state machine used for the iterator block. Table 9-1 lists the states used in the <Power>d__0 state machine for the iterator block.

Table 9-1. *States of the State Machine*

States	Value
Before	0
Running	-1
Suspended	1
After	Any positive values

State Transition

In the state transition of the <Power>d__0 state machine, the CLR executes specific tasks defined for the state, as shown in Table 9-2.

Table 9-2. *<Power>d__0 State Machine and the CLR-Specific Tasks*

State	Description
Before	The CLR changes the state of the state machine from before (0) into running (−1) to continue iteration of the collection. It initializes the parameters of the iterator block to the argument values and instance values saved when the enumerator object was initialized. In this state, the CLR executes the iterator block from the beginning until the execution is interrupted.
Suspended	The CLR changes the state into the running (-1) state to continue iteration of the collection and restores the state from suspended (1) to running. The CLR restores all the values saved when execution of the iterator block was last suspended. It resumes execution of the iterator block immediately following the yield return statement suspend the execution and continues until execution interrupted.
After running	In this state, invoking MoveNext returns false. The result of invoking MoveNext is unspecified in this state.

The MoveNext method of <Power>d__0 state machine is responsible for the state transition in the state machine to process the collection. Let's explore the MoveNext method, as presented in Figure 9-4, which shows the state transition of the <Power>d__0 state machine. The MoveNext method of the <Power>d__0 state machine is extracted from the executable produced from the code in Listing 9-3 using the .Net Reflector tool.

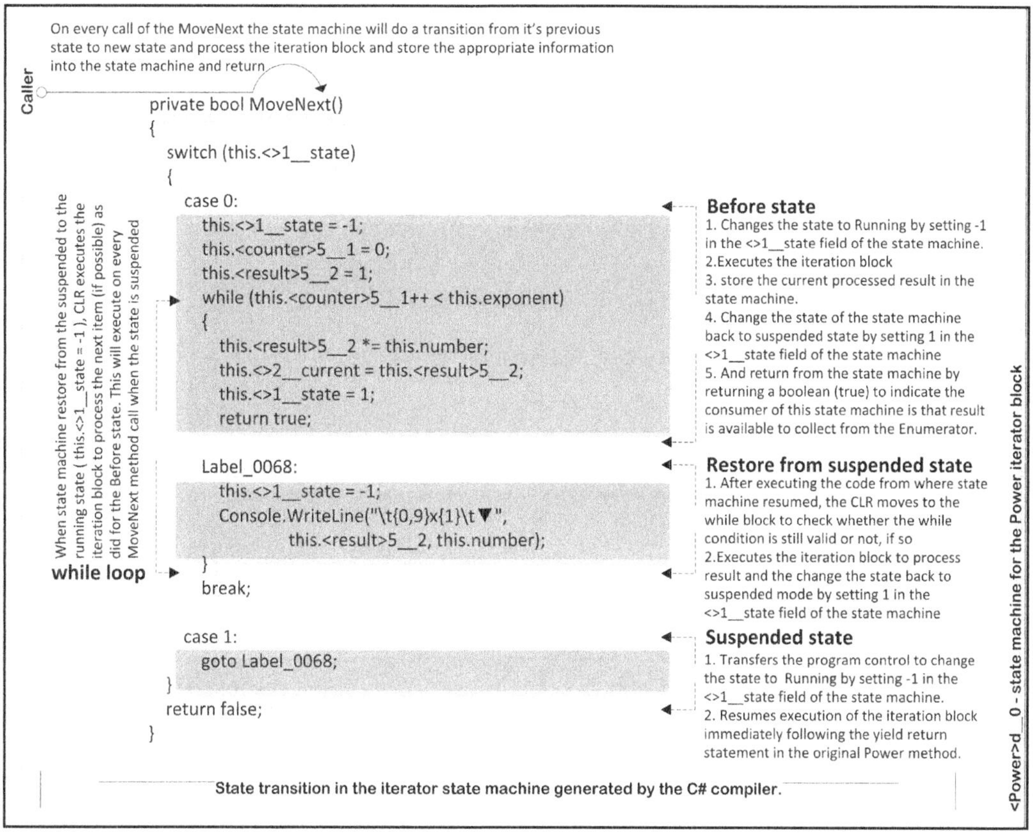
On every call of the MoveNext the state machine will do a transition from it's previous state to new state and process the iteration block and store the appropriate information into the state machine and return
Caller
private bool MoveNext()
{
switch (this.<>1__state)
{
case 0:
this.<>1__state = -1;
this.<counter>5__1 = 0;
this.<result>5__2 = 1;
while (this.<counter>5__1++ < this.exponent)
{
this.<result>5__2 *= this.number;
this.<>2__current = this.<result>5__2;
this.<>1__state = 1;
return true;
Label_0068:
this.<>1__state = -1;
Console.WriteLine("\t{0,9}x{1}\t▼",
this.<result>5__2, this.number);
}
break;
case 1:
goto Label_0068;
}
return false;
}
When state machine restore from the suspended to the running state (this.<>1__state = -1), CLR executes the iteration block to process the next item (if possible) as did for the Before state. This will execute on every MoveNext method call when the state is suspended
while loop
Before state
1. Changes the state to Running by setting -1 in the <>1__state field of the state machine.
2.Executes the iteration block
3. store the current processed result in the state machine.
4. Change the state of the state machine back to suspended state by setting 1 in the <>1__state field of the state machine
5. And return from the state machine by returning a boolean (true) to indicate the consumer of this state machine is that result is available to collect from the Enumerator.
Restore from suspended state
1. After executing the code from where state machine resumed, the CLR moves to the while block to check whether the while condition is still valid or not, if so
2.Executes the iteration block to process result and the change the state back to suspended mode by setting 1 in the <>1__state field of the state machine
Suspended state
1. Transfers the program control to change the state to Running by setting -1 in the <>1__state field of the state machine.
2. Resumes execution of the iteration block immediately following the yield return statement in the original Power method.
<Power>d__0 - state machine for the Power iterator block
State transition in the iterator state machine generated by the C# compiler.

Figure 9-4. *State transition of the state machine <Power>d__0*

Explore the State Machine <Power>d__0

Let's decompile the code in Listing 9-3 using the `ildasm.exe` tool to understand the underlying works of the iterator. The decompiled IL code is divided into three categories:

- *`Foreach`*: In this decompiled IL code block (Listing 9-4), you can see how the CLR iterates through the `Enumerator` object returned from the iterator block.
- *Instantiation of the state machine* (`<Power>d__0`): This method (Listing 9-5) instantiates an instance of the state machine `<Power>d__0`.
- *State machine* (`<Power>d__0`): The decompiled IL code (Listing 9-6) of the `<Power>d__0` state machine shows the internal implementation of the state machine.

Process Iterator Block Using the Foreach Statement

Let's decompiled the IL code for the `Main` method, as shown in Listing 9-4.

Listing 9-4. *Decompiled Main Method*

```
.method private hidebysig static void Main(string[] args) cil managed
{
    .entrypoint
    .maxstack 4
    .locals init (
        [0] int32 currentExponent,
        [1] int32 iterationPhase,
        [2] int32 i,
        [3] class [mscorlib]System.Collections.IEnumerator CS$5$0000,
        [4] bool CS$4$0001,
        [5] class [mscorlib]System.IDisposable CS$0$0002)
    L_0000: nop

    /* Code removed */
    L_0020: ldc.i4.2
    L_0021: ldc.i4.4

    /* Initialize the state machine */
    /* Power method will return an instance of the of <Power>d__0 which
     * encapsulates the iterator */
    L_0022: call class [mscorlib]System.Collections.IEnumerable
                    Ch09.Program::Power(int32, int32)

    /* Get the  Enumerator from the collection/enumerable return in L_0022 */
    L_0027: callvirt instance class [mscorlib]System.Collections.IEnumerator
                    [mscorlib]System.Collections.IEnumerable::GetEnumerator()
    L_002c: stloc.3

    /* Transfer the program control to the L_005a to execute the MoveNext
     * method of the Enumerator to find out whether the iteration should
     * continue or not.  */
    L_002d: br.s L_005a
    L_002f: ldloc.3

    /*Get the Current item from the Enumerator */
    L_0030: callvirt instance object
                    [mscorlib]System.Collections.IEnumerator::get_Current()
    L_0035: unbox.any int32
    L_003a: stloc.2
    L_003b: nop
    L_003c: ldloc.2
    L_003d: stloc.0

    /* Process the return item from the Enumerator in L_0030
     * if there any exists */
    L_003e: ldstr "{0,9}\t{1,9}"
    L_0043: ldloc.1
    L_0044: ldc.i4.1
    L_0045: add
```

```
    L_0046: dup
    L_0047: stloc.1
    L_0048: box int32
    L_004d: ldloc.0
    L_004e: box int32
    L_0053: call void [mscorlib]System.Console::Write(string, object, object)
    L_0058: nop
    L_0059: nop

    /* Loads the Enumerator object (CS$5$0000) stored at position 3 */
    L_005a: ldloc.3

    /* Check whether there is any item in the list or not by
     * calling the MoveNext method which will make sure whether
     *there is any item in the list by return a boolean value
     * true or false*/
    L_005b: callvirt instance bool
                     [mscorlib]System.Collections.IEnumerator::MoveNext()
    L_0060: stloc.s CS$4$0001
    L_0062: ldloc.s CS$4$0001

    /* On true return the CLR will transfer the program control
     * to the L_002f to keep continue the processing */
    L_0064: brtrue.s L_002f

    /* On false CLR will execute nearest finally block which indicate the
     * end of iteration. */
    L_0066: leave.s L_0084
    L_0068: ldloc.3
    /* Code removed */
    L_0084: nop
    L_0085: ret
  /* try finally embedded by the C# compiler for the foreach statement. */
    .try L_002d to L_0068 finally handler L_0068 to L_0084
}
```

In Listing 9-4, the CLR calls the MoveNext method of the Enumerator to iterate through the collection. The Enumerator object extracted from the IEnumerable object is returned in L_0022, as you saw earlier, because the CLR finds the collection type for the expression used in the foreach statement. In this circumstance, it will be the C# compiler–generated enumerator or state machine.

In Listing 9-3, the expression Power(2,4) is used in the foreach statement, which instantiates an instance of the C# compiler–generated Enumerator object or the state machine for the iterator block. In IL_0027 and IL_002c, the CLR loads and stores the instance of the Enumerator object returned from the Power method. The CLR calls the MoveNext method to iterate through the Enumerator object to continue to call the MoveNext method until the MoveNext method returns false.

Instantiation of the State Machine (<Power>d__0)

The C# compiler generates the stub method shown in Listing 9-5, which is used to instantiate the state machine <Power>d__0. Let's decompiled the stub method in IL for the Power method, which was used to instantiate an instance of the state machine <Power>d__0.

Listing 9-5. Decompiled Power Method

```
.method public hidebysig static class [mscorlib]System.Collections.IEnumerable
        Power(int32 number, int32 exponent) cil managed
{
    .maxstack 2
    .locals init (
        [0] class Ch09.Program/<Power>d__0 d__,
        [1] class [mscorlib]System.Collections.IEnumerable enumerable)
    L_0000: ldc.i4.s -2

    /* Instantiate the state machine generated by the C# compiler */
    L_0002: newobj instance void Ch09.Program/<Power>d__0::.ctor(int32)
    /* Code removed */

    L_000a: stfld int32 Ch09.Program/<Power>d__0::<>3__number
    /* Code removed */

    L_0011: stfld int32 Ch09.Program/<Power>d__0::<>3__exponent
    /* Code removed */
}
```

This stub method instantiates the state machine, sets the initial values for the state machine, and calls the MoveNext method from the state machine <Power>d__0 to start it. In the following section, we will explore in detail how this works in state machine.

State Machine (<Power>d__0)

Listing 9-6 shows the C# compiler-generated state machine <Power>d__0 for the iterator block defined in the Power method of Listing 9-3. The heart of the state machine <Power>d__0 is the MoveNext method, which is used to control the transition of the state. The MoveNext method will do following:

- It maintains the state of the Enumerator.

- It returns an indicator flag to determine whether the iteration is possible, and if not, by returning true when possible and false otherwise. It also sets the Current item from the Enumerator so the consumer of the Enumerator object can get the current item. It changes the state into suspended by setting a state value of 1 and returning to the caller with an indicator flag to indicate the possibility of iteration.

- On the next iteration, the CLR calls the MoveNext method, which loads the previous state of state machine. The CLR changes the state of the state machine from suspended to running and executes the associated code for the iterate item, for example, L_0068 to L_00ac as shown in Listing 9-6. Depending on the looping condition specified in the while statement, it will update the relevant state. This will continue until it finishes the iteration.

Let's look at the decompiled IL code for the <Power>d__0, as shown in Listing 9-6.

Listing 9-6. Decompiled State Machine <Power>d__0

```
.class auto ansi sealed nested private beforefieldinit <Power>d__0
    extends [mscorlib]System.Object
```

```
    implements
    [mscorlib]System.Collections.Generic.IEnumerable'1<object>,
    [mscorlib]System.Collections.IEnumerable,
    [mscorlib]System.Collections.Generic.IEnumerator'1<object>,
    [mscorlib]System.Collections.IEnumerator, [mscorlib]System.IDisposable
{
    { /*Code removed*/ }
    .method public hidebysig specialname rtspecialname instance void
        .ctor(int32 <>1__state) cil managed
    { /*Code removed*/ }

    .method private hidebysig newslot virtual final instance bool
        MoveNext() cil managed
    {
        .override [mscorlib]System.Collections.IEnumerator::MoveNext
        .maxstack 3
        .locals init (
            [0] bool CS$1$0000,
            [1] int32 CS$4$0001,
            [2] int32 CS$0$0002,
            [3] bool CS$4$0003)
        L_0000: ldarg.0
        L_0001: ldfld int32 Ch09.Program/<Power>d__0::<>1__state
        L_0006: stloc.1
        L_0007: ldloc.1

        /* Depending on the State of the State machine CLR will
         * switch between State 0 and State 1. For the first time or
         * first iteration, state of the State machine will be 0,
         * The CLR will  transfer the program control to the L_0019.*/
        L_0008: switch (L_0019, L_0017)
        L_0015: br.s L_001b
        L_0017: br.s L_0068
        L_0019: br.s L_0020
        L_001b: br L_00af

        /* The CLR start executing  from L_0020 to L_0066 while the state
         * of the state machine is 0.The CLR will store related information
         * in the state machine.*/
        L_0020: ldarg.0
        L_0021: ldc.i4.m1
        L_0022: stfld int32 Ch09.Program/<Power>d__0::<>1__state
        L_0027: nop
        L_0028: ldarg.0
        L_0029: ldc.i4.0
        L_002a: stfld int32 Ch09.Program/<Power>d__0::<counter>5__1
        L_002f: ldarg.0
        L_0030: ldc.i4.1
        L_0031: stfld int32 Ch09.Program/<Power>d__0::<result>5__2
        L_0036: br.s L_0091
```

```
L_0038: nop
L_0039: ldarg.0
L_003a: ldarg.0
L_003b: ldfld int32 Ch09.Program/<Power>d__0::<result>5__2
L_0040: ldarg.0
L_0041: ldfld int32 Ch09.Program/<Power>d__0::number
L_0046: mul
L_0047: stfld int32 Ch09.Program/<Power>d__0::<result>5__2
L_004c: ldarg.0
L_004d: ldarg.0
L_004e: ldfld int32 Ch09.Program/<Power>d__0::<result>5__2
L_0053: box int32
L_0058: stfld object Ch09.Program/<Power>d__0::<>2__current
L_005d: ldarg.0
L_005e: ldc.i4.1
L_005f: stfld int32 Ch09.Program/<Power>d__0::<>1__state
L_0064: ldc.i4.1
L_0065: stloc.0
L_0066: br.s L_00b3

/* The CLR start executing  from L_0068 to L_00ac while the state
 * of the state machine is 1.*/
L_0068: ldarg.0
L_0069: ldc.i4.m1
L_006a: stfld int32 Ch09.Program/<Power>d__0::<>1__state
L_006f: ldstr "\t{0,9}x{1}\t\u25bc"
L_0074: ldarg.0
L_0075: ldfld int32 Ch09.Program/<Power>d__0::<result>5__2
L_007a: box int32
L_007f: ldarg.0
L_0080: ldfld int32 Ch09.Program/<Power>d__0::number
L_0085: box int32
L_008a: call void
        [mscorlib]System.Console::WriteLine(string, object, object)
L_008f: nop
L_0090: nop

/* For State 1, CLR will keep continue to execute the
 * IL instruction from L_0091 to L_00ac (while loop) to
 * check the whether the <counter>5__1++ < this.exponent
 * condition meet*/
L_0091: ldarg.0
L_0092: dup
L_0093: ldfld int32 Ch09.Program/<Power>d__0::<counter>5__1
L_0098: dup
L_0099: stloc.2
L_009a: ldc.i4.1
L_009b: add
L_009c: stfld int32 Ch09.Program/<Power>d__0::<counter>5__1
L_00a1: ldloc.2
L_00a2: ldarg.0
```

```
    L_00a3: ldfld int32 Ch09.Program/<Power>d__0::exponent
    L_00a8: clt
    L_00aa: stloc.3
    L_00ab: ldloc.3

    /* On true transfer the control to the L_0038 */
    L_00ac: brtrue.s L_0038

    L_00ae: nop
    L_00af: ldc.i4.0
    L_00b0: stloc.0
    L_00b1: br.s L_00b3
    L_00b3: ldloc.0
    L_00b4: ret
}

.method private hidebysig newslot virtual final instance class
    [mscorlib]System.Collections.Generic.IEnumerator'1<object>
    System.Collections.Generic.IEnumerable<System.Object>.GetEnumerator()
    cil managed                                                         {}

.method private hidebysig newslot virtual final instance class
    [mscorlib]System.Collections.IEnumerator
    System.Collections.IEnumerable.GetEnumerator() cil managed          {}

.method private hidebysig newslot virtual final instance void
    System.Collections.IEnumerator.Reset() cil managed                  {}

.method private hidebysig newslot virtual final instance void
    System.IDisposable.Dispose() cil managed                            {}

.property instance object
        System.Collections.Generic.IEnumerator<System.Object>.Current
{
    .get instance object Ch09.Program/<Power>d__0::
    System.Collections.Generic.IEnumerator<System.Object>.get_Current()
}

.property instance object System.Collections.IEnumerator.Current
{
    .get instance object Ch09.Program/<Power>d__0::
        System.Collections.IEnumerator.get_Current()
}

.field private    int32         <>1__state
.field private    object        <>2__current
.field public     int32         <>3__exponent
.field public     int32         <>3__number
.field private    int32         <>l__initialThreadId
.field public     int32         <counter>5__1
.field public     int32         <result>5__2
```

```
    .field public    int32        exponent
    .field public    int32        number
}
```

Listing 9-6 shows the state machine <Power>d__0 that shows the state controlling is taken care of by the CLR in runtime. In the following section, we will explore the runtime behavior of Listing 9-6 that is taken of care by the CLR.

Before State (0)

In the before state (0), the CLR transfers the program control in L_0020 and executes the instructions up to L_0066 to process the results. In the beginning of this process, the CLR sets the state of the state machine in running state -1 in L_0021 and continues the processing. The CLR checks the state of the looping condition before it starts any further processing by transferring the program control in L_0091 from L_0036. While the CLR executes the instructions, it compares <counter>5__1 with the exponent in L_00a8. On a true return in L_00a8, the CLR moves the program control to the L_0038 from the L_00ac to start processing the result. Otherwise, it transfers the program control in L_00ae to L_00b4 to return from the MoveNext method.

On the other hand, when it finishes the processing to calculate the results, it sets the state of the state machine to suspended state (1) in L_005e and in L_0066, and the CLR again transfers the control to the L_00b3, which returns from the MoveNext method to terminate this round of iteration.

Figure 9-5 will help you understand the state transition of <Power>d__0 in more depth.

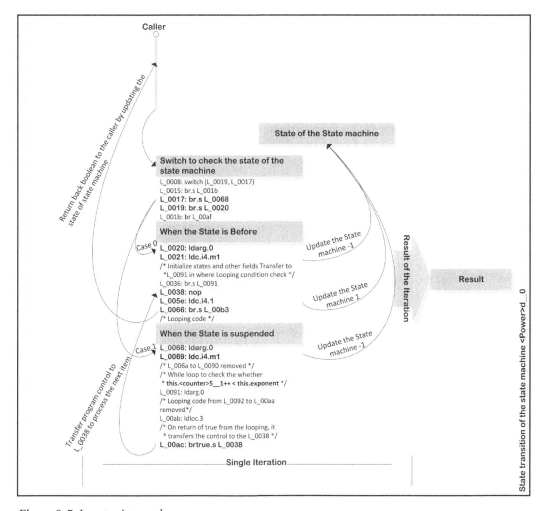

Figure 9-5. *Iterator internal*

Suspended State (1)

On the next iteration, when CLR calls the MoveNext method, it will determine that the state of the state machine is suspended (1), which was set earlier. The CLR executes the code block defined for suspended state (1), which is in L_0068. In the following instruction of L_0068, the CLR changes the state of state machine to running (-1) in L_0069. It starts processing with the result processed in the previous iteration from L_006a to L_0090. The CLR does the following processing and produces the following result:

```
Console.WriteLine("\t{0,9}x{1}\t\u25BC", result, number);
```

After finishing it, the CLR continues the execution and comes to L_0091. In between L_0091 to L_00ac, the CLR will check the loop condition as to whether or not it is possible to iterate through the iterator. In L_00a8, the clt instruction compares the <counter>5__1 with the exponent. On return of true, the CLR moves the program control to the L_0038 from L_00ac to process the next iterated item. The CLR stores the result in the state machine for the next processing and sets the state of the state machine back into suspended (1) in L_0064. It returns from the MoveNext method to the caller from L_0066.

■ **Note:** `ldc.i4.m1`: Push -1 onto the stack as int32.

`ldc.i4.1`: Push 1 onto the stack as int32.

`Clt`: Push 1 if value1 is less than value2, or else push 0.

Examine Memory of the State Machine

Figure 9-6 presents the memory information captured while debugging the executable produced from Listing 9-3 using the `windbg.exe` tool. It shows the state of the `<Power>d__0` state machine while it iterates through the enumerator in the `foreach` statement used in the `Main` method and the stack information of the `Main` method of each iteration.

The following command is run in the `windbg.exe` tool to set the breakpoint while running the executable code of Listing 9-3.

```
!bpmd Ch09.exe Ch09.Program.Main
!bpmd Ch09.exe Ch09.Program.Power
!bpmd Ch09.exe Ch09.Program+<Power>d__0.MoveNext
!g
```

The breakpoint is being set following the Run command in the `windbg.exe` tool on each iteration to get the state of the state machine `<Power>d__0` and `Main` method.

```
!clrstack -a
/* 0x018a4224 is the address of the <Power>d__0 instance */
!dumpobj 0x018a4224
p
```

Let's look at the captured memory information of the executable of Listing 9-3, as shown in Figure 9-6.

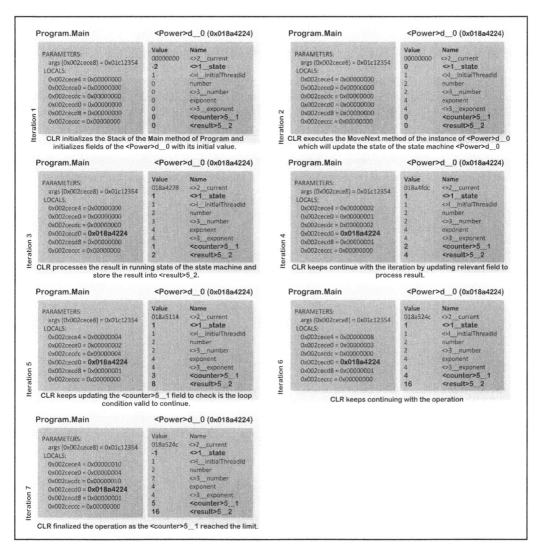

Figure 9-6. *Memory information while debugging Listing 9-3 using the windbg.exe tool*

Figure 9-6 illustrates that on every iteration except for iteration 1 and 2, CLR sets the state if the State machine 1 is suspended. Also, following every iteration the CLR uses an instance of the <Power>d__0 to store the state of the state machine.

Summary

In this chapter we have learned about the usage of the foreach statement and iterators block through a sample program. The C# compiler wraps the code block used in the foreach statement using a try catch block. It iterates through the collection based on a boolean indicator return from the MoveNext method of the enumerator object. You also learned how the state machine the C# compiler generates for the iterator block maintains the state of the iteration while iterating a collection. In the next chapter we will explore the string data type.

■ ■ ■

CHAPTER 10

The String Data Type

This chapter will discuss the string data type in Microsoft .NET Framework using C# language. First I will show how the CLR manages to instantiate a string in .NET. I will then discuss string immutability through which CLR ensures that when a string is created, it can't be changed, and examine its contents, chaining operations in string, and various concatenation techniques used in .NET Framework for the string.

Throughout the chapter, I reference StringBuilder, which is a class that can be used to generate string efficiently. It can also be used to manipulate string, such as append, insert, or remove string. You will see this class used in several examples, but it's not until later in the chapter that I detail the internal workings of the StringBuilder class. There we will examine the constructor of the StringBuilder and the addition, insertion, and remove operations to see how CLR deals with string when using StringBuilder to generate it.

String in .NET

In C#, you can represent numbers such as 1, 2, 3, and so forth using Int32 data type as characters, such as 'A','B', or 'C' using char data type. If you want to represent a word, a sentence, and so on, you can use String data type. In .NET, C# string is a sealed class defined in the System namespace of the mscorlib.dll assembly (located in C:\Windows\Microsoft.NET\Framework\v4.0.30319\mscorlib.dll), as shown in Figure 10-1.

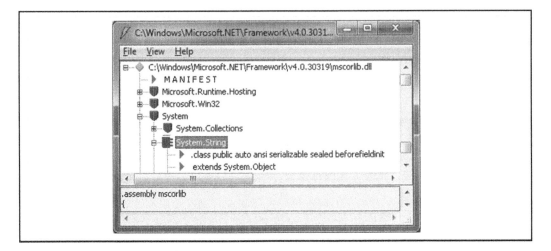

Figure 10-1. String class in System.String namespace

The class definition of the String is extracted using the ildasm.exe, as shown in Listing 10-1.

Listing 10-1. Definition of the String Class in .NET

```
.class public auto ansi serializable sealed beforefieldinit String
    extends
        System.Object
    implements
        System.IComparable, System.ICloneable, System.IConvertible,
        System.IComparable'1<string>, System.Collections.Generic.IEnumerable'1<char>,
        System.Collections.IEnumerable, System.IEquatable'1<string>
```

So based on the class definition, you can see that string class is derived from the System.Object. It is not possible to inherit a type from the String class as it is sealed. As the String class implements the IEnumerable'1<char> interface, you will be able to use the Linq (discussed in the Chapter 12) functionality over the String. Listing 10-2 gives an example of the String in .NET using C#.

Listing 10-2. An Example of String

```
using System;
using System.Text;
namespace Ch10
{
    class Program
    {
        static void Main(string[] args)
        {
            string bookName = "Expert C# 5.0: with the .NET 4.5 Framework";
            /* CLR will create a String with - by repeating the number
             * of the Length of the bookName string .*/
            string dashedLine = new string('-', bookName.Length);
            StringBuilder sb = new StringBuilder("by Mohammad Rahman");
```

```
Console.WriteLine("{0}\n{1}\n{2}",
    bookName,                    /* C# Compiler include the String Literal
                                  * used in bookName in metadata */
    dashedLine,                  /* C# Compiler does not include the
                                  * String Literal used in dashedLine
                                  * in metadata */
    sb.ToString());              /* C# Compiler include the String Literal
                                  * used in the constructor in metadata and
                                  * will construct the String at runtime
                                  * using StringBuilder */
        }
    }
}
```

In Listing 10-2, the bookName is declared as a String type and assigned the string literal Expert C# 5.0: with the .NET 4.5 Framework to it as a value, dashedLine has been constructed using a char, and the StringBuilder is used to construct the string. When this program executes, it will produce the following output:

```
Expert C# 5.0: with the .NET 4.5 Framework
------------------------------------------------------
by Mohammad Rahman
```

Let's open the executable of the program in Listing 10-2 using ildasm.exe to see the metadata information. When the C# compiler compiles the code in Listing 12-2, it embed the string literal used in the Program class into the User Strings section of the executable file, as you can see in Figure 10-2.

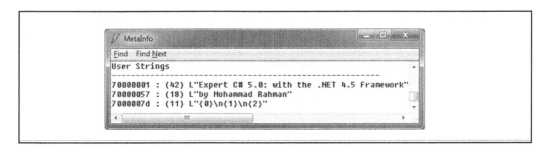

Figure 10-2. String literals in the User Strings section of the MetaInfo

The C# compiler embed Expert C# 5.0: with the .NET 4.5 Framework, by Mohammad Rahman, and {0}\n{1}\n{2} String literally into the metadata of the executable, and this will be used by the CLR when it is required.

Instantiation of a String Object

As you saw earlier, String class is derived from the System.Object, so the String is a reference type and it will live in the Heap while executing a program that uses String. However, in comparison to other reference types, CLR will handle this a bit differently to instantiate an instance of the String. Let's explore this further using the example in Listing 10-3.

Listing 10-3. Demonstration of the C# String Creation

```
using System;

namespace Ch10
{
    class Program
    {
        static void Main(string[] args)
        {
            string book = LoadStringLiteral();
        }
        static string LoadStringLiteral()
        { return "Expert C# 5.0: with the .NET 4.5 Framework"; }
    }
}
```

The decompiled IL code of the Listing 10-3 program using the ildasm.exe to .NETReflector is given in Listing 10-4.

Listing 10-4. IL Code of the Program in Listing 10-3

```
.class private auto ansi beforefieldinit Program
    extends [mscorlib]System.Object
{
    /* Code removed */
    .method private hidebysig static string LoadStringLiteral() cil managed
    {
        .maxstack 1
        .locals init (
            [0] string CS$1$0000)
        L_0000: nop
         /* String literal embedded by the C# compiler */
        L_0001: ldstr "Expert C# 5.0: with the .NET 4.5 Framework"
        L_0006: stloc.0
        L_0007: br.s L_0009
        L_0009: ldloc.0
        L_000a: ret
    }

    .method private hidebysig static void Main(string[] args) cil managed
    {
        .entrypoint
        .maxstack 1
        .locals init (
            [0] string book)
        L_0000: nop
        L_0001: call string Ch10.Program::LoadStringLiteral()
        L_0006: stloc.0
        L_0007: ret
    }
}
```

How the CLR Handles String Instantiation

Let's analyze the code in Listing 10-4 to better understand the concept of the String creation in the C#.

First, in runtime, while the CLR executes the Main method, it will Jit the IL code for the Main method, but the LoadStringLiteral method will not be Jitted at that point, as demonstrated below.

Let's see the MethodDesc Table for the Program class in Listing 10-3 while debugging using the windbg. exe.

```
MethodDesc Table
Entry           MethodDesc      JIT             Name
55c8a7e0        55a64934        PreJIT          System.Object.ToString()
55c8e2e0        55a6493c        PreJIT          System.Object.Equals(System.Object)
55c8e1f0        55a6495c        PreJIT          System.Object.GetHashCode()
55d11600        55a64970        PreJIT          System.Object.Finalize()
001dc019        001d3808        NONE            Ch10.Program..ctor()
003b0070        001d37f0        JIT             Ch10.Program.Main(System.String[])
003b00c0        001d37fc        NONE            Ch10.Program.LoadStringLiteral()
```

As you can see, for the MethodDesc Table of the Program class, the LoadStringLiteral method has not yet been Jitted, so there will not be any address in the Heap in regard to the String literal Expert C# 5.0: with the .NET 4.5 Framework.

Second, as soon as the CLR starts executing the Jitted LoadStringLiteral method, it will instantiate an instance of the String using String literal Expert C# 5.0: with the .NET 4.5 Framework and store it in the Heap and then pass the address of that String back to the Stack of the LoadLiteralString method as a reference, as shown in Figure 10-3.

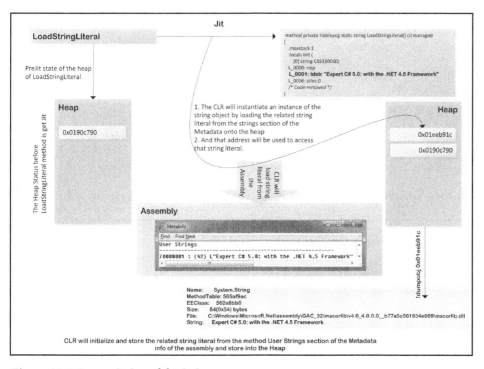

Figure 10-3. Instantiation of the String

From Figure 10-3, you can see that in the Heap there isn't any address for the string literal Expert C# 5.0: with the .NET 4.5 Framework in the pre-Jit state of the method LoadStringLiteral. While the CLR Jits the LoadStringLiteral and starts executing, it instantiates an instance of the string using the literal into the Heap and passes the reference (address 0x01eeb91c) back to the LoadStringLiteral method where it will be stored in the local variable CS$1$0000, as shown in Listing 10-4.

■ **Note**   ldstr: The ldstr instruction pushes a new string object representing the literal stored in the metadata as string (which is a string literal).

Analyzing the Stack information while executing Listing 10-3 will provide further understanding of the string creation in the .NET. Figure 10-4 shows the Stack information while executing the Main and LoadStringLiteral methods of the Program class in Listing 10-3.

Examining the Memory While the CLR Loads String into the Heap

The locals section of the Main method contains the variable for the book string (variable location 0x001ef09c) that is used to store the data it gets from the LoadStringLiteral method. When the CLR starts executing the LoadStringLiteral method, it will store the address (0x01eeb91c) of the book string from the Heap to the local variable (0x001ef08c refers to the CS$1$0000 of Listing 10-4), as demonstrated in Figure 10-4.

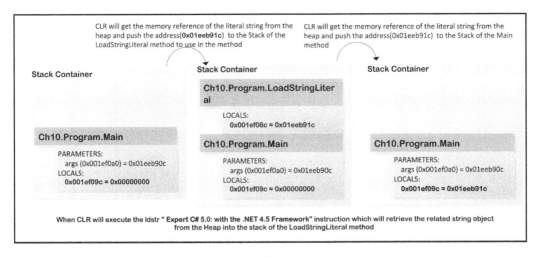

Figure 10-4. Stack information while executing Listing 10-3

From Figure 10-4, we can see that the address 0x01eeb91c from the Heap refers to the string literal Expert C# 5.0: with the .NET 4.5 Framework while executing the dumpobj command in the windbg.exe.

```
0:000> !dumpobj 0x01eeb91c
Name:          System.String
MethodTable:   565af9ac
EEClass:       562e8bb0
Size:          84(0x54) bytes
```

File: C:\Windows\Microsoft.NET\assembly\GAC_32\mscorlib\
                         v4.0_4.0.0.0__b77a5c561934e089\mscorlib.dll
String: **Expert C# 5.0: with the .NET 4.5 Framework**

In .NET, you can instantiate a string object using a char array, as demonstrated in Listing 10-5.

Listing 10-5. *Construct String Using Char Array*

```
using System;
namespace Ch10
{
    class Program
    {
        static void Main(string[] args)
        {
            string book = new String(new char[]
            {
                'E',    'x',    'p',    'e',    'r',    't',    ' ',    'C',    '#',
                ' ',    '5',    '.',    '0',    ':',    ' ',    'w',    'i',    't',
                'h',    ' ',    't',    'h',    'e',    ' ',    '.',    'N',    'E',
                'T',    ' ',    '4',    '.',    '5',    ' ',    'F',    'r',    'a',
                'm',    'e',    'w',    'o',    'r',    'k'
            });
            Console.WriteLine(book);
        }
    }
}
```

This program will produce the following output:

```
Expert C# 5.0: with the .NET 4.5 Framework
```

To understand the string construction using a char array, you need to look into the IL code the C# compiler produced for Listing 10-5.

String Instantiation Using Char Array

The decompiled IL code in Listing 10-6 shows how the CLR instantiates the string object in runtime using a char array.

Listing 10-6. *IL Code for the Source Code in Listing 10-5*

```
.class private auto ansi beforefieldinit Program
    extends [mscorlib]System.Object
{
    .method public hidebysig specialname rtspecialname instance void
            .ctor() cil managed
    {
        /*Code removed*/
    }

    .method private hidebysig static void Main(string[] args) cil managed
```

```
    {
        .entrypoint
        .maxstack 3
        .locals init (
            [0] string book)
        L_0000: nop
        L_0001: ldc.i4.s 0x2a

        L_0003: newarr char
        /* Code removed */

        /* The CLR creates a new instance of the string object
         * and pass the address to the Evaluation stack.*/
        L_0013: newobj instance void [mscorlib]System.String::.ctor(char[])

        /* Store the address from the top of the evaluation stack and store
         * into the book variable at position 0 of the Locals section
         * of the Main method Stack.*/
        L_0018: stloc.0

        /* Load the address of the local variable book from the method stack
         * to the evaluation stack */
        L_0019: ldloc.0

        L_001a: call void [mscorlib]System.Console::WriteLine(string)
        L_001f: nop
        L_0020: ret
    }
}
```

Let's analyze the code in Listing 10-6 to understand the String instantiation using char array.

How the CLR Handles String Instantiation from Char Array

The L_0003 label in the Main method will create an array of char with the size of 0x2a (42) and store all the related characters, for instance 'E', 'x', and so on in it. The CLR will use this array in the L_0013 to instantiate an instance of the string object using newobj instruction.

■ **Note**   newobj: The newobj instruction allocates a new instance of the class into the Heap and pushed the initialized object reference onto the stack.

Figure 10-5 shows the string instantiation using char array as input to the string class.

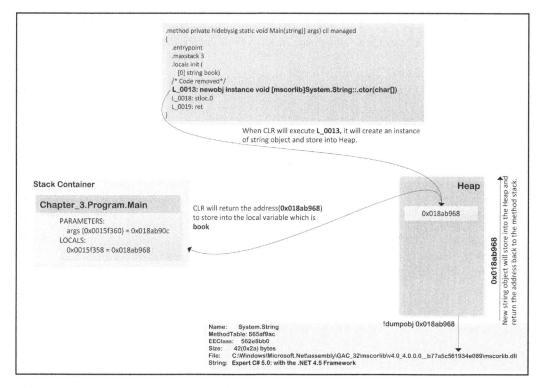

Figure 10-5. String instantiation using char array

HOW MANY CHARACTERS CAN STRING HOLD?

In the `string` type, you can store almost 2 billion characters if you look into the constructor of the `string` class:

```
/* count - refers to the number of times to repeat char c to
 *   construct new string object*/
public extern String (char c, int count);
```

where the `count` is a type of `int`. The maximum value of the `int` is 0x7fffffff (2147483647), which is approximately 2 billion, and this amount of characters can be stored into a `string` object.

String and Chaining

The method of chaining uses mechanisms through which you can call a series of method (each of the methods returns the same type where it is being defined) in one line. For example, if a class C defines methods Ma to Mz and each of the methods returns type C, then according to the method chaining mechanism, you call each of the methods as:

```
Ma().Mb().Mc()……Mz()
```

Listing 10-7 shows how method chaining has been implemented on the Book class.

Listing 10-7. Example of the Method Chaining for the String Type

```
using System;

namespace Ch10
{
    class Program
    {
        static void Main(string[] args)
        {
            Book book = new Book();
            Console.WriteLine(
                book.
                SetBookName("Expert C# 5.0: with the .NET 4.5 Framework").
                SetPublishedYear(2012).ToString());
        }
    }

    public class Book
    {
        private string bookName = default(string);
        private Int32 publishedYear = default(int);

        public Book SetBookName(string nameOfTheBook)
        {
            bookName = nameOfTheBook;
            return this;
        }

        public Book SetPublishedYear(int yearOfThePublication)
        {
            publishedYear = yearOfThePublication;
            return this;
        }

        public override string ToString()
        {
            return string.Format("{0}:{1}", bookName, publishedYear);
        }
    }
}
```

The Book class has SetBookName and SetPublishedYear methods, and these methods return Book as the return type, as demonstrated in Figure 10-6.

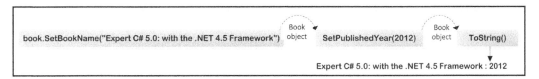

Figure 10-6. Method chaining

As a result, you can call `SetBookName` and `SetPublishedYear` methods as a series of the method call, for example:

```
book.SetBookName("Jupiter").SetPublishedYear(9999)
```

This program will produce the following output:

```
Expert C# 5.0: with the .NET 4.5 Framework : 2012
```

Strings Are Immutable

An immutable object refers to an object whose state cannot be altered after it is instantiated. Similarly, the string is by default immutable (i.e., whenever you create a `string` object, it is not possible to modify the contents of that string unless you create a new instance of it). This section will explore more detail about the immutable behavior of the string in .NET by analyzing the runtime behavior of the `string` object.

Listing 10-8 shows that when you try to modify the contents of the `string` object, the C# compiler raises a compilation error.

Listing 10-8. Modify the String Content

```
using System;

namespace Ch10
{
    class Program
    {
        static void Main(string[] args)
        {
            string bookName = "A book name.";

            /* replace the whole string */
            bookName = "Expert C# 5.0: with the .NET 4.5 Framework";

            /* Compiler will generate error in here. */
            bookName[2] = 'A';
        }
    }
}
```

In Listing 10-8, a `bookName` variable has been declared as `string` with the literal value of A book name. It is possible to replace the whole contents of the `bookName` variable, but it is not possible to modify the first, second, or any individual character or part of the `bookName` string. The C# compiler will produce the following error when you try to compile the code in the Listing 10-8:

```
Error    107    Property or indexer 'string.this[int]' cannot be assigned to -- it is read only
J:\Book\ExpertC#2012\SourceCode\BookExamples\Ch10\Program.cs    11    13    Ch10
```

Based on the compiler-generated error message, you can see that the string class has an index property, which will take an int type input and return a character from that specified position. Let's explore the index of the string class using the ildasm.exe to NETReflector, and you will see the code for the index property of the string class. Listing 10-9 shows the index property of the string class and the converted version of the C# code from the IL code of the string class.

Listing 10-9. Index of the String Class

```
public char this[int index]
{
    get; /* There is no set as a result it becomes readonly property */
}
```

The index property of the string class shows that it is readonly, and only the get method is defined. So in .NET, whenever it requires modification to a string to do an operation, it will copy the string-required modification into a new string, apply the change on the new string, and return it as the result of the operation. Listing 10-10 presents an example so we can see the string immutable behavior in .NET for the C#.

Listing 10-10. String Immutable Example

```
using System;

namespace Ch10
{
    class Program
    {
        static void Main(string[] args)
        {
            string myString =
                " Expert C# 5.0: with the .NET 4.5 Framework by Mohammad A Rahman ";
            myString = myString.ToUpper().ToLower().Trim();
            Console.WriteLine(myString);
        }
    }
}
```

Listing 10-10 will produce the following output:

```
expert c# 5.0: with the .net 4.5 framework by mohammad a rahman
```

Let's explore the internal workings of how CLR handles the string modification task. Listing 10-10 shows that ToUpper and ToLower functionality apply over the myString. Internally, CLR will instantiate a new instance of the string using the literal of the previous operation (such as ToUpper or ToLower), continue the operation, and finally produce the result as demonstrated in Figure 10-7.

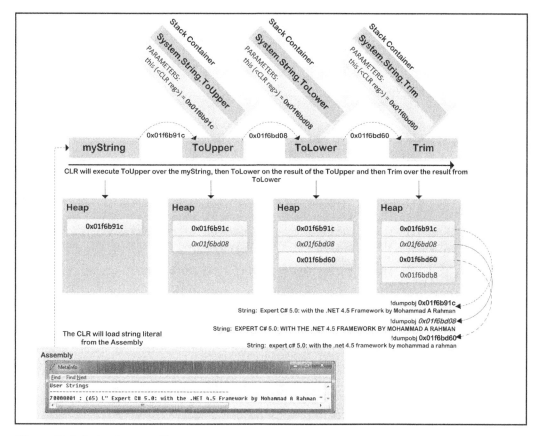

Figure 10-7. *String immutable*

The CLR will pass the address of the myString (0x01f6b91c) to the ToUpper method, which instantiates a new string (0x1f6bd08) object with the value of the myString. It will change the case of the new string (0x1f6bd08), pass to the ToLower method, which will do the same as ToUpper except make it lower case, and pass this new string (0x01f6bd60) to the Trim method and so on. Let's see the object information of those newly created strings, as shown in Listing 10-10, using windbg.exe.

```
!dumpobj 0x01f6b91c - Expert C# 5.0: with the .NET 4.5 Framework by Mohammad A Rahman
!dumpobj 0x01f6bd08 - EXPERT C# 5.0: WITH THE .NET 4.5 FRAMEWORK BY MOHAMMAD A RAHMAN
!dumpobj 0x01f6bd60 - expert c# 5.0: with the .NET 4.5 framework by mohammad a rahman
```

String Concatenation

String concatenation refers to joining two strings; for example, the concatenation between two string objects Sa and Sb will produce SaSb. In everyday programming life, you might need to deal with the string concatenation operation somehow. In .NET, there are many ways to perform this concatenation operation, such as using string concatenation operator +, the concatenation method provided by .NET Framework, or the StringBuilder class. Usage of these different techniques of string concatenation depends on the situation and number of items to concatenate. Table 10-1 shows the different concatenation techniques used in the C#.

Table 10-1. String Concatenation Techniques

Type	Signature
Concatenation operator	+

Concat method	```public static string Concat<T>(IEnumerable<T> values)```
	```public static string Concat(params object[] args)```
	```public static string Concat(params string[] values)```
	```public static string Concat(IEnumerable<string> values)```
	```public static string Concat(object arg0)```
	```public static string Concat(object arg0, object arg1)```
	```public static string Concat(string str0, string str1)```
	```public static string Concat(object arg0, object arg1, object arg2)```
	```public static string Concat(string str0, string str1, string str2)```
	```public static string Concat(object arg0, object arg1, object arg2, object arg3, __arglist)```
	```public static string Concat(string str0, string str1, string str2, string str3)```

StringBuilder	```public StringBuilder Append(bool value)```
	```public StringBuilder Append(byte value)```
	```public StringBuilder Append(char value)```
	```public StringBuilder Append(decimal value)```
	```public StringBuilder Append(double value)```
	```public StringBuilder Append(char[] value)```
	```public StringBuilder Append(short value)```
	```public StringBuilder Append(int value)```
	```public StringBuilder Append(long value)```
	```public StringBuilder Append(object value)```
	```public StringBuilder Append(sbyte value)```
	```public StringBuilder Append(float value)```
	```public StringBuilder Append(string value)```
	```public StringBuilder Append(ushort value)```
	```public StringBuilder Append(uint value)```
	```public StringBuilder Append(ulong value)```
	```public StringBuilder Append(char value, int repeatCount)```
	```public StringBuilder Append(string value, int startIndex, int count)```
	```public StringBuilder Append(char[] value, int startIndex, int charCount)```

Let's see how each of these operations is performed in the .NET.

+ Operator

The concatenation operator + can be used to concatenate multiple strings into one. Listing 10-11 provides an example that will concatenate a few strings into one using the concatenation operator +. The ConcatUsingOperator method will add three string literals into one and return the results as shown in Listing 10-11.

Listing 10-11. String Concatenation Using Concatenation Operator +

```
using System;

namespace Ch10
{
    class Program
    {
        static void Main(string[] args)
        {
            Console.WriteLine(ConcatUsingOperator());
            Console.WriteLine(ConcatUsingOperator("One,", "Two,", "Three"));
        }

        static string ConcatUsingOperator()
        {
            return "One," + "Two," + "Three.";
        }

        static string ConcatUsingOperator(string one, string two, string three)
        {
            return one + two + three;
        }
    }
}
```

This program will produce the following output:

```
One,Two,Three.
One,Two,Three
```

When the C# compiler finds any string literals in the source code while compiling, it will embed those string literals into the User Strings section of the meta info of that executable. If you build the program in Listing 10-11 and open the produced executable using the ildasm.exe to see the metadata info, you will find the string literals shown in Listing 10-12 embedded in the metadata.

Listing 10-12. User String Section of the Metadata

```
User Strings
-------------------------------------------------------
70000001 : ( 4) L"One,"
7000000b : ( 4) L"Two,"
70000015 : ( 5) L"Three"
70000021 : (14) L"One,Two,Three."
```

The CLR will use these string literals to execute the ConcatUsingOperator() and ConcatUsingOperator(string one, string two, string three) methods. The decompiled IL code for Listing 10-11, as shown in Listing 10-13, will demonstrate how the internally concatenation operator is used by the C# compiler.

Listing 10-13. IL code for the ConcatUsingOperator Method Shown in Listing 10-11

```
.class private auto ansi beforefieldinit Program
    extends [mscorlib]System.Object
{
    /* Code removed */
    .method private hidebysig static string
        ConcatUsingOperator() cil managed
    {
        .maxstack 1
        .locals init (
            [0] string CS$1$0000)
        L_0000: nop

        /* The C# compiler Concat all the string at the compile time. */
        L_0001: ldstr "One,Two,Three."
        L_0006: stloc.0
        L_0007: br.s L_0009
        L_0009: ldloc.0
        L_000a: ret
    }

    .method private hidebysig static string
        ConcatUsingOperator(
            string one, string two, string three) cil managed
    {
        .maxstack 3
        .locals init (
            [0] string CS$1$0000)
        L_0000: nop
        L_0001: ldarg.0
        L_0002: ldarg.1
        L_0003: ldarg.2

        /* The Concatenation operator will be replaced by the Concat method */
        L_0004: call string [mscorlib]System.String::Concat(string, string, string)
        L_0009: stloc.0
        L_000a: br.s L_000c
        L_000c: ldloc.0
        L_000d: ret
    }

    .method private hidebysig static void Main(string[] args) cil managed
    {
        /* Code removed */
        L_0001: call string Ch10.Program::ConcatUsingOperator()
        L_0006: call void [mscorlib]System.Console::WriteLine(string)
        L_000b: nop

        L_000c: ldstr "One,"
        L_0011: ldstr "Two,"
```

```
        L_0016: ldstr "Three"
        L_001b: call string Ch10.Program::ConcatUsingOperator(string, string, string)
        L_0020: call void [mscorlib]System.Console::WriteLine(string)
        L_0025: nop
        L_0026: ret
    }
}
```

The Main method will call the ConcatUsingOperator method while executing the instruction in the L_0001. Inside the ConcatUsingOperator method, the C# compiler declared a local variable CS$1$0000 in the stack, which will be used to store string One, Two, Three, as shown in the L_0006 instruction.

The CLR will extract string literal from the metadata info and include it into the labels L_000c, L_0011, L_0016 of the Main method, which will use the ldstr instruction to load the string and pass it as the parameter to the ConcatUsingOperator method in the L_001b. The CLR will execute the L_001b instruction from the Main method, which will call ConcatUsingOperator(string, string, string) with the argument value One, Two, and Three. This ConcatUsingOperator method calls the Concat method internally to concatenate the strings (you will find the details of the Concat method later in this chapter). From the overloaded ConcatUsingOperator method, CLR will call the Concat method and store the results in the local variable CS$1$0000 at position 0 of the method stack, as shown in L_0009 and it will be returned as output at L_000c.

Concat IEnumerable<T>

To concatenate the items from the IEnumerable<T>, you can use this method, the signature of which is shown below:

```
public static string Concat<T>(IEnumerable<T> values)
public static string Concat(IEnumerable<string> values)
```

The program in Listing 10-14 shows a list of string object listOfNumbers used to concatenate the items from that list.

Listing 10-14. Concat List of String Object

```
using System;
using System.Collections;
using System.Collections.Generic;

namespace Ch10
{
    class Program
    {
        static void Main(string[] args)
        {
            IList<string> listOfNumbers = new List<string>()
            {
                "One,", "Two,", "Three."
            };
            Console.WriteLine("{0}", ConcateUsingConcate(listOfNumbers));
        }

        static string ConcateUsingConcate(IEnumerable<string> enumerable)
```

```
        {
            return string.Concat<string>(enumerable);
        }
    }
}
```

Listing 10-14 will produce the following output:

```
One,Two,Three.
```

The code in Listing 10-14 uses the Concat<T>(IEnumerable<T> values) method to concatenate a list of strings. While the CLR executes this method, it will check whether the given list is null or not. If null, then it throws an ArgumentNullException, otherwise it will process the list to concatenate into one string object. The CLR will take the following steps to process the concatenation operation:

- Create an instance of StringBuilder type where it will store the entire string object to concatenate.

- Retrieve the Enumerator object from the IEnumberable<T>.

- Loop through the Enumerator object to get each of the items from the list and append them to the StringBuilder object it instantiated earlier.

- Call the ToString method of the StringBuilder object to get the final concatenated string and return it as output.

The implementation of the Concat<string>(IEnumberable<string> values) method is shown in Listing 10-15.

Listing 10-15. *The Implementation of Concat<string>(IEnumberable<string> values)*

```
public static string Concat(IEnumerable<string> values)
{
    StringBuilder builder = new StringBuilder();
    using (IEnumerator<string> enumerator = values.GetEnumerator())
    {
        while (enumerator.MoveNext())
        {
            if (enumerator.Current != null)
            {
                builder.Append(enumerator.Current);
            }
        }
    }
    return builder.ToString();
}
```

Concat Array of Objects

To concatenate the string representations of the elements in a given Object array, you can use one of the following methods:

```
public static string Concat(params object[] args)
public static string Concat(params string[] values)
```

Listing 10-16 shows the usage of the first method, and it will be used to explain the Concat method.

Listing 10-16. Usage of the Concat(params object[] args)

```
using System;

namespace Ch10
{
    class Program
    {
        static void Main(string[] args)
        {
            Console.WriteLine("{0}", ConcatUsingConcat(new[]
            {
                "One,", "Two,", "Three."
            }));
        }

        static string ConcatUsingConcat(params object[] args)
        {
            return string.Concat(args);
        }
    }
}
```

This program will produce the following output:

```
One,Two,Three.
```

To execute the Concat operation of the object array, the CLR will perform the following operations:

1. *Step 1*: Check whether the args(object array) is null or not. If null, it will throw an ArgumentNullException, otherwise it continues to process the operation.

2. *Step 2*: Call the ConcatArray method to process the further concatenation operation. The code for the Concat method shows how the CLR internally calls the ConcatArray method, as shown in Listing 10-17.

Listing 10-17. The Implementation of the Concat Method

```
public static string Concat(params object[] args)
{
    /* Code removed- This section does the Initial check as demonstrated in the Step 1.*/
    if (args == null)
    {
        throw new ArgumentNullException("args");
    }
    /* Code removed - This section described in the Step 2. */
    return ConcatArray(values, totalLength);
}
```

3. *Step 3*: The ConcatArray takes an array of string objects and the total length of the array. It will then allocate a string of size total length using the FastAllocateString method. This new string will be filled with the value from

the input array using the FillStringChecked method, as shown in Listing 10-18.
The implementation of the ConcatArray method of the System.String class from
the mscorlib.dll assembly is shown in Listing 10-18.

Listing 10-18. *The Implementation of the ConcatArray*

```
private static string ConcatArray(string[] values, int totalLength)
{
    string dest = FastAllocateString(totalLength);
    int destPos = 0;
    for (int i = 0; i < values.Length; i++)
    {
    FillStringChecked(dest, destPos, values[i]);
    destPos += values[i].Length;
    }
    return dest;
}
```

4. *Step 4*: Finally, the concatenated string will return an output.

Concat Objects

To concatenate one to three strings represented in the three objects, you can use one of the following
Concat methods in C#:

```
public static string Concat(object arg0)
public static string Concat(object arg0, object arg1)
public static string Concat(object arg0, object arg1, object arg2)
```

Listing 10-19 shows the usage of the first method, and this will be used to explain the Concat method.

Listing 10-19. *Using Concat(object arg0, object arg1)*

```
using System;

namespace Ch10
{
    class Program
    {
        static void Main(string[] args)
        {
            Console.WriteLine("{0}",
                ConcatUsingConcat( "Expert C# 5.0: with the .NET 4.5 Framework ",
                                    " by Mohammad Rahman"));
        }

        static string ConcatUsingConcat(object args0, object args1)
        {
            return string.Concat(args0, args1);
        }
    }
}
```

This program will produce the following output:

```
Expert C# 5.0: with the .NET 4.5 Framework  by Mohammad Rahman
```

The Concat operation works as follows:

1. *Step 1*: The CLR will load both of the object arguments and call their ToString method.

2. *Step 2*: It will then call the Concat(string, string) method to do the Concat operation.

The implementation of the Concat method is shown in Listing 10-20.

Listing 10-20. The Implementation of the Concat Method

```
.method public hidebysig static string  Concat(
      object arg0, object arg1) cil managed
{
  // Code size  38 (0x26)
  .maxstack  8
  IL_0000:  ldarg.0
  IL_0001:  brtrue.s IL_000a

  /* Following IL_0003 to L_0008 instruction will execute while there is no
   * argument value or null value for the argument at position 0 */
  IL_0003:  ldsfld    string System.String::Empty
  IL_0008:  starg.s  arg0        /* Store value at argument position 0 */

  IL_000a:  ldarg.1
  IL_000b:  brtrue.s IL_0014

  /* Following IL_000d to L_0012 instruction will execute while there is no
   * argument value or null value for the argument at position 0 */
  IL_000d:  ldsfld    string System.String::Empty
  IL_0012:  starg.s  arg1        /* Store value at argument position 1 */


  IL_0014:  ldarg.0
  IL_0015:  callvirt instance string System.Object::ToString()
  IL_001a:  ldarg.1
  IL_001b:  callvirt instance string System.Object::ToString()

  /* Concat method will be called to do the concat operation */
  IL_0020:  call string System.String::Concat(string,string)
  IL_0025:  ret
}
```

3. *Step 3*: This method will return the concatenated string object as a result.

Concat Strings

To concatenate a specified number of string instances, you can use one of the following methods:

```
public static string Concat(string str0, string str1)
public static string Concat(string str0, string str1, string str2)
public static string Concat(string str0, string str1, string str2, string str3)
```

Listing 10-21 shows the usage of the first method, and this will be used to explain the Concat method.

Listing 10-21. *An Example of Concat(string str0, string str1)*

```
using System;

namespace Ch10
{
    class Program
    {
        static void Main(string[] args)
        {
            Console.WriteLine("{0}",
                ConcatUsingConcat("Expert C# 5.0: with the .NET 4.5 Framework ",
                                  " by Mohammad Rahman"));
        }

        static string ConcatUsingConcat(string str0, string str1)
        {
            return string.Concat(str0, str1);
        }
    }
}
```

This will produce the following output:

```
Expert C# 5.0: with the .NET 4.5 Framework  by Mohammad Rahman
```

The Concat operation works as follows:

1. *Step 1*: Internally the CLR will check whether the arguments are empty or not.
    The logic is if the str0 is null or empty, then the compiler will check the str1. If
    str1 is null or empty, it will return the string.Empty, otherwise str1, as a result.
    On the other hand, if the str0 is not null or empty, or if str1 is null or empty,
    then the compiler will return the str0 as a result of the Concat method.

```
if (IsNullOrEmpty(str0))
{
    if (IsNullOrEmpty(str1))
    {
        return Empty;
    }
    return str1;
}
if (IsNullOrEmpty(str1))
{
```

```
    return str0;
}
```

    2.   *Step 2*: The CLR will determine the length of the str0 and str1. It will then call the FastAllocateString method with the sum of the str0 and str1's length as the total length of the new string instance. It will subsequently call the FillStringChecked method to do the concatenation operation. The implementation of these operations might be as demonstrated below:

```
int length = str0.Length;
string dest = FastAllocateString(length + str1.Length);
FillStringChecked(dest, 0, str0);
FillStringChecked(dest, length, str1);
return dest;
```

    3.   *Step 3*: Finally, the concatenation result will return as output.

StringBuilder

The StringBuilder class can be used to represent editable or mutable string in the .NET. You have already seen how you can use the StringBuilder class to construct the string in .NET. In this section, you will learn more details about the StringBuilder class and also explore how the CLR handles the StringBuilder class to do the Append, Insert operation.

    The StringBuilder class is defined in the String.Text namespace of the mscorlib.dll assembly, as shown in Figure 10-8.

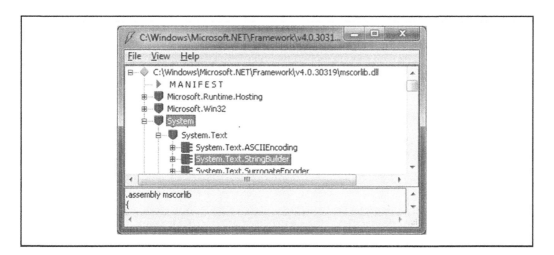

Figure 10-8. *StringBuilder class in System.Text namespace*

The StringBuilder is a sealed class defined with the following definition:

```
public sealed class StringBuilder : ISerializable
```

    The StringBuilder class can do append, insert, remove, replace, and clear operations over the string literals. In .NET, the StringBuilder class has the methods as demonstrated in Listing 10-22.

Listing 10-22. *The StringBuilder Class Definition*

```
public sealed class StringBuilder : ISerializable
{
    /* 6 overloaded constructors */
    public StringBuilder()                                                      {}

    /* 19 overloaded Append method*/
    public StringBuilder Append(bool value)                                     {}

    /* 5 overloaded AppendFormat method*/
    public StringBuilder AppendFormat(string format, object arg0)               {}

    /* 2 overloaded AppendFormat method*/
    public StringBuilder AppendLine()                                           {}

    public StringBuilder Clear()                                                {}
    public void CopyTo(int sourceIndex, char[] destination, int destinationIndex, int count)
                                                                                {}
    public int EnsureCapacity(int capacity)                                     {}
    public bool Equals(StringBuilder sb)                                        {}

    /* 18 overloaded AppendFormat method*/
    public StringBuilder Insert(int index, char[] value)                        {}

    public StringBuilder Remove(int startIndex, int length)                     {}

    /* 4 overloaded AppendFormat method*/
    public StringBuilder Replace(char oldChar, char newChar)                    {}

    /* 2 overloaded AppendFormat method*/
    public overide unsafe string ToString()                                     {}

    /*Properties*/
    public int Capacity                                                         {}
    public char this[int index]                                                 {}
    public int Length                                                           {}
    public int MaxCapacity                                                      {}
}
```

Listing 10-22 shows the definition of the `StringBuilder` class in .NET. In the following section, you will explore the internal workings of the `StringBuilder` class to learn how the CLR instantiates an instance of the `StringBuilder` class and how it does the Append, Insert operation in the `StringBuilder` class.

Internal of StringBuilder

The `StringBuilder` class internally maintains a few private fields to do its job. One of the important fields is the `m_ChunkChars`, which is a `char` array. Unless otherwise defined, the CLR will set the initial size of this array as 0x10 (16), which is defined internally as `const` of `int` called `DefaultCapacity`. Listing 10-23 provides an example of the use of the Append and Insert methods of the `StringBuilder` class.

Listing 10-23. An Example of StringBuilder

```
using System;
using System.Text;

namespace Ch10
{
    class Program
    {
        static void Main(string[] args)
        {
            StringBuilder sb = new StringBuilder();
            sb.Append("Expert C# 5.0: with the .NET 4.5 Framework ");
            sb.Insert(sb.Length, "by Mohammad A Rahman");
            Console.WriteLine(sb.ToString());
        }
    }
}
```

Listing 10-23 will produce the following output:

```
Expert C# 5.0: with the .NET 4.5 Framework by Mohammad A Rahman
```

Listing 10-23 shows how to instantiate an instance of the StringBuilder class and how to use the Append and Insert methods of the StringBuilder class to append and insert string. Figure 10-9 demonstrates the instantiation of the StringBuilder class and the Append, Insert, and ToString operations of the StringBuilder class.

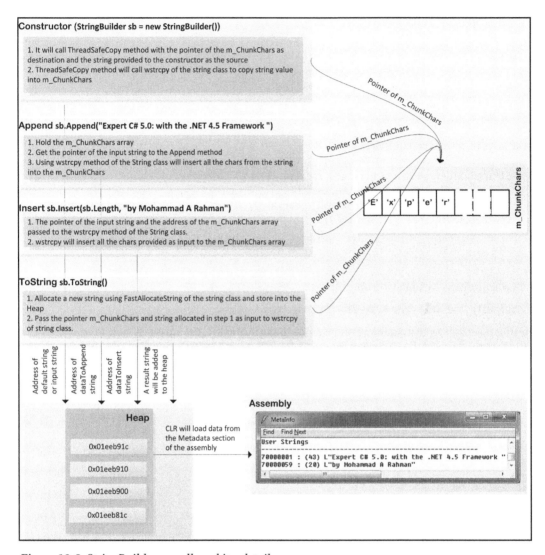

Figure 10-9. *StringBuilder overall working details*

In the following sections, you will explore in detail the StringBuilder instantiation and the Append and Insert operations in the StringBuilder class that is shown in Figure 10-9.

Instantiation of the StringBuilder

While CLR executes the constructor of the StringBuilder, it will initialize the m_ChunkChars array and call the ThreadSafeCopy method, which will copy the input string literal (if any provided as input) to the m_ChunkChars array, as shown in Listing 10-24.

Listing 10-24. The Implementation of the StringBuilder Constructor

```
public unsafe StringBuilder(string value, int startIndex, int length, int capacity)
{
    this.m_ChunkChars = new char[capacity];
    this.m_ChunkLength = length;
    fixed (char* str = ((char*) value))
    {
        char* chPtr = str;
        ThreadSafeCopy(
            chPtr + startIndex,         /* Source pointer */
            this.m_ChunkChars,          /* Destination char array */
            0,                          /* Destination index */
            length);                    /* Total length to copy. */
    }
}
```

Listing 10-24 demonstrates the internal workings of the StringBuilder instantiation that uses the ThreadSafeCopy method. The implementation of the ThreadSafeCopy method will be discussed in the next section. You can append data to the instance of the StringBuilder class using the Append method. In the following section, you will also explore the internal workings of the Append method of StringBuilder.

Append Operation in the StringBuilder

While executing the Append method, the CLR will use the ThreadSafeCopy method to copy the contents of the input to the m_ChunkChars array. The implementation of the ThreadSafeCopy method is shown in Listing 10-25. Interestingly, the ThreadSafeCopy method uses the wstrcpy method from the string class to handle copy operations of the input string to the m_ChunkChars array.

Listing 10-25. The Implementation of the ThreadSafeCopy

```
private static unsafe void ThreadSafeCopy(
    char* sourcePtr,
    char[] destination,
    int destinationIndex,
    int count)
{
    fixed (char* chRef = &(destination[destinationIndex]))
    {
        string.wstrcpy(chRef, sourcePtr, count);
    }
}
```

Listing 10-25 demonstrates the internal workings of the Append method of the StringBuilder class. You can insert data into the instance of the StringBuilder class using the Insert method of the StringBuilder class, which is examined in the next section.

Insert Operation in the StringBuilder

In the insertion time, the CLR checks the availability of the empty cells in the m_ChunkChars array and depending on the need the CLR will resize the m_ChunkChars array. It will then place the new value into the specified index using the ReplaceInPlaceAtChunk method. The implementation of the Insert method is shown in Listing 10-26.

Listing 10-26. *The Code for the Insert Method*

```
private unsafe void Insert(int index, char* value, int valueCount)
{
    this.MakeRoom(index, valueCount, out builder, out num, false);
    this.ReplaceInPlaceAtChunk(ref builder, ref num, value, valueCount);
}
```

Internally, ReplaceInPlaceAtChunk method will use the ThreadSafeCopy method to insert value into the m_ChunkChars array. The implementation of the ReplaceInPlaceAtChunk method is shown in Listing 10-27.

Listing 10-27. *Implementation of the ReplaceInPlaceAtChunk Method*

```
private unsafe void ReplaceInPlaceAtChunk(
    ref StringBuilder chunk,
    ref int indexInChunk,
    char* value, int count)
{
    /* Code removed */
    ThreadSafeCopy(value, chunk.m_ChunkChars, indexInChunk, num2);
    /* Code removed */
}
```

You've seen how to instantiate an instance of the StringBuilder class and how to append and insert data into the StringBuilder. Next you'll see how to get the string out of StringBuilder class using the ToString method.

Getting String from the StringBuilder

While the CLR executes the ToString method of the StringBuilder class, it will do the following:

1. Allocate a new string object with the current length of the m_ChunkChars array of the StringBuilder class.

2. Pass this newly allocated string and the current m_ChunkChars array of the StringBuilder class as pointers to the wstrcpy method of the string class. The wstrcpy method copies the characters from the m_ChunkChars array into the string object. This string will be returned as a result of the ToString method of the StringBuilder class.

Listing 10-28 presents an example that will show the usage of Append and ToString methods of the StringBuilder class.

Listing 10-28. *Concat Strings Using StringBuilder*

```
using System;
using System.Text;

namespace Ch10
{
```

```csharp
class Program
{
    static void Main(string[] args)
    {
        Console.WriteLine("{0}", ConcatUsingStringBuilder(
            "Expert C# 5.0: with the .NET 4.5 Framework ",
            "by Mohammad Rahman"));
        Console.WriteLine("{0}", ConcatUsingStringBuilder());
    }

    static string ConcatUsingStringBuilder(string str0, string str1)
    {
        StringBuilder builder = new StringBuilder();
        builder.Append(str0).Append("\t");
        builder.Append(str1).Append("\t");
        return builder.ToString();
    }

    static string ConcatUsingStringBuilder()
    {
        StringBuilder builder = new StringBuilder();

        bool boolValue = true;
        byte byteValue = 1;
        char charValue = 'A';
        decimal decimalValue = 10;
        double doubleValue = 100;
        short shortValue = 1000;
        char[] charArrayValue = new char[] { 'A', 'B', 'C' };
        int intValue = 10000;
        long longValue = 100000;
        object objectValue = new object();
        sbyte sByteValue = 2;
        float floatValue = 200;
        string stringValue = "Expert C# 5.0: with the .NET 4.5 Framework";
        ushort ushortValue = 10;
        uint uintValue = 4;
        ulong ulongValue = 400;

        builder
            .Append(boolValue).Append("\t")
            .Append(byteValue).Append("\t")
            .Append(charValue).Append("\t")
            .Append(decimalValue).Append("\t")
            .Append(doubleValue).Append("\t")
            .Append(shortValue).Append("\t")
            .Append(charArrayValue).Append("\t")
            .Append(intValue).Append("\t")
            .Append(longValue).Append("\t")
            .Append(objectValue).Append("\t")
            .Append(sByteValue).Append("\t")
```

```
                    .Append(floatValue).Append("\t")
                    .Append(stringValue).Append("\t")
                    .Append(ushortValue).Append("\t")
                    .Append(uintValue).Append("\t")
                    .Append(ulongValue).Append("\t")
                    .Append(charValue, 10).Append("\t")
                    .Append(stringValue, 1, 2).Append("\t")
                    .Append(charArrayValue, 1, 2);

            return builder.ToString();
        }
    }
}
```

This program will produce the following output:

```
Expert C# 5.0: with the .NET 4.5 Framework       by Mohammad Rahman
True    1       A               10      100     1000    ABC     10000   100000  System.0
bject   2       200             Expert C# 5.0: with the .NET 4.5 Framework       10
4       400     AAAAAAAAAA      xp      BC
```

Listing 10-28 shows the Append operation using the StringBuilder class, which appends different kinds of value types into an instance of the StringBuilder class.

Summary

In this chapter we have examined the internal workings of string in .NET, such as how the CLR instantiates an instance of the string object and how the string object relates to the Heap storage. You have also learned about the different string concatenation techniques that can be used. You learned the internal implementation of the different concatenation methods of the string class, which will help you understand the string concatenation. This chapter also explored the StringBuilder class and examined the internal behavior of the StringBuilder. Finally, we explored details about the Append, Insert, and ToString methods in the StringBuilder class. The next chapter will examine about the Collections in .NET.

.

CHAPTER 11

■ ■ ■

Collections Explained

This chapter will discuss the different collection types in .NET—Array, List<T>, ArrayList, Stack, Queue, Hashtable, and Dictionary—which are used for storing and managing data in an application. We will look at the internal workings of the List<T> class and how the CLR instantiates an instance of the List<T> class, how it adds items into it, and how it expands its internal array to accommodate more items. We will also examine the internal workings of the ArrayList, Stack, Queue, Hashtable, and Dictionary classes to see how CLR handles these classes to store information.

Collections in .NET

The System.Collections namespace in the .NET contains data structures that can be used in C# to define different kinds of collection types. All collection classes implement the interface ICollection with additional functionality. Figure 11-1 shows the different collection classes in the .NET.

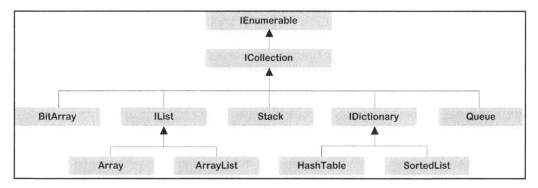

Figure 11-1. Different collections class used in .NET

Each of these classes has its own functionality and usage. Table 11-1 summarizes the different types of collection shown in Figure 11-1.

Table 11-1. *Summary of the Collection Types*

Types	Description
Array	Data structures that store collections of data and allow access to the elements by using simple index operations
ArrayList	Implements the IList interface using an array whose size is dynamically increased as required
List	Represents a collection of objects that can be individually accessed by the index and whose size is dynamically increased as required
BitArray	Manages a compact array of bit values, which are represented as Booleans, in where true is represented as one and false is represented as zero
Stack	The storage structure with insert (Push) and erase (Pop) operations occurs at one end, called the top of the Stack; the last element in is the first element out of the stack, so a stack is a LIFO (Last In First Out) structure
Queue	A first-come-first-served–data structure, so a queue is a FIFO (First In First Out) structure. Insertion operations (Enqueue) occur at the back of the sequence. Dequeue operations occur at the front of the sequence.
Hashtable	Represents a collection of key and value pairs that are organized based on the hash code of the key
SortedList	Represents a collection of key and value pairs that are sorted by the keys and are accessible by key and by index
IDictionary	Represents a collection of key and value pairs

Array Class

The Array class is the implicit base class for all single and multidimensional arrays, and it is one of the most fundamental types in implementing the standard collection interfaces. The Array class provides type unification, so a common set of methods is available to all arrays, regardless of their declaration or underlying element type.

Array Class in .NET

The Array class provides methods for creating, manipulating, searching, and sorting arrays. It serves as the base class for all arrays in the CLR. It has been defined in the mscorlib.dll (C:\Windows\Microsoft.NET\ Framework\v4.0.30319) assembly in .NET as shown in Figure 11-2.

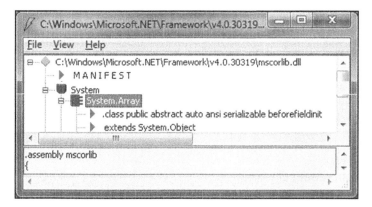

Figure 11-2. *Array class in the System namespace*

The signature of the Array class is:

```
public abstract class Array : ICloneable, IList, ICollection, IEnumerable
```

The Array class is an abstract type, which implements the ICloneable, IList, ICollection, and IEnumberable interfaces.

Array Class Members

The Array class has different public properties and methods that can be used to manipulate data stored in the Array class. In the next section, we will explore the different properties and methods of the Array class.

Properties

Table 11-2 lists the different properties of the Array class.

Table 11-2. *Public Properties of the Array Class*

Property	Description
IsFixedSize	Always true for all arrays, to get a value indicating whether the array has a fixed size
IsReadOnly	Always false for all arrays, to get a value indicating whether the array is read-only
IsSynchonized	Always false for all arrays, to get a value indicating whether the access to the array is synchronized
Length	Total number of elements (Int32) in all the dimensions of the array
LongLength	Total number of elements (Int64) in all the dimensions of the array
Rank	Number of dimensions of the array

Methods

The Array class has different methods that can be used to do different operations. Table 11-3 lists the different methods of the Array class.

Table 11-3. Public Methods of the Array Class

Method	Description
BinarySearch	**/* 8 overloaded*/** `public static int BinarySearch(Array a, object value)` Searches an entire one-dimensional sorted array for a specific value and returns the index of the specified value if it is found or a negative number otherwise
Clear	`public static void Clear(Array a, int index, int length)` Sets a range of elements in the array to zero, to `false`, or to a `null` reference, depending on the element type
Clone	`public virtual object Clone()` Creates and returns a shallow copy of the array

Copy	`public static void Copy(Array sourceArray, Array destinationArray, int length)`
	`public static void Copy(Array sourceArray, Array destinationArray, long length)`
	`public static void Copy(Array sourceArray, int sourceIndex, Array destinationArray, int destinationIndex, int length)`
	`public static void Copy(Array sourceArray, long sourceIndex, Array destinationArray, long destinationIndex, long length)`
	Copies a section of one array to another array and performs type casting and boxing as required
	`Array source = new int[] { 1,2,3,4};`
	`Array destin = new int[] {5,6,7,8 };`
	`/* startCopyFromSource - define from where in the source array`
	` * the copy operation will start*/`
	`int startCopyFromSource =2;`
	`/* startCopyIntoDestin – define in where in the destination`
	` * array the item will be copied over*/`
	`int startCopyIntoDestin =1;`
	`/* 2 – Define how many item will be copied from the source`
	` * array to the destination array. The copy will start from`
	` * the source array at position define by startCopyFromSource`
	` * and copy over in the destin array at position define by`
	` * startCopyIntoDestin */`
	`Array.Copy(source, startCopyFromSource, destin, startCopyIntoDestin,2);`
	`//Output: destin array will contain now 5,3,4,8`

CopyTo	**/* 2 overloaded*/** `public virtual void CopyTo(Array a, int index)` Copies all the elements of the current one-dimensional array to the specified one-dimensional array, starting at the specified destination Array index
CreateInstance	**/* 6 overloaded*/** `public static Array CreateInstance(Type t, int len)` Initializes a new instance of the Array class and creates and returns a new one-dimensional array of the specified type and length, with zero-based indexing
Equals	`public virtual bool Equals(object obj)` Determines whether two object instances are equal and returns true if the specified object is equal to the current object; otherwise, `false`
GetEnumerator	`public virtual IEnumerator GetEnumerator()` Returns an IEnumerator for the array: note that enumerators only allow reading the data in the array and cannot be used to modify the underlying array
GetHashCode	`public virtual int GetHashCode()` Serves as a hash function for a particular type, suitable for use in hashing algorithms and data structures such as a hash table, and returns a hash code for the current object

Method	Description
GetLength	`public int GetLength(int dimension)` Gets a 32-bit integer that represents the number of elements in the specified dimension of the array.
GetLongLength	`public long GetLongLength(int dimension)` Gets a 64-bit integer that represents the number of elements in the specified dimension of the array
GetValue	`public object GetValue(int index) /* 8 overloaded*/` Gets the value at the specified position in the one-dimensional array
GetType	`public Type GetType(int index)` Gets the type of the current instance

IndexOf	`/* 6 overloaded*/`
	`public static int IndexOf(Array a, object value)`
	Returns the index of the first occurrence of a value in a one-dimensional array or in a portion of the array

LastIndexOf	`/* 6 overloaded*/`
	`public static int LastIndexOf(Array a, object value)`
	Returns the index of the last occurrence of a value in a one-dimensional array or in a portion of the array

Initialize	`public void Initialize()` Initializes every element of the value-type array by calling the default constructor of the value type
Reverse	`public static void Reverse(Array a) /* 2 overloaded*/` Reverses the order of the elements in a one-dimensional array or in a portion of the array
SetValue	`/* 8 overloaded*/` public void SetValue(object value, int index) Sets the specified element in the current array to the specified value
Sort	`public static void Sort(Array a) /* 17 overloaded*/` Sorts the elements in an entire one-dimensional array using the IComparable interface implemented by each element of the array
ToString	`public virtual string ToString()` Returns a string that represents the current object

List

The List<T> class used in .NET represents a collection of objects. This class exposes different methods and properties used to manipulate the objects stored in it. This section will examine the List<T> class.

Capacity and Size of the List<T>

The List<T> is a dynamic array whose size increases as required. The number of elements that List<T> can hold is referred to as the capacity of the List<T> class. If the initial capacity (number of items it can hold) of the List<T> is N, then on every phase of List<T> expansion to accommodate more items, the CLR adds extra N empty slots in the internal array of the List<T> or increases to 2N. Figure 11-3 demonstrates the size and expansion of the List<T> class.

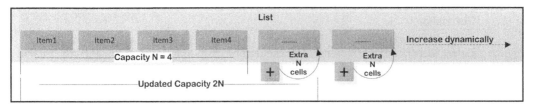

Figure 11-3. List<T> basics

When you instantiate the List<T> class without specifying the capacity, the initial capacity of the List<T> is zero. On the first Add operation to the List<T> instance, it will increase the capacity with the default capacity being four (N), which is stored in the internal field _defaultCapacity of the List<T> class. The capacity of the List<T> will be increased when needed to accommodate more items in the List<T> instance—such as 4(N) × 2 = 8 (2N), 8(N) × 2 = 16 (2N), 16(N) × 2 = 32 (2N), and so on. It means on every expansion of the List<T> class, a new capacity of the List<T> will be calculated and it will be two times that of the previous capacity. The actual items occupied in the List<T> are referred by the Count property (internally the _size field) of the List<T> class, and the total items can be added to the List<T> referred by the Capacity property. The value of the capacity is updated when the capacity of the List<T> is expanded to accommodate more items. For example, if you consider an instance of the List<T> class whose current capacity is eight (refers by the Capacity property) but it actually contains five items, then the Count property of that instance of the List<T> refers five (internally the _size field) and the Capacity is eight. The capacity of the List<T> can also be set:

- Explicitly by setting the Capacity property

- In the instantiation time of the List<T>

- When the List<T> class is instantiated based on another list of type ICollection, where the size of that list is used as the initial capacity of the List<T> class

The capacity of the List<T> can be decreased by calling the TrimExcess method. If an instance of the List<T> has the capacity N (where N = 4) and only two items have been stored in that instance of the List<T>, calling the TrimExcess method of the CLR will decrease the capacity of the List<T> to two by removing N-2 cells from the internal array of the List<T> class.

List Declaration

The List<T> class is defined in the System.Collections namespace of the mscorlib.dll (C:\Windows\ Microsoft.NET\ Framework\v4.0.30319) assembly in .NET as demonstrated in Figure 11-4.

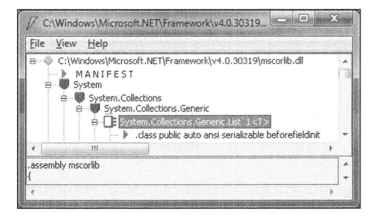

Figure 11-4. *List<T> class in the System.Collections.Generic namespace*

The signature of the List<T> class would be:

```
public class List<T> : IList<T>, ICollection<T>, IEnumerable<T>, IList,  ICollection,
IEnumerable
```

Let's look at an example where the List<T> class has been used to create an instance of the numbers object, as shown in Listing 11-1.

Listing 11-1. *Example of the List<T> Class*

```
using System;
using System.Collections;
using System.Collections.Generic;

namespace Ch11
{
    class Program
    {
        static void Main(string[] args)
        {
            List<int> numbers = new List<int>();
            numbers.Add(0);
            numbers.Add(1);
            ShowResult(numbers);
        }
        public static void ShowResult(IEnumerable aList)
        {
            foreach (var item in aList)
                Console.Write("{0}\t", item);
            Console.WriteLine();
        }
    }
}
```

This program will produce the output:

```
0       1
```

Instantiation of the List<T>

The List<T> comes to life when you call one of the following three overloaded constructors:

```
public List()                           {}
public List(int capacity)               {}
public List(IEnumerable<T> collection)  {}
```

When the CLR executes the first version of the List<T> constructor, it initializes the internal _items array with the default size zero, but on the first Add operation, it will be increased to four. In the second version of the constructor, it initializes the _items array with a given size provided as the parameter capacity. The CLR gets the size from the parameter collection via the Count property of the input collection. For the third version, the constructor initializes the internal _items array and copies the entire contents of the collection into the _items array. Figure 11-5 demonstrates the instantiation of the List<T> class.

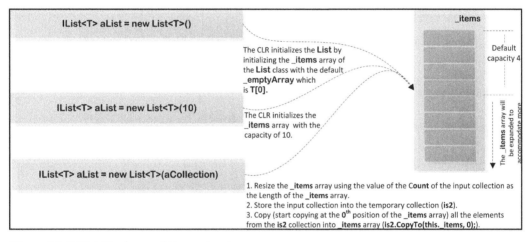

Figure 11-5. *List<T> class and its constructors*

Addition Operation in the List<T>

To add any item into the List<T>, the CLR checks whether the item can be stored in the internal _items array. The CLR ensures this by checking the number of the elements in the _items array of the List<T> using the EnsureCapacity method of the List<T> class. If the size is ensured by the EnsureCapacity method, the CLR adds that item (which has to be same type because the T refers to the List<T>) to the _items array. Figure 11-6 shows the basic Add and AddRange operations of the List<T> class.

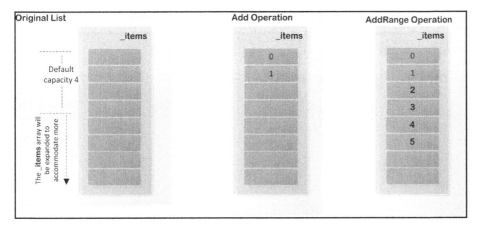

Figure 11-6. Addition operation in the List<T>class

The EnsureCapacity method does the entire back-end job to make sure that the List<T> is able to hold the required number of data (based on the available memory) in the _items array. The CLR calls this method with the value of the current _size field of the List<T> + 1. The EnsureCapacity method calculates the new capacity for the _items array and sets this new capacity value into the Capacity property of the List<T> class. The implementation of the EnsureCapacity method of the List<T> class is shown in the Listing 11-2.

Listing 11-2. The Implementation of the EnsureCapacity Method of the List<T> Class

```
/* min = (current size (value of the _size) of the List<T> + 1) */
private void EnsureCapacity(int min)
{
    /* The _items.Legth refers to the current total length of the _items
     * array or total cells of the _items array where as _size field of
     * the List<T> class refers to the currently used cells from the
     * _items array of the List<T> class. To able to add any new item into
     * the List<T>, _size has to be < _items.Length */
    if (this._items.Length < min)
    {
        int num = (this._items.Length == 0) ? 4 : (this._items.Length * 2);
        if (num >  0x7fefffff)
        {
            num = 0x7fefffff;
        }
        if (num < min)
        {
            num = min;
        }
        this.Capacity = num;
    }
}
```

The Capacity property of the List<T> class creates a new array using the new capacity value (num from Listing 11-2) as the total length of this new array. It copies the existing contents of the _items array to this new array. The new array will contain all the existing items and four new empty cells for storing extra items. Finally, this new array will replace the existing _items array. Let's examine the implementation of the Capacity property, as shown in Listing 11-3.

Listing 11-3. The Implementation of the Capacity Property of the List<T> Class

```
public int Capacity
{
    get
    {
        return this._items.Length;
    }
    set
    {
        /*.....*/
        /* value refers to the new Capacity value ensured by the
         * EnsureCapacity method.*/
        if (value > 0)
        {
            /* Temporary array to hold existing item and new empty items.*/
            T[] destinationArray = new T[value];
            if (this._size > 0)
            {

                /* Copy the existing items into the new array. */
                Array.Copy(
                    this._items,        /* It refers the source array from
                                         * where items will be copied */
                    0,                  /* The position of the source array
                                         * from where the copy will start */
                    destinationArray,   /* It refers the destination array in
                                         * where items will be copied into*/
                    0,                  /* The position of the destination array
                                         * in where the item will be
                                         * placed after copying*/
                    this._size          /* Total number of item will be copied
                                         * from the source array.*/

                    );
            }

            /* Replace _items with the temporary array which currently holding
             * existing contents of the _items array and empty items
             * for the expanded cells. */
            this._items = destinationArray;
        }
        else
        {
            /* Otherwise set _items with 0 items as _emptyArray hold 0 items. */
            this._items = List<T>._emptyArray;
        }
        /*.....*/
```

```
        }
}
```

Insert Operation in the List<T>

The InsertRange method works a bit differently in comparison to the Add method. The InsertRange method adds a series of items into the List<T>, starting from a given position of the _items array. From Listing 11-4, you can see that the values {22, 33, 77} are inserted by copying the existing items {3} from the numbers into a new location of the numbers. It started copying items from position 3 of the numbers list and continued until the number of items to copy was equal to the size (4) of the numbers (original sequence) list—the number of items to insert (3). It is also important to calculate the new index where the item will be copied over. The position 6 is calculated using the index plus count, where index refers to the start position of the copy from the source array (provided as input to the InsertRange, which is 3), and count refers to the number of items provided in the InsertRange method to be inserted into the original list. As a result, items {3} will be copied into the array position 6, but the capacity of the original list numbers is four. So it needs to expand the capacity to accommodate more items. After the expansion of the original list, the cell at position {3,4,5} of the expanded original list new values {22,33,77} will be copied. Listing 11-4 shows the usage of the InsertRange method.

Listing 11-4. Example of the InsertRange Method of the List<T> Class

```csharp
using System;
using System.Collections;
using System.Collections.Generic;

namespace Ch11
{
    class Program
    {
        static void Main(string[] args)
        {
            List<int> numbers = new List<int>()
            {
                0,1, 2, 3
            };
            numbers.InsertRange(3, new List<int>() { 22, 33, 77 });
            ShowResult(numbers);
        }

        public static void ShowResult(IEnumerable aList)
        {
            foreach (var item in aList)
                Console.Write("{0}\t", item);
            Console.WriteLine();
        }
    }
}
```

The program will produce this output:

```
0       1       2       22      33      77      3
```

The InsertRange method works as demonstrated in Figure 11-7.

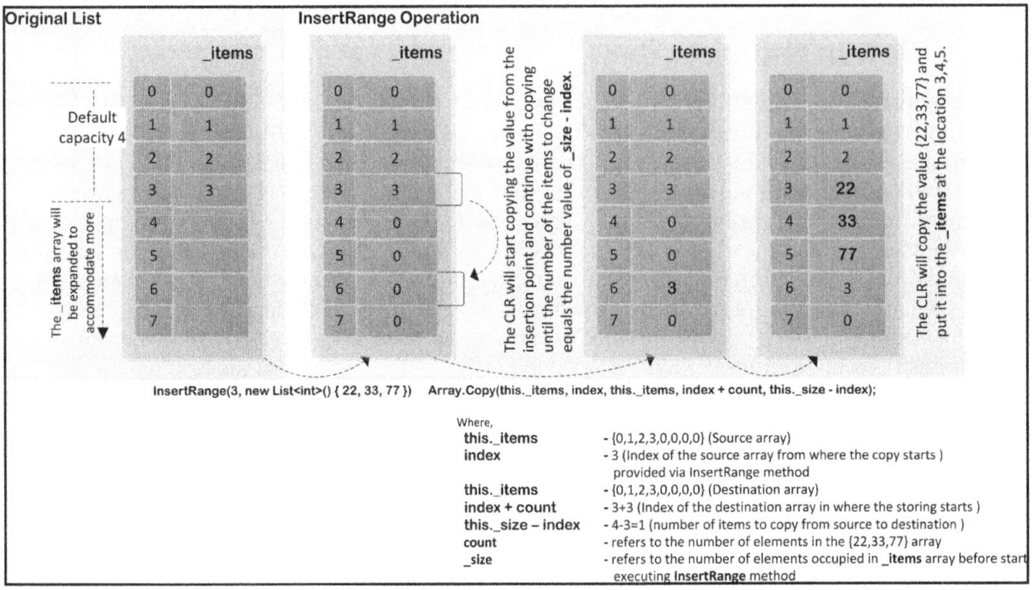

Figure 11-7. *InsertRange operation in the List<T> class.*

From Figure 11-7, you can see that:

- The CLR will copy the items from the original list, starting from the given position (3) (for Listing 11-4) until it reaches the number of items to copy, which is one, because it is calculated using this._size-index, which is (4 - 3) = 1. So it will copy the item from position 3 and store it in position 6 from the _items array in position 6.

- Insert the new values into cells three to five of the _items array, which will overwrite existing {3, 0, 0} items with new values {22, 33, 77}.

Deletion Operation in the List<T>

In List <T> class, you can use the Remove, RemoveAll, or Clear method to do the deletion operation or clear operation to the items from the list. Let's see how Remove method works internally:

- When the CLR executes the Remove method, it takes an item that is going to be removed as the argument. It looks for the index position of that item in the _items array, using the IndexOf method. This will return the index of that item, and the CLR passes this index as input to the RemoveAt method.

- The RemoveAt method copies items from the position of the item index (which is going to remove) plus one until the number of items to copy reaches the current size of the _items array—the position of the item to be removed (index of the item to be removed)—in the destination array at the position of the index of the item to be removed.

- The CLR will set the default value of the type T to the last item of the _items array.

The implementation of the RemoveAt method is shown in Listing 11-5.

Listing 11-5. The Implementation of the RemoveAt Method of the List<T> Class

```
public void RemoveAt(int index)          /* index - The position of the item which is going to
                 remove */
{
    if (index >= this._size)
    {
        ThrowHelper.ThrowArgumentOutOfRangeException();
    }
    this._size--;
    if (index < this._size)
    {
        Array.Copy(
                this._items,         /* Source array - from where
                                      * items will be copied */
                index + 1,           /* Source index - the position from where
                                      * the item will start copying */
                this._items,         /* Destination array - to where items will
                                      * be copied over */
                index,               /* Destination index - the position in where
                                      * the item will be placed after copied */
                this._size - index   /* Total number of item will be copied */
                    );
    }
    this._items[this._size] = default(T); /* Set the last item with the
                                           * default value */
    this._version++;
}
```

List<T> Class Members

This section examines different fields, constructors, and members used in the List<T>.

Constructors

The List<T> class has three overloaded constructors to initialize an instance of the List<T> class. Table 11-4 lists the three constructors that are used to instantiate the List<T> class.

Table 11-4. Public Constructors of the List<T> Class

Constructor	Description
List<T>()	Initializes a new instance of the List<T> class that is empty (i.e., it will be initialized with zero capacity) but the default capacity of the List<T> is four, which is referred by the _defaultCapacity field of the List<T> class. It will be set to the default capacity on the first Add operation to the List<T> instance. If the number of elements added to the list reaches the current capacity, the CLR increases its capacity to double. /* Initialize an instance of the List<T>*/ List<int> numbers = new List<int>();

Constructor	Description

List<T>(Int32)	Initializes a new instance of the List<T> class with the specified initial capacity
	`/* Initialize an instance of the List<T> with`
	`* the capacity 10 */`
	`List<int> numbers = new List<int>(10);`

List<T>(IEnumerable<T>)	Initializes a new instance of the List<T> class and copies elements from the IEnumerable<T> to the instance
	`List<int> numbers = new List<int>(new List<int>{ 0, 1 });`
	`/* 0        1 */`

Properties

Table 11-5 lists the different properties of the List<T> class.

Table 11-5. Public Properties of the List<T> Class

Property	Description

Capacity	Gets or sets the number of elements that the List<T> can contain
	`/* It will output the current capacity of the`
	`* List<T>  instance */`
	`int capacity = numbers.Capacity;`

Count	Returns the number of elements contained in the List<T>
	`/* It will output the current Count of the`
	`* List<T> instance */`
	`int count = numbers.Count;`

Item	Gets or sets the element at the specified index; in C#, this property is the indexer for the ArrayList class
	`/* 0, assuming the numbers hold 0 at its 0`th
	`* position */`
	`int itemAtPositionZero = numbers[0];`

Methods

The List<T> class has different methods that can be used to do different operations. Table 11-6 lists the different methods of the List<T> class.

Table 11-6. Public Methods of the List<T> Class

Method	Description

Add	`public void Add(T item)`
	Adds an item of type T to the end of the List<T>; the method returns the index at which the value has been added
	`numbers.Add(0); /* Add 0 to the numbers list */`

AddRange	`public virtual void AddRange(ICollection c)`
	Adds the elements of an ICollection to the end of the List<T>; assumes numbers contain 0,1
	`numbers.AddRange(new List<int>() { 2, 3 });`
	`/* 0        1       2       3 */`

Method	Description

AsReadOnly	`public ReadOnlyCollection<T> AsReadOnly()`
	Returns a read-only IList<T> for the current collection
	`var readOnlyNumbers =numbers.AsReadOnly();`
	`readOnlyNumbers[0] = 10; /* Compile time error */`

BinarySearch	`/* 3 overloaded*/`
	`public virtual int BinarySearch(T item)`
	Searches the entire sorted List<T> for an element using the default comparer and returns the zero-based index of the element if it is found or a negative number otherwise
	`var result = numbers.BinarySearch(0); /* 0 */`

Clear	`public virtual void Clear()`
	Removes all elements from the ArrayList
	`numbers.Clear();`
	`/* CLR throws an exception as there is no items in the numbers.*/`
	`var itemAtPositionZero = numbers[0];`

Contains	`public virtual bool Contains(T item)`
	Determines whether an element is in the List<T>
	`var containZero = numbers.Contains(0); /* true */`

CopyTo	`public virtual void CopyTo(T[] array, int index) /* 3 overloaded*/`
	Copies the entire List<T> or part of it to a compatible one-dimensional array, starting at the specified index of the target array; assumes numbers contain 0,1
	`int[] numberArray = new int[] { 2, 3, 4, 5 };`
	`numbers.CopyTo(numberArray, 1);`
	`/* numberArray: 2        0        1        5 */`

ConvertAll<TOutput>	`public List<TOutput> ConvertAll<TOutput>(Converter<T, TOutput> converter)` Converts the elements in the current List<T> to another type and returns a list containing the converted elements
Equals	`public virtual bool Equals(object obj)` Determines whether two object instances are equal and returns true if the specified object is equal to the current object; otherwise, false

Exists	Determines whether the List<T> contains elements that match the conditions defined by the specified predicate
	`var itemsLargerThanZero=numbers.Exists(item => item > 0);`
	`/* true*/`

Find	Searches for an element that matches the conditions defined by the specified predicate and returns the first occurrence within the entire List<T>
	`var itemsLargerThanZero=numbers.Find(item => item < 0);`
	`/* 0 */`

FindAll	Retrieves all the elements that match the conditions defined by the specified predicate
	`var itemsLargerThanZero=numbers.FindAll(item => item > 0);`
	`/* 1 */`

Method	Description

FindIndex(Predicate<T>)	Searches for an element that matches the conditions defined by the specified predicate and returns the zero-based index of the first occurrence within the entire List<T>
	`var itemsLargerThanZero=numbers.FindIndex(item => item > 0);`
	`/* 1 */`

FindLast	Searches for an element that matches the conditions defined by the specified predicate and returns the last occurrence within the entire List<T>
	`var itemsLargerThanZero=numbers.FindLast(item => item > 0);`
	`/* 1 */`

FindLastIndex(Predicate<T>)	Searches for an element that matches the conditions defined by the specified predicate and returns the zero-based index of the last occurrence within the entire List<T>
	`var itemsLargerThanZero=numbers.FindLastIndex(item => item > 0);`
	`/* 1 */`

ForEach	Performs the specified action on each element of the List<T>
	`numbers.ForEach(item => Console.Write("{0}\t", item));`
	`/* 0        1 */`

GetEnumerator	Returns an enumerator that iterates through the List<T>
GetHashCode	`public virtual int GetHashCode()` Serves as a hash function for a particular type, and it is suitable for use in hashing algorithms and data structures such as a hash table; returns a hash code for the current object

GetRange	`public virtual List<T> GetRange(int index, int count)`
	Creates a shallow copy of a range of elements in the source List<T>
	`numbers = numbers.GetRange(0, 2);   /* 0        1 */`

GetType	`public Type GetType()` Gets the type of the current instance

IndexOf	`public virtual int IndexOf(object value) /* 3 overloaded */`
	Searches for the specified object and returns the zero-based index of the first occurrence within the entire List<T>
	`var itemAtPosition = numbers.IndexOf(1) ; /* 1 */`

Insert	`public virtual void Insert(int index, object value)`
	Inserts an element into the List<T> at the specified index
	`numbers.Insert(1,100) ; /* 0        100     1 */`

InsertRange	`public virtual void InsertRange(int index, ICollection c)`
	Inserts the elements of a collection into the List<T> at the specified index
	`numbers.InsertRange(0, numbers); /* 0        1    0      1 */`

LastIndexOf	`public virtual int LastIndexOf(object value) /* 3 overloaded*/`
	Searches for the specified object and returns the zero-based index of the last occurrence within the entire List<T>
	`var itemLastIndexOf = numbers.LastIndexOf(0, 1); /* 0 */`

MemberwiseClone	Creates a shallow copy of the current object (inherited from the object)

Remove	`public virtual void Remove(object value)`
	Removes the first occurrence of a specific object from the List<T>
	`numbers.Remove(0); /* 1 */`

RemoveAt	`public virtual void RemoveAt(int index)`
	Removes the element at the specified index of the List<T>
	`numbers.RemoveAt(0); /* 1 */`

Method	Description
RemoveAll	Removes all the elements that match the conditions defined by the specified predicate
RemoveRange	public virtual void RemoveRange(int index, int count) Removes a range of elements from the List\<T\>
Reverse	public virtual void Reverse() /* 2 overloaded*/ Reverses the order of the elements in an List\<T\> numbers.Reverse(); /* 1 0 */
Sort	public virtual void Sort() /* 4 overloaded*/ Sorts the elements in an entire List\<T\> using the IComparable interface implemented by each element of the List\<T\> numbers.Sort(); /* 0 1 */
ToArray	public virtual Array ToArray(Type type) Copies the elements of the List\<T\> to a new array
ToString	public virtual string ToString() Returns a string that represents the current object
TrimExcess	public virtual void TrimExcess () Sets the capacity to the actual number of elements in the List\<T\>, if that number is less than a threshold value
TrueForAll	Determines whether every element in the List\<T\> matches the conditions defined by the specified predicate

ArrayList

The ArrayList class is another type of collection of the .NET. This section will explore in more detail the ArrayList class.

Capacity and Size of the ArrayList in .NET

The ArrayList is a dynamic array whose size dynamically increases as required. The number of elements that an ArrayList can hold refers to the capacity of the ArrayList. If the initial capacity (number of items it can hold) of the ArrayList is N on every phase of internal _items array expansion to accommodate more items, the CLR adds extra N items or increases to 2N. For example, the default capacity of the ArrayList is four, and it will be increased as 4 × 2 = 8, 8 × 2 = 16, 16 × 2 = 32, and so on. Figure 11-8 demonstrates the size and expansion of the ArrayList class.

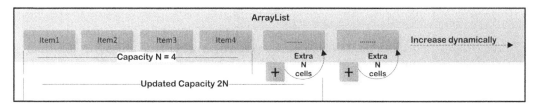

Figure 11-8. ArrayList basics

When you instantiate the ArrayList class without specifying the initial Capacity, the capacity of the ArrayList is zero. On the first Add operation with the instance of the ArrayList, it will increase the capacity with the value of four (N), which is stored in the internal field _defaultCapacity of the ArrayList class. It will be increased when needed to accommodate more items in the ArrayList instance, such as $4(N) \times 2 = 8$ (2N), $8(N) \times 2 = 16$ (2N), $16(N) \times 2 = 32$ (2N), and so on (as Figure 11-8 demonstrates). It means on every expansion of the ArrayList class, a new capacity of the ArrayList will be calculated and it will be two times that of the previous capacity. The actual items occupying the ArrayList are referred to as the Count property (internally the _size field) of the ArrayList class, and the total of the items can be added to the ArrayList referred by the Capacity property. The value of the capacity is updated when the CLR expands the capacity of the ArrayList to accommodate more items. For example, if you consider an instance of the ArrayList class whose current capacity is eight (refers by the Capacity property) but it actually contains five items, then the Count property of that instance of the ArrayList refers five (internally the _size field) and the capacity is eight. The capacity of the ArrayList can also be set:

- Explicitly by setting the required value in the Capacity property

- In the instantiation time of the ArrayList

- When the ArrayList will be instantiated based on another list of type ICollection, where the size of that list will be used as the initial capacity of the ArrayList

The capacity of the ArrayList can be decreased by calling the TrimToSize method. If an instance of the ArrayList has the capacity N (where N = 4) and only two items have been stored in that instance, then calling the TrimToSize method CLR will decrease the capacity of the ArrayList by two by removing N-2 cells from the internal array of the ArrayList class.

ArrayList Declaration

The ArrayList class defined in the System.Collections namespace of the mscorlib.dll (C:\Windows\ Microsoft.NET\ Framework\v4.0.30319) assembly in .NET is demonstrated in Figure 11-9.

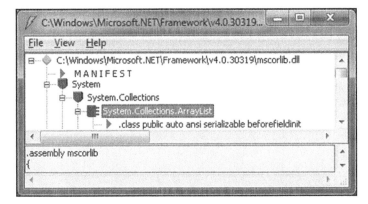

Figure 11-9. ArrayList class in the System.Collections namespace

The signature of the ArrayList class is:

```
public class ArrayList : IList, ICollection, IEnumerable, ICloneable
```

Let's look at an example of the ArrayList usage, as shown in Listing 11-6.

Listing 11-6. Example of the ArrayList Class

```
using System;
using System.Collections;

namespace Ch11
{
    class Program
    {
        static void Main(string[] args)
        {
            ArrayList terrestrialPlanets = new ArrayList();
            terrestrialPlanets.Add("Mercury");    /* Default capacity is 4.*/
            terrestrialPlanets.Add("Venus");
            terrestrialPlanets.Add("Earth");
            terrestrialPlanets.Add("Mars");

            ShowResult(terrestrialPlanets);
        }

        public static void ShowResult(
                        IEnumerable aList, char mySeparator = ' ')
        {
            foreach (string item in aList)
                Console.Write("{0}{1}", mySeparator, item);
            Console.WriteLine();
        }
    }
}
```

This program will produce the output:

```
Mercury Venus Earth Mars
```

Instantiation of the ArrayList

ArrayList comes to life when you call one of the following three overloaded constructors:

```
public ArrayList()                      {}
public ArrayList(int capacity)          {}
public ArrayList(ICollection c)         {}
```

When the CLR executes the first version of the ArrayList constructor, it initializes the internal _items array with the default size zero. But on the first Add operation, it will be increased to four. For the second version of the constructor, it initializes the _items array with the given size provided as input to the capacity parameter. The CLR gets the size of the parameter c (refers to a collection) via the Count property of the c collection for the third version of the constructor and uses this size to initialize the _items array. It copies the entire contents of the c into the _items array. Figure 11-10 demonstrates the ArrayList instantiation using the different constructors.

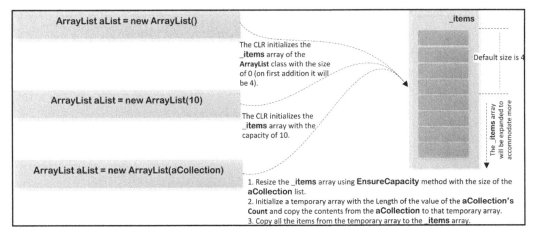

Figure 11-10. ArrayList class and its constructors

Addition and Insertion Operations in the ArrayList Class

To add any item into the ArrayList, the CLR checks whether the item can be stored in the _items array. The CLR ensures this by checking the current number of elements inside the ArrayList class using the EnsureCapacity method of the ArrayList class. If the size is ensured by the EnsureCapacity method, the CLR adds that item into the expanded _items array. Figure 11-11 demonstrates the Add and Insert operations in the ArrayList.

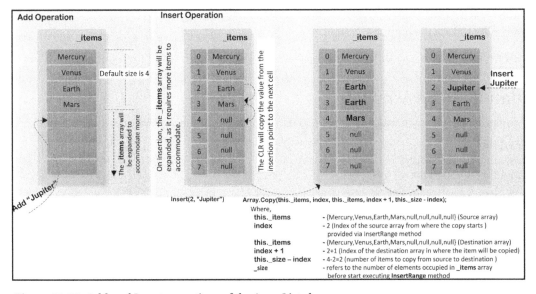

Figure 11-11. Add and Insert operations of the ArrayList class

The implementation of the Add method of the ArrayList class is demonstrated in Listing 11-7.

Listing 11-7. The Implementation of the Add Method of the ArrayList Class

```
public virtual int Add(object value)
{
    if (this._size == this._items.Length)
    {
        this.EnsureCapacity(this._size + 1);
    }
    this._items[this._size] = value;
    this._version++;
    return this._size++;
}
```

The EnsureCapacity method will do the entire back-end job to make sure that the ArrayList is able to hold the required number (based on the available memory) of data inside it. The CLR calls this EnsureCapacity method with the value of the current _size field of the ArrayList + 1. The EnsureCapacity method calculates the current new capacity for the _items array, which sets this new value into the Capacity property of the ArrayList class. The implementation of the EnsureCapacity method for the ArrayList class is shown in Listing 11-8.

Listing 11-8. The Implementation of the EnsureCapacity Method of the ArrayList Class

```
/* min is current size (_size) of the List<T> + 1 */
private void EnsureCapacity(int min)
{

    /* The _items.Legth refers to the current total length of the _items
     * array or total. cells of the _items array where as _size field of
     * the ArrayList refers to the currently used cells from the _items
     * array of the ArrayList class. To able to add any item into
     * the ArrayList, _size has to be < _items.Length */
    if (this._items.Length < min)
    {
        int num = (this._items.Length == 0) ? 4 : (this._items.Length * 2);
        if (num < 0x7fefffff)
        {
            num = 0x7fefffff;
        }
        if (num < min)
        {
            num = min;
        }
        this.Capacity = num;
    }
}
```

The Capacity property of the ArrayList class creates a new array with the size of the new capacity value calculated using the EnsureCapacity method. It copies the existing items from the _items array into this new array. The new array will contain all the existing items from the _items array and four new empty cells. Finally, this new array will replace the existing _items array. Let's look at the implementation of the Capacity property, as shown in Listing 11-9.

Listing 11-9. The Implementation of the Capacity Property of the ArrayList Class

```
public virtual int Capacity
{
    get
    {
        return this._items.Length;
    }
    set
    {
        if (value != this._items.Length)
        {
            /*  value refers to the new Capacity value ensured by
             * the EnsureCapacity method.*/
            if (value > 0)
            {
                /* Temporary array to hold existing item and new empty items.*/
                object[] destinationArray = new object[value];

                if (this._size > 0)
                {
                    /* Copy the existing items into the new array. */
                    Array.Copy(
                        /* It refers the source array from where items
                         * will be copied */
                        this._items,
                        /* The position of the source array from where
                         * the copy will start */
                        0,
                        /* It refers the destination array in  where items
                         * will be copied into */
                        destinationArray,
                        /* The position of the destination array
                         * in where the item will be placed after copying */
                        0,
                        /* Total number of item will be copied from the
                         * source array */
                        this._size
                    );
                }
                /* Replace _items with the temporary array which currently
                 * holding existing contents of the  _items array and empty
                 * items for the expanded cells. */
                this._items = destinationArray;
            }
            else
            {
                this._items = new object[4]; /* Otherwise set _items with 4
```

```
                                            * items. */
                    }
                }
            }
        }
```

Insert a Range of Items in the ArrayList

The InsertRange method works a bit differently from the Add method. The InsertRange method adds a series of items into the ArrayList, starting from a given position of the _items array. It started copying from the position 3 (as provided to the InsertRange method) of the numbers and continued until the number of items to copy was equal to the size (4) of the numbers (original sequence), that is, the number of items to insert (3). It is also important to calculate the new index from the items that will be copied. Position 6 is calculated using the index plus count, where the index refers to the start position of the copy from the source array (provided as of input to add to the InsertRange, which is 3), and count refers to the number of items provided in the InsertRange method to insert into the original list. As a result, item {3} will be copied at the array in position 6, but the capacity of the original list is four, so it needs to expand the capacity to accommodate more items. After the expansion of the original list, for the cell at position {3,4,5} from the expanded list, new values {22,33,77} will be copied. Listing 11-10 illustrates the InsertRange method.

Listing 11-10. Example of InsertRange Method of the ArrayList Class

```
using System;
using System.Collections;
using System.Collections.Generic;

namespace Ch11
{
    class Program
    {
        static void Main(string[] args)
        {
            ArrayList numbers = new ArrayList()
            {
                0,1, 2, 3
            };
            numbers.InsertRange(3, new List<int>() { 22, 33, 77 });
            ShowResult(numbers);
        }

        public static void ShowResult(IEnumerable aList)
        {
            foreach (var item in aList)
                Console.Write("{0}\t", item);
            Console.WriteLine();
        }
    }
}
```

The program will produce the output:

| 0 | 1 | 2 | 22 | 33 | 77 | 3 |

This work is shown in Figure 11-12.

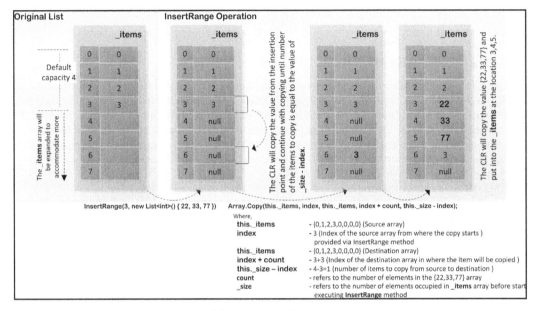

Figure 11-12. InsertRange operation of the ArrayList class

From Figure 11-12, you can see that:

- The CLR copies the items from the original list and it starts from the given position (3 for Listing 11-10) until it reaches the number of items to copy (which is 1, because it is calculated using the _size - index, which is (4 - 3) = 1. So it will copy the item from position 3 and store it in the _items array at position 6.

- The CLR will insert the new values into the empty cells in positions 3 to 5 of the _items array.

Deletion Operation in the ArrayList

If you want to remove any item from the ArrayList, you can use the Remove method. The program in Listing 11-11 shows the usage of the Remove method of the ArrayList class.

Listing 11-11. Remove Item from the ArrayList

```
using System;
using System.Collections;

namespace Ch11
{
    class Program
    {
```

```
static void Main(string[] args)
{
    ArrayList terrestrialPlanets = new ArrayList();
    terrestrialPlanets.Add("Mercury");
    terrestrialPlanets.Add("Venus");
    terrestrialPlanets.Add("Earth");
    terrestrialPlanets.Add("Mars");

    terrestrialPlanets.Remove("Venus");
    ShowResult(terrestrialPlanets);
}

public static void ShowResult(IEnumerable aList)
{
    foreach (string item in aList)
        Console.Write("{0}\t",item);
    Console.WriteLine();
}
    }
}
```

This program will produce the output:

```
Mercury Earth    Mars
```

The CLR takes the following steps to execute terrestrialPlanets.Remove("Venus") statement:

1. *Step 1*: From the Remove method, the CLR will try to find the index of the Venus object from the internal array _items of the ArrayList class. It will then call the RemoveAt method internally with the index found for the Venus item.

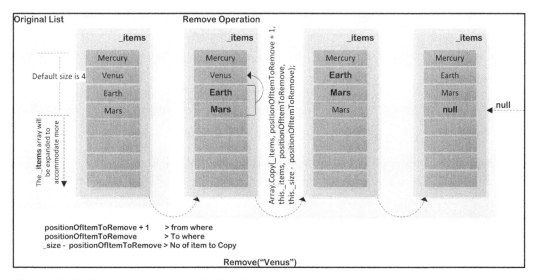

Figure 11-13. Remove operation in the ArrayList class

2. *Step 2*: Inside the RemoveAt method, the CLR calls the Copy method of the Array class with a related argument such as calculated index of the item to remove and the _size field of the ArrayList class. This copy operation replaces one item at a time. The CLR copies the Earth and Mars to replace Venus and Earth of the _items array. The _items array will no longer have Venus in it. The CLR will set the contents of the position Mars (last occurrence) in the _items array with null. Figure 11-13 shows the removed last item set with a null value and (unless you call the TrimToSize method) the internal array _items holds the null value for the removed items. The implementation of the RemoveAt method is demonstrated in Listing 11-12.

Listing 11-12. The Implementation of the RemoveAt Method of the ArrayList Class

```
/* index - The position of the item which is going to remove */
public virtual void RemoveAt(int index)
{
    this._size--;
    if (index < this._size)
    {
        Array.Copy(
                this._items,        /* It refers the source array - from where
                                     * items will be copied   */
                index + 1,          /* The position of the source array from
                                     * where the copy will start */
                this._items,        /* It refers the destination array in where
                                     * items will be copied over */
                index,              /* The position of the destination array
                                     * in where the item will be
                                     * placed after copying */
                this._size - index  /* Total number of item will be copied from
                                     * the source array */
            );
    }
    this._items[this._size] = null;
    this._version++;
}
```

ArrayList Class Members

This section will explore the different fields, constructors, and members used in the ArrayList.

Fields

Table 11-7 lists the different fields from the ArrayList class that the ArrayList class uses internally to implement the ArrayList functionality.

Table 11-7. *ArrayList Fields*

Field	Description
_defaultCapacity	This variable is an int-type constant, which will ensure the default capacity of the internal array used to store the item in the ArrayList.
object[] _items	The _items array will store data of the object type inside the ArrayList.
_size	The _size variable usage in the ArrayList keeps track of the current number of items stored in the _items array.

object[] emptyArray	This is a read-only object-type array, which does not contain any element inside it. It is just an array declaration. This array is used when the default constructor of the ArrayList is being called, for example:
	.method public hidebysig specialname rtspecialname instance void .ctor() cil managed
	{
	　IL_0001:　call　　instance void System.Object::.ctor()
	　IL_0006:　ldarg.0
	　IL_0007:　ldsfld　object[]
	　　　　　　System.Collections.ArrayList::emptyArray
	　IL_000c:　stfld　object[]
	　　　　　　System.Collections.ArrayList::_items
	　IL_0011:　ret
	}
	This IL code shows that the C# compiler will store the emptyArray object in the _items field in the default constructor of the ArrayList in IL_000c.

Constructors

The ArrayList class has three overloaded constructors to initialize an instance of the ArrayList class. Table 11-8 lists the three constructors that can be used to instantiate the ArrayList class.

Table 11-8. *Public Constructors of the ArrayList Class*

Constructor	Description
ArrayList()	A parameter-less constructor that initializes an instance of the ArrayList class that is empty **/* Initial capacity is 0.*/** ArrayList terrestrialPlanets = new ArrayList();
ArrayList(int capacity)	Initializes a new instance of the ArrayList class that has the specified initial capacity **/* The capacity has been set to 10.*/** ArrayList terrestrialPlanets = new ArrayList(10);
ArrayList(ICollection c)	Initializes a new instance of the ArrayList class and copies elements from the ICollection c to the instance ArrayList terrestrialPlanets = new ArrayList(new List<string>() { 　　"Mercury", "Venus" }); /* Mercury Venus */

Properties

Table 11-9 lists the different properties of the `ArrayList` class.

Table 11-9. *Public Properties of the ArrayList Class*

Property	Description
Capacity	The public property that gets or sets the number of elements the `ArrayList` can contain
Count	Used to get the number of elements contained in the `ArrayList`
IsFixedSize	Refers to whether the `ArrayList` has a fixed size
IsReadOnly	Refers to whether the `ArrayList` is read-only
IsSynchonized	Refers to whether the access to the `ArrayList` is synchronized
Item	In C#, this property is the indexer for the `ArrayList` class, which gets or sets the element at the specified index.
SyncRoot	Returns an object that can be used to synchronize access to the `ArrayList`

Methods

The `ArrayList` class has different methods that can be used to do different operations. Table 11-10 lists the different methods of the `ArrayList` class.

Table 11-10. *Public Methods of the ArrayList Class*

Method	Description

Adapter	`public static ArrayList Adapter(IList list)`
	Creates an `ArrayList` based on the provided list
	* Using the terrestrialPlanets ArrayList object from the Listing 11-11*/
	`var wrapper = ArrayList.Adapter(terrestrialPlanets);`
	`wrapper.Add("Neptune");`

Add	`public virtual int Add(object value)` Adds an object to the end of the `ArrayList` and will return the index at which the value been added
AddRange	`public virtual void AddRange(ICollection c)` Adds all the elements of an `ICollection` to the end of the `ArrayList`
BinarySearch	`public virtual int BinarySearch(object value) /* 3 overloads */` In `ArrayList` class, there are three overloaded `BinarySearch` methods to search the entire sorted `ArrayList` for an element using the default comparer. If the item is found, it returns the zero-based index, or a negative number otherwise.
Clear	`public virtual void Clear()` Used to remove all elements from the `ArrayList`
Clone	`public virtual object Clone()` Used to do a shallow copy of the existing `ArrayList`
Contains	`public virtual bool Contains(object item)` Used to find the existence of an item in the `ArrayList`
CopyTo	`public virtual void CopyTo(Array a, int index)/* 3 overloads */` Used to copy the entire `ArrayList` into an array

Method	Description
Equals	public virtual bool Equals(object obj) Used to determine whether two object instances are equal

FixedSize	public static ArrayList FixedSize(ArrayList list) /* 2 overloads */
	In ArrayList class, there are two overloaded FixedSize methods, which disable, add, or remove an item from the existing ArrayList, except for updating the contents of the existing items
	/* Using the terrestrialPlanets ArrayList object from the Listing 11-11*/
	var fixedSizeAL = ArrayList.FixedSize(terrestrialPlanets);
	/* The CLR throws exception (with **Collection was of a fixed size** message)
	 * when tries to add item to the fixedSizeAL Collection */
	fixedSizeAL.Add("Milky way");

GetEnumerator	public virtual IEnumerator GetEnumerator() /* 2 overloads */ Returns an IEnumerator for the ArrayList
GetHashCode	public virtual int GetHashCode() Returns a hash code for the current object
GetRange	public virtual ArrayList GetRange(int index, int count) Returns a subset of the elements in the source ArrayList
GetType	public Type GetType() Gets the type of the current instance
IndexOf	public virtual int IndexOf(object value) /* 3 overloads */ Returns the first occurrence of a value in an ArrayList
Insert	public virtual void Insert(int index, object value) Inserts an element into the ArrayList at the specified index
InsertRange	public virtual void InsertRange(int index, ICollection c) Inserts the elements of a collection into the ArrayList at the specified index
LastIndexOf	public virtual int LastIndexOf(object value) /* 3 overloads */ In ArrayList class, there are three overloaded LastIndexOf methods, which search for the specified object and return the last occurrence within the entire ArrayList /* if terrestrialPlanets contains {"Venus", "Earth", "Mercury", "Mars" }*/ terrestrialPlanets.LastIndexOf("Mercury"); /* output: 2 */
Remove	public virtual void Remove(object value) Removes the first occurrence of a specific object from the ArrayList
RemoveAt	public virtual void RemoveAt(int index) Removes the element at the specified index of the ArrayList
RemoveRange	public virtual void RemoveRange(int index, int count) Removes a range of elements from the ArrayList
Repeat	public static ArrayList Repeat(object value, int count) Returns an ArrayList whose elements are copies of the specified value var repeatedList = ArrayList.Repeat(".", 5); /* . . . . . */
Reverse	public virtual void Reverse() /* 2 overloads */ Reverses the order of the elements in an ArrayList or in a portion of it
SetRange	public virtual void SetRange(int index, ICollection c) Copies the elements of a collection over a range of elements in the ArrayList
Sort	public virtual void Sort() /* 3 overloads */ Sorts the elements in an entire ArrayList using the IComparable interface implemented by each element of the ArrayList

Method	Description
Synchonized	public static ArrayList Synchonized(ArrayList list) /* 2 overloads */ Returns a list wrapper that is synchronized
ToArray	public virtual Array ToArray(Type type) /* 2 overloads */ Copies the elements of the ArrayList to a new array
ToString	public virtual string ToString() Returns a string that represents the current object
TrimToSize	public virtual void TrimToSize() Sets the capacity to the actual number of elements in the ArrayList

Array vs. ArrayList

An ArrayList is a sophisticated version of an array. Most situations that call for an array can use an ArrayList instead. In general, ArrayList is easier to use and has performance similar to an array of type object. Table 11-11 lists the elements of an Array and the ArrayList.

Table 11-11. Array vs. ArrayList

Element	Array	ArrayList
Namespace	System	System.Collections
Element	Gets or sets the value of only one element at a time	Add, insert, or remove a range of elements
Method	Does not provide methods that return read-only and fixed-size wrappers	Provides methods that return read-only and fixed-size wrappers
Capacity	Fixed	Automatically expanded as required. If the value of the ArrayList Capacity property is changed, the memory reallocation and copying of elements are automatically done.
Dimension	Can have multiple dimensions	Always has exactly one dimension
Lower bound	The lower bound can be set	The lower bound is always zero
Type	An array of a specific type other than Object has better performance than an ArrayList	Elements of ArrayList are of type Object, and boxing and unboxing typically occur if storing or retrieving a value type
Synchronization	Up to the user to implement synchronization	Easy to create using the Synchronized method

Stack

A Stack is a sequence of items that are accessible at only one end of the sequence. The last data item placed into the sequence is the first processed. All activity occurs at the top of the Stack. The Push operation places a data item on top of the Stack, but Pop removes a data item from top of the Stack.

Stack in .NET

When you instantiate the Stack class without specifying the capacity, the initial capacity of the Stack is ten. The initial capacity of the Stack will be set with the default capacity N (= 10), which is stored in the internal field _defaultCapacity of the Stack class by default or otherwise provided the different initial capacity. The Stack class uses the _size field internally to represent how many items the internal _array currently holds. If the current capacity of the Stack is ten and it holds three items, the _size field will be three. The capacity will be increased to 2N to expand the internal _array when needed. Figure 11-14 demonstrates the behavior of the Stack operation.

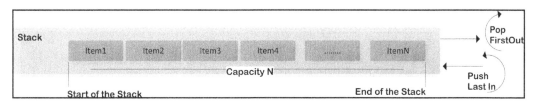

Figure 11-14. Stack basics

If the stack's current capacity is ten and it needs to add another item, it will increase the capacity to 10 × 2 = 20 (it will be 20 × 2 = 40, 40 × 2 = 80, 80 × = 160, 160 × 2 = 320, 320 × 2 = 640, and so on to accommodate more items into the Stack). After adding the new item to the Stack, it will update the _size field by one, so after the addition the _size field will be 11.

Stack Declaration

In .NET, Stack class is defined in the System.Collections namespace of the mscorlib.dll (C:\Windows\ Microsoft.NET \Framework\v4.0.30319) assembly, as shown in Figure 11-15.

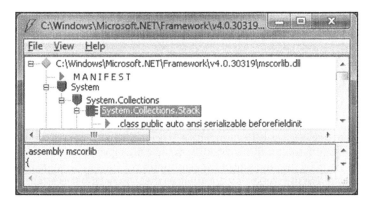

Figure 11-15. Stack class in the System.Collections namespace

The signature of the Stack class would be:

```
public class Stack : ICollection, IEnumerable, ICloneable
```

Let's look at an example of Stack usage, as shown in Listing 11-13.

Listing 11-13. An Example of Stack Class

```
using System;
using System.Collections;

namespace Ch11
{
    class Program
    {
        static void Main(string[] args)
        {
            Stack terrestrialPlanets = new Stack();
            terrestrialPlanets.Push("Mercury");
            terrestrialPlanets.Push("Venus");
            terrestrialPlanets.Push("Earth");
            terrestrialPlanets.Push("Mars");

            ShowResult(terrestrialPlanets);
        }

        public static void ShowResult(IEnumerable aList)
        {
            foreach (string item in aList)
                Console.Write("{0}\t",item);
            Console.WriteLine();
        }
    }
}
```

This program will produce the output:

```
Mars    Earth   Venus   Mercury
```

Instantiation of the Stack

The Stack comes to life when you call one of the three overloaded constructors:

```
public Stack()                      {}
public Stack(int initialCapacity)   {}
public Stack(ICollection col)       {}
```

When the CLR executes the first version of the Stack constructor, it initializes the internal _array with the default value ten. The second version of the constructor initializes the _array with a given size provided as the parameter initialCapacity. The CLR gets the size of the parameter col (using the value of the Count property of the col) for the third version of the constructor, initializes the _array with this size, and copies the entire contents of the col into the _array. Figure 11-16 demonstrates instantiation of the Stack constructors.

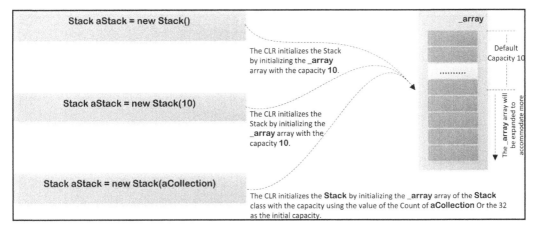

Figure 11-16. Stack class and its constructors

The implementation of the Stack constructor is shown in Listing 11-14.

Listing 11-14. The Implementation of the Overloaded Stack Constructor

```
public Stack()
{
    this._array = new object[10];
    this._size = 0;
    this._version = 0;
}

public Stack(int initialCapacity)
{
    if (initialCapacity < 10)
    {
        initialCapacity = 10;
    }
    this._array = new object[initialCapacity];
    this._size = 0;
    this._version = 0;
}
```

From the second constructor, you can see that it takes the initialCapacity to define the size of the internal _array. The third version of the Stack constructor accepts a Collection object as input and initializes the Stack object based on the given Collection object. Listing 11-15 demonstrates the implementation of this third constructor of the Stack class.

Listing 11-15. The Implementation of the Stack Constructor that Accepts a Collection as Input

```
public Stack(ICollection col) : this((col == null) ? 0x20 : col.Count)
{
    if (col == null)
    {
```

```
        throw new ArgumentNullException("col");
    }
    IEnumerator enumerator = col.GetEnumerator();
    while (enumerator.MoveNext())
    {
        this.Push(enumerator.Current);
    }
}
```

Push Operation in the Stack

When the CLR pushes the element into the Stack, it checks whether the _size field and the length of the internal _array are the same. If they are equal, then the CLR:

- Creates a new temporary array locally with the size of the current _array x 2

- Copies the contents of the existing _array into this new array

- Copies this temporary local array into the _array

Figure 11-17 demonstrates the Push and Pop operation of the Stack class based on the internal _array of the Stack class where the CLR stores the item added to the Stack.

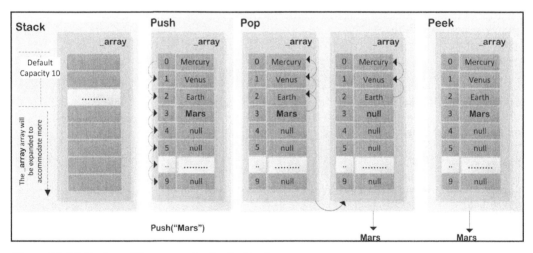

Figure 11-17. Push and Pop operation in the Stack

The implementation of the Push method is demonstrated in Listing 11-16.

Listing 11-16. The Implementation of the Push Method of the Stack Class

```
public virtual void Push(object obj)
{
    /* _size refers to the number of cells from _array is being used. */
    if (this._size == this._array.Length)
    {
```

```
        object[] destinationArray = new object[2 * this._array.Length];
        Array.Copy(this._array, 0, destinationArray, 0, this._size);
        this._array = destinationArray;
    }
    this._array[this._size++] = obj;
    this._version++;
}
```

Peek and Pop Operation in the Stack

While the CLR executes the Peek method, it returns a copy of the top item from the _array of the Stack class, as demonstrated in Listing 11-17 using the implementation of the Peek method.

Listing 11-17. The Implementation Code for the Peek Method of the Stack Class

```
public virtual object Peek()
{
    /* It copies the item stored at position (_size -1) from  _array*/
    return this._array[this._size - 1];
}
```

On the other hand, the Pop method will return the top-most items from the _array of the Stack and set the value as null for that position to remove the contents of the value at that position. Listing 11-18 demonstrates the implementation of the Pop method of the Stack class.

Listing 11-18. The Implementation of the Pop Method of the Stack Class

```
public virtual object Pop()
{
    /* Copy the top most value from the _array into the obj2 */
    object obj2 = this._array[--this._size];
    /* Set the value as null at the top most position of the _array */
    this._array[this._size] = null;
    return obj2;
}
```

Clear Operation in the Stack

The Clear method of the Stack class resets all the existing items stored in the _array with their default values and sets the _size of the Stack class to zero. The Clear method does not resize the _array but removes all the values stored in the _array. The implementation of the Clear method is shown in Listing 11-19.

Listing 11-19. The Implementation of the Clear Method of the Stack Class

```
public virtual void Clear()
{
    Array.Clear(
        this._array, /* The original array which to reset */
        0,           /* The starting index from where the reset will start */
        this._size   /* Total number of item to reset which is the size of
```

```
                             * the _array */
            );
    this._size = 0;   /* Set the size of the Stack as 0 which makes the Count
                       * property as 0 as the Count property is return
                       * this._size; */
    this._version++;
}
```

Stack Class Members

The Stack class provides several methods for Push and Pop items in a list.

Fields

Table 11-12 lists the different fields the Stack class uses internally to implement the stack functionality.

Table 11-12. Internal Fields of the Stack Class

Field	Description
_array	An object type array that is used by the Stack class to store the objects for the Stack
_defaultCapacity	Used to set the capacity of the _array field internally
_size	Used to define the number of element currently stored in the Stack (i.e., inside the _array object)

Constructors

The Stack class has three overloaded constructor to initialize an instance of the Stack class. Table 11-13 lists the three constructors that can be used to instantiate the Stack class.

Table 11-13. Public Constructors of the Stack Class

Constructor	Description
Stack()	Initializes a new instance of the Stack class with the default capacity of ten Stack terrestrialPlanets = new Stack();
Stack(int initialCapacity)	Initializes a new instance of the Stack class with the specified initial capacity Stack terrestrialPlanets = new Stack(320); /* 320 is the capacity*/
Stack(ICollection c)	Initializes a new instance of the Stack class and copies elements from the ICollection c to the instance. The new instance has the same initial capacity as the number of elements copied. Stack terrestrialPlanets = new Stack(new List<string>() { "Mercury", "Venus" ," Earth"," Mars" }); /* Mars Earth Venus Mercury */

Properties

Table 11-14 lists the different properties of the Stack class.

Table 11-14. Public Properties of the Stack Class

Property	Description
Count	Returns the number of elements contained in the Stack `var totalItems = terrestrialPlanets.Count; /* 4 */`
IsSynchonized	Determines whether access to the Stack is synchronized
SyncRoot	Gets an object that can be used to synchronize access to the Stack

Methods

The Stack class has different methods that can be used to do different operations. Table 11-15 lists the different methods used in the Stack class.

Table 11-15. Public Methods of the Stack Class

Method	Description

Clear	`public virtual void Clear()`
	Removes all elements from the Stack
	`terrestrialPlanets.Clear();`
	`var totalItems = terrestrialPlanets.Count; /* 0 */`

Clone	`public virtual object Clone()` Creates and returns a shallow copy of the Stack

Contains	`public virtual bool Contains(object item)`
	Determines whether an element is in the Stack
	`var contains = terrestrialPlanets.Contains("Mercury"); /* true */`

CopyTo	`public virtual void CopyTo(Array a, int index)`
	Copies the entire Stack to an existing one-dimensional array, starting at the specified array index
	`string[] copyTo = new string[] { string.Empty, string.Empty, string.Empty, string.Empty, };`
	`terrestrialPlanets.CopyTo(copyTo, 0);`
	`/* Mars    Earth    Venus    Mercury */`

Equals	`public virtual bool Equals(object obj)` Determines whether two Object instances are equal and returns true if the specified object is equal to the current object; otherwise, false
GetEnumerator	`public virtual IEnumerator GetEnumerator()` Returns an IEnumerator for the Stack. Note that enumerators only allow reading the data in the Stack. Enumerators cannot be used to modify the underlying Stack.
GetHashCode	`public virtual int GetHashCode()` Serves as a hash function for a particular type, suitable for use in hashing algorithms and data structures, such as a hash table. It returns a hash code for the current object.
GetType	`public Type GetType()` Gets the type of the current instance

Peek	`public virtual object Peek()`
	Returns the object at the top of the Stack without removing it
	`var result = terrestrialPlanets.Peek(); /* Mars */`

Pop	`public virtual object Pop()`
	Removes and returns the object at the top of the Stack
	`var result = terrestrialPlanets.Pop(); /* Mars */`

Method	Description
Push	public virtual void Push(object obj) Inserts an object at the top of the Stack terrestrialPlanets.Push("Vesta");
Synchonized	public static Stack Synchonized(Stack stk) Returns a synchronized wrapper for the Stack
ToArray	public virtual object [] ToArray() Copies the elements of the Stack to a new array
ToString	public virtual string ToString() Returns a string that represents the current object

Queue

The Queue is the data structure that enables the CLR to enter data into the list in a way that ensures that the item first in will be the first out. A data item enters the Queue at the rear and leaves from the front. When an item is added to the end of the Queue, it is said to be Enqueue; but when it removes an item at the beginning of the Queue, it is said to be Dequeue.

Size of the Queue in .NET

The size of the Queue is represented by N, where N is 32, which is the default size of the Queue unless different values are defined for the size. Figure 11-18 demonstrates the Queue class.

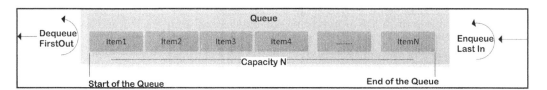

Figure 11-18. Queue class basics

Queue Declaration

The Queue class defined in the System.Collections namespace of the mscorlib.dll assembly is demonstrated in Figure 11-19.

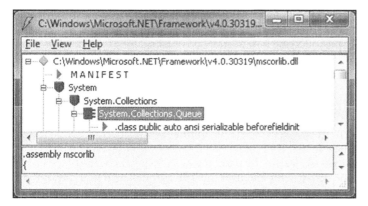

Figure 11-19. Queue in the System.Collections namespace

The signature of the Queue class is:

```
public class Queue : ICollection, IEnumerable, ICloneable
```

Let's look at an example of the usage of the Queue class, as shown in Listing 11-20.

Listing 11-20. Example of the Queue Class

```
using System;
using System.Collections;

namespace Ch11
{
    class Program
    {
        static void Main(string[] args)
        {
            Queue terrestrialPlanets = new Queue();
            terrestrialPlanets.Enqueue("Mercury");
            terrestrialPlanets.Enqueue("Venus");
            terrestrialPlanets.Enqueue("Earth");
            terrestrialPlanets.Enqueue("Mars");
            ShowResult(terrestrialPlanets);
        }

        public static void ShowResult(IEnumerable aList)
        {
            foreach (string item in aList)
                Console.Write("{0}\t", item);
            Console.WriteLine();
        }
    }
}
```

This program will produce the output:

```
Mercury    Venus    Earth    Mars
```

Instantiation of the Queue

The Queue comes to life when you call one of the following four overloaded constructors:

```
public Queue()                                          {}
public Queue(int capacity)                              {}
public Queue(ICollection col)                           {}
public Queue(int capacity, float growFactor)            {}
```

When the CLR executes the first version of the Queue constructor, it initializes the internal _array with the default value 32. The second version of the constructor initializes the _array with a given size provided as input to the capacity parameter. The CLR gets the size of the parameter col (using the value of the Count property of the col) for the third version of the constructor and uses this size to initialize the _array. It then copies the entire contents of the col into the _array. Figure 11-20 demonstrates the internal workings of the Queue constructors.

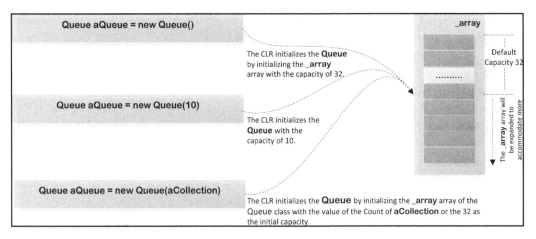

Figure 11-20. Queue class and its constructors

The implementation of the Queue constructors is shown in Listing 11-21.

Listing 11-21. The Implementation of the Constructor of the Queue Class

```
public Queue() : this(0x20, 2f){}
public Queue(ICollection col) : this((col == null) ? 0x20 : col.Count)
{
    IEnumerator enumerator = col.GetEnumerator();
    while (enumerator.MoveNext())
    {
        this.Enqueue(enumerator.Current);
    }
}
public Queue(int capacity) : this(capacity, 2f){}
public Queue(int capacity, float growFactor)
{
    this._array = new object[capacity];
```

```
    this._head = 0;
    this._tail = 0;
    this._size = 0;
    this._growFactor = (int) (growFactor * 100f);
}
```

Enqueue and Dequeue Operation in the Queue

When the CLR enqueues an element into the Queue, it checks whether the _size field and the length of the internal _array are the same. If they are equal, then the CLR:

- Ensures the capacity of the internal _array with the new length using the new length, which is the current length of the _array plus four

- Calls the SetCapacity method internally to set this new value for the Queue

- Puts the element at the top of the _array

Figure 11-21 demonstrates the Enqueue and Dequeue operations of the Queue class.

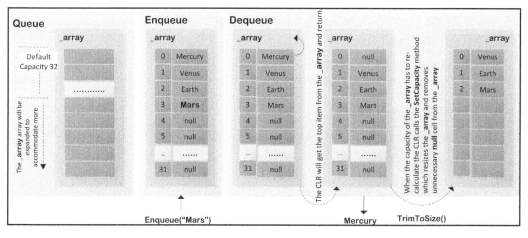

Figure 11-21. Enqueue and Dequeue operations in the Queue class

The implementation of the Dequeue method is demonstrated in Listing 11-22.

Listing 11-22. The implementation of the Dequeue Method of the Queue Class

```
public virtual object Dequeue()
{
    object obj2 = this._array[this._head];
    this._array[this._head] = null;
    this._head = (this._head + 1) % this._array.Length;
    this._size--;
    this._version++;
    return obj2;
}
```

The implementation of the Enqueue method is demonstrated in Listing 11-23.

Listing 11-23. The Implementation of the Enqueue Method of the Queue Class

```
public virtual void Enqueue(object obj)
{
    if (this._size == this._array.Length)
    {
        int capacity = (int) ((this._array.Length * this._growFactor) / 100L);
        if (capacity < (this._array.Length + 4))
        {
            capacity = this._array.Length + 4;
        }
        this.SetCapacity(capacity);
    }
    this._array[this._tail] = obj;
    this._tail = (this._tail + 1) % this._array.Length;
    this._size++;
    this._version++;
}
```

Clear Operation in the Queue

The Clear method of the Queue class resets all the existing items stored in the _array with its default value, and it sets the _size, _head, and _tail of the Queue class with zero. The Clear method does not remove all the items stored in the _array but resets them with the default values. The implementation of the Clear method is demonstrated in Listing 11-24.

Listing 11-24. The Implementation of the Clear Method of the Queue Class

```
public virtual void Clear()
{
    /*.........*/
    Array.Clear(
        this._array,   /* The original array which to reset */
        _head, ,       /* The starting index from where the reset will start */
        this._size,    /* Total number of item to reset*/
        );
    /*.........*/
    this._head = 0;
    this._tail = 0;
    this._size = 0;
    this._version++;
    this._size = 0; , /* Set the size of the Queue as 0 which makes the Count,
                       * property as 0 as the Count property is return
                       * this._size; */
    this._version++;
}
```

Queue Class Members

This section will explore the different fields, constructors, and members used in the Queue.

Fields

Table 11-16 lists the different fields the Queue class uses internally to implement queue functionality.

Table 11-16. Queue Internal Fields Used to Maintain the Size of the Queue

Field	Description
_array	Holds the entire item for the Queue class
_head	Holds the position of the Queue head
_tail	Holds the position of the Queue tail
_size	Holds the number of cells being used from the Queue class

Constructors

The Queue class has four overloaded constructors to initialize an instance of the Queue class. Table 11-17 lists the four constructors that can be used to instantiate the Queue class.

Table 11-17. Public Constructors of the Queue Class

Constructor	Description
Queue()	Initializes a new instance of the Queue class with the default initial capacity 32 and uses the default growth factor 2.0 `Queue terrestrialPlanets = new Queue();`

Queue(ICollection c)	Initializes a new instance of the Queue class that contains elements copied from the specified collection
	`Queue terrestrialPlanets = new Queue(new List<string>`
	`{`
	`    "Mercury", "Venus", "Earth", "Mars"`
	`}); /* Mercury Venus    Earth   Mars */`

Queue(int capacity)	Initializes a new instance of the Queue class with the specified initial capacity and uses the default growth factor `Queue terrestrialPlanets = new Queue(10);`
Queue(int capacity, float growFactor)	Uses capacity and growth factor to initialize itself

Properties

Table 11-18 lists the different properties of the Queue class.

Table 11-18. Public Properties of the Queue Class

Property	Description
Count	Returns the number of elements contained in the Queue `var totalItems = terrestrialPlanets.Count; /* 4 */`
IsSynchonized	Determines whether access to the Queue is synchronized
SyncRoot	Returns an object that can be used to synchronize access to the Queue

Methods

The Queue class has different methods that can be used to do different operations. Table 11-19 lists the different methods used in the Queue class.

Table 11-19. Public Methods of the Queue Class

Method	Description
Clear	public virtual void Clear() Removes all elements from the Queue terrestrialPlanets.Clear(); var totalItems = terrestrialPlanets.Count; /* 0 */
Clone	public virtual object Clone() Creates and returns a shallow copy of the Queue
Contains	public virtual bool Contains(object item) Determines whether an element is in the Queue var contains = terrestrialPlanets.Contains("Mercury"); /* true */
CopyTo	public virtual void CopyTo(Array a, int index) Copies the entire Queue to an existing one-dimensional Array, starting at the specified array index string[] copyTo = new string[] { string.Empty, string.Empty, string.Empty, string.Empty, }; terrestrialPlanets.CopyTo(copyTo, 0); /* Mercury Venus Earth Mars */
Dequeue	public virtual object Dequeue() Removes and returns the object at the beginning of the Queue var aItem = terrestrialPlanets.Dequeue(); /* Mercury */
Enqueue	public virtual void Enqueue(object obj) Adds an object to the end of the Queue terrestrialPlanets.Enqueue("Mercury");
Equals	public virtual bool Equals(object obj) Determines whether two Object instances are equal
GetEnumerator	public virtual IEnumerator GetEnumerator() Returns an IEnumerator for the Queue
GetHashCode	public virtual int GetHashCode() Serves as a hash function for a particular type, suitable for use in hashing algorithms and data structures, such as a hash table; returns a hash code for the current Object
GetType	public Type GetType() Gets the type of the current instance
Peek	public virtual object Peek() Returns the object at the beginning of the Queue without removing it var aItem = terrestrialPlanets.Peek(); /* Mercury */
Synchonized	public static Queue Synchonized(Queue q) Returns a synchronized wrapper for the Queue
ToArray	public virtual object [] ToArray() Copies the elements of the Queue to a new array
ToString	public virtual string ToString() Returns a string that represents the current Object
TrimToSize	public virtual void TrimToSize() Sets the capacity to the actual number of elements in the Queue

Hashtable

A Hashtable class consists of the buckets array, which contains the elements of the collection. A bucket is a virtual subgroup of elements within the Hashtable, which makes searching and retrieving easier and faster than in most collections. The Hashtable in .NET represents a collection of key and value pairs that are organized based on the hash code of the key. A *hash function* is an algorithm that returns a numeric hash code based on a key. A hash function must always return the same hash code for the same key, and it also could generate the same hash code for two different keys (collision). But a hash function that generates a unique hash code for each unique key results in better performance when retrieving elements from the hash table.

Size of the Hashtable in .NET

The initial size of the Hashtable is three (the first prime number as shown in Table 11-20), and it will resize to accommodate more items using one of the values shown in Table 11-20 to resize the buckets array.

Table 11-20. List of the Prime Numbers Used in the Hashtable Class

Prime numbers used in the Hashtable class					
3	7	11	0x11	0x17	0x1d
0x25	0x2f	0x3b	0x47	0x59	0x6b
0x83	0xa3	0xc5	0xef	0x125	0x161
0x1af	0x209	0x277	0x2f9	0x397	0x44f
0x52f	0x63d	0x78b	0x91d	0xaf1	0xd2b
0xfd1	0x12fd	0x16cf	0x1b65	0x20e3	0x2777
0x2f6f	0x38ff	0x446f	0x521f	0x628d	0x7655
0x8e01	0xaa6b	0xcc89	0xf583	0x126a7	0x1619b
0x1a857	0x1fd3b	0x26315	0x2dd67	0x3701b	0x42023
0x4f361	0x5f0ed	0x72125	0x88e31	0xa443b	0xc51eb
0xec8c1	0x11bdbf	0x154a3f	0x198c4f	0x1ea867	0x24ca19
0x2c25c1	0x34fa1b	0x3f928f	0x4c4987	0x5b8b6f	0x6dda89

The CLR initializes its default size with the three from the primes array as shown in Table 11-20 and progressively adds the next prime number from the primes array to expand the size to accommodate more items. Otherwise, the CLR generates a new prime number manually to resize the Hashtable.

Hashtable Declaration

The Hashtable class is defined in the System.Collections namespace of the mscorlib.dll (C:\Windows\ Microsoft.NET\ Framework\v4.0.30319) assembly in .NET, as shown in Figure 11-22.

Figure 11-22. *Hashtable class in the System.Collections namespace*

The signature of the Hashtable class is:

```
public class Hashtable :
                IDictionary, ICollection, IEnumerable, ISerializable,
                IDeserializationCallback, ICloneable
```

An example of the Hashtable is shown in Listing 11-25.

Listing 11-25. *Example of the Hashtable Class*

```csharp
using System;
using System.Collections;

namespace Ch11
{
    class Program
    {
        static void Main(string[] args)
        {
            Hashtable terrestrialPlanets = new Hashtable();
            terrestrialPlanets.Add("Mercury",
                                "The innermost of the eight planets.");
            terrestrialPlanets.Add("Venus",
                                "The second planet from the Sun.");
            terrestrialPlanets.Add("Earth",
                                "The third planet from the Sun.");
            terrestrialPlanets.Add("Mars",
                                "The fourth planet from the Sun.");
            terrestrialPlanets.Add("Vesta",
                        "One of the largest asteroids in the Solar System.");

            Console.WriteLine(
                "Mercury\t{0}\nVenus\t{1}\nEarth\t{2}\nMars\t{3}\nVesta\t{4}",
                terrestrialPlanets["Mercury"],
                terrestrialPlanets["Venus"],
                terrestrialPlanets["Earth"],
```

```
                terrestrialPlanets["Mars"],
                terrestrialPlanets["Vesta"]);
        }
    }
}
```

This program will produce the output:

```
Mercury                 The innermost of the eight planets.
Venus                   The second planet from the Sun.
Earth                   The third planet from the Sun.
Mars                    The fourth planet from the Sun.
Vesta                   One of the largest asteroids in the Solar System.
```

Instantiation of the Hashtable

The Hashtable comes to life when you call one of the following 15 overloaded constructors:

```
public Hashtable()                                                      {}
public Hashtable(bool trash)                                            {}
public Hashtable(IDictionary d)                                         {}
public Hashtable(IEqualityComparer equalityComparer)                    {}
public Hashtable(int capacity)                                          {}
public Hashtable(IDictionary d, IEqualityComparer equalityComparer)     {}
public Hashtable(IDictionary d, float loadFactor)                       {}
public Hashtable(IHashCodeProvider hcp, IComparer comparer)             {}
public Hashtable(int capacity, IEqualityComparer equalityComparer)      {}
public Hashtable(IDictionary d, IHashCodeProvider hcp,
                                            IComparer comparer){}
public Hashtable(IDictionary d, float loadFactor, IEqualityComparer
                                            equalityComparer){}
public Hashtable(int capacity, IHashCodeProvider hcp,
                                            IComparer comparer){}
public Hashtable(int capacity, float loadFactor, IEqualityComparer
                                            equalityComparer){}
public Hashtable(IDictionary d, float loadFactor, IHashCodeProvider hcp,
                                    IComparer comparer) {}
public Hashtable(int capacity, float loadFactor, IHashCodeProvider hcp,
                                    IComparer comparer){}
```

When the CLR executes the first version of the Hashtable constructor, it initializes the internal array buckets with the default size of three. In the Add operation, the CLR checks whether or not the item can be store in the buckets array by checking the current number of the elements in the Hashtable or otherwise increasing the size of the Hashtable to accommodate the new item in it.

Addition Operation in the Hashtable

When you add a new item into the Hashtable, CLR calculates the hash code for the associated key of the given item by calling the InitHash method:

```
/* num3 refers to the Hashcode of the key of the given item */
uint num3 = this.InitHash(key, this.buckets.Length, out num, out num2);
```

The InitHash method calculates the hash code for the key of the given item. The implementation of the InitHash method would be:

```
/*incr hold the value for the num2*/
private uint InitHash(object key, int hashsize, out uint seed, out uint incr)
{
    uint num = (uint) (this.GetHash(key) & 0x7fffffff);
    seed = num;
    incr = 1 + ((uint) (((seed * 0x65) + 1) % (hashsize - 1)));
    return num;
}
```

The CLR uses the num3 variable (contains hash code) to generate the slot index (referring to the position of the buckets array where the item will be added) of the buckets table where it stores the item (buckets is a one-dimensional array, with each of the cells referred to as a slot of the buckets). Each of the items of the buckets array contains a bucket, which is defined as a type of struct, as shown in Listing 11-26.

Listing 11-26. The Implementation of the Bucket Struct Used in the Hashtable Class

```
private struct bucket
{
    public int        hash_coll; /* To hold the Hash code of the Key */
    public object     key;       /* To store the Key */
    public object     val;       /* To store the associated value of the Key*/
}
```

The slot index will be calculated using the hash code of the given key and the current length of the buckets array:

```
/* num6 refers to the slot index of the buckets table. */
int num6 = (int) (num % this.buckets.Length);
```

The CLR uses this slot index as the position of the buckets table to add an item to the buckets table. After calculating the slot index, the CLR tries to add the item to the buckets based on three conditions: no collision, collision, and duplication checking. The next sections will explore each of these in detail.

No Collision While Adding an Item to the Hashtable

The CLR looks for the free slot in the buckets using the slot index (num6) to see whether it is already taken or if there is any duplicate key. If there is no collision, CLR adds the key and value into an instance of the bucket stored in the buckets array at the position referred by the slot index (num6), as shows in this implementation:

```
/* To check whether the item in the position of slot index (num6) of the
 * buckets array contains any key or not by checking the bucket, return
 * from the buckets array at position num6, holds null for the Key field */
if ((this.buckets[num6].key == null) ||
    ((this.buckets[num6].key == this.buckets) &&
    ((this.buckets[num6].hash_coll & 0x80000000L) == 0L)))
{
    if (index != -1)
```

```
    {
        num6 = index;
    }
    Thread.BeginCriticalRegion();
    this.isWriterInProgress = true;

   /* Stores the value of the item into buckets array at the position of the
    * slot index num6 calculated earlier */
    this.buckets[num6].val = nvalue;

   /* Stores the key of the item into buckets array at the at the position of
    * the slot index num6 calculated earlier */
    this.buckets[num6].key = key;

    /* num3 refers the hash code generated from the Key */
    this.buckets[num6].hash_coll |= (int) num3;

    /* Increase the count which refers the total number of items stored in
     * the buckets array.*/
    this.count++;
    this.UpdateVersion();
    this.isWriterInProgress = false;
    Thread.EndCriticalRegion();
}
```

As a result, the CLR adds the item at the slot index position (num6) of the buckets array.

Collision While Adding an Item to the Hashtable

If the slot at the position of the index (num6) from the buckets is already taken, CLR regenerates the slot index using the old slot index (so the value of the num6 will be regenerated). It also modifies the hash_coll value for the item stored at the position of the old generated slot index (num6) in the buckets array by doing the (OR operation) for the old hash_coll value:

```
/* Updates the hashcoll value by doing the OR */
this.buckets[num6].hash_coll    |= -2147483648;
```

This newly computed slot index (num6-regenerated) is used to check whether the buckets has a free slot at that position. If the CLR finds any free slot in the buckets, then it adds the given item to that slot or otherwise repeatedly looks for an available slot in the buckets. The implementation for this would be:

```
{
    if ((index == -1) && (this.buckets[num6].hash_coll >= 0))
    {
        /* Change the old slot item's hash code value */
        this.buckets[num6].hash_coll |= -2147483648;
        this.occupancy++;
    }

    /* Generates new slot index and stores into num6. num2 refers in the
     * InitHash method discussed earlier */
```

```
        num6 = (int) ((num6 + num2) % ((ulong) this.buckets.Length));
        if (++num4 < this.buckets.Length)
        {
            /* Go to the code block in where CLR will check for the availability
             * of the empty slot */
        }
    }
}
```

When you try to add more items into the Hashtable but the total items in the Hashtable begins to exceeds the limit of the size of the Hashtable, the buckets size has to expand (the current buckets size is three and the program tries to add more, as shown in Listing 11-25). The CLR uses the next prime number (for example, 7) from the primes array and calls the rehash method to redistribute the existing items from the old buckets into new expanded buckets with new slot indexes calculated based on the new buckets length and hash code value for each of the existing keys stored in the buckets array. In this phase, CLR replaces all the negative hash_coll values (when the index has been taken CLR updates the hash_coll of that item, as discussed earlier) by doing the OR by 0x7fffffff, which rolls back the previous hash_coll value for that item:

```
bucket.hash_coll & 0x7fffffff
```

Duplicate Item While Adding to the Hashtable

When the CLR adds an item to the Hashtable, if there is any duplicate key found, the CLR throws an exception, because Hashtable does not allow a duplicate key. Figure 11-23 demonstrates the execution of the Add operation the CLR does in the Hashtable.

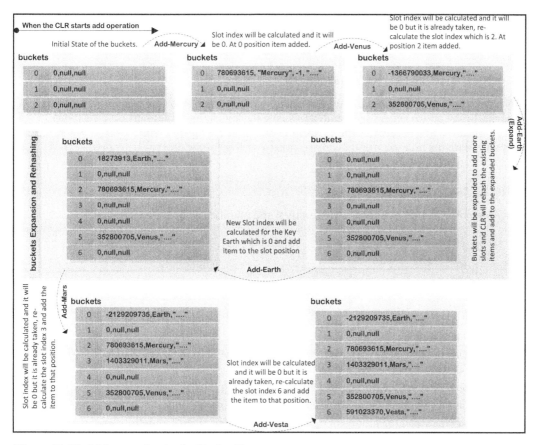

Figure 11-23. Add operation in the Hashtable.

From Figure 11-23, you can see that:

- The CLR initializes the buckets size with default value three and each of the buckets in the buckets is initialized with its default value. For instance, bucket struct has int of hash_coll, object of key, and val, so it is initialized as {0, null, null} for each of the buckets in the buckets.

- The first item, Mercury, is added to the buckets array at position 0 as the index 0 has been calculated.

- In the iteration of the Venus addition, the CLR generated the slot index 0 for Venus, but it is already taken by Mercury. So a new slot index is generated, which is 2, and the item Venus has been added at position 2 of the buckets array. In addition, the hash_coll value for the index 0 has been ORed by 0x7fffffff, and this ORed value will be rolled back on the buckets expansion and rehashing time.

- When CLR tries to add Earth into the Hashtable, it finds that it needs to expand the existing buckets. It expands the buckets, rehashes the existing items, and adds all the existing items into the buckets with updated slot index information. The new slot index is calculated again based on the new buckets to add the Earth item.

- Based on this addition rule, `Mars` and `Vesta` items are added to the buckets of the Hashtable.

Deletion Operation in the Hashtable

When you try to remove any item stored in the `Hashtable` based on its key, the CLR calculates the hash code and uses this hash code to generate the index to locate the key in the buckets array. If the index contains the key you are trying to remove, the CLR sets the key and `val` for that item stored at that position of the buckets array with the null value and decreases the `count` field of the `Hashtable` by one.

Hashtable Class Members

This section will explore the different fields, constructors, and members used in the `Hashtable`.

Properties

Table 11-21 lists the different properties of the `Hashtable` class.

Table 11-21. Public Properties of the Hashtable Class

Property	Description
Count	Gets the number of key-and-value pairs contained in the Hashtable `var totalItems = terrestrialPlanets.Count; /* 5 */`
IsFixedSize	Gets a value indicating whether the Hashtable has a fixed size
IsReadOnly	Gets a value indicating whether the Hashtable is read-only
IsSynchronized	Gets a value indicating whether access to the Hashtable is synchronized (thread-safe)
Item	Gets or sets the value associated with the specified key (in C#, this property is the indexer for the Hashtable class)
Keys	Gets an ICollection containing the keys in the Hashtable
SyncRoot	Gets an Object that can be used to synchronize access to the Hashtable
Values	Gets an ICollection containing the values in the Hashtable

Methods

The `Hashtable` class has different methods that can be used to do different operations. Table 11-22 lists the different methods of the `Hashtable` class.

Table 11-22. Public Methods of the Hashtable Class

Method	Description
Add	Adds an element with the specified key and value into the Hashtable `terrestrialPlanets.Add("Mercury", "The innermost of the eight planets.");`

Clear	Removes all elements from the Hashtable.
	`terrestrialPlanets.Clear();`
	`var totalItems = terrestrialPlanets.Count; /* 0 */`

Method	Description
Clone	Creates a shallow copy of the Hashtable
Contains	Determines whether the Hashtable contains a specific key `var isContainMercury = terrestrialPlanets.Contains("Mercury"); /* true */`
ContainsKey	Determines whether the Hashtable contains a specific key `var isKeyMercury = terrestrialPlanets.ContainsKey("Mercury"); /* true */`

ContainsValue	Determines whether the Hashtable contains a specific value
	`var valueExists = terrestrialPlanets.ContainsValue("The fourth planet from the Sun.");`
	`/* true */`

CopyTo	Copies the Hashtable elements to a one-dimensional Array instance at the specified index
	`string[] copyTo = new string[]`
	`{`
	`        string.Empty, string.Empty, string.Empty, string.Empty, string.Empty,`
	`};`
	`terrestrialPlanets.Keys.CopyTo(copyTo, 0);`
	`/* copyTo: Venus Mars Vesta Mercury Earth */`
	`terrestrialPlanets.Values.CopyTo(copyTo, 0);`
	`/* copyTo:`
	`* The second planet from the Sun.`
	`* The fourth planet from the Sun.`
	`* One of the largest asteroids in the Solar System.`
	`* The innermost of the eight planets.`
	`* The third planet from the Sun. */`

Equals	Determines whether two Object instances are equal
GetEnumerator	Returns an IDictionaryEnumerator that can iterate through the Hashtable
GetHashCode	Gets a hash code for an object
GetObjectData	Implements the ISerializable interface and returns the data needed to serialize the Hashtable
GetType	Gets the type of the current instance

Remove	Removes the element with the specified key from the Hashtable
	`int before = terrestrialPlanets.Count; /* 5 */`
	`terrestrialPlanets.Remove("Mercury");`
	`int after = terrestrialPlanets.Count;  /* 4 */`

Synchronized	Returns a synchronized (thread-safe) wrapper for the Hashtable
ToString	Returns a String that represents the current Object

Dictionary

The Dictionary<TKey,TValue> is a generic data structure that represents a collection of Key, Value in C#. It maintains a buckets and entries table to implement the Dictionary functionality. The entries table contains an array of a struct entry to hold the key and value information, and the buckets table maintains indexes or position of the items on the basis of keys stored in the entries table. Figure 11-24 demonstrates the relationship between the buckets and entries table in the Dictionary<TKey,TValue> class.

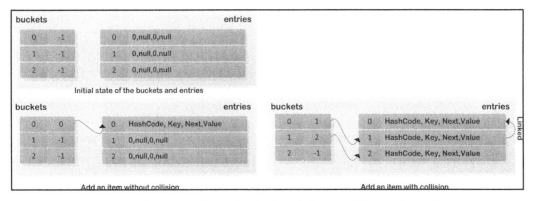

Figure 11-24. Buckets and Entries Relationship in the Dictionary<TKey, TValue> Class

Size of the Dictionary in .NET

The Dictionary<TKey, TValue> class initializes the buckets and entries table with the default size three, but the size varies to accommodate more items placed into it. The CLR uses one of the values (prime numbers) shown in Table 11-23 to resize the buckets and entries table. Otherwise, the CLR generates a prime number manually to resize the buckets and entries table.

Table 11-23. List of the Prime Numbers Used in the Dictionary Class

Prime numbers used in the Dictionary class					
3	7	11	0x11	0x17	0x1d
0x25	0x2f	0x3b	0x47	0x59	0x6b
0x83	0xa3	0xc5	0xef	0x125	0x161
0x1af	0x209	0x277	0x2f9	0x397	0x44f
0x52f	0x63d	0x78b	0x91d	0xaf1	0xd2b
0xfd1	0x12fd	0x16cf	0x1b65	0x20e3	0x2777
0x2f6f	0x38ff	0x446f	0x521f	0x628d	0x7655
0x8e01	0xaa6b	0xcc89	0xf583	0x126a7	0x1619b
0x1a857	0x1fd3b	0x26315	0x2dd67	0x3701b	0x42023
0x4f361	0x5f0ed	0x72125	0x88e31	0xa443b	0xc51eb
0xec8c1	0x11bdbf	0x154a3f	0x198c4f	0x1ea867	0x24ca19
0x2c25c1	0x34fa1b	0x3f928f	0x4c4987	0x5b8b6f	0x6dda89

Dictionary Declaration

The Dictionary<TKey, TValue> class defined in the System.Collections.Generic namespace of the mscorlib.dll assembly in .NET is demonstrated in Figure 11-25.

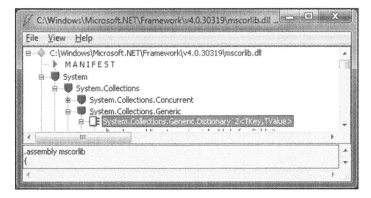

Figure 11-25. Dictionary<TKey, TValue> in the System.Collections.Generic namespace

The signature of the Dictionary<TKey, TValue> class would be:

```
public class Dictionary<TKey, TValue> :
    IDictionary<TKey, TValue>,
    ICollection<KeyValuePair<TKey, TValue>>,
    IEnumerable<KeyValuePair<TKey, TValue>>,
    IDictionary,
    ICollection,
    IEnumerable,
    ISerializable,
    IDeserializationCallback
```

Listing 11-27 presents an example of the Dictionary<TKey, TValue> class.

Listing 11-27. Example of the Dictionary<TKey,TValue> Class

```
using System;
using System.Collections.Generic;

namespace Ch11
{
    class Program
    {
        static void Main(string[] args)
        {
            IDictionary<string, string> terrestrialPlanets =
                                    new Dictionary<string, string>();

            terrestrialPlanets.Add("Mercury",
                                "The innermost of the eight planets.");
            terrestrialPlanets.Add("Venus",
                                "The second planet from the Sun.");
            terrestrialPlanets.Add("Earth",
                                "The third planet from the Sun.");
            terrestrialPlanets.Add("Mars",
                                "The fourth planet from the Sun.");
```

```
            terrestrialPlanets.Add("Vesta",
                        "One of the largest asteroids in the Solar System.");
            terrestrialPlanets.Add("Ceres",
                            "The dwarf planet in the inner Solar System.");
            terrestrialPlanets.Add("Pallas",
                            "One of the largest in the Solar System.");

            Console.WriteLine(                  "Mercury\t{0}\nVenus\t{1}\nEarth\t{2}\nMars\t{3}\
nVesta\t{4}\nCeres\t{5}\nPallas\t{6}\n",
                terrestrialPlanets["Mercury"      ],
                terrestrialPlanets["Venus"        ],
                terrestrialPlanets["Earth"        ],
                terrestrialPlanets["Mars"         ],
                terrestrialPlanets["Vesta"        ],
                terrestrialPlanets["Ceres"        ],
                terrestrialPlanets["Pallas"       ]);
        }
    }
}
```

The program in the Listing 11-27 will produce this output:

```
Mercury                 The innermost of the eight planets.
Venus                   The second planet from the Sun.
Earth                   The third planet from the Sun.
Mars                    The fourth planet from the Sun.
Vesta                   One of the largest asteroids in the Solar System.
Ceres                   The dwarf planet in the inner Solar System.
Pallas                  One of the largest in the Solar System
```

Instantiation of the Dictionary

The Dictionary<TKey, TValue> comes to life when you call one of the following six overloaded constructors:

```
public Dictionary()                                              {}
public Dictionary(IDictionary<TKey, TValue> dictionary)          {}
public Dictionary(IEqualityComparer<TKey> comparer)              {}
public Dictionary(int capacity)                                  {}
public Dictionary(IDictionary<TKey, TValue> dictionary,
                            IEqualityComparer<TKey> comparer){}
public Dictionary(int capacity, IEqualityComparer<TKey> comparer)  {}
```

When the CLR executes the constructor of the Dictionary, it initializes its internal data structure buckets and entries. The buckets table holds the indexes of the entries table, and the entries table holds the {Key, Value} information based on the index computed using the Key. The Key and Value information is stored in the entries table using the Entry struct. The implementation of the Entry struct is shown in Listing 11-28.

Listing 11-28. The Implementation of the Entry Struct Used in the Dictionary Class

```
private struct Entry
{
    public int        hashCode;    /* It holds the hash code for the Key */
    public TKey       key;         /* It holds the key of the item */
    public int        next;        /* It holds the index of an Entry from
                                     * the entries table */
    public TValue     value;       /* It holds the value of the item */
}
```

Addition Operation in the Dictionary

In the Add operation in Dictionary, the CLR first initializes two internal data structure buckets and entries. After initialization of these data structures, the CLR calculates the index of the buckets table, and in that position the entry of the buckets table points to the entries table that contains the key and values. The CLR will then add the related items in the Dictionary and store the key and values.

Bucket and Entry Initialization

When the CLR executes the Add operation in the Dictionary<TKey, TValue> for the first time, it initializes two data structures—buckets and entries—with its default value. For example, each of the items of the buckets initializes with -1 and each of the items in the entries table with its default value:

```
{
    0          /* hashCode */,
    null       /* key */,
    0          /* next item in the entry */,
    null       /* value */
}
```

Index Calculation

The CLR computes the hash code (Hc) for the given Key (Ki) using this statement:

```
/* Calculates the Hashcode */
int num = this.comparer.GetHashCode(key) & 0x7fffffff;
```

The CLR then computes the index using the Hc (num) and the length of the buckets with this statement:

```
int index = num % this.buckets.Length;   /* Calculates the index */
```

This index Ib is used to find the available free cells (which have a value -1) in the buckets table, and if it finds any, it will store the position of the item from the entries table (where the related item was stored based on the count field of the Dictionary) as an index in the buckets table at the position of the Ib.

The index Ib is used as the position of the buckets table in which to store the position of the entries table, where the Key-associated value (for which the index Ib has been computed) has been stored.

No Collision, Collision, and Duplication Checking While Adding to the Dictionary

The CLR calculates the index of the buckets to store related items during this process where some collision has occurred. The following sections explore this in greater detail.

No Collision While Adding an Item to the Dictionary

The CLR checks whether there is any free cell for the index Ib (it used it as the position number to lookup in the buckets table) in the buckets table or whether the value of that index Ib position from the buckets has already been populated, as shown in the statement:

int i = this.buckets[index];   i >= 0;   i = this.entries[i].next

The I > 0 expression indicates whether there is any item in the buckets at the position of the computed index Ib. If the result of the array look up (this.buckets[index]) is -1 (-1 has been set by the CLR to initialize the bucket of buckets table), the bucket (cell) at that index position has not yet been used. Therefore, -1 means the related bucket cell has been initialized but not yet used. The CLR will use this cell to store the position of the item (associate item with the Key for which the Ib is computed) in the entries table (based on the freeList field of the Dictionary class uses as the position).

The CLR uses the current count (freeList uses the value of the count) of the Dictionary class as the position (which is 0 for the Key Mercury int as shown in Listing 11-27) to store the item in the entries table:

```
/* freeList holds the value of the count of the  Dictionary */
this.entries[freeList].hashCode = num;
/* The value of buckets at position index Ib stores into the next  to do the
 * linked with collide data*/
this.entries[freeList].next        = this.buckets[index];
this.entries[freeList].key         = key;
this.entries[freeList].value       = value;
/* Update the value of the buckets at position of the computed index Ib with
 * the current count (freeList) value. So now the entries and buckets holding
 * the same index for the Key */
this.buckets[index]          = freeList;
```

The CLR also increases the count of the Dictionary class by one, and it will be used later as the position of the entries table to add the next item to the Dictionary.

Each of the items in the buckets table has the index information, which refers back to an index of the entries table where items associated with keys have been stored.

Collision and Duplication Checking While Adding an Item to the Dictionary

If the return value of the array look up (buckets[index]) is greater than -1, that means the cell of the buckets is being occupied. Therefore, there is an entry in the entries table, and the array look up return value refers to the position of the entries table in which an entry can be found. This is referred to as a *collision*. To resolve the collision, the CLR will first iterate through the entry (Ec) stored in the entries table at the position that stored (as value) the index Ib in the buckets table. It then checks whether the hash code of the Key is stored in the entry Ec item in the entries table and whether or not the related hash code for the current key (associated with the item to add) is the same. If it is the same, CLR throws the exception about this duplication.

Collision While Adding an Item to the Dictionary

If there is any collision for the given item (Gi), the CLR will then get the current count value of the Dictionary class via the freeList variable and add the item Gi at that position (freeList) into the entries table as an entry. For the next field of this entry, the CLR puts the entry located in the entries table at the position of the result of buckets[index], as shown in the code:

```
/* It adds the index of the entry from the entries table at position of
 * the result of the buckets[index] into the next field of the current
 * entry item stored in the entries table at position of the freeList*/
this.entries[freeList].next = this.buckets[index];
```

The CLR then updates the information stored in the current index Ib position of the buckets table with the value of the current freeList, which is the latest place where the current item Gi has been stored in the entries table:

```
/* It updates the information stored in the buckets at position of index (Ib)
 * with the current freeList which is the latest count value. */
this.buckets[index] = freeList;
```

As a result, this ensures the buckets are stored with the right mapping indexes for all items in the entries table. Figure 11-26 demonstrates the Add operation in the Dictionary<TKey,TValue>.

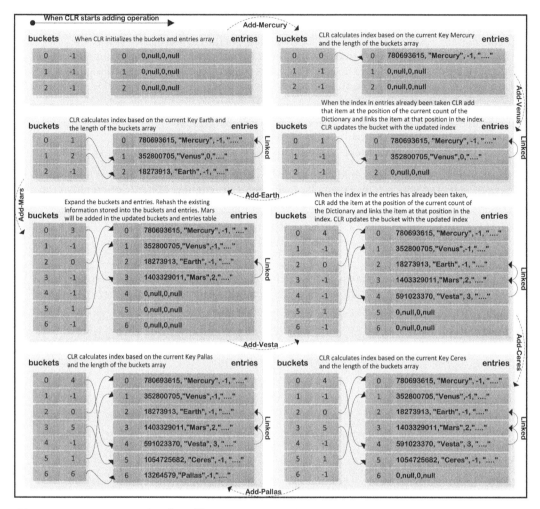

Figure 11-26. *CLR executing the Add operation in runtime*

From Figure 11-26, you can see what the CLR does to add items in the Dictionary:

- The CLR initializes the buckets data with -1 and {0, null, 0, null} for each of the items in the entries table.

- When the CLR tries to add the key Mercury, it calculates the index to use to look up the buckets and check availability of that cell to store the index information of the entries table for the Mercury item. The Mercury-associated item will be stored in the entries table at position 0 and also stored at position 0 in the buckets array of the index.

- When the CLR tries to add Venus, it will calculate the index position, which is position 0, but it has already been taken by the Mercury entry. Therefore, the CLR will increase the current count field of the Dictionary, which then becomes position 1, and adds the Venus information at that position of the count of the Dictionary in the entries array and also links the item at position 0 with it (resolve collisions). The CLR stores the index information in the buckets table at position 0 with this updated new position information in the entries table. The item at position 0 in the buckets table will now be 1 instead of 0.

- When the CLR tries to add the Mars key in the Dictionary, it finds that it needs to expand the buckets and entries array. So after expansion, the CLR rehashs the existing item and mapping information stored in the buckets and entries tables. It will recalculate the index based on the Mars key and update the length of the buckets array. Finally, it adds Mars to the right position in the entries array and updates the mapping information at the buckets array.

- These same steps are repeat to add other items in the array.

Dictionary Look Up

The CLR follows several steps when it looks for an item based on the Key in the Dictionary. First, it accesses the index property to look up the Dictionary by providing the Key. It calls the FindEntry method where it will check whether or not the buckets is null. It will then compute the hash code for the given key (num) and compute the index to look up the buckets table using the hash code and the length of the buckets:

num % this.buckets.Length

The return value of the bucket [num % this.buckets.Length] will be the related index of the entries table used to find the key to match. Using the value returned from the bucket [num % this.buckets.Length] statement, CLR loops through until it is > = 0; if it is not > 0, then it is -1, which means there is no other associated entry with this entry. As we learned in the initialization, when there is no item in the buckets, the default value is -1, as shown in the implementation of the Dictionary look up based on the Key in Listing 11-29.

Listing 11-29. The Implementation of the FindEntry Method of the Dictionary Class

```
private int FindEntry(TKey key)
{
    if (this.buckets != null)
    {
        int num = this.comparer.GetHashCode(key) & 0x7fffffff;
        for (int i = this.buckets[num % this.buckets.Length]; i >= 0;
                                    i = this.entries[i].next)
        {
            if ((this.entries[i].hashCode == num) &&
                this.comparer.Equals(this.entries[i].key, key))
            {
                return i;
            }
        }
    }
    return -1;
}
```

In this iteration, it will check whether the item from the entries has the same hash code and key as the look up Key, and if so the CLR stops iteration and returns the value of i, which refers to the index of the entries table. Using this position value, CLR returns an Entry from the entries table, with the implementation of the Index property as shown in Listing 11-30.

Listing 11-30. The Implementation of the Index of the Dictionary<TKey, TValue> Class

```
public TValue this[TKey key]
{
    get
    {
        int index = this.FindEntry(key);
        if (index >= 0)
        {
            return this.entries[index].value;
        }

        return default(TValue);
    }
    set {.....}
}
```

Dictionary Class Members

The Dictionary<TKey, TValue> class provides methods for creating, manipulating, and searching Keys and Values of items. The sections that follow explore the different fields, constructors, and members used in the Dictionary class.

Properties

Table 11-24 lists the different properties of the Dictionary class.

Table 11-24. Public Properties of the Dictionary Class

Property	Description
IsFixedSize	When implemented by a class, gets a value indicating whether the IDictionary has a fixed size
IsReadOnly	When implemented by a class, gets a value indicating whether the IDictionary is read-only

Item	When implemented by a class, gets or sets the element with the specified key. In C#, this property is the indexer for the IDictionary class.
	`var item = terrestrialPlanets["Mercury"];`
	`/* The innermost of the eight planets. */`

Keys	When implemented by a class, gets an ICollection containing the keys of the IDictionary
Values	When implemented by a class, gets an ICollection containing the values in the IDictionary
Comparer	Gets the IEqualityComparer<T> that is used to determine equality of keys for the Dictionary
Count	Gets the number of key/value pairs contained in the Dictionary<TKey, TValue>

Methods

The Dictionary class has different methods that can be used to do different operations. Table 11-25 lists the different methods of the Dictionary class.

Table 11-25. Public Methods of the Dictionary Class

Method	Description
Add	When implemented by a class, adds an element with the provided key and value to the IDictionary `terrestrialPlanets.Add("Mercury", "The innermost of the eight planets.");`

Clear	When implemented by a class, removes all elements from the IDictionary
	`var before = terrestrialPlanets.Count; /* 7 */`
	`terrestrialPlanets.Clear();`
	`var after = terrestrialPlanets.Count;  /* 0 */`

Contains	When implemented by a class, determines whether the IDictionary contains an element with the specified key
	`var itemExists = terrestrialPlanets.Contains(`
	`    new KeyValuePair<string,string>("Mercury","The innermost of the eight planets."));`
	`/* true*/`

GetEnumerator	When implemented by a class, returns an IDictionaryEnumerator for the IDictionary
Remove	When implemented by a class, removes the element with the specified key from the IDictionary `var status = terrestrialPlanets.Remove("Mercury"); /* true */`
ContainsKey	Determines whether the Dictionary<TKey, TValue> contains the specified key
ContainsValue	Determines whether the Dictionary<TKey, TValue> contains a specific value
TryGetValue	Gets the value associated with the specified key

Summary

In this chapter, we have learned about the different collection types in .NET, such as Array, List, ArrayList, Stack, Queue, Hashtable, and Dictionary. You have learned how each of these classes dynamically ensures the capacity to accommodate required amounts of data, and you have learned how these classes have been implemented internally by using the array. In the next chapter, you will explore in depth the Linq in C#.

CHAPTER 12

Linq in C#

This chapter will discuss the Language Integrated Query (Linq) in .NET and explore in detail the extension methods defined in the Enumerable class that are provided to do the Linq operation using C#. First, you will learn the basics of Linq and then examine the behind-the-scenes operations of each of the extension methods provided in the Enumerable class. Based on their delegate-based query syntax, you will learn the internal implementation of these extension methods using the help of ildasm.exe and .NET Reflector tool.

First Look into Linq in .NET

In .NET, any data structure that implements IEnumerable<T> from the System.Collections.Generic namespace of the mscorlib.dll assembly is able to access all the extension methods defined in the Enumerable class of the System.Linq namespace of the System.Core.dll assembly. I should mention before you dive into this that the delegate-based Linq query operators are defined in the Enumerable class of the System.Core.dll assembly, and a complete list of these operators is shown in Table 12-1. An example is provided in the following code, where the series has three items:

```
List<string> series = new List<string>(){"One", "Two", "Three"};
```

You can use the Where method to filter the list or Select to project into the output. Because List<T> type implements the IEnumerable interface and Where and Select extension method defined in the Enumerable class, it is the type IEnumerable<T>. For example, the Where extension method is a type of IEnumerable<TSource> as shows in the following code:

```
public static IEnumerable<TSource> Where<TSource>(
    this IEnumerable<TSource> source, Func<TSource, bool> predicate)
```

Any type that implements IEnumerable<T> is able to use the extension methods defined in the Enumerable class. For example, List<T> class implements IEnumerable<T> as the signature of the List<T> class as shown in the code:

```
public class List<T> :
    IList<T>,ICollection<T>,IEnumerable<T>,IList,ICollection,IEnumerable
```

The Enumerable class is a static noninheritable class. The definition of the Enumerable class is demonstrated in the code:

```
.class public abstract auto ansi sealed beforefieldinit
    System.Linq.Enumerable extends [mscorlib]System.Object
```

It is defined in the System.Linq namespace of the System.Core.dll assembly, as shown in Figure 12-1.

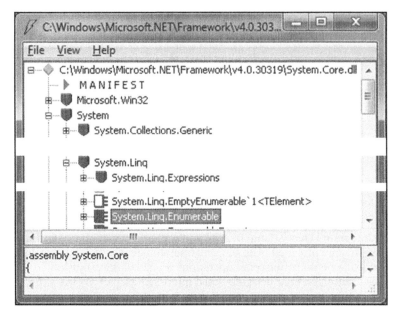

Figure 12-1. *System.Linq.Enumberable class in the System.Linq*

The static `Enumerable` class is a container for the different extension method types of `IEnumerable<T>`, for example:

```
public static bool Contains<TSource>(
    this IEnumerable<TSource> source, TSource value)                    {}
public static int Count<TSource>(this IEnumerable<TSource> source)      {}
public static IEnumerable<TSource> Distinct<TSource>(
    this IEnumerable<TSource> source, IEqualityComparer<TSource> comparer){}
  /* and many more */
```

Extension Method

The extension method is the heart of the delegate-based Linq query operation. You can find more detail about the extension method in Chapter 4.

Lambda Expressions and Expression Trees in Linq

In .NET, Linq query methods (referring to those extension methods that are defined in the `Enumerable` class) allow you to perform different operations, such as, filtering, projection, key extraction, or grouping, over a sequence of items. In query operation, you can use the concept of the lambda expression in place of these functions (i.e., filtering, projecting), which will provide a convenient way to write functions that can be passed as arguments for subsequent evaluation. Lambda expression is a kind of CLR-delegated function, and it must encapsulate a method that is defined by a delegate type. Lambda expressions are similar to CLR delegates, and they must adhere to a method signature defined by a delegate type. For example:

```
string expressionName = "Lambda Expression";
Func<string, int> filter = item => item.Length >3;
```

We can use this filter lambda in the Where method, for example:

```
/* To filter the string in expressionName variable */
expressionName.Where(filter);
```

You could also write this:

```
expressionName.Where( item => item.Length >3 );
```

In general, you are free to use named methods, anonymous methods, or lambda expressions with query methods. Lambda expressions have the advantage of providing the most direct and compact syntax for authoring. Linq also allows you to use Expression<T> (defined in the System.Expresion namespace of the System.core.dll assembly) to define the lambda expression. When you use this Expression<T> to create a lambda expression, the C# compiler generates an expression tree for the lambda expression rather than defining the method body. An example of the expression tree using Expression<T> would be:

```
Expression<Predicate<int>> expression = n => n < 10;
```

In compile time, the C# compiler would determine whether to emit an IL instruction or an expression tree, depending on the usage of the lambda expression in the query operator. The compiler determines whether to generate an expression tree or the method based for the query methods using the following basic rules:

- When a lambda expression is assigned to a variable, field, or parameter whose type is a delegate, the compiler emits IL that is identical to that of an anonymous method.

- When a lambda expression is assigned to a variable, field, or parameter whose type is Expression<T>, the compiler emits an expression tree instead.

This chapter will explore the Linq query methods that can be used for delegate-based method.

Deferred Execution in Linq

Deferred execution is a pattern of the execution model by which the CLR ensures a value will be extracted only when it is required from the IEnumerable<T>-based information source. When any Linq operator uses the deferred execution, the CLR encapsulates the related information, such as the original sequence, predicate, or selector (if any), into an iterator, which will be used when the information is extracted from the original sequence using ToList method or ForEach method or manually using the underlying GetEnumerator and MoveNext methods in C#. Figure 12-2 demonstrates the deferred execution in Linq.

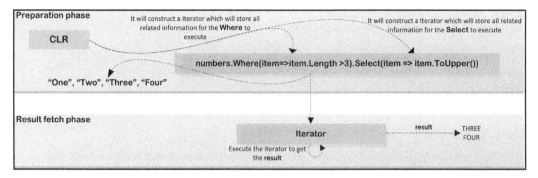

Figure 12-2. *Example of the Deferred Execution*

For example, as you can see in Figure 12-2, in order to extract data from the sequence numbers the CLR prepares related information for an Iterator object, and in the result fetch phase it will actually execute the iterator to get data from the sequence using the predicate and/or selector, which was encapsulated in the preparation phase.

In C#, the deferred execution is supported by directly using the yield keyword within the related iterator block. Table 12-1 lists the iterators in C# that use the yield keyword to ensure the deferred execution.

Table 12-1. *Iterators in Linq*

Method	Iterator	Class Definition
Cast	CastIterator	private sealed class <ConcatIterator>d__71<TSource>
Concat	ConcatIterator	private sealed class <ConcatIterator>d__71<TSource>
DefaultIfEmpty	DefaultIfEmptyIterator	private sealed class <DefaultIfEmptyIterator>d__a5<TSource>
Distinct	DistinctIterator	private sealed class <DistinctIterator>d__81<TSource>
Except	ExceptIterator	private sealed class <ExceptIterator>d__99<TSource>
GroupJoin	GroupJoinIterator	private sealed class <GroupJoinIterator>d__6a<TOuter, TInner, TKey, TResult>
Intersect	IntersectIterator	private sealed class <IntersectIterator>d__92<TSource>
Join	JoinIterator	private sealed class <JoinIterator>d__61<TOuter, TInner, TKey, TResult>
OfType	OfTypeIterator	private sealed class <OfTypeIterator>d__aa<TResult>
Range	RangeIterator	private sealed class <RangeIterator>d__b8
Repeat	RepeatIterator	private sealed class <RepeatIterator>d__bc<TResult>
Reverse	ReverseIterator	private sealed class <ReverseIterator>d__a0<TSource>
Select	SelectIterator	private sealed class <SelectIterator>d__7<TSource, TResult>
SelectMany	SelectManyIterator	private sealed class <SelectManyIterator>d__14<TSource, TResult>
Skip	SkipIterator	private sealed class <SkipIterator>d__4d<TSource>
SkipWhile	SkipWhileIterator	private sealed class <SkipWhileIterator>d__52<TSource>

Method	Iterator	Class Definition
Take	TakeIterator	private sealed class <TakeIterator>d__3a<TSource>
TakeWhile	TakeWhileIterator	private sealed class <TakeWhileIterator>d__40<TSource>
Union	UnionIterator	private sealed class <UnionIterator>d__88<TSource>
Where	WhereIterator	private sealed class <WhereIterator>d__0<TSource>
Zip	ZipIterator	private sealed class <ZipIterator>d__7a<TFirst, TSecond, TResult>

Query Methods in Linq

Here we will examine the behind-the-scenes operation of the Linq query methods that implement delegate-based syntax. All the query methods have categories, as shown in Table 12-2, which summarizes all the extension methods and their associated categories.

Table 12-2. Linq Query Methods Classification

Category	Extension Methods
Filtering- and projection-based methods	Where Select
Partitioning-based methods	Skip SkipWhile Take TakeWhile
Concatenation methods	Concat
Ordering methods	ThenBy Reverse
Grouping- and joining-based methods	Join GroupJoin GroupBy
Set-based methods	Distinct Except Union Intersect Sum LongCount
Aggregation-based methods	Max Min Count Average Aggregate
Quantifiers-based methods	All Any Contains

Category	Extension Methods
Element-based methods	First
	FirstOrDefault
	Last
	LastOrDefault
	Single
	SingleOrDefault
	ElementAt
	ElementAtOrDefault
	DefaultIfEmpty
Generation-based methods	Empty
	Range
	Repeat
Conversion-based methods	Cast
	ToArray
	OfType
	ToDictionary
	ToList
	ToLookup
Miscellaneous methods	Zip

Filtering- and Projection-Based Methods

The filtering method Where and the projection method Select will be explored in this section.

Where and Select

The Where and Select are two of the common extension methods of the IEnumerable<TSource> to filter and project data of a list or sequence. The list works with these two extension methods and are needed to implement IEnumerable<T>. The signature of the Where and Select extensions would be:

```
public static IEnumerable<TSource> Where<TSource>(
    this IEnumerable<TSource> source, Func<TSource, bool> predicate)
public static IEnumerable<TSource> Where<TSource>(
    this IEnumerable<TSource> source, Func<TSource, int, bool> predicate)
```

Listing 12-1 demonstrates the use of the Where and Select extension methods.

Listing 12-1. Example of Where and Select Clause

```
using System;
using System.Collections;
using System.Collections.Generic;
using System.Linq;

namespace Ch12
{
    class Program
    {
        static void Main(string[] args)
```

```
    {
        IList<string> numbers = new List<string>()
        {
            "One", "Two", "Three", "Four", "Five", "Six", "Seven"
        };

        var numbersLengthThree =
            numbers.Where(x => x.Length == 3).Select(x => x).ToList();

        numbersLengthThree.ForEach(x => Console.WriteLine(x));
    }
  }
}
```

Listing 12-1 creates a sequence of strings and stores them in numbers, which is a type of IList<string>, and then filters those items from the numbers whose total number of characters is equal to three and projects the results into a new list numbersLengthThree. Using the ForEach method, it iterates through the new list and displays the output on the console. The output of Listing 12-1 would be:

```
One
Two
Six
```

Internal Operation of the Where and Select Execution

Let's analyze the code in Listing 12-1 carefully to really understand how the CLR handles the Where and Select extension method while executing the program. Focus on the following line from Listing 12-1 to see how CLR handles it:

```
numbers.Where(x => x.Length == 3).Select(x => x).ToList()
```

This line of code is used to filter and project data from the numbers sequence. Figure 12-3 demonstrates the Where and Select extension method based on Listing 12-1.

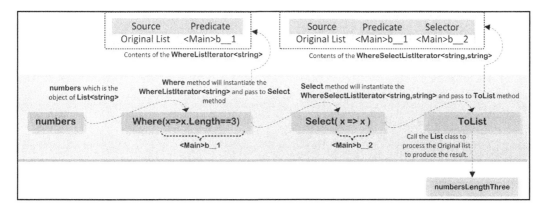

Figure 12-3. How the Where and Select extension methods work

From Figure 12-3, you can see that:

- The CLR passes the numbers sequence as input to the Where method along with an instance of the MulticastDelegate, which holds the information about the <Main>b__1 method compiled by the C# compiler for an anonymous method block (x=>x.Length == 3) in the compile time.

- The Where method returns an instance of the WhereListIterator<string> iterator, which is then used in the Select method along with another instance of the MulticastDelegate, which holds the information about the method <Main>b__2 created from an anonymous method (x=>x) in the compile time.

- The Select method instantiates the relevant iterator based on the input enumerable; for example, the WhereSelectListIterator<string, string> iterator for the program in Listing 12-1. Until this point, CLR will not process the original list due to the deferred execution.

- The CLR passes this iterator instance as input to the ToList method, which finally processes the original list by iterating through the sequence using filtering criteria (<Main>b__1) to get a new list as output using the projection(<Main>b__2).

Execution of the Where Method

This section examines the steps the CLR takes when executing the Where method.

1. *Step 1*: The C# compiler compiles an anonymous method block x => x.Length == 3 from the Where method into <Main>b__1. Following the decompiled IL code the C# compiler generates for the anonymous method x => x.Length == 3:

```
.method private hidebysig static bool <Main>b__1(string x) cil managed
{
    /* Code removed */
    L_0000: ldarg.0

    /* To get the Length of the string */
    L_0001: callvirt instance int32 [mscorlib]System.String::get_Length()
    L_0006: ldc.i4.3

    /* Check the equality of the length */
    L_0007: ceq
    L_0009: stloc.0
    L_000a: br.s L_000c
    L_000c: ldloc.0
    L_000d: ret
}
```

The equivalent C# code would be:

```
private static bool <Main>b__1(string x)
{
    return (x.Length == 3);
}
```

The CLR instantiates an instance of the `MulticastDelegate` using the method `<Main>b__1` that will be used as the delegate to filter items from the sequence. In the compile time, the C# compiler also created another method, `<Main>b__2`, for the `(x=>x)`, as demonstrated in the following IL code:

```
.method private hidebysig static string <Main>b__2(string x) cil managed
{
    /* Code removed */
    L_0000: ldarg.0
    L_0001: stloc.0
    L_0002: br.s L_0004
    L_0004: ldloc.0
    L_0005: ret
}
```

Or with the equivalent C# code:

```
private static string <Main>b__2(string x)
{
    return x;
}
```

The CLR used `<Main>b__2` to instantiate another instance of the `MulticastDelegate`, and it will be used as the projector to project items from the filtered sequence.

2. *Step 2*: When the CLR starts execution of the program in Listing 12-1, it starts execution of the `Where` method. It passes the original sequence numbers and instance of `MulticastDelegate` (created in step 1) as input, as demonstrated in the following decompiled IL code of the `Main` method from Listing 12-1:

```
.method private hidebysig static void Main(string[] args) cil managed
{
    .entrypoint
    .maxstack 4
    .locals init (
        [0] class [mscorlib]System.Collections.Generic.IList'1<string> numbers
        /* Code removed */)
    L_0000: nop

    /* Step 1: Created List<string> object for the numbers */
    L_0001: newobj instance void
            [mscorlib]System.Collections.Generic.List'1<string>::.ctor()
    /* Code removed */
    L_005c: stloc.0

    /* Step 2: Load the numbers variable into the evaluation stack */
    L_005d: ldloc.0
    L_005e: ldsfld class
            [mscorlib]System.Func'2<string, bool>  /*Field type */
            Ch12.Program::CS$<>9__CachedAnonymousMethodDelegate4
    L_0063: brtrue.s L_0078
    L_0065: ldnull
    L_0066: ldftn bool Ch12.Program::<Main>b__1(string)
```

```
L_006c: newobj instance void
        [mscorlib]System.Func'2<string, bool>::.ctor(object, native int)

L_0071: stsfld class
        [mscorlib]System.Func'2<string, bool>
        /* It is holding the <Main>b__1 now */
        Ch12.Program::CS$<>9__CachedAnonymousMethodDelegate4

L_0076: br.s L_0078
L_0078: ldsfld class
        [mscorlib]System.Func'2<string, bool>
        Ch12.Program::CS$<>9__CachedAnonymousMethodDelegate4

/* Step 3: CLR will call the Where extension by passing numbers retrieved
 * into the evaluation stack at L_005c and the delegate object of
 * System.Func'2<string, bool> (inherited from MulticastDelegate)
 * at L_0078 */
L_007d: call
        /* return type of the Where */
        class [mscorlib]System.Collections.Generic.IEnumerable'1<!!0>
        [System.Core]System.Linq.Enumerable::Where<string>(
            /* First parameter type, CLR will pass value for this */
            class [mscorlib]System.Collections.Generic.IEnumerable'1<!!0>,
            /* Second parameter type CLR will pass value for this   */
            class [mscorlib]System.Func'2<!!0, bool>
        )
/* Code removed */
}
```

3. *Step 3*: Based on the data type of the numbers, the Where method returns the appropriate iterator instance as output. The implementation of the Where method to return an appropriate iterator is demonstrated in Listing 12-2.

Listing 12-2. *The Implementation of the Where Method*

```
public static IEnumerable<TSource> Where<TSource>(
    this IEnumerable<TSource> source, Func<TSource, bool> predicate)
{
    if (source is Iterator<TSource>)
        return ((Iterator<TSource>) source).Where(predicate);
    if (source is TSource[])
        return new WhereArrayIterator<TSource>((TSource[]) source, predicate);
    if (source is List<TSource>)
        return new WhereListIterator<TSource>(
                (List<TSource>) source, predicate);
    return new WhereEnumerableIterator<TSource>(source, predicate);
}

public static IEnumerable<TSource> Where<TSource>(
    this IEnumerable<TSource> source, Func<TSource, int, bool> predicate)
{
```

```
    return WhereIterator<TSource>(source, predicate);
}
```

You can find the complete list of iterator classes used by the different extension methods in the Linq in the System.Core.dll assembly. Figure 12-4 shows the iterator used for the Where method.

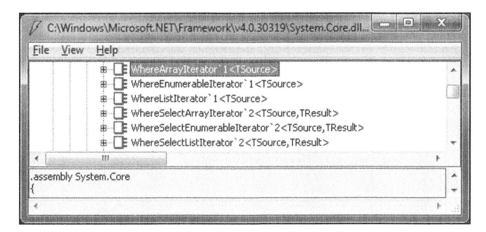

Figure 12-4. Iterator classes used in the Enumerable class of the System.Core.dll assembly

For example, the CLR returns the WhereListIterator<TSource> iterator from the Where method, which contains the original list as the source sequence and <Main> b__1 as the predicate. The CLR passes this WhereListIterator<TSource> as input to the Select method.

Execution of the Select Method

While executing the Select method, the CLR instantiates the relevant iterator based on the input of the IEnumerable object and the selector delegate. For the program in Listing 12-1, the CLR will return an instance of the WhereSelectListIterator<TSource,TResult> as output from the Select method. The implementation of the Select method to return an appropriate iterator is demonstrated in Listing 12-3.

Listing 12-3. Implementation Code for the Select Method

```
public static IEnumerable<TResult> Select<TSource, TResult>(
    this IEnumerable<TSource> source, Func<TSource, TResult> selector)
{
    if (source is Iterator<TSource>)
        return ((Iterator<TSource>) source).Select<TResult>(selector);
    if (source is TSource[])
        return new WhereSelectArrayIterator<TSource, TResult>(
            (TSource[]) source, null, selector);
    if (source is List<TSource>)
        return new WhereSelectListIterator<TSource, TResult>(
            (List<TSource>) source, null, selector);

    return new WhereSelectEnumerableIterator<TSource, TResult>(source, null, selector);
}
```

```
public static IEnumerable<TResult> Select<TSource, TResult>(
    this IEnumerable<TSource> source, Func<TSource, int, TResult> selector)
{
    return SelectIterator<TSource, TResult>(source, selector);
}
```

The iterator returned by the Select method contains the original list, the predicate delegate (<Main>b__1), and the selector or projector delegate (<Main>b__2).

4. *Step 4*: The CLR will not process the sequence until the program calls the ToList method or uses the ForEach method due to the deferred execution. The CLR passes this WhereSelectListIterator<string,string> iterator instance as input to the ToList method. In the ToList method, the CLR instantiates an instance of the List<string> by passing the WhereSelectListIterator<string,string> iterator as input to it.

5. *Step 5*: The CLR iterates through the enumerator to get the item from the input parameter collection (WhereSelectListIterator<string,string>) and applies the filtering criteria on it and adds the result into a dynamic _items array (a field of the List<TSource> class). This list object is returned as a result for the original list. The implementation of the List<TSource> constructor is demonstrated in the new list instantiation process for the Where and Select methods, as shown in Listing 12-4.

Listing 12-4. Constructor of the List<TSource>

```
public list(ienumerable<t> collection)
{
    /* copy the original list into is2 */
    icollection<t> is2 = collection as icollection<t>;
    if (is2 != null)
    {
        int count = is2.count;

        /* Initialize the _items using number of item in the original list.*/
        this._items = new t[count];
        is2.copyto(this._items, 0);
        this._size = count;
    }
    else
    {
        this._size = 0;
        this._items = new t[4];
        using (ienumerator<t> enumerator = collection.getenumerator())
        {
            /* iterate through each of the item from the sequence and execute
             * the filtering function Predicate over that item if it returns
             * true then that item will be add to the new list. */
            while (enumerator.movenext())
            {
            /* This add method internally work as dynamic array by making
             * sure the size of the array using EnsureCapacity method
```

```
        * (See Chapter 11 for the more about the
        * EnsureCapacity method).*/
        this.add(enumerator.current);
        }
      }
    }
  }
}
```

You have explored in detail the Where and Select extension method to filter and project data from a sequence. The following section will examine the partition-based extension methods of the Linq that can be used to manipulate the sequence.

Partitioning-Based Methods

This section will explore the partitioning-based methods, such as Skip, SkipWhile, Take, and TakeWhile.

Skip

The Skip method is used to bypass a specified number of elements from a sequence and then return the remaining elements as output. Due to the deferred execution, the immediate return value is an object of the relevant iterator type that stores all the information that is required to perform the skip operation. The Skip method iterates through the list and skips the specified number of items from the beginning of the list. The specified number is provided as a parameter of this method. The signature of the Skip extension method is:

```
public static IEnumerable<TSource> Skip<TSource>(this IEnumerable<TSource> source, int count)
```

The program in Listing 12-5 creates a sequence of strings into the numbers that holds One, Two, Three, Four, and Five as items of this sequence.

Listing 12-5. Example of the Skip Method

```
using System;
using System.Collections;
using System.Collections.Generic;
using System.Linq;

namespace Ch12
{
    class Program
    {
        static void Main(string[] args)
        {
            IList<string> numbers = new List<string>()
            {
                "One","Two","Three", "Four","Five"
            };

            var result = numbers.Skip(2);
            result.ToList().ForEach(number => Console.WriteLine(number));
        }
```

```
        }
}
```

The program in Listing 12-5 will produce the output:

```
Three
Four
Five
```

Internal Operation of the Skip Method of Execution

Let's look at how the CLR executes the `numbers.Skip(2)` from the code in Listing 12-5.

1. *Step 1*: The CLR returns the `SkipIterator<TSource>` (which holds the original list and the count to define the number of items to skip) from the `Skip` method.

2. *Step 2*: Due to the deferred execution pattern, this `SkipIterator<TSource>` is executed by the CLR while, for example, iterating the sequence used for the `ToList` method, as shown in Listing 12-5. Inside the `SkipIterator<TSource>`, the CLR runs a loop and it continues until the number of items to skip becomes zero. During this iteration, the CLR moves the current position of the inner Enumerator object. When the number of items becomes zero, it loops through the list again to return the remaining items from the original sequence as output, as demonstrated in Listing 12-6.

Listing 12-6. Implementation Code for the Skip Method

```
private static IEnumerable<TSource> SkipIterator<TSource>(
    IEnumerable<TSource> source,
    int count)
{
    using (IEnumerator<TSource> iteratorVariable0 = source.GetEnumerator())
    {
        /* Skip items from the begin of the list as long as count > 0 */
        /* Outer loop */
        while ((count > 0) && iteratorVariable0.MoveNext())
            count--;
        /* As soon as count becomes 0 CLR returns the rest of the item
         * as output. */
        if (count <= 0)
        {
            /* The CLR will start iterating the original list from the point
             * the CLR left from the outer loop */
            /* Inner loop */
            while (iteratorVariable0.MoveNext())
                yield return iteratorVariable0.Current;
        }
    }
}
```

SkipWhile

The SkipWhile extension method bypasses elements from the sequence as long as a specified condition is true and it returns the remaining elements as output. The signature of this extension method is:

```
public static IEnumerable<TSource> SkipWhile<TSource>(
    this IEnumerable<TSource> source, Func<TSource, bool> predicate)
public static IEnumerable<TSource> SkipWhile<TSource>(
    this IEnumerable<TSource> source, Func<TSource, int, bool> predicate)
```

An example of the use of the SkipWhile method is provided in Listing 12-7.

Listing 12-7. *Example of the SkipWhile Method*

```csharp
using System;
using System.Collections;
using System.Collections.Generic;
using System.Linq;

namespace Ch12
{
    class Program
    {
        static void Main(string[] args)
        {
            IList<string> numbers = new List<string>()
            {
                "One","Two","Three", "Four","Five"
            };

            var result = numbers.SkipWhile(number => number.Length == 3);
            result.ToList().ForEach(number => Console.WriteLine(number));
        }
    }
}
```

The program in Listing 12-7 will produce the output:

```
Three
Four
Five
```

Internal Operation of the SkipWhile Method of Execution

The output shows that the SkipWhile method excluded those items whose length is equal to three in the output sequence. Let's analyze the code in Listing 12-7 in detail to understand what's happening when the CLR executes the SkipWhile method.

1.   *Step 1*: The C# compiler constructs a method <Main>b__1 using the anonymous method (number => number.Length == 3) in the compile time. The CLR will instantiate an instance of MulticastDelegate using the <Main>b__1 method as a predicate to the SkipWhile. The CLR instantiates an instance of the SkipWhileIterator iterator using the original list and the predicate <Main>b__1.

Due to the deferred execution, the SkipWhileIterator will not execute until the CLR calls the ToList or uses the ForEach method to iterate through.

2. *Step 2*: The CLR executes the ToList method over the SkipWhileIterator return from the SkipWhile method, and inside the SkipWhileIterator, the CLR loops through the original list one by one and executes the predicate over each of the items. If the predicate returns false, then the SkipWhileIterator returns that item as a result of the SkipWhile method; or if it returns true, then it continues through the list until it finishes. The implementation of the SkipWhileIterator used by the CLR at runtime is shown in Listing 12-8.

Listing 12-8. Implementation Code of the SkipWhileIterator

```
private static IEnumerable<TSource> SkipWhileIterator<TSource>(
    IEnumerable<TSource> source,
    Func<TSource, bool> predicate)
{
    bool iteratorVariable0 = false;
    foreach (TSource iteratorVariable1 in source)
    {
        if (!iteratorVariable0 && !predicate(iteratorVariable1))
            iteratorVariable0 = true;

        if (iteratorVariable0)
            yield return iteratorVariable1;
    }
}
```

Take

The Take method is used to return the specified number of elements from the list. An example of the Take method is shown in Listing 12-9.

Listing 12-9. Example of the Take Method

```
using System;
using System.Collections.Generic;
using System.Linq;
using System.Text;

namespace Ch12
{
    class Program
    {
        static void Main(string[] args)
        {
            IList<int> series = new List<int>()
            {
                1,2,3,4,5,6,7
            };
```

```
        series.Take(4)
            .ToList()
            .ForEach(number =>
                    Console.Write(string.Format("{0}\t",number)));
        }
    }
}
```

This program will produce the output:

1   2   3   4

It will return the TakeIterator, which will encapsulate the original list and the count that holds the number of elements to take. This will execute as soon as the ToList or Foreach method is executed by the iterator.

TakeWhile

The TakeWhile method is used to extract those items from a sequence that meet a provided condition. Listing 12-10 shows the use of the TakeWhile method.

Listing 12-10. Example of the TakeWhile Method

```
using System;
using System.Collections.Generic;
using System.Linq;
using System.Text;

namespace Ch12
{
    class Program
    {
        static void Main(string[] args)
        {
            IList<int> series = new List<int>()
            {
                1,2,3,4,5,6,7
            };
            Console.WriteLine("When the condition is true");
            series.TakeWhile(number => number < 3)
                .ToList()
                .ForEach(number => Console.Write(string.Format("{0}\t",
                                                        number)));

            Console.WriteLine("\nOn first false return iteration will stop ");
            series.TakeWhile(number => number > 3)
                .ToList()
                .ForEach(number => Console.Write(string.Format("{0}\t",
                                                        number)));
        }
    }
}
```

This program produced the output:

```
When the condition is true
1       2
On first false return iteration will stop
```

Internal Operation of the TakeWhile Method of Execution

The TakeWhile method will return TakeWhileIterator with the original list and the predicate and it will pass this iterator to the List class while executing the ToList method over it. ToList will create a new List and in the List constructor it will loop through the iterator, which is TakeWhileIterator. It will return the items from the original list based on several steps. As long as the condition is true for the item in the list, it will continue down the list to take the item from it. But with the first occurrence of a false return from the predicate, the CLR will stop iterating the original list to take the item and return with whatever it has found so far (i.e., whatever items from the list meet the condition and only those). The code for implementing this would be:

```
private static IEnumerable<TSource> TakeWhileIterator<TSource>(
    IEnumerable<TSource> source,
    Func<TSource, bool> predicate)
{
    foreach (TSource iteratorVariable0 in source)
    {
        /* While the predicate return false for a item from the original list it will break the
iteration*/
        if (!predicate(iteratorVariable0))
        {
            break;
        }
        /* Otherwise return that item from the original list */
        yield return iteratorVariable0;
    }
}
```

Concatenation Methods

This section discusses the operations of the Concat method in detail.

Concat

The Concat extension method concatenates two sequences into one sequence. This method differs from the Union method because the Concat<TSource> returns all the original elements in the input sequences regardless of the duplicates, whereas the Union method returns only unique elements from the sequences. The signature for this extension method would be:

```
public static IEnumerable<TSource> Concat<TSource>(
    this IEnumerable<TSource> first, IEnumerable<TSource> second)
```

The program in Listing 12-11 demonstrates the Concat method.

Listing 12-11. Example of the Concat Method

```csharp
using System;
using System.Collections;
using System.Collections.Generic;
using System.Linq;

namespace Ch12
{
    class Program
    {
        static void Main(string[] args)
        {
            IList<int> listOne = new List<int>()
            {
                1,2,3,4,5,6
            };

            IList<int> listTwo = new List<int>()
            {
                6,7,8,9,10
            };

            var result = listOne.Concat(listTwo).ToList();
            result.ForEach(x => Console.Write(string.Format("{0}\t",x)));
        }
    }
}
```

The program in Listing 12-11 will produced the output:

```
1       2       3       4       5       6       6       7       8       9
10
```

Internal Operation of the Concat Method of Execution

The CLR concatenates items from the sequence listOne and listTwo into a new sequence that holds all the items, for example, { 1,2,3,4,5,6,6,7,8,9,10 }, with duplicated values. Figure 12-5 demonstrates how the Concat method works internally.

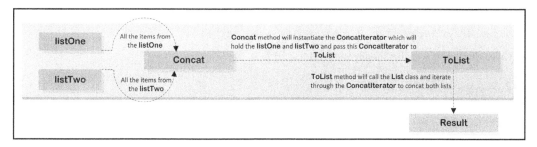

Figure 12-5. How the Concat extension method works

Figure 12-5 shows that the CLR passes the listOne and listTwo sequences as input to the Concat method and returns an instance of ConcatIterator<int> as output to the caller. Due to the deferred execution pattern used by the Concat method, the ToList method iterates through the items from the sequence and ConcatIterator<int> Concat listOne and listTwo sequences based on concatenate logic to produce the final output sequence. Let's analyze the code in Listing 12-11 to help explain what's happening when the CLR executes the Concat method.

1. *Step 1*: The CLR passes the original lists listOne and listTwo to the Concat<TSource> method as input.

2. *Step 2*: In the Concat method, the CLR instantiates the ConcatIterator<int> iterator, which holds the listOne and listTwo and returns to the caller of the Concat method. The implementation of the Concat method would be:

```
public static IEnumerable<TSource> Concat<TSource>(
    this IEnumerable<TSource> first,
    IEnumerable<TSource> second)
{
    return ConcatIterator<TSource>(first, second);
}
```

3. *Step 3*: The ToList method loops through the lists, such as listOne and listTwo, via the Enumerator object returned from the ConcatIterator<int> instance and inserts each of the items from listOne and listTwo into a new list and returns this new list as a result of the Concat extension.

Ordering Methods

This section will explore the ThenBy and Reverse ordering methods.

ThenBy

The ThenBy method performs a subsequent ordering of the elements in a sequence in ascending order. Because it follows the deferred execution pattern in ThenBy, the immediate return value is an object of the relevant type that stores all the information, such as the original list, key selector, and so forth. The signature of the ThenBy extension method is:

```
public static IOrderedEnumerable<TSource> ThenBy<TSource, TKey>(
    this IOrderedEnumerable<TSource> source, Func<TSource, TKey> keySelector)
public static IOrderedEnumerable<TSource> ThenBy<TSource, TKey>(
    this IOrderedEnumerable<TSource> source,
    Func<TSource, TKey> keySelector, IComparer<TKey> comparer)
```

Listing 12-12 demonstrates the ThenBy method.

Listing 12-12. Example of the ThenBy Extension Method

```
using System;
using System.Collections;
using System.Collections.Generic;
using System.Linq;
```

```csharp
namespace Ch12
{
    class Program
    {
        static void Main(string[] args)
        {
            IList<Person> persons = new List<Person>()
            {
                new Person(){ Name="Person F", Address= "Address of F",
                            Id= 111116},
                new Person(){ Name="Person G", Address= "Address of G",
                            Id= 111117},
                new Person(){ Name="Person C", Address= "Address of C",
                            Id= 111113},
                new Person(){ Name="Person B", Address= "Address of B",
                            Id= 111112},
                new Person(){ Name="Person D", Address= "Address of D",
                            Id= 111114},
                new Person(){ Name="Person A", Address= "Address of A",
                            Id= 111111},
                new Person(){ Name="Person E", Address= "Address of E",
                            Id= 111115}
            };

            var result =
                persons.OrderBy(person => person.Id).ThenBy(person => person);

            foreach (Person person in result)
            {
                Console.WriteLine("{0,-15} {1,-20}{2,-20}",
                    person.Name,
                    person.Address,
                    person.Id);
            }
        }
    }

    public class Person
    {
        public string Name
        {
            get;
            set;
        }

        public string Address
        {
            get;
            set;
        }
```

```
        public double Id
        {
            get;
            set;
        }
    }
}
```

This program produced the output:

```
Person A        Address of A        111111
Person B        Address of B        111112
Person C        Address of C        111113
Person D        Address of D        111114
Person E        Address of E        111115
Person F        Address of F        111116
Person G        Address of G        111117
```

Internal Operation of the ThenBy Method of Execution

This method works as demonstrates in the steps that follow.

1. *Step 1*: It will call the CreateOrderedEnumerable method, as shown in Listing 12-13.

Listing 12-13. *Implementation of the ThenBy Method*

```
public static IOrderedEnumerable<TSource> ThenBy<TSource, TKey>(
    this IOrderedEnumerable<TSource> source,
    Func<TSource, TKey> keySelector)
{
    return source.CreateOrderedEnumerable<TKey>(keySelector, null, false);
}
```

2. *Step 2*: CreateOrderedEnumerable method instantiates an instance of the OrderedEnumerable, as shown in Listing 12-14.

Listing 12-14. *Implementation of the CreateOrderedEnumerable Method*

```
IOrderedEnumerable<TElement> IOrderedEnumerable<TElement>.CreateOrderedEnumerable<TKey>(
    Func<TElement, TKey> keySelector,
    IComparer<TKey> comparer,
    bool descending)
{
    return new OrderedEnumerable<TElement, TKey>(
        this.source,
        keySelector,
        comparer, descending)
    { parent = (OrderedEnumerable<TElement>) this };
}
```

3. *Step 3*: The OrderedEnumerable class is implemented, as shown in Listing 12-15.

Listing 12-15. Implementation for the OrderedEnumerable Class

```
internal class OrderedEnumerable<TElement, TKey> : OrderedEnumerable<TElement>
{
    /* Code removed*/
    internal OrderedEnumerable(
        IEnumerable<TElement> source,
        Func<TElement, TKey> keySelector,
        IComparer<TKey> comparer, bool descending)    {  /*Code removed*/ }

    internal override EnumerableSorter<TElement> GetEnumerableSorter(
        EnumerableSorter<TElement> next)
    {
        EnumerableSorter<TElement> enumerableSorter = new
            EnumerableSorter<TElement, TKey>(
                this.keySelector,
                this.comparer,
                this.descending, next);
        if (this.parent != null)
        {
            enumerableSorter =
                    this.parent.GetEnumerableSorter(enumerableSorter);
        }
        return enumerableSorter;
    }
}
```

Reverse

The Reverse method inverts the order of the elements in a sequence. This method follows the deferred execution pattern. Unlike OrderBy, this sorting method does not consider the actual values themselves in determining the order. Rather, it just returns the elements in the reverse order from which they are produced by the underlying source. The signature of the Reverse extension method is:

```
public static IEnumerable<TSource> Reverse<TSource>(this IEnumerable<TSource> source)
```

In the example provided in Listing 12-16, the Reverse method reverses the original sequence.

Listing 12-16. Example of the Reverse Method

```
using System;
using System.Collections.Generic;
using System.Linq;

namespace Ch12
{
    class Program
    {
        static void Main(string[] args)
        {
            IList<int> numbers = new List<int>() { 1, 2, 3, 4, 5 };
```

```
            var reverseNumbers = numbers.Reverse();

            var result = reverseNumbers.ToList();

            result.ForEach(x => Console.Write("{0}\t", x));
            Console.WriteLine();
        }
    }
}
```

The program in Listing 12-16 will produce the output:

```
5       4       3       2       1
```

Internal Operation of the Reverse Method of Execution

Let's analyze the code in Listing 12-16 carefully to really understand what's happening when the CLR executes the Reverse method.

1. *Step 1*: The CLR will pass the original sequence, in this case the numbers, as input to the Reverse method and it instantiates an instance of the ReverseIterator<TSource>, which holds the related information to execute by the ToList or ForEach method.

2. *Step 2*: The CLR will pass the ReverseIterator<TSource> instance to the ToList method, which passes this iterator to the List class and processes the operation based on the iteration logic implemented in the ReverseIterator<TSource>. Finally, this method produces the reversed sequence as output, as shown in Listing 12-17.

Listing 12-17. Implementation of the ReverseIterator<TSource>

```
private static IEnumerable<TSource> ReverseIterator<TSource>(
    IEnumerable<TSource> source)
{
    /* Copy the original list into this Buffer instance. Buffer is a struct
     * which hold input list into a internal array. */
    Buffer<TSource> iteratorVariable0 = new Buffer<TSource>(source);

    /* index will hold the last index of the buffer */
    int index = iteratorVariable0.count - 1;

    while (true)
    {
        if (index < 0)
            yield break;

        /* So the item at the last index from internal array of the Buffer
         * will be return and index will be decremented as long as the
         * while loop continue. */
        yield return iteratorVariable0.items[index];
```

```
            index--;
        }
    }
}
```

The Buffer struct has the definition:

```
.class private sequential ansi sealed beforefieldinit Buffer<TElement>
    extends [mscorlib]System.ValueType
{

    .method assembly hidebysig specialname rtspecialname instance void
        .ctor(class
            [mscorlib]System.Collections.Generic.IEnumerable'1<!TElement>
            source) cil managed                    { /* Code removed */ }

    .method assembly hidebysig instance !TElement[] ToArray() cil managed
                                                   { /* Code removed  */ }
    .field assembly int32 count

    /* items array will hold the data from the sequence*/
    .field assembly !TElement[] items
}
```

Grouping- and Joining-Based Methods

This section will examine different grouping- and joining-based methods, such as Join, GroupJoin, and GroupBy.

Join

The Join operator is used to merge two sequences into one based on the joining condition. Figure 12-6 demonstrates the Join operation.

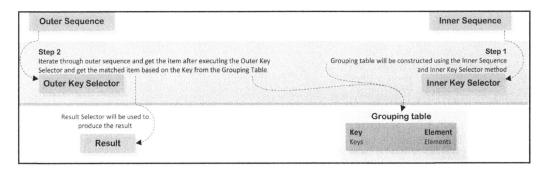

Figure 12-6. Join basic operation

The Join operation works through the following steps:

1. *Step 1*: It constructs a grouping table using the inner sequence and inner key selector.

2. *Step 2*: It will iterate through the outer sequence and match with the grouping table to determine the matched item, and the matched item will then be passed to the result selector to processed the matched item and store it in the list of <>f__AnonymousType0<string,string> type. The type <>f_ AnonymousType0<string,string> is constructed based on the anonymous type passed into the result selector.

The signature of the Join operator is:

```
public static IEnumerable<TResult> Join<TOuter, TInner, TKey, TResult>(
    this IEnumerable<TOuter> outer, IEnumerable<TInner> inner,
    Func<TOuter, TKey> outerKeySelector, Func<TInner, TKey> innerKeySelector,
    Func<TOuter, TInner, TResult> resultSelector)

public static IEnumerable<TResult> Join<TOuter, TInner, TKey, TResult>(
    this IEnumerable<TOuter> outer, IEnumerable<TInner> inner,
    Func<TOuter, TKey> outerKeySelector, Func<TInner, TKey> innerKeySelector,
    Func<TOuter, TInner, TResult> resultSelector, IEqualityComparer<TKey> comparer
)
```

An example of the Join operation is presented in Listing 12-18.

Listing 12-18. Implementation of the Join Operation

```
using System;
using System.Collections.Generic;
using System.Linq;

namespace Ch12
{
    class Program
    {
        static void Main(string[] args)
        {
            List<Person> persons;
            List<Address> addresses;

            InitializeData(out persons, out addresses);

            /* persons - Outer Sequence */
            var result = persons.Join(
                /*addresses - Inner Sequence*/
                addresses,
                /* Outer Key Selector */
                person => person,
                /* Inner Key Selector */
                address => address.AddressOf,
                /* Result Selector */
```

```
            (person, address) =>
                new
                {
                    PersonName = person.PersonName,
                    AddressDetails = address.AddressDetails
                }
            );

        result.ToList().
            ForEach(personAddress =>
                Console.WriteLine("{0} \t{1}",
                personAddress.PersonName, personAddress.AddressDetails));
    }

    private static void InitializeData(
        out List<Person> persons, out List<Address> addresses)
    {
        var personA = new Person
            { PersonID = "PA_01", PersonName = "A" };
        var personB = new Person
            { PersonID = "PB_01", PersonName = "B" };
        var personC = new Person
            { PersonID = "PC_01", PersonName = "C" };

        var addressOne = new Address
            { AddressOf = personA,
              AddressDetails = "Mystery Street,Jupiter" };
        var addressTwo = new Address
            { AddressOf = personA, AddressDetails = "Dark Street,Mars" };
        var addressThree = new Address
            { AddressOf = personB, AddressDetails = "Sun Street,Jupiter" };
        var addressFour = new Address
            { AddressOf = personC, AddressDetails = "Dry Street,Neptune" };

        persons = new List<Person>
            { personA, personB, personC };
        addresses = new List<Address>
            { addressOne, addressTwo, addressThree, addressFour };
    }
}

public class Person
{
    public string PersonID { get; set; }
    public string PersonName { get; set; }
}

public class Address
{
    public Person AddressOf { get; set; }
    public string AddressDetails { get; set; }
```

```
        }
}
```

The program in the Listing 12-18 produced the output:

```
A        Mystery Street,Jupiter
A        Dark Street,Mars
B        Sun Street,Jupiter
C        Dry Street,Neptune
```

Internal Operation of the Join Method of Execution

Let's analyze the code in Listing 12-18 to help us understand in depth what's happening while the CLR executes Join. Figure 12-7 demonstrates the inner details of the Join method.

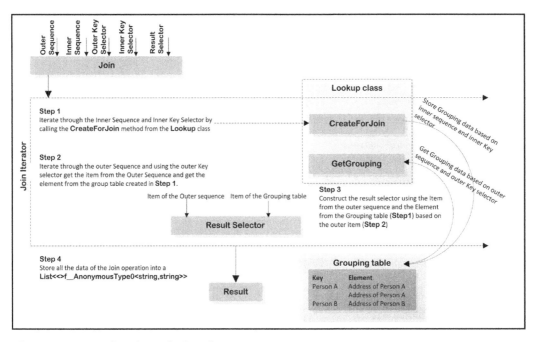

Figure 12-7. *How the Join method works*

Each of the steps illustrated in Figure 12-7 will be explored in details in the following discussion.

1. *Step 1*: The CLR passes the related data, such as outer sequence, inner sequence, key, and result selectors, into the Join method, which selects the appropriate iterator, as demonstrated in Listing 12-19.

Listing 12-19. *Implementation of the Join Method*

```
public static IEnumerable<TResult> Join<TOuter, TInner, TKey, TResult>(
    this IEnumerable<TOuter> outer,
    IEnumerable<TInner> inner,
```

```
    Func<TOuter, TKey> outerKeySelector,
    Func<TInner, TKey> innerKeySelector,
    Func<TOuter, TInner, TResult> resultSelector,
    IEqualityComparer<TKey> comparer)
{

    /* JoinIterator will be returned which holds all the necessary information
     * to   execute while enumerated either via ToList() or ForEach method*/
    return JoinIterator<TOuter, TInner, TKey, TResult>(
        outer,
        inner,
        outerKeySelector,
        innerKeySelector,
        resultSelector,
        comparer);
}
```

Listing 12-19 shows that the Join method returns the JoinIterator to the caller that encapsulates related information. The caller of the Join method will not execute the JoinIterator immediately.

2. *Step 2*: Due to the deferred execution, as soon as the caller of the Join method calls the ToList method, the CLR will start executing the JoinIterator. Listing 12-20 shows the implementation code for the JoinIterator.

Listing 12-20. Implementation of the Join Operation

```
private static IEnumerable<TResult> JoinIterator<TOuter, TInner, TKey, TResult>(
    IEnumerable<TOuter> outer,
    IEnumerable<TInner> inner,
    Func<TOuter, TKey> outerKeySelector,
    Func<TInner, TKey> innerKeySelector,
    Func<TOuter, TInner, TResult> resultSelector,
    IEqualityComparer<TKey> comparer)
{
    Lookup<TKey, TInner> iteratorVariable0 =
        Lookup<TKey, TInner>.CreateForJoin(inner, innerKeySelector, comparer);

    foreach (TOuter iteratorVariable1 in outer)
    {
        Lookup<TKey, TInner>.Grouping grouping =
            iteratorVariable0.GetGrouping(outerKeySelector(iteratorVariable1),
                                          false);

        if (grouping != null)
        {
            for (int i = 0; i < grouping.count; i++)
                yield return resultSelector(iteratorVariable1,
                                            grouping.elements[i]);
        }
    }
}
```

Listing 12-20 shows that the CLR will initialize a Lookup class using the CreateForJoin method, which holds the default initialized groupings array of Grouping type. The CLR will iterate through the original inner sequence and, based on the inner keySelector, add the iterated item into the groupings array of the Lookup class. The implementation of the CreateForJoin method is:

```
internal static Lookup<TKey, TElement> CreateForJoin(
    IEnumerable<TElement> source,
    Func<TElement, TKey> keySelector,
    IEqualityComparer<TKey> comparer)
{
    /* It will initialize an array of Grouping into the groupings
     * with the default size 7 */
    Lookup<TKey, TElement> lookup = new Lookup<TKey, TElement>(comparer);
    foreach (TElement local in source)
    {
        TKey key = keySelector(local);
        if (key != null)
        {
            /* Add the relevant key into the groupings array */
            lookup.GetGrouping(key, true).Add(local);
        }
    }
    return lookup;
}
```

3. *Step 3*: The CLR will iterate through the outer sequence and, using the outer key selector, it will get relevant items from the grouping table created for the inner sequence.

4. *Step 4*: The CLR yields the resultSelector to get the result.

GroupJoin

GroupJoin works the same as the Join operator but it produces the hierarchy output. The signature of the GroupJoin method is:

```
public static IEnumerable<TResult> GroupJoin<TOuter, TInner, TKey, TResult>(
    this IEnumerable<TOuter> outer, IEnumerable<TInner> inner,
    Func<TOuter, TKey> outerKeySelector, Func<TInner, TKey> innerKeySelector,
    Func<TOuter, IEnumerable<TInner>, TResult> resultSelector)

public static IEnumerable<TResult> GroupJoin<TOuter, TInner, TKey, TResult>(
    this IEnumerable<TOuter> outer, IEnumerable<TInner> inner,
    Func<TOuter, TKey> outerKeySelector, Func<TInner, TKey> innerKeySelector,
    Func<TOuter, IEnumerable<TInner>, TResult> resultSelector, IEqualityComparer<TKey> comparer)
```

The modified version of a Join example is used to demonstrate the use of the GroupJoin operator, as showing in Listing 12-21.

Listing 12-21. Example of the GroupJoin

```
static void Main(string[] args)
{
```

```
        List<Person> persons;
        List<Address> addresses;
        InitializeData(out persons, out addresses);

        /* persons - Outer Sequence */
        var result = persons.GroupJoin(
            /*addresses - Inner Sequence*/
            addresses,
            /* Outer Key Selector */
            person => person,
            /* Inner Key Selector */
            address => address.AddressOf,
            /* Result Selector */
            (person, address) =>
                new
                {
                    PersonName = person.PersonName,
                    AddressDetails =
                    address.Select(innerAddress=>innerAddress.AddressDetails)
                }
        );

    var rr = result.ToList();
    foreach (var item in result)
    {
        Console.WriteLine("{0}", item.PersonName);
        item.AddressDetails.ToList().ForEach(
            address => Console.WriteLine(address));
    }
}
```

It will produce the output:

```
A
Mystery Street,Jupiter
Dark Street,Mars
B
Sun Street,Jupiter
C
Dry Street,Neptune
```

GroupBy

The GroupBy method groups the elements of a sequence based on the specified key selector. This method has eight overloaded methods, and one of those is:

```
public static IEnumerable<TResult> GroupBy<TSource, TKey, TElement, TResult>(
    this IEnumerable<TSource> source, Func<TSource, TKey> keySelector,
    Func<TSource, TElement> elementSelector, Func<TKey, IEnumerable<TElement>, TResult>
resultSelector,
    IEqualityComparer<TKey> comparer)
```

An example of the GroupBy method is shown in Listing 12-22.

Listing 12-22. Example of the GroupBy Method

```
using System;
using System.Collections.Generic;
using System.Linq;

namespace Ch12
{
    class Program
    {
        static void Main(string[] args)
        {
            List<Person> persons;
            InitializeData(out persons);

            var result = persons.GroupBy(
                person => person.PersonAge,
                person => person.PersonID,
                (Age, Id) =>
                    new
                    {
                        PersonAge = Age,
                        PersonID = Id
                    }
                );

            Console.WriteLine("Age group \t No of person \t Persons are");
            result.ToList().ForEach(item =>
                Console.WriteLine(
                    string.Format("{0,5} \t {1,15} \t {2,-33}",
                        item.PersonAge,
                        item.PersonID.Count(),
                        string.Join(",", item.PersonID))));
        }

        private static void InitializeData(
            out List<Person> persons)
        {
            persons = new List<Person>
            {
                new Person { PersonID = "PA_01", PersonAge = 6 },
                new Person { PersonID = "PB_01", PersonAge = 7 },
                new Person { PersonID = "PC_01", PersonAge = 7 },
                new Person { PersonID = "PD_01", PersonAge = 4 },
                new Person { PersonID = "PE_01", PersonAge = 7 },
                new Person { PersonID = "PF_01", PersonAge = 5 },
                new Person { PersonID = "PG_01", PersonAge = 5 },
                new Person { PersonID = "PH_01", PersonAge = 9 },
                new Person { PersonID = "PI_01", PersonAge = 9 }
```

```
            };
        }
    }

    public class Person
    {
        public string PersonID { get; set; }
        public int PersonAge   { get; set; }
    }
}
```

This program will produce the output:

```
Age group       No of person    Persons are
    6                1           PA_01
    7                3           PB_01,PC_01,PE_01
    4                1           PD_01
    5                2           PF_01,PG_01
    9                2           PH_01,PI_01
```

Internal Operation of the GroupBy Method of Execution

Let's analyze Listing 12-22 to help us understand what's happening while the CLR executes the GroupBy method. Figure 12-8 demonstrates the details about the GroupBy method.

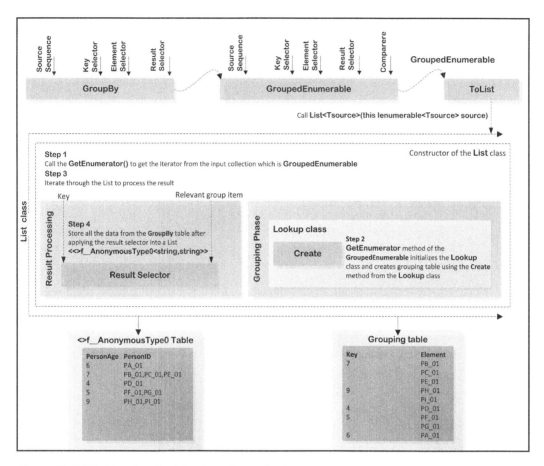

Figure 12-8. *Working details of the GroupBy method*

Each of the steps in Figure 12-8 will be explored in detail in the following discussion.

1. *Step 1*: The C# compiler will construct a method `<Main>b__1` using the anonymous method `person => person.PersonAge.Name`, `<Main>b__2` using the anonymous method `person => person.PersonID`, and `<Main>b__3` using the anonymous method as shows below,

```
(Age, Id) =>
new
{
    PersonAge = Age,
    PersonID = Id
}
```

The CLR will instantiate three instances of the `MulticastDelegate` object using the `<Main>b__1`, `<Main>b__2`, and `<Main>b__3` methods to pass this into the `GroupedEnumerable` class as input to `keySelector`, `elementSelector`, and the `resultSelector` from the `GroupBy` method:

```
public static IEnumerable<TResult> GroupBy<TSource, TKey, TElement, TResult>(
    this IEnumerable<TSource> source,
```

```
    Func<TSource, TKey> keySelector,
    Func<TSource, TElement> elementSelector,
    Func<TKey, IEnumerable<TElement>, TResult> resultSelector)
{
    return new GroupedEnumerable<TSource, TKey, TElement, TResult>(
        source,
        keySelector,
        elementSelector,
        resultSelector, null);
}
```

2. *Step 2*: While the CLR instantiates the GroupedEnumerable class in the constructor, it will initialize related data structures such as source (original sequence), keySelector, elementSelector, and resultSelector and will hold the keySelector, elementSelector, and resultSelector from the input of the constructor.

3. *Step 3*: Due to the deferred execution pattern followed by the GroupBy method, the CLR calls the ToList method, which will initialize a new list using the enumerator by calling the GetEnumerator from the GroupedEnumerable class instantiated in step 1. The implementation of the GetEnumerator method is:

```
public IEnumerator<TResult> GetEnumerator()
{
/* source              - refers the Original sequence
 * keySelector         - refers The Key selector
 * elementSelector     - refers The Element selector
 * comparer            - refers The comparer
 * ApplyResultSelector - apply the result selector to extract the result */
    return Lookup<TKey, TElement>.Create<TSource>(
        this.source,
        this.keySelector,
        this.elementSelector,
        this.comparer).
        /* Apply the result selector to extract the result */
        ApplyResultSelector<TResult>(this.resultSelector).GetEnumerator();
}
```

The GetEnumerator method shows that the Lookup class will hold the grouped result after executing the Create and ApplyResultSelector.

4. *Step 4*: Internally the Create method of the Lookup class will instantiate an instance of the Lookup class, which will initialize a data structure groupings (an array with default size 7) with the type Grouping, as shown in the partial code of the constructor of the Lookup class:

```
private Lookup(IEqualityComparer<TKey> comparer)
{
    /* Code removed */
    this.groupings = new Grouping<TKey, TElement>[7];
}
```

This `groupings` array will initially hold default values of the specified type. The CLR then iterates through the original list. Based on the `KeySelector` and `ElementSelector`, it will extract data from the original list and add these iterated items into the groupings array:

```
foreach (TSource local in source)
{
    lookup.GetGrouping(keySelector(local), true).Add(elementSelector(local));
}
```

On return of the `Create` method, the CLR will return the instance of the `Lookup` class that holds the Lookup table for the original sequence. The implementation of the code for the `Create` method in the Lookup class is:

```
internal static Lookup<TKey, TElement> Create<TSource>(
    IEnumerable<TSource> source,
    Func<TSource, TKey> keySelector,
    Func<TSource, TElement> elementSelector,
    IEqualityComparer<TKey> comparer)
{
    Lookup<TKey, TElement> lookup = new Lookup<TKey, TElement>(comparer);
    foreach (TSource local in source)
    {
        lookup.GetGrouping(keySelector(local),
                        true).Add(elementSelector(local));
    }
    return lookup;
}
```

Set-Based Methods

This section will explore the different set-based methods, such as `Distinct`, `Except`, `Union`, and `Intersect`.

Distinct

The `Distinct` method returns distinct elements from a sequence. The signature of this extension method is:

```
public static IEnumerable<TSource> Distinct<TSource>(this IEnumerable<TSource>
                                             source)
public static IEnumerable<TSource> Distinct<TSource>(this IEnumerable<TSource>
                              source, IEqualityComparer<TSource> comparer)
```

These extension methods use the default equality comparer to compare values. The first method returns distinct elements from a sequence, and the second method returns distinct elements from a sequence by using a specified `IEqualityComparer<T>` to compare values.

The `Distinct` extension method returns identical items from the list, for example, the program in Listing 12-23 determines the `Distinct` items from the sequence {1,1,1,2,2,2,3,3,3}.

Listing 12-23. Example of the Distinct Method

```
using System;
using System.Collections;
```

```
using System.Collections.Generic;
using System.Linq;

namespace Ch12
{
    class Program
    {
        static void Main(string[] args)
        {
            IList<int> numbers = new List<int>()
            {
                1,1,1,2,2,2,3,3,3
            };

            var distinctedNumbers = numbers.Distinct().ToList();
            distinctedNumbers.ForEach(x => Console.Write(string.Format("{0}\t", x)));
        }
    }
}
```

This program will produce the output:

```
1       2       3
```

Internal Operation of the Distinct Method of Execution

Let's analyze Listing 12-23 to help us understand what's happening while the CLR executes the Distinct method. Figure 12-9 demonstrates the details of the Distinct method in Linq.

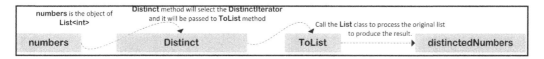

Figure 12-9. *Distinct method working details*

Each step from Figure 12-9 will be explored in further detail in the following discussion.

1. *Step 1*: The CLR will pass the original list to the Distinct method as input, which will later instantiate an instance of DistinctIterator by encapsulating the original list.

2. *Step 2*: From the ToList method, the CLR calls the List class by passing the DistinctIterator instance, instantiated in step 1, as input to it. Inside the List class, it will instantiate an instance of the Set<TSource>, which will be used for temporary sequence storage and iterates it through the DistinctIterator, as demonstrated in Listing 12-24.

Listing 12-24. *Implementation Code of the Distinct Method*

```
private static IEnumerable<TSource> DistinctIterator<TSource>(
    IEnumerable<TSource> source, IEqualityComparer<TSource> comparer)
```

```
{
    Set<TSource> iteratorVariable0 = new Set<TSource>(comparer);
    foreach (TSource iteratorVariable1 in source)
    {
        if (iteratorVariable0.Add(iteratorVariable1))
        {
            /* Only execute this line when able to add item in the Set */
            yield return iteratorVariable1;
        }
    }
}
```

While the CLR iterates through the original list, it will add the iterated item in the Set<TSource> instance it created earlier. Internally the Set<TSource> class uses the Add and Find methods to add the item from the given sequence into the internal array slots only when there is no duplicate item in the slots array.

The slots is an array of the Slot type, which is defined in the System.Linq namespace of the System.Core.dll assembly. The following code was extracted via the ildasm.exe:

```
.class sequential ansi sealed nested assembly beforefieldinit
    Slot<TElement>
    extends [mscorlib]System.ValueType
{
    .field assembly int32 hashCode
    .field assembly int32 next
    /* This field will hold the value */
    .field assembly !TElement value
}
```

When there is a duplicate item in the Set, the Add method does not add that item in the slots and it will continue until the CLR reaches the end of the list iteration and produces a list with distinct items.

Except

The Except extension method is used to remove a list of items from another list of items. It produces the set difference of two sequences. For example, if you have a list of items {1,2,3,4,5,6,7} and another one with {1,2,3}, the Except of these two list will produce {4,5,6,7}.

The signature of this extension method is:

```
public static IEnumerable<TSource> Except<TSource>(
    this IEnumerable<TSource> first, IEnumerable<TSource> second)
public static IEnumerable<TSource> Except<TSource>(
    this IEnumerable<TSource> first, IEnumerable<TSource> second, IEqualityComparer<TSource>
comparer)
```

These two extension methods will use the default equality comparer to compare values. The first version produces the set difference of two sequences, and the second version produces the set difference of two sequences by using the specified IEqualityComparer<T> to compare values.

The program in Listing 12-25 demonstrates the use of the Except method.

Listing 12-25. Example of the Except Method

```
using System.Collections;
using System.Collections.Generic;
using System.Linq;
using System;

namespace Ch12
{
    class Program
    {
        static void Main(string[] args)
        {
            IList<int> firstNumbers = new List<int>()
            {
                1,2,3,4,5,6,7
            };
            IList<int> secondNumbers = new List<int>()
            {
                1,2,3
            };

            var result = firstNumbers.Except(secondNumbers).ToList();
            result.ForEach(x => Console.Write(string.Format("{0}\t",x)));
        }
    }
}
```

The program in Listing 12-25 will produce the output:

4   5   6   7

Internal Operation of the Except Method of Execution

Let's analyze Listing 12-25 to help us understand what's happening when the Except method is executed. Figure 12-10 demonstrates the inner details of the Except method.

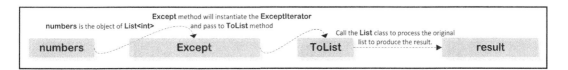

Figure 12-10. Except method working details

Each of the steps from Figure 12-10 will be explored in detail in the following discussion.

1. *Step 1*: The CLR passes the original list to the Except method, which will internally instantiate the ExceptIterator<TSource> by encapsulating the original list inside the iterator. This iterator will not execute due to the deferred execution until it calls the ToList method or ForEach method applied over the iterator object.

2. *Step 2*: When the CLR executes the ToList method, it calls the List class by passing the ExceptIterator instance created in step 1 as input. The List class calls the ExceptIterator method while it iterates through the list.

The ExceptIterator method creates a new instance of the Set<TSource> and adds all the items from the second list, as demonstrated in Listing 12-26.

Listing 12-26. Implementation Code of the ExceptIterator

```
private static IEnumerable<TSource> ExceptIterator<TSource>(
    IEnumerable<TSource> first,
    IEnumerable<TSource> second,
    IEqualityComparer<TSource> comparer)
{
    Set<TSource> iteratorVariable0 = new Set<TSource>(comparer);
    foreach (TSource local in second)
        iteratorVariable0.Add(local);
    foreach (TSource iteratorVariable1 in first)
    {
        if (!iteratorVariable0.Add(iteratorVariable1))
            continue;
        yield return iteratorVariable1;
    }
}
```

In the second loop, the CLR iterates through the first list and tries to add iterated items in the set. If the item of the second list does not exist (!iteratorVariable0.Add(iteratorVariable1)) in the set, it will then return that item and continue until it finishes the first list.

Union

The Union method (denoted as ∪) sets the union in two sequences. The Union method excludes duplicates from the output sequence. For example, if you have two sets, A = {1,2,3,4,5,6,7} and B = {5,6,7,8,9}, the union of these sets is A ∪ B = {1,2,3,4,5,6,7,8,9}, as demonstrated in Figure 12-11.

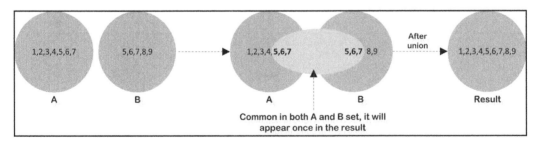

Figure 12-11. Union operation

The signature of the Union method is:

```
public static IEnumerable<TSource> Union<TSource>(
    this IEnumerable<TSource> first, IEnumerable<TSource> second)
```

CHAPTER 12 ▪ LINQ IN C#

```
public static IEnumerable<TSource> Union<TSource>(
    this IEnumerable<TSource> first, IEnumerable<TSource> second, IEqualityComparer<TSource>
comparer)
```

The program in Listing 12.27 demonstrates the usage of the Union operation.

Listing 12-27. Example of the Union Operation Using the Union Method

```
using System;
using System.Collections;
using System.Collections.Generic;
using System.Linq;

namespace Ch12
{
    class Program
    {
        static void Main(string[] args)
        {
            IList<int> firstList = new List<int>()
            {
                1,2,3,4
            };

            IList<int> secondList = new List<int>()
            {
                7,9,3,4,5,6,7
            };

            var result = firstList.Union(secondList);
            result.ToList().ForEach(x =>
                        Console.Write(string.Format("{0}\t",x)));
        }
    }
}
```

The program in Listing 12-27 will produce the output:

```
1       2       3       4       7       9       5       6
```

Internal Operation of the Union Method of Execution

To execute the Union method, the CLR will follow these steps:

1. *Step 1*: The Union method returns the UnionIterator<TSource>, which holds the firstList and the secondList, null for the IEqualityComparer, because the program in Listing 12-27 does not use a comparer to compare the items.

2. *Step 2*: Due to the deferred execution, the UnionIterator<TSource> will be executed when the CLR starts executing the ToList method. Inside the UnionIterator<TSource>, a new instance of the Set<TSource> class is instantiated, which will be used to find the distinct items from both lists, as demonstrated in Listing 12-28.

Listing 12-28. Implementation Code for the UnionIterator

```
private static IEnumerable<TSource> UnionIterator<TSource>(
    IEnumerable<TSource> first,
    IEnumerable<TSource> second,
    IEqualityComparer<TSource> comparer)
{
    Set<TSource> iteratorVariable0 = new Set<TSource>(comparer);

    foreach (TSource iteratorVariable1 in first)
    {
        /* If the CLR able to add the iterated item from the first List
         * in the Set it will yield that iterated item and keep continue
         * the loop. This will make sure only the identical items from the
         * first list is being returned.*/
        if (iteratorVariable0.Add(iteratorVariable1))
            yield return iteratorVariable1;
    }
    foreach (TSource iteratorVariable2 in second)
    {
        /* If the CLR not able to add iterated item from the second list
         * (to make sure  there is no duplicate between first list and second
         * list) it will continue the loop until able to add the iterated
         * item from the second list into the Set. If so then that item will
         * be returned and it will continue the iteration until finish
         * the Second List.*/
        if (!iteratorVariable0.Add(iteratorVariable2))
            continue;
        yield return iteratorVariable2;
    }
}
```

Intersect

The Intersect extension method produces the set intersection of two sequences. For example, if you have a list A with items {1,2,3,4,5} and B with {4,5}, the intersection of these two list A and B is {4,5}, as shown in Figure 12-12.

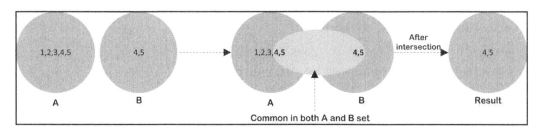

Figure 12-12. Intersect operation

The method signature for this extension method is:

```
public static IEnumerable<TSource> Intersect<TSource>(
    this IEnumerable<TSource> first, IEnumerable<TSource> second)
public static IEnumerable<TSource> Intersect<TSource>(
    this IEnumerable<TSource> first, IEnumerable<TSource> second,IEqualityComparer<TSource>
comparer)
```

This extension method produces the set intersection of two sequences by using the default equality comparer to compare values, and it will produce the set intersection of two sequences by using the specified IEqualityComparer<T> to compare values.

The program in Listing 12-29 creates two list: listA with 1,2,3,4,5 and listB with 4,5. It shows the intersect operation between these two list.

Listing 12-29. Example of the Intersect Method

```
using System;
using System.Collections.Generic;
using System.Linq;

namespace Ch12
{
    class Program
    {
        static void Main(string[] args)
        {
            IList<int> listA = new List<int>() { 1, 2, 3, 4, 5 };
            IList<int> listB = new List<int>() { 4, 5 };

            var intersectResult = listA.Intersect(listB);

            intersectResult.ToList().ForEach(x => Console.Write("{0}\t",x));
        }
    }
}
```

This program produced the output:

```
4       5
```

Internal Operation of the Intersect Method of Execution

While executing the Intersect method, the CLR follows these steps:

1. *Step 1*: The CLR initialize the IntersectIterator<TSource> with the original lists and returns to the caller the instance of the IntersectIterator<TSource>. Due to the deferred execution, this iterator will not execute until the ToList method is called.

2. *Step 2*: While executing the IntersectIterator<TSource>, the CLR instantiates an instance of the Set<TSource> that is used to hold the second list, demonstrated in the implementation of the IntersectIterator as shown in Listing 12-30.

Listing 12-30. Implementation Code of the InteresectIterator Method

```
private static IEnumerable<TSource> IntersectIterator<TSource>(
    IEnumerable<TSource> first,
    IEnumerable<TSource> second,
    IEqualityComparer<TSource> comparer)
{
    Set<TSource> iteratorVariable0 = new Set<TSource>(comparer);

    /* The CLR will add all the items from the second list to the Set.*/
    foreach (TSource local in second)
        iteratorVariable0.Add(local);

    /* Iterate though the first list */
    foreach (TSource iteratorVariable1 in first)
    {
    /* If the CLR able to remove based on the iterated item from the first
     * list i.e. there is a same item in the second list and that will
     * return otherwise continue the operation.*/
        if (!iteratorVariable0.Remove(iteratorVariable1))
            continue;

        yield return iteratorVariable1;
    }
}
```

The CLR will then iterate through the first list and try to remove each of the items of the first list from the Set<TSource> that is holding the items of the second list, as mention earlier. If it can remove it, it will then return that item of the first list, otherwise it will continue to iterate through the first list until it finishes the first list.

Aggregation-Based Methods

This section will explore in detail the different aggregation-based methods, such as Sum, LongCount, Max, Min, Count, Average, and Aggregate.

Sum

To do the sum operation over the items of a list, you can use the Sum method. The Sum method has 20 overloaded methods of which 10 are instance and rest static methods. The signature of the Sum methods is:

```
public static int Sum( this IEnumerable<int> source)
public static int Sum<TSource>(this IEnumerable<TSource> source, Func<TSource, int> selector)
```

An example of the Sum extension method is presented in Listing 12-31.

Listing 12-31. Example of the Sum Method

```
using System;
using System.Collections;
using System.Collections.Generic;
using System.Linq;
```

```
namespace Ch12
{
    class Program
    {
        static void Main(string[] args)
        {
            IList<int> numbers = new List<int>()
            {
                1,2,3,4,5,6,7,8,9,10
            };

            Console.WriteLine("Sum of the numbers :{0}", numbers.Sum());

            Console.WriteLine("Sum of the original numbers x 2 :{0}",
                numbers.Sum(x => x * 2));
        }
    }
}
```

This program produces the output:

```
Sum of the numbers :55
Sum of the original numbers x 2 :110
```

Internal Operation of the Sum Method of Execution

To execute the first overloaded Sum extension method used in Listing 12-31, the CLR follows these steps:

1. *Step 1*: The CLR passes the original list as input to the Sum extension method.

2. *Step 2*: The Sum method loops through the list, performs the summation of each of the items, and produces the result, as demonstrated in this implementation code:

```
public static int Sum(this IEnumerable<int> source)
{
    int num = 0;
    foreach (int num2 in source)
        num += num2;
    return num;
}
```

Let's analyze Listing 12-31 to help us understand what's happening while the CLR executes the second overloaded Sum extension method. Figure 12-13 demonstrates the details of the Sum method.

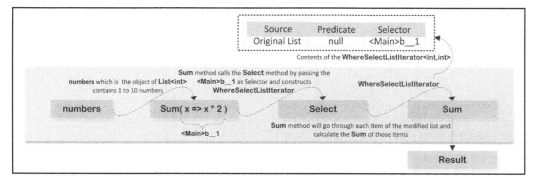

Figure 12-13. *How the Sum method works*

Each of the steps in Figure 12-13 will be explored in detail in the following discussion.

1. *Step 1*: The C# compiler constructs the method <Main>b__1 for the anonymous method block (x => x * 2), as shown in the following IL code:

```
.method private hidebysig static int32 <Main>b__1(int32 x) cil managed
{
    /* Code removed   */
    L_0000: ldarg.0
    L_0001: ldc.i4.2
    /* Multiply the argument at position 0 of the evaluation stack by 2*/
    L_0002: mul
    L_0003: stloc.0
    L_0004: br.s L_0006
    L_0006: ldloc.0
    L_0007: ret
}
```

The CLR creates a MulticastDelegate instance using the method <Main>b__1, as shown in the following IL code extracted from the decompiled Main method of the program in Listing 12-31 using the .NET Reflector tool:

```
L_007f: ldftn
        int32
        Ch12.Program::<Main>b__1(int32)
L_0085: newobj instance
        void
        [mscorlib]System.Func'2<int32, int32>::.ctor(object, native int)
```

■ **Note:** The System.Func<TSource,TResult> is derived from the MulticastDelegate.

2. *Step 2*: The CLR passes the original list and MulticastDelegate instance created in step 1 as input to the Sum method, which calls the Select method with the original list and the instance of the MulticastDelegate as input. The CLR instantiates the relevant iterator, for example, WhereSelectListIterator<TSource, TResult>, from the Select method and returns it back to the Sum method, for

example, WhereSelectListIterator<TSource, TResult>. The CLR then calls the overloaded Sum method. The implementation of this overloaded Sum would be:

```
public static float Sum(
    this IEnumerable<float> source)
{
    double num = 0.0;
    foreach (float num2 in source)
        num += num2;
    return (float) num;
}
```

3. *Step 3*: The CLR gets the iterator from the IEnumerable object passed to the Sum method, for example, the instance of the WhereSelectListIterator, as shown in the following decompiled Sum method code:

```
.method public hidebysig static int32 Sum(
    class [mscorlib]System.Collections.Generic.IEnumerable'1<int32> source)
    cil managed
{
    /* Code removed   */
    /* Load the argument which is the IEnumerable passed one evaluation
     * stack from the caller */
    L_0010: ldarg.0

    L_0011: callvirt instance
            /* return type of the GetEnumerator method */
            class [mscorlib]System.Collections.Generic.IEnumerator'1<!0>
            [mscorlib]System.Collections.Generic.IEnumerable'1<int32>::
            GetEnumerator()
    /* Code removed   */
}
```

4. *Step 4*: Using this Enumerator, the CLR iterates through the items from the original list. While the CLR executes the iterator, it iterates through each of the items by calling the MoveNext method from the relevant enumerator and executes the relevant selector method passed as input to it. The following anonymous method is used to modify the item while it is being retrieved from the original list and just before committing to the sum for that item:

```
( x => x * 2 )   /* compiled as <Main>b__1 used in the MoveNext method
                  * as Selector */
```

The implementation of the MoveNext method of WhereSelectListIterator<TSource, TResult> class would be:

```
public override bool MoveNext()
{
    while (this.enumerator.MoveNext())
    {
        TSource current = this.enumerator.Current;
        if ((this.predicate == null) || this.predicate(current))
        {
            /* selector(current) will actually execute as
```

```
        * <Main>b__1(current) */
        base.current = this.selector(current);
        return true;
      }
    }
    return false;
  }
}
```

From there you find that the this.selector(current) statement executes the selector for the current item from the original list and continues unless it has finished the iteration of the original list.

LongCount

The LongCount method can be used to return an Int64 that represents the number of elements in a sequence. The method signature for this extension method is:

```
public static long LongCount<TSource>(this IEnumerable<TSource> source)
public static long LongCount<TSource>(this IEnumerable<TSource> source,
                                      Func<TSource, bool> predicate)
```

This extension method will return an Int64 that represents the total number of elements in a sequence, and it will return an Int64 that represents how many elements in a sequence satisfy a condition.

Listing 12-32 presents an example of the LongCount method.

Listing 12-32. Example of the LongCount Method

```
using System;
using System.Collections;
using System.Collections.Generic;
using System.Linq;

namespace Ch12
{
    class Program
    {
        static void Main(string[] args)
        {
            IList<int> firstList = new List<int>()
            {
                1,2,3,4
            };

            Console.WriteLine(firstList.LongCount());
        }
    }
}
```

This program will produce the output:

```
4
```

Internal Operation of the LongCount Method of Execution

The implementation of the first version of the LongCount method shows that the CLR will iterate through the original list and sum each of the items and store the results in the num variable:

```
public static long LongCount<TSource>(this IEnumerable<TSource> source)
{
    long num = 0L;
    using (IEnumerator<TSource> enumerator = source.GetEnumerator())
    {
        while (enumerator.MoveNext())
        {
            num += 1L;
        }
    }
    return num;
}
```

The implementation of the second version of the LongCount extension method shows that the CLR iterates through the original list and selects items from the list based on a provided predicate (which will return those item that meet the condition) and sums up and stores this in the num variable:

```
public static long LongCount<TSource>(this IEnumerable<TSource> source, Func<TSource, bool> predicate)
{
    long num = 0L;
    foreach (TSource local in source)
    {
        if (predicate(local))
            num += 1L;
    }
    return num;
}
```

Max

The Max extension method is used to determine the maximum number from a list. The signature of the Max method has 22 overloaded methods, with two of those being:

```
public static int Max(this IEnumerable<int> source)
public static decimal Max<TSource>(this IEnumerable<TSource> source,
                          Func<TSource, decimal> selector)
```

Listing 12-33 presents an example of the Max method.

Listing 12-33. Example of Max Method

```
using System;
using System.Collections;
using System.Collections.Generic;
using System.Linq;

namespace Ch12
```

```
{
    class Program
    {
        static void Main(string[] args)
        {
            IList<int> numbers = new List<int>()
            {
                1,2,3,4,5,6,7,8,9,10
            };

            Console.WriteLine("Max of the numbers :{0}", numbers.Max());
            Console.WriteLine("Max of the original numbers x2 :{0}",
                numbers.Max(x => x * 2));
        }
    }
}
```

This program produces the output:

```
Max of the numbers :10
Max of the original numbers x2 :20
```

Internal Operation of the Max Method of Execution

The CLR performs the followings steps to execute the Max operation:

1. *Step 1*: The CLR pass the original list as input to the Max method.

2. *Step 2*: The Max method loops through the list and performs the Max operation, as demonstrated here by the implementation of the Max:

```
public static int Max(
    this IEnumerable<int> source)
{
    int num = 0;
    bool flag = false;
    foreach (int num2 in source)
    {
        if (flag)
        {
            if (num2 > num)
                num = num2;
        }
        else
        {
            num = num2;
            flag = true;
        }
    }
    return num;
}
```

The second overloaded method of the Max extension method works as demonstrated in Figure 12-14.

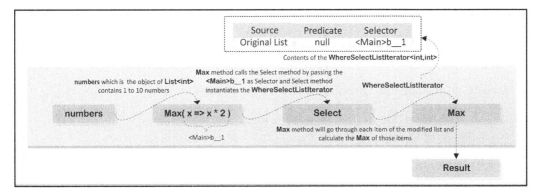

Figure 12-14. *How the Max method works*

The CLR follows these steps in executing the Max method:

1. *Step 1*: The C# compiler constructs a method <Main>b__1 using the anonymous method (x => x * 2). The CLR passes this <Main>b__1 method to the MulticastDelegate class to instantiate an instance of it and calls the Select method of the list, which takes the original list and the instance of the MulticastDelegate as input and returns the relevant iterator instance, for example, WhereSelectListIterator<TSource,TResult>, for the list as output.

2. *Step 2*: The CLR then calls the overload Max method, which accepts only the iterator returned from step 1. In this overload Max method, a ForEach method is forced to iterate through the list and perform the Max operation based on the Selector condition.

Min

The Min extension method will determine the minimum of the list. Two signatures of the extension methods Min (of the 22 overloaded methods) are:

```
public static int Min(this IEnumerable<int> source)
public static int Min<TSource>(this IEnumerable<TSource> source, Func<TSource, int> selector)
```

The program in Listing 12-34 demonstrates the usage of the Min extension method.

Listing 12-34. Example of Min Method

```
using System;
using System.Collections;
using System.Collections.Generic;
using System.Linq;

namespace Ch12
{
    class Program
    {
        static void Main(string[] args)
        {
```

```
ILIst<int> numbers = new List<int>()
{
    1,2,3,4,5,6,7,8,9,10
};

Console.WriteLine("Min of the numbers :{0}", numbers.Min());

Console.WriteLine("Min of the original numbers x2 :{0}",
    numbers.Min(x => x * 2));
    }
  }
}
```

This program will produce the output:

```
Min of the numbers :1
Min of the original numbers x2 :2
```

Internal Operation of the Min Method of Execution

When the CLR finds the first version of the Min extension method, as shown in Listing 12-34, it follows the steps to perform the operation. The CLR passes the original list as input to the Min extension method. The Min method then loops through the list and performs the minimum calculation operation.

The second version of the Min extension method is demonstrated in Figure 12-15.

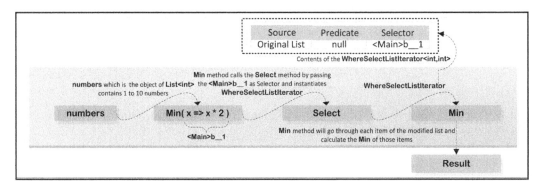

Figure 12-15. Min method working details

The CLR follows these steps:

1. *Step 1*: The C# compiler constructs a method <Main>b__1 using the anonymous method (x => x * 2) and passes this <Main>b__1 method to the MulticastDelegate class to instantiate an instance of it. It will then call the Select method by passing the original list and the instance of the MulticastDelegate as input, which returns the relevant iterator instance, for example, WhereSelectListIterator<TSource,TResult>, for the list as output.

2. *Step 2*: The CLR will call the overloaded Min method, which accepts only the iterator returned in step 1. In this overload Min method, a ForEach method forces it to iterate the list using the provided Selector and performs the Min operation.

Count

The Count method returns the number of elements in a sequence. The method signature for this method is:

```
public static int Count<TSource>(this IEnumerable<TSource> source)
public static int Count<TSource>(this IEnumerable<TSource> source,
                                 Func<TSource, bool> predicate)
```

The first version returns the number of elements in a sequence. The second version returns a number that represents how many elements are in the specified sequence that satisfy a condition.

The Count method determines how many items are in the list. For example, the program in Listing 12-35 determines how many items are in listOne and also determines how many items in listOne have more than three characters.

Listing 12-35. Example of the Count Method

```
using System;
using System.Collections;
using System.Collections.Generic;
using System.Linq;

namespace Ch12
{
    class Program
    {
        static void Main(string[] args)
        {
            IList<string> listOne = new List<string>()
            {
                "One","Two","Three"
            };

            var result = listOne.Count();

            var fourOrMoreCharacters = listOne.Count(item => item.Length > 3);
            Console.WriteLine("{0}\n{1}", result,fourOrMoreCharacters);
        }
    }
}
```

The program in Listing 12-35 will produce the output:

```
3
1
```

Internal Operation of the Count Method of Execution

Let's analyze the code in Listing 12-35 to help us understand what's happening when we use the Count method.

When the CLR finds the first overloaded instance of the Count method, it tries to determine the enumerator of the given list and iterates through the items (using the iterator of the list), unless the MoveNext method of the enumerator returns false.

The implementation of the Count method shown in Listing 12-36 returns the number of iteration as the output for a list when using the Count method.

Listing 12-36. Example of the Count Method

```
public static int Count<TSource>(this IEnumerable<TSource> source)
{
    int num = 0;
    using (IEnumerator<TSource> enumerator = source.GetEnumerator())
    {
        while (enumerator.MoveNext())
        {
            /* num will be increased as per the iteration of the while*/
            num++;
        }
    }
    return num;
}
```

Figure 12-16 demonstrates the second version of the Count method.

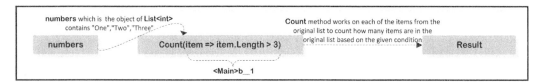

Figure 12-16. Count method working details

The second version of the Count method will take the original list and a predicate to filter the items from the list and count based on the filtered items. The predicate will be created in the compile time based on the anonymous method provided (item => item.Length > 3). The CLR loops through the items of the list and executes the predicate over each of the items. If the predicate meets the condition over the items on iteration, it increases the item count.

Finally, it returns the item count as the total number of items that meet the condition. The implementation of the Count method is:

```
public static int Count<TSource>(
    this IEnumerable<TSource> source,
    Func<TSource, bool> predicate)
{
    foreach (TSource local in source)
        if (predicate(local))
            num++;
    return num;
}
```

Average

The Average method calculates the average of a sequence of numeric values. Two (of a total of 11 overloaded methods) of the signatures for this extension method are:

```
public static double Average(this IEnumerable<int> source)
public static decimal Average<TSource>(
    this IEnumerable<TSource> source, Func<TSource, decimal> selector)
```

Listing 12-37 presents an example of the Average method.

Listing 12-37. *Example of Average Method*

```
using System;
using System.Collections;
using System.Collections.Generic;
using System.Linq;

namespace Ch12
{
    class Program
    {
        static void Main(string[] args)
        {
            IList<int> numbers = new List<int>()
            {
                1,2,3,4,5,6,7,8,9,10
            };
            Console.WriteLine("Average of the numbers :{0}",
                numbers.Average());

            Console.WriteLine("Average of the original numbers x2 :{0}",
                numbers.Average((x => x * 2)));
        }
    }
}
```

This program produces the output:

```
Average of the numbers :5.5
Average of the original numbers :11
```

Internal Operation of the Average Method of Execution

Listing 12-37 shows that the CLR passes the list numbers as input to the Average method. This method processes the original list by iterating through it and calculates the average of items of the numbers and returns the average of the items as output. The CLR performs the first version of the Average method using these steps to execute it:

1. *Step 1*: The CLR pass the original list, for example, numbers for Listing 12-37, as input to the Average method.

2.   *Step 2*: The Average method loops through the list and performs the average. The implementation of the Average method is shown in Listing 12-38.

Listing 12-38. *Internal Operation of the Average Method*

```
public static double Average(this IEnumerable<int> source)
{
    long num = 0L;
    long num2 = 0L;
    foreach (int num3 in source)
    {
    num += num3;
    num2 += 1L;
    }

    /* total of the numbers / to no of items in list */
    return (((double) num) / ((double) num2));
}
```

The second version of the Average extension method follows the steps outlined in Figure 12-17 to perform the operation.

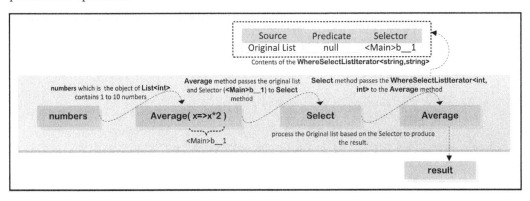

Figure 12-17. *Average extension method working details*

Figure 12-17 shows that the CLR passed the list numbers to the Average method along with the instance of MulticastDelegate class instantiated in the compile time using the anonymous method (x=>x*2). The CLR will pass this instance of the MulticastDelegate to the Select method from which the appropriate iterator will be instantiated. For the program in Listing 12-37, the WhereSelectListIterator<int,int> iterator will be instantiated and it will hold the original list and the selector inside. The CLR will iterate through the list and calculate the average based on the filtering criteria provided in the selector.

Let's analyze Listing 12-37 to understand what's happening when the CLR executes the second version of the Average method.

1.   *Step 1*: The CLR passes the original list and the instance of the MulticastDelegate using the <Main>b__1 method (which is generated in the compile time by the C# compiler using the Anonymous method (x=>x*2)) as input to the Average method.

2.   *Step 2*: While executing the Average method, the CLR calls the Select method, which instantiates the WhereSelectListIterator<int, int> iterator returned from the Select method.

3. *Step 3*: The CLR then calls the overloaded Average method by passing the WhereSelectListIterator<int, int> instantiated in step 2 as input. This iterator contains the original list and the instance of the MulticastDelegate as the selector.

4. *Step 4*: In the Average method, the ForEach method iterates through the list and performs the average calculation as demonstrated in the implementation code for the foreach block and performs the average calculation:

```
foreach (int num3 in source)
{
    num += num3;
    num2 += 1L;
}
```

Aggregate

The Aggregate method combines a series of items from the sequence, for example, if you have a sequence with One, Two, Three, Four and apply the Aggregate method over the sequence, the CLR then performs the operation as demonstrated in Figure 12-18.

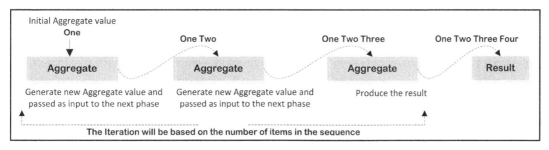

Figure 12-18. Basics of the Aggregate operation

The signature of this method is:

```
public static TSource Aggregate<TSource>(
    this IEnumerable<TSource> source, Func<TSource, TSource, TSource> func)
public static TAccumulate Aggregate<TSource, TAccumulate>(
    this IEnumerable<TSource> source,
    TAccumulate seed, Func<TAccumulate, TSource, TAccumulate> func)
public static TResult Aggregate<TSource, TAccumulate, TResult>(
    this IEnumerable<TSource> source, TAccumulate seed,
    Func<TAccumulate, TSource, TAccumulate> func, Func<TAccumulate, TResult> resultSelector)
```

Listing 12-39 demonstrates an example of the Aggregate method.

Listing 12-39. Example of the Aggregate Method

```
using System;
using System.Collections.Generic;
using System.Linq;
```

```
namespace Ch12
{
    class Program
    {
        static void Main(string[] args)
        {

            List<string> numbers = new List<string>()
            {
                "One", "Two", "Three", "Four"
            };

            var result = numbers.Aggregate(
                (aggregatedValue, nextItem) =>
                nextItem + aggregatedValue);

            Console.WriteLine("Aggregated value : {0}", result);
        }
    }
}
```

This program produces the output:

```
Aggregated value : FourThreeTwoOne
```

The output is different from that of the original list because of `nextItem + aggregatedValue`. Stated another way, the output would read as:

```
Aggregated value : OneTwoThreeFour
```

Internal Operation of the Aggregate Method of Execution

Figure 12-19 demonstrates the internal operation of the Aggregate method.

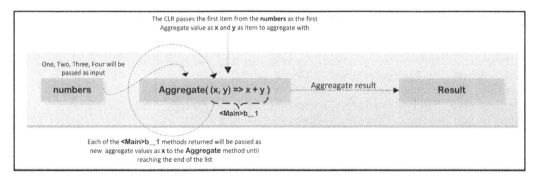

Figure 12-19. *How the Aggregate method works*

Let's analyze the code in Listing 12-39 to understand what's happening as we initiate the Aggregate method.

1.   *Step 1*: The C# compiler creates the <Main>b__1 method to encapsulate the
     anonymous method body (aggregatedValue, nextItem) => nextItem +
     aggregatedValue) as <Main>b__1, which will be used as the Aggregator func of the
     Aggregate method. The CLR uses this anonymous method to execute Aggregate.
     The contents of the compiled <Main>b__1 method would be:

```
.method private hidebysig static string <Main>b__1
    (string aggregatedValue, string nextItem) cil managed
{
    /* Code removed  */
    L_0000: ldarg.1
    L_0001: ldarg.0
    L_0002: call string [mscorlib]System.String::Concat(string, string)
    L_0007: stloc.0
    L_0008: br.s L_000a
    L_000a: ldloc.0
    L_000b: ret
}
```

2.   *Step 2*: When the CLR executes the Aggregate function, it takes the original list
     and anonymous method created in step 1 as input. It iterates through each of the
     items from the list and uses the first item from the list as the current aggregate
     value:

```
TSource current = enumerator.Current;
```

The second item (using enumerator.Current) from the list is used as input to the anonymous method
(i.e., the aggregator to generate new aggregate value). This new value will be used as a new aggregated
value for the next iteration and continues the iteration until it finishes the list. The implementation of the
Aggregate method used in Listing 12-39 is shown in Listing 12-40.

Listing 12-40. Implementation Code for the Aggregate Method

```
public static TSource Aggregate<TSource>(
    this IEnumerable<TSource> source,
    Func<TSource, TSource, TSource> func)
{
    using (IEnumerator<TSource> enumerator = source.GetEnumerator())
    {
        /* current as the initial seed */
        TSource current = enumerator.Current;
        /* enumerator will move forward and start looping from the
         * second item */
        while (enumerator.MoveNext())
        /* seed and iterated item will be passed to the Aggregator which
         * is func to generate new seed. */
            current = func(current, enumerator.Current);

        return current;
    }
}
```

The following discussion will explore the overloaded method of the Aggregate, which will take a value as input for the initial aggregate value. So the CLR will not take the first item from the list as the initial aggregate value as it did for the first version of the Aggregate method discussed earlier. Listing 12-41 demonstrates the use of the Aggregate method that takes an aggregate value as input.

Listing 12-41. Modified Version of Listing 12-39

```csharp
using System;
using System.Collections.Generic;
using System.Linq;

namespace Ch12
{
    class Program
    {
        static void Main(string[] args)
        {
            List<string> items = new List<string>()
            {
                "One", "Two", "Three", "Four"
            };
            var result = items.Aggregate(
                    /* Zero as seed, to use as the initial aggregate value */
                    "Zero",
                    (temporaryAggregatedValue, nextItem) =>
                    {
                        Console.WriteLine(temporaryAggregatedValue);
                        return nextItem + temporaryAggregatedValue;
                    },
                    aggregatedResult =>
                    string.Format("Final result : {0}",
                                    aggregatedResult.ToUpper())
                );
            Console.WriteLine(result);
        }
    }
}
```

This program will produce the output:

```
Zero
OneZero
TwoOneZero
ThreeTwoOneZero
Final result : FOURTHREETWOONEZERO
```

The Aggregate method generated the seed using the Aggregator method based on the initial seed and iterated item. The final results will be produced with a specific format, for example, for the code in Listing 12-41, the anonymous method <Main>b__2 format of the aggregated method produces the final result as demonstrated in Figure 12-20.

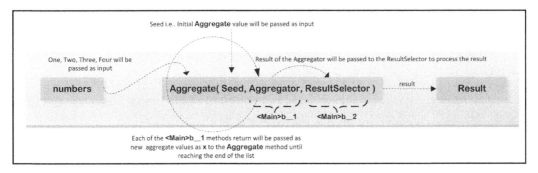

Figure 12-20. *How the Aggregate method works*

The CLR will pass the initial aggregate value as input and the first item from the original list (for the first pass) to the <Main>b__1 to create the aggregate value, as shown in Listing 12-41. After performing the initial aggregate operation, <Main>b__1 will return the new aggregate value. After first pass while iterating the list, the CLR will replace the old aggregate value with the new one created using <Main>b__1 and continue until it finishes iterating the original list. The implementation of the Aggregate method is shown in Listing 12-42.

Listing 12-42. *Implementation Code for the Aggregate Method*

```
public static TAccumulate Aggregate<TSource, TAccumulate>(
    this IEnumerable<TSource> source, TAccumulate seed, Func<TAccumulate, TSource, TAccumulate>
func)
{
    TAccumulate local = seed;
    foreach (TSource local2 in source)
        local = func(local, local2);
    return local;
}
```

The aggregate seed generated using the initial seed is:

```
(temporaryAggregatedValue, nextItem) =>
{
    Console.WriteLine(temporaryAggregatedValue);
    return nextItem + temporaryAggregatedValue;
}
```

This code is compiled into <Main>b__1:

```
.method private hidebysig static string <Main>b__1(
    string temporaryAggregatedValue, string nextItem) cil managed
{
    /* Code removed  */
    L_000a: call string [mscorlib]System.String::Concat(string, string)
    L_000f: stloc.0
    L_0013: ret
}
```

The result selector method aggregatedResult =>string.Format("Final result : {0}", aggregatedResult.ToUpper()) is compiled as:

```
.method private hidebysig static string <Main>b__2(string aggregatedResult) cil managed
{
    /* Code removed */
    L_000b: call string [mscorlib]System.String::Format(string, object)
    L_0014: ret
}
```

Quantifier-Based Methods

This section will explore in detail the All, Any, and Contains extension methods.

All

The All extension method determines whether all of the elements of a sequence satisfy a condition, if every element of the source sequence passes the condition in the specified predicate, or if the sequence is empty and returns true; otherwise, false. The signature of this extension method is:

```
public static bool All<TSource>(this IEnumerable<TSource> source, Func<TSource, bool> predicate)
```

Listing 12-43 shows how to find those items from the sequence that have at least three characters.

Listing 12-43. Example of the All Method

```
using System;
using System.Collections;
using System.Collections.Generic;
using System.Linq;

namespace Ch12
{
    class Program
    {
        static void Main(string[] args)
        {
            IList<string> numbers = new List<string>()
            {
                "One", "Two", "Three", "Four", "Five", "Six", "Seven"
            };

            if (numbers.All<string>(x => x.Length >= 3))
                Console.WriteLine(
                        "All numbers have at least three characters.");
        }
    }
}
```

The program in Listing 12-43 will produce the output:

```
All numbers have at least three characters.
```

Internal Operation of the All Method of Execution

The All method will match the specified filtering condition to find items from the sequence. Figure 12-21 demonstrates the details of the All method in Linq.

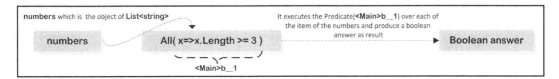

Figure 12-21. Working details of the All method

From Figure 12-21 you can see that the CLR passes the numbers list as input to the All method along with the instance of the MulticastDelegate class instantiated using the anonymous method (x=>x.Length >= 3). In the All method, CLR processes the list to find whether each of the items satisfies the condition provided as a predicate.

Let's analyze the code in Listing 12-43 to understand what's happening while the CLR uses the All method over a list.

1. *Step 1*: The CLR uses the method <Main>b__1 (x => x.Length >= 3) to instantiate the instance of the MulticastDelegate. The CLR passes the original list and the instance of the MulticastDelegate class created in this step as input to the extension method All.

2. *Step 2*: The All method will loop through the list and try to determine whether any element in the sequence does not meet the condition and it then returns false, otherwise a true value, as a result of the operation. The implementation of the All method is:

```
public static bool All<TSource>(
    this IEnumerable<TSource> source,
    Func<TSource, bool> predicate)
{
    foreach (TSource local in source)
        if (!predicate(local))
            return false;
    return true;
}
```

Any

The Any method determines whether any element of a sequence exists or satisfies a condition provided as a predicate. The method signatures for this extension method are:

```
public static bool Any<TSource>(this IEnumerable<TSource> source)
public static bool Any<TSource>(this IEnumerable<TSource> source,
                        Func<TSource, bool> predicate)
```

The first version of the Any extension method will determine whether or not the sequence of items contains any element in it. The second version of the Any extension method will determine if there is any element in the sequence that matches the criteria provided in the predicate.

Listing 12-44 demonstrates the use of the Any method.

Listing 12-44. Example of the Any Extension Method

```csharp
using System;
using System.Collections;
using System.Collections.Generic;
using System.Linq;

namespace Ch12
{
    class Program
    {
        static void Main(string[] args)
        {
            IList<string> numbers = new List<string>()
            {
                "One", "Two", "Three", "Four", "Five", "Six", "Seven"
            };

            if (numbers.Any<string>())
                Console.WriteLine("Contains");

            if (numbers.Any<string>(x => x.Length >= 3))
                Console.WriteLine("Contains");
        }
    }
}
```

This program produced the output:

```
Contains
Contains
```

Internal Operation of the Any Method of Execution

When the CLR executes the first version of the Any method, it performs the following steps:

1. *Step 1*: The CLR will send the original sequence or the list, in this case numbers, to the Any<TSource>(this IEnumerable<TSource> source) method as input.

2. *Step 2*: This method loops through the list via the Enumerator object returned from the list of numbers and checks whether the enumerator returned a true value while calling the MoveNext method of it and returns true, otherwise false (i.e., the sequence does not have any element in it). The implementation of the Any method is shown in Listing 12-45.

Listing 12-45. Example of the Any Extension Method

```csharp
public static bool Any<TSource>(this IEnumerable<TSource> source)
{
    using (IEnumerator<TSource> enumerator = source.GetEnumerator())
    {
        if (enumerator.MoveNext())
            return true;
```

```
    }
    return false;
}
```

The overloaded version of the Any method will execute as demonstrated in Figure 12-22.

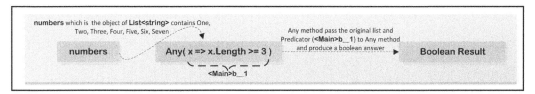

Figure 12-22. Example of the Any statement

The CLR follows these steps in executing the Any method:

1. *Step 1*: The CLR instantiates an instance of MulticastDelegate using method <Main>b__1 (constructed using the anonymous method (x => x.Length >= 3) in the compile time) as the predicate along with the original list to the Any extension method.

2. *Step 2*: The CLR loops through the list to execute the predicate using each item as input to the predicate. The predicate returns true while iterating the list, otherwise it will continue until it finds a match. The implementation of the Any method is shown in Listing 12-46.

Listing 12-46. Implementation of the Any Method

```
public static bool Any<TSource>(
    this IEnumerable<TSource> source,
    Func<TSource, bool> predicate)
{
    foreach (TSource local in source)
    {
        if (predicate(local))
            return true;
    }
    return false;
}
```

Contains

The Contains method determines whether or not a sequence contains a specified element in it, for example, if a sequence contains 1,2,3,4 and you use Contains(4), it will then return the availability of 4 in the list. This method determines whether a sequence contains a specified element by using the default equality comparer, and it determines whether a sequence contains a specified element by using a specified IEqualityComparer<T>.

The method signature for this extension method is:

```
public static bool Contains<TSource>(this IEnumerable<TSource> source, TSource value)
public static bool Contains<TSource>(this IEnumerable<TSource> source, TSource value,
    IEqualityComparer<TSource> comparer)
```

Listing 12-47 demonstrates the use of the Contains method.

Listing 12-47. *Example of Contains Method Over the List<int> Type*

```
using System;
using System.Collections;
using System.Collections.Generic;

namespace Ch12
{
    class Program
    {
        static void Main(string[] args)
        {
            IList<int> listOne = new List<int>()
            {
                1,2,3,4,5
            };

            var resultAsTrue = listOne.Contains(2);
            var resultAsFalse = listOne.Contains(200);
            Console.WriteLine("{0}\n{1}", resultAsTrue, resultAsFalse);
        }
    }
}
```

This program will produce the output:

```
True
False
```

Internal Operation of the Contains Method of Execution

While executing the Contains method, the CLR will search a particular item from the list. This search will have two directions: if the input is a null value, it will then loop through the list to match the item with the null from the list and return true if one of the items from the list is null; otherwise, it will return false. Other than null value, the CLR will compare the value (provided to match as input) with each of the items from the list, and depending on a match, it will return a Boolean answer. The implementation of the Contains method is shown in Listing 12-48.

Listing 12-48. *Implementation of the Contains Method*

```
public bool Contains(T item)
{
    /* First way of search */
    if (item == null)
    {
        for (int j = 0; j < this._size; j++)
        {
            if (this._items[j] == null)
                return true;
        }
```

```
        return false;
    }

    /* Second way of search when the First does not execute */
    EqualityComparer<T> comparer = EqualityComparer<T>.Default;
    for (int i = 0; i < this._size; i++)
    {
        if (comparer.Equals(this._items[i], item))
            return true;
    }
    return false;
}
```

Element-Based Methods

This section will examine the different element-based extension methods, such as `First`, `FirstOrDefault`, `Last`, `LastOrDefault`, `Single`, `SingleOrDefault`, `ElementAt`, `ElementAtOrDefault`, and `DefaultIfEmpty`.

First

The `First` method returns the first element of a sequence. The method signatures of this extension are:

```
public static TSource First<TSource>(this IEnumerable<TSource> source)
public static TSource First<TSource>(this IEnumerable<TSource> source, Func<TSource, bool>
predicate)
```

The first version of this extension method finds the first item from the sequence of items. The second version of this extension method finds the first item of a list that meets the predicate condition.

Listing 12-49 demonstrates the use of the `First` method.

Listing 12-49. *Example of the First Extension Methods*

```
using System.Collections;
using System.Collections.Generic;
using System.Linq;
using System;

namespace Ch12
{
    class Program
    {
        static void Main(string[] args)
        {
            IList<int> numbers = new List<int>()
            {
                1,2,3,4,5,6,7
            };

            var firstItem = numbers.First();
            var firstItemBasedOnConditions = numbers.First(item => item > 3);
```

```
            Console.WriteLine("{0}\n{1}",
                firstItem,
                firstItemBasedOnConditions);
        }
    }
}
```

This program produces the output:

```
1
4
```

Internal Operation of the First Method of Execution

When the CLR executes the first version of the First method, it follows these steps to execute the operation:

1.   *Step 1*: The CLR sends the original list to the First <TSource>(this IEnumerable<TSource> source) method as an input parameter.

2.   *Step 2*: This method will return the first item from the original list or iterate through the original list and return the first item from the iteration as a result.

The implementation of the First method is shown in Listing 12-50.

***Listing 12-50.** Implementation of the First Method*

```
public static TSource First<TSource>(this IEnumerable<TSource> source)
{
    IList<TSource> list = source as IList<TSource>;
    if (list != null)
    {
        if (list.Count > 0)
            return list[0];
    }
    else
    {
        using (IEnumerator<TSource> enumerator = source.GetEnumerator())
        {
            if (enumerator.MoveNext())
                return enumerator.Current;
        }
    }
}
```

To execute the overloaded method of the First method, which takes a predicate to filter the list, the CLR will instantiate an instance of the MulticastDelegate using the method <Main>b__1 (item => item > 3). It will then loop through the list and match with each element in the sequence based on the predicate. This returns on the first match, otherwise it will continue until it finds a match.

The implementation of the First method would be:

```
public static TSource First<TSource>(
    this IEnumerable<TSource> source,
    Func<TSource, bool> predicate)
```

```
{
    foreach (TSource local in source)
    {
        if (predicate(local))
            return local;
    }
}
```

FirstOrDefault

The `FirstOrDefault` method returns the first element of a sequence or a default value if no element is found. The signature for the `FirstOrDefault` method is:

```
public static TSource FirstOrDefault<TSource>(this IEnumerable<TSource> source)
public static TSource FirstOrDefault<TSource>(
    this IEnumerable<TSource> source, Func<TSource, bool> predicate)
```

These two methods will return the first element of a sequence or a default value if the sequence contains no elements. The default value will be the value of the generic type for which the list will be instantiated. For example, if the list is the type int, the default value will be zero if there is no element in it. It returns the first element of the sequence that satisfies a condition or a default value if no such element is found.

Listing 12-51 presents an example to demonstrate the use of the `FirstOrDefault` method.

Listing 12-51. Example of FirstOrDefault Method

```
using System;
using System.Collections;
using System.Collections.Generic;
using System.Linq;

namespace Ch12
{
    class Program
    {
        static void Main(string[] args)
        {
            IList<int> firstNumbers = new List<int>();

            IList<int> secondNumbers = new List<int>()
            {
                1,2,3,4,5,6,7
            };

            var firstItemOfFirstList = firstNumbers.FirstOrDefault();
            var firstItemIfFirstListBasedOnConditions =
                firstNumbers.FirstOrDefault(item => item > 3);

            var firstItemOfSecondList = secondNumbers.FirstOrDefault();
            var firstItemOfSecondListBasedOnConditions =
                secondNumbers.FirstOrDefault(item => item > 3);
```

```
            Console.Write(string.Format("{0}\t{1}\t{2}\t{3}",
                firstItemOfFirstList,
                firstItemIfFirstListBasedOnConditions,
                firstItemOfSecondList,
                firstItemOfSecondListBasedOnConditions
                ));
        }
    }
}
```

The program in Listing 12-51 produced the output:

```
0        0        1        4
```


Internal Operation of the FirstOrDefault Method of Execution

The implementation of the first overloaded FirstOrDefault method is shown in Listing 12-52.

Listing 12-52. Implementation of the First FirstOrDefault Method

```
public static TSource FirstOrDefault<TSource>(this IEnumerable<TSource> source)
{

    IList<TSource> list = source as IList<TSource>;
    if (list != null)
    {
        if (list.Count > 0)
            return list[0];
    }
    else
    {
        using (IEnumerator<TSource> enumerator = source.GetEnumerator())
        {
            if (enumerator.MoveNext())
                return enumerator.Current;
        }
    }
    return default(TSource);
}
```

The implementation of the second overloaded FirstOrDefault method is shown in Listing 12-53.

Listing 12-53. Implementation of the Second FirstOrDefault Method

```
public static TSource FirstOrDefault<TSource>(
    this IEnumerable<TSource> source,
    Func<TSource, bool> predicate)
{
    foreach (TSource local in source)
    {
        if (predicate(local))
            return local;
```

```
    }
    return default(TSource);
}
```

Last

The Last method is used to find the last element of a sequence. The method signature for this extension method is:

```
public static TSource Last<TSource>(this IEnumerable<TSource> source)
public static TSource Last<TSource>(this IEnumerable<TSource> source, Func<TSource, bool>
predicate)
```

The first version of this method will find the last item from the sequence of items. The second version of this method will find the last item from a list that meets the predicate condition.

The program in Listing 12-54 demonstrates the use of the Last extension method.

Listing 12-54. Example of the Last Extension Methods

```
using System;
using System.Collections;
using System.Collections.Generic;
using System.Linq;

namespace Ch12
{
    class Program
    {
        static void Main(string[] args)
        {
            IList<int> numbers = new List<int>()
            {
                1,2,3,4,5,6,7
            };

            var lastItem = numbers.Last();
            Console.WriteLine(lastItem);
            var lastItemBasedOnConditions = numbers.Last(item => item > 3);
            Console.WriteLine(lastItemBasedOnConditions);
        }
    }
}
```

The code produced the output:

```
7
7
```

Internal Operation of the Last Method of Execution

When the CLR executes the first overloaded Last method, the original list will be passed to the Last <TSource> (this IEnumerable<TSource> source) method as input. This method will iterate through the list

419

via the Enumerator object it gets from the original list, keeping the current item from the Enumerator and checking whether the enumerator returns a true value while calling the MoveNext. As long as this MoveNext returns, the iteration will continue and the current item from the enumerator will hold locally. If the MoveNext returns false, the iteration will end and the current value will be return as the last item of the list. The implementation of this constructor is shown in Listing 12-55.

Listing 12-55. Implementation of the Last Method

```
public static TSource Last<TSource>(this IEnumerable<TSource> source)
{
    IList<TSource> list = source as IList<TSource>;
    if (list != null)
    {
        int count = list.Count;
        if (count > 0)
            return list[count - 1];
    }
    else
    {
        using (IEnumerator<TSource> enumerator = source.GetEnumerator())
        {
            if (enumerator.MoveNext())
            {
                TSource current;
                do
                {
                    /* Hold the Current item from the original list */
                    current = enumerator.Current;
                }while (enumerator.MoveNext());
                return current;
            }
        }
    }
    throw Error.NoElements();
}
```

To execute the overloaded version of the Last method, as used in Listing 12-55, the C# compiler will construct a method <Main>b__1 using the anonymous method (item => item > 3) in the compile time and the CLR will instantiate an instance of the MulticastDelegate using the <Main>b__1. The CLR passes this instance to the Last method. The CLR will loop through the list and match with each element in the sequence based on the condition provided in the predicate. This will return the last element that satisfies the condition, otherwise the default value of the type is provided as a generic type, as shown in the implementation of the Last method in Listing 12-56.

Listing 12-56. Implementation of the Last Method

```
public static TSource Last<TSource>(
    this IEnumerable<TSource> source,
    Func<TSource, bool> predicate)
{
    TSource local = default(TSource);
    bool flag = false;
```

```
    foreach (TSource local2 in source)
    {
        if (predicate(local2))
            local = local2;
            flag = true;
    }
    return local;
}
```

LastOrDefault

The LastOrDefault method returns the last element of a sequence or a default value if no element is found. The method signature for this extension method is:

```
public static TSource LastOrDefault<TSource>(this IEnumerable<TSource> source)
public static TSource LastOrDefault<TSource>(
    this IEnumerable<TSource> source, Func<TSource, bool> predicate)
```

Listing 12-57 demonstrates the use of the LastOrDefault method.

Listing 12-57. Example of the LastOrDefault Method

```
using System;
using System.Collections;
using System.Collections.Generic;
using System.Linq;

namespace Ch12
{
    class Program
    {
        static void Main(string[] args)
        {
            IList<int> firstNumbers = new List<int>();

            IList<int> secondNumbers = new List<int>()
            {
                1,2,3,4,5,6,7
            };

            var lastItemOfFirstList = firstNumbers.LastOrDefault();
            var lastItemIfFirstListBasedOnConditions =
                firstNumbers.LastOrDefault(item => item > 3);

            var lastItemOfSecondList = secondNumbers.LastOrDefault();
            var lastItemOfSecondListBasedOnConditions =
                secondNumbers.LastOrDefault(item => item > 3);

            Console.Write(string.Format("{0}\t{1}\t{2}\t{3}",
                lastItemOfFirstList,
                lastItemIfFirstListBasedOnConditions,
```

```
                    lastItemOfSecondList,
                    lastItemOfSecondListBasedOnConditions
                    ));
        }
    }
}
```

This program will produce the output:

```
0        0        7        7
```


Internal Operation of the LastOrDefault Method of Execution

The implementation code for the first version of the LastOrDefault method is:

```
public static TSource LastOrDefault<TSource>(this IEnumerable<TSource> source)
{
    IList<TSource> list = source as IList<TSource>;
    if (list != null)
    {
        int count = list.Count;
        if (count > 0)
            return list[count - 1];
    }
    else
    {
        using (IEnumerator<TSource> enumerator = source.GetEnumerator())
        {
            if (enumerator.MoveNext())
            {
                TSource current;
                do
                {
                    current = enumerator.Current;
                }
                while (enumerator.MoveNext());
                return current;
            }
        }
    }
    return default(TSource);
}
```

The implementation of the second version of the LastOrDefault extension method is:

```
public static TSource LastOrDefault<TSource>(
    this IEnumerable<TSource> source,
    Func<TSource, bool> predicate)
{
    TSource local = default(TSource);
    foreach (TSource local2 in source)
    {
```

```
        if (predicate(local2))
            local = local2;
    }
    return local;
}
```

Single and SingleOrDefault

The Single method returns a single, specific element of a sequence. The method signature for the extension method is:

```
public static TSource Single<TSource>(this IEnumerable<TSource> source)
public static TSource Single<TSource>(this IEnumerable<TSource> source,
                                    Func<TSource, bool> predicate)
public static TSource SingleOrDefault<TSource>(this IEnumerable<TSource>
                                            source)
public static TSource SingleOrDefault<TSource>(
    this IEnumerable<TSource> source, Func<TSource, bool> predicate)
```

This method returns the only element of a sequence and throws an exception if there is not exactly one element in the sequence. It returns the only element of a sequence that satisfies a specified condition and throws an exception if more than one such element exists.

Listing 12-58 presents a program that uses the Single extension method. In this program, the Single method works over the numbers that contains only an item and returns One as the output.

Listing 12-58. Use of the Single Extension Method

```
using System;
using System.Collections;
using System.Collections.Generic;
using System.Linq;

namespace Ch12
{
    class Program
    {
        static void Main(string[] args)
        {
            IList<string> numbers = new List<string>
            {
                "One"
            };
            var result = numbers.Single();
            Console.WriteLine("{0}", result);
        }
    }
}
```

The program in Listing 12-58 will produce the output:

```
One
```

Internal Operation of the Single and SingleOrDefault Methods of Execution

If you modify the code in Listing 12-58 and add one more item in the numbers list, the CLR will then throw an exception:

```
Unhandled Exception: System.InvalidOperationException: Sequence contains more than one element
    at System.Linq.Enumerable.Single[TSource](IEnumerable'1 source)
    at Ch12.Program.Main(String[] args) in J:\Book\ExpertC#2012\SourceCode\BookExamples\Ch12\
Program.cs:line 16
```

Let's find out how this works behind the scenes. While executing the Single method, the CLR will make a new List<string> using a copy of the original list and check whether or not the new list is null. If it is not null, then it will check the number of items in the list. If the number of items in the list is zero, then the CLR will throw an exception, otherwise if it is one, it will return the first and only item from the list. The implementation of the Single method is shown in Listing 12-59.

Listing 12-59. Implementation of the Single Method

```
public static TSource Single<TSource>(this IEnumerable<TSource> source)
{
    IList<TSource> list = source as IList<TSource>;
    if (list != null)
    {
        switch (list.Count)
        {
            case 0:
                throw Error.NoElements();

            case 1:
                return list[0];
        }
    }
    else
    {
        using (IEnumerator<TSource> enumerator = source.GetEnumerator())
        {
            TSource current = enumerator.Current;
            if (!enumerator.MoveNext())
                return current;
        }
    }
    throw Error.MoreThanOneElement();
}
```

Let's try the Single extension method with a predicate function, as demonstrated in Listing 12-60.

Listing 12-60. Usage of the Single Method

```
using System;
using System.Collections;
using System.Collections.Generic;
using System.Linq;
```

```
namespace Ch12
{
    class Program
    {
        static void Main(string[] args)
        {
            IList<string> numbers = new List<string>
            {
                "One","Four"
            };
            var result = numbers.Single(x => x.Length > 3);
            Console.WriteLine("{0}", result);
        }
    }
}
```

This program produces the output:

Four

Let's analyze Listing 12-60 to understand what's happening while we are executing the Single method, as demonstrated in Figure 12-23.

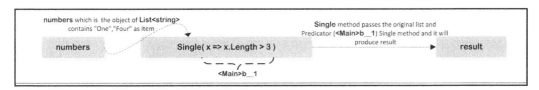

Figure 12-23. *How the Single method works*

If you modify the program in Listing 12-60 by adding one more items whose length is more than three characters, the program will fail by throwing an exception.

SingleOrDefault works much the same way as the Single extension method, but instead of throwing an exception when there is no item, it returns the default value of the type defined in the method call as generic type. Let's look at the example in Listing 12-61 of the use of the SingleOrDefault method.

Listing 12-61. Example of SingleOrDefault Method

```
using System;
using System.Collections;
using System.Collections.Generic;
using System.Linq;

namespace Ch12
{
    class Program
    {
        static void Main(string[] args)
        {
            IList<string> listStringWithoutItem = new List<string>();
            IList<string> listStringWithItem = new List<string>() { "One" };
```

```
IList<int> listInt = new List<int>();
IList<char> listChar = new List<char>();
IList<long> listLong = new List<long>();
IList<double> listDouble = new List<double>();

Console.WriteLine("string   : {0}",
                     listStringWithoutItem.SingleOrDefault());
Console.WriteLine("string   : {0}",
                     listStringWithItem.SingleOrDefault());
Console.WriteLine("int      : {0}", listInt.SingleOrDefault());
Console.WriteLine("char     : {0}", listChar.SingleOrDefault());
Console.WriteLine("long     : {0}", listLong.SingleOrDefault());
Console.WriteLine("double   : {0}", listDouble.SingleOrDefault());
        }
    }
}
```

The program in Listing 12-61 will produce the output:

```
string      :
string      : One
int         : 0
char        :
long        : 0
double      : 0
```

Let's analyze the code in Listing 12-61 to understand what's happening when the CLR executes the SingleOrDefault method.

The CLR makes a copy of the original list in a temporary list. It then checks the number of items in the list, if it is zero then the CLR will return the default value of the provided type, for example, the string listStringWithoutItem.SingleOrDefault<string>(), or inferred type from the list (for example, listStringWithoutItem is a type of IList<string> so the inferred type will be string). The implementation of the SingleOrDefault method is demonstrated in Listing 12-62.

Listing 12-62. Implementation of SingleOrDefault Method

```
public static TSource SingleOrDefault<TSource>(this IEnumerable<TSource> source)
{
    IList<TSource> list = source as IList<TSource>;
    if (list != null)
    {
        switch (list.Count)
        {
            case 0:
                return default(TSource);

            case 1:
                return list[0];
        }
    }
    else
    {
```

```
        using (IEnumerator<TSource> enumerator = source.GetEnumerator())
        {
            if (!enumerator.MoveNext())
                return default(TSource);

            TSource current = enumerator.Current;

            if (!enumerator.MoveNext())
                return current;
        }
    }
    throw Error.MoreThanOneElement();
}
```

ElementAt

The ElementAt extension method returns the element at a specified index in a sequence. The method signature for this extension method is:

```
public static TSource ElementAt<TSource>(this IEnumerable<TSource> source, int index)
```

Listing 12-63 presents the program for use of the ElementAt method.

Listing 12-63. Example of the ElementAt Method

```
using System;
using System.Collections.Generic;
using System.Linq;

namespace Ch12
{
    class Program
    {
        static void Main(string[] args)
        {
            IList<string> numbers = new List<string>()
            {
                "One","Two","Three"
            };

            var elementAt = numbers.ElementAt(1);

            Console.WriteLine(elementAt);
        }
    }
}
```

This program produces the output:

```
Two
```

Internal Operation of the ElementAt Method of Execution

Let's analyze the code in Listing 12-63 carefully to understand what's happening when we execute the ElementAt method.

1. *Step 1*: The CLR calls the get_Item method from the System.Collections. Generic.List'1<T> while executing the ElementAt<TSource>() extension method. Listing 12-64 has been extracted from the ElementAt method of the System.Linq. Enumerable class of the mscorlib.dll assembly using the ildasm.exe, as shown in Listing 12-64.

Listing 12-64. *Example of the ElementAt Method*

```
.method public hidebysig static !!TSource ElementAt<TSource>(
        class [mscorlib]System.Collections.Generic.IEnumerable'1<!!TSource> source,
        int32 index) cil managed
{
  IL_0018: ldloc.0
  /* Load the argument which is used as the index to retrieve item from
   * the array */
  IL_0019: ldarg.1
  IL_001a: callvirt    instance !0 class
             [mscorlib]System.Collections.Generic.IList'1<!!TSource>::
             get_Item(int32)
  IL_001f: ret
} // end of method Enumerable::ElementAt
```

From this code you can see that the CLR calls the get_Item(int32) method of the System.Collections. Generic.List'1<T> class with the index (input of the ElementAt method).

2. *Step 2*: The get_Item(int32) method will load the _items array of this class(label IL_000f in the following IL code) and will load the argument(label IL_0014 in the following IL code) to get the index, which will later be used to access the item from the _items array based on the index. The IL code in Listing 12-65 of the get_Item(int32) method is extracted from the System.Collections.Generic. List'1<T> class from the mscorlib.dll using ildasm.exe.

Listing 12-65. *Example of the ElementAt Method*

```
.method public hidebysig newslot specialname virtual final
        instance !T  get_Item(int32 index) cil managed
{
  IL_000e:  ldarg.0
  /* It will load the _items array */
  IL_000f:  ldfld       !0[] class System.Collections.Generic.List'1<!T>::_items
  IL_0014:  ldarg.1

  /* CLR will load an item based on the index value provided into !T  */
  IL_0015:  ldelem      !T
  IL_001a:  ret
} // end of method List'1::get_Item
```

In Listing 12-65, the ldfld IL instruction used in the IL_000f will load the _items field of the List<T> class, and on the IL_0014 label it will load argument 1, which is the index of the array that will be used to access the item from the _items array using the IL instruction ldelem used in the IL_0015.

■ ldfld filedName: It will push the value of the field specified in the specified to the method's (get_item) stack.

■ ldelem indexPosition: It will load an element from the position specified in indexPosition from the array.

ElementAtOrDefault

The ElementAtOrDefault method returns the element at a specified index in a sequence or a default value if the index is out of range. The method signature is:

```
public static TSource ElementAtOrDefault<TSource>(this IEnumerable<TSource> source, int index)
```

Listing 12-66 presents an example of the ElementAtOrDefault method.

Listing 12-66. Example of the ElementAtOrDefault Method

```
using System;
using System.Collections.Generic;
using System.Linq;
using System.Linq.Expressions;
namespace Ch12
{
    public struct MyStruct
    {
        public string Name { get; set; }
    }
    public class Person
    {
        public string PersonID { get; set; }
        public int PersonAge { get; set; }
    }
    class Program
    {
        static void Main(string[] args)
        {
            List<string> series = new List<string> { "One", "Two", "Three" };
            List<MyStruct> names = new List<MyStruct>
            {
                new MyStruct{ Name="A"},
                new MyStruct{ Name="B"},
            };
            List<Person> persons = new List<Person>
            {
                new Person { PersonID = "PA_01", PersonAge = 6 },
                new Person { PersonID = "PB_01", PersonAge = 7 },
```

```
            };
            // output will be null
            var item = series.ElementAtOrDefault(8);
            // Output contain an instnce of MyStruct in where Name will be null
            var name = names.ElementAtOrDefault(8);
            //Output will be null
            var person = persons.ElementAtOrDefault(8);
        }
    }
}
```

Internal Operation of the ElementAtOrDefault Method of Execution

For the ElementAtOrDefault method, the CLR will pass the original list and the index into the ElementAtOrDefault method. It will then find the item from the specified index or otherwise return the default values, for example, the default value for reference and nullable types is null, or the default value for the value type (see Chapter 1).

DefaultIfEmpty

The DefaultIfEmpty method returns the elements of an IEnumerable<T> or a default valued singleton collection if the sequence is empty. The signature for this extension method is:

```
public static IEnumerable<TSource> DefaultIfEmpty<TSource>(this IEnumerable<TSource> source)
public static IEnumerable<TSource> DefaultIfEmpty<TSource>(
    this IEnumerable<TSource> source, TSource defaultValue)
```

The first version returns the elements of the specified sequence or the type parameter's default value in a singleton collection if the sequence is empty. The second version returns the elements of the specified sequence or the specified value in a singleton collection if the sequence is empty.

This method can be used on a list that does not have items in it. If we call the extension method over this list, it will return the default value of the item. Listing 12-67 presents a program using the DefaultIfEmpty method.

Listing 12-67. Use of the DefaultIfEmpty Method

```
using System.Collections;
using System.Collections.Generic;
using System.Linq;

namespace Ch12
{
    class Program
    {
        static void Main(string[] args)
        {

            IList<Person> persons = new List<Person>();
            IList<int> numbers = new List<int>();
            IList<string> names = new List<string>();
            /* Output: A list with 1 item with the null value */
            var defaultPersons = persons.DefaultIfEmpty();
```

```
            /*Output: A list with 1 item with the 0 value */
             var defaultNumbers = numbers.DefaultIfEmpty().ToList();
            /* Output: A list with 1 item with the null value */
             var defaultNames = names.DefaultIfEmpty();
        }
    }

    class Person
    {
        public string Name
        {
            get;
            set;
        }

        public string Address
        {
            get;
            set;
        }

        public int Age
        {
            get;
            set;
        }
    }
}
```

Internal Operation of the DefaultIfEmpty Method of Execution

Listing 12-67 has three lists, such as persons, numbers, and names, of type Person, int, and string, respectively. These three lists do not have any items, as the Count Property of this list returns zero. When the DefaultIfEmpty method is called over any of this list, the CLR will then:

- Copy the list to this DefaultIfEmpty method. From this method the CLR will return the instance of the DefaultIfEmptyIterator<TSource> iterator, which will hold the default value and source value for the related type. The defaultvalue property will contain the default value of the type of list it is processing, and the source will be the original list.

- Pass the DefaultIfEmptyIterator to the ToList method, which will call the List class passing the object of the DefaultIfEmptyIterator as input. In this class, CLR will iterate through the original list and process the result.

The implementation of the DefaultIfEmptyIterator is shown in Listing 12-68.

Listing 12-68. *Implementation of the DefaultIfEmptyIterator Method*

```
private static IEnumerable<TSource> DefaultIfEmptyIterator<TSource>(
    IEnumerable<TSource> source,
    TSource defaultValue)
```

```
{
    using (IEnumerator<TSource> iteratorVariable0 = source.GetEnumerator())
    {
        if (iteratorVariable0.MoveNext())
            do
            {
                yield return iteratorVariable0.Current;
            }
            while (iteratorVariable0.MoveNext());
        else
            yield return defaultValue;
    }
}
```

From Listing 12-68, you can see that the iterator is not be able to iterate through, and as a result, the CLR will return the value of defaultValue of the DefaultIfEmptyIterator. In this circumstance, the defaultValue of the DefaultIfEmptyIterator for the persons.DefaultIfEmpty() will hold null (because persons is a type IList<Person>), zero for the numbers (because it is a type of IList<int>), and null for the names (because it is a type of the IList<string>).

Generation-Based Methods

This section will examine the Empty, Range, and Repeat extension methods.

Empty

The Empty method returns an empty IEnumerable<T>. The method signature for this extension is:

```
public static IEnumerable<TResult> Empty<TResult>()
```

Listing 12-69 shows the use of the Empty method.

Listing 12-69. Example of the Empty Method

```
using System;
using System.Linq;

namespace Ch12
{
    class Program
    {
        static void Main(string[] args)
        {
            var emptyList = Enumerable.Empty<int>();

            Console.WriteLine(emptyList.Count());
        }
    }
}
```

The program in Listing 12-69 produces the output:

```
0
```

Internal Operation of the Empty Method of Execution

When the CLR executes the Empty method, as shown in Listing 12-69, it creates an empty list of int. Let's analyze the code in the Listing 12-69 to help us understand what's happening as we execute this program.

1. *Step 1*: The CLR calls the get_Instance method of the EmptyEnumerable'1<!!TResult> (an internal class from the System.Linq namespace of the System.Core.dll assembly) while executing the Empty<TResult> method. This class has an array field of given type (!!TResult) and a property instance that returns the array field. The IL code in Listing 12-70 of the Empty method (decompiled from the System.Core.dll assembly) demonstrates how the get_Instance method is being called.

Listing 12-70. Example of the Empty Method

```
.method public hidebysig static class
        [mscorlib]System.Collections.Generic.IEnumerable'1<!!TResult>
        Empty<TResult>() cil managed
{
  IL_0000:  call class [mscorlib]System.Collections.Generic.IEnumerable'1<!0>
             class System.Linq.EmptyEnumerable'1<!!TResult>::get_Instance()
  IL_0005:  ret
} // end of method Enumerable::Empty
```

2. *Step 2*: The instance property from the System.Linq. EmptyEnumerable'1<!!TResult> will call the get_Instance method. The get_Instance method will create an array with zero items. The CLR will first push zero onto the stack as int32 type using the ldc.i4.0 IL instruction from the label IL_0007 as shown in Listing 12-71. Using the newarr IL instruction, the CLR will create a new array with the zero item and will push it onto the Stack. In the label IL_000d, the CLR will use stsfld to replace the value of the field value (i.e., instance field's value using the value from the Stack).

Listing 12-71. Internal Operation of the get_Instance Method

```
.method public hidebysig specialname static
        class [mscorlib]System.Collections.Generic.IEnumerable'1<!TElement>
        get_Instance() cil managed
{
  // code size       24 (0x18)
  .maxstack  8
  IL_0000:  ldsfld     !0[] class
             System.Linq.EmptyEnumerable'1<!TElement>::'instance'
  IL_0005:  brtrue.s   IL_0012
  IL_0007:  ldc.i4.0
  IL_0008:  newarr     !TElement
  IL_000d:  stsfld     !0[] class
             System.Linq.EmptyEnumerable'1<!TElement>::'instance'
  IL_0012:  ldsfld     !0[] class
             System.Linq.EmptyEnumerable'1<!TElement>::'instance'
  IL_0017:  ret
} // end of method EmptyEnumerable'1::get_Instance
```

Range

The Range method generates a sequence of integral numbers within a specified range, implemented by using deferred execution. The immediate return value is an instance of the relevant iterator instance that stores all the information required to perform the action. The method signature for this method is:

```
public static IEnumerable<int> Range(int start, int count)
```

This method will create a list of int items based on the start number until the number of times is defined in the count. Listing 12-72 demonstrates the use of the Range method.

Listing 12-72. Example of the Range Method

```
using System;
using System.Linq;

namespace Ch12
{
    class Program
    {
        static void Main(string[] args)
        {
            Enumerable.Range(1, 10).ToList().ForEach(x =>
                    Console.Write("{0}\t", x));
        }
    }
}
```

The program in Listing 12-72 will produce the output:

```
1       2       3       4       5       6       7       8       9       10
```

Internal Operation of the Range Method of Execution

Figure 12-24 demonstrates how the CLR executes the Range method.

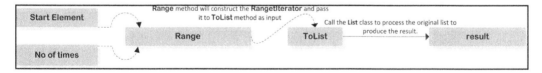

Figure 12-24. How the Range method works

The CLR follows these steps to execute the Range operation:

1. *Step 1*: The CLR passes the start element and the length of the generated sequence to the Range method as input. The code in Listing 12-73 demonstrates that the CLR will return the RangeIterator<int>, which will hold all the related information such as the start element and length of the sequence inside it as a return.

Listing 12-73. Implementation of the Range Method

```
public static IEnumerable<int> Range(int start, int count)
{
    long num = (start + count) - 1L;
    return RangeIterator(start, count);
}
```

The RangeIterator<int> will not be executed (due to the deferred execution) until the CLR calls the ToList method.

2. *Step 2*: The CLR will pass this RangeIterator<int> to the ToList method to the List class and process the operation based on the iteration logic implemented in the RangeIterator<int> class and produce the ranged sequence as output. The implementation of the RangeIterator<int> is shown in Listing 12-74.

Listing 12-74. Implementation of the RangeIterator Method

```
private static IEnumerable<int> RangeIterator(int start, int count)
{
    int iteratorVariable0 = 0;
    while (true)
    {
        if (iteratorVariable0 >= count)
            yield break;

        yield return (start + iteratorVariable0);
        iteratorVariable0++;
    }
}
```

Repeat

The Repeat method generates a sequence that contains one repeated value as implemented by using deferred execution. The immediate return value is an object of the relevant iterator type that stores all the information that is required to perform the action. The method signature of this extension method is:

```
public static IEnumerable<TResult> Repeat<TResult>(TResult element, int count)
```

It will generate a sequence of a number defined by the TResult type of a number of times measured by the count, as shown in Listing 12-75.

Listing 12-75. Example of the Repeat Method

```
using System;
using System.Collections.Generic;
using System.Linq;

namespace Ch12
{
    class Program
    {
        static void Main(string[] args)
```

```
        {
            Enumerable.Repeat(1, 5).ToList().
                    ForEach(x=>Console.Write("{0}\t",x));
        }
    }
}
```

The Repeat method of the Enumerable class will generate a sequence of 1 five times. It will produce the output:

```
1       1       1       1       1
```

Internal Operation of the Repeat Method of Execution

The CLR will follow the following steps in executing the Repeat method:

1. *Step 1*: The CLR will pass the element to repeat and number of times to repeat the element to the Repeat method as input. Inside the Repeat method, it will construct the RepeatIterator<TResult> iterator, which will hold the related information to generate the sequence.

2. *Step 2*: The CLR will pass this RepeatIterator<TResult> instance to the ToList method, which will pass this iterator to the List class and process the operation based on the iteration logic implemented in the RepeatIterator<TResult> and produce the repeated sequence as output. The implementation of the Repeat method is:

```
private static IEnumerable<TResult> RepeatIterator<TResult>(TResult element, int count)
{
    int iteratorVariable0 = 0;
    while (true)
    {
        if (iteratorVariable0 >= count)
            yield break;

        yield return element;
        iteratorVariable0++;
    }
}
```

Conversion-Based Methods

This section will examine the different conversion-based extension methods, such as Cast, ToArray, OfType, ToDictionary, ToList, and ToLookup.

Cast

The Cast method casts the elements of a sequence to the specified type. This method is implemented by using deferred execution. Listing 12-76 presents an example of the Cast method.

Listing 12-76. Example of the Cast Method

```
using System;
using System.Collections;
using System.Linq;
namespace Ch12
{
    class Program
    {
        static void Main(string[] args)
        {
            ArrayList numbers = new ArrayList();
            numbers.Add("One");
            numbers.Add("Two");
            numbers.Add("Three");
            numbers.Cast<string>().Select(number => number).ToList().ForEach(
                number => Console.Write("{0}\t", number));
        }
    }
}
```

The program will produce the output:

```
One      Two       Three
```

Internal Operation of the Cast Method of Execution

Let's analyze the code in the Listing 12-76 to understand what's happening, when the CLR executes the Cast method. Figure 12-25 demonstrates that the numbers will be passed as input to the Cast method internally.

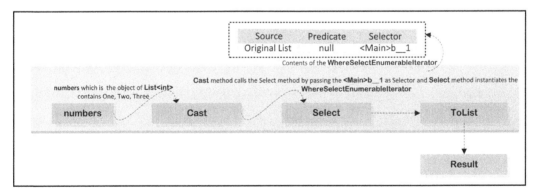

Figure 12-25. Internal operation of the Cast method

The CLR follows several steps in executing the Cast method:

1. *Step 1*: It encapsulates the original list numbers into the CastIterator and passes this to the Select method.

2. *Step 2*: The Select method will construct the WhereSelectEnumerableIterator and pass it to the ToList method, and this will iterate through the enumerator

and cast the iterated item with the inferred type, for example, for the code in Listing 12-76, it is string. The implementation of the CastIterator is:

```
private static IEnumerable<TResult> CastIterator<TResult>(IEnumerable source)
{
    IEnumerator enumerator = source.GetEnumerator();
    while (enumerator.MoveNext())
    {
        object current = enumerator.Current;
        yield return (TResult) current;
    }
}
```

ToArray

The ToArray method will create an array from the given list. The program in Listing 12-77 shows the use of the ToArray method. ToList<TSource> has similar behavior, but it returns a List<T> instead of an array. The method signature is:

```
public static TSource[] ToArray<TSource>(this IEnumerable<TSource> source)
```

Listing 12-77. Example of the ToArray Method

```
using System;
using System.Collections;
using System.Collections.Generic;
using System.Linq;

namespace Ch12
{
    class Program
    {
        static void Main(string[] args)
        {
            IList<int> firstList = new List<int>()
            {
                1,2,3,4
            };

            var result = firstList.ToArray();
            result.ToList().ForEach(x =>
                        Console.Write(string.Format("{0}\t",x)));
        }
    }
}
```

This program will produce the output:

```
1       2       3       4
```

Internal Operation of the ToArray Method of Execution

Let's analyze the code in Listing 12-77 to understand what's happening when the CLR executes the ToArray method.

1. *Step 1*: The CLR passes the original list as input to the ToArray<TSource> method. Inside the ToArray method it will create an instance of the Buffer<TSource> type by passing the original list object as input.

2. *Step 2*: The CLR will copy each of the items from the original list to an internal array named items. The implementation of the ToArray method is:

```
public static TSource[] ToArray<TSource>(this IEnumerable<TSource> source)
{
    Buffer<TSource> buffer = new Buffer<TSource>(source);

    return buffer.ToArray();
}
```

The internal struct of the Buffer<TSource> is:

```
internal struct Buffer<TElement>
{
    internal TElement[] items;
    internal int count;
    internal Buffer(IEnumerable<TElement> source)
    {
        TElement[] array = null;
        int length = 0;
        ICollection<TElement> i.= source as ICollection<TElement>;
        if (i.!= null)
        {
            length = i..Count;
            if (length > 0)
            {
                array = new TElement[length];
                i..CopyTo(array, 0);
            }
        }
        else
        {
            foreach (TElement local in source)
            {
                if (array == null)
                {
                    array = new TElement[4];
                }
                else if (array.Length == length)
                {
                    TElement[] destinationArray = new TElement[length * 2];
                    Array.Copy(array, 0, destinationArray, 0, length);
                    array = destinationArray;
                }
```

```
                array[length] = local;
                length++;
            }
        }
        this.items = array;
        this.count = length;
    }
}
```

3. *Step 3*: When the CLR calls the ToArray method, it will return the items.

The implementation of the ToArray method is:

```
internal TElement[] ToArray()
{
    if (this.count == 0)
        return new TElement[0];

    if (this.items.Length == this.count)
        return this.items;

    TElement[] destinationArray = new TElement[this.count];
    Array.Copy(this.items, 0, destinationArray, 0, this.count);
    return destinationArray;
}
```

From this source code we can see that a copy of the items array is returned as output of the ToArray method.

OfType

The OfType extension method filters the elements of an IEnumerable based on a specified type using the deferred execution. The immediate return value is an object of the iterator class, which stores all the information that is required to perform the action. The signature of this extension method is:

```
public static IEnumerable<TResult> OfType<TResult>(this IEnumerable source)
```

Listing 12-78 presents an example of use of the OfType method.

***Listing 12-78.** Example of the OfType<TResult> Method*

```
using System;
using System.Collections.Generic;
using System.Linq;

namespace Ch12
{
    class Program
    {
        static void Main(string[] args)
        {
            IList<object> numbers = new List<object>()
            {
```

```
                    "One",
                    "Two",
                    1,
                    2,
                    "Three",
                    new Person
                    {
                        Name="A Person"
                    }
            };

            var filteredNumbers = numbers.OfType<string>();

            filteredNumbers.ToList().ForEach(x => Console.Write("{0}\t", x));
            Console.WriteLine();
        }
    }

    public class Person
    {
        public string Name { get; set; }
    }
}
```

This program will filter string values from the numbers list as string type used in OfType method. The program will produce the output:

```
One     Two     Three
```

Internal Operation of the OfType Method of Execution

Let's analyze the code in Listing 12-78 to really understand what's happening when the CLR executes the OfType method.

1. *Step 1*: The CLR will pass the sequence, for example, numbers in this example, to the OfType method as input. Inside the OfType method, the CLR will instantiate the OfTypeIterator, which will hold the original sequence inside it. The implementation of the OfType method is:

```
public static IEnumerable<TResult> OfType<TResult>(this IEnumerable source)
{
    return OfTypeIterator<TResult>(source);
}
```

2. *Step 2*: The CLR will pass the instance of the OfTypeIterator<TResult> class to the ToList method, which will pass this iterator to the List class and process the operation based on the iteration logic implemented in the OfTypeIterator and produce the ranged sequence as output. The implementation of the RangeIterator is:

```
private static IEnumerable<TResult> OfTypeIterator<TResult>(IEnumerable source)
{
    IEnumerator enumerator = source.GetEnumerator();
```

```
        while (enumerator.MoveNext())
        {
            object current = enumerator.Current;
            if (current is TResult)
                yield return (TResult) current;
        }
    }
}
```

ToDictionary

The ToDictionary method creates a Dictionary<TKey, TValue> from an IEnumerable<T>. If you want to create a dictionary object based on the data in a list, this method will take care of it, but you need to specify a field from the list data as a key. The signature of this method is:

```
public static Dictionary<TKey, TSource> ToDictionary<TSource, TKey>(
    this IEnumerable<TSource> source, Func<TSource, TKey> keySelector)
public static Dictionary<TKey, TSource> ToDictionary<TSource, TKey>(
    this IEnumerable<TSource> source,
    Func<TSource, TKey> keySelector, IEqualityComparer<TKey> comparer)
public static Dictionary<TKey, TElement> ToDictionary<TSource, TKey, TElement>(
    this IEnumerable<TSource> source,
    Func<TSource, TKey> keySelector, Func<TSource, TElement> elementSelector)
public static Dictionary<TKey, TElement> ToDictionary<TSource, TKey, TElement>(
    this IEnumerable<TSource> source, Func<TSource, TKey> keySelector,
    Func<TSource, TElement> elementSelector, IEqualityComparer<TKey> comparer)
```

Listing 12-79 presents an example to explain the use of the ToDictionary method.

Listing 12-79. Example of ToDictionary Method

```
using System;
using System.Collections;
using System.Collections.Generic;
using System.Linq;

namespace Ch12
{
    class Program
    {
        static void Main(string[] args)
        {
            IList<Person> persons = new List<Person>()
            {
                new Person(){ Name="Person A", Address= "Address of A",
                            Id= 111111},
                new Person(){ Name="Person B", Address= "Address of B",
                            Id= 111112},
                new Person(){ Name="Person C", Address= "Address of C",
                            Id= 111113},
                new Person(){ Name="Person D", Address= "Address of D",
                            Id= 111114},
```

```
        };

        var result = persons.ToDictionary(person => person.Id);

        foreach (KeyValuePair<double, Person> person in result)
        {
            Console.WriteLine("{0,-15} {1,-20}{2,-20}{3,-20}",
                person.Key,
                person.Value.Name,
                person.Value.Address,
                person.Value.Id);
        }
    }
}


public class Person
{
    public string Name
    {
        get;
        set;
    }

    public string Address
    {
        get;
        set;
    }

    public double Id
    {
        get;
        set;
    }
}
}
```

The program in Listing 12-79 produces the output:

```
111111          Person A        Address of A        111111
111112          Person B        Address of B        111112
111113          Person C        Address of C        111113
111114          Person D        Address of D        111114
```

Internal Operation of the ToDictionary Method of Execution

From the code in Listing 12-79 you can see that a list of Person objects was created and stored in persons and then converted persons into a dictionary using the ToDictionary method. ToDictionary takes an anonymous method as input. This anonymous method is actually a key selector that will select the key from the list and set it as the key in the dictionary object. For example, Id from the Person is selected as the key for the result in the dictionary and the value is the person object itself. Interestingly, the Id property will be used as the key for the dictionary and it will also be stored as part of the person object as it was initialized. Let's analyze Listing 12-79 to help us understand what's happening when the CLR executes the ToDictionary method.

1. *Step 1*: If we open the System.Linq.Enumerable namespace from the System.core.dll assembly using ildasm.exe, you can see that the ToDictionary method internally calls the internal ToDictionary method, which has the signature:

```
public static Dictionary<TKey, TElement> ToDictionary<TSource, TKey, TElement>(
    this IEnumerable<TSource> source, Func<TSource, TKey> keySelector,
    Func<TSource, TElement> elementSelector, IEqualityComparer<TKey> comparer)
```

Before the CLR calls the internal ToDictionary method from the ToDictionary extension method, it will create an element selector function. Although we haven't provided any element selector in Listing 12-79, the CLR will use the default element selector, which is IdentityFunction<TSource>.Instance, which is an internal class that will be used as an element selector for the ToDictionary method. Figure 12-26 shows this class from the System.Core.dll assembly.

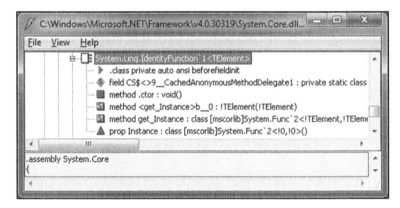

Figure 12-26. IdentityFunction in the System.Linq

The implementation of the ToDictionary method is presented in Listing 12-80.

Listing 12-80. Implementation of the ToDictionary Method

```
public static Dictionary<TKey, TSource> ToDictionary<TSource, TKey>(
    this IEnumerable<TSource> source,
    Func<TSource, TKey> keySelector)
{
    return source.ToDictionary<TSource, TKey, TSource>(
        keySelector, IdentityFunction<TSource>.Instance, null);
}
```

2. *Step 2*: When the CLR goes to the above method, it calls the overloaded ToDictionary as shown in Listing 12-81.

Listing 12-81. Implementation of the ToDictionary Method

```
public static Dictionary<TKey, TElement> ToDictionary<TSource, TKey, TElement>(
    this IEnumerable<TSource> source, Func<TSource, TKey> keySelector,
    Func<TSource, TElement> elementSelector, IEqualityComparer<TKey> comparer)
{
    Dictionary<TKey, TElement> dictionary =
            new Dictionary<TKey, TElement>(comparer);

    foreach (TSource local in source)
        dictionary.Add(keySelector(local), elementSelector(local));
    return dictionary;
}
```

This will instantiate an instance of the Dictionary<TKey, TElement> class. It will then iterate through the original list, and each of the iterate values will pass to the KeySelector and ElementSelector functions to extract the Key and Value from the iterate value. The anonymous method (person => person.Id) will be used as the KeySelector. The C# compiler will generate an anonymous method <Main>b_5 and pass it to the KeySelector, which will return the Id from the person object, and the compiler will compile the ElementSelector (x=>x as in the IdentityFunction<TElement> where x=>x will be converted as <get_Instance>b__0), which will return the value itself (i.e., the person object with Name, Address and Id value inside).

ToList

The ToList method creates a List<T> from an IEnumerable<T>. The method signature for this extension method is:

```
public static List<TSource> ToList<TSource>(this IEnumerable<TSource> source)
```

Listing 12-82 provides the working details of the ToList method.

Listing 12-82. Example of the ToList() Extension Method

```
using System.Collections;
using System.Collections.Generic;
using System.Linq;
using System;

namespace Ch12
{
    class Program
    {
        static void Main(string[] args)
        {
            IList<int> numbers = new List<int>()
            {
                1,2,3,4,5,6,7,8,9,10
            };

            var result = numbers.Where(x => x > 3).ToList();

            result.ForEach(x => Console.Write("{0}\t", x));
```

```
        Console.WriteLine();
      }
    }
}
```

This program will produce the output:

4	5	6	7	8	9	10

Internal Operation of the ToList Method of Execution

Let's analyze the code in Listing 12-82 to really understand what's happening when the CLR executes the ToList method.

1. *Step 1*: The ToList method will accept an IEnumerable<TSource> object as input.
    It will pass this IEnumerable object as input to the List<TSource> type:

```
public static List<TSource> ToList<TSource>(this IEnumerable<TSource> source)
{
    return new List<TSource>(source);
}
```

Step 2: The List<IEnumerable<TSource>> type will accept an IEnumerable<TSource> collection as input of the constructor. Inside the constructor, the CLR will initialize the _items array with the type as TSource and define the initial size of the array with 4 by default. It will then iterate through the enumerator of the input list as demonstrated in Listing 12-83.

Listing 12-83. Implementation for the List Constructor

```
public List(IEnumerable<T> collection)
{
    ICollection<T> i. = collection as ICollection<T>;
    if (i. != null)
    {
        int count = i..Count;
        this._items = new T[count];
        i..CopyTo(this._items, 0);
        this._size = count;
    }
    else
    {
        this._size = 0;
        this._items = new T[4];
        using (IEnumerator<T> enumerator = collection.GetEnumerator())
        {
            while (enumerator.MoveNext())
                this.Add(enumerator.Current);
        }
    }
}
```

3. *Step 3*: The CLR passes each of the items from the iteration phase in step 2 to the Add(TSource item) method to add them into the _items array initialized in step 2. The implementation of the Add method is:

```
public void Add(T item)
{
    if (this._size == this._items.Length)
        this.EnsureCapacity(this._size + 1);

    this._items[this._size++] = item;
    this._version++;
}
```

In the Add method, the most important code is the line this.EnsureCapacity(this._size + 1). The size of this _items array is dynamic and it will be ensured by the EnsureCapacity method.

4. *Step 4*: After finishing the iteration, the CLR will return the list object as the output of the ToList method, which will contain elements returned from the given IEnumerable<TSource> object inside the _items array.

ToLookup

The ToLookup method creates a lookup based on the specified key selector. The method signature for this extension method is:

```
public static ILookup<TKey, TSource> ToLookup<TSource, TKey>(
        this IEnumerable<TSource> source, Func<TSource, TKey> keySelector)
public static ILookup<TKey, TSource> ToLookup<TSource, TKey>(
        this IEnumerable<TSource> source,
        Func<TSource, TKey> keySelector, IEqualityComparer<TKey> comparer)
public static ILookup<TKey, TElement> ToLookup<TSource, TKey, TElement>(
        this IEnumerable<TSource> source,
        Func<TSource, TKey> keySelector, Func<TSource, TElement> elementSelector)
public static ILookup<TKey, TElement> ToLookup<TSource, TKey, TElement>(
        this IEnumerable<TSource> source, Func<TSource, TKey> keySelector,
        Func<TSource, TElement> elementSelector, IEqualityComparer<TKey> comparer)
```

The ToLookup method will create a mapping of the Key and Value for a given list. In comparison to the Dictionary, this method will map one to many (i.e., Dictionary maps one key vs. one value), whereas the ToLookup method maps one key vs. many values. For example, if you have a list such as:

```
/* Before: applying the ToLookup Key and Data combination */
{ A, { A1.1,    A1.1  } }
{ A, { A2.2,    A2.2  } }
{ A, { A3.3,    A3.3  } }

{ B, { B1.1,    B1.1  } }

{ C, { C1.1,    C1.1  } }
{ C, { C2.1,    C2.2  } }
```

the ToLookup will produce the output:

```
/* After: applying the ToLookup Key and Data combination */
{ A,    { A1.1,    A1.1 } }
{       { A2.2,    A2.2 } }
{       { A3.3,    A3.3 } }

{ B,    { B1.1,    B1.1 } }

{ C,    { C1.1,    C1.1 } }

{       { C2.1,    C2.2 } }
```

So in the ToLookup method group, the entire set of items is based on the Key:

- All the data in A category groups under A

- All the data in B category groups under B

- All the data in C category groups under C

Figure 12-27 demonstrates the basics of the ToLookup method.

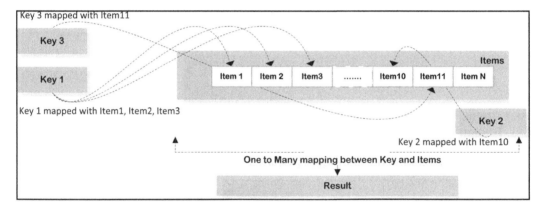

Figure 12-27. *Basic operation for the ToLookup method*

Listing 12-84 presents an example of the ToLookup method.

Listing 12-84. *Example of the ToLookup Method*

```
using System;
using System.Collections.Generic;
using System.Linq;

namespace Ch12
{
    class Program
    {
        static void Main(string[] args)
        {
            List<Person> persons = CreatePersonList();
```

```
        var result = persons.ToLookup(
            (key) => key.Name,
            (groupItem) => groupItem.Address);

        result.ToList().ForEach(item =>
        {
            Console.Write("Key:{0,11}\nValue:\t{1,12}\n",
                item.Key,
                string.Join("\n\t", item.Select(groupItem =>
                    groupItem).ToArray()));
        });
    }

    private static List<Person> CreatePersonList()
    {
        return new List<Person>()
        {
            new Person{ Name="APerson",     Address="APerson's Address"},
            new Person{ Name="AAPerson",    Address="AAPerson's Address"},
            new Person{ Name="APerson",
                        Address="APerson's Second Address"},
            new Person{ Name="BPerson",     Address="BPerson's Address"},
            new Person{ Name="BBPerson",    Address="BBPerson's Address"},
            new Person{ Name="BPerson",
                        Address="BPerson's Second Address"},
            new Person{ Name="CPerson",     Address="CPerson's Address"},
            new Person{ Name="CCPerson",    Address="CCPerson's Address"},
            new Person{ Name="CPerson",
                        Address="CPerson's Second Address"},
        };
    }
}

public class Person
{
    public string Name { get; set; }
    public string Address { get; set; }
}
}
```

This program will produce the output:

```
Key:    APerson
Value:  APerson's Address
        APerson's Second Address
Key:    AAPerson
Value:  AAPerson's Address
Key:    BPerson
Value:  BPerson's Address
        BPerson's Second Address
Key:    BBPerson
```

```
Value:  BBPerson's Address
Key:    CPerson
Value:  CPerson's Address
        CPerson's Second Address
Key:    CCPerson
Value:  CCPerson's Address
```

Internal Operation of the ToLookup Method of Execution

Let's analyze the code in Listing 12-84 to understand what's happening when the CLR executes the ToLookup method.

1. *Step 1*: The C# compiler will construct a method <Main>b__1 using the anonymous method (key) => key.Name and <Main>b__2 using the anonymous method (groupItem) => groupItem.Address. The CLR will instantiate two instances of the MulticastDelegate object using the <Main>b__1 and <Main>b__2 methods to pass them into the Lookup class as input to keySelector and elementSelector:

```
public static ILookup<TKey, TElement> ToLookup<TSource, TKey, TElement>(
        this IEnumerable<TSource> source,
        Func<TSource, TKey> keySelector, Func<TSource, TElement> elementSelector)
{
        return (ILookup<TKey, TElement>) Lookup<TKey, TElement>.Create<TSource>(
                source,             /* Original list */
                keySelector,        /* <Main>b__1 */
                elementSelector,    /* <Main>b__2 */
                null);              /* Comparer */
}
```

2. *Step 2*: Internally the Create method of the Lookup class will instantiate an instance of the Lookup class, which will initialize a data structure groupings (an array with default size 7) with the type Grouping and, as shown in this partial code, of the constructor of the Lookup class:

```
private Lookup(IEqualityComparer<TKey> comparer)
{
        /* Code removed */
        this.groupings = new Grouping<TKey, TElement>[7];
}
```

This groupings array will initially hold default values of the specified type. The CLR will then iterate through the original list and, based on the KeySelector and ElementSelector, it will add iterated items into the groupings array:

```
foreach (TSource local in source)
{
    lookup.GetGrouping(keySelector(local), true).Add(elementSelector(local));
}
```

On return of the Create method, the CLR will return the instance of the Lookup class, which will hold the lookup table for the original sequence. The implementation code for the Create method in the Lookup class is:

```
internal static Lookup<TKey, TElement> Create<TSource>(
    IEnumerable<TSource> source, Func<TSource, TKey> keySelector,
    Func<TSource, TElement> elementSelector, IEqualityComparer<TKey> comparer)
{
    Lookup<TKey, TElement> lookup = new Lookup<TKey, TElement>(comparer);
    foreach (TSource local in source)
    {
        lookup.GetGrouping(keySelector(local),
                        true).Add(elementSelector(local));
    }
    return lookup;
}
```

Miscellaneous Methods

This section explores the Zip method.

Zip

The Zip method applies a specified function to the corresponding elements of two sequences, producing a sequence of the results. The method iterate through the two input sequences, applying the function resultSelector to the corresponding elements of the two sequences. The method returns a sequence of the values, which are returned by the resultSelector. If the input sequences do not have the same number of elements, the method combines elements until it reaches the end of one of the sequences. For example, if one sequence has three elements and the other one has four, the result sequence has only three elements. This method is implemented by using deferred execution. The immediate return value is an object that stores all the information required to perform the action.

The Zip extension method will combine two list items based on the provided combination logic. Looking at the method signature provided, we can see it is an extension of the IEnumerable<TFirst> type and accepts IEnumerable<TSecond> second, Func<TFirst, TSecond, TResult> resultSelector items as input:

```
public static IEnumerable<TResult> Zip<TFirst, TSecond, TResult>(
    this IEnumerable<TFirst> first, IEnumerable<TSecond> second,
    Func<TFirst, TSecond, TResult> resultSelector)
```

So the items of first and second lists will be combined item by item to produce a new list based on the combination logic provided in the resultSelector Func. So you can see in Figure 12-28 that the Zip method will combine each of the items in the list.

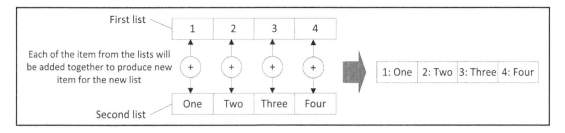

Figure 12-28. Basic operation of the Zip method

From Figure 12-28 you can see that the Zip method combined the items in the first list, which contains {1, 2, 3, 4}, with the items in the second list, which contains {"One","Two","Three","Four"} with combination logic: item from the first list + ":\t" + item from the second list. Listing 12-85 presents an example of the use of the Zip method.

Listing 12-85. Example of the Zip Method

```
using System;
using System.Collections;
using System.Collections.Generic;
using System.Linq;

namespace Ch12
{
    class Program
    {
        static void Main(string[] args)
        {
            IList<int> firstList = new List<int>()
            {
                1,2,3,4
            };

            IList<string> secondList = new List<string>()
            {
                "One","Two","Three","Four"
            };

            var result = firstList.Zip(secondList, (x, y) => x + ":\t" + y);

            result.ToList().ForEach(x => Console.WriteLine(x));
        }
    }
}
```

This program will produce the output:

```
1:      One
2:      Two
3:      Three
4:      Four
```

Internal Operation of the Zip Method of Execution

When the C# compiler finds the Zip method, it will follow these steps:

1. *Step 1*: The C# compiler will construct a method <Main>b__2 using the anonymous method (x, y) => x + ":\t" + y. The CLR will pass this <Main>b__2 method to the MulticastDelegate class to instantiate an instance of it. The C# compiler compiles the (x, y) => x + ":\t" + y code block into the method, as shown in Listing 12-86.

Listing 12-86. <Main>b__2 Method Contents

```
.method private hidebysig static string  '<Main>b_2'(int32 x,
                                                      string y) cil managed
{
  // code size        22 (0x16)
  .maxstack  3
  .locals init ([0] string CS$1$0000)
  IL_0000:  ldarg.0
  IL_0001:  box          [mscorlib]System.Int32
  IL_0006:  ldstr        ":\t"
  IL_000b:  ldarg.1
  IL_000c:  call         string [mscorlib]System.String::Concat(object,
                                                                object,
                                                                object)
  IL_0011:  stloc.0
  IL_0012:  br.s         IL_0014
  IL_0014:  ldloc.0
  IL_0015:  ret
} // end of method Program::'<Main>b_2'
```

2. *Step 2*: The CLR will pass the instance of the MulticastDelegate created in step 1 to the Zip method, which will return the ZipIterator<TFirst, TSecond, TResult> instance after doing a few basic checks internally. The ZipIterator<TFirst, TSecond, TResult> instance will hold the first and second list and resultSelector (instance of the MulticastDelegate created in step 1) inside it, as illustrated in Figure 12-29.

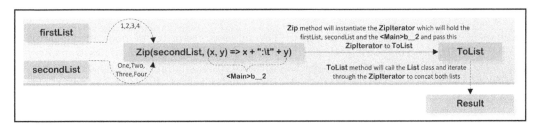

Figure 12-29. Operation details for the Zip method

3. *Step 3*: Because this Zip extension method will execute using a deferred execution pattern, whenever the CLR executes the ToList method it will iterate through the ZipIterator enumerator. Inside the ZipIterator enumerator the CLR will iterate through each of the lists and get the Current item from each list. It will pass that Current item as input to the resultSelector Func as the input.

4. *Step 4*: The resultSelector will then combine each of the provided items into one single item (for example, 1 from the firstList and One from the secondList will be combined as 1: One) and return it. This will continue until both lists have finished.

In this iteration process, if one of the lists has less items than the other list, this method will then only return the same amount of items from both lists. For example, if list A has {A1, B1, C1, D1} items and B has {A2, B2, C2} items, then the result will be based on combination logic (+) processed, with the result

{A1A2, B1B2, C1C2}. The D1 from the A list will be deducted. The implementation of the Zip extension is presented in Listing 12-87.

Listing 12-87. Implementation of the Zip Extension

```
private static IEnumerable<TResult> ZipIterator<TFirst, TSecond, TResult>(
    IEnumerable<TFirst> first,
    IEnumerable<TSecond> second,
    Func<TFirst, TSecond, TResult> resultSelector)
{
    using (IEnumerator<TFirst> iteratorVariable0 = first.GetEnumerator())
    {
        using (IEnumerator<TSecond> iteratorVariable1 = second.GetEnumerator())
        {
            while (iteratorVariable0.MoveNext() &&
                    iteratorVariable1.MoveNext())
            {
                yield return resultSelector(
                    iteratorVariable0.Current,
                    iteratorVariable1.Current);
            }
        }
    }
}
```

Summary

In this chapter, we have learned about the Linq in C# with the different extension methods provided from the Enumerable class for Linq. All of the methods discussed in this chapter were delegated based on query syntax. Examination of the internal operations of each of these extension methods has provided a better understanding of these methods and will help you to use these methods more efficiently. The next chapter will discuss exception management.

CHAPTER 13

■ ■ ■

Exception Management

This chapter will discuss the exception and exception handling in .NET using C#. The chapter begins with the definition of exception and then explains how the CLR manages the exception in .NET by discussing exception-handling information in the Method Description table and how the CLR uses this exception-handling information to manage the exception. I will then discuss exception handling in .NET by examining the protected block and throw and rethrow statements in .NET. The chapter then explores the stack overwrite by discussing how the CLR manages the exception throughout the method call chain using the throw statement in addition to exception matching.

What Is an Exception?

A program consists of a sequence of instructions that are used to execute a specific operation based on the given data (if any) to produce an expected outcome of the operation. If in the execution time the instruction cannot do its operation based on the provided data, it will raise either an error or an exception for that operation to let the user know about this unexpected behavior. There are many possible situations for the system to raise an exception for an operation. In a system, there should be a proper mechanism to handle this unexpected behavior. Before we go further, let's examine the example in Listing 13-1 to get a better understanding of the concept of the exception in the .NET application.

Listing 13-1. An Example of Division Operation

```
using System;

namespace Ch13
{
    class Program
    {
        static void Main(string[] args)
        {
            int a = 10, b = 5;
            Division div = new Division();
            Console.WriteLine("{0}/{1}={2}", a, b, div.Divide(a, b));
        }

        public class Division
        {
```

```
        public int Divide(int a, int b)
        {
            return a / b;
        }
    }
  }
}
```

The program in Listing 13-1 is doing a divide operation based on the data passed via parameter a, b. For example, if a = 10 and b = 5, then it will return 2 as a result of the operation, and so on. Let's test Listing 13-1 with the set of values given in Table 13-1.

Table 13-1. Sample Data Used for Listing 13-1

a	b	Result
10	5	2
100	50	2
100	0	Undefined

This program will work normally with the values (10, 5) and (100, 50). When this program uses (100, 0) as input to do the divide operation, it will not work because anything divided by zero returns infinity. For this reason, in runtime the CLR will not be able to handle infinity as a result, so it will raise a notification with the reason for this unexpected behavior. This behavior is called *exceptional behavior* for a type, and in the point of view of .NET, it is an *exception*. For example, while you run the division program in Listing 13-1 with the value (100, 0) as input, the CLR will produce an error notification to describe the unexpected behavior of the division program, as demonstrated in Figure 13-1.

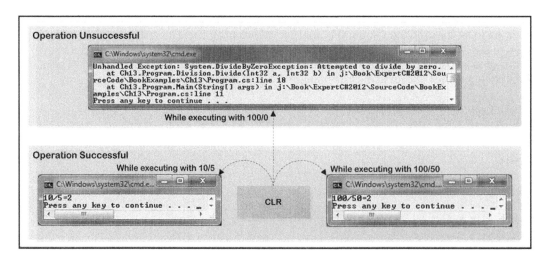

Figure 13-1. Example of the exception that occurred in the division program given in Listing 13-1

Therefore, the exception types of *handled* or *unhandled* are key concepts for defining the exceptional or unexpected behavior for a program in .NET, as demonstrated in Figure 13-1. When the CLR executes the division program from Listing 13-1 with the values 100 and 0, it cannot process the operation, and it shows the detailed information about this unexpected behavior of the program to let the user know about the unexpected behavior of the program.

In .NET, you use an exception-handling mechanism to manage unexpected behavior of the application. This mechanism is based on a simple rule, for example, mark the relevant code as a protected block and define some handlers associated with the protected block, which will be activated when any unexpected behavior is raised from the protected block (i.e., the handler block will deal with any unexpected behavior for the application). The protected block can be declared using the try statement and the handler blocks by using the catch and finally statements.

When an instance of the exception is instantiated, it contains the information regarding the exception. In runtime, the CLR transfers the program control from the point where the exception was raised to the appropriate handler block of the program that is the best match for the type of exception object that was instantiated. The CLR executes the matched handler block. If the CLR cannot find any matching handler block in the method, the program control moves back to the caller of the method to find the relevant handler block. It will keep continuing the search all the way up to the top of the method chain. If it does not find a handler block, the CLR will log the exception to the Windows log(which can be seen by the event viewer). It will leave the program control to the Windows error report, which will also write it to the Windows log.

Exception and .NET Framework

In .NET, the Exception class is defined in the System namespace of the mscorlib.dll assembly, as demonstrated in Figure 13-2.

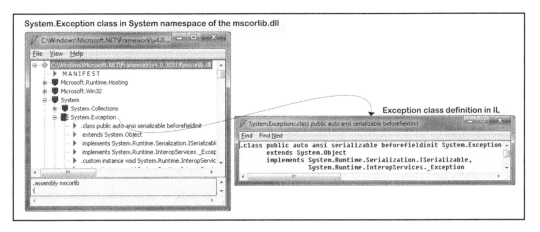

Figure 13-2. System.Exception class in the mscorlib.dll assembly

The Exception class has the following definition:

```
public class Exception : ISerializable, _Exception
{
    public Exception()                                                      {}
    public Exception(string message)                                        {}
    protected Exception(SerializationInfo info, StreamingContext context) {}
    public Exception(string message, Exception innerException)              {}
```

```
    public virtual Exception GetBaseException()                              {}
    public virtual void
        GetObjectData(SerializationInfo info, StreamingContext context)     {}
    public Type GetType()                                                    {}
    public override string ToString()                                        {}
    public virtual IDictionary Data                                          {}
    public virtual string HelpLink                                           {}
    public Exception InnerException                                          {}
    public virtual string Message                                            {}
    public virtual string Source                                             {}
    public virtual string StackTrace                                         {}
    public MethodBase TargetSite                                             {}
}
```

The System.Exception is a base class for all other Exception classes, such as DivisionByZeroException or NullReferenceException. The definition of the Exception class shows that it is implemented through the ISerializable and _Exception interfaces (defined in the System.Runtime.InteropService namespace of the mscorlib.dll) and inherited from the System.Object (as are all classes in .NET). The _Exception interface contains most of the important properties for the Exception class, and this is discussed in the next section.

_Exception Interface

Let's examine the _Exception interface, as shown in Listing 13-2, extracted via ildasm.exe from the mscorlib.dll.

Listing 13-2. *Definition of the _Exception Interface*

```
.class public interface abstract auto ansi _Exception
{
    /* Code removed */
    /* Defined property in the _Exception interface*/
    .property instance string HelpLink                                      {}
    .property instance class System.Exception InnerException                {}
    .property instance string Message                                       {}
    .property instance string Source                                        {}
    .property instance string StackTrace                                    {}
    .property instance class System.Reflection.MethodBase TargetSite        {}
}
```

The System.Exception class has a few important properties that are used to manage the exception details when an exception is raised by the CLR. In Table 13-2, these properties show where the CLR stores these properties to manage the exception.

Table 13-2. *Internal Fields of the Exception Class(Property Defined in the _Exception Interface)*

Property	Internal field	Description
Message	_message or CLR will retrieve the resource string based on the _className filed	It will contain the high-level description of an exception, for example, for the code in Listing 13-1 the Division operation exception description, attempted to divide by zero, which resides in the Message property.
StackTrace	_stackTraceString or contacted value of _stackTraceString and _remoteStackTraceString	It will contain the most important bit of the exception object, such as all the information regarding the exception, where it occurred, what its chain is (i.e., from the caller to the point where the exception occurred).
HelpLink	_helpURL	This property uses to get or set a link to the help file associated with the exception.
Source	_source	It will contain the namespace information for the program.
InnerException	_innerException	It will contain the inner exception details if there are any, otherwise null.
TargetSite	_exceptionMethod	The method where the unexpected behavior occurred (for the division program example above you can see it is {Int32 Divide(Int32, Int32)}).
Data	_data	This is an IDictionary type internal data structure for the Exception class where it is possible to provide additional user-defined information about the exception. This will return either an EmptyReadOnlyDictionaryInternal object or a ListDictionary Internal object.

Table 13-2 demonstrates that _message, _stackTraceString, _remoteStackTraceString, _helpURL, _source, _innerException, _exceptionMethod, and _data are the internal fields of the Exception class that is used by the CLR to encapsulate all the information related to the exception when it is raised.

How C# Compiler Handles Exception in Compile Time

In the compile time of a C# program, the C# compiler creates a Method State Description table for each of the methods defined in the class of a program. In the Method State Description table, the compiler sets an empty entry or possibly an array block of the Exception Handling Information Block (depending on the try...catch block presence in the code), and each of the methods in the Method State Description table will be linked with the Method table of the class. Figure 13-3 demonstrates the association between the Method table, Method State Description table, and Exception Handling Information Block or the Exception Entry.

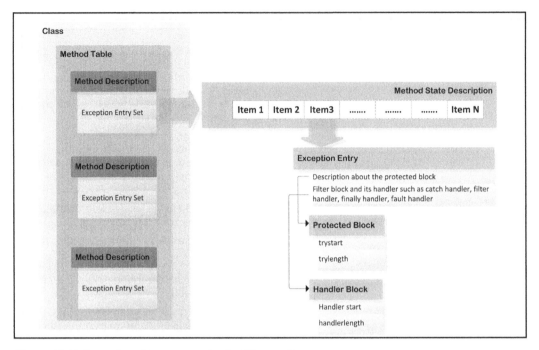

Figure 13-3. *Exception object process by the C# compiler*

Figure 13-3 demonstrates how the C# compiler includes exception-handling information (if the code block in the method has been guarded using try...catch) in the Method State Description table to the method of a class. In the Method State Description table, there will be an empty entry or an array of the exception entry. Each of these items (exception entry) contains information about the protected, guarded, or try block, associate filters, and its handlers, such as catch handler, filter handler, finally handler, or a fault handler.

In .NET, each of the methods of a type (class) could possibly have an exception entry (if there is a try...catch block in the code or nothing if there is no try...catch block defined in the code), which will contain the exception-handling information regarding that method. The protected or guarded block is defined using the trystart and trylength properties, and the filter/handler block is defined using handlerstart and handlerlength. Table 13-3 presents the definitions of the handlers data structure and the different exception-handler regions in a program.

Table 13-3. *Handlers in Exception*

Region	Fields	Description
Protected region	trystart	The address of the first instruction to be protected
	trylength	The length of the protected region
Handler region	handlerstart	The address of the first instruction of the handler
	handlerlength	The length of the handler region

The next section will explore how the CLR handles an exception in runtime.

Exploring Exception Details in Runtime

Let's do a bit of research to determine how the C# compiler generates and uses the `Method State Description` table to store the exception-handling information used in the program. You can use `windbg.exe` to explore the exception-handling information for the method used in the code given in Listing 13-3.

Listing 13-3. An Example to Demonstrate Method Description Table Information in a Class

```
using System;

namespace Ch13
{
    class MainClass
    {
        static void Main(string[] args)
        {
            ExceptionInMethodStateDescription exInMSD =
                new ExceptionInMethodStateDescription();
            exInMSD.MethodOne();
            exInMSD.MethodTwo();
            exInMSD.MethodThree();
        }
    }

    public class ExceptionInMethodStateDescription
    {
        public void MethodOne()
        {
            try                                                     {}
            catch (IndexOutOfRangeException indexOutOfRangeException) {}
        }
        public void MethodTwo()
        {
            try                                                     {}
            catch (ArgumentException argumentException)              {}
        }
        public void MethodThree()
        {
            try                                                     {}
            catch (Exception exception)                             {}
        }
    }
}
```

When the C# compiler compiles the code as given in Listing 13-3, the `MainClass` and `ExceptionInMethodStateDescription` classes will have a `Method` table. The `Method` table of the `MainClass` will hold the `Method Description` table information for the `MainClass` and the same for the `ExceptionInMethodStateDescription` class. The number of methods in the `MethodDescription` table depends on the number of methods defined in the class. Each of these methods from the `Method Description` table from the class can be used to determine the associated exception-handling information for the methods demonstrated in the code given in Listing 13-3.

461

Let's debug the executable (produced from Listing 13-3) using windbg.exe to explore the exception-handling information defined by the C# compiler in the compile time.

The executable file (Ch13.exe) produced from Listing 13-3 can be used in the windbg.exe to determine the related information about the Method table and method description and to find out how exception-handling information is stored in the method description table for an executable program (for example, the Ch13.exe). You will find the following information when you run the executable program using windbg.exe.

1. You will extract the Method Table address of the MainClass and ExceptionInMethodStateDescription class from the executable.

2. You will extract the Method Description Table information for each of the methods defined in the type, using the Method Table address information extracted the Step 1.

3. Using the Method Description Address retrieved from Step 2, you will retrieve the exception-handling information (if there is any) associated with each of the methods defined in the classes used in Listing 13-3.

Let's debug the executable using the windbg.exe program.

1. *Step 1*: Extract the MethodTable address for the MainClass and ExceptionInMethodStateDescription using the Name2EE command in the windbg.exe.

```
!Name2EE Ch13.exe Ch13.MainClass
!Name2EE Ch13.exe Ch13.ExceptionInMethodStateDescription
```

These commands will return the MethodTable address information for MainClass and ExceptionInMethodStateDescription class shown here (output might vary when you run this locally):

```
Module:       00142e9c
Assembly:     Ch13.exe
Token:        02000003
MethodTable:  00143834
EEClass:      0014145c
Name:         Ch13.MainClass

Module:       00142e9c
Assembly:     Ch13.exe
Token:        02000004
MethodTable:  001438b8
EEClass:      001414c8
Name:         Ch13.ExceptionInMethodStateDescription
```

The MethodTable address of the MainClass is 00143834, and 001438b8 is the address for the ExceptionInMethodStateDescription class that was used in Step 2 to determine the associated Method Description table information for the MainClass and ExceptionInMethodStateDescription class.

2. *Step 2*: Retrieve the Method Description table information for the MainClass and ExceptionInMethodStateDescription classes using the MethodTable address from Step 1 using the dumpmt command in the windbg.exe. You can use 00143834 as the address of the MethodTable of the MainClass to determine the method description table for each of the methods defined in the MainClass (output might vary when you run it locally).

```
!dumpmt -MD 00143834
EEClass:        0014145c
Module:         00142e9c
Name:           Ch13.MainClass
mdToken:        02000003
File:           J:\Book\ExpertC#2012\SourceCode\BookExamples\Ch13\bin\Debug\Ch13.exe
BaseSize:               0xc
ComponentSize:          0x0
Slots in VTable:        6
Number of IFaces in IFaceMap: 0
----------------------------------------
MethodDesc Table
Entry           MethodDesc      JIT     Name
54efa7e0        54cd4934        PreJIT  System.Object.ToString()
54efe2e0        54cd493c        PreJIT  System.Object.Equals(System.Object)
54efe1f0        54cd495c        PreJIT  System.Object.GetHashCode()
54f81600        54cd4970        PreJIT  System.Object.Finalize()
0014c015        0014382c        NONE    Ch13.MainClass..ctor()
002a0070        00143820        JIT     Ch13.MainClass.Main(System.String[])
```

This output shows that MethodDesc Table address 00143820 is for the Main method of the MainClass class and so on.

In addition, you can use 001438b8 as the address of the MethodTable of the ExceptionInMethodStateDescription to determine the method description table for each of the methods defined in the ExceptionInMethodStateDescription class (output might vary when you run it locally).

```
!dumpmt -MD 001438b8
EEClass:        001414c8
Module:         00142e9c
Name:           Ch13.ExceptionInMethodStateDescription
mdToken:        02000004
File:           J:\Book\ExpertC#2012\SourceCode\BookExamples\Ch13\bin\Debug\Ch13.exe
BaseSize:               0xc
ComponentSize:          0x0
Slots in VTable:        8
Number of IFaces in IFaceMap: 0
----------------------------------------
MethodDesc Table
Entry       MethodDesc  JIT     Name
54efa7e0    54cd4934    PreJIT  System.Object.ToString()
54efe2e0    54cd493c    PreJIT  System.Object.Equals(System.Object)
54efe1f0    54cd495c    PreJIT  System.Object.GetHashCode()
54f81600    54cd4970    PreJIT  System.Object.Finalize()
002a00f0    001438b0    JIT     Ch13.ExceptionInMethodStateDescription..ctor()
002a0130    0014388c    JIT     Ch13.ExceptionInMethodStateDescription.MethodOne()
002a01a0    00143898    JIT     Ch13.ExceptionInMethodStateDescription.MethodTwo()
002a0210    001438a4    JIT     Ch13.ExceptionInMethodStateDescription.MethodThree()
```

The output shows that the Method Description table address for MethodOne, MethodTwo, and MethodThree is 0014388c, 00143898, and 001438a4, respectively, for the ExceptionInMethodStateDescription class, which will be used later in Step 3 to determine the exception-handling information associated with each of the methods for the ExceptionInMethodStateDescription class.

3.   *Step 3*: Get the Exception Handling Block information for each of the methods associated with MainClass and ExceptionInMethodStateDescription class using the respective method description table addresses. For example, 00143820 is the method description table address of the Main method of the MainClass, as retrieved in Step 2.

!EHInfo 00143820

The EHInfo command will return the exception-handling block information about the Main method of the MainClass class, as demonstrated in Figure 13-4.

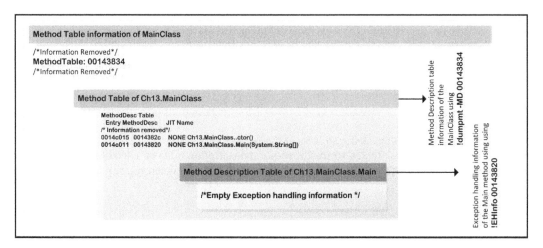

Figure 13-4. *Exception handling information of the Main method in the MainClass*

Figure 13-4 shows that in the Main method there is no exception-handling block information associated by the C# compiler in the compile time as in Listing 13-3. The Main method hasn't defined any exception-handling code (try...catch block) in the MainClass. For the ExceptionInMethodStateDescription class, 0014388c, 00143898, and 001438a4 are the addresses for MethodOne, MethodTwo, and MethodThree, respectively, retrieved in Step 2.

!EHInfo 0014388c
!EHInfo 00143898
!EHInfo 001438a4

The EHInfo command will return the exception-handling block information for MethodOne, MethodTwo, and MethodThree of the ExceptionInMethodStateDescription class as shown in Figure 13-5.

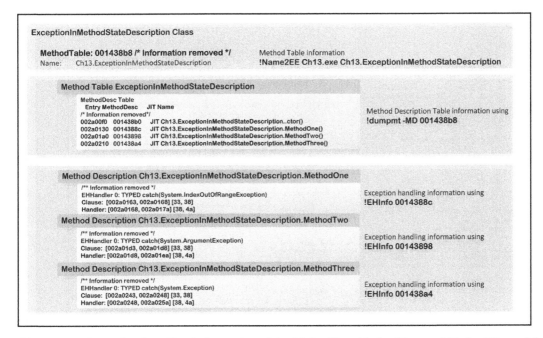

Figure 13-5. *Exception-handling information of the MethodOne, MethodTwo, and MethodThree of the ExceptionInMethodStateDescription class*

Figure 13-5 demonstrates that the C# compiler added the exception-handling information for MethodOne with the IndexOutOfRangeException as the exception type, MethodTwo with the ArgumentException as the exception type, and Exception as the exception type for MethodThree for the ExceptionInMethodStateDescription class.

In the .NET application, if you define any exception handler block in a method for the class, the C# compiler will then add an exception-handling information block for each of the methods defined in the class, as demonstrated in Figure 13-6. It shows each of the methods of the MainClass and ExceptionInMethodStateDescription class associated with the exception-handling information in it.

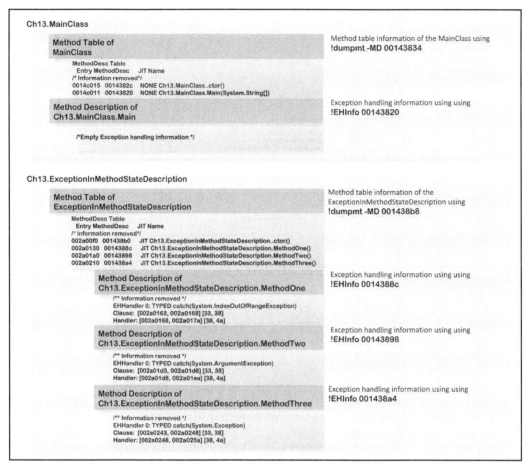

Figure 13-6. Exception-handling information of the MainClass and ExceptionInMethodStateDescription class

Exception Handling in .NET

When an exception occurs in a program, the CLR will handle this exception in one of three ways:

- It will search the exception-handling information array (if it exists) associated with the method to determine the related catch block or the handler block. If the CLR finds a matching one in the current method, it will then execute code from that handler block.

- Otherwise, it will continue to search for a relevant handler block to the calling method and so on.

- Finally, if the CLR does not find any matching exception handling block in the program, it will then log the stack trace information contained in the exception in the Windows log and abort the program, as demonstrated in Figure 13-7. The CLR will search for the exception-handling information from MethodA if an exception occurred in `MethodA` and continue searching `MethodB` to `MethodC` until it finds any information. If it finds an exception, it will execute and return from the program or dump the exception information in the Windows log as an unhandled exception.

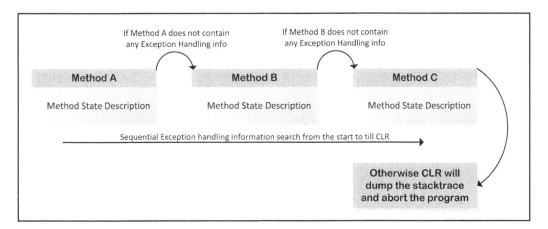

Figure 13-7. Exception-handling information searching from Method State to Method State

So far, we have seen the way CLR handles an exception in a program in the place it occurred. There are many possibilities where you do not want to handle the exception in the place where it occurred but instead want to pass back this exception information to the caller of this method. Figure 13-8 shows what happens when a method call sequence (`MethodA` calls `MethodB` and `MethodB` calls `MethodC`) has happened.

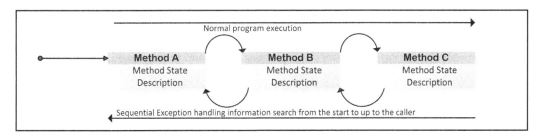

Figure 13-8. Method call bubble up when an exception has occurred

Let's modify the code in Listing 13-1 to do the following:

- The exception is handled by the method itself.
- The exception is handled by the CLR.

So the first version of this modified division program will handle the exception itself using the exception-handler block, and second version will not handle the exception by itself but rather let the application or Windows handle the exception, as demonstrated in Listing 13-4.

Listing 13-4. First Version of the Exception Handling

```
/* First version of the Exception handling */

using System;

namespace Ch13
{
    class MainClass
    {
        static void Main(string[] args)
        {
            Division div = new Division();
            div.Divide(100, 0);
        }
    }
    public class Division
    {
        public int Divide(int a,
            int b)
        {
            try
            {
                return a / b;
            }
            /* Exception is handled in here by catching all the exception. */
            catch (Exception exception)
            {
                Console.WriteLine(
                    exception.StackTrace);
                 return -1;
            }
        }
    }
}
```

This would be the second version of the exception handling:

```
using System;

namespace Ch13
{
    class MainClass
    {
        static void Main(string[] args)
        {
            Division div = new Division();
            div.Divide(100, 0);
        }
    }

    public class Division
```

CHAPTER 13 ■ EXCEPTION MANAGEMENT

```
    {
        public int Divide(int a,
            int b)
        {
            return a / b;
        }
    }
}
```

When the first version of the program from Listing 13-4 is compiled, the C# compiler will create an exception entry for the Method State Description table of the Divide method of the Division class. In execution of the first program from Listing 13-4, if any exception occurs in the Divide method, the CLR will then search the Method State Description table for this method to determine the exception-handler block information (if any exists). It will execute it and show the StackTrace information of the exception by accessing the exception object and return and finish the program execution, as shown in Figure 13-9.

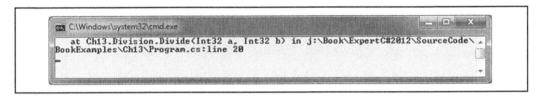

Figure 13-9. Exception handled by the program itself

For the second version of the program in Listing 13-4, the compiler will not create any ExceptionEntry (it will create an empty array for the exception handling) for the Method State Description table of the Divide method of the Division class. There is no defined exception handler for this method. In execution of the second program from Listing 13-4, if any exception occurs the CLR will search the Method State Description table for this method but it will not find an exception handler associated with it. This program will then crash and let Windows take care of this exception by writing exception information to the Event Viewer, as demonstrated in Figure 13-10.

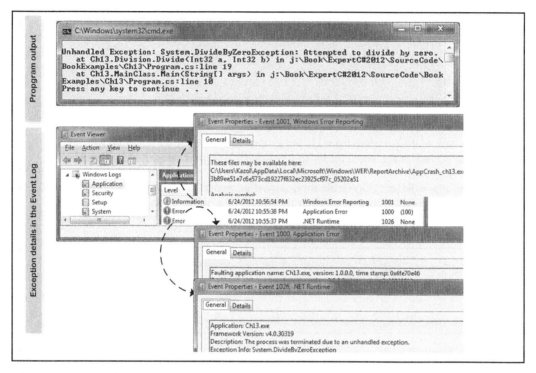

Figure 13-10. *Windows Logs in the Event Viewer*

From Figure 13-10 you can see that the CLR wrote the exception details to the Windows log and the Windows Error Reporting also takes care of it by writing the exception details into the Windows log.

Exception Handling and Bubble Up

As shown in Figure 13-8, the CLR will search through each of the methods in the method chain to match an appropriate exception-handler block. If it finds one, it will execute it or otherwise continue searching. Listing 13-5 presents an example of this.

Listing 13-5. *Example of Salary Calculation*

```
using System;

namespace Ch13
{
    class Program
    {
        static void Main(string[] args)
        {
            try
            {
                Salary salary = new Salary();
                salary.CalculateSalary(10, 0);
```

```
            }
            catch (Exception exception)
            {
                Console.WriteLine("An error occured.");
            }
        }
    }
}

public class Salary
{
    public int CalculateSalary(int week, int rate)
    {
        try
        {
            Calculator calculator = new Calculator();
            return week * calculator.Divide(week, rate);
        }
        catch (DivideByZeroException divideByZeroException)
        {
            throw;
        }
    }
}

public class Calculator
{
    public int Divide(int a, int b)
    {
        try
        {
            return a / b;
        }
        catch
        {
            throw;
        }
    }
}
}
```

In Listing 13-5, each of the handler blocks defined in the Calculator and Salary classes handles the exception by returning the exception details from the Divide method to the CalculateSalary method of the Salary class, which is finally return to the Main method of the Program class. This whole concept is called the *bubble up*, where the exception is returned all the way up to the caller of the method from where the exception was raised. Figure 13-11 illustrates the bubble up concept using stack trace information extracted in the runtime while the code in Listing 13-5 is executing.

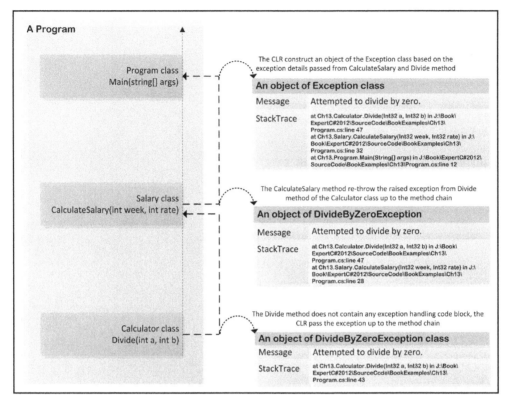

Figure 13-11. Exception Bubble up

When the exception occurred in the Divide method of the Calculator class in Listing 13-5, the CLR produced an instance of the DivideByZeroException type with the details shown in Figure 13-11. The CLR then passes these exception details back to the CalculateSalary method of the Salary class. The CLR modifies the StackTrace to combine the information it gets from the Exception object DivideByZeroException from the divide method and passes this back to the Main method of the Program class. The CLR will modify the StackTrace of the Exception object to capture the most up-to-date information about the exception and handle the exception as if there were a handler block defined.

While the CLR executes the program in Listing 13-5, the program pointer will move into the Divide method of the Calculator class. As soon as an exception is raised, the CLR will bubble up this exception all the way to the Main method of the Program class, which can be seen by looking at the stack trace of this call using windbg.exe, as demonstrated here:

```
0:000> !clrstack -a
OS Thread Id: 0xd08 (0)
Child SP IP       Call Site
0039ee08 00400295 Ch13.Calculator.Divide(Int32, Int32) [J:\Book\ExpertC#2012\SourceCode\
BookExamples\Ch13\Program.cs @ 40]
    PARAMETERS:
        this (0x0039ee10)     = 0x0153b688
        a (0x0039ee0c)        = 0x0000000a
        b (0x0039ee3c)        = 0x00000000
    LOCALS:
```

```
0x0039ee08                    = 0x00000000
```

```
0039ee40 004001d4 Ch13.Salary.CalculateSalary(Int32, Int32) [J:\Book\ExpertC#2012\SourceCode\
BookExamples\Ch13\Program.cs @ 28]
    PARAMETERS:
        this (0x0039ee60)     = 0x0153b67c
        week (0x0039ee5c)     = 0x0000000a
        rate (0x0039ee8c)     = 0x00000000
    LOCALS:
        0x0039ee4c            = 0x0153b688
        0x0039ee48            = 0x00000000
        0x0039ee58            = 0x00000000
```

```
0039ee90 004000d7 Ch13.Program.Main(System.String[]) [J:\Book\ExpertC#2012\SourceCode\
BookExamples\Ch13\Program.cs @ 12]
    PARAMETERS:
        args (0x0039eea0)     = 0x0153b63c
    LOCALS:
        0x0039ee9c            = 0x0153b67c
        0x0039ee98            = 0x00000000
```

```
0039f0fc 5a8a21db [GCFrame: 0039f0fc]
```

This windbg.exe output shows the stack information while CLR executes the program in Listing 13-5. The stack of each of the methods is stacked one upon the other, for instance, CalculateSalary is on top of the Main method and Divide is on top of the CalculateSalary method. If any exception occurs, for example, in the Divide method, the CLR would search for the exception-handling information in that method, and if it cannot find it, it would then search CalculateSalary and lastly Main as they are stacked. Figure 13-12 demonstrates the exception searching and bubble up after an exception occurred in the Divide method of the Calculator class.

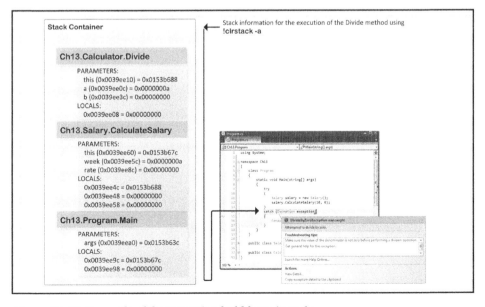

Figure 13-12. Example of the Exception bubble up in code

Figure 13-12 demonstrates that the program pointer has come back to the exception handler section of the Main method of the Program class from the Divide method of the Calculator class.

Protected Block

A protected or guarded block is declared using the try keyword; the handler block is defined using the catch or finally keyword. A catch block is declared using the catch keyword. This specifies the type of exception object the clause is going to handle and the handler code itself. A finally block is declared using the finally keyword. Using these try, catch, and finally statements, you can handle all the exceptional behavior of any program in the .NET application. The general structure of the try...catch statements while using a .NET program is shown in Figure 13-13.

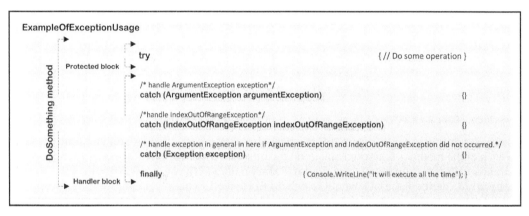

Figure 13-13. Handler and protected block defined in the class

From Figure 13-13, you can see that the protected block is defined using the try block, and the handler block is defined using the catch and finally blocks. An example of the declaration of the protected and handler blocks is shown in Listing 13-6.

Listing 13-6. An Example of try.catch.finally in .NET

```
using System;

namespace Ch13
{
    class MainClass
    {
        static void Main(string[] args)
        {
            ExampleOfExceptionUsage eeu = new ExampleOfExceptionUsage();
        }
    }

    public class ExampleOfExceptionUsage
    {
```

```
public void DoSomething()
{
    try
    {
        /* Do some operation */
    }

    catch (ArgumentException argumentException)
    {
        /* handle ArgumentException exception */
    }

    catch (IndexOutOfRangeException indexOutOfRangeException)
    {
        /*handle IndexOutOfRangeException */
    }

    catch (Exception exception)
    {
        /* handle exception in general in here if ArgumentException
         * and IndexOutOfRangeException did not occurred. */
    }

    finally
    {
        Console.WriteLine("It will execute all the time");
    }
    }
  }
}
```

In the code in Listing 13-6, the try block is the place where we need to put the entire operation block, which will do the actual functional operation of the method. This is referred to as the protected or guarded block. In the protected block, if there is any situation where the argument has not been provided, the index of the array is not in range, or any other kind of unexpected behavior, the program will handle that unexpected behavior using the catch block or the finally block, referred to as handler blocks. However, the finally block will execute regardless of the exceptional behavior raised in the method. To explain how the code in Listing 13-6 works, let's look at the decompiled IL code in the Listing 13-7, extracted using ildasm. exe from the executable produced by Listing 13-6.

Listing 13-7. IL Code of the DoSomething Method Defined in Listing 13-6

```
.method public hidebysig instance void  DoSomething() cil managed
{
  // Code size       39 (0x27)
  .maxstack  1
  .locals init (
    [0] class [mscorlib]System.ArgumentException
            argumentException,
    [1] class [mscorlib]System.IndexOutOfRangeException
            indexOutOfRangeException,
```

```
    [2] class [mscorlib]System.Exception
             exception)
  IL_0000:  nop
  .try
  {
    .try
    {
      IL_0001:  nop
      IL_0002:  nop
      IL_0003:  leave.s    IL_0014
    } // end .try
    catch [mscorlib]System.ArgumentException
    {
      IL_0005:  stloc.0
      IL_0006:  nop
      IL_0007:  nop
      IL_0008:  leave.s    IL_0014
    } // end handler
    catch [mscorlib]System.IndexOutOfRangeException
    {
      IL_000a:  stloc.1
      IL_000b:  nop
      IL_000c:  nop
      IL_000d:  leave.s    IL_0014
    } // end handler
    catch [mscorlib]System.Exception
    {
      IL_000f:  stloc.2
      IL_0010:  nop
      IL_0011:  nop
      IL_0012:  leave.s    IL_0014
    } // end handler
    IL_0014:  nop
    IL_0015:  leave.s    IL_0025
  } // end .try

  finally
  {
    IL_0017:  nop
    IL_0018:  ldstr      "It will execute all the time"
    IL_001d:  call       void [mscorlib]System.Console::WriteLine(string)
    IL_0022:  nop
    IL_0023:  nop
    IL_0024:  endfinally
  } // end handler

  IL_0025:  nop
  IL_0026:  ret
} // end of method ExampleOfExceptionUsage::DoSomething
```

In this IL code, you can see that there are two blocks of try...catch, one for the inner execution block and the exception-handler block and the other for the outer try...catch, which is executed by the finally block regardless of whether the exception is raised. Let's analyze the code carefully to really understand what's going on in this IL code.

Where no unexpected behavior has occurred in the program, the CLR will execute the IL code as described here:

- The program will execute IL instruction from the label IL_0000 and keep executing until IL_0003, where it will find the instruction leave.s IL_0014, which will move the program control to the label IL_0014 as well as look for the surrounding finally block. However, there is none, so it will move the program control to the IL_0014 label.

- The program control will move into the IL_0014 and continue to the IL_0015, where it will find the instruction leave.s IL_0025. While executing the leave.s IL_0025 instruction, it will try to determine if there is any matching finally block. In this case there is one, so it will execute that first and then move the program pointer to the IL_0025 label and continue the program from there.

Where an exception occurs in the program, the CLR will execute the above IL code as described here:

- The program will execute IL instruction from the label IL_0000 and keep executing until IL_0003. While the instruction from IL_0000 to IL_0003 is executing, if any unexpected behavior is raised by the CLR, it will then instantiate a relevant exception object and try to determine if there is any matching handler section that is accepting the type of exception object the CLR is trying to match with. If there is, then the program will move to that point. For example, if the CLR instantiated an object of ArgumentException, then the program pointer will move into the IL_0005 and start executing instructions from that point up to IL_0008. In this location the CLR will find the leave.s IL_0014 instruction, from which it will then look for the related finally block to execute or else move the program control into IL_0014. Alternatively, if there is no matching exception object defined in the exception-handler section in the program, then it will execute the catch (Exception exception) handler section and continue the execution from there.

- When the program finishes executing the handler section of the program, it will continue to execute the instruction and it will find the IL_0015: leave.s IL_0025 instruction. This leave.s instruction will try to determine if there is any matching finally block, and if so it will execute that first and then move the program pointer to the IL_0025 and continue the program from there.

In both circumstances, the CLR will end up executing the IL_0025 and IL_0026 labels, regardless of the exception handler's finally block, which will execute anyway.

Throw and Rethrow

The throw statement from the C# code and the rethrow IL instruction the C# compiler generates are used in the .NET application to rethrow an exception. The throw and rethrow instructions can be define as:

- The throw instruction throws the exception object on the stack.

- • The rethrow instruction is permitted within the body of a catch handler, and it throws the same exception that was caught by this handler. The rethrow IL instruction does not change the stack trace in the object.

All the examples presented so far have used the exception raised by the CLR while executing the program to determine any exceptional behavior not expected while running the program. Let's see how an exception can be raised in a program using the throw and rethrow statements, which is demonstrated in Listings 13-8 and 13-9.

Listing 13-8. *Example of Throw Statement*

```
using System;

namespace Ch13
{
    class Program
    {
        static void Main(string[] args)
        {
            throw new Exception("An exception object");
            Console.WriteLine("This will never execute.");
        }
    }
}
```

While executing this program, the CLR creates an instance of the Exception type with the An exception object string literal. Using the throw instruction, the CLR raises an exception using the exception object, instantiating an instance of the Exception type. If you examine the following IL code from the executable of the program in Listing 13-8 generated using the .NETReflector program, you will see the C# compiler used the throw IL instruction to throw an exception, as shown in Listing 13-9.

Listing 13-9. *IL Code While Using Throw Statement*

```
.class private auto ansi beforefieldinit Program
    extends [mscorlib]System.Object
{
    .method public hidebysig specialname rtspecialname instance void
        .ctor() cil managed                                              {}

    .method private hidebysig static void Main(string[] args) cil managed
    {
        .entrypoint
        .maxstack 8
        L_0000: nop
        L_0001: ldstr "An exception object"
        L_0006: newobj instance void [mscorlib]System.Exception::.ctor(string)

        /* CLR will raise an Exception using the exception instance
         * created in L_0006*/
        L_000b: throw
    }
}
```

In the IL code, the L_000b label has the throw IL instruction, which will instruct the program to throw the exception instance created in L_0006 label. On the other hand, rethrow is not directly usable in the C# code or it is not a C# keyword, because it is an IL instruction that will be generated by the C# compiler while the compiler compiles a particular pattern of the C# code for the exception handling block, as demonstrated in Listing 13-10.

Listing 13-10. An Example of Divide Operation

```
using System;

namespace Ch13
{
    class Program
    {
        static void Main(string[] args)
        {
            try
            {
                ExampleOfRethrow();
            }
            catch (Exception exception)
            {
                Console.WriteLine(exception.StackTrace);
            }
        }

        static void ExampleOfRethrow()
        {
            try
            {
                int a = 10, b = 0;
                var result = a / b;
            }
            catch
            {
                throw;
            }
        }
    }
}
```

In Listing 13-10, you will see that in the handler block there hasn't been anything done besides catching the exception object and letting the exception go by using the throw statement to be handled by the caller of this method. The decompiled IL code shown in Listing 13-11 of the executable of the Listing 13-10 demonstrates how the C# compiler used the rethrow instruction to rethrow the existing exception.

Listing 13-11. IL Code for the Code in Listing 13-10

```
.class private auto ansi beforefieldinit Ch13.Program
       extends [mscorlib]System.Object
{
  .method private hidebysig static void  Main(string[] args) cil managed
```

```
{
  .entrypoint
  // Code size       30 (0x1e)
  .maxstack  1
  .locals init ([0] class [mscorlib]System.Exception exception)
  IL_0000:  nop
  .try
  {
    IL_0001:  nop
    IL_0002:  call        void Ch13.Program::ExampleOfRethrow()
    IL_0007:  nop
    IL_0008:  nop
    IL_0009:  leave.s     IL_001c

  }  // end .try
  catch [mscorlib]System.Exception
  {
    IL_000b:  stloc.0
    IL_000c:  nop
    IL_000d:  ldloc.0
    IL_000e:  callvirt    instance string
              [mscorlib]System.Exception::get_StackTrace()
    IL_0013:  call void [mscorlib]System.Console::WriteLine(string)
    IL_0018:  nop
    IL_0019:  nop
    IL_001a:  leave.s     IL_001c

  }  // end handler
  IL_001c:  nop
  IL_001d:  ret
} // end of method Program::Main

.method private hidebysig static void  ExampleOfRethrow() cil managed
{
  // Code size       20 (0x14)
  .maxstack  2
  .locals init ([0] int32 a,
           [1] int32 b,
           [2] int32 result)
  IL_0000:  nop
  .try
  {
    IL_0001:  nop
    IL_0002:  ldc.i4.s    10
    IL_0004:  stloc.0
    IL_0005:  ldc.i4.0
    IL_0006:  stloc.1
    IL_0007:  ldloc.0
    IL_0008:  ldloc.1

    /* The CLR does the div operation
```

```
  * 1. if successful then it will store the result at position
  * 2 of method stack 2. Or otherwise move the execution in IL_00e */
  IL_0009:  div

  /*It stores the result at position 2 of method stack */
  IL_000a:  stloc.2

  IL_000b:  nop
  IL_000c:  leave.s    IL_0012

} // end .try
catch [mscorlib]System.Object
{
  /* If any exception raised by the CLR while doing the div operation
   * it creates an Exception (Or relevant type) object with the
   * exception details on the Heap and put that exception object
   * reference on top of the Evaluation Stack. Following pop
   * instruction loads that exception object from the Evaluation Stack and
   * rethrow it inIL_0010*/
  IL_000e:  pop

  IL_000f:  nop

  /* This rethow instruction does not reset the stack trace of
   * the original exception object*/
  IL_0010:  rethrow

} // end handler
  IL_0012:  nop
  IL_0013:  ret
} // end of method Program::ExampleOfRethrow

.method public hidebysig specialname rtspecialname
        instance void  .ctor() cil managed
{
  /* code removed */
} // end of method Program::.ctor

} // end of class Ch13.Program
```

From this IL code, the IL_0010: rethrow instruction will rethrow the current exception without altering the starting point of the exception object. Another usage of the throw statement is presented in the code given in Listing 13-12.

Listing 13-12. *An Example of Divide Operation*

```
using System;

namespace Ch13
{
    class Program
```

```
    {
        static void Main(string[] args)
        {
            try
            { ExampleOfRethrow(); }

            catch (Exception exception)
            { Console.WriteLine(exception.StackTrace); }
        }

        static void ExampleOfRethrow()
        {
            try
            {
                int a = 10, b = 0;
                var result = a / b;
            }
            catch (Exception ex) { throw; }
        }
    }
}
```

In this example, the ExampleOfRethrow method is doing a division operation and protecting that code by handling the unexpected behavior using the catch block. This catch block will accept an exception object of Exception type. In the catch block, I use the throw statement, which will actually rethrow the original exception instance created by the CLR in runtime without altering the starting point of the exception. Let's analyze the IL code in Listing 13-13, generated from Listing 13-12 using ildasm.exe.

Listing 13-13. IL Example of Throw in IL Code

```
.class private auto ansi beforefieldinit Ch13.Program
       extends [mscorlib]System.Object
{
  .method private hidebysig static void  Main(string[] args) cil managed
  {
    .entrypoint
    // Code size       30 (0x1e)
    .maxstack  1
    .locals init ([0] class [mscorlib]System.Exception exception)
    IL_0000:  nop
    .try
    {
      IL_0001:  nop
      IL_0002:  call       void Ch13.Program::ExampleOfRethrow()
      IL_0007:  nop
      IL_0008:  nop
      IL_0009:  leave.s    IL_001c

    }  // end .try
    catch [mscorlib]System.Exception
    {
```

```
    IL_000b:  stloc.0
    IL_000c:  nop
    IL_000d:  ldloc.0
    IL_000e:  callvirt    instance string
              [mscorlib]System.Exception::get_StackTrace()
    IL_0013:  call        void [mscorlib]System.Console::WriteLine(string)
    IL_0018:  nop
    IL_0019:  nop
    IL_001a:  leave.s     IL_001c

  }  // end handler
  IL_001c:  nop
  IL_001d:  ret
} // end of method Program::Main

.method private hidebysig static void  ExampleOfRethrow() cil managed
{
  // Code size       20 (0x14)
  .maxstack  2
  .locals init ([0] int32 a,
           [1] int32 b,
           [2] int32 result,
           [3] class [mscorlib]System.Exception ex)
  IL_0000:  nop
  .try
  {
    IL_0001:  nop
    IL_0002:  ldc.i4.s    10
    IL_0004:  stloc.0
    IL_0005:  ldc.i4.0
    IL_0006:  stloc.1
    IL_0007:  ldloc.0
    IL_0008:  ldloc.1

    /*  The CLR does the div operation
     * 1. if successful then it will store the result on top of the
     * Evaluation Stack
     * 2. Or otherwise move the execution in IL_000e*/
    IL_0009:  div

    /* If div operation successful pop the output of the div from
     * the Evaluation Stack and store into result (at position 2
     * of the Locals section of this method stack) .*/
    IL_000a:  stloc.2
    IL_000b:  nop
    IL_000c:  leave.s     IL_0012

  }  // end .try
  catch [mscorlib]System.Exception
  {
    IL_000e:  stloc.3
```

```
    IL_000f:  nop

    /* If any exception raised by the CLR while doing the div operation
     * it creates an Exception object (Or relevant type)  with the
     * exception details on the Heap and re-throw the original
     * exception (without reset the original stack trace) in IL_0010.*/
    IL_0010:  rethrow

  }  // end handler
  IL_0012:  nop
  IL_0013:  ret
} // end of method Program::ExampleOfRethrow

.method public hidebysig specialname rtspecialname
        instance void  .ctor() cil managed
{
  /* code removed */
} // end of method Program::.ctor
} // end of class Ch13.Program
```

The CLR will execute the IL code as demonstrated below:

1. *Step 1*: The program will call the ExampleOfRethrow method from the IL_0002 of the Main method, and the program will move to the method ExampleOfRethrow and continue by executing the instruction from there.

2. *Step 2*: If everything goes normally in the ExampleOfRethrow method, then the CLR stores the div result in IL_000a and returns from that method back to the Main method to finish the execution of the program.

3. Step 3: If the execution from the IL_0009 does not go normally, then the CLR will instantiate a relevant exception object on the Heap and put that exception reference on top of the evaluation stack. The program will come to IL_0010, which loads the current exception details from the top of the evaluation stack, and rethrows the exception, which is caught by this handler without modifying the starting point of the exception. The CLR will then pass this exception to caller.

If you modify the code in Listing 13-12 as shown in Listing 13-14, the C# compiler will then generate different IL instructions, as shows in Listing 13-15.

Listing 13-14. Modified Version of the Code in Listing 13-12

```
using System;

namespace Ch13
{
    class Program
    {
        static void Main(string[] args)
        {
            try
            { ExampleOfRethrow(); }
```

```
        catch (Exception exception)
        { Console.WriteLine(exception.StackTrace); }
    }

    static void ExampleOfRethrow()
    {
        try
        {
            int a = 10, b = 0;
            var result = a / b;
        }
        catch (Exception ex)
        {
            throw ex;
        }
    }
  }
}
```

In the code in Listing 13-14, the throw ex statement is used instead of using just the throw statement. While the CLR executes the throw ex statement, it will override some of the property of the exception object, as shown in Listing 13-15.

Listing 13-15. IL for the Code in Listing 13-14

```
.class private auto ansi beforefieldinit Ch13.Program
      extends [mscorlib]System.Object
{
  .method private hidebysig static void  Main(string[] args) cil managed
  {
    .entrypoint
    // Code size       30 (0x1e)
    .maxstack  1
    .locals init ([0] class [mscorlib]System.Exception exception)
    IL_0000:  nop
    .try
    {
      IL_0001:  nop
      IL_0002:  call         void Ch13.Program::ExampleOfRethrow()
      IL_0007:  nop
      IL_0008:  nop
      IL_0009:  leave.s      IL_001c

    }  // end .try
    catch [mscorlib]System.Exception
    {
      IL_000b:  stloc.0
      IL_000c:  nop
      IL_000d:  ldloc.0
      IL_000e:  callvirt     instance string
                [mscorlib]System.Exception::get_StackTrace()
```

```
      IL_0013:  call       void [mscorlib]System.Console::WriteLine(string)
      IL_0018:  nop
      IL_0019:  nop
      IL_001a:  leave.s    IL_001c

   }  // end handler
   IL_001c:  nop
   IL_001d:  ret
} // end of method Program::Main

.method private hidebysig static void  ExampleOfRethrow() cil managed
{
  // Code size       20 (0x14)
  .maxstack  2
  .locals init ([0] int32 a,
           [1] int32 b,
           [2] int32 result,
           [3] class [mscorlib]System.Exception ex)
  IL_0000:  nop
  .try
  {
    IL_0001:  nop
    IL_0002:  ldc.i4.s   10
    IL_0004:  stloc.0
    IL_0005:  ldc.i4.0
    IL_0006:  stloc.1
    IL_0007:  ldloc.0
    IL_0008:  ldloc.1

    /*  The CLR does the div operation
     * 1. if successful then it will store the result on top of the
     * Evaluation Stack
     * 2. Or otherwise move the execution into IL_000e*/
    IL_0009:  div

    /* Stores the output of the div operation from the evaluation stack into
     * the result (at position 2) of the Locals section of this method
     * stack. */
    IL_000a:  stloc.2
    IL_000b:  nop
    IL_000c:  leave.s    IL_0012

  }  // end .try
  catch [mscorlib]System.Exception
  {
    /* When any exception occurred, the CLR will store that exception
     * from the evaluation stack into the ex object of the Locals
     * section of this method stack.  */
    IL_000e:  stloc.3
    IL_000f:  nop
```

```
    /* Load the local variable at position 3 from the Local section
     * of this method stack which is ex on the top of the evaluation
     * stack */
    IL_0010:  ldloc.3

    /* The CLR will throw exception using the ex object store
     * into the Locals section at position 3 which will reset the
     * starting point of the original exception and the CLR will
     * set the exception as it raised from here instead of
     * the original location.*/
    IL_0011:  throw

  } // end handler
  IL_0012:  nop
  IL_0013:  ret
} // end of method Program::ExampleOfRethrow

.method public hidebysig specialname rtspecialname
        instance void  .ctor() cil managed
{
  /* code removed */
} // end of method Program::.ctor
} // end of class Ch13.Program
```

The CLR will execute this IL code as described here:

1. *Step 1*: The program will call the ExampleOfRethrow method from the IL_0002 of the Main method of the Program class and will move to the ExampleOfRethrow method and continue by executing the instruction from there.

2. *Step 2*: If everything goes normally, then the IL_000c: leave.s IL_0012 instruction will be executed from the ExampleOfRethrow method. At this time, the leave.s instruction will not find any finally block, so it will move to the IL_0012: nop and continue from there.

3. *Step 3*: If the div operation in IL_0009 from the ExampleOfRethrow method does not go normally, the program will come to the IL_000e, which will load the current exception details from the evaluation stack and store it in the local variable at position 3 of the ExampleOfRethrow method. In the instruction L_0010: ldloc.3 load, the value from the local variable at position 3 is moved into the top of the evaluation stack. The CLR then throws it (in the IL_0011) by resetting the starting point of the original exception raised position, in other words, it overwrites the stack information. You will see an example of the stack overwrite in the next section.

Figure 13-14 demonstrates how the CLR changes the exception information while using the following code:

```
catch(Exception ex)
{
        throw;
}
catch
```

```
{
        throw;
}
OR
catch(Exception ex)
{
        throw ex;
}
```

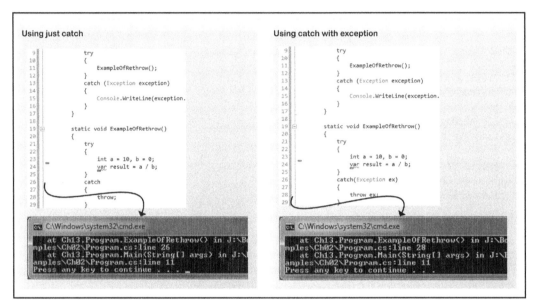

Figure 13-14. Example of just throw

The CLR changes the exception details, and the caller of this method will not get the right information or the information about the original starting point of the exception, which will make the application debugging a bit more difficult. So use of the just throw statement will not change the starting point of the exception, whereas using the throw exceptionObject statement will change the starting point of the exception, as discussed above.

Stack Overwrite

Let's look at an example where we will see how CLR overwrites the exception details. This program will give the month name based on the month index in the year, as shown in Listing 13-16.

Listing 13-16. An Example of Stack Overwrite

```
using System;

namespace Ch13
{
```

```csharp
class Program
{
    static void Main(string[] args)
    {
        try
        {
            Year year = new Year();
            year.GetMonth(22);
        }
        catch (Exception exception)
        {
            Console.WriteLine("{0}", exception.StackTrace);
        }
    }
}

public class Year
{
    public string GetMonth(int position)
    {
        try
        {
            MonthNameFinder monthFinder = new MonthNameFinder();
            return monthFinder.Find(position);
        }
        catch (Exception exception)
        {
            throw;
        }
    }
}

public class MonthNameFinder
{
    private string[] months =
    {
        "January",          "February",
        "March",            "April",
        "May",              "June",
        "July",             "August",
        "September",        "October",
        "November",         "December"
    };

    public string Find(int whichMonth)
    {
        try
        {
            return months[whichMonth];
        }
        catch (Exception exception)
```

```
                    {
                        throw;
                    }
                }
            }
        }
    }
```

Running this program will show the details provided in Figure 13-15.

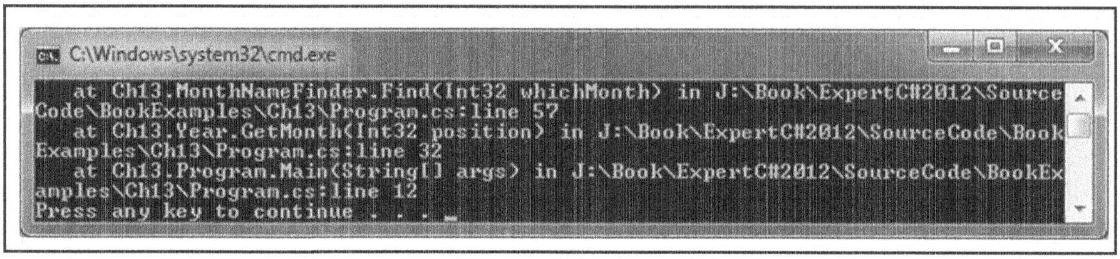

Figure 13-15. *While using only a throw statement*

Listing 13-17 shows the modified version of the GetMonth method of the Year class.

Listing 13-17. *Modified Code of the GetMonth(int position) of the Year Class*

```
public class Year
{
    public string GetMonth(int position)
    {
        try
        {
            MonthNameFinder monthFinder = new MonthNameFinder();
            return monthFinder.Find(position);
        }
        catch (Exception exception)
        {
            throw exception;
        }
    }
}
```

The program will produce the exception details as shown in Figure 13-16.

Figure 13-16. *While using the throw statement with exception object*

How the CLR Matches Exception in Runtime

When you define exception-handling blocks in a program, you can use different types of the exception type as input of the catch blocks. These are called *handler blocks*. In runtime, the CLR will choose which block of the handler it should invoke (depending on the exception type) when an exception is raised, otherwise the CLR will choose the catch-handling block, which is defined in Exception as the type by default. If no matching catch-handling block is defined or found in the class, then the program control will bubble up all the way to the caller of the method to determine the best-matched exception type. This catch block searching or matching maintains the hierarchy (i.e., most of the derived exception types). In Listing 13-18, IndexOutOfRangeException is the defined catch block (the best match), and it will be the first one in the chain, and the topmost (for the following example, Exception) one will be the last one.

Listing 13-18. *An Example of the Exception Type Matching for the Exception Handler Block*

```
using System;

namespace Ch13
{
    class Program
    {
        static void Main(string[] args)
        {
            Division div = new Division();
            div.Divide(100, 0);
            Console.ReadLine();
        }

        public class Division
        {
            public int Divide(int a, int b)
            {
                try
                {
                    return a / b;
                }

                catch (IndexOutOfRangeException indexOutOfRangeException)
                {
                    Console.WriteLine("IndexOutOfRangeException");
                }
                catch (ArgumentException argumentException)
                {
                    Console.WriteLine("ArgumentException");
                }
                catch (DivideByZeroException divideByZeroException)
                {
                    Console.WriteLine("{0}\n{1}",
                        "DivideByZeroException",
                        "This handler block will execute.");
                }
                catch (Exception exception)
```

```
            {
                Console.WriteLine("{0}",
                    "It will execute when there is no best matched found.");
            }
            return -1;
        }
    }
}
}
```

So while this program executed by the CLR will raise the exception in the Divide method, as shown in Listing 13-18, it will try to match it with the relevant exception-handler block, as demonstrated in Figure 13-17.

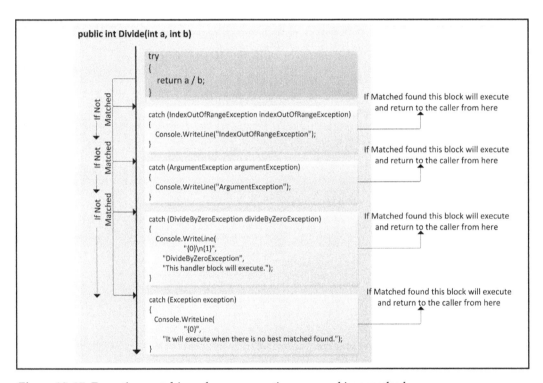

Figure 13-17. Exception matching when an exception occurred in a method

In the program in Listing 13-18, IndexOutOfRangeException, ArgumentException, DivideByZeroException, and Exception type have been used for the handler blocks. When the CLR raises an exception in the Divide method while executing the a/b statement with the value 10/0, for example, it will first search the handler block defined in the Divide method to match the exception type raised and the exceptions defined in the handler block to execute the code in the matched exception-handler block. The best match exception type is DivideByZeroException, so the CLR will execute the handler block for the DivideByZeroException and show the output:

```
DivideByZeroException
This handler block will execute.
```

If you modify this program by removing the DivideByZeroException handler block and then execute the program, the CLR will try to match the best-matched handler block and execute the best-matched handler block, which is the Exception block, and produce the following output:

```
It will execute when there is no best matched found.
```

Unhandled Exception

If you remove the catch block that handled the Exception type exception in the Main method and Exception type and DivideByZeroException from the Divide method, when an exception occurs in the Divide method the CLR will try to match the raised exception with the catch block. However, it will not find any, as there is no longer a DivideByZeroException or Exception type handler block in the Divide method. The CLR will try to determine a possible handler block for the exception it raised. If there is any handler block defined in the caller of the method (e.g., here in the Main method of the Program class), the CLR will move the execution pointer to that point and try to match the type of the exception defined in the handler block. If it does not find a match, then the handler block will execute, as shown in Figure 13-18.

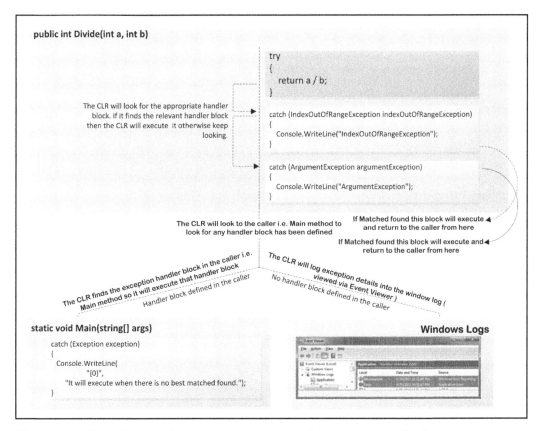

Figure 13-18. Exception matching when there is no match in executing method.

If there is no handler block defined in the Main method of the Program class or there is no best-matched exception type defined in the handler block of the Main method in the Program class, the CLR will then write the exception information to the Windows log.

Using Statement

The using statement in C# allows you to specify for the CLR when objects that use resources should release them. The object provided to the using statement must implement the IDisposable interface, and this interface provides the Dispose method. Listing 13-19 demonstrates the usage of the using statement.

Listing 13-19. Example of Using Statement

```
using System;
using System.Text;
using System.IO;

namespace Ch13
{
    class Program
    {
        static void Main(string[] args)
        {
            StringBuilder sb = new StringBuilder();
            sb.Append("StringBuilder\n");

            using (StringWriter sw = new StringWriter(sb))
            {
                sw.WriteLine("StringWriter");
            }
            Console.WriteLine("{0}", sb.ToString());
        }
    }
}
```

The decompiled IL code for the program in Listing 13-19 is shown in Listing 13-20.

Listing 13-20. IL Code for Listing 13-19

```
.method private hidebysig static void  Main(string[] args) cil managed
{
  .entrypoint
  // Code size       77 (0x4d)
  .maxstack  2
  .locals init (
          [0] class [mscorlib]System.Text.StringBuilder sb,
          [1] class [mscorlib]System.IO.StringWriter sw,
          [2] bool CS$4$0000)

  /* Code removed */

  IL_0013:  ldloc.0
  IL_0014:  newobj     instance void
          [mscorlib]System.IO.StringWriter::.ctor(
              class [mscorlib]System.Text.StringBuilder)
  IL_0019:  stloc.1
```

```
  /* using statement has been replaced with the try as protected block
   * and finally as the handler block  */
  .try
  {
    IL_001a:  nop
    IL_001b:  ldloc.1
    IL_001c:  ldstr      "StringWriter"
    IL_0021:  callvirt   instance void
              [mscorlib]System.IO.TextWriter::WriteLine(string)
    IL_0026:  nop
    IL_0027:  nop
    IL_0028:  leave.s    IL_003a
  }  // end .try
  finally
  {
    IL_002a:  ldloc.1
    IL_002b:  ldnull
    IL_002c:  ceq
    IL_002e:  stloc.2
    IL_002f:  ldloc.2
    IL_0030:  brtrue.s   IL_0039
    IL_0032:  ldloc.1
    IL_0033:  callvirt   instance void
              [mscorlib]System.IDisposable::Dispose()
    IL_0038:  nop
    IL_0039:  endfinally
  }  // end handler

  /* Code removed */
}
```

The IL code of the label IL_0024 will look for the surrounding finally code block, and if it finds it, it will then execute that finally block and continue the execution from label IL_0030 until it finishes the execution.

Summary

In this chapter we have learned about the C# exception, the exception-handling mechanism, and how the CLR handles the exception in runtime. The C# compiler embeds the exception-handling–related information in the Method State Description table, which is later used by the CLR to handle exceptions. You have explored these methods in detail by analyzing the runtime Method State Description information of the methods defined in a type. The throw statement and rethrow IL instruction have been discussed in depth to explain different scenarios and explain how the CLR works differently in different circumstances. The chapter also explored the unhandled exception. The next chapter will discuss about the asynchronous programming using async and await.

CHAPTER 14

■ ■ ■

Asynchrony

A powerful new feature has been added for asynchronous programming in C# language 5.0. This new feature comes in the form of two new keywords—async and await—which are used to make the synchronous method asynchronous. When you use these two keyword in your method, the C# compiler performs a transformation of your method code to generate the appropriate code, such as stub method and state machine, to do the asynchronous operation behind the scenes. This new feature makes asynchronous programming much easier than the exiting asynchronous pattern used in .NET.

This chapter will define the basics of synchronous and asynchronous programming and then explain asynchronous programming using the Task class introduced in .NET Framework 4.0. It will explain how to add a continuation block in the Task class and use different options such as TaskStatus and TaskContinuationOptions. Exception handling in the Task class is discussed to show how this has been made easier. The chapter will also explain in detail async and await, how to use them, and how the C# compiler takes care of these two keywords to implement the necessary code behind the scenes. Finally, the chapter will show how to use Task-based asynchronous patterns using the async and await keywords.

Synchronous and Asynchronous Programming

A synchronous operation does not return to its caller until it finishes its job. For example, in synchronous context, if Method1 calls Method2, the program control does not return to Method1 until the CLR finishes with Method2, and this makes the synchronous operation a blocking operation. In synchronous context, the program will only be allowed to do one thing at a time.

Figure 14-1 demonstrates the behavior of the synchronous operation of a program, where Method1, Method2, Method3, Method4, and Method5 are called from a program one after another. Each of the methods takes approximate 10 milliseconds to finish its operation, so the program will be blocked for about 50 milliseconds to finish execution of the five methods.

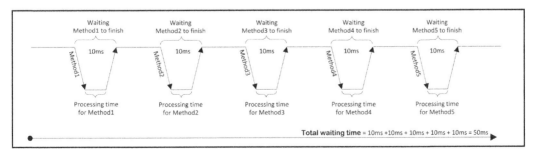

Figure 14-1. Synchronous method call

Listing 14-1 shows an example of the synchronous method called in a program and shows that the synchronous operation takes about 50 milliseconds to finish its execution.

Listing 14-1. *Example of synchronous method call*

```
using System;
using System.Diagnostics;
using System.Threading;

namespace Ch14
{
    class Program
    {
        static void Main()
        {
            Stopwatch stopwatch = new Stopwatch();
            stopwatch.Start();
            Method1();
            Method2();
            Method3();
            Method4();
            Method5();
            stopwatch.Stop();
            Console.WriteLine("Elapsed time: {0}ms",
                            stopwatch.ElapsedMilliseconds);
            Console.ReadKey();
        }
        static void Method1() { Thread.Sleep(10); }
        static void Method2() { Thread.Sleep(10); }
        static void Method3() { Thread.Sleep(10); }
        static void Method4() { Thread.Sleep(10); }
        static void Method5() { Thread.Sleep(10); }
    }
}
```

This program will produce the output (output might vary when you run it locally):

```
Elapsed time: 50ms
```

Asynchronous programming is the opposite of synchronous programming: you write long running functions asynchronously rather than synchronously. The difference with the asynchronous approach is that concurrency is initiated inside the long-running function, rather than from outside the function. Asynchronous programming is used in many programs, especially writing (typically server-side) applications that deal efficiently with a lot of concurrent input/output (I/O). The second use is to make the thread safety in rich-client applications easier.

Figure 14-2 demonstrates the behavior of the asynchronous programming, from which you can see that if Method1 starts asynchronously, then it will return the program control immediately to the place where it left to continue with other operations. When Method1 finishes its execution sometime later, it returns (or executes the callback if there is any) to the caller. While Method1 is executing, the program can deal with Method2, Method3, Method4, and Method5, as demonstrated in the Figure 14-2.

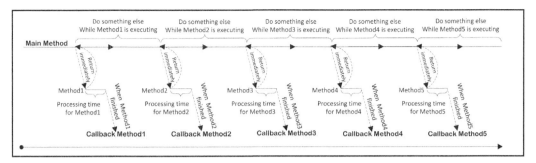

Figure 14-2. Asynchronous method call

As a result, while you need to wait about 50 milliseconds to finish the execution of five methods using synchronous programming, in asynchronous programming you do not need to block the program that long to continue with some other operation.

The .NET Framework allows you to execute some methods asynchronously without blocking the calling program, and these asynchronous methods might be executed on different threads, thus allowing the calling program to do its own job after the other method has been invoked.

In these kinds of asynchronous programming scenarios, in general you expect the following features to be implemented:

- Allowed to perform certain tasks (execute methods) in a different thread without blocking the calling thread

- Allowed to execute another method as a callback or continuation on completion of the asynchronous method

- Allowed to check the status of the task to determine whether the task is ready to run, it is complete, or if a fault occurred during execution

- Allowed to get information about the progress status of the task

- Allowed to cancel the task that is running

- Allowed to handle the exceptions raised during the asynchronous operation

To implement asynchronous methods using the .NET Framework, you can use the following techniques:

- Asynchronous programming model (APM)

- Event-based asynchronous pattern

- Task-based asynchronous programming

- Async-await–based asynchronous programming

This chapter will explore the asynchronous programming using `async`- and `await`-based techniques in .NET Framework 4.5. The `async`-based asynchronous programming works based on the `Task`-based asynchronous pattern using the `async` and `await` keywords. This chapter will explore `Task`-based programming to help you understand the beauty of the `async`- and `await`-based asynchronous programming.

Asynchronous Programming Using Task

The Task class is used to represent the asynchronous operation in .NET and was introduced in .NET Framework 4.0 as part of the parallel programming library. The Task class has a higher level of abstraction, which is used for the asynchronous operation. The tasks are compositional and use a thread pool to manage the task that is being assigned.

When you instantiate the Task class, you pass the job as an Action block and call the Start method from it to schedule the task to execute depending on the available threads. Alternatively, you can pass the instance of the Task class to some other method (which accepts Task) as a parameter to execute from there.

The Thread class can be used to perform an asynchronous operation by initiating new threads for the new operation, but it has some limitations, for example, it is hard to get data back from the thread you are waiting to Join unless you configure a shared field to pass the data around. The thread you will start cannot start a new thread by itself when it has finished its task. In addition, and most importantly, exception handling is not easy to do in concurrent programming using threading. Therefore, using the thread to write asynchronous operations becomes quite tedious and complex, and synchronization also becomes another issue. The use of the Thread also slows the performance due to the context switching from thread to thread.

The Task class eliminates most of these problems. When you instantiate the Task class, the instance of the Task will be scheduled to execute by the TaskScheduler (discussed later on this chapter), therefore, you do not need to maintain the Thread creation.

Task Class in .NET

The Task class is defined in the System.Threading.Tasks namespace of the mscorlib.dll assembly, as shown in Figure 14-3.

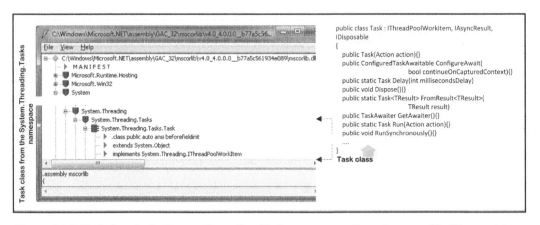

Figure 14-3. *Task class in the System.Threading.Tasks namespace from the mscorlib.dll assembly*

Listing 14-2 shows the methods and properties from the Task class.

Listing 14-2. *Definition of the Task Class*

```
public class Task : IThreadPoolWorkItem, IAsyncResult, IDisposable
{
```

```
    /* 8 overloaded */
    public Task(Action action)                              {}
    /* 21 overloaded */
    public ConfiguredTaskAwaitable ConfigureAwait(
            bool continueOnCapturedContext)                 {}
    /* 4 overloaded */
    public static Task Delay(int millisecondsDelay)         {}
    public void Dispose()                                   {}
    public static Task<TResult> FromResult<TResult>
                            (TResult result)                {}
    public TaskAwaiter GetAwaiter()                         {}
    /* 8 overloaded */
    public static Task Run(Action action)                   {}
    /* 2 overloaded */
    public void RunSynchronously()                          {}
    /* 2 overloaded */
    public void Start()                                     {}

    /* 5 overloaded */
    public void Wait()                                      {}
    /* 5 overloaded */
    public static void WaitAll(params Task[] tasks)         {}
    /* 5 overloaded */
    public static int WaitAny(params Task[] tasks)          {}
    /* 4 overloaded */
    public static Task WhenAll(IEnumerable<Task> tasks)     {}
    /* 4 overloaded */
    public static Task<Task> WhenAny(IEnumerable<Task> tasks)  {}
    public static YieldAwaitable Yield()                    {}
    public object AsyncState                                {}
    public TaskCreationOptions CreationOptions              {}
    public static int? CurrentId                            {}
    public AggregateException Exception                     {}
    public static TaskFactory Factory                       {}
    public int Id                                           {}
    public bool IsCanceled                                  {}
    public bool IsCompleted                                 {}
    public bool IsFaulted                                   {}
    public TaskStatus Status                                {}
}
```

Creation/Wait of the Task

To create a task you can use the Run method from the Task class, as shown in Listing 14-3.

Listing 14-3. Task Creation Using the Run Method

```
using System;
using System.Threading.Tasks;
```

```
namespace Ch14
{
    class Program
    {
        static void Main()
        {
            /* A task will be instantiated and scheduled to run sometime
             * later on and
             * return the instance of the Task to displayTask variable. */
            Task displayTask = Task.Run(() =>
                                    Console.WriteLine("async in C# 5.0"));

            /* Continue until the task completes */
            while (true)
            {
                /* To check whether the task has completed or not */
                if (displayTask.IsCompleted)
                {
                    Console.WriteLine("Task completed!");
                    break;
                }
            }
            Console.ReadLine();
        }
    }
}
```

The program will produce the output:

```
async in C# 5.0
Task completed!
```

You could also use the Start method from the Task class to start a task, as demonstrated in Listing 14-4.

Listing 14-4. Task Creation Using the Task Constructor

```
using System;
using System.Threading.Tasks;

namespace Ch14
{
    class Program
    {
        static void Main()
        {
            /* An instance of the Task will be instantiated. */
            Task displayTask = new Task(
                /* The Task will execute the Action block */
                () => Console.WriteLine("async in C# 5.0"),
                /* Task creation options */
                TaskCreationOptions.None
```

```
        );

        displayTask.Start();
        /* The Task will execute sometimes later */
        displayTask.Wait();
        /* Explicitly wait for the task to finish */
        Console.ReadLine();
    }
  }
}
```

This will produce the output:

```
async in C# 5.0
```

Details About the Task Creation Options in Task

In Listing 14-4, the instance of the Task class displayTask was instantiated using the constructor of the Task class, which takes an Action block (the Action block contains the code of the operation the Task class will execute), and a value of the TaskCreationOptions enum, which controls the behavior for the task creation and execution. When you instantiate a task, you can use different values of the TaskCreationOptions enum, as defined in the System.Threading.Tasks namespace of the mscorlib.dll assembly. Listing 14-5 shows the different values of the TaskCreationOptions enum that can be used.

Listing 14-5. TaskStatus Enum

```
public enum TaskCreationOptions
{
    /* It indicates that the created Task will be attached to the
     * parent in the Task hierarchy */
    AttachedToParent            = 4,

    /* It indicates to throw an InvalidOperationException when a
     * child task try to attach */
    DenyChildAttach             = 8,

    /* It prevents the immediate scheduler from being seen as the
     * current scheduler in the created task.*/
    HideScheduler               = 0x10,

   /* It indicates that the newly created Task will be long running task. */
    LongRunning                 = 2,

   /* It indicates to use the default behavior when the Task will created.*/
    None                        = 0,

    /* It indicates that the Task scheduled to run sooner will run sooner
     * and the Task scheduled to run later will run later. */
    PreferFairness              = 1
}
```

Listing 14-6 demonstrates the use of the TaskCreationOptions enum.

Listing 14-6. *Return Value from the Task*

```
using System;
using System.Threading.Tasks;

namespace Ch14
{
    class Program
    {
        static void Main()
        {
            Task<string> displayTask = new Task<string>(
                        () => "async in C# 5.0", TaskCreationOptions.None);
            displayTask.Start();
            Console.WriteLine("Result from the Task : {0}",
                            displayTask.Result);
            Console.ReadLine();
        }
    }
}
```

This program will produce the output:

```
Result from the Task : async in C# 5.0
```

Details About the Status of the Task

In Listing 14-6 we instantiated the Task, which is scheduled by the CLR to execute sometime later. The Task initiator needs to know whether or not the Task has completed, is being canceled, or is being faulted while executing. To determine this, the TaskStatus enum keeps track of the status of the Task you initiated. The TaskStatus enum is defined in the System.Threading.Tasks namespace of the mscorlib.dll assembly. Listing 14-7 shows the different values of the TaskStatus enum you can use.

Listing 14-7. *TaskStatus Enum*

```
public enum TaskStatus
{
    /* It indicates that the task has been canceled.*/
    Canceled                = 6,

    /* It indicates that the CLR sets this status when the task has been
     * initialized but has not been scheduled yet. */
    Created                 = 0,

    /* It indicates that the CLR sets Faulted status if there is any
     * unhandled exception.*/
    Faulted                 = 7,

    /* It indicates that the task completed successfully.*/
    RanToCompletion         = 5,

    /* It indicates that the Task is Running but has not completed yet.*/
```

```
    Running                     = 3,

    /* It indicates that the CLR scheduled the Task internally but waiting
     * to be activated.*/
    WaitingForActivation        = 1,

    /* It indicates that the CLR finished executing the Task but waiting
     * for the attached child tasks to finish (if there is any).*/
    WaitingForChildrenToComplete = 4,

    /* It indicates that the CLR scheduled the task for execution still
     * waiting to execute.*/
    WaitingToRun                = 2
}
```

The Created status is set by the CLR when you first instantiate a task, and as soon as the task starts it changes the status to WaitingToRun. The started task will be executed sometime later based on the allocated schedule for the task, and when it starts running, the CLR changes its status to Running. It will get WaitingForChildrenToComplete status if it stops running or it is waiting for any child tasks. The CLR will assign one of three statuses when it has finished the operation of the task completely:

- RanToCompletion
- Canceled
- Faulted

RanToCompletion indicates when the task has been completed successfully, Canceled indicates the task has been canceled, and Faulted indicates any exception that has occurred during the task execution. Listing 14-2 shows that the Task class has three properties:

- IsCompleted
- IsCanceled
- IsFaulted

It uses these, respectively, to determine the status of the RanToCompletion, Canceled, or Faulted properties from the Task class. Listing 14-8 shows the use of the IsCompleted, IsCanceled, and IsFaulted properties of the Task class to determine the task completion status.

Listing 14-8. *Example of the IsCompleted, IsCanceled, and IsFaulted*

```
using System;
using System.Threading.Tasks;

namespace Ch14
{
    class Program
    {
        static void Main()
        {
            Task<string> displayTask = Task.Run(() =>
            {
                /* To simulate as doing something.*/
```

```
                for (int i = 0; i <= Int16.MaxValue; ++i) ;
                return "async in C# 5.0";
        });
        Console.WriteLine("Result from the Task : {0}",
                          displayTask.Result);

        if (displayTask.IsCompleted)
            Console.Write(TaskStatus.RanToCompletion.ToString());
        if (displayTask.IsCanceled)
            Console.Write(TaskStatus.Canceled.ToString());
        if (displayTask.IsFaulted)
            Console.Write(TaskStatus.Faulted.ToString());
        Console.ReadLine();
        }
    }
}
```

This program will produce the output:

```
Result from the Task : async in C# 5.0
RanToCompletion
```

If you use the ContinueWith, ContinueWhenAll, ContinueWhenAny, or FromAsync method to instantiate a task, the CLR will use WaitingForActivation as the status of this task instance. Alternatively, if you instantiate a task using the TaskCompletionSource<TResult> object, the CLR also sets WaitingForActivation status. Listing 14-9 demonstrates the use of the different statuses of the task.

Listing 14-9. Example of the TaskStatus

```
using System;
using System.Threading.Tasks;

namespace Ch14
{
    class Program
    {
        static void Main()
        {
            Task displayTask = Task.Run(() =>
            {
                Task.Delay(500000);
                for (int i = 0; i < byte.MaxValue; ++i) ;
                Console.WriteLine("async in C# 5.0");
            });

            while (true)
            {
                Console.WriteLine(displayTask.Status.ToString());
                if (displayTask.IsCompleted)
                    break;
            }
            Console.WriteLine(displayTask.Status.ToString());
```

```
            Console.ReadLine();
        }
    }
}
```

This program will produce the output:

```
WaitingToRun
Running
Running
Running
async in C# 5.0
Running
RanToCompletion
```

You have seen how to initiate an instance of the Task class and leave the instance of the task to the scheduler to execute when it has been scheduled. When the task is being scheduled, you can continue with other operations without even waiting for the task to finish. Otherwise, you can use the Wait method of the Task class to explicitly wait for the scheduled task to finish. Listing 14-10 shows the use of the Wait method from the Task class.

Listing 14-10. Wait for the Task to Finish

```
using System;
using System.Threading.Tasks;

namespace Ch14
{
    class Program
    {
        static void Main()
        {
            Task displayTask = Task.Run(
                () => Console.WriteLine("async in C# 5.0"));

            Console.WriteLine(
                    "Task completion status : {0}, waiting to finish....",
                    displayTask.IsCompleted);
            displayTask.Wait();
            Console.ReadLine();
        }
    }
}
```

This program will produce the output:

```
Task completion status : False, waiting to finish....
async in C# 5.0
```

Continuation of the Task

In asynchronous programming, the continuation code block refers to those statements that will execute after finishing the asynchronous operation. Figure 14-4 refers to that at statement 5; the program control moves to another location to execute some operations asynchronously. It was intended that when this asynchronous operation finishes its operation, the program control will return to statement 6 to finish statements 6 to 10. This can be achieved by remembering statements 6 to 10 as a continuation code block that will be executed after the asynchronous operation has finished its operation.

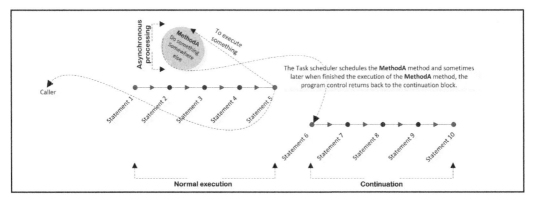

Figure 14-4. Continuation in asynchronous method

Statements 6 through 10 will be set as a continuation code block and will execute when the program has finished the asynchronous operation defined in MethodA, as shown in Figure 14-4. You can set up the continuation of the task using the following techniques:

- Using the OnCompleted method
- Using the ContinueWith method
- Using the await statement

In the following section, we will explore these options except for the await statement, which we will explore later in this chapter.

Using the OnCompleted Method

In asynchronous programming using the Task class, you can define the continuation code block in the task to execute when the original task finishes its execution. A continuation is a callback function, which executes upon completion of the operation defined in the Task class. You can define the continuation using the OnCompleted method of the TaskAwaiter by setting the Action block of the continuation in the OnCompleted method. Listing 14-11 demonstrates the continuation of a task using the OnCompleted method.

Listing 14-11. Example of the Continuations Using Task

```
using System;
using System.Linq;
using System.Runtime.CompilerServices;
using System.Threading.Tasks;

namespace Ch14
{
```

```
class Program
{
    static void Main()
    {
        ShowEvenNumbers();
        Console.WriteLine("Waiting.....");
        for (int i = 0; i <= Int16.MaxValue * 100; ++i) ;
        Console.ReadLine();
    }

    static void ShowEvenNumbers()
    {
        /* A Task is instantiated*/
        Task<int> evenNumbersTask = Task.Run(
                () => Enumerable.Range(1,
                new Random().Next(Int16.MaxValue)).Count(
                item => item % 2 == 0));

        /* Retrieved the awaiter from the Task instantiated earlier */
        TaskAwaiter<int> awaiter = evenNumbersTask.GetAwaiter();

        /* Setup the continuation block in the awaiter of the Task
         * evenNumbersTask */
        awaiter.OnCompleted(() =>
        {
            /* Continuation code block */
            Console.WriteLine("Complete, Total no of even : {0}",
                            awaiter.GetResult());
        });

        /* Following line or lines is not part of the continuation
         * code block in relation to the Task  evenNumbersTask */
        Console.WriteLine("Schedule to complete...");
    }
}
```

This program will produce the output:

```
Schedule to complete...
Waiting.....
Complete, Total no of even : 10652
```

When the CLR executes the executable produced from Listing 14-11, it works as shown in Figure 14-5. The Figure 14-5 demonstrates that:

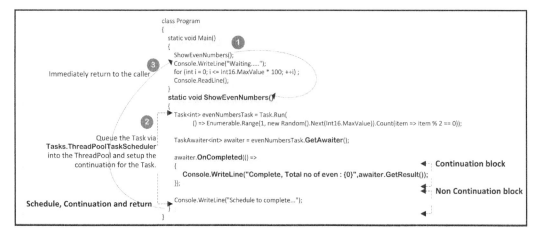

Figure 14-5. *Continuation and Task*

1. The program control moves to the ShowEvenNumbers method.

2. It instantiates the task and gets the awaiter type TaskAwaiter<int> from the task by calling the GetAwaiter method of the task. The OnCompleted method from the TaskAwaiter<TResult> (the awaiter for the evenNumbersTask Task) is used to set the continuation code block for the task that will be executed after the job assigned to the task finishes its execution. The TaskAwaiter or TaskAwaiter<TResult> struct is defined in the System.Runtime.CompilerServices namespace of the mscorlib.dll assembly.

Listing 14-12 shows the definition of the TaskAwaiter<TResult> struct.

Listing 14-12. *The TaskAwaiter Struct*

```
public struct TaskAwaiter<TResult> :
                        ICriticalNotifyCompletion, INotifyCompletion
{
    public bool        IsCompleted                           {}
    public void        OnCompleted(Action continuation)      {}
    public void        UnsafeOnCompleted(Action continuation) {}
    public TResult     GetResult()                           {}
}
```

The OnCompleted method from the TaskAwaiter<TResult> struct is used to set the continuation of the task to execute when the task should complete its execution. The OnCompleted method internally calls the OnCompletedInternal method from the TaskAwaiter<TResult> struct, as shown in Listing 14-13.

Listing 14-13. *OnCompletedInternal Method*

```
internal static void OnCompletedInternal(
    Task task,  Action continuation,  bool continueOnCapturedContext,
    bool flowExecutionContext)
{
    if (continuation == null)
```

```
    {
        throw new ArgumentNullException("continuation");
    }
    StackCrawlMark lookForMyCaller = StackCrawlMark.LookForMyCaller;
    if (TplEtwProvider.Log.IsEnabled(EventLevel.Verbose, ~EventKeywords.None))
    {
        continuation = OutputWaitEtwEvents(task, continuation);
    }

    /* Setup the continuation for the Task */
    task.SetContinuationForAwait(
            continuation, /* continuation - represents continuation code
                           * block which execute after finishing the Task.*/
            continueOnCapturedContext,
            flowExecutionContext,
            ref lookForMyCaller);
}
```

The OnCompletedInternal method is set up in the continuation code block along with other parameters, for example, the current captured execution context (which is discussed later in this chapter), for the task. This continuation code block will execute when the original job assigned to the task finishes its execution.

3. After the CLR sets up the continuation for the task, the program control immediately returns to the initiator of the task.

We have seen how the OnCompleted method of the TaskAwaiter<TResult> struct is used to set up the continuation for the task. In addition to the OnCompleted method, you can also use the ContinueWith method from the Task class, as discussed in the next section.

Using the ContinueWith Method

To set up the continuation for the task, you can also use the ContinueWith method from the Task class. The ContinueWith method internally sets up the continuation code block for the task. Listing 14-14 shows an example of the ContinueWith method.

Listing 14-14. Example of the ContinueWith

```
using System;
using System.Linq;
using System.Threading.Tasks;

namespace Ch14
{
    class Program
    {
        static void Main()
        {
            ShowEvenNumbers();
            Console.WriteLine("Waiting.....");
            for (int i = 0; i <= Int16.MaxValue * 100; ++i) ;
            Console.ReadLine();
```

```
        }

        static void ShowEvenNumbers()
        {
            Task<int> evenNumbersTask = Task.Run(
                    () => Enumerable.Range(1,
                                    new Random().Next(Int16.MaxValue)).
                                    Count(item => item % 2 == 0));

            evenNumbersTask.ContinueWith(task =>
            {
                Console.WriteLine("Complete, Total no of even : {0}",
                                                    task.Result);
            });

            Console.WriteLine("Schedule to complete...");
        }
    }
}
```

This program will produce the output:

```
Schedule to complete...
Waiting.....
Complete, Total no of even : 12896
```

So we have seen two different ways to set up the continuation code block for a task. We can use TaskCreationOptions to specify the behavior of the task creations; or we can specify the behavior of the task continuation using the TaskContinuationOptions enum when we set up the continuation for the task.

Details About the Task Continuation Options

The TaskContinuationOptions enum are defined in the System.Threading.Tasks namespace of the mscorlib.dll assembly, and they define the continuation behavior of the task. Listing 14-15 demonstrates the different values of the TaskContinuationOptions enum that can be used to set the continuation.

Listing 14-15. TaskContinuationOptions Enum

```
public enum TaskContinuationOptions
{
    AttachedToParent         = 4,
    DenyChildAttach          = 8,
    ExecuteSynchronously     = 0x80000,
    HideScheduler            = 0x10,
    LazyCancellation         = 0x20,
    LongRunning              = 2,
    None                     = 0,
    NotOnCanceled            = 0x40000,
    NotOnFaulted             = 0x20000,
    NotOnRanToCompletion     = 0x10000,
    OnlyOnCanceled           = 0x30000,
    OnlyOnFaulted            = 0x50000,
```

```
    OnlyOnRanToCompletion           = 0x60000,
    PreferFairness                  = 1
}
```

Schedule the Task Using the TaskScheduler

The CLR uses the TaskScheduler to schedule the tasks. The default task scheduler is based on the .NET Framework 4.0 ThreadPool. However, if you require a special functionality, you can create a custom scheduler and enable it for specific tasks or queries. The TaskScheduler class is defined in the System. Threading.Tasks namespace of the mscorlib.dll assembly. Listing 14-16 shows the definition of the TaskScheduler class.

Listing 14-16. *Definition of the TaskScheduler Class*

```
public abstract class TaskScheduler
{
    protected TaskScheduler()                                        {}
    public static TaskScheduler FromCurrentSynchronizationContext()  {}
    protected internal virtual bool TryDequeue(Task task)            {}
    protected bool TryExecuteTask(Task task)                         {}

    /* abstract methods */
    protected abstract bool TryExecuteTaskInline(Task task,
                          bool taskWasPreviouslyQueued);
    protected abstract IEnumerable<Task> GetScheduledTasks();
    protected internal abstract void QueueTask(Task task);

    /* Properties */
    public static TaskScheduler Current                              {}
    public static TaskScheduler Default                              {}
    public int Id                                                    {}
    public virtual int MaximumConcurrencyLevel                       {}

    /*Event in TaskScheduler class */
    public static event EventHandler<UnobservedTaskExceptionEventArgs>
        UnobservedTaskException                                      {}
}
```

In .NET, there are two kinds of task schedulers:

- The thread pool task scheduler

- A synchronization context task scheduler

In .NET, all the applications by default use the ThreadPool task scheduler, which maintains a global FIFO (first-in-first-out) work queue. The FIFO is maintained for threads in each of the application domains. On call of the QueueUserWorkItem (or UnsafeQueueUserWorkItem) method, the CLR keeps the task on this shared queue, which will be dequeued to process later.

When the CLR queues the task into the queue, it follows two threads:

- Top-level tasks, which are tasks that are not created in the context of another task, are put on the global queue.

- Child or nested tasks, which are created in the context of another task, are put on a local queue that is specific to the thread on which the parent task is executing. The local queue works as LIFO (last-in-first-out).

When the thread is ready to work, the CLR looks in the local queue first, and if there are any work items waiting to be executed, the CLR will accessed those. Figure 14-6 shows the TaskScheduler queue strategy for the top level tasks and child task that has been instantiated in context of another task.

The use of local queues not only reduces pressure on the global queue, but it also takes advantage of data locality.

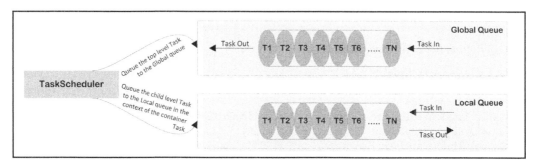

Figure 14-6. TaskScheduler

ExecutionContext to Capture the Context

Every thread has an execution context data structure associated with it, which is the ExecutionContext class that defines in the System.Threading namespace of the mscorlib.dll assembly. The ExecutionContext class allows the user code to capture and transfer the context of the execution across a user-defined asynchronous point. This captured context can be accesses from somewhere else and used later to execute the operation. Listing 14-17 shows the definition of the ExecutionContext class.

Listing 14-17. Definition of the ExecutionContext Class

```
public sealed class ExecutionContext : IDisposable, ISerializable
{
    public      static ExecutionContext Capture()                        {}
    public      ExecutionContext CreateCopy()                            {}
    public      void Dispose()                                           {}
    public      void GetObjectData(SerializationInfo info,
                           StreamingContext context)                     {}
    public      static bool IsFlowSuppressed()                           {}
    public      static void RestoreFlow()                                {}
    public      static void Run(ExecutionContext executionContext,
                    ContextCallback callback, object state)              {}
    public      static AsyncFlowControl SuppressFlow()                   {}
}
```

The execution context includes all the information relevant to a logical thread execution, for example, security settings (compressed stack, thread's principal property, and Windows identity), host settings, and logical call context data. The ExecutionContext is used to capture the current execution context and pass it to relevant places to execute from there. For example, you can pass captured ExecutionContext to the asynchronous point to execute some action block on the captured execution context. Transferring the execution context by setting it from one thread to another causes exceptions unless you copy across the execution context. Listing 14-18 demonstrates where a state machine is running in the captured execution context.

Listing 14-18. Example of the State Machine Run on the Captured Execution Context

```
using System;
using System.Threading;

namespace Ch14
{
    class Program
    {
        static void Main()
        {
            /*Instantiates an instance of the State machine */
            StateMachine sm = new StateMachine();

            /*Initialize the State machine with it's default value*/
            sm.State = 1;

            /* Start the State machine */
            sm.MoveNext();

            /* Queue the captured execution context with the workitem in the
             * ThreadPool to process later. */
            ThreadPool.QueueUserWorkItem(state =>
                RunLaterOn<object>(
                    /* Get the current execution context */
                    CaptureExecutionContext(),
                    /* pass the callback code block */
                    new Action<object>(Callback),
                    /* The State machine which maintains the state */
                    sm));

            /* Do something else. */
            for (int i = 0; i <= Int16.MaxValue; ++i)
                if (i % byte.MaxValue == 0)
                    Console.Write(".");
            Console.ReadLine();
        }

        /* This code block capture the current execution context */
        static ExecutionContext CaptureExecutionContext()
        {
            return ExecutionContext.Capture();
        }

        /* This code block will run the callback code block on the
```

```
         * captured execution context*/
        static void RunLaterOn<T>(
                    ExecutionContext context, Action<T> callback, object state)
        {
            ExecutionContext.Run(context,
                                new ContextCallback(Callback), state);
        }

        /* This code block used as the callback */
        static void Callback(object state)
        {
            ((StateMachine)state).MoveNext();
        }
    }

    /* The State machine used to maintain the state of the operation */
    public class StateMachine
    {
        public int State { get; set; }

        public void MoveNext()
        {
            switch (State)
            {
                case 0:
                    Console.Write("State 0");
                    State = 1;
                    break;
                case 1:
                    Console.Write("State 1");
                    for (int i = 0; i <= byte.MaxValue; ++i) ;
                    State = 0;
                    break;
                default:
                    Console.Write("State -1");
                    State = 10;
                    break;
            }
        }
    }
}
```

This program will produce the output:

State 1...State 0.
....

In Listing 14-18, a state machine has been instantiated with its initial state 1 in the Main method of the Program class. The CLR then calls the MoveNext method from the instance of the State Machine to change the state of the state machine. The current execution context has been captured using the CaptureExecutionContext method. This captured execution context and a callback method have been passed to the ThreadPool to queue a new work item to schedule to run later. As soon as it is queued in the

ThreadPool to run later, the program control will return to the caller (i.e., Main method) to finish the rest of the code, which is the for loop block.

When the item queued in the ThreadPool executes, it will run the callback method and change the state of the state machine based on the state it was in before using the captured execution context.

Exceptions of the Task

One of the main reasons to use the Task class is to make exception handling in the concurrent programming easy. When you use the Task class, the CLR propagates the unhandled exception thrown from the code block that is running inside a task back to the thread from which the task was instantiated. If you use the Wait method from the task or the Task<TResult> class in the program, the CLR will propagate the exceptions, which you can handle using the try-catch block. The task calling code block will be inside the try block and exception handling will be inside the catch block.

The CLR aggregates all the exceptions in an AggregateException class, which is defined in the System namespace of the mscorlib.dll assembly. Listing 14-19 shows the definition of the AggregateException class.

Listing 14-19. Definition of the AggregateException Class

```
public class AggregateException : Exception
{
    /* 7 overloaded constructors*/
    public AggregateException()                                     {}
    public AggregateException Flatten()                             {}
    public override Exception GetBaseException()                    {}
    public override void GetObjectData(
        SerializationInfo info, StreamingContext context)           {}
    public void Handle(Func<Exception, bool> predicate)            {}
    public override string ToString()                              {}
    public ReadOnlyCollection<Exception> InnerExceptions           {}
}
```

The AggregateException class contains the InnerExceptions property where the CLR puts all the aggregated exceptions. You can get all the original exceptions back after enumerating in the InnerExceptions from the AggregateException class. Listing 14-20 shows the use of the AggregateException class.

Listing 14-20. Exception Handling in the Task

```
using System;
using System.Linq;
using System.Threading.Tasks;

namespace Ch14
{
    class Program
    {
        static void Main()
        {
            int limit = new Random().Next(Int32.MaxValue);
```

```
            Task<int> evenNumbersTask = Task.Run(
                () => Enumerable.Range(1, limit).Count(item =>
                {
                    if (item == Int16.MaxValue)
                        /* Out of Range will be concat with the original
                         * Framework given exception message */
                        throw new ArgumentOutOfRangeException(
                                                "Out of Range....");
                    return item % 2 == 0;
                }));
            try
            {
                evenNumbersTask.Wait(); /* Wait for the Exception to occur. */
            }
            catch (AggregateException aggregateException)
            {
                aggregateException
                    .InnerExceptions
                    .Where(item => item is ArgumentOutOfRangeException)
                    .ToList()    /* Contains ArgumentOutOfRangeException */
                    .ForEach(age => Console.WriteLine(age.Message));
            }
        }
    }
}
```

This program will produce the output:

```
Specified argument was out of the range of valid values.
Parameter name: Out of Range....
```

UnobservedTaskException of the Task

You use the UnobservedTaskException event from the TaskScheduler class at a global level to subscribe to unobserved exceptions. The handler of this event can be used to log the error.

Exception of the Task that Attached with Child

Listing 14-21 shows an example of the exception handling for the task that attached with child.

Listing 14-21. Example of the Exception for the Task that Attached with Child

```
using System;
using System.Linq;
using System.Threading.Tasks;

namespace Ch14
{
    class Program
    {
        static void Main()
```

```
    {
        int limit = new Random().Next(Int32.MaxValue);

        var evenNumbersTask = Task.Factory.StartNew(() =>
        {
            var r = Task.Factory.StartNew(() =>
            {
                Enumerable.Range(1, limit).Count(item =>
                {
                    if (item == Int16.MaxValue)
                        /* Out of Range will be concat with the original
                         * Framework given exception message */
                        throw new ArgumentOutOfRangeException(
                                                "Out of Range....");
                    return item % 2 == 0;
                });
            }, TaskCreationOptions.AttachedToParent);
        }, TaskCreationOptions.AttachedToParent);

        try
        {
            evenNumbersTask.Wait();   /* Wait for the Exception to occur. */
        }
        catch (AggregateException aggregateException)
        {
            aggregateException
                .Flatten()
                .InnerExceptions
                .Where(item => item is ArgumentOutOfRangeException)
                .ToList()    /* Contains ArgumentOutOfRangeException */
                .ForEach(age => Console.WriteLine(age.Message));
        }
    }
  }
 }
}
```

This program will produce the output:

```
Specified argument was out of the range of valid values.
Parameter name: Out of Range....
```

Exception of the Task that Detached with Child

Listing 14-22 shows an example of the exception handling for the task that detached with child.

Listing 14-22. Example of the Exception of the Task that Detached with Child

```
using System;
```

```csharp
using System.Linq;
using System.Threading.Tasks;

namespace Ch14
{
    class Program
    {
        static void Main()
        {
            int limit = new Random().Next(Int32.MaxValue);

            var evenNumbersTask = Task.Factory.StartNew(() =>
            {
                var r = Task.Factory.StartNew(() =>
                {
                    Enumerable.Range(1, limit).Count(item =>
                    {
                        if (item == Int16.MaxValue)
                            /* Out of Range will be concat with the original
                             * Framework given exception message */
                            throw new ArgumentOutOfRangeException(
                                                    "Out of Range....");
                        return item % 2 == 0;
                    });
                });
                r.Wait();
            });

            try
            {
                evenNumbersTask.Wait(); /* Wait for the Exception to occur. */
            }
            catch (AggregateException aggregateException)
            {
                aggregateException
                    .Flatten()
                    .InnerExceptions
                    .Where(item => item is ArgumentOutOfRangeException)
                    .ToList()    /* Contains ArgumentOutOfRangeException */
                    .ForEach(age => Console.WriteLine(age.Message));
            }
        }
    }
}
```

This program will produce the output:

```
Specified argument was out of the range of valid values.
Parameter name: Out of Range....
```

Asynchronous Programming Using Async and Await

Earlier in this chapter you learned how you can write asynchronous method using the Task class by setting the continuation code block manually. In this section, you will explore how to use the new features of C# 5.0—async and await keywords—to write the asynchronous method without having to manually set up the continuation code block. Using these keywords, you will be able to write asynchronous code that has the same structure and simplicity as the synchronous code you would write.

Asynchronous functions in C# 5.0 are easy to write and handle in application, for example, I/O-bound and CPU-bound applications. As discussed earlier, when you use the Task class for asynchronous operations, you can assign continuation of the asynchronous operation, but you need to set that up manually. When using the await expression in the asynchronous function, you can leave the continuation set up to the C# compiler who will set up the continuation code block for you. The C# compiler implements the continuation code block using the rest of the code after the first await statement it finds. Therefore, the responsibility goes to the C# compiler, not you, to set up the continuation block for the asynchronous functions.

Because you are able to leave this task to the C# compiler, you can write code that maintains its logical structure and eliminate many flow issues you would have in asynchronous operations. Asynchronous function uses async and await keywords, which need to have a few elements in them:

- An asynchronous function defined by async and await in C# must have possible return types of either void or one of the types of Task or Task <T>.

- If you want to create a function, an asynchronous function needs to be marked with the async modifier; without the async modifier, a function would be called synchronous.

- The execution of the asynchronous methods is different from synchronous methods because their execution is discontinuous. Using the await statement, the execution of the asynchronous method can be suspended and can resume the execution using the continuation.

The following sections will explore more in depth about the async and await keywords and their usage, and later we will explore the behind-the-scenes operation of the asynchronous implementation mechanism in C# 5.0, for example, how the asynchronous behavior is implemented using the state machine and how the asynchronous task gets scheduled to the ThreadPool.

The Async Modifier

The async is the modifier used to mark a method as an asynchronous function, so a function without the async modifier is called a synchronous function. The grammar for the async modifier is:

- When the async modifier is used in a method: **async(optional) with method signature**

- When the async modifier is used in a lambda expression: **async (optional) with anonymous-function-signature => anonymous-function-body**

- When the async modifier is used in anonymous method expression: **async(optional) with delegate explicit-anonymous-function-signature (optional) block**

Listing 14-23 shows an example of asynchronous method defined using the async modifier.

***Listing 14-23.** Example of the Async*

```
using System;
using System.Threading.Tasks;

namespace Ch14
{
    class Program
    {
        static void Main()
        {
            Task showNumber = ShowEvenNumbers();
            Console.ReadLine();
        }

        /* The async modifier used to define the asynchronous method */
        public static async Task ShowEvenNumbers()
        {
            await Task.Run(() => Console.WriteLine("Async Function"));
        }
    }
}
```

This program will produce the output:

```
Async Function
```

Listing 14-24 shows another example of the asynchronous method that used the async modifier to define it and it returns Task.

***Listing 14-24.** Example of the Asynchronous Method with Different Return Statement*

```
using System;
using System.Threading.Tasks;

namespace Ch14
{
    class Program
    {
        static void Main()
        {
            Task showNumber = ShowEvenNumbers();
            Console.ReadLine();
        }

        /* The async modifier used to define the asynchronous method */
        public static async Task<int> ShowEvenNumbers()
        {
            return await Task.Run(() =>
            {
                Console.WriteLine("Async Function");
            });
        }
    }
```

```
        }
}
```

Listing 14-24 produced the following compile time error, as the return statement does not return any integer value from the ShowEvenNumbers method.

```
Error   150   Cannot implicitly convert type 'void' to 'int'
```

If you use the Task<T> as the return type from the asynchronous method, the return expression must be implicitly convertible to type of T, for example, if the return is Task<string>, then the return expression of the asynchronous method must be string.

Invocation of the task returning asynchronous method initially is the same as the synchronous function until the CLR finds the first await expression.

The Await

The await expression is used to suspend the execution of an asynchronous function until the awaited task completes its operation. In Listings 14-23 and 14-24, the await keyword is used in the asynchronous method. The grammar of the await expression is:

```
unary-expression:

        …
        await-expression
        await-expression:
                await unary-expression
        statement-expression:

                …
                await-expression
```

The await expression is allowed when the await is used in a method marked with the async modifier, otherwise the compiler generates a compile time error:

```
The 'await' operator can only be used within an async method
```

The await keyword is used to await a task if the Task (T) is used in an await expression (AE), for example:

```
AE = await T
```

The T then has to have a GetAwaiter method with no parameter but it returns a type of R, which has the following accessible members:

```
bool IsCompleted                        {get;}
void OnCompleted (Action);
void GetResult(); or
o    GetResult(); where o refers to a type
```

When the C# compiler finds an await keyword in source code, it compiles the await statement, for example:

```
Get a awaiter (A) from the Task (T)
If A exists in T then
        Set the continuation using the OnCompleted method from the A.
```

The C# compiler then evaluates the await expression:

1. An awaiter A of type TaskAwaiter is obtained from the expression followed by the await Task T. The TaskAwaiter is used to set up the continuation for the asynchronous function and gets the result from the asynchronous function. The TaskAwaiter is defined as a struct in the mscorlib.dll assembly, with the definition shown in Listing 14-25.

Listing 14-25. Definition of the TaskAwaiter

```
public struct TaskAwaiter : ICriticalNotifyCompletion, INotifyCompletion
{
    public bool IsCompleted                             {}
    public void OnCompleted(Action continuation)        {}
    public void UnsafeOnCompleted(Action continuation)  {}
    public void GetResult()                             {}
}
```

2. The CLR then checks the status of the task by checking the IsCompleted property from the awaiter A to see whether or not the task has completed.

3. On return of true from the IsCompleted property, the associated continuation will execute, otherwise on false, the execution will suspended and the program control will be returned to the method that invoked this asynchronous method.

4. When the awaited task completes, the CLR executes the GetResult method from the TaskAwaiter struct and returns the result to the caller of the asynchronous function, otherwise the result is nothing.

Analysis of the Async- and Await-Based Asynchronous Program

We have explored two of the key feature in C#, async and await, in the previous section. This section will explore this in more detail how the C # compiler compiles async- and await-based asynchronous methods.

Listing 14-26 demonstrates the async- and await-based asynchronous methods. This program determines the number of even numbers from a specified range of numbers. While the program executes the asynchronous operation in the ShowEvenNumbers method, the for loop block of the Main method will act as if it were doing some other long running operation to let you get the output from the asynchronous operation.

Listing 14-26. Example of the Asynchronous Program

```
using System;
using System.Linq;
using System.Threading;
using System.Threading.Tasks;

namespace Ch14
{
    class Program
    {
        static void Main()
        {
            Console.WriteLine("{0,15}{1,46}{2,15}",
                            "Method", "Description", "Thread Id");
```

```
    Console.WriteLine("{0,15}{1,46}{2,15}",
        "Main", "Start Processing.....",
        Thread.CurrentThread.ManagedThreadId);

    /* Call an async method */
    Task showNumber = ShowEvenNumbers();

    /* The for loop used to simulate as something else is executing
     * while the asynchronous operation is executing it's task.*/
    for (int i = 0; i < Int64.MaxValue; ++i)
        if (i % Int32.MaxValue == 0)
            Console.WriteLine("{0,15}{1,46}{2,15}",
                "Main", "something else is doing......",
                Thread.CurrentThread.ManagedThreadId);
    /* Checking the Task whether it's completed or not */
        else if (showNumber.IsCompleted)
            break;

    Console.WriteLine("{0,15}{1,46}{2,15}",
        "Main", "Finished execution",
        Thread.CurrentThread.ManagedThreadId);
    Console.ReadLine();
}

public static async Task ShowEvenNumbers()
{
    Console.WriteLine("{0,15}{1,46}{2,15}", "ShowEvenNumbers",
        "Processing is continuing.....",
        Thread.CurrentThread.ManagedThreadId);
    int limit = new Random().Next(Int32.MaxValue);
    string range = string.Format("({0},{1})", 1, limit);

    /* Initialize and schedule a Task to run sometime later on.*/
    Task<int> evenNumbersTask = Task.Run(
        () => Enumerable.Range(1, limit).Count(item => item % 2 == 0));

    /* The await statement await the Task to complete later by
     * set up the continuation code block to execute after the
     * Task finishes it's job.*/
    int count = await evenNumbersTask;

    /* Following code block will be used as the continuation code
     * block for the evenNumbersTask and it will be setup by
     * the C# compiler. */
    Console.WriteLine("{0,15}{1,46}{2,15}", "ShowEvenNumbers",
        string.Format("In {0} Total: {1} On Thread", range, count),
        Thread.CurrentThread.ManagedThreadId);
    Console.WriteLine("{0,15}{1,46}{2,15}", "ShowEvenNumbers",
        "Processing is finished.....",
        Thread.CurrentThread.ManagedThreadId);
}
```

```
        }
    }
```

This program will produce the output.

```
          Method                              Description  Thread Id
            Main                     Start Processing.....          1
 ShowEvenNumbers              Processing is continuing.....          1
            Main              something else is doing......          1
            Main              something else is doing......          1
            Main              something else is doing......          1
 ShowEvenNumbers   In (1,1507146102) Total: 753573051 On Thread      3
 ShowEvenNumbers                 Processing is finished.....          3
            Main                        Finished execution          1
```

From the output of Listing 14-26, you can see that the Main method starts the processing and calls the ShowEvenNumbers method, which begins the process by assigning the Task to the scheduler to execute when it is able to and then returning to the Main method to do something else. All these operations are executing in the same thread, as shown in the output of Listing 14-26. You can see that sometime later the ShowEvenNumbers method shows it has processed the result and continues executing its remaining operation, for example, to display the "Processing is finished" on the console from the continuation of the ShowEvenNumbers method. All the processing for the ShowEvenNumbers was executing in thread 3, which is different from others, but the scheduler control continues to allocate the scheduled task on the available thread. Figure 14-7 demonstrates the basic control flow of the async method in C#.

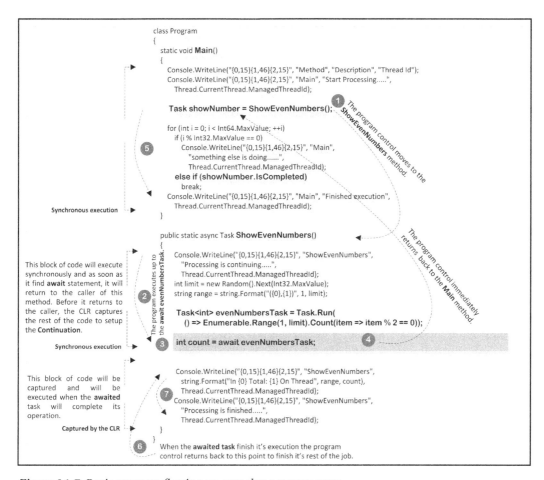

Figure 14-7. *Basic program flowing an asynchronous program*

When Listing 14-26 starts execution, it starts from the Main method and continues the execution until it comes to step 1. From there the CLR executes the program as described in these steps, as shown with the numbers in Figure 14-7:

1. The program control moves to the ShowEvenNumbers method.

2. The CLR continues executing the statement from the ShowEvenNumbers method, for example, displaying the initial "Processing is continuing" message on the console, generating the Random number, and instantiating the task.

3. As soon as the CLR comes to the await expression, to execute the task, it assigns the continuation to the awaiter of the task and suspends the execution.

4. The program control immediately returns to the Main method, to the point from which it left, to the ShowEvenNumbers method in step 1.

5. The CLR will continue with the rest of the statements from the Main method.

6. Sometimes later, when the awaited task (in step 3) has been completed, it will come to the point marked as step 6 in Figure 14-7 to finish the execution of the rest of its operation, which includes all the statements after the await expression in the ShowEvenNumbers method set up, as the continuation in step 3.

7. The CLR finishes the ShowEvenNumbers method.

This explains the very basic high-level workflow used in the async- and await-based asynchronous programming in C#. The following sections will explore more about the operations of these asynchronous methods in C#.

Async Behind the Scenes

In the .NET Framework 4.5, any method marked with the async keyword is considered an asynchronous method in C#. The C# compiler will perform the necessary transformations to implement the method asynchronously using the task asynchronous pattern (TAP).

The C# compiler compiles the asynchronous method into two important code blocks:

- *Stub method* contains the initial set up information for the asynchronous method, including generating the code related to the AsyncTaskMethodBuilder class, and starts the state machine generated by the C# compiler for the async-based method.

- *State machine* maintains the state of the asynchronous method, for example, as discussed earlier, the async-based method resumes its execution by assigning the continuation to process it later. This state machine maintains the state in which the method was before the resume was initiated, where this will be after the resume is initiated, or what it will do when it finishes its execution.

This section will explore the details how the C# compiler generates the necessary code for the async-based method and how this generated code works in runtime.

Async in Compile Time

Figure 14-8 demonstrates how the async-based method is recompiled by the C# compiler. The .NET Reflector tool is used to decompile the executable produced from Listing 14-26 to explore the stub method and state machine generated for the ShowEvenNumbers method, as demonstrated in Figure 14-8.

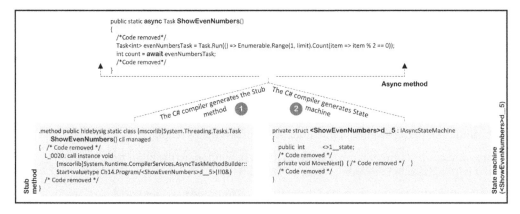

Figure 14-8. *The C# compiler generated code for the async method*

Figure 14-8 demonstrates that the C# compiler compiles the ShowEvenNumbers method into two code blocks:

- Stub method is used to initiate the state machine that the C# compiler generated for the ShowEvenNumbers method. It will initiate the state machine with the default value –1 and start the state machine.

- State machine, which is the heart of the ShowEvenNumbers asynchronous method, maintains the state of the operation to use later when it resumes the operation.

The following section explores the C# compiler–generated stub method and the state machine for the ShowEvenNumbers method.

Stub Method of the Async Method

The C# compiler generates the stub method, as shown in Listing 14-27, for the ShowEvenNumbers asynchronous method presented in Listing 14-26.

Listing 14-27. IL Version of the Stub Method

```
.method public hidebysig static class
        [mscorlib]System.Threading.Tasks.Task
        ShowEvenNumbers() cil managed
{
    /* Code removed */
    .maxstack 2
    .locals init (
        [0] valuetype Ch14.Program/<ShowEvenNumbers>d__5 d__,
        [1] class [mscorlib]System.Threading.Tasks.Task task,
        [2] valuetype
            [mscorlib]System.Runtime.CompilerServices.AsyncTaskMethodBuilder
            builder)

    L_0000: ldloca.s d__

    /* It creates AsyncTaskMethodBuilder and store into
     * the  <>t__builder  field */
    L_0002: call valuetype
            [mscorlib]System.Runtime.CompilerServices.AsyncTaskMethodBuilder
            [mscorlib]System.Runtime.CompilerServices.AsyncTaskMethodBuilder::
            Create()

    L_0007: stfld valuetype
            [mscorlib]System.Runtime.CompilerServices.AsyncTaskMethodBuilder
            Ch14.Program/<ShowEvenNumbers>d__5::<>t__builder

    L_000c: ldloca.s d__

     /* Initiates the state machine with it's default value -1 */
    L_000e: ldc.i4.m1
    L_000f: stfld int32 Ch14.Program/<ShowEvenNumbers>d__5::<>1__state
```

```
L_0014: ldloca.s d__
L_0016: ldfld valuetype
        [mscorlib]System.Runtime.CompilerServices.AsyncTaskMethodBuilder
        Ch14.Program/<ShowEvenNumbers>d__5::<>t__builder
L_001b: stloc.2
L_001c: ldloca.s builder
L_001e: ldloca.s d__

/* Start the state machine by executing the Start method from
 * the AsyncTaskMethodBuilder*/
L_0020: call instance
        void
        [mscorlib]System.Runtime.CompilerServices.AsyncTaskMethodBuilder::
        Start<valuetype Ch14.Program/<ShowEvenNumbers>d__5>(!!0&)

L_0025: ldloca.s d__
L_0027: ldflda valuetype
        [mscorlib]System.Runtime.CompilerServices.AsyncTaskMethodBuilder
        Ch14.Program/<ShowEvenNumbers>d__5::<>t__builder

/* Get the Task which has been initialized and scheduled to execute
 * later on */
L_002c: call instance class
        [mscorlib]System.Threading.Tasks.Task
        [mscorlib]System.Runtime.CompilerServices.AsyncTaskMethodBuilder::
        get_Task()

L_0031: stloc.1
L_0032: br.s L_0034
L_0034: ldloc.1
L_0035: ret
}
```

This stub method is an important bit of code that the C# compiler generates for the ShowEvenNumbers async-based method, which is responsible for initiating the generated state machine <ShowEvenNumbers>d__5 with its initial value –1 set in L_000f by setting it to the <>1__state field of the state machine. In L_0020, it will call the Start method from the AsyncTaskMethodBuilder class to start the state machine <ShowEvenNumbers>d__5. Later it calls the get_Task method from the AsyncTaskMethodBuilder class to get the task (whether or not it is completed), which will be used to access the result if there is any from the Task class or to get the status of the task.

State Machine of the Async Method

Listing 14-28 shows the C# compiler–generated state machine <ShowEvenNumbers>d__5 for Listing 14-26.

Listing 14-28. The Compiler-Generated State Machine

```
private struct <ShowEvenNumbers>d__5 : IAsyncStateMachine
{
    public  int                              <>1__state;
    public  AsyncTaskMethodBuilder           <>t__builder;
```

```
private object                              <>t__stack;
private TaskAwaiter<int>                     <>u__$awaiter9;
public  int                                  <count>5__8;
public  Task<int>                            <evenNumbersTask>5__7;
public  string                               <range>5__6;
public  Program.<>c__DisplayClass2          CS$<>8__locals3;

private void MoveNext()
{
    try
    {
        TaskAwaiter<int> CS$0$0001;
        bool <>t__doFinallyBodies = true;

        switch (this.<>1__state)
        {
            case -3:
                goto Label_0196;

            case 0:
                break;

            default:
                this.CS$<>8__locals3 = new Program.<>c__DisplayClass2();

                Console.WriteLine("{0,15}{1,46}{2,15}", "ShowEvenNumbers",
                    "Processing is continuing.....",
                    Thread.CurrentThread.ManagedThreadId);

                this.CS$<>8__locals3.limit = new Random().Next(0x7fffffff);
                this.<range>5__6 = string.Format("({0},{1})",
                            1, this.CS$<>8__locals3.limit);

                this.<evenNumbersTask>5__7 = Task.Run<int>(
                    new Func<int>(
                            this.CS$<>8__locals3.<ShowEvenNumbers>b__0));

                CS$0$0001 = this.<evenNumbersTask>5__7.GetAwaiter();

                if (CS$0$0001.IsCompleted)
                {
                    goto Label_0104;
                }
                this.<>1__state = 0;
                this.<>u__$awaiter9 = CS$0$0001;

                this.<>t__builder.AwaitUnsafeOnCompleted<TaskAwaiter<int>,
                        Program.<ShowEvenNumbers>d__5>(
                                    ref CS$0$0001, ref this);
                <>t__doFinallyBodies = false;
```

```
                return;
            }

            CS$0$0001 = this.<>u__$awaiter9;
            this.<>u__$awaiter9 = new TaskAwaiter<int>();
            this.<>1__state = -1;

        Label_0104:
            int introduced6 = CS$0$0001.GetResult();

            CS$0$0001 = new TaskAwaiter<int>();

            int CS$0$0003 = introduced6;
            this.<count>5__8 = CS$0$0003;
            Console.WriteLine("{0,15}{1,46}{2,15}", "ShowEvenNumbers",
                string.Format("In {0} Total: {1} On Thread",
                    this.<range>5__6, this.<count>5__8),
                    Thread.CurrentThread.ManagedThreadId);
            Console.WriteLine("{0,15}{1,46}{2,15}", "ShowEvenNumbers",
                "Processing is finished.....",
                Thread.CurrentThread.ManagedThreadId);
        }
        catch (Exception <>t__ex)
        {
            this.<>1__state = -2;
            this.<>t__builder.SetException(<>t__ex);
            return;
        }
    Label_0196:
        this.<>1__state = -2;
        this.<>t__builder.SetResult();
    }

    /* Code removed */
}
```

Fields in the State Machine

The C# compiler will generate fields for the state machine for each of the fields it owns, as demonstrated in Table 14.1.

Table 14.1. *Fields Generated for the State Machine* <ShowEvenNumbers>d__5

Field	Task
<>1__state	Uses to keep track of the state of the state machine
<>t__builder	Used to hold an AsyncTaskMethodBuilder in the state machine
<>t__stack	Used for the state that needs to be persisted based on what was on the evaluation stack when the method was suspended
<>u__$awaiter9	Used to hold the TaskAwaiter

Field	Task
<count>5__8	Local variable
<evenNumbersTask>5__7	Holds the Task return from the Task.Run
<range>5__6	Local variable
CS$<>8__locals3	Contains the Func used to execute the task

Depending on the circumstances and number of local variable used in the async method, the fields may be different.

Methods in the State Machine

The C# compiler generates two methods for the state machine:

- MoveNext: This method contains the switch block to control the operation based on the state of the state machine.

- SetStateMachine: This method is used to set the state machine.

Async in Runtime

When the CLR starts executing the async-based asynchronous method, it starts execution from the stub method to initiate and start the state machine, schedule the task, and set up the continuation for the task if there is any and leaves the asynchronous task to the scheduler to execute later when it is scheduled. The CLR:

- Starts the state machine

- Schedules the task

- Sets up the Continuation

- Executes the task

- Executes the continuation

This section will explore the details involved in these steps to show how the CLR executes the async-based asynchronous method in runtime. The CLR instantiates an instance of the AsyncTaskMethodBuilder class in L_0002, shown in Listing 14-27, by calling the Create method of the AsyncTaskMethodBuilder class. The Create method then instantiates an instance of the AsyncTaskMethodBuilder class:

```
public static AsyncTaskMethodBuilder Create()
{
    return new AsyncTaskMethodBuilder();
}
```

After instantiating the AsyncTaskMethodBuilder class, the CLR executes the rest of the asynchronous code as described in the sections that follow.

Start the State Machine

The CLR uses the AsyncTaskMethodBuilder created earlier to start the state machine <ShowEvenNumbers>d__5 by calling the Start method from it (step 1 in Figure 14-9). The CLR passes the initialized state machine <ShowEvenNumbers>d__5 from the stub method as input to the Start method of the AsyncTaskMethodBuilder class. Listing 14-29 shows the Start method from the AsyncTaskMethodBuilder class.

Listing 14-29. Start Method from the AsyncTaskMethodBuilder Class

```
.method public hidebysig instance void Start<(System.Runtime.CompilerServices.
IAsyncStateMachine) TStateMachine>(!!TStateMachine& stateMachine) cil managed
{
    .custom instance void
    System.Diagnostics.DebuggerStepThroughAttribute::.ctor()
    .custom instance void __DynamicallyInvokableAttribute::.ctor()
    .maxstack 8
    L_0000: ldarg.0
    L_0001: ldflda valuetype
        System.Runtime.CompilerServices.AsyncTaskMethodBuilder'1
        <valuetype System.Threading.Tasks.VoidTaskResult>
        System.Runtime.CompilerServices.AsyncTaskMethodBuilder::m_builder
    L_0006: ldarg.1
    L_0007: call instance void
        System.Runtime.CompilerServices.AsyncTaskMethodBuilder'1
        <valuetype System.Threading.Tasks.VoidTaskResult>::
        Start<!!TStateMachine>(!!0&)
    L_000c: ret
}
```

The Start method internally calls the Start method from AsyncTaskMethodBuilder<VoidTaskResult> class in L_0007 from Listing 14-29. The Start method of AsyncTaskMethodBuilder<VoidTaskResult> class is demonstrated in Listing 14-30.

Listing 14-30. Start Method from the AsyncTaskMethodBuilder<TResult> Class

```
.method public hidebysig instance void Start
        <(System.Runtime.CompilerServices.IAsyncStateMachine) TStateMachine>
        (!!TStateMachine& stateMachine) cil managed
{
    .custom instance void System.Diagnostics.DebuggerStepThroughAttribute::.ctor()
    .custom instance void __DynamicallyInvokableAttribute::.ctor()
    .maxstack 8
    L_0000: ldarg.0

    L_0001: ldflda valuetype
            System.Runtime.CompilerServices.AsyncMethodBuilderCore
            System.Runtime.CompilerServices
                .AsyncTaskMethodBuilder'1<!TResult>::m_coreState
    L_0006: ldarg.1

    /* Call the Start method of the AsyncMethodBuilderCore which will
     * start the given state machine.*/
    L_0007: call instance
            void System.Runtime.CompilerServices.AsyncMethodBuilderCore::
            Start<!!TStateMachine>(!!0&)
```

```
    L_000c: ret
}
```

From Listing 14-30, the CLR calls the Start method of the AsyncMethodBuilderCore class in L_0007 by passing the state machine it received as input. The Start method internally works as demonstrated in the decompiled Start method code, as shown in Listing 14-31.

Listing 14-31. Start Method from the AsyncMethodBuilderCore Class

```
.method assembly hidebysig instance void Start
    <(System.Runtime.CompilerServices.IAsyncStateMachine) TStateMachine>
    (!!TStateMachine& stateMachine) cil managed
{
    .custom instance void
            System.Security.SecuritySafeCriticalAttribute::.ctor()
    .custom instance void
            System.Diagnostics.DebuggerStepThroughAttribute::.ctor()
    .maxstack 3
    .locals init (
        [0] class System.Threading.Thread thread,
        [1] valuetype System.Threading.ExecutionContextSwitcher switcher)
    /* Code removed */

    /* The CLR calls the MoveNext method from the state machine to do a
     * transition in the state machine */
    L_003b: callvirt instance void
            System.Runtime.CompilerServices.IAsyncStateMachine::MoveNext()

    /* Code removed */
    .try L_002b to L_0042 finally handler L_0042 to L_004b
}
```

The Start method of the AsyncMethodBuilderCore class calls the MoveNext method from the state machine passed to it. Figure 14-9 demonstrates the execution of the stub method and state machine <ShowEvenNumbers>d__5 in runtime.

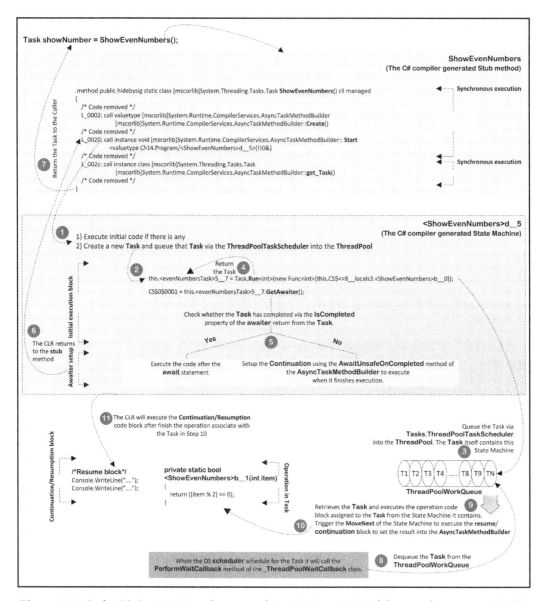

Figure 14-9. *Stubs (Listing 14-27) and state machine (Listing 14-28) of the asynchronous method in runtime*

In step 2 of Figure 14-9, the CLR comes to the state machine with its default value –1 (set from the stub method) and executes the default section of the switch block from the state machine <ShowEvenNumbers>d__5. The CLR instantiated an instance of the Task class with the provided operation it has to complete via the Run method of the Task class, which internally calls the StartNew method from the Task class:

```
public static Task<TResult> Run<TResult>(Func<TResult> function)
{
    StackCrawlMark lookForMyCaller = StackCrawlMark.LookForMyCaller;
```

```
    return Task<TResult>.StartNew(
            null,
            function,
            new CancellationToken(),
            TaskCreationOptions.DenyChildAttach,
            InternalTaskOptions.None,
            TaskScheduler.Default,
            ref lookForMyCaller);
}
```

The StartNew method initiates a task and schedules the newly created task by calling the ScheduleAndStart method from the Task class:

```
internal static Task<TResult> StartNew(
    Task parent,
    Func<TResult> function,
    CancellationToken cancellationToken,
    TaskCreationOptions creationOptions,
    InternalTaskOptions internalOptions,
    TaskScheduler scheduler,
    ref StackCrawlMark stackMark)
{
  /*Code removed*/
    Task<TResult> task = new Task<TResult>(
        function,
        parent,
        cancellationToken,
        creationOptions,
        internalOptions | InternalTaskOptions.QueuedByRuntime,
        scheduler,
        ref stackMark);

    /* Schedules the Task to execute when it is scheduled or sometime
     * later on */
    task.ScheduleAndStart(false);
    return task;
}
```

Schedule the Task

In step 3 in Figure 14-9, the ScheduleAndStart method from the Task class queues the task using the QueueTask method of the ThreadPoolTaskScheduler class, which it inherited from the TaskScheduler class. The m_taskScheduler field from the Task class holds the TaskScheduler class. The QueueTask is an abstract method defined in the TaskScheduler class:

```
protected internal abstract void QueueTask(Task task);
```

Let's look at the implementation of the QueueTask method from the ThreadPoolTaskScheduler class:

```
protected internal override void QueueTask(Task task)
{
    TplEtwProvider log = TplEtwProvider.Log;
    if (log.IsEnabled(EventLevel.Verbose, ~EventKeywords.None))
    {
```

```
            Task internalCurrent = Task.InternalCurrent;
            Task parent = task.m_parent;
            log.TaskScheduled(base.Id,
                (internalCurrent == null) ? 0 : internalCurrent.Id,
                task.Id,
                (parent == null) ? 0 : parent.Id,
                (int) task.Options);
        }
        if ((task.Options & TaskCreationOptions.LongRunning) !=
                                    TaskCreationOptions.None)
        {
            new Thread(s_longRunningThreadWork)
                    { IsBackground = true }.Start(task);
        }
        else
        {
            bool forceGlobal = (task.Options & TaskCreationOptions.PreferFairness)
                                    != TaskCreationOptions.None;
            ThreadPool.UnsafeQueueCustomWorkItem(task, forceGlobal);
        }
    }
```

The implementation of the UnsafeQueueCustomWorkItem method of the ThreadPool class is:

```
internal static void UnsafeQueueCustomWorkItem
                        (IThreadPoolWorkItem workItem, bool forceGlobal)
{
    EnsureVMInitialized();
    try
    {
    }
    finally
    {
        ThreadPoolGlobals.workQueue.Enqueue(workItem, forceGlobal);
    }
}
```

The field workQueue is from the ThreadPoolWorkQueue class, which calls the Enqueue method and eventually queues the task into the ThreadPool:

```
public void Enqueue(IThreadPoolWorkItem callback, bool forceGlobal)
{
    /* Code removed */
    else
    {
        QueueSegment queueHead = this.queueHead;
        while (!queueHead.TryEnqueue(callback))
        {
            Interlocked.CompareExchange<QueueSegment>(
                            ref queueHead.Next, new QueueSegment(), null);
            while (queueHead.Next != null)
            {
                Interlocked.CompareExchange<QueueSegment>(
```

```
                           ref this.queueHead, queueHead.Next, queueHead);
                queueHead = this.queueHead;
            }
        }
    }
    this.EnsureThreadRequested();
}
```

Setting Up the Continuation

In step 4 of Figure 14-9, the CLR returns the initialized task. In step 5, after finishing the task initialization and scheduling, the CLR checks whether or not the task has been completed by checking the awaiter return from the task in step 4. If the task has not completed, then it sets up the continuation or resumption code, or callback code block in the task.

In step 6, the program control immediately transfers back to the async stub method at the point from which the CLR called the Start method (in L_0020 from the stub method code in Listing 14-27).

In step 7, the CLR gets the task from the AsyncTaskMethodBuilder by calling the get_Task method in L_002c and returns it to the caller of the async method ShowEvenNumbers. The CLR then continues with the operation (if there is any) from the caller method, which is the Main method.

In step 8, sometime later, the task scheduled in the ThreadPool will be triggered by the operating system (OS) scheduler to start execution, as demonstrated in the code:

```
internal static class _ThreadPoolWaitCallback
{
    [SecurityCritical]
    internal static bool PerformWaitCallback()
    {
        return ThreadPoolWorkQueue.Dispatch();
    }
}
```

Executing the Scheduled Task

In step 9, the CLR dequeues the task from the ThreadPool and executes the operation assigned to the task, for example, the b__1 method, as shows in the code:

```
private static bool <ShowEvenNumbers>b__1(int item)
{
    return ((item % 2) == 0);
}
```

In step 10, the CLR executes the b__1 method and sets the new state into the state machine. It calls the MoveNext method of the state machine to move into the next state and executes the relevant code with the associate state.

In step 11, the continuation or resumption code block will be executed to finalize the async method processing. The state transition for the state machine will then be working, as demonstrated in Figure 14-10.

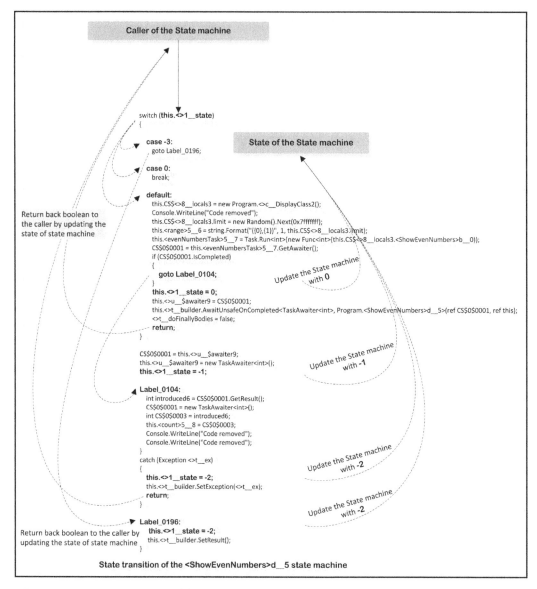

Figure 14-10. State transition of the state machine

When the CLR executes the state machine, it comes with the default value –1, which executes the default section of the switch block and updates the state with 0, sets up the continuation, and returns to the caller. The state machine value is currently set at 0 and each time the CLR tries to do another transition by calling the MoveNext method from the state machine, it will start with the state value 0. So it executes the case 0, which will break the switch block and execute the code block at Label_0104 to get the awaiter and to update the state with –1. On input of –3 as the state from the CLR, the program control transfers to Label_0196 to update the state of the state machine by –2 and sets the results to get by the caller of the state machine.

Test Cases

The following sections will explore a few common scenarios of the asynchronous method that are based on the async and await keywords.

When There Is No Return Type

When you design a program, it might require you to trigger a task and not wait for that task to finish and return to you. When you do an asynchronous operation, you can achieve this by using the FireAndForget task. To write a FireAndForget task, you need to return void instead of the Task or Task<TResult> from an async-based method. In the FireAndForget task, the C# compiler does not produce and return any task when it generates the stub method for it, therefore, it is not possible for the caller to track the completion or status of the FireAndForget-based task. Listing 14-32 shows an example of the FireAndForget task using the async and await statements.

Listing 14-32. Example of the Void Return from the Async Method

```
using System;
using System.Linq;
using System.Threading.Tasks;

namespace Ch14
{
    class Program
    {
        static void Main()
        {
            FireAndForget();

            for (int i = 0; i < Int32.MaxValue; ++i)
            {
                if (i % (Int16.MaxValue*999) == 0)
                    Console.Write(".");
            }
            Console.ReadLine();
        }

        public static async void FireAndForget()
        {
            var evenNumbersTask = Task.Run(
                () =>
                {
                    Enumerable.Range(1, 5).ToList().ForEach(itemOuter =>
                    {
                        int limit = new Random().Next(Int16.MaxValue * 999);
                        var result = Enumerable.Range(
                        itemOuter, limit).Count(item =>
                        {
                            return item % 2 == 0;
                        });
```

```
                    Console.WriteLine(
                        "\nProcessing and processed result {0}.", result);
                });
            });
        await evenNumbersTask;
    }
}
}
```

This program will produce the output:

```
..
Processing and processed result 7689415.
Processing and processed result 335471.
..
Processing and processed result 6208074.
Processing and processed result 3476038.
.
Processing and processed result 1138061.
.............................................................
```

The difference between a void return and task return from the asynchronous method is that the asynchronous method that returns void cannot be awaited. If you were to add another method to Listing 14-32:

```
 public static async void FireAndForget2()
{
    await FireAndForget();
}
```

the C# compiler will complain and show the following errors:

```
'Ch14.Program.FireAndForget()' does not return a Task and cannot be awaited. Consider changing
it to return Task.
```

If you want to await for any asynchronous method, that asynchronous method needs to return either Task or Task<TResult>. The C# compiler–generated stub method does not return Task for the void return async method, as a result, there is nothing to wait for. So you can see that with the FireAndForget method there is nothing to wait for as the FireAndForget method does not return Task.

Let's look at the stub method the C# compiler generates for the FireAndForget method of the Listing 14-32, as shown in Listing 14-33.

Listing 14-33. The C# Compiler–Generated Stub Method for Listing 14-32

```
.method public hidebysig static void FireAndForget() cil managed
{
    /* code removed */
    .maxstack 2
    .locals init (
        [0] valuetype Ch14.Program/<FireAndForget>d__6 d__,
        [1] valuetype
            [mscorlib]System.Runtime.CompilerServices.AsyncVoidMethodBuilder
            builder)
    L_0000: ldloca.s d__
```

```
    L_0002: call valuetype
            [mscorlib]System.Runtime.CompilerServices.AsyncVoidMethodBuilder
             [mscorlib]System.Runtime.CompilerServices.AsyncVoidMethodBuilder::
            Create()
    L_0007: stfld valuetype
            [mscorlib]System.Runtime.CompilerServices.AsyncVoidMethodBuilder
               Ch14.Program/<FireAndForget>d__6::<>t__builder
    L_000c: ldloca.s d__

    L_000e: ldc.i4.m1
    L_000f: stfld int32 Ch14.Program/<FireAndForget>d__6::<>1__state
    L_0014: ldloca.s d__

    L_0016: ldfld valuetype
            [mscorlib]System.Runtime.CompilerServices.AsyncVoidMethodBuilder
               Ch14.Program/<FireAndForget>d__6::<>t__builder
    L_001b: stloc.1
    L_001c: ldloca.s builder
    L_001e: ldloca.s d__

  /* State machine has  been started */
    L_0020: call instance void
            [mscorlib]System.Runtime.CompilerServices.AsyncVoidMethodBuilder::
                Start<valuetype Ch14.Program/<FireAndForget>d__6>(!!0&)

  /* There has not been return any Task from this Stub method */
    L_0025: br.s L_0027

  /* This method does not return  */
    L_0027: ret
}
```

Listing 14-33 shows that the CLR will not return Task as a result, so it is not possible to get the status from the FireAndForget method. It is only used as a call and leaves everything to that calling method.

When There Are Multiple Await Statements in Asynchronous Method

Listing 14-34 shows an example of the use of multiple await statements in a program.

Listing 14-34. Multiple Await Statements

```
using System;
using System.Linq;
using System.Threading.Tasks;

namespace Ch14
{
    class Program
    {
```

```csharp
        static void Main()
        {
            MultipleAwait();

            for (int i = 0; i < Int16.MaxValue * 8; ++i)
            {
                if (i / byte.MaxValue==0)
                    Console.Write(">");
            }
            Console.WriteLine("Operation is completed.");
            Console.ReadLine();
        }
        public static async void MultipleAwait()
        {
            await EvenNumbers();
            await EvenNumbers();
        }

        public static async Task EvenNumbers()
        {
            int limit = new Random().Next(Int16.MaxValue);
            Task<int> evenNumbersTask = Task.Run(
                () => Enumerable.Range(1, limit).Count(
                item => item % 2 == 0));
            await evenNumbersTask;
            Console.WriteLine("\n" + evenNumbersTask.Result);
        }
    }
}
```

This program will produce the output:

```
>>>>>>>>>>>>>>>>>>>>>>>>>>>>>>>>>>>>>>>>>>>>>>>>>>>>>>>>
11635
>>>>>>>>>>>>>>>>>>>>>>>>>>>>>>>>>>>>>>>>>>>>>>>>>>>>>>>>>>
8954
>>>>>>>>>>>>>>>>>>>>>>>>>>>>>>>>>>>>>>>>>>>>>>>>>>>>>>>>>>>>>>>
>>>>>>>>>>>>>>>>>>>>>>>>>>>>>>>>>>>>>>Operation is completed.
```

When Async in the User Interface

So far, you have seen the async method used in the console application. Listing 14-35 shows an example of the async method used in the graphic user interface (GUI) application.

Listing 14-35. Example of the GUI Async

```csharp
using System;
using System.Linq;
using System.Threading.Tasks;
using System.Windows.Forms;
```

```
namespace Ch14_GUI
{
    public partial class EvenNumberDisplayWindow : Form
    {
        public EvenNumberDisplayWindow()
        {
            InitializeComponent();
        }

        private void btnProcess_Click(object sender, EventArgs e)
        {
            ShowEvenNumbers();
        }
        public async Task ShowEvenNumbers()
        {
            int limit = new Random().Next(Int32.MaxValue);
            string range = string.Format("({0},{1})", 1, limit);

            Task<int> evenNumbersTask = Task.Run(
                () => Enumerable.Range(1, limit).Count(item => item % 2 == 0));

            int count = await evenNumbersTask;
            txtEvenNumbers.Text = count.ToString();
        }

        private void btnCurrentTime_Click(object sender, EventArgs e)
        {
            txtCurrentTime.Text = DateTime.Now.ToLongTimeString();
        }
    }
}
```

This program will produce the output shown in Figure 14-11.

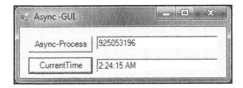

Figure 14.11. *Output produced using the GUI async method*

Task-Based Asynchronous Pattern

The task-based asynchronous pattern (TAP) is used to implement the asynchronous methods in the .NET Framework. It is built on the basics of the Task and Task<TResult> types. When you define a method that follows the TAP, it needs to follow some rules, for example, it has to return Task or Task<TResult> and a method marks async except for the task combinators, such as WhenAll, WhenAny. In the TAP method you can also set the cancellation to cancel while it is running using the CancellationToken, or you can get the progress status of the running task using the IProgress<T>. The following section will explore Cancellation and IProgress.

Usage of the Cancellation to Cancel a Running Task

It is common behavior for a responsive system while it is doing a long-running operation to allow cancellation of the task whenever the user wants to. For the asynchronous operation, we also expected to have the option to cancel the task whenever we want to. You can achieve this by using the cancellation flag, for example, CancellationToken, a type introduced in the System.Threading namespace of the mscorlib. dll assembly. Listing 14-36 shows the CancellationToken struct definition.

Listing 14-36. CancellationToken Struct

```
public struct CancellationToken
{
    public static CancellationToken None                                        {}
    public bool IsCancellationRequested                                         {}
    public bool CanBeCanceled                                                   {}
    public System.Threading.WaitHandle WaitHandle                               {}
    public CancellationToken(bool canceled)                                     {}
    public CancellationTokenRegistration Register(Action callback)              {}
    public CancellationTokenRegistration Register
            (Action callback, bool useSynchronizationContext)                   {}
    public CancellationTokenRegistration Register(Action<object> callback,
                                    object state)                               {}
    public CancellationTokenRegistration Register(
        Action<object> callback, object state, bool useSynchronizationContext){}
    public bool Equals(CancellationToken other)                                 {}
    public override bool Equals(object other)                                   {}
    public override int GetHashCode()                                           {}
    public static bool operator ==
            (CancellationToken left, CancellationToken right)                   {}
    public static bool operator !=
            (CancellationToken left, CancellationToken right)                   {}
    public void ThrowIfCancellationRequested()                                  {}
}
```

A CancellationToken is created through a CancellationTokenSource, which is also defined in the System.Threading namespace of the mscorlib.dll assembly. Listing 14-37 shows the definition of the CancellationTokenSource struct.

Listing 14-37. CancellationTokenSource Struct

```
public class CancellationTokenSource : IDisposable
{
    static CancellationTokenSource()                                {}
    public CancellationTokenSource()                                {}
    public CancellationTokenSource(int millisecondsDelay)           {}
    public CancellationTokenSource(TimeSpan delay)                  {}
    public void Cancel()                                            {}
    public void Cancel(bool throwOnFirstException)                  {}
```

```
public void CancelAfter(int millisecondsDelay)             {}
public void CancelAfter(TimeSpan delay)                    {}
public static CancellationTokenSource
    CreateLinkedTokenSource(params CancellationToken[] tokens) {}
public static CancellationTokenSource
    CreateLinkedTokenSource(CancellationToken token1,
                            CancellationToken token2)      {}
public void Dispose()                                      {}
public bool IsCancellationRequested                        {}
public CancellationToken Token                             {}
}
```

The source's Token property returns the CancellationToken, which can be used to signal when the source's Cancel method is invoked, as shown in Listing 14-38.

Listing 14-38. Example of the Task Cancellation in the Asynchronous Method

```
using System;
using System.Linq;
using System.Threading;
using System.Threading.Tasks;

namespace Ch14
{
    class Program
    {
        static void Main()
        {
            CancellationTokenSource cancelSource = new CancellationTokenSource();

            /* Initialize the Task with the cancel Token from
             * the CancellationTokenSource */
            Task showNumber = ShowEvenNumbers(cancelSource.Token);

            /* Following for-loop simulates as something else is going on */
            for (int i = 0; i < Int64.MaxValue; ++i)
                if (i == byte.MaxValue)
                {
                    /* Call the Cancel method to cancel the task in sometime
                     * when the Task was executing it's Task*/
                    cancelSource.Cancel();
                    break;
                }
            Console.WriteLine("Cancel");
            Console.ReadLine();
        }

        public static async Task ShowEvenNumbers(CancellationToken cancelToken)
        {
            int limit = new Random().Next(Int32.MaxValue);
            string range = string.Format("({0},{1})", 1, limit);
```

```
                /* Pass the cancel token to the Task   */
                Task<int> evenNumbersTask = Task.Run(
                    () => Enumerable.Range(1, limit).Count(
                   item => item % 2 == 0), cancelToken);
                int count = await evenNumbersTask;
            }
        }
}
```

This program will produce the output:

```
Cancel
```

Usage of the IProgress<T> and Progress to Show Progress of a Running Task

When you use the asynchronous method, it is helpful to be able to view the progress status of the operation. To achieve this, you can use the Report method of the Progress<T> class by passing an Action delegate that fires whenever progress changes in the task. The Progress<T> class implements IProgress<T>, which is defined in the System namespace of the mscorlib.dll assembly. Listing 14-39 shows the definition of the IProgress<T> and Progress<T> classes.

Listing 14-39. Usage of the IProgress<in T> and Progress<T>

```
public interface IProgress<in T>
{
    void Report(T value);
}

public class Progress<T> : IProgress<T>
{
    public event EventHandler<T> ProgressChanged          {}
    public Progress()                                      {}
    public Progress(Action<T> handler)                     {}
    protected virtual void OnReport(T value)               {}
    void IProgress<T>.Report(T value)                      {}
}
```

Listing 14-40 shows an example of the progress report.

Listing 14-40. Example of the Progress Report

```
using System;
using System.Linq;
using System.Threading;
using System.Threading.Tasks;

namespace Ch14
{
    class Program
    {
        static void Main()
```

```
    {
        CancellationTokenSource cancelSource = new
                            CancellationTokenSource();
        Progress<int> progressReport = new Progress<int>((status) =>
        {
            Console.Clear();
            Console.WriteLine(status + " %");
        });
        Task showNumber = ShowEvenNumbers(cancelSource.Token,
                                    progressReport);

        for (int i = 0; i < Int64.MaxValue; ++i)
            if (i == Int32.MaxValue)
            {
                cancelSource.Cancel();
                break;
            }
        Console.WriteLine("Cancel");
        Console.ReadLine();
    }

    public static async Task ShowEvenNumbers(
        CancellationToken cancelToken,
        IProgress<int> onProgressChanged)
    {
        int limit = new Random().Next(Int32.MaxValue);
        string range = string.Format("({0},{1})", 1, limit);

        Task<int> evenNumbersTask = Task.Run(
            () => Enumerable.Range(1, limit).Count(item =>
            {
                onProgressChanged.Report((item * 100) / limit);
                return item % 2 == 0;
            }), cancelToken);
        int count = await evenNumbersTask;
    }
    }
}
```

Combinators

In task-based asynchronous patterns, combinators refers to the creation, manipulation, or combination of tasks, for example, WhenAll, WhenAny, or Delay. The following sections will explore these combinators.

Task WhenAll

The WhenAll method is used to wait asynchronously for a task that represents multiple asynchronous operations. This method returns a task that completes when all of the tasks assigned to this method have been completed. The WhenAll method has the following overloaded signatures:

```
public static Task WhenAll(IEnumerable<Task> tasks)                            {}
public static Task<TResult[]> WhenAll<TResult>(
                              IEnumerable<Task<TResult>> tasks)                {}
public static Task WhenAll(params Task[] tasks)                                {}
public static Task<TResult[]> WhenAll<TResult>(params Task<TResult>[] tasks){}
```

Listing 14-41 demonstrates the use of the WhenAll method.

Listing 14-41. Example of the WhenAll Method

```
using System;
using System.Linq;
using System.Threading.Tasks;

namespace Ch14
{
    class Program
    {
        static void Main()
        {
            Task<int> combinedResult = TestWhenAll();
            while (true)
            {
                if (combinedResult.IsCompleted)
                {
                    Console.WriteLine("Finished : {0}", combinedResult.Result);
                    break;
                }
                Console.Write(".");
            }
            Console.ReadLine();
        }

        public static async Task<int> TestWhenAll()
        {
            int[] combinedResult =
            await Task.WhenAll(CountEvenNumbers(),
                        CountEvenNumbers(), CountEvenNumbers());
            return combinedResult.Sum();
        }

        public static async Task<int> CountEvenNumbers()
        {
            return await Task.Run(
            () => Enumerable.Range(1, Int16.MaxValue).Count(x => x % 2 == 0));
        }
    }
}
```

This program will produce output:

```
.................Finished : 49149
```

If any exception occurred in the above example code, such as if one of the methods throws an exception, the CLR will continue with other tasks assigned in the WhenAll method and, when finished, return to the task with the related exceptions in the InnerException property of the Exception. Listing 14-42 shows an example when an exception(s) occurred in the task assigned to the WhenAll method.

Listing 14-42. Exception in the WhenAll Method

```
using System;
using System.Linq;
using System.Threading.Tasks;

namespace Ch14
{
    class Program
    {
        static void Main()
        {
            Task<int> combinedResult = TestWhenAll();
            while (true)
            {
                if (combinedResult.IsCompleted)
                {
                    Console.WriteLine("Finished : {0}", combinedResult.Result);
                    break;
                }
                Console.Write(".");
            }
            Console.ReadLine();
        }

        public static async Task<int> TestWhenAll()
        {
            int[] combinedResult =
                await Task.WhenAll(CountEvenNumbers(),
                    ThrowAnException(), CountEvenNumbers());
            return combinedResult.Sum();
        }

        public static async Task<int> ThrowAnException()
        {
            return await Task.Run(() =>
            {
                throw new Exception(
                        "There is something wrong in the processing....");
                return Enumerable.Range(1, Int16.MaxValue).Count(
                                        x => x % 2 == 0);
            });
        }
        public static async Task<int> CountEvenNumbers()
        {
            return await Task.Run(() =>
```

```
        {
            int result = Enumerable.Range(1, Int16.MaxValue).Count(
                                          x => x % 2 == 0);
            Console.WriteLine(result);
            return result;
        });
    }
  }
}
```

This will produce the output:

```
16383
16383
...
Unhandled Exception: System.AggregateException: One or more errors occurred. ---
> System.Exception: There is something wrong in the processing....
   at Ch14.Program.<ThrowAnException>b__4()

/* Rest of the error details removed */
```

This output shows that the CLR process with the CountEvenNumbers methods returns the result as 16383 and 16383. On the other hand, while processing the ThrowAnException method, it throws an exception that the CLR passes as AggregateException.

Task WhenAny

The WhenAny method is used when any one of the methods (assigned to the WhenAny method) from the assigned method completes its operation. The WhenAny method has the following overloaded signatures:

```
public static Task<Task> WhenAny(IEnumerable<Task> tasks)          {}
public static Task<Task<TResult>> WhenAny<TResult>(
        IEnumerable<Task<TResult>> tasks)                          {}
public static Task<Task> WhenAny(params Task[] tasks)              {}
public static Task<Task<TResult>> WhenAny<TResult>(
                        params Task<TResult>[] tasks)              {}
```

Listing 14-43 demonstrates the use of the WhenAny method.

Listing 14-43. Example of the WhenAny Method

```
using System;
using System.Linq;
using System.Threading.Tasks;

namespace Ch14
{
    class Program
    {
        static void Main()
        {
            Task<int> result = TestWhenAny();
            while (true)
```

```
        {
            if (result.IsCompleted)
            {
                Console.WriteLine("Finished : {0}", result.Result);
                break;
            }
            Console.Write(".");
        }
        Console.ReadLine();
    }

    public static async Task<int> TestWhenAny()
    {
        Task<int> firstCompleted=
    await Task.WhenAny(CountEvenNumbers(),
                    CountEvenNumbers(), CountEvenNumbers());
        return firstCompleted.Result;
    }

    public static async Task<int> CountEvenNumbers()
    {
        return await Task.Run(() => Enumerable.Range(1,
                            Int16.MaxValue).Count(x => x % 2 == 0));
    }
  }
}
```

This program produced the output:

```
.........................................................................................
..............................................................Finished : 16383
```

Task Delay

The Delay method from the Task class is used to set the pauses into an asynchronous method while it is executing. This method can be used to create a task that will complete after a time delay. The Delay method has the following overloaded signatures:

```
public static Task Delay(int millisecondsDelay)                                {}
public static Task Delay(TimeSpan delay)                                       {}
public static Task Delay(int millisecondsDelay,
            System.Threading.CancellationToken cancellationToken)              {}
public static Task Delay(TimeSpan delay,
            System.Threading.CancellationToken cancellationToken)              {}
```

Listing 14-44 demonstrates the use of the WhenAny method.

Listing 14-44. Example of the Delay

```
using System;
using System.Threading.Tasks;
```

```
namespace Ch14
{
    class Program
    {
        static void Main()
        {
            Task combinedResult = TestDelayWithWhenAny();

            while (true)
            {
                if (combinedResult.IsCompleted)
                {
                    Console.WriteLine("Finished waiting");
                    break;
                }
                Console.Write(".");
            }
            Console.ReadLine();
        }

        public static async Task TestDelayWithWhenAny()
        {
            await Task.WhenAny(Task.Delay(1), Task.Delay(2000));
        }
    }
}
```

This program produced the output.

```
...................................................................................................
...................................................Finished waiting
```

Summary

In this chapter we have explored asynchronous programming using the Task class that has been introduced in the .NET Framework. You have learned how to set up the continuation in the Task class, how to set different options when instantiating the Task class, and how to set different continuation options while setting up the continuation in the Task. You have also learned about exception handling while doing asynchronous operation using the Task class.

The keywords async and await were introduced to show how you do asynchronous operation using these new features. Then async and await were explore in depth to learn how the C# compiler generates the stub method and state machine to handle the asynchronous operation by scheduling the task to execute the asynchronous operation using the operating system's available schedule instead of blocking the execution of the program. You also learned how these new features improve asynchronous programming by handling the set up in the continuation block, keeping the flow and structure of the program simple.

Finally, this chapter introduced the Task-based asynchronous pattern to show the different built-in combinators you can use in asynchronous programming as well as how to set up the cancellation and progress reports of a task in .NET using the C#. The final chapter will look at diagnostic tool in .NET for debugging.

CHAPTER 15

■ ■ ■

Diagnostic Tools in .NET

This chapter will discuss the different debugging tools used in the .NET Framework to analyze an application and its performance and to explore the source code of the application. This chapter will explore the use of many debugging tools for applications written in .NET, such as Windbg, ILDasm, .NET Reflector, and CLR Profiler.

These tools are discussed to show you how to analyze the memory, stack, and Heap, which were discussed in this book, in relation to the different features of C# language.

Windbg and Son of Strike Debugging Extension DLL

Windbg is a debugging tool that is used for user and kernel mode debugging. This tool comes from Microsoft as part of the Windows Driver Kit (WDK). Windbg is a GUI built in the Console Debugger (CDB), NT Symbolic Debugger (NTSD), and Kernel Debugger (KD) along with debugging extensions. The Son of Strike (SOS) debugging extension DLL (Dynamic Link Library) helps to debug managed assembly by providing information about the internal operation of the CLR environment. Windbg is a powerful tool that can be used to:

- Debug managed assembly by allowing you to set a breakpoint

- View source code using symbol files

- View stack trace information

- View Heap information

- Examine the parameters of a method, memory, and registers

- Examine the exception handling information

Let's see how to download and install the Windbg.

Download and Installation

Windbg comes as part of the Windows debugging tools; it is free and available for download at http://msdn.microsoft.com/en-us/windows/hardware/gg463009.aspx. Once you have downloaded and installed the installation package, open the windbg.exe from the installed directory. When you open it, it will look much like the screenshot in Figure 15-1.

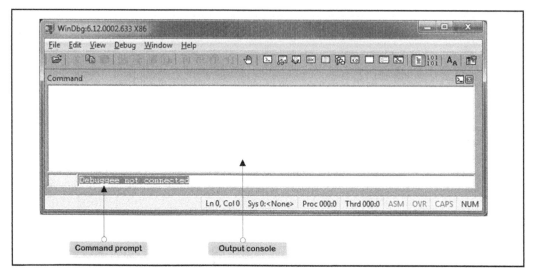

Figure 15-1. *The windbg.exe tool*

Figure 15-1 demonstrates that the Command prompt section is used to write the command for Windbg to execute, and in the output console section, you can see the output generated from the executed command. When you install the Windbg, it is not ready to use right away. It requires a few other steps to make it ready to debug the managed assembly. One of the first steps is to set up the symbol path, and the second is to ensure you are using the right version of the SOS debugging extension DLL, which we will explore further in the following sections.

Setting Up the Symbol Path

The symbol file contains a variety of data that can be used in the debugging process. The symbol file might contain:

- Global variables

- Local variables

- Function names and the addresses of their entry points

- Frame pointer omission (FPO) records

- Source line numbers

When the debugger tool, such as Windbg, has to have access to the related symbol files, it requires you to set the symbol file location. Microsoft has provided a symbol server for that purpose, so it is good to point the debugger to that symbol server. In Windbg, in order to point to that symbol server, you use the srv command along with the local cached folder (where the symbol files will be downloaded) and the server location from which the symbol files will be downloaded. It is just as easy to use the symbol server through the srv command as it is to use the appropriate syntax in your symbol path. Typically, the syntax takes the following format:

```
SRV*your local cached folder*http://msdl.microsoft.com/download/symbols
```

In your local cached folder, there is a drive or shared drive that can be used as the symbol destination. For example, to set the symbol path in the Windbg, type the following command in the command window of the debugger:

```
.sympath SRV*C:\symbols*http://msdl.microsoft.com/download/symbols
```

Alternatively, you can set the symbol path location via the Symbol File Path under the File menu of the Windbg, as demonstrated in Figure 15-2.

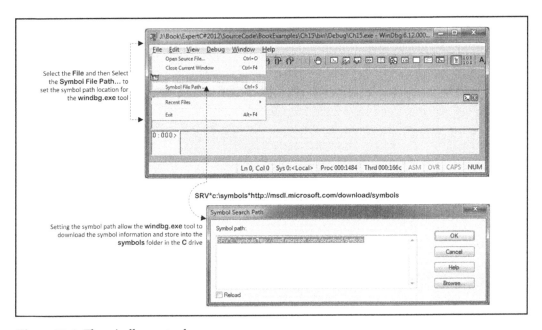

Figure 15-2. *The windbg.exe tool*

Figure 15-2 shows that in the Symbol Search Path window, the symbol path location has been set as:

```
SRV*c:\symbols*http://msdl.microsoft.com/download/symbols
```

Here `c:\symbols` refers to the local cached folder in where the symbol file will be downloaded, the location being specified as `http://msdl.microsoft.com/download/symbols`.

Another important step requires that you finish the Windbg set up using the correct version of the SOS debugging extension DLL. This will be explored in the following section.

Son of Strike Debugging Extension DLL

The SOS debugging extension DLL helps you to debug a managed assembly. When using SOS, you will be able to:

- Display managed call stacks
- Set breakpoints in managed code
- Find the values of local variables

- Dump the arguments to method calls

- Perform most of the inspection and control debugging actions that you can use in native-code debugging without the convenience of source-level debugging

When the SOS is used with the Windbg tool, it requires that you to use the correct version of it. The next section will explain how to set that version of the SOS.dll extension while debugging an executable.

Loading SOS Debugging Extension DLL in Windbg

To load the SOS debugging extension DLL into Windbg, you need to first load a managed assembly. The executable from Listing 15-1 can be used to do this.

Listing 15-1. An Example Program

```
using System;

namespace Ch15
{
    class Program
    {
        static void Main(string[] args)
        {
            Person aPerson = new Person()
            {
                Name = "A"
            };
            aPerson.ShowDetails();
        }
    }

    public class Person
    {
        public string Name { get; set; }
        public void ShowDetails()
        {
            Console.WriteLine(Name);
        }
    }
}
```

Listing 15-1 produced the output:

```
A
```

The executable produced from Listing 15-1 needs to load into the Windbg. Figure 15-3 demonstrates how to do this. Let's open the executable produced from Listing 15-1 in the Windbg, as shown in Figure 15-3.

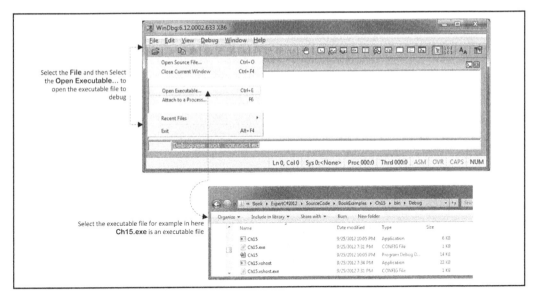

Figure 15-3. *Using the windbg.exe tool*

Figure 15-3 demonstrates that Open Executable... under the File menu produces a dialog window from which you can choose the location of the executable file produced from Listing 15-1 and select it. The Windbg tool is now ready to load the SOS debugging extension DLL.

The following commands (executing g command might throw an exception but please ignore it) need to be run to load the SOS.dll, which will initiate the debugging environment in Windbg:

```
sxe ld clrjit
g
.loadby sos clr
.load sos.dll
```

The .load sos.dll command is used to load the SOS, but if Windbg cannot find the right version of the SOS, it throws an exception.

In .NET, every version of the CLR has its own copy of the SOS extension DLL. You must always load the correct version of the SOS that comes with the CLR. To load this version of the SOS, you need to use the full path of the SOS (installed in your system) using the .load command. The path syntax is:

```
.load <full path to sos.dll>
```

Or you can use:

```
.load %windir%\Microsoft.NET\Framework\<version>\sos.dll
```

For example, if the SOS that is installed in the directory is C:\Windows\Microsoft.NET\Framework\ v4.0.30319\, you might need to execute the command:

```
.load C:\Windows\Microsoft.NET\Framework\v4.0.30319\sos.dll
```

The complete list of the commands would be:

```
sxe ld clrjit
g
```

```
.loadby sos clr
.load C:\Windows\Microsoft.NET\Framework\v4.0.30319\sos.dll
```

Figure 15-4 demonstrates that the SOS is loaded in the Windbg.

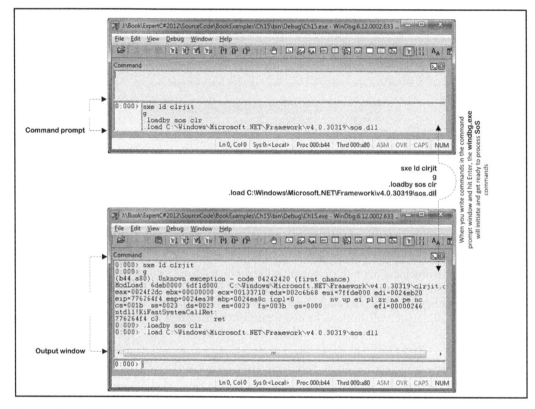

Figure 15-4. *SOS debugging extension DLL loading in the Windbg tool*

The Windbg tool is now able to execute the SOS commands to debug the loaded Ch15.exe executable. In the following section, you will use different test cases to explore the power of the SOS commands and get an idea of how to debug the managed assembly in the Windbg along with SOS debugging extension DLL.

Use of the SOS Debugging Extension DLL in Windbg

The following section will explore different scenarios to show how different SOS commands can be used to debug the managed assembly using the Windbg.

Type Information Using name2ee

If you want to explore the type information, such as the address of the MethodTable of an object or the address of the EEClass of a loaded module, you can use the name2ee command. The name2ee command takes a module and type name as input and displays the relevant information about the given type as output.

Before you do anything, load the type information to set a breakpoint:

```
!bpmd Ch15.exe Ch15.Person.ShowDetails
```

Then execute the command:

```
g
```

Then execute the following command, which takes Ch15.exe as the module name and Ch15.Person as the type name. This command is executed against the loaded executable from Listing 15-1:

```
!name2ee Ch15.exe Ch15.Person
```

When the name2ee command has successfully executed, it will produce the following output (throughout the chapter, the output might vary when you run a command locally):

```
Module:        00232e94
Assembly:      Ch15.exe
Token:         02000003
MethodTable:   002337bc      /* later used in the dumpmt command */
EEClass:       002312d8
Name:          Ch15.Person
```

The output shows information about the MethodTable of the Person type that contains information about all of the methods in the Person class. You can use the address of the MethodTable to explore the methods information of the Person class. Later we will learn how to use the dumpmt command to do that.

The name2ee command can also be useful to explore information about a method of a type, for example, if you execute the following command to explore the ShowDetails method of the Person class:

```
!name2ee Ch15.exe Ch15.Person.ShowDetails
```

This will produce the output:

```
Module:               00232e94
Assembly:             Ch15.exe
Token:                06000005
MethodDesc:           0023379c
Name:                 Ch15.Person.ShowDetails()
JITTED Code Address:  004f0148  /* Later used to explore the native code */
```

The output contains important information, for example, the MethodDesc address 0023379c, which can be used to explore more details about the method if you execute the command:

```
!dumpmd 0023379c
```

It will produce output that shows the details about the ShowDetails method:

```
Method Name:      Ch15.Person.ShowDetails()
Class:            002312d8
MethodTable:      002337bc
mdToken:          06000005
Module:           00232e94
IsJitted:         yes
CodeAddr:         004f0148
Transparency:     Critical
```

You can use the MethodDesc address to see the IL code of the ShowDetails method. The dumpil command with the MethodDesc address will display the IL code of the specified method.

Let's execute the dumpil command as shown:

```
!dumpil 0023379c
```

This will produce the IL version of the ShowDetails method:

```
ilAddr = 00f720a4
IL_0000: nop
IL_0001: ldarg.0
IL_0002: call Ch15.Person::get_Name
IL_0007: call System.Console::WriteLine
IL_000c: nop
IL_000d: ret
```

The Jitted code address (from the output of name2ee Ch15.exe Ch15.Person.ShowDetails) can be used to explore the native code for the method that has Jitted using the u command. For example:

```
/* 004f0148  refers the JITTED Code Address extracted
 * when explore the ShowDetails method using the name2ee */
!u 004f0148
```

It produces the output:

```
Normal JIT generated code
Ch15.Person.ShowDetails()
Begin 004f0148, size 37

j:\Book\ExpertC#2012\SourceCode\BookExamples\Ch15\Program.cs @ 28:
>>> 004f0148 55                push         ebp
004f0149 8bec                  mov          ebp,esp
004f014b 83ec08                sub          esp,8
004f014e 33c0                  xor          eax,eax
004f0150 8945f8                mov          dword ptr [ebp-8],eax
004f0153 894dfc                mov          dword ptr [ebp-4],ecx
004f0156 833d6031230000        cmp          dword ptr ds:[233160h],0
004f015d 7405                  je           004f0164
004f015f e80b6a840f            call         clr!JIT_DbgIsJustMyCode (0fd36b6f)
004f0164 90                    nop

j:\Book\ExpertC#2012\SourceCode\BookExamples\Ch15\Program.cs @ 29:
004f0165 8b4dfc                mov          ecx,dword ptr [ebp-4]
004f0168 ff158c372300          call         dword ptr ds:[23378Ch] (Ch15.Person.get_Name(),
mdToken: 06000003)
004f016e 8945f8                mov          dword ptr [ebp-8],eax
004f0171 8b4df8                mov          ecx,dword ptr [ebp-8]
004f0174 e827a3b178            call         mscorlib_ni+0x2fa4a0 (7900a4a0) (System.Console.
WriteLine(System.String), mdToken: 0600098f)
004f0179 90                    nop

j:\Book\ExpertC#2012\SourceCode\BookExamples\Ch15\Program.cs @ 30:
004f017a 90                    nop
004f017b 8be5          mov            esp,ebp
```

```
004f017d 5d                    pop          ebp
004f017e c3                    ret
```

You can use the name2ee command to explore the method table information of the different types from .NET Framework assembly. If you want to explore the String class from the mscorlib.dll assembly, you need to execute the command:

```
!name2ee mscorlib.dll System.String
```

This will show you the type information about the String class:

```
Module:        536b1000
Assembly:      mscorlib.dll
Token:         0200004c
MethodTable:   53aab808        /* This used later in the dumpmt command */
EEClass:       536b4ec8
Name:          System.String
```

The following section will explore the dumpmt command that can be used to find the information about the method of a type. The dumpmt command will use the method table address 002337bc of the Person class, which we saw in the name2ee command earlier.

Method Table Information of an Object dumpmt

If you want to explore method table information using the method table address returned from the Person class, we can execute the dumpmt command along with the method table address 002337bc. The dumpmt command has an MD option that is used to display information about the method description:

```
!dumpmt -MD 002337bc
```

This produces the output:

```
EEClass:                          002312d8
Module:                           00232e94
Name:                             Ch15.Person
mdToken:                          02000003
File:                             J:\Book\ExpertC#2012\SourceCode\BookExamples\Ch15\bin\
Debug\Ch15.exe
BaseSize:                         0xc
ComponentSize:                    0x0
Slots in VTable:                  8
Number of IFaces in IFaceMap:     0
---------------------------------------
MethodDesc Table
Entry          MethodDe    JIT      Name
78ff99d0       78d16a08    PreJIT   System.Object.ToString()
78fe4b70       78d16a10    PreJIT   System.Object.Equals(System.Object)
78fe4c80       78d16a30    PreJIT   System.Object.GetHashCode()
78fe1500       78d16a44    PreJIT   System.Object.Finalize()
004f00d0       002337a8    JIT      Ch15.Person..ctor()
004f0190       00233784    JIT      Ch15.Person.get_Name()
004f0108       00233790    JIT      Ch15.Person.set_Name(System.String)
004f0148       0023379c    JIT      Ch15.Person.ShowDetails()
```

The dumpmt command can also be used to explore the method table for the .NET Frameworks' type. For example, the method table address 53aab808 of the string class (explore early) in the mscorlib.dll assembly would be:

```
!dumpmt -MD 53aab808
```

It produces the output:

```
EEClass:       536b4ec8
Module:        536b1000
Name:          System.String
mdToken:       0200004c
File:             C:\Windows\Microsoft.Net\assembly\GAC_32\mscorlib\v4.0_4.0.0.0__
b77a5c561934e089\mscorlib.dll
BaseSize:                               0xc
ComponentSize:                          0x2
Slots in VTable:                        193
Number of IFaces in IFaceMap:    7
---------------------------------------
MethodDesc Table
   Entry MethodDe    JIT Name
539a2cd0 5373f874 PreJIT System.String.ToString()
/* information removed */
539dfca0 5373fbd0 PreJIT System.String.ConcatArray(System.String[], Int32)
```

Explore Heap Using dumpheap

The CLR stores all the reference types, for example, the instance of the Person class from Listing 15-1, onto the Heap. Using the dumpheap command, we can find the current state of the Heap for the Person object:

```
!dumpheap -type Person
```

This will produce the output:

```
Address        MT             Size
016c2374       002937bc       12
total 0 objects
Statistics:
MT             Count          TotalSize       Class Name
002937bc       1              12              Ch15.Person
Total 1 objects
```

Setting the Breakpoint of a Method to Pause Execution

The bpmd command is used to set the breakpoint in a method of a loaded type. For example, if you want to set a breakpoint in the ShowDetails method, execute the command:

```
!bpmd Ch15.exe Ch15.Person.ShowDetails
```

This will set the breakpoint to the ShowDetails method and display the following output to show the status of the bpmd execution:

```
Found 1 methods in module 00142e94...
MethodDesc = 0014379c
Adding pending breakpoints...
```

The bpmd command can also be used to set the breakpoint in the .NET Framework method, for example, the ToUpper method of the String class using the bpmd command:

```
!bpmd mscorlib.dll System.String.ToUpper
!bpmd mscorlib.dll System.String.ToLower
!bpmd mscorlib.dll System.String.Trim
```

This command will produce the output:

```
Found 2 methods in module 536b1000...
MethodDesc = 5373f850
MethodDesc = 5373f85c
Setting breakpoint: bp 53999956 [System.String.ToUpper(System.Globalization.CultureInfo)]
Setting breakpoint: bp 539A0ECC [System.String.ToUpper()]
Adding pending breakpoints...

Found 2 methods in module 536b1000...
MethodDesc = 5373f82c
MethodDesc = 5373f838
Setting breakpoint: bp 539A3936 [System.String.ToLower(System.Globalization.CultureInfo)]
Setting breakpoint: bp 53986690 [System.String.ToLower()]
Adding pending breakpoints...

Found 2 methods in module 536b1000...
MethodDesc = 5373f490
MethodDesc = 5373f88c
Setting breakpoint: bp 539AF41C [System.String.Trim()]
Setting breakpoint: bp 5399BF63 [System.String.Trim(Char[])]
Adding pending breakpoints...
```

The bpmd command is very useful when you want to explore the stack information of the method execution.

Stack Information for an Application

The dumpstack command can be used to find the status of the stack:

```
!dumpstack
```

It will produce the output:

```
0:000> !dumpstack
OS Thread Id: 0xa80 (0)
Current frame: ntdll!KiFastSystemCallRet
ChildEBP RetAddr  Caller, Callee
/* information removed */
0024ff50 7763b3f5 ntdll!__RtlUserThreadStart+0x70
0024ff90 7763b3c8 ntdll!_RtlUserThreadStart+0x1b, calling ntdll!__RtlUserThreadStart
```

To analyze the stack information, you need to use the `clrstack` command, which is one of most important commands to explore the stack information of a method:

```
!clrstack
```

It will produce the output:

```
OS Thread Id:   0x450 (0)
Child SP        IP              Call Site
0028f4a8        002b0164        Ch15.Person.ShowDetails() [j:\Book\ExpertC#2012\SourceCode\
BookExamples\Ch15\Program.cs @ 24]
0028f4b8        002b00b6        Ch15.Program.Main(System.String[]) [j:\Book\ExpertC#2012\
SourceCode\
BookExamples\Ch15\Program.cs @ 17]
0028f64c        6cd03dd2        [GCFrame: 0028f64c]
```

The `clrstack` command takes p option to display the parameters section of the method call. You have to set the breakpoint to the `ShowDetails` method and program control, which is currently in the `Main`. Let's execute the g command and `!clrstack` with the p option:

```
!clrstack -p
```

It produces the output:

```
OS Thread Id: 0xb7c (0)
Child SP IP     Call Site
0039f318 00610164 Ch15.Person.ShowDetails()
[j:\Book\ExpertC#2012\SourceCode\BookExamples\Ch15\Program.cs @ 28]
    PARAMETERS:
        this (0x0039f31c) = 0x016c2374
0039f328 006100b6 Ch15.Program.Main(System.String[])
[j:\Book\ExpertC#2012\SourceCode\BookExamples\Ch15\Program.cs @ 17]
    PARAMETERS:
        args (0x0039f334) = 0x016c2354
0039f4bc 0f593dd2 [GCFrame: 0039f4bc]
```

The l option can be used in the `clrstack` command to show the LOCALS section of the method stack:

```
!clrstack -l
```

It produces the output:

```
OS Thread Id: 0xb7c (0)
Child SP        IP              Call Site
0039f318        00610164        Ch15.Person.ShowDetails() [j:\Book\ExpertC#2012\SourceCode\
BookExamples\Ch15\Program.cs @ 28]

0039f328        006100b6        Ch15.Program.Main(System.String[]) [j:\Book\ExpertC#2012\
SourceCode\BookExamples\Ch15\Program.cs @ 17]
    LOCALS:
        0x0039f330 = 0x016c2374
        0x0039f32c = 0x016c2374
0039f4bc        0f593dd2        [GCFrame: 0039f4bc]
```

The p and l options can be combined with the a option, which can be used to get the full details about the method stack:

```
!clrstack -a
```

This will produce the output:

```
OS Thread Id: 0xb7c (0)
Child           SP                    IP Call Site
0039f318        00610164       Ch15.Person.ShowDetails() [j:\Book\ExpertC#2012\SourceCode\
BookExamples\Ch15\Program.cs @ 28]
    PARAMETERS:
        this (0x0039f31c) = 0x016c2374
0039f328        006100b6       Ch15.Program.Main(System.String[]) [j:\Book\ExpertC#2012\
SourceCode\BookExamples\Ch15\Program.cs @ 17]
    PARAMETERS:
        args (0x0039f334) = 0x016c2354
    LOCALS:
        0x0039f330 = 0x016c2374 /* Used later to explore object information*/
        0x0039f32c = 0x016c2374
0039f4bc        0f593dd2 [GCFrame: 0039f4bc]
```

From this output, we can see the PARAMETERS and LOCALS sections use some addresses, for example, 0x016c2374, to refer to some objects on the Heap. You can use the dumpobj command to explore information about these objects. The next section will discuss the dumpobj command.

Exploring Object Information of a Type Using dumpobj

The dumpobj command, along with the address of an object, shows details about the object stored in the Heap:

```
/* address taken from the LOCALS section of the above output which
 * refers the instance of the Person*/
!dumpobj 0x016c2374
```

It produced the output:

```
Name:           Ch15.Person
MethodTable:    002937bc
EEClass:        002912d8
Size:           12(0xc) bytes
File:           J:\Book\ExpertC#2012\SourceCode\BookExamples\Ch15\bin\Debug\Ch15.exe
Fields:
MT        Field     Offset  Type            VT  Attr      Value     Name
7957b808  4000001   4       System.String   0   instance  016c2364  <Name>k__BackingField
```

Current Object in the Stack

Using the dumpstackobjects command, you can get the current object information from the stack:

```
!dumpstackobjects
```

It produces the output:

```
OS Thread Id: 0xb7c (0)
ESP/REG          Object          Name
ecx              016c2374        Ch15.Person
0039F31C         016c2374        Ch15.Person
0039F328         016c2374        Ch15.Person
0039F32C         016c2374        Ch15.Person
0039F330         016c2374        Ch15.Person
0039F334         016c2354        System.Object[]    (System.String[])
0039F3B0         016c2354        System.Object[]    (System.String[])
0039F50C         016c2354        System.Object[]    (System.String[])
0039F544         016c2354        System.Object[]    (System.String[])
```

For example, you can use the address of the instance of the Person class 016c2374 to find object information using the dumpobject (do is short for dumpobject):

```
!do 016c2374
```

It produces the output:

```
Name:           Ch15.Person
MethodTable:    002937bc
EEClass:        002912d8
Size:           12(0xc) bytes
File:           J:\Book\ExpertC#2012\SourceCode\BookExamples\Ch15\bin\Debug\Ch15.exe
Fields:
MT       Field   Offset Type          VT  Attr     Value     Name
7957b808 4000001 4      System.String 0   instance 016c2364  <Name>k__BackingField
```

So far we have explored the instance of a type. If you want to explore the static class that does not have any instance, you can use the dumpclass command, which shows information about the static class, as described in the next section.

Static Class Information

The dumpclass command can be used to explore the static class. For example, the Console class is a static class within the system namespace:

```
!name2ee mscorlib.dll System.Console
```

It produces the output:

```
Module:         536b1000
Assembly:       mscorlib.dll
Token:          020000af
MethodTable:    53a9d1f8
EEClass:        53716970                 /* used by the dumpclass */
Name:           System.Console
```

The dumpclass command along with the address of the EEClass 53716970 shows information about the static class console:

```
!dumpclass 53716970
```

It produces the output:

```
Class Name:                      System.Console
mdToken:                         020000af
File:                            C:\Windows\Microsoft.Net\assembly\GAC_32\
                    mscorlib\v4.0_4.0.0.0__b77a5c561934e089\mscorlib.dll
Parent Class:                    536b4f7c
Module:                          536b1000
Method Table:                    53a9d1f8
Vtable Slots:                    4
Total Method Slots:              5
Class Attributes:                100181  Abstract,
Transparency:                    Transparent
NumInstanceFields:               0
NumStaticFields:                 16
MT     Field   Offset        Type VT    Attr     Value Name
53aad758  40002aa       60 ...t.UnicodeEncoding  0    shared    static StdConUnicodeEncoding
    >> Domain:Value  00083d70:018223d4 <<
53a9fcd8  40002ab       64 System.IO.TextReader  0    shared    static _in
    >> Domain:Value  00083d70:00000000 <<
53aae768  40002ac       68 System.IO.TextWriter  0    shared    static _out
    >> Domain:Value  00083d70:01824024 <<
/* Information removed */
```

Exception Handling Analysis Using name2ee and ehinfo

The SOS debugging extension DLL provides another way to examine the exception handling mechanism in .NET. The program in Listing 15-2 will be used to help us explore exception handling.

Listing 15-2. Example of Exception Handling

```
using System;

namespace Ch15
{
    class Program
    {
        static void Main(string[] args)
        {
            try
            {
                int a = 100, b = 0;
                Console.WriteLine(a / b);
            }
            catch (DivideByZeroException dbze)
            {
                Console.WriteLine(dbze.Message);
            }
        }
    }
}
```

This program will produce the output:

Attempted to divide by zero.

To debug the executable from Listing 15-2, you need to start from scratch (i.e., stop the previous debug session in the Windbg and load the executable produced from Listing 15-2). You need to load the SOS.dll (just to clarify, you do not need to load the symbols again for the windbg.exe), as we did earlier in the chapter, but this time with the new executable produced from Listing 15-2. To refresh your mind, you would execute as follows:

```
sxe ld clrjit
g
.loadby sos clr
.load C:\Windows\Microsoft.NET\Framework\v4.0.30319\sos.dll
```

These commands will allow you to execute further commands to analyze the exception handling information embedded within the method in compile time. To explore the exception handling, you need to execute the name2ee, dumpmt, and ehinfo commands. The name2ee command will show the method table information for the Program class:

```
0:000> !name2ee  Ch15.exe Ch15.Program
Module    : 00332e94
Assembly    : Ch15.exe
Token    : 02000002
MethodTable : 00333724
EEClass    : 00331264
Name    : Ch15.Program
```

To explore the method description table for the program, you need to use the dumpmt command, which produces the output:

```
0:000> !dumpmt -md 00333724
EEClass : 00331264
Module  : 00332e94
Name    : Ch15.Program
mdToken : 02000002
File    :J:\Book\ExpertC#2012\SourceCode\
        BookExamples\Ch15\bin\Debug\Ch15.exe
BaseSize        : 0xc
ComponentSize   : 0x0
Slots in VTable : 6
Number of IFaces in IFaceMap: 0
--------------------------------------
MethodDesc Table
Entry           MethodDesc      JIT     Name
78e499d0        78b66a08        PreJIT  System.Object.ToString()
78e34b70        78b66a10        PreJIT  System.Object.Equals(System.Object)
78e34c80        78b66a30        PreJIT  System.Object.GetHashCode()
78e31500        78b66a44        PreJIT  System.Object.Finalize()
0033c015        0033371c        NONE    Ch15.Program..ctor()
0033c011        00333710        NONE    Ch15.Program.Main(System.String[])
```

From the Jitted status of the Main method, you can see that it has not yet been Jitted, so to Jit the Main method you need to execute the g command. It will execute the Main method and return to the caller. As a result, you be unable to explore details about the Main method. It requires pausing the execution of the Main method to add a breakpoint to the Main method using the bpmd command:

```
!bpmd  Ch15.exe Ch15.Program.Main
```

It produces the output:

```
Found 1 methods in module 00332e94...
MethodDesc = 00333710
Adding pending breakpoints...
```

Now execute the g command, and this will start Jitting the process, and the Jit compiler will compile the Main method. To find out more about it, execute the following:

```
0:000> !dumpmt -md 00333724
EEClass : 00331264
Module  : 00332e94
Name      : Ch15.Program
mdToken : 02000002
File      : J:\Book\ExpertC#2012\SourceCode\BookExamples\Ch15\bin\Debug\Ch15.exe
BaseSize              : 0xc
ComponentSize   : 0x0
Slots in VTable : 6
Number of IFaces in IFaceMap: 0
--------------------------------------
MethodDesc Table
Entry           MethodDesc      JIT        Name
78e499d0        78b66a08        PreJIT     System.Object.ToString()
78e34b70        78b66a10        PreJIT     System.Object.Equals(System.Object)
78e34c80        78b66a30        PreJIT     System.Object.GetHashCode()
78e31500        78b66a44        PreJIT     System.Object.Finalize()
0033c015        0033371c        NONE       Ch15.Program..ctor()
0033c011        00333710        JIT        Ch15.Program.Main(System.String[])
```

The Main method has been Jitted so you can explore the exception handling information about the Main method using the MethodDesc reference exception handling information that is extracted using the EHInfo command:

```
0:000> !EHInfo 00333710
It produces the output:
MethodDesc:     00333710
Method Name:    Ch15.Program.Main(System.String[])
Class:          00331264
MethodTable:    00333724
mdToken:        06000001
Module:         00332e94
IsJitted:       yes
CodeAddr:       003b0050
Transparency:   Critical

EHHandler 0: TYPED
Clause  :  [003b0089, 003b00a9] [39, 59]
Handler :  [003b00a9, 003b00d2] [59, 82]
```

The output produces the exception handling information regarding the Main method. You can explore this a bit further in native code level using the following command for the MethodDesc address 00333710:

```
!u -ehinfo -n 00333710
```

It produces the output:

```
Normal JIT generated code
Ch15.Program.Main(System.String[])
Begin   003b0050, size 8b
003b0050         55                          push     ebp
003b0051         8bec                        mov      ebp,esp
003b0053         57                          push     edi
003b0054         56                          push     esi
003b0055         83ec2c                      sub      esp,2Ch
003b0058         8bf1                        mov      esi,ecx
003b005a         8d7dcc                      lea      edi,[ebp-34h]
003b005d          b90a000000                 mov      ecx,0Ah
003b0062         33c0                        xor      eax,eax
003b0064         f3ab                        rep stos dword ptr es:[edi]
003b0066         8bce                        mov      ecx,esi
003b0068         894de0                      mov      dword ptr [ebp-20h],ecx
003b006b         833d6031330000             cmp      dword ptr ds:[333160h],0
003b0072         7405                        je       003b0079
003b0074         e8f66afd0e                  call     clr!JIT_DbgIsJustMyCode (0f386b6f)
003b0079         33d2                        xor      edx,edx
003b007b         8955d4                      mov      dword ptr [ebp-2Ch],edx
003b007e         33d2                        xor      edx,edx
003b0080         8955d8                      mov      dword ptr [ebp-28h],edx
003b0083         33d2                        xor      edx,edx
003b0085         8955dc                      mov      dword ptr [ebp-24h],edx
003b0088         90                          nop


/* Exception Catch block start from here */
EHHandler 0: TYPED CLAUSE BEGIN
003b0089         90              nop
003b008a c       745dc64000000   mov      dword ptr [ebp-24h],64h
003b0091         33d2            xor          edx,edx
003b0093         8955d8          mov      dword ptr [ebp-28h],edx
003b0096         8b45dc          mov      eax,dword ptr [ebp-24h]
003b0099         99              cdq
003b009a         f77dd8          idiv     eax,dword ptr [ebp-28h]
003b009d         8bc8            mov      ecx,eax
003b009f         e8d4661679      call     mscorlib_ni+0x9b6778 (79516778) (System.
Console.WriteLine(Int32), mdToken: 0600098a)
003b00a4         90              nop
003b00a5         90              nop
003b00a6         90              nop
003b00a7         eb29            jmp      003b00d2
EHHandler 0: TYPED CLAUSE END
/* End of the  Exception Catch block*/


/* Start of the Exception handling block */
EHHandler 0: TYPED HANDLER BEGIN
```

```
003b00a9          8945d0                     mov      dword ptr [ebp-30h],eax
003b00ac          8b45d0                     mov      eax,dword ptr [ebp-30h]
003b00af          8945d4                     mov      dword ptr [ebp-2Ch],eax
003b00b2          90                         nop
003b00b3          8b4dd4                     mov      ecx,dword ptr [ebp-2Ch]
003b00b6          8b01                       mov      eax,dword ptr [ecx]
003b00b8          8b4028                     mov      eax,dword ptr [eax+28h]
003b00bb          ff5010                     call     dword ptr [eax+10h]
003b00be          8945cc                     mov      dword ptr [ebp-34h],eax
003b00c1          8b4dcc                     mov      ecx,dword ptr [ebp-34h]
003b00c4          e8d7a3aa78                 call     mscorlib_ni+0x2fa4a0 (78e5a4a0) (System.Console.
WriteLine(System.String), mdToken: 0600098f)
003b00c9          90                         nop
003b00ca          90                         nop
003b00cb          e8f53dd20e                 call     clr!JIT_EndCatch (0f0d3ec5)
003b00d0          eb00                       jmp      003b00d2
EHHandler 0: TYPED HANDLER END
/* End of the Exception handling block */

003b00d2          90                         nop
003b00d3          90                         nop
003b00d4          8d65f8                     lea      esp,[ebp-8]
003b00d7          5e                         pop      esi
003b00d8          5f                         pop      edi
003b00d9          5d                         pop      ebp
003b00da          c3                         ret
```

Clear the Output Window

The .cls command is helpful to clear the command output window in the windbg.exe.

Complete List of Command

To get information about an individual command, for example, to get more information about clrstack command, execute the command:

```
!help clrstack
```

Intermediate Language Disassembler

The Intermediate Language Disassembler (ILDasm) tool is used to examine .NET Framework assemblies in IL format, such as mscorlib.dll, as well as other .NET Framework assemblies provided by a third party or that you created. The ILDasm parses any .NET Framework–managed assembly. The ILDasm can be used:

- To explore Microsoft intermediate language (MSIL) code

- To displays namespaces and types, including their interfaces

- To explore the executable header information

Download and Installation

The ILDasm comes with the .NET Framework Software Development Kit, so you do not need to download it and it will be installed as part of the Visual Studio installation.

How to Use the ILDasm

After opening any executable in the ILDasm, the generated IL code would be displayed as shown in Figure 15-5.

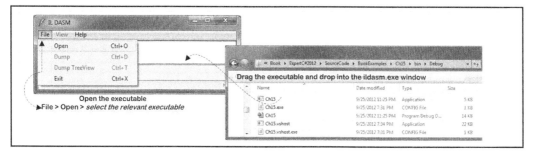

Figure 15-5. Open an executable via the ILDasm.exe

After opening the executable in the ILDasm, the generated IL code would be displayed as shown in Figure 15-6.

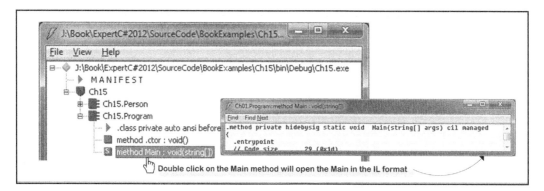

Figure 15-6. Main method in IL view

Figure 15-6 demonstrates that you can explore the contents of the method by double-clicking the method name from the explored assembly contents in the ILDasm. The contents of the method will be in IL format.

The following sections will explore different scenarios to show how the ILDasm tool can be used to explore the managed assembly, metadata information of the managed assembly, and much more.

Exploring .ctor and .cctor Using ildasm.exe

The C# compiler compiles the constructors of a type and names the constructors with the `.ctor` and `.cctor` extensions in the compiled IL code. Listing 15-3 is used to explain the `.ctor` and `.cctor` compiled by the C# compiler for the constructors of a class in C#.

Listing 15-3. *Example of the Universe Class*

```
namespace Ch15
{
    class Program
    {
        static void Main(string[] args)  {}
    }

    public class Universe
    {
        static double ageOfTheUniverse;
        public Universe()          {}     /* Compiled as .ctor */
        public Universe(double age) {}     /* Compiled as .ctor */
        static Universe()
        { ageOfTheUniverse = 13.75e+10; } /* Compiled as .cctor */
        public void EmtpyMethod()   {}     /* Method declaration */
    }
}
```

Let's decompiled the executable produced from Listing 15-3 using the ILDasm. Open the Universe class, which will show you the compiled IL code as shown in Figure 15-7.

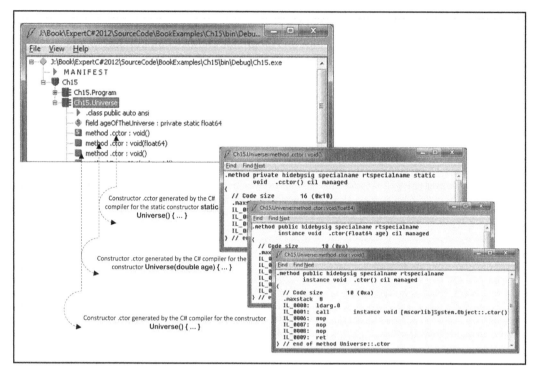

Figure 15-7. *Decompiled IL code via ildasm.exe*

Following the decompiled IL code shows how the C# compiler compiled the constructor's `.cctor` and `.ctor` including overloaded, as shown in Listing 15-4.

Listing 15-4. *Decompiled IL Code for Listing 15-3*

```
.class public auto ansi Universe extends [mscorlib]System.Object
{
    /* Type Initializer */
    .method private hidebysig specialname rtspecialname
     static void .cctor() cil managed
    {
        .maxstack 8
        L_0000: nop
        L_0001: ldc.r8 137500000000
        L_000a: stsfld float64 Ch15.Universe::ageOfTheUniverse
        L_000f: ret
    }

    /* Instance constructor */
    .method public hidebysig specialname rtspecialname instance
     void .ctor() cil managed
    {
        .maxstack 8
```

```
    L_0000: ldarg.0
    L_0001: call instance void [mscorlib]System.Object::.ctor()
    L_0006: nop
    L_0007: nop
    L_0008: nop
    L_0009: ret
}

/* Instance constructor */
.method public hidebysig specialname rtspecialname instance
 void .ctor(float64 age) cil managed
{
    .maxstack 8
    L_0000: ldarg.0
    L_0001: call instance void [mscorlib]System.Object::.ctor()
    L_0006: nop
    L_0007: nop
    L_0008: nop
    L_0009: ret
}

/* Method declaration */
.method public hidebysig instance void EmtpyMethod() cil managed
{
    .maxstack 8
    L_0000: nop
    L_0001: ret
}
.field private static float64 ageOfTheUniverse
}
```

From Listing 15-4, you can see that while C# compiler compiles the constructor for the Universe class from Listing 15-3, it compiles the instance constructors with the .ctor extension and type initializers with the .cctor extension.

.ctor

From Listing 15-4, you can see that two methods have been named as .ctor. These are the instance constructors. According to the CLI specification Partition II (Metadata Definition and Semantics), the instance constructors are named as .ctor and marked with instance, rtspecialname, and specialname.

.cctor

From Listing 15-4, you can see that a method has been named as .cctor. It is the type initializer, which is used to initialize the type itself. According to the CLI specification Partition II (Metadata Definition and Semantics), this method will be static, take no parameters, return no value, be marked with rtspecialname and specialname, and be named .cctor. Besides the constructors, Listing 15-4 contains a field declaration with the .field extension and a method named EmptyMethod.

Exploring Metadata Information of an Assembly Using ILDasm

The ILDasm tool can be used to explore the metadata information of an assembly, for example, you can see the String Heap addresses, user strings section, and so forth, as demonstrated in Figure 15-8.

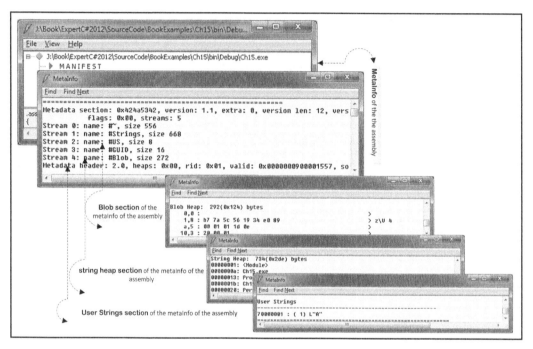

Figure 15-8. *Metadata information using ILDasm.exe tool*

Exploring .NET Framework Source Code in IL Code

Let's open ToUpper method from the String class of the mscorlib.dll assembly via ildasm.exe:

- Drag the mscorlib.dll assembly onto the ILDasm.

- Locate the string class from the mscorlib.dll and double-click the ToUpper method from the string class.

This will show the IL implementation of the ToUpper method, as shown in Figure 15-9.

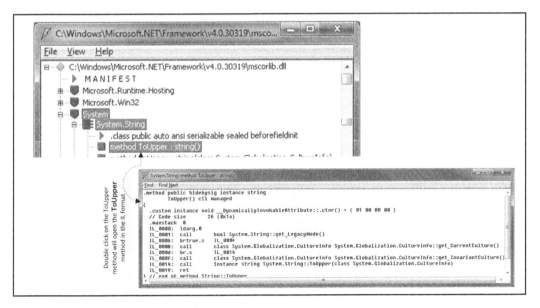

Figure 15-9. Open string class via ildasm.exe

The .NET Reflector: Source Code Explorer

The .NET Reflector tool is used to explore .NET assembly's source code in C# or in IL format, which shows the inner implementation of the .NET assemblies. To analyze this, browse and debug the .NET components, for example, the executable or the DLL in different .NET languages. This tool can be used to:

- See the metadata

- See the IL code of the assembly

- View resources and XML documentation

- View and debug the .NET Framework code

Its Analyzer option can be used to find assembly dependencies and even Windows DLL dependencies. Once the .NET Reflector tool is combined with other add-ins, it can become a tool to facilitate testing and make teamwork more effective.

Download and Installation

This tool can be download from http://www.reflector.net/. After installing the Reflector, you open it from the installed directory. Figure 15-10 shows the source code of the string class from the mscorlib.dll assembly that was opened using the Reflector.

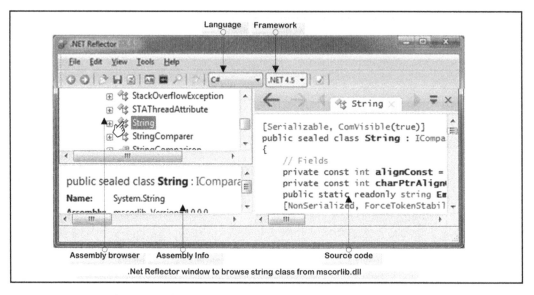

Figure 15-10. *Introduction of the .Net Reflector tool*

The .NET Reflector, ILasm, and ILDasm

Microsoft supplies two tools for investigating assemblies:

- ILasm, the Microsoft IL Assembler. It will take an ASCII assembly language source code file and produce binary IL (MSIL) code.

- ILDasm, the .NET disassembler. This is part of the .NET Framework that works the other way around. It will produce an "assembly" file from an IL file.

The ILDasm tools are useful, but not sufficient by themselves. Unfortunately, ILDasm works best only with CLI assembly sections. The tool will show method signatures and member variables of an assembly, but the code will be in .NET IL code.

To be able to extract everything you want from a .NET assembly, in the language that was used originally to create the assembly, you will need .NET Reflector. This will also allow you to browse and inspect the other resources in the assembly, even the XML documentation used by the IDE (Integrated Development Environment) that created the assembly.

Exploring .NET Framework Source Code in C# or IL View

The Reflector can be used to explore the source code of the assembly in C# or IL language. Figure 15-11 shows the source code of the String class in the mscorlib.dll in .NET Framework.

You can also explore the source code of the executable produced from Listing 15-1. This tool is very handy when you have a managed assembly but not the source code.

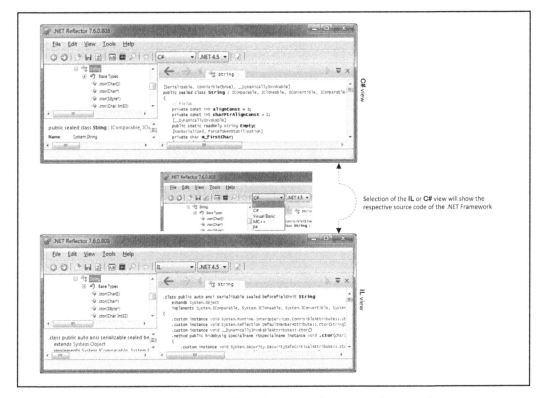

Figure 15-11. .NET Framework source code explore using the .NET Reflector tool

CLR Profiler: A Memory Profiler

The CLR Profiler is a memory profiler for the .NET Framework. It allows you to analyze the contents of the managed Heap and the garbage collector. This tool can also be used to analyze different information about the execution, allocation, and memory consumption of your application and to analyze the performance of your application. Figure 15-12 shows the CLR Profiler tools.

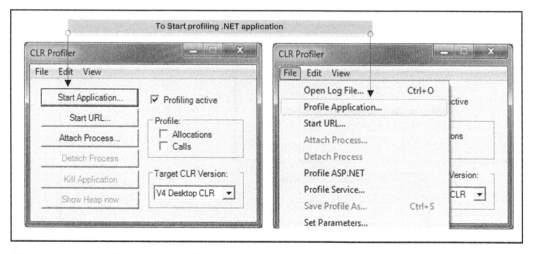

Figure 15-12. *Introducing CLR Profiler 4.0*

Download and Installation

The CLR Profiler is downloaded as a self-extracting executable file. The expanded contents include the source code and the executable file (CLRProfiler.exe). The download also contains a comprehensive document that provides detailed information on CLR Profiler. This can be download from http://www.microsoft.com/en-us/download/details.aspx?id=16273.

Views in CLR Profiler

The CLRProfiler.exe has different views that can be used to analyze the application, as discussed in the sections that follow.

Histogram Allocated Types

This shows the high-level view of object type's allocation (by allocation size) during the application lifetime. It also shows the large object Heap (objects larger than 85KB).

Histogram Relocated Types

It shows that those objects that survived in the garbage collection move to different generation, for example, Gen0, Gen1, and Gen2.

Objects By Address

It shows the managed Heap status at any given time.

Histogram By Age

By this view, you can see the lifetime of the objects on the managed Heap.

Allocation Graph

This view displays the call stack and shows how objects were allocated. You can use this view to:

- See the cost of each allocation by method

- Isolate allocations you were not expecting

- View possible excessive allocations by a method

- View assembly, module, function, and class graphs

Heap Graph

It shows the objects on the managed Heap and their connections.

Call Graph

This view help you to see which methods call other methods and how frequently. You can use this graph to get a feel for the cost of library calls and to determine how many calls are made to methods and which methods are called.

Time Line

This view displays what the garbage collector does over the lifetime of the application. You can use this view to:

- Analyze the behavior of the garbage collector

- Explore the three generations (Gen0, Gen1, and Gen2) and how frequently they occur.

- Determine which objects survive garbage collection and are promoted to the next generation.

You can select time points or intervals and right-click to show who allocated memory in the interval.

Call Tree View

This view can be used to explore text-based, chronological, and hierarchical views of your application's execution. You can use this view to:

- See what types are allocated and their size

- See which assemblies are loaded as a result of method calls

Memory Profiling

Let's do a memory profiling for the program in Listing 15-5 using the CLR Profiler.

Listing 15-5. *Example of a Memory Profile*

```
using System;
namespace Ch15
{
    class Program
    {
        static void Main(string[] args)
        {
            double result = default(double);
            for (int i = 0; i < Int16.MaxValue; ++i)
                result += i;
        }
    }
}
```

If you open the executable produced from Listing 15-5 via the ClrProfiler.exe tool, you will see the statistics of the memory while the CLR executes the executable, as shown in Figure 15-13.

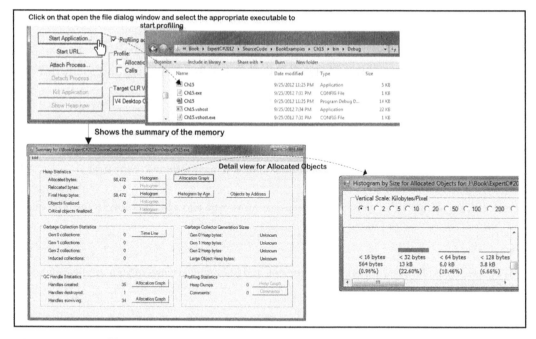

Figure 15-13. *Profile and application*

Figure 15-13 demonstrates that when the program in Listing 15-5 is loaded by the CLR Profiler, it shows you the Heap statistics, such as how many bytes have been allocated, how much is in the final Heap, and what the status of the garbage collector is.

Summary

Debugging is one of the most important keys to understanding the internal operations of the C# language features. Using the debugger, you will better understand how the C# actually works. This book has explored the stack and Heap, parameter passing in method call, automatic property declaration, how the enum type is handled by the CLR, the state machine in iterator, and much more. This chapter has brought these different concepts together by exploring the use of debugging tools such as Windbg, ILDasm, .NET Reflector, and CLR Profiler.

Index

E

S

CPSIA information can be obtained at www.ICGtesting.com
Printed in the USA
LVOW022006211212

312806LV00002B/2/P